S

A HISTORY
of
ENGLAND

A HISTORY
of
ENGLAND

by

W. FREEMAN GALPIN, Ph.D.

PROFESSOR OF HISTORY
SCHOOL OF CITIZENSHIP AND PUBLIC AFFAIRS
SYRACUSE UNIVERSITY

NEW YORK
PRENTICE-HALL, INC.
1941

Preface

IN THE preparation of this volume, the needs of the student have been kept uppermost in my mind. No attempt has been made to include all of the personalities or events that may be of peculiar significance to Englishmen. Important as these are to the students of Great Britain, they appear to have less value to the American student of British history. For this reason the reader will not encounter detailed statements concerning the various ministers and cabinet members who have advised the Crown. It has been my purpose to write a history of England for American students. Moreover, this volume does not seek to exalt "Drum and Trumpet." Military and naval history has not been ignored, but the emphasis has been placed upon the antecedents of these activities, the essential features of wars, and the consequences that have followed. Instead of reciting the heroic deeds of generals and admirals and of the battles they won or lost, attention has been given to those whose life and treasure were spent in these conflicts.

It will also be noticed that while considerable space is devoted to political, constitutional, and foreign affairs, it is not done at the expense of social, economic, and intellectual activities. A history of England is not a record of kings and queens; it is not a narrative of statesmen who have directed the conduct of foreign affairs, fought wars, or promoted legislation. Rather, it is a record of the English people, of their struggle for democratic government, their desire to gain economic security and to advance the spiritual and intellectual opportunities of their children. For this reason material has been presented that reflects the political and social aspirations of the English people. Selected material also appears relative to travel, entertainment, amusement, diet, and dress.

In the field of English literature no attempt has been made to duplicate that which the student experiences in other college courses; nor is much attention given to such well-known writers as Bacon, Shakespeare, and Browning. In every age the great mass of the reading public has found relaxation and entertainment in lighter and less well-known writings. Although these may not be rated as classics and seldom are referred to in the standard works or courses on English literature, they, nevertheless, captured the imagination of the reading public and should be viewed as an integral part of the literary history of England.

My indebtedness to the contributions of other writers is most apparent, and I trust that sufficient recognition of their help appears in the text and bibliographical notes. In preparing the bibliography, it was decided to include only those works of special distinction and merit. Moreover, in citing the date of publication I have used, in most cases, the latest date rather than that of original publication. No special consideration has been given to pamphlet and magazine material. Government publications and original sources are mentioned only when they may be of special value. In general, English pounds have been computed in terms of American dollars.

I wish to thank The Travel and Industrial Development Association of Great Britain and Ireland, of New York City, for permission to reproduce many of the illustrations which appear in this volume. The cartoons from *Punch* were "reproduced by permission of the Proprietors of *Punch*." I am obligated to Dr. Philip Taylor of Syracuse University for reading and correcting those chapters relating to recent foreign affairs. I am also greatly indebted to Dean Carl Wittke of Oberlin College for guidance and counsel. With a patience that has often surprised me, he has smoothed many an awkward passage and has offered valuable suggestions as to content and interpretation.

W. Freeman Galpin

Contents

Genealogical Tables, Maps and Charts, Illustrations

GENEALOGICAL TABLES

MAPS AND CHARTS

ILLUSTRATIONS

CHAPTER I

England Before the Saxons

FEW nations, since the seventeenth century, have played as large a rôle in the history of mankind as Great Britain. Much of this preëminence is due to England's insular position. Although only a narrow ribbon of water separates her from the Continent, this barrier has been sufficient to check all foreign invasions since 1066. On the other hand, while insularity has not prevented Britain from engaging in European disputes, the fact remains that the Channel has kept her out of many of the squabbles that have caused Europeans so much suffering. Relative isolation, moreover, has aided in the growth and development of a civilization which few states have equalled and from which many have borrowed. Through trade, commerce, and imperialistic tendencies, this culture has been carried to all parts of the globe. There is scarcely a nation that has not reaped some benefit from England's numerous contributions. None, however, is more indebted to that nation than the United States of America. For this reason, if for no other, Americans have ample cause to study the history of a people in which so much of their political, social, and economic fabric had its beginnings.

Salient Geographic Features of the British Isles

England is but a part of an island group which is known geographically as the British Isles. Of these the largest is called Great Britain and includes within its area Scotland, Wales, and England. Next, in size and importance, is Ireland. In addition there are a number of smaller units like the Isles of Wight and Man, and to the far north, the Hebrides and Shetland groups. From a geological point of view all of these islands rest on an extension of the European shore line, which is known as the Continental Shelf. The seas that wash the British Isles are relatively shallow and generally are less than six hundred feet in depth. On the other hand, though there are hills and mountains, the elevation is rather low, a feature which permits easy access to the interior by a number of tidal rivers and bays. Indeed, there is no place in Great Britain that is as much as a hundred miles from tidal water. As a result there is a very extensive coastline dotted, chiefly on the eastern side, by many excellent harbors. The total area enclosed by the coastline is less than ninety thousand square miles, of which England alone embraces over half. Add to this figure the thirty-three thousand square miles of Ireland, and one has the approximate size of the British Isles.

Looking more closely at England, one notes that if a line were drawn from Exeter in the southwest to Durham in the northeast, the area to the left would be marked by hills and mountains while that to the right would be characterized by lowlands. The latter half has a soil that is suitable in most places for farming, while the former is rough and rocky. Bisecting this diagonal line is the Pennine Ridge, which sweeps down from the north and forms what might be called the backbone of the island. The presence of this ridge has materially affected the life of the English people. In the first place it has permitted a relatively easy penetration into Scotland as the lowland to the right and, save for the Cheviot Hills and the Tweed River, continues unbroken from England into Scotland. There have been frequent tribal and national wars between the people who have lived in these separate states. At the same time, trade, communication, and culture have passed freely back and forth, thereby creating a greater degree of similarity between southern Scotland and northern England than between the Highlands and Lowlands of Scotland. Again, flowing from the Pennine Ridge are many streams, few of which are swift enough to develop electrical power. Most of these streams flow east and have their outlets in waters that are also fed by the Seine, Scheldt, Elbe, and Rhine, a fact in itself of great commercial value to England. These eastward-flowing streams cross an area which is rich in arable- and pasture-land. Wheat is grown in abundance northeast of the Thames, a section which is also suitable for oats, barley, peas, and beans. All these grains are likewise raised south of the Thames, along whose banks rises many a busy factory. Industrial pursuits today engage the attention of thousands in the Lowlands while London itself has become one of the world's greatest commercial centers.

Most of the manufacturing in modern England, however, is found to the left of the Exeter-Durham line. The rich coal and iron fields in this area account for this industrial activity, though the moist temperature and the commercial advantages of the valley of the Mersey should not be forgotten. Shipbuilding, textiles, pottery, hardware, chemicals, machinery, and iron and steel goods are produced in large quantities within this area. Of agriculture there is relatively little. The firm and rocky nature of the soil, plus a very heavy rainfall, makes farming generally unprofitable. The warm and moist westerlies, sweeping in from the southwest, encounter the hills and ranges of west and northwest England and yield a precipitation that exceeds sixty inches a year in some localities. Even to the right of this mountainous area, a generous rain falls. Were it not for the westerlies and the warm waters of the North Atlantic, England would experience rather low temperatures. The presence of these moderating influences has been a fortunate and decisive factor in the history of England. Seldom does the temperature within the Lowlands fall below forty degrees or rise above seventy-five. Western and southern England is even warmer. In both areas, winter is in no way comparable to a winter in Michigan or Minnesota, although these states are in about the same degree of latitude. Seldom if ever do the English rivers become completely frozen, while the presence of a snow storm is sufficient to warrant articles and pictures in the daily papers.

Scotland in general has many of the characteristics of England, though the temperature is relatively cooler, particularly in the Highlands, while the rainfall is usually heavier. Manufacturing, shipbuilding, fishing, and agriculture occupy the attention of the inhabitants of this country today. The great port of Glasgow is the chief city. Ireland, on the other hand, has little manufacturing outside of its well-known linens. Its agriculture, moreover, is limited by reason of the excessive rains which fall upon this saucer-like island. Oats are grown in considerable abundance, but wheat does not thrive to any marked extent. This moisture has resulted in the growth of a dairying activity that bulks large in the export of that island.

Prehistoric Man

These salient geographic and economic factors are common knowledge and are often viewed as having always been active in the life of the people of the British Isles. Every schoolboy knows that England is an island, but not every one knows that Britain, at one time, was an integral part of a greater European continent. Today, a visitor to Calais may look across the Channel and see, if the weather is favorable, the historic white cliffs of Dover; he may also, if so minded, tour through Picardy and see similar geological formations. Centuries ago, the chalk ranges of England ran in an unbroken line to those of France, and over these hills, through the dense forests that extended far to the west, roamed many a wild animal, such as the hyena, hippopotamus, and the mammoth.

The Thames, moreover, flowed at a higher level than it does today and emptied itself into a mighty Rhine, which had its outlet far to the north. Into this primitive and prehistoric Britain came Palaeolithic man. Whence he came, no one knows, although it was probably a quest for food that prompted these rugged hunters to cross a plateau that is now washed by the Channel. Southeastern England, which seems to have been favored then as now with a genial climate, was peopled by this race whose average height was only a little over five feet. Although their skeletons dot this area, remains have been found as far north as Lincolnshire and west as far as the Severn. Tools made chiefly of flint and rough stone also have been found, as has a single pictorial representation of a horse crudely sketched on a bone. Interesting and inviting as these records are to the imagination, they are actually of little value in the history of England, as Palaeolithic man left no cultural traits that have influenced to any extent those who followed him in Britain.

Exactly what happened to these "old stone age" men, for so the Palaeolithic race has been called, no one knows. Their decline and disappearance were gradual and are clouded with mystery and uncertainty. The advances of an ice sheet must have made life difficult to sustain. Battle and murder, moreover, meted out by a more vigorous invading race, doubtless hurried the end of these earlier inhabitants. Finally, it should be observed that an amalgamation of these two races resulted in an absorption of the former by the latter. When this process was completed, the "old stone age" man had gone; and in his place there ruled a "new stone age" man, or, as he is also known, Neolithic man.

Neolithic man, of European origin, was probably in England before the bridgeland connecting England with the Continent gave way to the Channel. The greater part of these invaders arrived in England after this geological change and in the course of time swarmed over all parts of the British Isles.

Their remains, as based upon an examination of many ancient tombs, reveal that they were taller than their predecessors, possessed elongated skulls, and had faces somewhat oval in shape. Equipped with tools made of stone, flint, bone, and reindeer antler, these people built rude dwellings of wood, dirt, and stone. Often their homes were located close to a quarry and were partly sunk in the ground, for which they have been called "pit dwellings." Flanked or faced by these protecting walls, Neolithic man defended himself against wild animals and the marauding bands of his own people. Hunters and fighters they were, with little interest in agriculture, gathering food and clothing from the game they caught or from the animals they domesticated, and building, by the toil of servants and slaves, sepulchral chambers in which they buried or burned their dead with the weirdest of funeral rites. Probably these rites, the knowledge of which is based upon the deposits of bones, charred or otherwise, and on weapons and pottery that have been found in these graves, indicate some type of a religious faith. Of their political life nothing is known. National and even tribal life does not seem to have existed, although a village of pit dwellings, like that discovered on Hayes Common with its one hundred and sixty homes, must have had some form of local government. The coöperative construction of their elaborate burial chambers, the sinking of shafts for flint mining, and the possible erection of extensive hill-top fortifications add strength to the assumption that Neolithic man enjoyed some type of community life.

Neolithic man's domination in England must have lasted a long time. How long cannot be stated, though it is clearly established that before his power waned, a new order was in the making. In other words, the late "new stone age" was transitional in nature. A new race, possessed of superior culture, had entered the island and had slowly undermined the older civilization. Ultimately, the entire country was conquered by these invaders whose culture was characterized by the use of bronze. The arrival of these new people probably was not earlier than 2000 B.C.

Bronze Age man doubtless came from the lowlands of Europe and areas to the north. They probably were a mixed race composed of those who had round skulls and long bodies and of others who were shorter in stature but whose heads were more elongated. Of the two groups, however, the former were far more numerous, though the latter, as well as other types, were common. Southeastern England seems to have been the center of this culture, though remains of both groups have been found throughout the British Isles. Their homes were often mere pit dwellings, though circular stone huts topped either by timber or turf seem to have been common. Occasionally, a series of these huts were enclosed for defensive purposes, as war seems to have been largely the order of the day. Hill forts have been located into which neighboring people doubtless moved during periods of attack by some adjacent group or by invaders from across the sea. For weapons and tools, these early inhabitants used stone, flint, and bronze, the latter being most skillfully worked and fashioned. Bronze knives, daggers, saws, chisels, and the like have been found in large quantities. At times, these implements were ornamented with designs of gold and amber. Gold and amber were also used for rings, armlets, necklaces, and other bits of jewelry. Further indication of a growing culture may be seen in the drinking cups, food vessels, and cinerary urns, many of which bore decorations and designs of simple or complicated pattern.

The manufacturing of these various articles must have provided some degree of industrial activity and management. Further, bronze tools permitted the felling of trees and the cultivation of soil for agricultural purposes, an activity that must have grown as the population increased, as big game became scarcer and as the demand for pastureland developed. Agrarian life became more and more important as the bronze age advanced. Oxen and horses were used for ploughing and hauling, while sickles and stone mullers were employed for harvesting and grinding. From their domesticated animals, the fish that was caught, and the game that was killed, as well as from bronze, gold, and amber, came material from which pins, buttons, razors, tweezers, leather garments, and even woolen cloth was made. These and many other objects indicate the accumulation of a greater wealth and commonweal than had been enjoyed by their predecessors in Britain.

Much of the evidence for these observations has been gleaned from an examination of cairns, round barrows, and burial chambers. Within these tombs, students have found definite proof as to the religious beliefs and practices of Bronze Age man. Cremation and inhumation were both common, while the presence of animal remains, and even of human beings, indicates that some form of sacrifice accompanied the burial rites. Many of these chambers were surrounded by circular areas of stone, some of which, judging by those still extant, must have been of great size. Of these none is better known than Stonehenge. Probably, in the case of Stonehenge and certain others, these monoliths served a religious purpose. What these rites were or what crafty priests presided over them no one knows, any more than we know why these upright stones were reared. "Time-honored even when the Roman first landed . . . Stonehenge was standing in all its glory when the Greek explorer Pytheas came." Pytheas was the first to make known the existence of Britain to the civilized world. Very little is known concerning his actual discoveries, as most of his writings have come down to us in fragments, and even these seem to have been garbled by later writers. From these extracts, however, it is established that the ancient world was introduced to the present geographic features of the island as well as to some of the customs and habits of the Britains, for so Pytheas called the inhabitants. One of the most interesting comments made by this writer described the tin mines of Cornwall and the domestic and foreign trade in that article.

STONEHENGE, NEAR SALISBURY

From this statement, one is led to believe that an overseas traffic in this commodity had existed for some time preceding the advent of the Celt into Britain.

The Advent of the Celts

Scholars are by no means agreed as to when the Celts first appeared in England or from what part of the Continent they migrated. Some writers, pointing to certain similarities between Celtic culture and that of the eastern Mediterranean, hold to a theory that would credit the latter areas as the original home of the Celts. Others contend that these people swarmed out of central Asia, while again some insist that they were Alpine in origin. In any case those that crossed the Channel must have come from the western part of Europe. Equally contentious are the views as to the date of their arrival. Most historians, however, tend to agree that the earliest of these invaders did not touch the island before 1200 to 600 B.C. Others of the same race followed, the last being a tribe known as the Belgae, who appear to have crossed the Channel sometime before the middle of the last century before Christ. Between these two limits of time, the Bronze Age man was conquered by the Celt whose culture spread throughout the British Isles. More significant is the fact that this civilization has continued to influence the subsequent history of these islands from that day to this.

Celtic culture was characterized by the use of iron. Not that bronze, copper, or stone disappeared, but that this newer and stronger metal became more common. Iron was used freely to fashion weapons of war and tools for industry. It was also employed in the making of mirrors, brooches, pins, and bracelets. Iron axes and saws felled mighty trees, and plows, similarly constructed and drawn by oxen, turned virgin soil into arable land. Cereals supplemented by huge quantities of meat gained from the domesticated ox, pig, and wild animals, bulked large in the diet of these people. Milk was a staple article of food, while a rough and potent mead seems to have been generously used by all. The dependence of the Celtic farmer upon iron must have stimulated the mining of that article already in demand for other purposes. Mining must have been one of the chief industrial activities of these people. Skilled and unskilled labor was also used in the making of beads, bronze-mounted drinking cups, and pottery elaborately ornamented with bands, scrolls and curves, sometimes of coral and amber. Household utensils were mostly made by hand, although the potter's wheel was used for the cinerary urns and larger vases, and bowl-like dishes.

Celtic homes, nucleated or otherwise, were chiefly round huts crudely formed of stone and timber, though caves were used by the poorer classes. Those more fortunate in worldly goods lived in homes of several rooms. Judging from the remains of these more advanced dwellings it would appear that many were grouped in villages and small towns like Camulo-dunum (Colchester), Verulamium (St. Albans), Lundinium (London) and Glastonbury (the last being a lake or marsh village of wealth and culture). Hill forts, though chiefly used as places of refuge in time of war, seem to have been the permanent abode of others.

Military skill and physical strength, plus ownership of land and cattle, as well as religious prominence, became the basis for a social stratification. Lowest in this scale were the poorer classes, many of whom doubtless had strains of neolithic ancestry. Living in caves or miserable huts and dressed in skins or the coarsest of woolen cloths, these people must have furnished much of the labor that was needed on the farms or in the mines. Their lot must have been extremely unfortunate. Above these laborers, though considerably fewer in number, were the hunters, farmers, and traders, who in turn were topped by a noble class of chiefs, kings, and priests. And although this was an order made by man for men, women were by no means ignored. Here and there we encounter tribes that were ruled by queens. The practice of dowry and of polyandry also adds proof to this statement. Then again, the extensive use of costly and attractive articles of toilet, such as mirrors, rouges, and the like, indicates a feminine touch that seems to have been highly pleasing to man. The latter also showed signs of vanity as he often wore his hair long, shaved his face and carefully raised a most impressive moustache. Woolen and linen cloth, brilliantly colored or braided and held together by an elaborate pin or brooch, constituted the usual dress of the privileged class. These more fortunate people also enjoyed political power, though to what extent or in what manner is not known. It is established, however, that the Celts were in a tribal stage and were ruled over by kings or chieftains. In all probability, a group of elders or nobles assisted the king, for it seems difficult to believe that absolute authority rested in one man's hands.

Definite limitation upon royal power was present in a religious life that was highly polytheistic in nature and institutionalized by a crafty priesthood, the Druids. Formal theology did not exist, though belief in the transmigration of souls and even perhaps in immortality, strongly suggests some organized faith. In any case, whatever faith was adhered to, its ritual was zealously administered by the Druids. These priests were members of a sacerdotal hierarchy, whose secrets were closed to all outsiders. To stamp their power upon their subjects' superstitious minds, the Druids perpetrated crude and barbarous rites in the name of some deity. Further signs of their power may be seen in their immunity from military service and taxation; moreover, they constituted the educated class on the island. Whatever unity existed among the Celtic tribes must have centered in Druidism which was also the faith of the Gauls across the Channel.

Contact between Britain and Europe is evidenced in other ways. The presence of certain Continental objects of art points to some intercourse, while there was, in all probability, an export trade in tin. The bulk of this trade was in the hands of foreigners, though the Celts retained control of a coastwise trade. Most of this domestic traffic was inland and followed ancient paths or trails. Although the greater part of both foreign and domestic trade was conducted by barter and exchange, the use of money was not uncommon. Gold, silver, and bronze coins, many of which bore inscriptions, were used to facilitate commerce. Tin tokens were also employed, and iron bars appear to have passed for currency in the western parts of the island.

Celtic culture represented a social stage far advanced over that of the Stone Age. Government and commerce, religion and family life, seem to have had some basis of organization of which many evidences have been unearthed in burial grounds. Certain improvements in agriculture, such as the one-field system of farming, reflect more advanced methods in cultivation, methods which survived long after the Celt lost control in Britain. Beyond these remains, certain techniques in industry, the presence of place-names and a few words like "boast," "pot," and "down," and certain physical characteristics, there is little in modern English life that may safely be said to have had a Celtic origin.

Roman Britain

The growth of Celtic culture in Britain was paralleled by the rise of Rome, whose desire for world conquest led her into Britain. Roman writers and rulers had known of the island for some time. So busy, however, was that state in European affairs that it gave scant attention to the petty Celtic kingdoms beyond the Channel. It was not, therefore, until the middle of the last century before the Christian era that any expansion took place in that direction. At that time Julius Caesar was governor of Gaul. Caesar, it appears, was anxious to play a dominant rôle in Roman politics, but was well aware that he first must build for himself financial power and military reputation. Having conquered the Gauls, Caesar now turned his attention toward Britain, whose recent interference in Gaul had caused him considerable trouble. Convinced that Roman authority in Gaul was endangered by the Celts of Britain, Caesar laid plans for an invasion.

Accordingly, having destroyed the naval power of the Veneti, allies of the Britains, Caesar led an army into England during the summer of 55 B.C. Success did not attend this adventure, which after all was little more than a reconnoitering expedition in anticipation of a more thorough attack the next year. In July, 54 B.C., Caesar attacked Britain with a large force, and easily brushed aside the Celts who sought to check his march inland. The passage of the Stour and Thames, however, was more stubbornly resisted by the Celts, who also nearly succeeded in destroying Caesar's line of communications. By this time Caesar realized that an effective conquest would entail a greater outlay in men and money than he had expected. Reports, moreover, from Gaul indicated the need of his return. Having exacted tribute and hostages from those tribes he had conquered, Caesar crossed the Channel never again to return to Britain.

For nearly a century Britain was left to herself. Native rulers rose and fell, and no noticeable attempt was made towards political unification. Petty jealousy among the various tribes constantly checked any development along that line. Further, many a defeated chieftain hastened to Rome in the hope of gaining help and protection. At times Rome considered another invasion, but it was not until 43 A.D. that the Imperial Legions appeared in Britain. Then it was that the Emperor Claudius undertook what proved to be a conquest of most of the island. What Claudius started, others, notably Agricola, finished, with the result that by the close of the first century Roman power was well established over most of

England, Wales, and the Lowlands of Scotland. Later penetrations extended this control as far as the Clyde. Stout native resistance, however, forced the Romans to withdraw to the Tyne and Solway. Connecting these two points was Hadrian's wall, seventy-three and a half miles in length and faced by a ditch thirty-four feet wide and nine feet deep. In height the wall was sixteen feet, while in thickness it measured between seven and eight feet. Here and there at important points watch towers and military stations were erected.

The steady onward march of the Roman soldiers did not mean that peace prevailed in those parts that had been conquered. Indeed, there were several serious insurrections, of which that led by Boadicea, Queen of the Iceni, was the most important. In each case, however, the well-drilled legionnaires won the day. Ultimately most of the country south of Hadrian's wall saw the folly of further resistance and accepted Roman domination. Garrisons continued to be posted at strategic centers, but at no time, with the exceptions noted, did the Celts seek to overthrow the Imperial Government. Except for the presence of these troops or the passage of armies to the North or Welsh stations, the inhabitants of Britain seldom encountered the military. Nevertheless, it is apparent that the military formed the dominant element in Roman Britain and that behind this steel defense a Roman-British civilization developed. Governmental efficiency plus the influence of trade did much to further the spread of this culture which fastened itself quite firmly, particularly in southeastern England.

Concerning the actual extent and nature of this civilization, our sources are none too generous. Few written records appear, in consequence of which the historian is forced to lean heavily upon archaeological research. On the basis of this evidence, it may be asserted that Roman Britain was essentially non-urban in nature. Probably, there were not more than thirty towns, of which London, Colchester, Gloucester, York,

Canterbury, Aldborough, Exeter, and Winchester were the most important. Within these areas Roman officers, traders, and merchants so completely dominated life that the Celtic population largely lost its identity. Temples, forums, baths, and paved streets were to be found in each community. Cleanliness and order predominated, although comfort was not overlooked, as is attested by the fact that Roman and Celt heated

Courtesy Assoc. British and Irish Railways, Inc.

ROMAN BATH AT BATH.

their homes and bathed themselves in warm water. The tourist of today may, for a small fee, see one of these baths in the very heart of London, or visit the town of Bath where the original pedestals for the columns and the steps leading to the baths are in a state of splendid preservation. Outside the town and facing a paved highway was the cemetery in which the dead were buried in coffins of wood, stone, or lead. Cremation was also practiced. The remains of these burials as well as tombstones and inscriptions have been found in large numbers throughout the island. A few of the more prosperous centers may have had arenas at which the populace witnessed reproductions of the games and festivals of Rome.

Connecting these towns and crossing the island at different points were a number of roads. These highways were built primarily for military purposes and were constructed by trained engineers to withstand heavy usage and the ravages of time. Watling Street, which ran from Dover to Chester, was one of the most famous of these highways. Along these roads at centers like Canterbury or Rochester, as well as at stated intervals, horses might be exchanged and accommodations secured by the traveler. Stone markers, moreover, guided these people to their destination. Here and there as one rode over these highways, villages and villas came into view. The villa was a large landed estate owned and occupied by a Roman lord and worked by a group of dependent Celtic cultivators. The village, however, was an un-Romanized agricultural unit inhabited by a Celtic peasantry which clung tenaciously to primitive customs and traditions. Their homes were but one-roomed huts, and their holdings were limited to small enclosed plots of arable land. The villas cultivated large open areas surrounding a house that was constructed and equipped on approved Roman lines. Probably the greater part of southern Britain was covered by these villas, which should be viewed as the most characteristic feature of Roman Britain. In general the bulk of the rural population was Celtic, and while it accepted many Roman customs, it continued to adhere to its own culture. Latin, though written and spoken generally within the towns, was not commonly used in the country.

From a governmental point of view, Britain was a province under the control of a military governor. For administrative purposes the country was subdivided into districts and towns, the latter being accorded in some instances an independent status comparable to the continental *municipia*. Often the direction of local affairs was placed in the hands of some native prince, as Rome did not wish to interfere too much with local custom and law as long as no formidable opposition was encountered. Even in religious matters supervision was not exacting. Acceptance of the Emperor as God and of the state religion was required of all, though the presence of different faiths illustrates the tolerance of the government. Druidism alone suffered at the hands of Rome because its priestly caste was constantly seeking to arouse the Celts to rebellion. The smashing defeat of the latter at Anglesey by Paulinus in 60 A.D. marked the end of that creed. Other faiths arose in time, some of which were Oriental in origin and for a while had a numerous following. Mithraism, probably a form of sun worship and especially popular among the Roman soldiers on the frontier, had its adherents as did Christianity. Concerning the origin of the latter in Britain, there is a lack of information, though it is likely that Christianity reached the island in the wake of the Roman soldier and trader. By the fourth century, Christians in Britain must have constituted a large share of the total population. British bishops, moreover, attended a general church council at Arles while numerous remains of the Christian monogram X P have been found. Further evidence of the presence of the Christian faith exists in the visits of Germanus, Archbishop of Auxerre, to Britain in the fifth century. Germanus came to Britain to stamp out the heretical views of the British cleric, Pelagius. Reference should also be made to Patricius, a Christian and well-born Roman Britain, who was carried to Ireland by a band of Celtic pirates. Later Patricius, or St. Patrick to use his more common name, escaped from his captors, visited Gaul, and returned to his home in western Britain. In the meantime St. Patrick had become an ecclesiastic and, answering a call from Ireland, went there, where he did splendid work in converting the Celts. Finally, there should be noted the basilica at Silchester, which some authorities claim to be Christian in origin.

The growth of Christianity in Britain came at a time when Roman authority in that island reached its height. Shortly thereafter the Imperial Government was faced by a number of problems which ultimately led to its downfall. Internal disorder was matched by invasions from without. By the middle of the fourth century the situation was rendered acute by repeated invasions by the Picts and Scots and by the withdrawal of Roman troops to the Continent. At the same time roving bands of Saxons swept down upon the island. Ultimately, by the close of the fifth century, all semblance of Roman authority was destroyed, and England was at the mercy of the Teutonic invaders. Superior fighting ability enabled the latter to win the day over the Celt, who stubbornly resisted every inch of territory. Not until the opening of the seventh century were the Saxons supreme in most of England.

Concerning the story of this conquest there is little direct information at hand, though there can be no doubt of the disappearance of Roman-Celtic culture. A cross-sectional view of England in the seventh century doubtless would reveal many signs of this civilization which has long since disappeared. Chester must have still retained much of its former beauty and greatness. Its appearance, as late as the twelfth century, has been described by one writer as a city surrounded by walls of brick or tiles and composed of "immense palaces, a gigantic tower, beautiful baths, remains of temples and sites of theaters almost entirely surrounded by excellent walls in part remaining; also both within and without the circumference of the walls subterranean constructions, watercourses, vaults with passages . . . and furnaces constructed with wonderful art, the narrow sides of which exhale heat by concealed spiracles." It is also of interest to note that, in the middle of the eighteenth century, the citizens of Littleborough witnessed the destruction of a paved ford over the Trent. Probably many other Roman buildings and works escaped the ravages of the Teuton only to fall before the pick and shovel of later generations. Had medieval England been more careful of these treasures, our knowledge of Roman Britain would be more complete. Again, the sheer weight of numbers, the superior fighting ability and governmental organization of the Saxon must have ground those Celts who survived the conquest to a point where their blood and culture became lost in a developing English civilization. Roman law and administration largely disappeared even before this; and although present day legal institutions contain much that is Roman, they are probably a result of the Norman conquest of the eleventh century. The presence of the Norman explains most of the Latin words and forms in modern English, although a few of these may be traced back to Roman Britain. Certain students also credit the Roman with having influenced agricultural methods, and there seems to be little doubt that some of the fens and swamps of eastern England were drained in part by the Romans. The Romans also left behind them a number of tablets, inscriptions, bits of pottery, columns, and walls. Few of these remains have been found in Wales, Cornwall, or the Lake district. In these sections Celtic populations were able to withstand Saxon invasion. But even here it is reasonable to assume that, as the years passed, the Celt more and more lost his coating of Roman civilization, so that, with the exception of physical remains, little was left that had been Latin. One notable exception exists in the continuation and development of Christianity in western Britain, which was so influenced by native forces that historians have commonly called it Celtic Christianity. It may safely be said, therefore, that English life and customs of to-day owe little to the Roman who ruled in Britain longer than the United States has existed as an independent nation.

SELECTED BIBLIOGRAPHY

No attempt will be made in this volume to present an exhaustive list of references nor will much attention be given to periodical articles. Those desiring this type of information will find the following of help: C. Gross' *Sources and Literature of English History, from the earliest times to about 1485* (New York, 1915); *Bibliography of British History: Stuart Period, 1603–1714,* edited by G. Davies (Oxford, 1928); *Dictionary of English History,* edited by S. J. M. Low and F. S. Pulling (New York, 1928); H. L. Cannon's *Reading References for English History* (Boston, 1910), and *A Guide to Historical Literature* (New York, 1931). Leslie Stephen and Sir S. Lee have edited the *Dictionary of National Biography,* 36 vols. (London, 1885–1900). Several supplementary volumes have appeared.

For geographical, geological and racial material the student should consult H. J. Mackinder's *Britain and the British Seas* (New York, 1914); *The Clarendon Geography* (Oxford, 1919); H. F. Osborn's *Men of the Old Stone Age* (New York, 1915); W. Z. Ripley's *Races of Europe* (New York, 1910); N. Ault's *Life in Ancient Britain* (London, 1920); H. J. Peake's *English Villages* (London, 1922), and J. Rys' *Celtic Britain* (London, 1904). The literature on Roman Britain is most extensive. Valuable insight may be gained from: F. J. Haverfield's *Roman Occupation of Britain* (Oxford, 1924), and *Romanization of Roman Britain* (Oxford, 1912); B. C. A. Windle's *Romans in Britain* (London, 1923), and R. G. Collingwood's *Roman Britain* (London, 1923). The influence of the villa upon subsequent English history is reviewed by G. Seebohm's *The English Village Community* (London, 1883), and P. Vinogradoff's *Growth of the Manor* (London, 1925). The *Roman Era in Britain* by J. Ward (London, 1920) is rich in information as to archaeological findings. *Roman Britain* (Oxford, 1936), by R. G. Collingwood and J. N. L. Myres, is a recent study of merit.

General supplementary readings for this chapter and for those that follow may be found in the *Political History of England,* 12 vols., edited by W. Hunt and R. L. Poole (London, 1905–1910); *History of England,* 7 vols., edited by C. Oman (London, 1904–1913); *Cambridge Medieval History,* 7 vols. (Cambridge, 1911–1935); *Cambridge Modern History,* 14 vols. (Cambridge, 1902–1912); *Cambridge History of British Foreign Policy,* 3 vols. (Cambridge, 1922–1923); *Social England,* 6 vols., in 12, edited by H. D. Traill and J. S. Mann (London, 1909), and *The History of British Civilization* by E. Wingfield-Stratford (New York, 1930). In addition the student should introduce himself to J. A. Froude's *History of England* (New York, 1865–1870); Leopold von Ranke's *History of England* (Oxford, 1875), and the volumes by Sir James H. Ramsay which cover English history from the period of the

Roman occupation to the advent of the Tudors. P. H. Brown's *History of Scotland* (Cambridge, 1902–1909); J. E. Lloyd's *History of Wales* (London, 1912), and P. W. Joyce's *Short History of Ireland* (London, 1911) are standard works.

For constitutional and legal history, as well as political theory the following are of value: G. B. Adams' *Constitutional History of England* (New York, 1934); F. W. Maitland's *Constitutional History of England* (Cambridge, 1908); A. B. White's *Making of the English Constitution* (New York, 1925); W. Stubbs' *Constitutional History of England* (Oxford, 1874–1878); Sir W. A. Anson's *Law and Custom of the Constitution* (Oxford, 1909); W. S. Holdsworth's *History of English Law* (London, 1922–1923), and H. J. Laski's *Political Thought in England from Locke to Bentham* (New York, 1920).

Economic and social history is conveniently summarized by E. P. Cheyney's *Introduction to the Industrial and Social History of England* (New York, 1920); F. W. Tickner's *Social and Industrial History of England* (London, 1915); C. M. Waters' *Economic History of England* (Oxford, 1925); W. Cunningham's *Growth of English Industry and Commerce* (Cambridge, 1915–1921); E. Lipson's *Economic History of England* (London, 1929–1931), and W. Page's *Commerce and Industry* (London, 1919).

In the field of ecclesiastical history W. R. W. Stephens and W. Hunt have edited the *History of the English Church* (London, 1899–1910). Felix Makower's *Constitutional History and Constitution of the Church of England* (London, 1895); R. W. Dixon's *History of the Church of England from the Abolition of the Roman Jurisdiction* (Oxford, 1877–1902), and Henry O. Wakeman's *Introduction to the History of the Church of England* (London, 1920) are standard works.

W. V. Moody and R. M. Lovett have made a valuable contribution in their *History of English Literature* (New York, 1918). The most complete and authoritative work is the *Cambridge History of English Literature,* edited by A. W. Ward and A. R. Waller, (New York, 1907–1917). G. E. B. Saintsbury's *Short History of English Literature* (New York, 1898) is a manual of value.

Colonial expansion, imperialism and diplomacy are covered by H. Robinson's *The Development of the British Empire* (Boston, 1936); W. H. Woodward's *Short History of the Expansion of the British Empire* (New York, 1912); *Historical Geography of the British Colonies,* edited by C. P. Lucas (Oxford, 1888–1923); *Cambridge History of the British Empire,* edited by J. H. Rose, to be in eight volumes (Cambridge, 1930–   ); A. W. Tilby's *English People Overseas* (London, 1908–1914); *Oxford Survey of the British Empire,* edited by A. J. Herbertson (Oxford, 1914); J. R. Seeley's *Expansion of England* (London, 1895); R. Jebb's *Studies in Colonial Administration* (London, 1905); H. E. Egerton's *British Foreign Policy* (London, 1917), and G. P. Gooch and

J. H. B. Masterman's *Century of British Foreign Policy* (London, 1917). J. W. Fortescue's *History of the British Army* (London, 1899–1930), and W. L. Clowes' *Royal Navy* (London, 1897–1903) are the standard military and naval works.

CHAPTER II

The Saxon and Norman Conquests

The Saxons Invade Britain

THE advent of the Angles and Saxons into Britain was an event of supreme importance. Exactly when these people invaded the island is not known. The construction, in the late third century, of a chain of forts, "more imposing at the present day" than the ruined foundations of the Roman forts in northern Britain, from the Wash to Southampton, indicates that Britain was being attacked that early. Further raids followed in spite of these defenses, and by the fifth century this armed area was placed under the command of a Roman official, the Count of the Saxon Shore. No definite penetration, however, was undertaken until the middle of that century. Even then it is not clearly established whether the Teutons came as foes or friends, as tradition credits the Celts with having asked certain of these tribes to aid them in their wars against the Picts and Scots. In any event before many years had passed, the invader had gained a firm footing in southeastern England, while by the close of the sixth century most of eastern and central Britain was in the hands of the Saxons. One may picture the first attacks as having been those of an invading force with spoil and conquest as the chief motives. Closely akin to these factors was the restlessness which pervaded the tribes north of the Rhine, as well as the probable pressure of alien races to the east. Recent studies stress the scarcity of arable land in Germany as the primary factor in bringing about the Saxon invasion of Britain.

In examining the nature of this conquest one must be cautious in accepting the repeated accounts of the wholesale slaughter and extermination of the Celts. Armed resistance doubtless met fierce punishment, but it is hard to believe that the invaders slew men, women, and children merely for the sake of killing. Historical evidence, moreover, argues against this assumption. The continued existence of slavery throughout the Saxon age points to the persistency of Celtic blood. Again, the utilization of Celtic place-names by the aggressor should not be overlooked. An examination of Saxon burial grounds, reveals, in some cases, the presence of Celtic remains. Moreover, there is a school of historical writing which insists upon the survival of the villa to the eleventh century and to the continued presence of urban life; nor should it be forgotten that Wales was never conquered, and that Devon, Cornwall, and Cumberland retained much that was Celtic for several centuries. Probably the victories gained by the Celts under Ambrosius Aurelianus and the "King Arthur" made famous by legend did much to stay the Saxon and thus give deeper root to Celtic culture in western England.

Ultimately the "scoundrels," as the Celtic writer, Gildas, styled the invaders, gained supremacy over most of England. It is to Gildas, and to his fellow countryman Nennius, as well as to the Roman historian Tacitus, the authors of the *Anglo-Saxon Chronicle,* the writings of the Venerable Bede, and the researches of modern archaeologists, that we are indebted for most of the information concerning the invasion and conquest. Scholars, having studied these sources, agree that the invaders were the Angles and Saxons whose original homes had been around the mouth of the Elbe and in the area drained by the Weser, Ems, and Ysel. These tribes spoke dialects of the same tongue and had many political and social traits in common— factors which ultimately aided in the unification of England.

In addition to the Angles and Saxons, there were the Jutes whose original home Bede placed beyond that of the Angles. Recent investigation has qualified this conclusion by suggesting that some of the Jutes may have come from those sections of Europe opposite Kent.

The Anglo-Saxon conquest was not a national undertaking. No single executive or centralized state directed the invasion. Rather, it was the result of a general movement of a number of related tribes who entered Britain in various waves that ultimately swept over most of the island. Each group was under some king or chief who, having carved for himself a suitable domain, sought to protect his holdings from Celtic uprisings or from the attack of some other Teutonic ruler. Decades followed during which the smaller units were absorbed by the larger ones, thus laying the foundations for the kingdoms of the seventh century, Essex, Sussex, Wessex, Kent, East Anglia, Mercia, and Northumbria, which, collectively, have been called the *heptarchy*.

Of these states Kent, Northumbria, Mercia, and Wessex were most important. Each of these kingdoms in turn attempted to impose its authority over all England. War and conquest was the order of the day though Ethelbert of Kent, Edwin of Northumbria, Offa of Mercia, and Ine of Wessex made important contributions to the legal, religious, and financial life of that age. Ultimately it remained for Wessex, in the eighth and ninth centuries, to assume the leadership of Saxon England and make a bid for supremacy over Scotland. Kings Cadwalla, Ine, and Egbert were the outstanding monarchs who, by war and expansion, achieved some degree of political unification among the various Teutonic peoples.

Christianity Enthroned

Brute force was not the only factor which had made this possible. Indeed, the humble doctrines of the Prince of Peace did as much, if not more, in consolidating the English states into one kingdom. Ever since the appearance of Christianity during the Roman period, the Church had been seeking to unify all people under one common creed. The Saxon invasions disrupted this movement, but with the reintroduction of Christianity by Augustine, in 597, heathenism had steadily given ground. Doubtless, Christianity with its emphasis upon the fatherhood of God, the brotherhood of man, and of the life immortal did much to soften men's hearts and make more easy the spread of a common faith. More important was the organization and discipline of the Roman Church. Parishes with their priests and dioceses with their bishops were planted as one king after another, from Ethelbert of Kent to Penda of Mercia, embraced the faith of Christ. Much of this success was due to Theodore of Tarsus, chief primate of Canterbury (669–690), who extended the authority of his see over that of York and helped to spread church law and custom throughout the island. Theodore is also remembered for having developed missionary, monastic, and educational activities. The significance of these forces may be appreciated by observing the attitudes and habits of the common soldier as he marched north under the banners of a Wessex king. Reared in the faith of Rome, this soldier paused and worshipped at the churches, shrines, and cathedrals which he encountered on his march. In each he witnessed the same service and ritual, listened to similar music, and heard prayers said in Latin. By his side there stood a man from Kent or East Anglia and, though each had come from a different state, all felt completely at home. Through its common service and universal tongue, the Roman Church knit a delicate and complex pattern which drew men of different areas into one united people.

In the meantime, contact had been established with the Celtic Church which had its stronghold in Ireland; but in contrast to Rome, the Celtic Church was weak in organization. Deacons, priests, and bishops were loosely grouped under the authority of monastic heads in a way that prevented the growth and development of any central government. What this Church lacked in organization, however, it more than made up for in asceticism and learning. By the sixth century, Ireland was dotted with monasteries which excelled all others in Europe in scholarship and missionary zeal. Into England and Europe the Celtic Church poured a steady stream of missionaries and culture, which did much to enhance the standing of Christianity at a time when the moral tone of Rome was at a low ebb. The activities of the Celtic Church were well known at Rome when Gregory the Great dispatched Augustine to Kent where he soon succeeded in converting the King to Christianity. Having won this victory, Augustine attempted to effect a reconciliation with the Celtic Church, whose adherents were numbered by the thousands in Wales and northern England. Augustine and his immediate successors failed in this mission and allowed the Celtic priests to make headway in the north and midland areas. By the middle of the seventh century, Northumbria, Mercia, and Essex had been won by the Celts. Further success was halted by Oswy, King of Northumbria. Oswy's wife was a member of the Roman faith and through her, his loyalty to the Celtic Church was lessened. At the same time some of the younger members of the Celtic clergy, notably Wilfrid of York, were advocating union with Rome. Wilfrid and his followers recognized that while their beloved Church had much for which to commend itself, the cause of Christ could be advanced best by uniting with the splendidly organized faith of Rome.

It seems odd that these two historic branches of a common faith had not merged long before. Both had much in common as to belief and doctrine; yet the two had been unable to reconcile detailed and minor differences. That the shape of one's tonsure, the form of baptism, or whether Easter should be celebrated on this or that day should become matters of violent controversy, may seem peculiar today. However, these differ-

ences may be explained by remembering that the Celtic Church
had been cut off from the Continent from the time of the
withdrawal of the Roman legions until the middle of the
sixth century. During this interval the Celtic Church had
grown in structure and power and, unwilling to lose these advantages, refused to accept the overlordship of Canterbury.
Had Augustine and his followers been a trifle more tactful or
had the Celtic bishops been less headstrong, these differences
might have been bridged much earlier. It remained for Oswy
to take the lead in solving these problems by calling a general
church council at Whitby in 664. At this gathering both sides
of the question were debated with the result that Oswy finally
was persuaded to embrace the faith of Rome. Tradition has
it that the King was led to this decision by reason of the fact
that Rome claimed to have in its hands the keys to heaven.
While the primacy of Peter may have weighed in the mind
of Oswy, who declared for Rome lest "When I come before
the gates of heaven, he who holds the keys should not open
unto me," it is more likely that the influence of his wife and
Wilfrid had more to do with the final decision. The splendor,
skill, and ability of those who argued for a church which was
international in scope must have had its effect upon Oswy.

Following the Council of Whitby, the Roman faith · had
things much its own way in England. Celtic missionaries
gradually withdrew only to find that the priests and monks of
Rome had made definite headway in Wales and Ireland. By
the close of the eighth century, the Papacy had become generally recognized throughout the British Isles. The Celtic influence, however, continued to affect the life of the English
Church for many decades, as may be seen by examining the
liberalism which existed in English thought and letters, and
in the missionary zeal of the Saxon clergy. At the same time
the example of a unified and compact church organization
could not but help toward greater political consolidation, especially as all now worshipped in the same way. Furthermore,

from the point of view of Rome, it was far better to have one united kingdom in England than a series of smaller ones constantly contending for supremacy. Historically, therefore, it is important to note that in some respects an English Church preceded an English nation and that in the development of the latter the Church played an important rôle.

Alfred the Great

One more factor remains to be reviewed in an explanation of why the Saxon and Angle states finally accepted the domination of the house of Wessex. Sometime late in the eighth century, England experienced the first of a series of Danish invasions. Others followed during the next one hundred years. Self-protection, therefore, forced the English to unite in opposition to a common enemy. Wessex took the lead and under her kings, notably Egbert, Ethelwulf, and Alfred, struck many a telling blow. At times the invaders swept all before them, but then again, as at Ashdown Hills, they were thoroughly beaten. By the middle of the ninth century the Danes ceased their wanton pillaging and settled down in those places where their power had been established. Against these fortified areas Alfred led his troops and much ground was regained. Finally at Edington in Wiltshire the Danes were so soundly defeated that they were glad to accept the Peace of Wedmore (879). According to its terms, the Danes retired to an area north and east of Watling Street, commonly called the Danelaw. Here they lived for some time, but in 892 broke the peace by joining hands with an invading force from Scandinavia. Once again the island was harried by Danish attacks, but after a conflict which lasted close to five years, the English under Alfred were victorious. The Danes, however, remained within the Danelaw. Important as the defeat of the Danes was regarding the question whether England was to be Danish or English, the most significant result was the effect the conquest

THE BRITISH ISLES
ABOUT 885 A.D.

SCALE

0   50   100 Miles

░░░ Areas held by the Celts

▨▨▨ Danelaw

Northumbria shown as of the
Seventh Century

ORKNEYS

NORTH

58

PICTLAND

SEA

56

DALRIADA

IONA

STRATHCLYDE

Edinburgh

LINDISFARNE

NORTHUMBRIA

ROMAN WALL

R. Tyne

Jarrow

Whitby

54

Stamford Bridge

York
(Eboracum)

The Humber

IRELAND

IRISH SEA

Dublin

ANGLESEY

Chester

NORTH WALES

EAST

ANGLIA

Leicester

Limerick

MERCIA

Wexford

Worcester

Colchester
(Camulodunum)

Waterford

Hereford

ESSEX

SHEPPEY

Canterbury

THANET

Aclea

Stonehenge

Windsor

London

KENT

Folkstone

WESSEX

Winchester

SUSSEX

Exeter

Issbury

WEST WALES
CORNWALL

Hengestdun

ENGLISH CHANNEL

OCEAN

HEBRIDES

ATLANTIC

Latitude North

50

8   6   Longitude West 4 of Greenwich   2   0   2

Prepared for Prentice-Hall, Inc.   Copyright Rand McNally & Company, N. Y. 289

had had upon the question of unification. To preserve English identity was much more important than gaining the day over a kindred state. In order, therefore, to defeat a common foe, England not only accepted Wessex leadership but, when the peril was over, continued to follow where Wessex led.

Alfred's achievements in military affairs were more than equaled by his accomplishments in governmental and cultural matters. As a lawgiver he compiled what is known as the *Dooms of Alfred,* while his administrative skill brought greater order to all of England. His reputation, moreover, spread beyond the seas and important contacts were made with Rome and the Frankish Empire. With the latter state Alfred was on friendly terms, and from it, several scholars were obtained for the purpose of aiding educational development in England. A Court School, in imitation of that started by Charlemagne, was established to enable nobles' sons to fit themselves for a life of service to "God . . . Church and State." Reading and writing, both in Latin and English, occupied most of the time of these pupils. The instructors of these students, together with other learned men, aided Alfred in translating several works into the vernacular. Of these, Bede's *Ecclesiastical History* and the *Consolation of Philosophy* by Boethius should be mentioned. To Alfred also should be given credit for having conceived the *Anglo-Saxon Chronicle* from which much information of Teutonic England is derived. Alfred likewise was a devoted friend and patron of the Church and did much to promote the monastic system. Finally, Alfred is remembered for his interest in naval affairs, though his actual contributions have been overstated. All things considered, Alfred stands out as one of the ablest rulers of Anglo-Saxon England and as one of the most significant characters of his age.

Alfred's immediate successors, Edward the Elder and Athelstan, undertook to limit the power of the Dane still further and to extend the authority of the Wessex kingdom. Edward was able to gain control over the midland area, while Athelstan, thanks to his victory over a coalition of Scotch, Irish, and Danes at Brunanburh, paved the way for the conquest of the Danelaw. During the reign of Edgar (959–975) the Wessex monarchy reached its greatest height. Practically all of Teutonic and Danish England recognized his power, as did most of the Celtic princes in Wales and Scotland. Military success, together with skill in government, had made Wessex master of England but not the ruler of a united nation. Local and provincial loyalties still predominated.

Danish Domination

Internal dissensions within the Danelaw area, which had arisen as a result of certain ecclesiastical reforms introduced by Edgar, only added to the difficulties of the central government. Furthermore, in 980 England was again visited by the Danes. This time there was no Alfred to meet them and the invader made merry in southeast England. Northern England, which had distinct Anglian traditions as well as a Danish complexion, was luke warm in its loyalty to the English King, Ethelred. Hoping to stave off the enemy, Ethelred levied a land tax known as the Danegeld. The proceeds of this tax were given to the enemy with the understanding that the Danes would cease their attack. For a time the Danes kept the peace but within a few years were ravaging again. Had Ethelred been able to consolidate Saxon England, he might have defeated the enemy. As it was, he threw discretion to the winds and staked all upon a general massacre of the Danes within his kingdom. Sweyn, King of Denmark, avenged his people by invading England. Thrown back upon his own resources, Ethelred was unable to withstand the onslaughts of Sweyn, who carried the war into the very heart of Wessex. So successful were his efforts that Ethelred deserted his kingdom and fled to Normandy for safety. By 1014, England was in Sweyn's hands though his death in the same year gave Ethelred a chance to return and lead a counter attack against Cnut, who had succeeded his father, Sweyn, to the throne of England. After some desperate fighting, Cnut defeated Ethelred and his son Edmund Ironside so thoroughly that by the fall of 1016 Cnut ruled undisputedly throughout the land. In spite of occasional uprisings, Cnut was able to govern his domain without much serious trouble. His acceptance of the Christian faith and his skill in administration won the respect of many Englishmen.

Furthermore, in order to prevent local disturbances, Cnut divided his realm into several large earldoms over which he placed trusted officials. During his reign a brother, who was King of Denmark, died leaving to Cnut his continental holdings. A little later Norway was added, so that by 1028 England had become part of a Danish Empire. Cnut died in 1035 and was succeeded by his two sons who were unable to govern this far-flung empire. Civil war ensued, the Danish power in England was overthrown, and Edward, the youngest son of Ethelred, was restored to the throne in 1042. Much of Edward's earlier life had been spent in Normandy, whose feudal lord was related by blood to the House of Wessex. During these years of exile Edward had absorbed much of the culture of the Normans, who had developed rapidly since the days when their ancestors under the Viking, Rollo, had invaded and conquered this area.

Edward the Confessor and the Norman Conquest

Edward, whose reign lasted to January, 1066, bears the title of the Confessor, in recognition of his pious devotion to the Church. His loyalty to Rome was shown in a number of ways, none being more lasting than the impetus he gave to the building of churches and monasteries. Westminster Abbey, though not completed until a much later date, was begun by him. Possessed of a religious and gentle turn of mind,

Edward seems to have adopted the policy of trusting almost everyone. His ear was always open to those near at hand. In short he seems to have had very little will power of his own and to have leaned heavily upon the advice of his council. Some of the members of this body were English, but others were Normans who had come to England with Edward in 1042. This silent infiltration of aliens continued throughout his reign. Many of the Normans were given places of trust and confidence, a procedure which did much to alienate the good will of Edward's Saxon subjects. Among those who resented Edward's pro-Norman tendencies was the powerful Godwine, Earl of Wessex. Around Godwine and his sons, notably Harold, gathered a number of discontented nobles who wished to rid the land of foreign domination. The frequent visits of arrogant Norman barons tended only to aggravate the situation which finally led to an occasional clash of arms. Edward, however, was so completely under the control of his Norman advisers, chiefly Robert of Jumiéges, Archbishop of Canterbury, that steps were taken to drive Godwine and his family from England. In this the Norman party was successful; Godwine and his sons sought an asylum on the Continent. During this exile, Edward, it seems was visited by his kinsman, William of Normandy, whose presence at Winchester must have caused many misgivings in the minds of the English. Continued insolence on the part of the Normans at length led to an armed rebellion in 1052. Godwine and Harold at once returned to England and directed the movement which resulted in a rapid exodus of Norman officials. Their places were filled by Englishmen, one of whom, Stigand, Bishop of Winchester, became Primate of Canterbury.

Shortly thereafter, Godwine died and was succeeded in his earldom by Harold, who, to all intents and purposes, became the power behind the throne for the remainder of Edward's reign. It was during this period that Harold crossed the

Channel and fell into the hands of Guy, Count of Ponthieu
and vassal of William, Duke of Normandy. Guy held Harold
a prisoner until William asked for his release and to have
him brought to Normandy. The oft-repeated story of
Harold's having been shipwrecked and cast upon an enemy's
shore is probably pure fiction. That Harold was seized by
Guy and later handed over to William may be true. Harold,
moreover, was received most kindly by William and actually
aided the latter in a campaign in Brittany. At Bayeaux, however, William gained some sort of a promise from his visitor
to help him in obtaining the English throne upon Edward's
death. At least this is what Norman sources would suggest,
though there is no reason for accepting the tale of Harold's
having been tricked into taking an oath. Shortly after the
Bayeaux incident Harold returned to England. In less than
two years Edward died and the Witan, the Saxon body of
nobles, acting within its rights and in accordance with the
Confessor's last wishes, named Harold as their king.

In choosing the new monarch the Witan had passed over
Edgar, the grandson of Edmund Ironside. Edgar's blood
claim was beyond all question as he was clearly next in line
to the childless Edward. He was, however, but a lad, whereas
the situation in England demanded an experienced person on
the throne. Such a man was Harold, but Harold was not a
blood relative of the Confessor. On the other hand, William
of Normandy claimed the throne through his wife, Matilda,
a descendant of a former Saxon king. William, moreover,
according to Continental records, had been named by Edward
as his successor upon the occasion of the Duke's visit to the
island. This doubtful promise, if ever made, was clearly
repudiated by the Confessor's last act in naming Harold.
Even though Edward may have yielded as a result of the
pressure exerted by his English advisers, the King's nomina-
tion of Harold took precedence over any promise made to
William. In the last analysis, and in spite of all that William

might say to the contrary, Englishmen surely had the legal right to elect one of their own number.

William was not the man to allow his desires to be brushed aside so easily. From early childhood this monarch had been compelled to fight for his rights. Born out of wedlock, his political authority questioned on more than one occasion, William's rise to power had not been an easy affair. Possessed of a strong right arm and a mind steeled to realities, William gained his father's duchy and paved the way for the later conquest of Maine. William, however, seemed unwilling to settle down to life as a mere duke. Near relatives had risen to greater heights and the Conqueror, as he was later known, was keenly anxious to emulate their accomplishments. France, for the time being, offered no field for expansion, but directly across the Channel was a country which invited attack. Less than fifty years before, a kindred race, the Danes, had swept over England and had founded a kingdom of their own. What these Northmen had done William believed he could do as well if not better. Marriage contacts between his family and the house of Wessex had opened a possible line of approach, while the exile of the Wessex monarchs had been spent under the shelter of Normandy. The Confessor's pro-Norman policy quickened the hopes of William, while the recent sojourn of Harold at Bayeaux had given the Duke reason to believe that England in a short time would be his own. All that he had to do was to wait until Edward should die. This he had done only to find that England had plans which did not coincide with his own ambitions.

William immediately picked up the gauntlet which had been thrown at his feet. An appeal to Rome brought back the speedy reply that William was the rightful ruler of England. Supported by this action and unfurling a standard which had been blessed by the Pope, William girded himself for an invasion of England. Appealing to his vassals with promises of rich feudal holdings, a force was gathered which also included many adventurers and politically minded knights from France, Italy, and Sicily. Harold had never doubted that William would contest his accession to the English throne and accordingly threw his military strength into southeastern England and awaited the attack. In the meantime enemies had arisen in other quarters of the realm, none being more dangerous than Tostig, Harold's own brother. Tostig, jealous of his brother's power, joined hands with Hardrada, King of Norway, who at the time was contemplating an invasion of England. In due time Hardrada appeared in northern England, where he and Tostig brushed aside the feeble resistance of the local militia. Convinced that he could not allow these northern forces to attack him while William was entering the island and believing that the latter's fortunes would not permit an immediate crossing of the Channel, Harold broke camp and marched north with his army. Within five days he met Hardrada and Tostig at Stamford Bridge, where, after some bitter fighting, Harold won the day. This engagement was fought on Monday, September 25, and for the next few days Harold allowed his battle-worn men a well-deserved rest. In the meantime, William had landed in England. Harold at once rushed his troops southward, reaching London by October 11. Three days later the two forces joined in combat, with the Normans winning the day. Harold and a large number of the English lords lost their lives in this engagement, which is known as the Battle of Hastings.

William's success at Hastings was followed by the military occupation of the neighboring territory. Romney, Dover, Canterbury, and Rochester were taken without much difficulty, while Winchester, the capital of the Wessex rulers, recognized the power of the Normans. By this time William had reached the gates of London where Edgar, who had been elected king by the Witan, was ready for resistance. The rapid progress of Norman arms, the desertion of certain prominent Saxon leaders, notably Stigand, and the apathy of the northern earls convinced Edgar of the folly of any further opposition. Accordingly, he made his submission and allowed William to enter London. Prior to this event it may be said that William was a *de facto* monarch, but the act of Edgar and the Witan in accepting William made the latter King of England in accordance with existing law. Formal recognition of this fact was evidenced by William's coronation on Christmas day, 1066. The ceremony, moreover, was conducted in a manner which was entirely in keeping with both the spirit and the letter of time-honored Saxon rites.

William's accession to the throne was not altogether pleasing to many of the English, who on more than one occasion sought by force of arms to dispute Norman control. As a result William was busily engaged during the next few years in putting down one insurrection after another. The final stand of the Saxons was taken by Hereward the Wake at the island of Ely in 1071. In gaining this security William had relied not merely upon military strength but also upon a policy of brutality and frightfulness. Severe punishment was meted out to all who resisted his power. Symeon, a monk of Durham, provides a contemporary picture of the devastation wrought by the Normans in the north. "So great a famine arose that . . . they ate the flesh of human beings, horses, dogs and cats . . . some sold themselves into perpetual slavery . . . others started to go into exile but falling on the way lost their lives. It is horrible to see the dead bodies decaying in the houses, in the open spaces and on the streets. . . . Between York and Durham nowhere was there an inhabited village, while the dens of wild beasts and robbers caused terror to the travelers."

The degradation of the English, moreover, was not the only result which followed in the wake of the Normans who were described by William Malmesbury, some fifty years after the Conquest, as those who weighed treachery "by its chance of success" and who changed "their sentiments with money." This chronicler, however, admitted that the Norman conquest was not without benefits. English social and cultural life was turned into new channels. The language was modified by the infusion of Latin, and formal English today is more Latin in its origins than Saxon. On the other hand, the ordinary spoken or written word is still fundamentally Teutonic. England, moreover, was brought into the scheme of European things. Trade and commerce were stimulated while English lives and fortunes were guided to a great extent by monarchs who continued to be interested in their Continental holdings. In one sense it may be said that England was launched upon an imperial adventure which was not to end until the middle of the fifteenth century. English life and treasure were expended in numerous feudal and national wars that followed in a fruitless attempt to retain the French possessions of Norman rulers. For better or for worse, the English were tied to a Continental program as a result of William's victory at Hastings. At the same time the ecclesiastical position of the Church in England was materially changed. Papal authority was more firmly entrenched, though William and his immediate successors took pains to see that Rome never became superior to the monarchy. Finally, it may be noted that William's victory brought about a thorough reorganization of the governmental arrangements in England, a reorganization which was so well conceived and executed that even today the hands of these strong rulers may be seen in the legal and administrative machinery of the island kingdom.

RULERS OF ANGLO-SAXON ENGLAND, 871–1066

I. THE HOUSE OF WESSEX

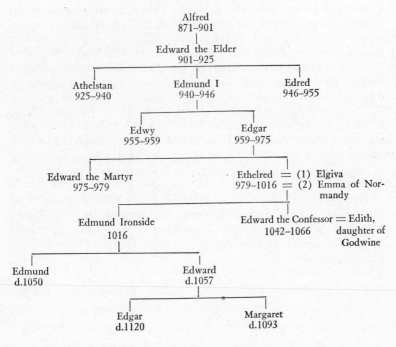

Alfred
871–901

Edward the Elder
901–925

Athelstan   Edmund I   Edred
925–940   940–946   946–955

Edwy   Edgar
955–959   959–975

Edward the Martyr   Ethelred = (1) Elgiva
975–979   979–1016 = (2) Emma of Nor-
                                             mandy

Edmund Ironside   Edward the Confessor = Edith,
1016   1042–1066   daughter of
                                                  Godwine

Edmund   Edward
d.1050   d.1057

Edgar   Margaret
d.1120   d.1093

II. THE DANISH KINGS

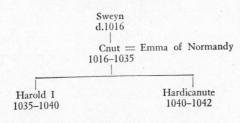

Sweyn
d.1016

Cnut = Emma of Normandy
1016–1035

Harold I   Hardicanute
1035–1040   1040–1042

III. THE EARLS OF WESSEX

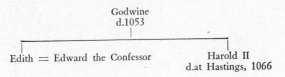

Godwine
d.1053

Edith = Edward the Confessor   Harold II
                                      d.at Hastings, 1066

SELECTED BIBLIOGRAPHY

General narrative information, clearly presented, may be found in J. R. Green's *Making of England* (New York, 1882) and his *Conquest of England* (New York, 1884). E. A. Freeman's monumental study, *History of the Norman Conquest* (Oxford, 1870) is of primary importance. Vinogradoff and Seebohm have suggestive material in their studies relative to Saxon England while H. M. Chadwick's *Origin of the English Nation* (Cambridge, 1907), and F. B. Gummere's *Germanic Origins* (New York, 1892) have scholarly accounts of the Saxons in their continental homes. Interesting biographical materials exist in C. Plummer's *Life and Times of Alfred the Great* (Oxford, 1902); L. M. Larson's *Canute the Great* (New York, 1912); S. A. Lee's *Alfred the Great* (New York, 1915), and F. M. Stenton's *William the Conqueror* (New York, 1908). Edward L. Cutts' *Augustine of Canterbury* (London, 1895) is of general value. S. J. Crawford's *Anglo-Saxon Influence on Western Christendom* (Oxford, 1933) and R. H. Hodgkin's *A History of the Anglo-Saxons* (Oxford, 1935) are recent studies of importance. C. H. Haskins' *Normans in European History* (Boston, 1915); M. W. Williams' *Social Scandinavia in the Viking Age* (New York, 1920), and J. A. Robinson's *Times of St. Dunstan* (Oxford, 1933) are of importance.

CHAPTER III

Anglo-Saxon England

Anglo-Saxon Thought and Letters

IMPORTANT as was the political development of Saxon England ending with Harold's death, its cultural and institutional growth was perhaps of greater significance. As early as the seventh century a wholesome intellectual life had shown itself in various parts of the island. Further progress followed. England was indebted to western Europe for much of the impetus which occasioned this insular awakening. On the other hand, there was much that was native and Celtic in origin. Gildas, the British monk of Strathclyde, and certain unknown writers of southwestern England have left definite proof that Roman-Celtic culture had not been totally erased by the Saxon conquest. More important, however, were the efforts of a number of Irish scholars during the sixth and seventh centuries. The most outstanding characteristic of the Celtic Church, of which these scholars were members, was a widespread monastic system. Each individual monastery became a living center of intellectual activity and through its gates passed a steady stream of missionaries who carried their culture into Scotland, northern England, and western Europe. "Self-exile," as one writer has described this movement, "for the sake of Christ and the Gospel" caused these hardy disciples to travel far and wide.

Most notable in this respect was Columba, who founded the

famous religious house on the Scottish island of Iona. Equally important was Columbanus whose zeal and devotion led him to Gaul, where he founded several outstanding monasteries. The life of Columba, as written by Adamnan, a later abbot of Iona, reveals much of the wisdom, scholarship, and generosity of the man. In recording these facts the author earned for himself a high place among medieval writers. His knowledge of Greek and Latin, as reflected in this and other works, as well as his style and methodology, indicate the relatively high standards maintained by the Celtic priests and teachers. Aidan, Colman, and others kept alive this learning and carried it south into Northumbria, whose king, Oswy, had been schooled at Iona.

Oswy's decision in favor of Rome at Whitby in 664 brought to an end any further extension of the Irish Church. The contributions which its followers had made, however, were not destroyed, and upon their efforts much that developed in the future was built. The intellectual leaders of Saxon England owed little to the teachings of Gregory or Augustine. They were, however, deeply indebted to Celtic ideas which became deeply rooted in Saxon ecclesiastical life. Those who directed church development after Whitby espoused the Roman form but followed Celtic thought. Wilfrid, Primate of York, and Biscop, founder of the monasteries at Wearmouth and Jarrow, were outstanding examples. Even Theodore of Canterbury, though loyal to Rome, was Greek in his training and outlook. These men and others encouraged learning and supplied their libraries with many valuable manuscripts. The York Library, for example, according to an extant catalogue, contained numerous theological works by Augustine, Jerome, Orosius, and Boethius; historical writings by Trogas; literary productions by Aristotle and Cicero; and grammatical compositions by prominent teachers of that age.

Similar activity took place in Wessex under the guidance of Aldhelm, who had been educated at the monastery of Malmesbury. In many ways Aldhelm was one of the leaders of thought and letters of his day. He appears to have studied many subjects and to have had a firm grasp upon the culture of the time. *De Virginitate* is the best known of his works. Greater than Aldhelm was Bede, the author of the famous *Ecclesiastical History of the English Nation*. In addition to this monumental study, Bede wrote other volumes dealing with religious, educational, and scientific topics. His knowledge of previous historical and literary writings was enormous. Bede was also an ardent student of Greek and Latin and, although not so critical as might be desired, did much to foster and extend intellectual activity in England.

Secular writing was paralleled by a widespread interest in the vernacular literature of the time. Some of this was religious in nature, like the poetical efforts of Caedmon and Cynewulf, both of Northumbria. *Beowulf* is also a product of this age and has been described by a recent scholar as the "only complete epic in an old Germanic tongue as well as the most substantial monument of Old English heroic poetry." Other bits of poetical writing, reflecting Saxon life and culture, are *Waldhere* and the *Battle of Maldon*. In the field of prose there was less activity. Alfred's writings have already been mentioned. To these might be added the legal compilations of Ethelbert, Ine, and Offa. Asser, a Welsh ecclesiastic, produced an interesting *Life of King Alfred*. Beyond these and one or two others, Anglo-Saxon literature has little to offer in the field of prose.

Educational Activities

Most of this intellectual awakening centered in the Church, which was an alien institution using a foreign tongue in its services and courts, a law which was colored by Roman influences, and a ritual and discipline which were European in origin. Impressed by the spiritual and temporal possibilities of this highly complicated international organization, its advocates sought to advance the power of Rome in many ways, but none was more important than that of education. Men trained in Latin, canon law, theology, and song were necessary if the Church was to achieve its mission in England. Accordingly, from the first, Augustine and his followers showed a deep interest in the founding of Church schools. King's School, Canterbury, doubtless had its origin in the labors of this missionary and served as a model for similar foundations at Dunwich, Rochester, York, and London. Augustine's efforts were ably seconded by Theodore, and Canterbury became the leading educational center of England. After the death of this great prelate the educational supremacy of Kent was lost to Wessex, where flourished the famous Winchester School. By the eighth century, however, the schools of southern England were eclipsed by those of Northumbria, notably that at York, which had been founded a century earlier by Paulinus, the first archbishop of that see. Other centers of learning existed at Hexham, Ripon, and Jarrow, at which the Venerable Bede labored for many years. Although Bede made an enviable reputation as a writer and teacher, it remained for Alcuin of York to establish Northumbria's intellectual supremacy throughout England and Europe. Alcuin's learning and insight soon reached the ear of the Frankish king who prevailed upon this scholar to leave his native land and undertake the founding of the celebrated Palace School of Charlemagne. While at York, Alcuin enriched the educational opportunities of that school by bringing to it many priceless manuscripts. The fame and reputation of the York Library were recognized throughout the continent. Alcuin's work was carried on by his successors, though the advent of the Danes checked further progress for the time being. Southern England, which escaped much of the devastation wrought by these invaders, waxed greater in educational work. Most prominent in this respect was the labor of Alfred and his school at Winchester. Mention should also be made of the efforts of Dunstan, Ethelwald, and Aelfric.

The curriculum of the Anglo-Saxon grammar school, using the term in the modern sense, followed the type employed in Europe. Students, many of whom were much older than those who now attend the secondary schools, were taught the *trivium* and the *quadrivium*. By the former was meant rhetoric, logic, and grammar, while the latter included arithmetic, geometry, music, and astronomy. None of these subjects were taught as they are today; arithmetic, for example, was studied primarily to aid the clergy (for most students entered the Church) in determining feast and fast days, while music was taught so as to drill the voice for the chanting of songs and the intonation of prayers and responses. In certain schools, law and theology played a prominent part. The proficiency or number of the pupils should not be overstated; on the other hand, accomplishments should not be undervalued. Thoroughness was insisted upon, and when a student showed an unwillingness to work a sound flogging soon convinced him of the error of his way. Skill in reading and writing Latin was matched by a proficiency in speaking which was remarkable for that day.

Considerable insight into educational policies and methods of Saxon schools may be gained from an examination of the Anglo-Saxon Grammar, Glossary, and Colloquy, all three the product of that great schoolmaster at Eynsham, Aelfric. Most of the students were recruited from noble families, though evidence exists that some of humble birth were also enrolled. The instructional staff usually consisted of a master, an usher and at times a monitor, though in the monastic schools one monk was assigned to every two or three students. Not all of the English schools were of the monastic type as has often been supposed. Indeed in the older ones at Canterbury and Winchester instruction was in the hands of the secular rather than the regular clergy, the latter being those who lived in a monastery subject to rules and regulations. Finally, it should be noted that not all of these institutions were of the grammar type. Many schools, particularly during the earlier decades, concentrated on singing. In these centers pupils were taught to carry on the ritualistic appeal of the religious service. Reading and speaking Latin also found a place in the program of the song schools. Nothing like universal education existed in Saxon England. The great majority of the people were illiterate. Relatively there were but few schools and the number of people that availed themselves of these institutions must have been small.

Monasticism

Most of the teachers in the song and grammar schools were secured from the monasteries, which by the close of the seventh century were relatively common throughout England. These religious houses were modeled after the famous monastery at Monte Cassino where St. Benedict in the sixth century founded the Benedictine order of monks. According to the discipline laid down by this leader, each monk was supposed to keep a three-fold vow of chastity, poverty, and obedience. Housed together under one roof and holding all things in common, they lived the simplest of lives. Hard manual work, long vigils and fastings, constant attendance at daily service, and simple, though hearty, food characterized the routine existence of those who had dedicated themselves to the service of God. At the head of each house there was an abbot or abbess (for women also embraced the monastic ideals) elected by members of the monastery, and to this head complete submission was due. Augustine, Theodore, Wilfrid, and many others were active in spreading the monastic system to all parts of the island. The rapid extension of the Christian faith, the progress in thought and letters, the development of the grammar and song schools bespeak the success of monasticism.

Continued prosperity, however, bred a false pride and an air of arrogance which paved the way for the entrance of evil influences. Wealth and good living supplanted the idea of poverty; internal strife weakened the duty of obedience; while immorality choked chastity. At the same time the decadence of the secular clergy encouraged the monks to seek worldly attractions, while the political squabbles of the Saxon kings, the ravages of the Dane and the growing force of feudalism did much to burden the monasteries with temporal goods and problems. The acquisition of wealth, moreover, stimulated misgivings and complaints on the part of the lower classes whose tithes and gifts to a well-endowed monastery contrasted sharply with their own poverty and want. Some earnest attempts at reform were made by Bede and others, while the Councils of Clovesho and Chelsea legislated in favor of a stricter monastic and Church life. Greater selection as to personnel was to be observed; the monastic dress was to be simple and not costly; excessive drinking was to be frowned upon and each monk was to labor at all times for God and the Rule.

In the eighth century as a result of these efforts, some improvement took place; but by the opening of the new century matters were worse than before. Against this decline, which was paralleled by a similar degradation among the secular clergy, no particular stand was taken until the days of Alfred. By this period monastic life was all but gone, learning was practically extinguished, celibacy (the rule which forbade the marriage of the clergy) was a dead letter, while earthly things had dimmed the value of being a humble disciple of Christ. Alfred's work did much to restore the Church to its former position. He also pointed the way toward a revival of the Benedictine ideal. This renaissance in ecclesiastical life, however, was not limited to England but was common throughout western Europe, where the Church had fallen into evil ways. Here as in Britain voices had been raised against the lax and immoral practices of both the clergy and laity. Slowly but certainly the Benedictine discipline appealed to these reformers as the one safe way out of the morass into which the world had fallen. Monasticism with its pristine habits was once more in the ascendency. Much of this reforming spirit centered in France, particularly at the monastery of Cluny, which became the mecca for those who sought to carry on this crusade against sin. More than one religious house in France and the adjoining states reorganized their life along the Cluniac lines. One of these was the Flemish monastery of Blandinium, to which an English exile by the name of Dunstan came in 956.

The earlier life of St. Dunstan, to adopt his better known name, centered about the monastery at Glastonbury. Here he received his education and here he became a monk. By reason of his birth, he was invited to the court of King Edmund, but life at the capital failed to interest Dunstan. His companions, moreover, looked down upon him and found fault with his learning, which seemed to them to be unholy. Forced to leave court as a result of these conditions, Dunstan returned to Glastonbury, where in due time he became abbot. Trouble, however, dogged his steps and his enemies were able to have him banished from the realm. It was while in exile that he encountered the Cluniac movement. The sensitive and alert mind of the abbot, who had already raised the moral tone at Glastonbury, was aroused and on his return to England in 957 he undertook to spread anew the ideals of St. Benedict. Fortune favored him in that his friend and patron, Edgar, became king and straightway Dunstan was recalled to court where he did splendid service for state and church. On the death of the Primate at Canterbury, Edgar placed Dunstan in charge of the English Church. Considerable headway was then made in raising the tone of the monasteries. Bitter opposition, however, was offered by those who were hostile to the movement, but the work begun by Dunstan and continued by his successors did much to elevate the moral tone of the entire nation. The Church was purged of many of its evil practices, while education and the fine arts received a helpful stimulus.

Architectural Growth

In gaining these ends considerable attention was given to the restoration of old monasteries and the building of new ones. Saxon ecclesiastical architecture was predominately Romanesque in that it followed the style laid down by the builders of the Roman Empire. Originally, the groundwork of a Saxon church was rectangular in shape with a semicircular end in which was placed the altar. This end or chancel, to use the church term, was usually short and high, and was separated by a lofty arch from a nave without aisles. Later, in order to provide room for the choir, the nave was lengthened, and aisles and transepts appeared. Further, the single apse with its wide arch was replaced by two and sometimes three apses, each with a characteristic Roman arch. Although this form was common in England, the Saxon showed a decided preference for a square-end church. Narrow windows, widely splayed, pierced the massive walls, while the roof or dome was supported by ornamental piers of large proportions. Stone structures were common through northern England but elsewhere wooden buildings predominated. Many of the Saxon churches stressed a western tower in which a belfry was placed. The perishable nature of these wooden churches plus the devastation of the Danes doubtless accounts for the disappearance of most of these edifices. Those few that remain were probably built in the eleventh century and show distinct Norman influences. Earls Barton in Northamptonshire with its rich pilaster strips reflects the Saxon influence, though there are liberal touches of the Norman present. Westminster Abbey, started by the Confessor, seems to be chiefly Norman in style. On the other hand there existed at Hexham a Saxon church which is described as follows: "The deeper part of this building was founded in the earth with chambers constructed of finely polished stones, and above the ground the structure was manifold, borne up by many columns and many side chapels." Although this picture is not so complete as one might desire, it is far better than anything available relative to domestic architecture. Wood was probably used and for the great mass of the population small and simple homes must have sufficed. In these rather crude dwellings iron and bronze tools and receptacles were used, while glass, gold, and silver were employed in the more spacious homes of the noble and wealthier classes.

Social Classes Among the Saxons

Socially, the Anglo-Saxons may be divided into several different groups, though probably none of these distinctions existed in the fifth and sixth centuries. The ancestors of the modern Englishman doubtless entered the island as freemen of the noble and non-noble type. The former group included the athelings, or kingly and princely type, and the earls, who formed the warrior class. Beneath these were the ceorls, who, though free, had no noble status. Tribal and intertribal contests as well as the Danish wars broke down these earlier classifications. Furthermore, economic and political forces shoved many unfortunates into an unfree class. By the seventh century, a new social order had appeared. At the bottom was the slave, originally a conquered Celt. Owing to economic forces and the growth of an order which in time rested on service and office, many of the ceorls became slaves. Some of the ceorls escaped this misfortune, but a goodly number lost their former status and became little more than serfs. Above the slaves, serfs, and independent ceorls there was a privileged group. Among those who made up this latter class were those who, by reason of military, political, or economic service to the king, formed the basis for a new nobility which was not based upon blood as had been true of the atheling and earl class. The new lords were known as thegns. The rise of this military class forced the earls to decline in importance. The atheling, or royal noble, topped all groups and enjoyed considerable power and influence. Finally, one should note the presence of an ecclesiastical element which exercised far-reaching power through its spiritual and temporal rights.

Bound to the soil as a dependent cultivator, or working in the home of a noble or churchman, the lot of the serf was by no means a happy one. Even though it must have been much better than that of the slaves, the distinction between the two classes was neither clear nor well defined. Neither had title to land, though society tacitly recognized the small garden plot of the serf, which surrounded a miserable hut, as belonging to the inmates by right of continual use. In return for this, the barest form of economic security, the serf was required to till the soil, grind the corn, and repair the roads, fences, and bridges of his lord. On the basis of this servile labor, the noble class was able to perform those duties required of it by the crown. Land and power, therefore, were rapidly gravitating into the hands of a small group who, on the eve of the Norman Conquest, formed the bulk of the governing, fighting, and priestly class. Commendation, that is, the binding of an individual to a lord in return for a promise of protection; the development of legal and judicial rights of a lord over his dependents, and the rise of a military class were factors which resulted in something much like the feudal system. Politically, Saxon feudalism never reached the perfection that existed in Europe though there is no reason for believing that if left to himself the Saxon would not have developed the feudal system proper. This assumption is borne out by certain well-defined economic factors which may be described as the manorial system, though the word manor was

not used in England until after the Conquest. Patterns, therefore, of both the feudal and manorial orders existed in Saxon
England. It remained, however, for the Norman to give these
systems the standardized shape and form generally understood
as feudalism.

Saxon Government and Law

The Norman also surpassed the Saxon in the art of government. Indeed, at no time were the Saxon rulers able to administer England in a manner which commanded the respect and
obedience of all. In part this was due to the decentralizing
influences of a growing feudal structure which may be illustrated by the great earldoms which existed in the eleventh
century. Powerful earls, like Godwine, did much to check
the rise of a strong central state. Again, the Saxon kings,
many of whom were weak rulers, had a very limited income.
Rents from personal holdings, fees and fines from judicial
actions, tolls, treasure trove, the salvage from wrecks, and the
danegeld, which was the only true tax the central government had, formed the chief sources of revenue. Some of these
were paid in specie, though payment in kind or service was by
far more common. Silver and gold might be brought to the
royal court, but in order to collect those goods which served
as taxes, the crown was forced to tour the country from one
manor to another. In many cases these assets were consumed at the time of royal visitation, a practice which was
known as purveyance. Lack of funds, moreover, prevented
the growth of an effective official class and seriously hampered
the state's police power. The Saxon army was notably weak.
A national militia, known as the fyrd, existed, but the experiences of Alfred and Harold show how unreliable this force
was in time of need. The thegns always gave good service,
but were not numerous enough to permit the growth of a
strong central state; nor is it clear that this class desired any

powerful overlordship. Finally, difficulties in communication and transportation added to the troubles of the Saxon monarch, who in the last analysis was more of a personal than a national ruler. Within a certain limited radius of the court some degree of authority existed, but the farther one went away from this center, the fewer evidences of a central government appeared.

At the head of the Saxon state was a king whose powers were limited and poorly defined. Nothing like a constitution existed, while most of the law, with the exception of the dooms, was unwritten and was based on custom rather than upon legislation. Probably a king might order in a personal way this or wish that, but he could not make law in the modern sense; nor was law made by any assembly for the simple reason that no national body existed. Within the limits of custom and tradition, the crown might collect taxes, raise an army, dispense justice, and administer law. In exercising these powers the king was bound to heed the voice of the Witan, which was an advisory body composed of the important and influential men of the country. One's title to membership in this assembly rested upon the choice of the crown, a fact which helps to explain the relative lack of power enjoyed by this body. On the other hand if the king was weak, the Witan was apt to play a more important rôle. A wise monarch governed with the help of this body, which met at least once a year, though there was nothing to prevent the king from ignoring the Witan altogether. In addition to being a group of counsellors, the Witan traditionally had a voice in determining royal succession. Free election, however, did not exist, as the Witan generally endorsed the hereditary rights of the next in line. Harold's and William's accession to the throne constitute important exceptions to this rule. Finally, it should be noted that the Witan acted as a court for the trial of the king's cases and those of important individuals.

Next in order of importance was the shire or county, as the Norman called this territorial unit. At the head of the shire in the early Saxon age was an earl, though by the eleventh century most of his duties had been absorbed by the royal officer, the sheriff. These officials tried to enforce the law, keep the peace, control the militia, and collect the taxes, and together with the bishop presided at the meetings of the shire-moot. Primarily, the shire-moot was a court which met twice a year and was composed of the chief property owners of the county. Originally all freemen had attended this assembly, but because of economic and political inequalities they were no longer present. In addition to being a court the shire-moot served as a medium for determining the local law. Each shire, moreover, for judicial and administrative purposes was broken up into smaller units known as hundreds. At the head of each hundred was a reeve who was in one sense the representative of the central government. The reeve also presided over the monthly meetings of the hundred-moot which like the shire court was both an administrative and judicial body composed of the important personages of the community.

Below the hundred was the vill which seems to have been the center of local agricultural life. Historical evidence is none too clear as to whether this body had any legal or corporate life. Possessed of a population which was small and engaged in an activity that required no special regulation or control, there seems to have been little need for anything like a court. Probably in some unknown manner decisions in minor disputes were arrived at by those concerned, but of this there is no tangible proof. It is established, however, that the local priest, reeve, and four freemen were allowed to attend the sessions of the hundred-moot, a function which can hardly be considered as constituting representation in the modern sense of the word. As time went on, some of these vills rose to the rank of boroughs and as such were governed by a port-reeve and a local gathering of important individuals. The borough-moot acted in a manner similar to that of the hundred.

It is important for the student, at this point, to divorce from his mind all present day concepts of law and court actions, as the great majority of these were totally unknown to the Saxons. Theirs was a simple life and there was no reason for an elaborate system of courts or laws. Criminal actions were chiefly limited to murder, arson, theft and house-breaking, while civil suits concerned title to property. The Saxon court, moreover, was minus many of the officials and ceremonies which are present today, and most of its meetings during the earlier centuries were held out of doors. Again, the moots had jurisdiction over both lay and ecclesiastical matters, though this was an exception to Continental practice. Moreover, there was nothing like appellate jurisdiction. Men of wealth and power, however, often gained this end by having their cases tried in a superior court, while all matters which concerned the shire or the crown were reserved for the shire-moot or Witan, even though the action itself had taken place in a hundred or vill. It should also be noted that the procedure used in one court was practically the same in all.

At the opening of the Saxon age there existed a primitive method of settling disputes known as the right of private vengeance. As society, however, became more complex, the need for greater security occasioned the development of a better order. In other words, the idea arose that a question of title to property or of personal injury was an offense against the community and not merely against the individual concerned. This concept did not imply that the local unit equipped itself with police or jails, as the matter of apprehending a criminal or of confining him until the time of trial was left largely to the plaintiff. Public opinion may have helped, but in the last analysis the plaintiff was responsible for bringing the defendant to court. Once this had been done, both parties proceeded to take a formal oath that was a recitation of a traditional statement which had been used by the Saxons for countless decades. The content of this oath had no bearing on the case in the sense that it threw any light or evidence as to guilt,

innocence, or title to property. The actual terminology of the
oath was little more than a statement as to human character
in general, and was used for all kinds of cases. The oath,
however, had a very important relation to the trial, for if the
defendant gave the same correctly without hesitation, then he
was judged innocent of the charge made against him. On the
other hand, if he failed or faltered in the slightest degree, and
the court determined him a failure, then he had to stand trial.
The plaintiff also had to take this oath. If both parties made
mistakes the court decided which of the two should stand
trial. This aspect of the procedure is of great significance as
it really disclosed the opinion of the community as to who
was the offender. In this sense it may be said that judgment
actually preceded trial.

Trial, according to Saxon customs, amounted to furnishing proof that one was not guilty, and differed as to procedure
in civil and criminal cases. Witnesses were not used and it
was not until the late Saxon age that evidence was introduced.
In a civil action a method known as compurgation was used,
according to which the accused was asked to furnish a number
of oath-helpers (compurgators) who by correctly repeating another formal oath purged the defendant of the charges which
had been made. The number of these oath-helpers varied in
respect to their rank and that of the accused. A thegn, for
example, was obliged to furnish fewer compurgators than a
ceorl, while the presence of a thegn as an oath-helper reduced
the total number required. If the accused could furnish sufficient oath-helpers, and if they could recite the oath correctly,
then the former won the case; if not, it was lost.

At first glance it might seem that this was an unsatisfactory
and unscientific way of handling a trial. Actually, for that day
it was a sound method and probably worked for justice in the
greater number of cases. The entire trial, it should be noted,
was viewed as an appeal to God who was known to have
wreaked vengeance upon those who had knowingly perjured

themselves. It took courage to defy the wrath of Providence unless one was quite certain of the innocence of the accused. Then again, the community knew almost for a certainty who was the offender, for the simple reason that each member of this area knew quite well the character and habits of everyone. Had the number been greater, this precise knowledge would not have existed, but in a community where everyone knew everybody and where title to property was an established fact generally known throughout the area, there could be little doubt as to who the offender was.

Public opinion and an appeal to heaven likewise explain why criminal procedure worked as well as it did in the Saxon age. In criminal actions, a method known as the ordeal was used to establish guilt or innocence. The ordeal was also employed in civil cases affecting strangers or those who were known to have a bad reputation. In either instance the accused submitted his body to pain and possible mutilation, such as carrying a red-hot iron, walking barefooted over heated plow-shares, or being thrown into a pond. In the event that one of the first two methods were used, the injured hand or foot was bandaged for several days, after which an examination took place. If no injury were apparent, and the court determined what constituted injury, the person was judged not guilty. However, if damage had been done, the individual was declared guilty. Generally speaking, the water ordeal was more frequently used. Floating, it was believed, was evidence of guilt, as the clean, pure spirit of the deity who dwelt within the pond would not harbor an evil person. What constituted floating rested entirely with the court who, already fairly well convinced of guilt or innocence, could be relied upon to give the proper decision. Needless to say no one was allowed to drown, as the procedure was one of trial and not of punishment.

Punishment itself was largely left in the hands of the plaintiff, though the community was supposed to pursue the guilty one in case he took to flight. This pursuit was known as hue and cry and was to be continued throughout the area controlled by the court. Actual punishment consisted of fines, outlawry, and in a few cases, death. The assessment of a fine was quite common and the Anglo-Saxon dooms are crowded with references to these. Each individual seems to have had a money value placed upon his life as well as upon the various parts of his body. The amount of the fine, moreover, varied in proportion to one's social rank in the community. A thegn's ear or life, therefore, was worth much more than that of a serf. In case of murder the fine was known as the *wergeld* and was payable to near relatives; otherwise, one paid what was called a *bot*. It was also understood that the accused should pay to the crown a fine known as the *wite*. In the event that neither *bot* nor *wergeld* could be collected, the injured party might then resort to personal vengeance. Finally, it should be noted that the Roman Church recognized these practices and actually assisted in the course of the trial.

Commerce and Industry

Of equal interest to the student of Saxon history is the economic basis upon which society rested. Most people during this age gained their livelihood from farming; hence ownership of land was the chief source of wealth and power. Most Saxons, however, were dependent cultivators and did not, therefore, have property in land. Moreover, England's population at that time was exceedingly small, and only an insignificant part of the total land was in a state of cultivation. Most of the rural inhabitants lived in small villages or tuns; isolated farms, such as exist in America, were not to be found. In the course of time many of these vills became manors on which lived a lord, a priest, and a number of dependent and independent farmers. The detail management of a manor was so much like that of the Norman period that the discussion of it will appear in a later chapter. Suffice it now to say that on the eve of the Conquest the manor was a conspicuous part of agricultural England and that from an economic point of view, it was practically self-sufficient.

The occasional visits of traders and merchants to these agrarian centers indicated that commerce flourished to some degree in Saxon England. Most of the trade, however, was foreign in nature and probably was chiefly in the hands of aliens. During the reign of Ethelred II, traders from Flanders, Normandy, and Picardy imported wines and fish into England. A trade also existed between England and the kingdom of Charles the Great. London, described by Bede as an "emporium for many peoples, coming by land and sea," seems to have been the chief port of entry. Finally, it should be noted that the advent of the Dane in the ninth century stimulated commerce and shipbuilding. Celts from Ireland also visited English markets while evidence exists of a Scandinavian trade in the early records of York, Lincoln, Norwich, Cambridge, and Thetford.

Imports included jewels, wines, oils, silks, iron goods, furs, fish, masts, ropes, and groceries, particularly pepper and vinegar. Exports consisted of tin, lead, wool, slaves, and certain foodstuffs like cheese. France, Ireland, the Lowlands, Scandinavia and even Rome received these commodities. Most of the trade, export or import, centered in those towns which were favored by easy access to the sea. Little industrial life existed in these towns or elsewhere for that matter. Some attention was paid to mining which was stimulated by the widespread use of iron. Brooches, pins, farm implements, combs and the like were made and decorated by a workmanship which reflected skill and ingenuity. Fishing seems to have engaged the efforts of some as did the making of salt. Glasswork, shipbuilding, milling, and masonry employed a number of hands. In general, industry was in the handicraft stage and most of the articles made were fashioned by those who used them. Here and there exceptions may be found, especially among the monks who seem to have specialized in certain activities.

Although Saxon England was predominately rural, urban centers developed at an early date. Several different views have been advanced concerning the genesis of these towns. One school of writers has argued that the Saxon borough was an outgrowth of the vill. This group rests its case chiefly upon the fact that rural rather than urban life characterized the activities of these centers for a long time. Another group holds to the view that towns arose from military posts and fortifications, which Saxon rulers erected during the course of their military excursions; others have credited the Danes, whose interest in trade presumes the founding of markets and towns. · In one or two cases it has been argued that urban life dates from the Roman period and was continued either because of commercial advantages or because of the location of a Roman mint. Available evidence, however, discredits this view with the possible exception of London. Probably no one theory is complete and definitive and it may be that a combination of these various forces resulted in the appearance of towns.

It is now believed that the earliest urban communities formed an agricultural group housed behind fortifications or walls, and to some extent engaged in trade. The ravages of the Dane gave a definite stimulus to urban life within fortified areas but this hardly justifies the conclusion that military needs resulted in the founding of towns. Nor is there any valid reason for believing that the vill developed into a borough. It is the influence of trade that may have molded a vill into a borough and most certainly led to urban aggregations within the abandoned wall towns of Roman origin. During Alfred's day and thereafter, trading activities resulted in the establishment of other boroughs which were fortified against the attack of the Danes. The Saxon borough, therefore, was a mercantile center possessed of a market and enjoying certain advantages that differentiated it from the agricultural unit, the vill. Town government, as far as it existed, rested in the hands of the leading traders under the general supervision of a royal reeve. These officers controlled whatever judicial or administrative work there was. Some of these duties related to the agricultural life of the town, as many of the inhabitants held and worked land within and without the borough's walls. More important were the jurisdictions held over trading activities. Most students agree that the post-Conquest association of traders, known as the merchant gild, was a Norman introduction. Recently, however, Professor Tait of the University of Manchester has shown that Canterbury and London had gilds during the Saxon age. "These societies," he states, "must have made for a stronger sense of community and their presence weakens the suggestion that the burgesses of an Anglo-Saxon borough were a mere fortuitous collection of disparate elements with no real bond or union." On the other hand most of the so-called Saxon gilds were probably no more than general fraternal associations.

SELECTED BIBLIOGRAPHY

Pertinent material relative to church life may be found in M. L. W. Laistner's *Thought and Letters in Western Europe* (New York, 1931). M. R. James' *Two Ancient English Scholars* (Glasgow, 1931); J. J. Jusserand's *Literary History of the English People,* Vol. I (New York, 1917); A. F. Leach's *Schools of Medieval England* (London, 1915); C. Plummer's *Life and Times of Alfred the Great* (Oxford, 1902) and his edition of Bede's *Ecclesiastical History* (Oxford, 1906) are works of decided merit. A. W. Clapham's *English Romanesque Architecture before the Conquest* (Oxford, 1930) and W. R. Godfrey's *The Story of Architecture in England* (New York, 1928) are valuable for architectural history.

For constitutional material the student should consult the works by White and Adams. In addition there are T. P. Taswell-Langmead's *English Constitutional History* (Boston, 1929); W. A. Morris' *The Medieval Sheriff* (London, 1927), and H. C. Lea's *Superstition and Force* (Philadelphia, 1870). Agriculture, trade and industry are covered by Vinogradoff's *English Society in the Eleventh Century* (Oxford,

1908); J. E. A. Jolliffe's *Pre-Feudal England* (Oxford, 1933); A. Ballard's *Domesday Boroughs* (Oxford, 1904); C. Stephenson's *Borough and Town* (Cambridge, 1933), and J. Tait's *The Medieval English Borough* (Manchester, 1936). See L. F. Salzman's *English Industries of the Middle Ages* (Oxford, 1923) for material on Saxon industry.

CHAPTER IV

Norman and Angevin Government

The Feudal System

THE Norman Conquest marked the beginning of a new England. Though Saxon culture stubbornly contended against the infiltration of alien custom and thought, it lost ground on every front. This was due in part to a policy of frightfulness which beat down all opposition. By confiscating the estates of those who resisted him and by distributing their land to his followers, William placed the control of wealth in the hands of the Normans. Saxons, moreover, no longer held important judicial and administrative posts. "To the victor belong the spoils" was practiced then as today. More significant than any one of these factors was the introduction of European feudalism. From a constitutional point of view, the advent of this type of feudalism was the most important result of the Conquest. European feudalism was more highly institutionalized than that which existed in Saxon England. On the other hand, economic feudalism, as has been shown, was well advanced in England before 1066, though much less had been accomplished toward the building of political feudalism. The Norman, therefore, on entering the island, recognized the presence of these two factors and placed upon the Saxon base merely a Continental form in which the political element was much more perfectly developed. The union of these two forms—Saxon and Continental—made for the growth of what has been called English feudalism.

Saxon feudalism, like the Continental type, had its genesis in the chaos and disorder which had followed in the wake of Rome's decline and fall. Rome, however, through its culture contributed the sources out of which European feudalism was born. Generally speaking, feudalism represents a social arrangement in which two important elements are present. One of these, a personal relationship which existed between a lord and his vassal, was a product of the Roman system of *patrocinium*; the other, a political nexus, was the outgrowth of the *precarium,* also Roman in origin. Under the *patrocinium,* a Roman, because of political and economic pressure, placed himself under the legal protection of some more fortunate person. On the other hand, an individual who, through the operation of similar forces, was in danger of losing his property, handed it over to a powerful person. By this practice (*precarium*) the original owner forfeited title but retained the use of the property, subject to certain restrictions and limitations. Both of these legal processes survived the fall of Rome and were employed by the Teutonic invaders during the decades which followed. Had the central government of Rome or the Germanic kingdoms been strong enough to protect the small landowner, the growth of a feudal world might have been turned into other channels. As it was, individual after individual gave up his original status and entered into a dependent relationship with some powerful lord, who in return for title to land and services protected those who now became his vassals.

The procedure was speeded to a marked degree by the Mohammedan spear thrust through the Pyrenees in the eighth century. At that time, Charles Martel, leading figure in a disintegrating Merovingian state, sought to recruit horsemen to meet the crashing cavalry charges of the Moors. To achieve this end, Martel granted large sections of land on the express condition that hereafter the owners would furnish him military service. As land was the chief source of both political and economic power, Martel had many applicants and the Battle of Tours was turned into a Christian victory. Important as this conflict was for the future of Europe, its chief interest centers in the fact that the concept of military service was added to the older forms of *patrocinium* and *precarium*. And when at a later date the proud Carolingian state tottered and divided into many smaller units, with chaos and disorder appearing everywhere, the two Roman forms as modified by military service formed the basis upon which a feudal structure was reared. To what extent the Roman practices survived the Saxon conquest of England is not known. In any event, economic and political forces at work in Britain, produced an order feudal in nature. In all probability a feudal system would have developed in England regardless of the Conquest. The entrance of the Norman, therefore, merely speeded a process already in progress.

Feudal holdings, regardless of their size or the rank of the lord, were known as fiefs or tenures. The use of the word tenure was not accidental, as its Latin meaning conveyed precisely the idea of *holding* rather than *owning* land. Theoretically, therefore, all land was held and none was owned, though in the last analysis the crown was viewed as the owner of all land in England. In practice, however, time and custom transformed a tenure into ownership. Completely developed English feudalism had three basic forms of tenure of which the most important was the knight's fee, a term which may be used to describe any land or office held by one of noble rank. One of noble standing would not, of course, render any service beneath his social status. Consequently, military and court duties were the most common obligations assumed by the holder of a knight's fee. In return, the lord agreed to protect his vassal against hostile attack and to maintain his legal rights in the feudal courts. This arrangement, entered into by a lord and his vassal, was contractual in nature and was assumed voluntarily. Custom dictated that those of free noble birth should accept a feudal position, though there was no other factor which might compel a freeman to become a lord or vassal unless he so desired. This voluntary contractual arrangement, which the king as well as any noble assumed, represents one of the most important contributions made by the Norman to English history. By it the crown was definitely checked whenever it sought to transgress the rights of English lords. In other words the king was a feudal lord, and like all other lords, was supposed to live up to the terms of the contract. While all the English kings from William to John inclusive (1066–1216) frequently were able to place themselves above the law, neither the idea back of the law nor the law itself was lost sight of, and often these concepts were put to good use by the barons. Feudalism, although it contained much that worked for the growth of royal absolutism, also contained the highly significant restriction that even the king was subject to feudal law and custom.

Second to the knight's fee was the freehold. Here the purpose was partly economic and partly political, as services of both types were required of those who held fiefs of this kind. The tenants were free men, but they were not nobles, and though found chiefly in the boroughs, existed in large numbers throughout the rural areas. In return for this tenure and such protection as went with it, the freeholder gave services in kind, money, and labor. He was not, however, asked to do military duty, as the feudal order allowed only those of noble birth, except for mercenaries, to engage in this noble profession. Those who caused wars or sought to advance their economic position went forth to battle, while those who did not have this honorable standing remained at home, neither causing nor waging war. Modern concepts of patriotism or loyalty to a state or nation meant nothing to the great mass of the people during the feudal era, while even among the noble class these ideas were restricted in a realistic manner to an individual and not to an institution. Below the freeholder came the servile tenure in which the purpose was solely economic. The tenants, moreover, were dependent laborers—serfs or villeins—and in return for meagre protection gave services which were menial in nature. The serf bulked large in the total population and upon the fruit of his labor the entire superstructure rested.

Generally speaking, one is apt to view the feudal world as a pyramid with the king at the top and the serfs forming a broad base. Although this picture is a true one, it should be recalled that there was nothing to prevent either a noble from being a vassal to several different lords, regardless of their rank, or a lord being a vassal to someone below him. As a land-owner today may rent property of one of more humble stand-ing, so in the feudal world anyone from the knight class up might hold and give out land to another, irrespective of rank or standing.

Among the services required of a vassal, in addition to mili-tary and court duty, were aids and incidents. An aid was an assessment which any lord might levy upon his vassals under certain established conditions. Three of these aids became customary: one being assessed on the marriage of the eldest daughter; another upon the knighting of the eldest son; and a third, for ransoming the lord in the event of his having been captured by an enemy. Among the incidents there was the right of wardship by a lord over a tenure held by a minor; the right of relief or the payment of a sum to the lord by a vassal upon the latter's entrance into a state of vassalage; the right of marriage, whereby the lord controlled the matrimonial desires of an heiress so as to protect his rights; and finally, the incidents of escheat and forfeiture. By escheat was meant the return of the tenure to the original lord upon the death of a vassal without issue, while forfeiture implied a similar re-turn in case the vassal broke his obligation. Finally, it should be noted that the feudal lords were quite anxious to keep their estates intact. Consequently there developed a form of inheritance known as primogeniture whereby an estate passed at the death of a lord to his eldest heir.

In the case of the Church, which quite willingly adjusted itself to the feudal system, the principle of primogeniture did not operate except in respect to lay vassals who might hold land of an ecclesiastic. When the ecclesiastic was a vassal there was no question of primogeniture for the simple reason that canon law forbade the marriage of the clergy. When a church lord died the tenure was taken over by a new ecclesiastic. In this way, while lay fiefs might revert to the original donor, church holdings did not. Consequently, during the medieval period, ecclesiastical tenures were said to be held in *mortmain* (dead hand).

William's Laws and Government

The introduction of these various feudal forces and practices has been attributed to William, who directed the trend of English events from 1066 to 1087. Although these highly institutionalized devices amounted to the development of a new order and a new law, William was tactful enough not to irritate Saxon opinion by destroying all their customs and laws, particularly when he realized the inherent value of the same. Accordingly, many of the decrees and pronouncements of Alfred and Edward the Confessor were retained, as were the shire and hundred courts and the offices of earl and sheriff. To the ordeal and compurgation, however, William added a method of trial known as wager of battle or the judicial combat. This device had been employed by the Normans before the Conquest and consisted of a physical combat between the litigants in order to determine guilt or innocence. Wager of battle did not imply that the conflict was to continue until one or the other was slain, although severe injury was frequently inflicted; rather, it was contested until one of the two surrendered. And this act of yielding was interpreted by the courts as a sign of guilt. Again, William by his so-called Forest Laws set aside certain areas for private hunting purposes and woe unto him who might be found poaching on these preserves. Finally, there should be mentioned the law of Englishry. This innovation arose out of a peculiar situation. Normans, as may readily be appreciated, were none too well liked by the Saxons, especially as the former were often cruel in their conduct toward the latter. Naturally, therefore, murder frequently followed with no clue left to establish the guilty party. In order to put an end to this practice, William ruled that unless the hundred could produce the slayer or prove the dead man to be a Saxon, the hundred was legally responsible, on the assumption that the murdered individual was a Norman.

By means of these various regulations plus a generous dis-play of the military, William was able to keep his Saxon sub-jects in control. As for the Normans, he exacted complete obedience by the famous Oath of Salisbury Plain (1086). In that year William assembled all the feudal lords and required of them an oath of homage and fealty. In the main, however, the Conqueror's success in dealing with the Normans, as well as the Saxons, was largely due to the growth of a strong cen-tral government. Foremost in importance was the *Magnum Concilium* or Great Council. This body, which may be viewed constitutionally as the successor of the Witan, was a feudal assembly composed of those tenants, lay or ecclesiastic, who held lands directly of the king. The Great Council, therefore, was merely a lord's court, but because in this case it was the court of the greatest feudal lord in all England, it out-ranked all others and aided William in his program of establishing an absolute monarchy. The duties of this council consisted of assisting the crown in all matters of state, judicial or otherwise, and theoretically, at least, included the power of election to the throne. Further, as William frequently was compelled to spend much of his time in Normandy, the chief members of this body acted, during his absence, as the executive. This was particularly true of the Justiciar, who possessed vice-regal power while William was on the Continent.

The Great Council, moreover, usually met but two or three times a year, and in lieu of this body William relied upon the advice of those members who were either attached to his household or those, like the Primate of Canterbury, whose positions were closely related to the monarchy. These individuals made up what might be termed the Little Council, or the *Curia Regis*. This body had all-embracing functions and there was no conception of a separation of powers. Administrative duties occupied much of its time. Justice was rendered by this court, and its decisions amounted to law. In general, during the Norman period, law was found rather than made, and there were many bodies of law, each influenced by its own jurisdiction, such as the shire-moot, the forest-law and the canons of the church.

It was the *Magnum Concilium,* however, which executed William's order in 1085 to undertake an economic survey of the realm. William wanted this information to meet the growing need for a definite base upon which feudal assessments might be levied as well as for an extraordinary tax to meet an anticipated Danish invasion. At the same time the survey would provide the king with general knowledge as to the economic resources of the kingdom. Royal officers visited every shire and hundred and gained from each a precise statement as to the nature and wealth of every tenure. The findings of these agents were collected in what has been called the *Domesday Book,* from which is obtained much knowledge as to the social, political, and economic structure of eleventh-century England.

Among other things this survey or census throws light upon Church matters. William's relation to Rome was, on the whole, a happy one and proved to be of great benefit to both parties. From the first, the Pope had viewed William's enterprise with favor, as it was believed that the Church in England would thereby be brought into closer contact with the papacy. William, moreover, was heartily in accord with this plan and shortly after his coronation elevated to Canterbury his friend and adviser, Lanfranc. William also showed his gratitude and loyalty to Rome by building and endowing many churches and monasteries, and by allowing churchmen to have their own ecclesiastical courts, which had not been permitted during the Saxon age. On the other hand, William had no intention of allowing the papacy to advance so far as to endanger his own control. Accordingly, while canon law was recognized in England, it was definitely subordinated to royal law, a policy, moreover, which had the endorsement of the Archbishop himself. As evidence of this general attitude, attention should be paid to three of William's decrees relative to the Church. In the first place, no pope was to be recognized as having any authority in England without the King's consent; second, no papal bull or decree of any church council was to have any standing without William's approval; and third, none of his tenants-in-chief were to be excommunicated unless William agreed. As a result of this program, William was able to keep the Church within its own field of operation.

The Reigns of William II and Henry I

When William died in 1087, the consequences of the Norman invasion were not as yet complete, but enough had taken place to show that Norman control had come to stay. All of the innovations which the Conqueror had conceived were not only kept intact but were developed by his sons who ruled after him, William Rufus (1087–1100) and Henry I (1100–1135). While spending considerable time on the Continent, these kings kept their Saxon subjects in control and repelled, on occasion, the attacks of certain Norman lords who chafed under a government which did not allow them greater feudal rights and powers. Both William II and Henry I were exceedingly arbitrary at times and earned much criticism for their stern policies and heavy assessments. Notwithstanding this opposition, these kings developed a strong central government. Although William Rufus added little that was new, considerable credit is due him for the efficient manner in which he governed the realm. His reign, however, was characterized by such cruelty and despotism that his death caused no regret on the part of either Saxon or Norman.

According to his father's wishes and in keeping with the principle of primogeniture, William II should have been succeeded by his brother Robert. At this time, however, Robert was in the Near East engaged in the First Crusade and did not hear of his brother's death for some months. Conscious of the fact that circumstances were all in his favor, Henry determined to seize the throne and make amends to Robert later. Hurrying to Winchester, the ancient capital of Saxon England, Henry made himself master of the royal treasury and secured from those barons who could be relied upon, their consent to his elevation to the throne. In order to fortify his position, Henry then issued a Charter of Liberties in which he promised to undo the evil deeds of his brother, protect the Church, and rule wisely. Upon Robert's return, Henry defeated his brother in battle and placed him in confinement for the rest of his life. The issuing of the Charter of Liberties, which later became the basis upon which *Magna Carta* rested, the taking of the coronation oath, the penetrating influence of the feudal contract, and the force of Church opinion should be viewed as evidences of restrictions upon an absolute monarchy. These forces, however, for the time being were overshadowed by the many instances in which Henry added to the power of the central government. Henry was not as despotic as William II, though he often forgot his promises and frequently ignored the feudal rights of his barons. In the main, a greater sense of security and justice prevailed throughout England during his reign.

In gaining these ends Henry leaned heavily upon both the Great and Little Councils. Further, as the complexity of government increased, he assigned larger and more important duties to his carefully selected officers. Foremost among the work rendered by these men was that incident to finance. Financial matters, indeed, had become one of the most prominent features of government. The amount of revenue which poured into Henry's strongbox had become so large and the duties incident to financial matters so numerous that the King was forced to rearrange the functions of the *Curia Regis*. Selecting those men, therefore, who had already excelled in such matters, Henry established what has been known as the Court of the Exchequer. These men, notably the Treasurer, the Justiciar and the Chancellor, were assisted by others of the *Curia* as well as by a group of trained clerks. Doubtless, Henry did not intend to found a distinct new court and the presence of the same directing personnel lends strength to this assumption. In view of the increased fiscal work which had fallen upon the Little Council, Henry probably intended only to concentrate this activity both as to time and procedure. In this manner financial affairs would be handled more efficiently without impairing the performance of other duties.

Twice a year, therefore, in the spring and fall, certain royal officers of the *Curia* devoted most of their time and energies to matters affecting finance. At these sessions they received from the sheriffs a statement of receipts and expenditures, audited it and saw to it that the treasury received the amount due the King. The procedure by which this was done was extremely simple. The sheriff, having had his collections assayed, stood before a table which was marked off by horizontal and perpendicular lines forming columns. The column at one extreme was listed as the "penny" column, the next one as the "shilling" column, the next a "pound" column, while the remainder were allotted to larger denominations of pounds. Bisecting these columns was a broad horizontal line. While the sheriff was reciting his accounts, a clerk was tossing counters into the various columns, the number of counters agreeing with each item reported by the sheriff. Those counters which fell on the far side of the table represented the sheriff's receipts, while those which fell on the near side stood for his expenses. Having finished his report the clerk then proceeded to clear the various columns; for example, if there were eleven counters in the pound column, ten of these were removed while another was tossed into the "ten pound" column. In this manner, an exact statement was gained of the sheriff's return, a record of which in pounds, shillings, and pence was then cut into a short piece of wood (tally); a thin slice indicating a penny, a larger one a shilling and still larger ones, pounds. These slices went from one side of the stick to the other, a method which permitted the tally to be split in two so that both the sheriff and the Exchequer had receipts of the transaction much in the manner of a Chinese laundry ticket. It was because of this movement of counters on a table with its columns, which resembled a chessboard, that the Court received the name of Exchequer.

The Court of Exchequer was an important cog in the scheme of centralization which Henry pursued. Not only did it render the financial life of the state more precise by compelling the sheriff to appear in person before the court but it tended to make the relationship between the central and local governments more realistic. Further, the independence of the sheriff, which of late had become somewhat disturbing, was limited to a marked degree. The more one studies the administration of the Norman kings, the more one is impressed by the importance of financial matters. The fiscal needs of the King were enormous. In his desire, therefore, to make his revenue secure, rests the key for many of the innovations which were made in the central government.

Closely allied in purpose to the Exchequer were the itinerant justices. These men, all of whom were members of the Little Council, were sent by Henry at intervals into the local units for the primary purpose of bringing royal justice to these communities. Royal justice was more speedy and effective than the local courts and for that reason became immensely popular. These justices might preside over all suits of the King's tenants-in-chief, the pleas of the Crown, and such disputes as the local courts did not care to handle. Furthermore, litigants who were fortunate enough to have won the King's favor might upon a royal order known as the writ, have their cases handled by the itinerant justices. As a fee was always charged for both the writ and the use of royal justice, the Crown was none too backward about extending its courts and systems of law. Indeed, the presence of these justices, which really amounted to a function of the *Curia,* did much to weaken the power of the local courts, private or public, and to enhance the strength of the central government.

Ecclesiastical Problems

While these various reforms were being undertaken, Henry became engaged in a bitter contest with the Church. This conflict seems to have arisen during the reign of his brother as a result of the latter's refusal to fill a vacancy which had taken place in the office of the Archbishop of Canterbury. During this vacancy, William Rufus had reaped a golden harvest from the rich revenues of that holding. Probably William Rufus would have delayed longer in filling the office but for the fact that he was taken seriously ill. Interpreting this sickness as a sign of Divine disapproval for his past actions, William hastened to appoint Anselm, an Italian monk, whose piety and humility were of the highest order. Anselm accepted the office and immediately showed such strength of character that William must have regretted his selection on more than one occasion. Anselm, moreover, was in accord with Rome's desire to elevate the temporal and spiritual powers of the Church which, if carried to their logical conclusions, would have placed the state under papal control. Accordingly, canon law and the jurisdiction of Rome were advanced by Anselm in a manner which provoked royal protest. One thing led to another until a yawning gap separated the King from the Archbishop, who showed his feelings and fears by fleeing to the Continent.

On William's death Henry recalled Anselm, but in a short time the two were at swords' points over the general question whether the Church or state was to be supreme in England. The contest centered chiefly about the investing of an individual with the office of bishop once that individual had been elected to that position by the clerical staff of a vacated see. The act of investiture was ceremonial in nature and consisted of bestowing upon the candidate the pastoral ring and staff. The possessor of this power, therefore, naturally exercised a great influence over the future conduct of the bishop, as the latter was clearly indebted to the former for his office. Moreover, the position entailed feudal as well as ecclesiastical services and duties. This duality of function caused no end of trouble. For how could a bishop, or an archbishop for that matter, obey papal instructions if at the same time he were subject to the dictates of a lay lord? On the other hand, how could the state exact obedience to the feudal contract if the Church constantly interpreted this obligation to suit itself? Added to this political problem was the question of revenue which both state and Church were anxious to control. For several centuries investiture had often been conducted by laymen who frequently reminded the bishop that he owed everything to the hand which had placed him in office. Prior to 1075, although prominent ecclesiastics had condemned lay investiture, there had been no official action by the Church. In that year, however, Pope Gregory VII decreed that this practice was unsound and highly detrimental to the best interests of the Church.

Anselm proceeded without delay to carry out the Pope's wishes, only to meet unflinching resistance on the part of Henry. For several years a fierce contest was waged. Ultimately the Archbishop threatened the King with excommunication, whereupon Henry receded from his former position and accepted a compromise offered by his sister Adela. According to this agreement the state relinquished the right of bestowing the ring and the staff, a concession that was immediately taken over by the Church, which seemingly had won an important victory. In reality Rome had gained very little, for while the state could no longer invest, it continued to exact the oath of homage and fealty from the bishop as a feudal lord. More important was the fact that royal influence was powerful enough to force the clerical staff to elect one who was known to be friendly to the Crown. In this manner the state retained all that was vital and significant.

Henry's triumph over Anselm marked the end of his contest with the Church. Furthermore, it permitted him to give his whole attention to the growth of royal power throughout the realm. Success crowned his efforts. However, one thing arose which caused Henry much concern, and that was the death of his son, William, in 1120. Conscious of the fact that the barons would not take kindly to the succession of his daughter Matilda, Henry sought to make certain of the future by exacting from them an oath to accept her as their next ruler. Upon Henry's death in 1135, these promises were forgotten and Stephen, son of Adela, was made King of England. The new monarch realized that his position was insecure but hoped that his cousin Matilda would not dispute his right to the throne.

Civil War

Stephen's reign lasted from 1135 to 1154 and was marked by much chaos and disorder. In order to protect his title, which was being questioned by Matilda, Stephen was forced to grant concessions to both lay and Church lords who gained, thereby, enormous power at the expense of the splendid system of government which had been developed since the Conquest. Had Stephen possessed greater skill and ability, it is likely that much of the confusion which followed might have been avoided. He was unable to prevent the spread of feudal anarchy or check the rapid intrusion of the Church into state affairs. Furthermore, some of the very acts conceived in the hope of stopping this disorder made matters only worse. Stephen had to meet the repeated attacks of Matilda and her husband, Geoffrey of Anjou, who wished to gain the English throne in accordance with Henry's plans. Matilda's rights, moreover, were championed by her most able son, who, named after his grandfather, caused Stephen much concern. In the meantime feudal armies, assisted by mercenaries, marched back and forth over the island, spreading fire and destruction. The knight might find refuge from these attacks behind the castle walls, but the great mass of the population experienced unheard-of insolence and cruelty. Small wonder that a local scribe inserted the following in the *Anglo-Saxon Chronicle*: "In this king's time was all dissension and evil and rapine. . . . Never yet was there more wretchedness in the land."

By 1153 Stephen was ready to compromise with Henry, particularly as Eustace, Stephen's eldest son, had died. Stephen and Henry met at Wallingford and agreed to end the war and restore peace to a bewildered country. Stephen was allowed to retain his title and power while he and the barons agreed to accept Henry as king upon the death of Stephen. While Henry bided his time, Stephen tried to bring the realm back to peace and order. Castles that had been built during the civil war were to be destroyed, the mercenaries disbanded and banished, while property which had been seized was to be restored. It is also of interest to note that Stephen attempted to rehabilitate agriculture by granting what today would be termed governmental subsidies. To what extent Stephen might have succeeded in carrying out this program, no one knows, as he died within less than a year after Wallingford. Whereupon, Henry of Anjou, then in his twenty-first year, ascended the throne of England.

GENEALOGY OF THE NORMAN AND ANGEVIN KINGS

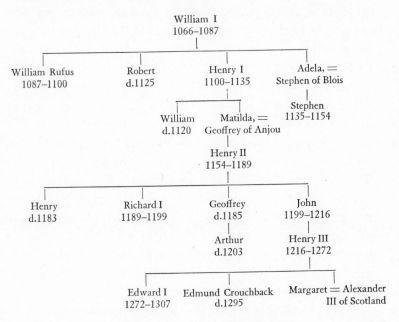

SELECTED BIBLIOGRAPHY

In addition to the volumes by White, Adams, Maitland and Stubbs, valuable suggestions may be found in G. B. Adams' *Council and Courts in Anglo-Norman England* (New Haven, 1926) and in the same author's work *The Origin of the English Constitution* (New Haven, 1912). J. H. Round's *Feudal England* (London, 1895), and R. L. Poole's *The Exchequer in the Twelfth Century* (Oxford, 1912) are of value. A convenient summary of the origins and nature of feudalism may be found in G. B. Adams' *Civilization During the Middle Ages* (New York, 1912).

Biographical and narrative accounts may be found in C. W. David's *Robert Curthose* (Cambridge, 1920); J. H. Round's *Geoffrey de Mandeville* (London, 1892); F. M. Stenton's *William the Conqueror* (New York, 1908); A. J. Macdonald's *Lanfranc* (New York, 1926), and R. W. Church's *Saint Anselm* (London, 1888).

CHAPTER V

Henry the State Maker

Imperial Growth

THE reign of Henry II (1154–1189) constitutes one of the most significant periods in English history. Particularly is this true when one reviews the contributions made by this monarch. Physically, Henry was possessed of a strong body and a mind steeled to the realities of life. Although not of great height, he became a powerful leader whose boundless energy and vitality command respect even today. Long hard hours in the saddle, either in battle or in hunting, were matched by arduous tasks at the council table. Exacting as this monarch could be in dealing with those who resisted his will—exacting even to the point of extreme cruelty—still he was unable to manage his own family and died heartbroken by the treachery of his sons. Unhappy as these contacts must have been, Henry probably realized before his death that he left England much better than when he had inherited it from Stephen.

When he ascended the throne in October, 1154, he was ruler of a kingdom that had rapidly grown in power and influence since 1066. Within five years after the Conquest, William's power was felt in all parts of the old Saxon monarchy and the way was paved for a penetration of Wales and Scotland. Heretofore all attempts of the Wessex kings to control these areas had failed. To protect his holdings from the Celts in Wales, William parcelled out extended domains in western England to his Norman followers. These lords, while subject to the King in a general way, were permitted to undertake a conquest of the frontier as independent adventures. Year after year the power of these barons was extended, while at times William II and Henry I supported their endeavors by military efforts when Celtic resistance became too stubborn. By 1135 Celtic independence was limited to North Wales. Stephen's misrule, however, permitted many a Celtic chieftain in south and central Wales to rebel against Norman domination. It is to the credit of Henry II that this bid for independence was brought speedily to an end. Southern Wales was brought once more into the scheme of English affairs, while the northern part was forced to render homage to the new monarch.

In the meantime Henry had his attention turned toward Scotland. At the time of the Conquest, Scotland was ruled by Malcolm III, whose ambition had already led him into conflict with the Saxon kings. Determined to push his domain across the Tweed, Malcolm joined hands with certain northern Saxon lords in an attempt to check the onward march of William. The military strength of the Norman, however, was too much for the Scottish king, who accepted the situation, so it is reported, by giving homage to the Conqueror. It is evident in the light of Malcolm's later invasions of England that he never took his promises to William and William II very seriously. Accordingly it was necessary for the latter monarch to mete out punishment to the Scottish king by driving him out of Cumberland, which heretofore he had held as a fief of the Norman. Henry I followed this gain by his marriage to the sister of the Scottish ruler. The advent of Stephen, however, undid all his predecessors had accomplished, and by 1154 Northumberland, Cumberland, and Westmoreland were subject to Scotland. To regain these lost provinces became an avowed object of Henry II who, taking advantage of internal dissension in Scotland, not only wrested these territories away but was able to compel the Scottish king to accept Scotland as a fief of England. The relationship thus established, actually amounted to little, as Scottish rulers governed their domain without much regard to their feudal contracts. On the other hand, a theoretical overlordship had been created, and the road was cleared for later and more successful English penetrations.

As far as Ireland is concerned, not until the days of Henry II did any ruler of England seek to conquer that island. Supported by the papacy, which eagerly sponsored a movement that might bring the Irish under greater ecclesiastical control, Henry permitted Richard, Earl of Pembroke, commonly known as Strongbow, to undertake a military penetration of Ireland. Strongbow was followed by others and by Henry himself in 1171. Before the superior fighting machine of the Normans, the poorly equipped Irish, sadly weakened by internal strife, were forced to yield. Most of the conquered territory centered about Dublin and Cork and has historically been called the Pale. Within this area Henry attempted to establish an orderly government which functioned as long as regular garrisons were maintained. The withdrawal of these forces and the inability of the civil officers to check the feudal tendencies of the Norman lords led to disorder. Henry tried to restore his authority by sending his son, John, to Ireland in 1185. John failed to accomplish his mission and returned to England. Left to themselves, the Norman lords reverted to their old policy of plunder and destruction unrestrained by the English kings. From a practical point of view, therefore, Henry's invasion did little beyond preparing the stage for future activity.

Henry's interest in Ireland never seems to have been very great, probably because he was more concerned with his Continental holdings. At his accession to the English throne Henry already held Normandy, Maine, Anjou, and Touraine, and was the overlord of Brittany. All these states were held by Henry as a vassal of the king of France, but so weak was this monarch that Henry ruled these possessions in much the

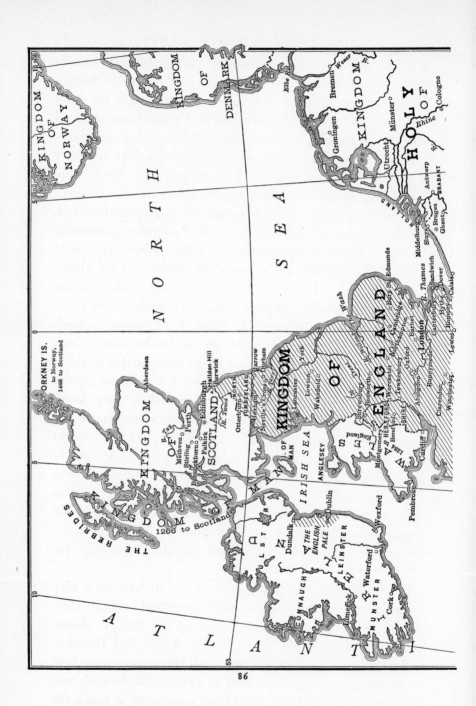

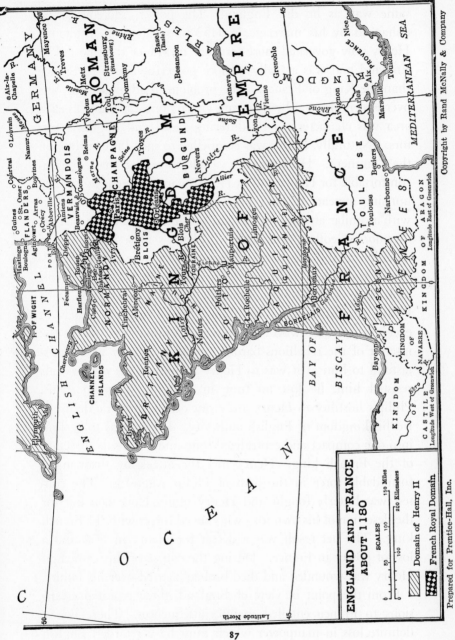

ENGLAND AND FRANCE
ABOUT 1180

SCALES

0   50   100   150 Miles

0   100   200 Kilometers

Domain of Henry II

French Royal Domain

Prepared for Prentice-Hall, Inc.

Copyright by Rand McNally & Company

GERMANY

ROMAN

EMPIRE

KINGDOM OF FRANCE

BURGUNDY

CHAMPAGNE

VERMANDOIS

FLANDERS

NORMANDY

BRITTANY

MAINE

TOURAINE

POITOU

AQUITAINE

GUIENNE

GASCONY

PROVENCE

KINGDOM OF NAVARRE

KINGDOM OF ARAGON

KINGDOM OF CASTILE

MEDITERRANEAN SEA

BAY OF BISCAY

ENGLISH CHANNEL

PYRENEES

same way as he did England. His power, moreover, was
enhanced by his marriage in 1152 to Eleanor of Aquitaine.
Henry now governed more territory in France than he did in
England and was actually a more powerful figure in France
than the King of France. The problem of administering this
overseas empire was by no means an easy one, especially as each
area was characterized by differing racial and linguistic factors. Naturally, Henry was compelled to spend much time on
the Continent. His European vassals, moreover, made life uncomfortable for Henry and in 1173 rose in open rebellion. The
uprising appears to have been well planned, as it coincided
with a similar attempt on the part of the English barons. Furthermore, Geoffrey and Richard, Henry's sons, joined in the
rebellion as did the King of France. In spite of this attack
Henry was able to hold together his domains. Another revolt
took place in 1181 followed by others in rapid succession, with
Philip Augustus, King of France, supporting the rebels in
every conceivable way. Philip's intervention was not in the
interest of the rebellious barons. Feudal anarchy was as distasteful to him as it was to Henry and when his own vassals
resisted him, he lost no time in bringing them to terms.
Philip's hostility to Henry arose out of the former's desire to
rid his kingdom of English authority. France was to be knit
into one compact and centralized state under the sole direction
of the French king. Henry met the attack by throwing a
formidable force in the path of Philip Augustus. The contest was bitterly fought and Henry might have won but for
the desertion of his own sons who joined forces with the French
king. The net result was a defeat for Henry in 1189 and a
loss of power in France. During the course of this campaign
Henry was wounded and died broken-hearted over his failure.

From the point of view of England, these repeated excursions to France entailed many consequences. There was a
definite loss in manpower which must have retarded English
social development in more ways than one. The English

barons, moreover, were repeatedly taxed to support these wars which ultimately gained nothing but defeat. Nor could they see any valid reason why their resources should be wasted in the feudal wars of France. Their interests lay in England and not in France. Financially, they gained nothing from these conflicts. From Henry's point of view the contest proved a poor investment, and the government was saddled with a burdensome debt for many years to come. English resources, which might have been profitably spent at home, were wasted in an ill-conceived French program.

Innovations in Government

Although Henry's attempt at building and maintaining the so-called Angevin Empire was none too successful, greater and more lasting triumphs were achieved at home in the fields of government and law. Little remains today of this pretentious empire. On the other hand, the descendants of his age, whether they reside in Great Britain, Australia, Canada, or the United States are reaping the benefits of Henry's legal and administrative reforms. And while it is true that the accomplishments of his predecessors gave him a firm and broad foundation, the fact remains that Henry not only perfected what he inherited but added many innovations of priceless value.

It will be recalled that when Henry became king, England was emerging from the ill effects of civil war and that many of the feudal lords had gained great power at the expense of the central government. To restore law and order as well as to place the barons under the strong hand of the monarchy became Henry's avowed policy. At first some of the lords scoffed at the young king's order to destroy their castles, but before many months had passed, their armed fortresses were leveled and their military power greatly reduced. Many an injustice, however, continued to be perpetrated by these men upon their vassals and serfs. Removed from the seat of government, and endowed with local wealth and prominence, these barons were able to challenge the authority of Henry. Furthermore, through their feudal courts they protected their soldiers and bore down hard upon the civil rights of their vassals, a procedure as painful to the local inhabitants as it was irritating to a king who wished to make his word law in England.

In seeking to break the power of the barons Henry developed the existing machinery of government. The *Curia Regis* was staffed by men who were punctilious in the performance of their duties and loyal to their leader, whose brilliancy in council won their deep respect. Well trained in law, the members of this body gradually took over most of the legal work which had rested in the Great Council. Not that the latter ceased to handle judicial matters or that any distinction existed in contemporary thought between it and the *Curia Regis,* but because of specialized activities and abilities the *Curia* tended to outdistance the other in importance and value. This body of experts, moreover, had their duties defined and separated in a manner which led to the creation in time of separate courts. The Exchequer, for example, devoted so much time and attention to fiscal matters that its staff became largely composed of members who had little relation to the *Curia,* of which they were still a part. Again, Henry delegated special judicial powers to five of his justices who were to handle any case whatsoever, although they might at any time request the advice and coöperation of the King and *Curia.* Ultimately this step led to the creation of the Court of Common Pleas, a body which did not take on an independent status until the thirteenth century.

Political considerations alone do not account for these changes in national or local government. Of equal importance was the desire to organize England so thoroughly that taxation could be handled more easily. It was imperative, if Henry was to assert his authority in England over local and private jurisdictions and to undertake his continental wars, that an orderly and secured income be established. The increased functioning of the Court of Exchequer illustrates this factor, while the extension of the judicial powers of the *Curia* brought a larger income of fees and fines. In the opinion of certain scholars, Henry's fiscal needs furnish the key to his many administrative and legal reforms.

As an example of this motivating force there are the itinerant Justices. Recruited from the *Curia,* these officials visited the local units at stated intervals. They were clothed with ample power to decrease the influence of the local and private courts. This was accomplished by the use of a writ which either transferred cases to the king's justices or else forced the local unit to render justice in a royal manner. When these officers appeared, they constituted a branch of the *Curia,* and being viewed as such, did much to overshadow the baronial and shire courts. Their method was so speedy and the justice administered so effective and fair that public opinion came to welcome their visitations. The law which was dispensed in one section was the same that was rendered in another, with the result that England in the course of time developed what is known as common law. Although common law—common in the sense that it was uniform throughout the realm—had other sources, such as the dooms of the Saxon kings and the legal writings of the great jurists of the twelfth and thirteenth centuries, the fact remains that Henry's practices did much to make it a priceless heritage. These justices, moreover, performed other duties of significance. Indeed it seems likely that their early use by William II and Henry I was for fiscal rather than judicial purposes. Not only did they assist in the collection of revenue, but they also saw to it that the feudal aids and incidents were properly rendered, that fortifications and bridges were maintained—in short, they gave attention to anything which concerned the king's rights or affected his interests.   Finally, it should be observed that these justices furthered the growth of the jury.

The Genesis of the Jury

The inception of the modern jury antedates the reign of Henry.   Its germs may be found in the practices of the Carolingian kings.   According to the desires of these monarchs, special officers, known as the *missi,* were sent into the local areas for the purpose of gaining some desired information. Perchance the king wished to know how much it might cost to construct a road, castle, or bridge; in which case the *missi* would summon a group of persons who were known to be honest, residents of the community and also possessed with technical knowledge.   To these men, who because they gave their information under oath were known as the *jurati* (jury), the *missi* put the question and from them received the required information.   The entire method was known as the *inquisitio* or inquisition and was commonly used in France when the Northmen under Rollo settled in Normandy.   Norman dukes employed the inquisition on more than one occasion and the institution was introduced into England by the Conqueror. The collection of material which appeared in the Domesday Survey is a classic illustration of the use of the inquisition. William's two sons, as well as Stephen, continued the practice as did Henry II.   Continental, therefore, rather than Saxon sources produced the germ out of which evolved the modern jury.

Doubtless the student has noticed that this device was royal in nature and was employed for non-judicial purposes.   Although there are earlier instances of its having been used in legal matters, it was Henry II who transformed it into the jury.   The earliest known use in this respect came in 1164 when Henry directed that in all disputes as to whether a fief was lay or ecclesiastical, the matter should be decided by the oath of twelve lawful men of the community. Two years later at Clarendon, it was decreed that a similar body was to present to the itinerant justices a list of names of all persons known or thought to have committed robbery, murder, or theft. In other words the older procedure which called for an individual challenge before a local court was abolished and in its place was substituted a form of the inquisition known as the jury of accusation or presentment. Henry had been led to this step by reason of the fraud and injustice which had taken place under the former method. Thus, Henry laid the foundations for the grand jury of today. It is to be noted that the presentment jury did not try the accused nor did they furnish evidence or witnesses to prove the truth of their charge. A simple statement on their part that they knew or believed an individual to have committed a crime was enough for the king's justices to order the defendant to stand trial according to the ordeal. It may be said that Henry would have liked to have done away with the ordeal, the validity of which was then being questioned by public opinion. Many a person of evil reputation and certain guilt had gone to the ordeal and been declared clean. This fact was patent to Henry and in order to make it more difficult for such individuals, he ruled at Clarendon that they were to be considered outlaws and given eight days to get out of the realm.

For ten years this procedure was followed, and at Northampton in 1176 Henry reissued these orders but added considerable that was important. In the first place the list of crimes was increased and in the second place it was decreed that if an accused was found guilty by the ordeal he was to suffer mutilation. Northampton, therefore, put teeth into the Clarendon provisions. No attempt, however, was made during his reign to try criminals by a jury. During the thirteenth century the courts endeavored to force persons to submit to jury trial, particularly after the Church, in 1215, had forbidden its clergy to participate in the ordeal. By this time compurgation and the ordeal by water or fire had gone into disuse; there still remained, however, wager of battle, a device which distinctly favored those of superior strength or skill. As a result the bench, which reluctantly allowed the challenger to resort to wager of battle, was alert for any technical slip on the part of the plaintiff. If an error were noted the court ruled that the accuser had lost his case. The courts, moreover, frequently placed the person under trial in a most uncomfortable prison or tortured him in various ways. Pain or misery finally was able to effect what the government could not, and, by the opening of the fourteenth century, the great share of criminals accepted jury trial. Torture, however, remained a practice until abolished in 1772, though it was not until 1819 that wager of battle was removed as a judicial procedure.

In the meantime Henry II had applied the inquisition to civil cases, and struck a severe blow at both the ordeal and compurgation. The procedure involved was simple. Any person who could convince the king's justices that a wrong might be committed in a trial following the old Saxon forms or who might gain the good will of these officers was allowed to purchase a writ. This document provided that the case should be settled on the oath of the lawful men of the community. To illustrate, if *A* claimed that he had been dispossessed illegally of his property and could gain a royal writ, the justices of the king then summoned before them a jury and asked whether or not *A* had been dispossessed. As the jury was one of the locality where the action had taken place and because such action ordinarily would have been observed in so small a community, it was assumed that this body would tell the truth. Upon their answers the justices rendered their decision. In time this body became known as the petit jury. It should be noticed, however, that the use of the trial jury was a royal right and could not be employed by any other court; further, that the jury presented no evidence nor summoned any witnesses. The extension of this procedure, which guaranteed jury trial to any person and introduced evidence and witnesses, came long after Henry's reign.

Henry made possible the use of the trial jury by a number of assizes, which in this case meant a royal act of legislation, though the term was also applied to a session of the itinerant justices. Among these assizes was that of *utrum* which was used in litigation involving the holding of church lands, and that of *novel disseisen* which concerned the question of dispossession. The importance of these and other assizes lay in the fact that in all cases relative to title, possession, or use, a jury trial might be employed instead of the Saxon forms. Because royal justice was speedier and more efficient, individuals eagerly sought writs so as to avail themselves of this newer method. Further, by serving on a jury the local personnel came vitally in contact with a growing central government, whose merits it readily appreciated, and from this participation secured valuable training in government. Henry's legal reforms, therefore, did much to stimulate interest and education in government, so that when the time came for the local units to participate in national affairs they did so with much success. Again, it should be noted that the use of the writs and trial jury checked arbitrary power on the part of the feudal courts and transferred many a feudal or local dispute to a royal court. Finally, it is of interest to note that the further development of the jury idea helped to bring about the House of Commons in the thirteenth century.

Henry Quarrels with Becket

As a result of Henry's judicial pronouncements, England became a better-ordered country. This gain had been made at the expense of the barons, whose unruly conduct Henry had sought to destroy. For much the same general reason this monarch was led into a contest with the Church. During Stephen's reign the power and influence of the Church had grown, owing to the ability of its leaders and the political disturbances of the time. Ecclesiastical growth had also been assisted by Rome's insistency upon temporal and spiritual jurisdiction. Canon law and the Church courts steadily encroached upon the central government. Henry met this attack by sponsoring the development of common law and by seeking to restrict the jurisdiction of the Church courts. Procedure in these courts differed in many respects from that employed by the central and local governments. Among these distinctions was a method followed by the Church in criminal trials. Even here, that which is of special importance relates to the punishments inflicted. Where the state administered mutilation, fine, imprisonment, and outlawry, the Church contented itself with imposing spiritual punishments in the form of fastings, pilgrimages, prayers, the burning of candles and, in extreme cases, removal from office. Believing that Christ's command should be obeyed, the Church courts refused to inflict any punishment which might draw blood.

As a result of this policy, Church officials, especially those of the lower orders, might commit crime and escape with very light sentences, which did little to advance the cause of orderly government in England. At this juncture (1161) Archbishop Theobald died, an event which gave Henry the opportunity of placing in that office someone who could be relied upon to carry out the King's wishes. To this office, Henry appointed his close friend and adviser, Thomas Becket, who on more than one occasion had been a loyal supporter of the King. Becket, it seems, was somewhat reluctant to accept this post but yielded to the persuasive pleas of his monarch. Once installed as primate, Becket completely reversed his entire mode of life. Where before he had taken his religious duties none too seriously, he now outdid all others in the punctilious manner in which he performed the tasks that faced him. Moreover, he constantly mortified the flesh so as to make himself an outstanding example of one who placed his God and

Pope above all others. Further, in order to indicate how completely he had altered his life and thought, he resigned the lucrative and important office of chancellor. Safely entrenched in his cathedral home and entirely in accord with the philosophy of Rome, Becket lost no time in challenging Henry's attacks on Church power. A crisis was reached over the question of ecclesiastical courts and the punishment which these bodies imposed.

To Henry the thought that a clerk of the Church, one whose duties were largely clerical and whose reputation may have been none too good, should be allowed to hide behind the Church for the violation of laws against murder, was as absurd as it was illogical. Why should a clerk of the Church escape the punishment which was inflicted upon one of his own clerks? Henry was aware, moreover, that every case tried before a Church court was a financial loss to the state and a positive gain to papal power and influence. For exactly the same reasons, though in reverse emphasis, Becket stoutly defended jurisdiction of the Church in all cases affecting the clergy. Repeated conversations between Becket and Henry failed to settle the dispute which rapidly assumed alarming proportions. At Clarendon, in 1164, Henry referred the entire affair to his barons and supported his views by a formidable array of facts in a document which is known as the *Constitutions of Clarendon*. In this document the King defined the limits of Church power. Among other things it was held that an accused cleric should be brought before the King's court, which was to decide whether the case was lay or ecclesiastic. If this body allocated the trial to the Church courts and if the latter found the defendant guilty, then the Church was to hand over the prisoner to the state for punishment. Becket refused to admit the legality of this procedure. Moreover, he called the barons' attention to the fact that while the point at issue concerned criminous clerks, the Constitutions affected the entire position of the Church. Eventually, however, Becket granted that there was nothing new in the various proposals advanced by Henry and agreed to observe them. He did, however, insist that in the event a state law conflicted with a Church ruling, the latter should be obeyed. By this time the atmosphere at Clarendon had become so charged that Becket yielded to the advice of his bishops and accepted the Constitutions.

If Henry believed that Becket had been sincere in his promise to obey these laws, he was speedily disillusioned by the Primate's actions. The Archbishop not only advanced a papal dispensation releasing him from his pledge but openly refused to allow the King's justices to try clerics accused of crime. Henry's anger rose to great heights, and Becket, in order to protect himself, crossed the Channel in haste. For six years Becket lived in France. During this period a number of fruitless negotiations were carried on between Henry and the Primate. Finally, Henry, who wished to arrange for the coronation of his son, met Becket and persuaded him to return to his see. Nothing was said about the Constitutions, as both parties were more than eager to arrive at some settlement even if it were only nominal. Back at home, Becket was soon in his old mood and aroused the King's ire by his high-handed actions. Those clerics who had supported Henry fell under the ban of excommunication, which was nothing less than an act of defiance to the king. Henry was in France when he heard of this action and demonstrated his feelings by bitterly upbraiding his followers for allowing "an upstart clerk" to set royal power aside. Several knights, present at this display of anger, believed that Henry's wish fathered a thought, if not a command. Accordingly, they crossed over to England and in a short time were thundering through Becket's home bent on murder. Becket's followers hurried the Archbishop into the cathedral but the pursuers were upon them. Eventually, after both sides had hurled sharp taunts at one another, the knights drew their swords and slew Becket.

Immediately throughout Canterbury, England, and Europe, fierce condemnation descended upon Henry, who was viewed as the real perpetrator of this unholy murder. Hoping to escape the effects of popular resentment, Henry hurried over to Ireland. Two years passed and while the deed was by no means forgotten much of the ill will had disappeared. Accordingly, Henry and the Pope, both of whom were anxious to heal the breach, came to an understanding. Henry gave his sacred word that he was not responsible for Becket's death and showed his regret by going to Canterbury as a humble and penitent pilgrim. Moreover, he promised to permit appeals to Rome and not to interfere with the freedom of the Church. On the other hand, Rome agreed not to receive appeals which might injure royal rights. As for criminous clerks, the Church was allowed, through what was known as benefit of clergy, to retain sole jurisdiction. It should be noted, however, that nothing was said in this agreement about the Constitutions of Clarendon, an omission which permitted Henry to advance some of the claims made in this document during the remainder of his reign. Neither party, therefore, had won a clear victory, both having to be content with a compromise. From the point of view of the state, the fact that benefit of clergy still existed was unfortunate.

Richard, the Crusader

In spite of the ultimate outcome of his contest with Becket, Henry left to his son Richard in 1189 a much better-ordered England than he had inherited from Stephen in 1154. Richard's reign lasted ten years, during which the machinery of government which Henry had forged was used over and over again with astonishing efficiency and success. Much of this was due to the King's ministers, as Richard spent most of his time on the Continent. Among these officers was Hubert Walter, an ecclesiastic, who had been schooled in the art of government by the great master, Henry. Hubert Walter ably administered the royal courts, and increased the power of the itinerant justices at the expense of the sheriff and the private and local courts. He is also credited with having conceived the office of coroner, though there is evidence that it had existed before this time. The coroner was empowered with duties which resulted in still further diminishing the influence of the sheriff, an office that had grown altogether too much for the well-being of the central government. Indeed, Henry had recognized this condition and by his celebrated Inquest of the Sheriffs had restricted the powers of this officer. Walter's action is of added significance in that it provided for the election of the coroner by the qualified suitors of the shire court. There was thus introduced the highly important principle of election, a function which did much toward educating the local units for greater participation in government in years to come.

Hubert Walter also found means of collecting the huge sums necessary to carry on Richard's wars in France and the Holy Land. Richard's rôle in the celebrated Third Crusade is one which fires enthusiasm for this monarch even today. The entire episode, shorn of its drama, cost England a large sum of money and many lives, and it may well be asked whether the effort was worth the price. The effects of this and other crusades will be discussed in a later chapter. For the present, however, it may be noticed that Richard's absence permitted the King of France to initiate a program that weakened England's position in France. In this, France was aided by no less a person than Richard's brother John, who had been left in charge of the English empire while Richard was away. John, it appears, had never been very loyal to his brother and he took advantage of the latter's absence to increase his own power. When John heard that Richard had been captured on his way back from the Near East by the Duke of Austria, John did nothing to hurry his release. Indeed he joined hands with

Philip Augustus, King of France, in trying to bribe the Duke to refuse Richard's ransom offer. Richard, however, raised his original offer and was accordingly released in 1194. Had John been other than a brother, Richard might have administered some form of punishment. As it was he pardoned the offender and, having raised an army, hurried across to France to fight it out with Philip Augustus. Neither monarch was able to win a decisive victory, and the contest dragged on until Richard's death in battle in 1199. In accordance with the principle of primogeniture, Richard should have been followed by his nephew Arthur, the son of Geoffrey. John, however, gained the support of Norman and English barons and was placed upon the English throne.

SELECTED BIBLIOGRAPHY

Interesting biographical material for the period covered by this chapter may be found in Mrs. J. R. Green's *Henry II* (London, 1888); L. F. Salzman's *Henry II* (Boston, 1914); K. Norgate's *Richard the Lion Hearted* (London, 1924) and *John Lackland* (London, 1902), and W. H. Hutton's *Thomas Becket* (Cambridge, 1926). F. M. Powicke's *Loss of Normandy, 1189–1204* (Manchester, 1913), and G. H. Orpen's *Ireland under the Normans* (Oxford, 1911–1920) are standard works of value. Kate Norgate's *England under the Angevin Kings* (London, 1887) is detailed but not so accurate as it should be. *Essays in Medieval History presented to Thomas Frederick Tout,* edited by A. G. Little and F. M. Powicke (Manchester, 1925) has material on the reign of Henry II. James H. Ramsay's *Angevin Empire, 1154–1216* (London, 1903) is a narrative history of merit.

CHAPTER VI

Baronial Conflicts

England Loses its Continental Empire

IT WAS during John's reign (1199–1216) that the absolute monarchy which the Norman kings had conceived reached its greatest heights. Little that was new was added by John, but when he summoned four discreet knights of each shire to meet him at St. Albans in November, 1213, he introduced an innovation crowded with meaning for the future. John's sole purpose in arranging for this meeting was to find some suitable way of strengthening the royal power. In taking this step he was following in spirit and form, the precedents established by his ancestors. Every monarch since the Conquest had viewed government as a means for developing an absolute monarchy. When Henry I and Henry II had conceived the system of itinerant justices, their sole purpose had been to extend royal power into the local units at the expense of the latter's institutions which were blocking the growth of the central government. Curia, exchequer, writs, coroner and the like were all created in the interests of a powerful king. At the same time, these monarchs were schooling their subjects in the art of self-government, and self-government is the very opposite of absolute power. Paradoxically, therefore, as it may seem, absolutism actually made possible the rise of democracy. In 1213, however, John was so blinded by his own strength that he failed to see the inherent possibilities which lay in the meeting of St. Albans. John's act, though motivated by selfish reasons, helped in a small way to pave the way for the future House of Commons.

When John came to the throne, he was the ruler not only of England but also of vast domains in France. To rid France of this alien domination had become the prime objective of the French king, Philip Augustus. During Richard's reign, a beginning had been made by sowing seeds of dissension between John and Richard, and upon the latter's death Philip immediately began to move against John. Taking advantage of John's dispute with Arthur over the English kingship, Philip showed his hand by openly supporting the latter. War ensued, but in 1200 Philip, by reason of a quarrel with Rome, asked for and obtained peace with England. Two years later, however, the French king was free to renew his feud with John upon the latter's marriage to Isabella of Angoulême This was not John's first marriage, but at the moment he was single because of a recent papal annulment. No one questioned the King's right to a second wife, though a goodly number believed his action inconsistent with the overtures he was then making for a marriage with a Portuguese princess. What alienated most people, however, was the fact that Isabella was already engaged to one of John's vassals. John's act, though approved by the girl's father, constituted a violation of the feudal rights which existed between lord and vassal.

John was too well informed of his duties as a feudal lord not to know that he had exposed himself to attack. Accordingly, he could not have been surprised when he heard the affair had been referred to Philip for settlement. Philip, as the superior lord, was perfectly within his rights when he summoned John to appear before a French court and stand trial. It was one thing, however, to summon and quite another to force John, an English king, to accept trial at the hands of a foreign court. Several times Philip ordered John to appear, but in every instance the latter found some reason for not accepting the invitation. Finally, Philip announced that John, by failing to answer the summons, had forfeited his French holdings. The next step was to compel his stubborn foe to relinquish these fiefs, and finding John unwilling to do so, Philip reopened the war.

The French troops had little difficulty in brushing aside the resistance offered by John, who seemed strangely apathetic. At times he was aroused to action, but so brutal were his tactics that he lost friends on every hand. On top of this came the death of Arthur, murdered, so it was believed, either by John himself or at his command. Everywhere in France English authority tottered, while John registered his fears by fleeing to England in 1204. Within another year, Philip's standards were flying from every castle in Normandy, Maine, Anjou, Touraine, and Brittany. Only in a part of Aquitaine was John's government recognized; elsewhere, Philip had won a complete victory. Within a little over five years John had lost, as a result of his mishandling, practically all of the empire which he had inherited from his brother. And while it would be quite erroneous to say that English honor had been touched to the quick by this disaster, the fact remains that John's reputation as a soldier and administrator had received a severe setback. Moreover, many an English baron had found fault with John's repeated campaigns abroad on the ground that they wasted life and treasure and had taken them away from their own interests in England. Others were disgruntled because of the excessive taxation, while still others suffered feudal losses in France as a result of John's defeat. There can be no doubt, therefore, that baronial opinion and feeling toward John in 1205 was decidedly hostile as a result of the ill-fated French wars.

John Defies Rome

In the meantime, affairs in England had turned against John, who became embroiled in a quarrel with the Church over a vacancy at Canterbury. According to past practices, the office of archbishop had been filled by the action of the cathedral chapter which possessed the right of electing its spiritual lord. However, because of the close relationship which existed between Canterbury and the Crown, the chapter had always chosen one acceptable to the King. Somewhat resentful of this royal interference and smarting under the pressure of the Episcopate of England, which was claiming a voice in these elections, a group within the chapter secretly elected one of their own number. This individual, sworn to absolute silence, immediately crossed the Channel and traveled to Rome to receive papal sanction. Success, however, turned his head and loosened his tongue, and long before he reached the Eternal City John heard what had happened. In haste and in anger this monarch forced the chapter to elect his own candidate, who was sent at once to Rome. Here ruled one of the greatest of popes, Innocent III, who ever since his accession to the papal throne had been marching along the trail which Gregory VII had blazed throughout Europe. Intent, therefore, on pushing the temporal jurisdiction of the papacy to the utmost, Innocent rejected both candidates and appointed one of his own choice, Stephen Langton. Stephen was an English cardinal, well-schooled in canon law and quite in agreement with the aims of the papacy. For this reason, as well as because Stephen's appointment set aside royal rights in elections to the archbishopric, John flatly refused to receive the man.

John's action at once precipitated a contest with Rome, a conflict which immediately broadened out as the monarch showed his ire by confiscating the primate's holdings. In addition, John proceeded to drive out of Canterbury those monks who questioned his authority. John's show of power was speedily matched by Innocent, who in 1208 laid England under a papal interdict. According to an interdict, church services as well as many of the precious sacraments were to be suspended. Today an edict of this type would hardly cause a

commotion except among the most faithful of the Roman
Church. In the thirteenth century, however, membership in
the Roman communion was the accepted order of the day.
From the time of one's birth until death, the Church exercised
a vital control over man's earthly existence, and only through
the medium of a priest might one hope to gain eternal life.
Accordingly, when England was placed under the interdict,
no one could marry, be confirmed, or ordained, as these rites
could be performed only by the Church. Moreover, those who
were so unfortunate as to die during the life of the interdict
were buried in unconsecrated ground and no church bells
tolled to frighten away the evil spirits who were ever on the
alert to seize the souls of the dead. Innocent, in other words,
finding that John refused to accept papal commands, had
plunged England into great misery. John, however, was quick
to retaliate by further confiscations and by abusing those
clerics who attempted to follow the dictates of Rome. The
net result of the conflict was that while some of the clergy tried
to enforce the interdict, much of the usual severity of its implications was lost.

Conscious that he had not gained his ends, Innocent next
hurled upon John a bull of excommunication. Unlike an interdict, which operated territorially, excommunication concerned only an individual. By this measure, John was denied
every privilege of the Church, while the faithful were forbidden to associate with the outlaw or aid him in any manner.
Accordingly, men trembled at performing any duty of state
or of availing themselves of any royal service. At the same
time the Church, which controlled many a civil function, like
probating an estate, withheld its kind offices. As for John,
he seemed to be utterly devoid of all fear, and visited his wrath
upon those who respected the Pope's commands. Once again,
therefore, Innocent had failed in bringing John to terms.

At John's court the King's authority seemed to be more
deeply entrenched than ever before. In England itself, beyond

the confines of the court, there were heard murmurs of discontent. Public opinion, in short, was becoming hostile to John despite the royal officers who executed the King's orders under protection of mercenaries. Where murmurs gave way to passive disobedience, the strong arm of John suddenly reached out and administered dire punishment. Property was confiscated, monasteries had their fine silver and gold plate taken away, while the more humble felt the arbitrary power of officers, many of whom were of foreign birth. Serfs and freemen knew not where to turn, but many a baron was bold enough to talk of open rebellion. So confident was John that he held England in his steel grasp, that he paid little attention to what reached his ears. Moreover, he had the courage even to summon his tenants to follow him into a Welsh war. Then it was that he first realized the seriousness of the situation. His officers told him in no uncertain terms that it would be sheer folly to undertake this expedition in the face of baronial opposition. Once John was out of England, so he was informed, civil war would follow. Thereupon John abruptly altered his plans while Innocent, who likewise was aware of what had taken place, threw his last thunderbolt. By a papal enactment in 1212, all of John's subjects were released from their allegiance, and early the next year, Innocent requested Philip of France to assert papal authority in England.

At once Philip, who was more than pleased to cross swords with an old rival, assembled an expeditionary force. In the meantime John, by one device or another, had prepared for resistance. He realized, however, that his troops had no confidence in him, and, dreading the prospect of Philip's marching into London behind the joint forces of France and the English barons, John hastened to make peace with Rome. Langton was received with open arms, while bountiful compensations for past wrongs were showered upon the clergy. Finally, John handed England and Ireland over to Innocent as a papal fief, in recognition of which John agreed to pay a yearly tribute of no small size. Though John's actions amounted to a complete reversal of policy towards Rome and gave to the Pope a most satisfying victory, the fact remains that the King had executed a clever arrangement. Philip, moreover, was informed by Rome that the invasion of what now was papal territory had been cancelled. Finally, John's position at home was greatly improved. Conscious of his good fortune and anxious to wreak vengeance upon Philip, John announced a war with France. At the same time he sought allies abroad, notably Otto IV of Germany, who joined with the English king in an attempt to check the rising power of Philip. In the meantime the French king had marched against Otto and defeated him at Bouvines in 1214. Philip then turned his armies against John, who had arrived in France. Realizing that his plans had failed, John made peace and returned home.

Magna Carta

During his absence, the English barons had prepared an armed protest against John's repeated misgovernment. Among other things they drafted a series of demands, patterned after the Charter of Liberties of Henry I, and presented them to John on his return. Realizing the seriousness of his situation, John obtained what was equivalent to a truce until Easter, 1215, when John promised to answer the barons. John, however, had no intention of yielding; and while the barons waited, the King sought to regain lost ground. The Church, freemen, townspeople, and even some of the barons were approached by John with concessions of various kinds. Mercenaries were brought over from the Continent and the Pope was asked to lend help. Aware of John's conduct the barons marched to London, where they received a cordial welcome. Encouraged by the support of this important city, the barons opened the war. After a short time, during which he maneuvered both for time and military position, John realized his

case was hopeless. Accordingly, on June 15, 1215, at Runnymede, John met his vassals in conference. The result of this
immortal gathering was John's consent to Magna Carta.

No document in all English history equals Magna Carta.
At the same time no document has been more misunderstood
and misinterpreted. Stripped of its verbiage, the Great Charter was little more than a treaty won by a victorious barony
from a defeated monarch. Moreover, in the last analysis, the
Charter meant simply that John, like all other Englishmen,
was subject to the spirit and the letter of the law. But what
law? Surely this law was none other than that which was
used in 1215; and since the parties to the treaty were nobles,
the bulk of the law was feudal. Keeping this pertinent fact
in mind, one may review the more salient features of the
Charter. That which first attracts attention is John's long list
of titles, his unquestioned devotion to Rome and his intense
desire to govern the realm for the well-being of his faithful
subjects. Most of this may well be considered as so much
rationalization, as John on many occasions had demonstrated
little regard for either God or man. On the other hand,
John's expressions of loyalty to the Church and the barons
constituted a definite commitment on his part which the
barons intended should not be forgotten. The rest of the
Charter concerns chiefly the feudal relations existing between
the King and his vassals and amounts to a confession on John's
part that he had violated these rights in the past. For example,
the right of the king to confiscate the property of those who
owed him debts was to be restricted in the future, while abuses
relative to wardship were to be discontinued. It should be
noted, however, that the barons in seeking to protect their own
position seriously cramped the further growth of the central
government. Not that they removed any of the important
devices which past kings had instituted, but by subjecting the
Crown to the will of the barons, they transferred considerable
power from the former to the latter. Moreover, the victors

created a committee of the barons to attend the Crown and watch over its conduct and their interests. Because of internal dissensions and the subsequent actions of John, this committee accomplished practically nothing. Accordingly, while the letter of Magna Carta made possible a system of baronial control, its enforcement was far from being successful.

It is important, nevertheless, to note that had the barons had their way the future development of government would, in all probability, have been retarded. Fortunately for future generations this movement was not realized. The simple fact that it did not take place, however, accounts in part for much of the misunderstanding which has grown about Magna Carta. The Charter, in short, has been viewed by many as a document of human liberties and the foundation upon which rests the British democracy of today. While it is true that some of the provisions of the Charter contain benefits which seeped down to the freeholders of 1215, the important thing to remember is that it contained a statement of feudal rights and privileges which did not concern the great mass of Englishmen of that day. None of the sources for the next three centuries refer to Magna Carta as a document drafted in the interests of the unprivileged classes. Indeed, though the Charter was repeatedly reissued during this period, it was gradually pushed into the background and ultimately forgotten. This was due in part to the many revisions that appeared, revisions which often left out certain clauses of the original charter. Again, the civil disturbances which attended the War of the Roses did much to blot out the memory of the document. These dissensions were followed by the rule of the Tudors, whose strong arms arrested further democratic growth. Contemporary literature of the Tudor period (1485–1603) is strangely silent about Magna Carta. Shakespeare in his play *King John* has no reference to what probably was the most important event in that king's public career. Had this

great dramatist known of the Charter, it seems most unlikely
that he would have passed over so significant an episode.

During the first half of the seventeenth century, however,
the Charter was discovered by the Puritans in their contest
with the Stuart kings. It was these Puritans who made the
Charter a document of human rights and liberties. Without
purposely misquoting or misinterpreting Magna Carta, they
read into it seventeenth-century ideas and meanings. Had
they possessed greater historical and critical sense they could
hardly have used the Charter as a check upon Stuart practices.
Thankful as one may be for their failure to read Magna Carta
correctly, one should not be blind to the fact that much of
their reasoning and interpretation was false. One or two
illustrations will make clear the errors of the Puritan lawyers.
On scanning the document they encountered a clause which
read that no scutage or aid, except the customary three, could
be levied but by the consent of the Great Council. This clause
was made to mean that no taxation could be imposed by the
king except by parliament's consent. Now the language of
Magna Carta is feudal and the levies referred to were not
taxes in the sense of the Stuart period. Again, parliament as
it existed then was quite a different thing from the Great
Council of John's reign. There was no parliament in 1215,
while the composition and constitution of the Great Council
as defined by Magna Carta relate in no way to the legislative
body known to the Puritans. Accordingly there is nothing in
the Charter which denies the right of taxation by the crown
without the consent of parliament.

The Puritans also declared that the Charter definitely mentioned rights granted by John to the freemen of England; in
this, they were entirely correct. What constituted a freeman
in 1215, however, was quite different from what it was in the
seventeenth century. In John's day not more than ten per
cent of the total population could be classed as freemen and

practically all these were among the noble class who, it will be recalled, had forced John to grant the Charter. Few, if any, of these nobles gave any thought to those below them; they were concerned solely in the protection of their own rights. Again, the Charter has been said to contain reference to jury trial in criminal cases, a procedure which was not common until after the middle of the fourteenth century and which did not exist in 1215. Hence the Puritans were quite wrong in attributing to the Charter a meaning which was not then thought of. It has also been argued by the seventeenth-century lawyers that the Charter guaranteed habeas corpus, but once again these men erred. Habeas corpus was not enacted into law until the Stuart period, although it is true that the writ had been in use for some time. It was not, however, employed in John's day.

It is also quite false to hold that Magna Carta contains any reference to an independent English Church. The language, to be sure, implies the existence of a national church but the use to which the term was then applied is quite different. In John's reign the Church in England was an integral part of the Roman faith, as was the Church in France or Germany. Writers, however, instead of speaking of the Roman Church in France, Scotland, or England adopted the practice of referring to the Church in respect to a country. Accordingly, when mentioning the ecclesiastical arrangement of England, the expression used was the English Church, which in no way implied the existence of a separate or distinct national organization.

These several illustrations will suffice to show how the interpretations made by the Puritans and others were erroneous and how public opinion as to the Charter has been built upon false reasoning and knowledge. Not until the nineteenth century did historians begin to point out the true meaning of Magna Carta. Many school texts and orators, however, still proclaim a greatness that is largely a myth. Surely no one would expect a person of the thirteenth century to employ words as they were to be used at a much later date.

Although Magna Carta was not a document of human liberty there is much within the Charter that is important. Having violated the feudal contract, John was forced to admit his guilt publicly and to promise not to abuse his rights in the future. In other words the power of an absolute monarch was definitely restricted in favor of a limited executive. Moreover, each succeeding king for the next two centuries was compelled to recognize this fact by reissuing the Charter. Custom, therefore, dictated the practice of referring to Magna Carta whenever the barons believed it necessary to check the crown or to enforce their rights. Through the repeated use of the Charter the idea gradually developed that a reissue was tantamount to a sacred and binding promise on the part of the king to rule in the interests of all. Such a promise John made, but subsequent events enabled him to disregard his oath. John was aided in this by the barons themselves, some of whom, in contradiction of the Charter, continued the war against him. Even those whose duty was to watch over the King's conduct quarreled among themselves and treated John with a haughtiness that aroused royal disfavor. At the first opportunity, therefore, John tried to free himself from his obligations. Messengers pleaded his case before the Pope, who lost no time in declaring the Charter void on the ground that it violated the rights of England's overlord, the Pope. Bulls of excommunication were showered upon those who resisted John, the Pope's vassal. A few of the more timid barons went over to the King's side, which was being strengthened daily by the arrival of mercenaries. The great majority of the barons, however, stood their ground and refused to be browbeaten by royal and spiritual thunderings. As a result the civil war was renewed. Conscious of the fact that John had gained in power, the barons offered the throne of England to Louis of France. Louis accepted the invitation and appeared in England, during the spring of 1216, with a force that won several victories. By the close of the summer, John's position was none too secure. His spirit, however, urged him on to greater efforts. During the course of the campaign that followed, everything was thrown into great disorder by the sudden death of the King.

Henry III and Simon de Montfort

John's death left the throne to his son Henry, who was but nine years old. In accordance with his father's wishes, Henry was placed under the care of certain loyal barons, notably William, Earl of Pembroke. William, supported by the Pope, had Henry crowned, and shortly thereafter reissued the Charter minus one or two clauses. A little later a general pardon was extended to the rebellious barons, most of whom, being assured of personal and political safety, flocked to the royal standards. By 1217 practically all of England was under the rule of its lawful king. But what of the fair promises to Louis and what of Louis himself? As far as the barons were concerned, their arrangement with the Frenchman was over, and if that ruler sought to maintain his cause, Louis would have to fight a united England. This is exactly what Louis determined to do, but after a brief campaign he made peace and retired to France. With Louis out of the way, the few remaining barons who had continued in revolt laid down their arms and the war came to an end. It should be noted, however, that in accepting Henry, the barons did not admit defeat. The reissuing of the Charter, void as it was of certain clauses, assured these men that the contest had not been in vain.

From 1217 to 1234, the English government rested in the hands of several different lords. This was due in part to Henry's age, although the desire of the barons to retain control should be remembered. First, in order, came William, Earl of Pembroke, who administered England until his death in 1219. For the next two years England was governed by the papal agent, Pandulph, who held an even balance between several baronial groups who wished to dominate. After his retirement Hubert de Burgh directed affairs until 1232, when he was dismissed by Henry, who since 1227 had occupied the throne in his own name. Henry then allowed his former tutor, Peter des Roches, to administer the realm. Peter was distinctly pro-Roman in his policies and accordingly alienated those Englishmen who were hostile to foreign influences in England. Peter also courted disfavor by giving preferment to his own countrymen, the Poitevins. Those who resented Peter's rule showed their feelings by joining with the Welsh, who had thrown the gauntlet at England's feet. In the face of a possible civil war, Henry finally yielded to pressure and dismissed his friend and tutor. Moreover, Henry rid the realm of the foreigners and in 1234 announced that from then on he was going to govern the kingdom himself.

From 1234 until his death in 1272, Henry tried to live up to this pronouncement. During these years much that is of interest to students of constitutional history took place. For the present it is sufficient to point out that Henry, in spite of occasional signs of ability alienated the good will of his subjects. Foreigners again poured into England, and upon these favorites Henry bestowed offices and wealth. Court life became extremely extravagant and the benefits fell largely to the King's alien advisers. The barons protested strenuously against this policy and against the trend of foreign affairs. Henry, it seems, ever faithful to Rome, had allowed papal tax collectors a free hand in England in the face of violent opposition from rich and poor alike. Further, when Henry heard that his son Edmund had been given the Sicilian throne by the Pope, England was asked to furnish men and money to see the affair through. Well-informed Englishmen knew that while the Pope was the feudal lord of Sicily his authority in that island amounted to nothing. Indeed, Rome's only reason for granting this state to Edmund was to gain English aid so as to make the Pope the real owner of Sicily. In the face of this common knowledge, the barons refused to furnish men or money. Moreover, they forced Henry, on threat of civil war, to accept baronial control.

Although Henry was still recognized as king, government actually rested in the hands of the barons. Detailed information of this arrangement may be found in the celebrated Provisions of Oxford. In substance these Provisions placed all officers of state under a baronial committee, part of which was to be in constant attendance upon Henry. The King was also required to gain this committee's approval for every important act, while the committee itself was to report to the Great Council three times a year. These Provisions were announced in 1258; but it was not until the following year that the new government was able to carry through certain reforms favoring the middle class, which had suffered greatly under Henry's misrule. The delay had been caused by a series of internal dissensions among the barons, who had been unable to agree upon how the realm should be governed once they had won a victory over the King. Taking advantage of these difficulties Henry had appealed to Rome, which quite willingly released him from his promises and ordinances. In 1261, therefore, he dismissed the committee of the barons and endeavored to rule as an absolute monarch.

For two years utter confusion existed in government. Taxes were as high as ever and foreign favorites held important offices. By this time the monarchy had become morally and financially bankrupt, while the barons were girding for open war. Their leader was no less a person than Simon de Montfort, a Frenchman and brother-in-law to the King. For some time past, Simon had been remonstrating with Henry as to the latter's conduct but earned for himself only insult and abuse. Simon, moreover, had come to realize that what England needed was a government ruled by Englishmen for Englishmen. Expressed in modern terms, Simon had become nationally minded; and when in 1265 a civil war seemed imminent, this defender of popular rights was hailed as the leader of the rebellious barons. Possessed of an unusual military skill, Simon crushed Henry's forces at Lewes and forced the King to accept what is known as the Mise of Lewes. According to this arrangement, Henry was to govern subject to the advice of nine barons, who were to function like the committee of 1258. These barons were able, during the course of 1265, to extend their control, and what is more important, to gain the good will of the commercial class by giving them a voice in the meetings of the Great Council. Simon's political innovations, however, aroused not only royal opposition but dissatisfaction from some of his own party who were unwilling to take so democratic a step. As a result Henry weaned away from Simon some of his former supporters and renewed the war. The royal forces were captained this time by Edward, Prince of Wales, who, while a hostage of Simon in 1263 and 1264, had received splendid training in military art. Edward met Simon at Evesham in 1265 and won the day; Simon was killed in the battle.

During the next five years Edward practically governed England, and upon the death of his father in 1272, ascended the throne by the consent of the barons. Edward received this support primarily because he had ruled England in a manner which did not displease the feudal classes. Although he had refused to accept the domination of a baronial group, Edward had gained their good will by not over-reaching his royal powers. The fact, moreover, that the barons had been unwilling to espouse the reforms of Simon, who probably would have progressed toward a more democratic form of government, illustrates how far Simon was ahead of his contemporaries. Subsequently, many of his ideas were woven into the very heart of English democracy and for this reason it may be said that the baronial wars of Henry III were not in vain.

SELECTED BIBLIOGRAPHY

General narrative material may be gained from Kate Norgate's *England under the Angevin Kings* (London, 1887) and her two biographies, *John Lackland* (London, 1902), and *Minority of Henry III* (London, 1912). C. Bemont's *Simon de Montfort* (Paris, 1884) is still of value though the recent work by S. Bateman, *Simon de Montfort* (Birmingham, 1923) is better. A. L. Smith's *Church and State in the Middle Ages* (Oxford, 1913) presents the ecclesiastical problems of this period.

The literature on Magna Carta is quite extensive. The following references will furnish insight into the background and influence of the Great Charter: W. S. McKechnie's *Magna Carta* (Glasgow, 1914); F. Thompson's *The First Century of Magna Carta* (Minneapolis, 1925); *Magna Carta Commemoration Essays,* edited by H. E. Malden (London, 1917), and G. B. Adams' *Origin of the English Constitution* (New Haven, 1912).

CHAPTER VII

The Medieval Manor

Merry Old England

A MERICAN tourists of today frequently refer to England as the garden spot of Europe. Blessed by a temperate climate and showered by moderate rains, England experiences neither the extreme cold nor heat that is common to certain parts of the United States. Furthermore, the great majority of the inhabitants of the island are today directly or indirectly engaged in manufacturing, mining, and commercial activities. Consequently, as one drives through rural England, palatial estates, picturesque villages, and well-ordered farms are encountered at every turn. The grass and the fields seem forever green. Sharp as is the contrast between this vista and American rural areas, few observers pause to think what England was like during the years the Norman and Angevin ruled with an iron hand. Were one to follow in the wake of William's march to the north or pursue the royal standard to Runnymede or Lewes, a different picture would be presented. The fields would still be fresh and attractive, the climate as pleasing, and the twilight as long as they are at present. The visitor, however, would note how his travels took him over rough and often impassable roads, through dark and foreboding forests and past dismal swamp land. Towns would be few and far between, with no comfortable hotel to greet his tired body after the torment of the day's journey. He would also notice the miserable lot of the farmer and how the great mass of the inhabitants were struggling to make ends meet by primitive and inefficient agricultural pursuits. Behind all this, he would see the domineering political and economic order of an age which distributed income in a manner that favored the feudal lord—lay or ecclesiastic.

Basically, therefore, medieval England was not a "Merry Old England"; rather, it was a land of striking inequalities and sordid conditions, a land weighed down by a feudal system. Feudalism, as has been noted, was a social order into which knights, freeholders and serfs were fitted in an amazing complexity. The discussion heretofore has centered largely about the noble class; it is now time to devote some attention to the others who, after all, bulked largest in the total population. Most of the serfs and a share of the freeholders lived in the rural areas and were an essential part of what is known as the manorial system. The word "manor" is of Roman origin and probably was not used in England until after the Conquest. As used in the Domesday Survey the word appears as a synonym for a tract of land. At times, the manor may signify a house, a mansion or a hall; but generally it may be defined as a piece of land held by a lord and worked by a group of dependent and semi-independent cultivators. In size the manor might be as small as twenty acres, though others existed which were many times larger. Often a manor was an estate which covered a large area, having on it several rural villages and hundreds of workers. In the north and east there seems to have been some uniformity of size, but for most of England no general or typical manor existed. Usually the total population did not exceed four hundred.

The question naturally arises at this point as to the genesis of the manor; in short, did it exist before 1066? The Domesday Book notes countless manors. Some of these show distinct age, others appear well under way, still others are but beginning to evidence the shape and form of the manorial system. Further, there were many tracts over which no landlord governed and on which no services were rendered. Clearly, there existed in Saxon England an economic arrangement much like the manor of Norman and Angevin times. But what was the origin of the Saxon manor; did it grow out of Roman or Teutonic sources? Both sides of the question have had able defenders, though the view generally accepted at present favors the Teutonic genesis. Regardless of the question of origin, the outstanding fact is the existence of a manor in medieval England.

The Manorial System

The most conspicuous part of a manor was the demesne, or that area of land withheld for the lord. The purpose of the demesne was to furnish the lord with food, clothing, and an income, the latter generally being in commodities though money payments were not infrequent. Often the demesne was a compact unit, but more frequently it was scattered among the land held by the manorial laborers. Again, the demesne might be either arable- or pasture-land. In addition to the demesne, the manor included the outland which consisted of arable, waste, pasture, and woodland. Crossing the pasture, or for that matter any part of the estate, was a highway which came from and led to some other manor or borough. Facing this road were the homes and farm yards of the laborers, while not far away but in a more desirable location, was the great hall of the lord. Around the manor house were the homes of the lord's officers and some of the more fortunate workers. Granaries, barns, stables, bake-ovens, wine-presses and workshops were also placed near the great hall. In another part of the manor was the mill, its location being determined by a stream or pond. Finally, most manors had some type of religious house or church. Physically, the manor was quite different from the modern agricultural village. The latter consists of scattered farm houses, each with its own barns and sheds, and possibly a general store or filling-station.

PLAN OF A MEDIEVAL MANOR

Prepared for Prentice-Hall, Inc.   Copyright Rand McNally & Company, N. Y. 289

There may or may not be a mill though in all probability there is at least one church. It does not, however, include the fenced areas devoted to farming or pasture and usually is somewhat removed from the woodland. Further differences may be seen by reviewing the agricultural methods employed and the type of people who lived on the manor.

The inhabitants of the manor consisted of privileged and

unprivileged individuals. First in power and importance was
the lord, and to him some form of service or payment was
owed by practically every one who lived on the manor.
Closely identified with the lord was the local priest or abbot.
Power, wealth and influence were the outstanding characteristics of a lord's position, which was restricted only by feudal or
local law. Assisting him in the management of the estate
were a number of officials and servants, free and unfree, who
were generally recruited from the local population. Chief
among these servants was the bailiff or manager, who was
personally responsible for the well-being of the manor. Certain definite tasks fell to his lot, such as selling surplus stock,
caring for the roads and barns, and inspecting the stock and
farm equipment. In most cases the bailiff was a freeman and
frequently held his office for but a year or two. The manorial
reeve, however, appears to have retained his position for an
indefinite period if not for life. He was probably a serf and,
as such, seldom left the manor except when his duties took
him to town. His name usually appeared on the account roll
of the manor. He prepared the items which the scribes entered upon this roll, relying upon memory or "from entries
on 'tally sticks' or on barn doors, where notches recorded various sums." At first he seems to have been appointed by the
lord, but by the close of the medieval period he stands as
the chosen representative of the serfs. In this capacity he
served as an intermediary between the serfs and the manorial
lord. Below the reeve came a group of minor officers like
the shepherds, waggoners, bakers, millers, and auditors. Most
of these servants were serfs though at times free tenants were
employed. A free tenant was a privileged individual in that
his social and economic position was usually higher than a serf.
He lived in a better home, possessed more worldly effects, and
was counted politically free. He was compelled, however, to
render certain services to the lord in the form of money payments. In addition he gave his master at certain times dur-

ing the year, some produce of his farm or an article of clothing. During the rush of plowing, planting, or harvesting, the free tenant labored on the demesne by the side of the serf.

Among the unprivileged classes none was more important than the serf. Politically he had no rights but those which custom or feudal law might grudgingly grant him. On the other hand, the serf was considered free before the law of the land, and, as such, served on the juries of Henry II. Practically, however, the life of the average serf began and ended as an unfree individual. He was the laborer *par excellence,* and upon his broad back fell most of the manual work performed on the manor. As a cultivator he tilled both the demesne and those strips of land which the lord permitted him to use. He was allowed to turn his scrawny stock out on the common pasture and gather hay from the hayland and loose wood from the forest. In return for the use and fruit of the land, the serf ploughed and planted the demesne, sheared the lord's sheep, transported his master about the country, cared for the roads and bridges, and performed a number of tasks too numerous to mention. During harvesting time he was required to render extra services, and at stated intervals he made special gifts in kind or money.

Below the serf came the cottage tenant (cotter) who was not asked to do as much as the serf, or villein, as he was also known. The cottage tenant enjoyed no special consideration but his economic status did not warrant such services. The cotter class was recruited from the younger sons of the serfs and possessed holdings barely large enough to sustain life. The cotter's home, which was often on the edge of the forest, was miserable. To the lord the cotter gave one day's work a week. Ordinarily the labor wants of the manor were met by the free tenant and serf. There were occasions, however, that called for additional labor, especially at harvest time. Anyone acquainted with American agriculture is aware of the transient number of hands employed during harvest. These men, moreover, move north with the season from the wheat fields of Oklahoma to those of western Canada. Medieval England, on the contrary, lacked this mobile supply of labor and to offset this want the lord availed himself of the cotter. The value of the cotter is also attested by the fact that his services frequently were used by the lord and free tenants in return for actual compensation. A wage-earning class, therefore, existed this early in English economic life.

Lowest down in the scale of unprivileged persons were the slaves, who were used by the lord as laborers to perform menial tasks about the manor, houses, barns, granaries, and workshops. At the time of the Conquest the slaves numbered about nine per cent of the total population and, contrary to usual belief, were not emancipated by William I; nor did the Church exert itself to better the lot of these people whose servitude was a constant source of profit. Slavery did not die out in England until the early part of the thirteenth century, ecclesiastical lords being the last to give up this un-Christian practice. The treatment accorded the slaves beggars description, though it was probably better than that followed on the Continent.

The lot of the English serf was little better. Difficult as was the work exacted of the serf, the insecurity attached to his tenure was what made his life hard. Politically, as has been pointed out, the serf had few rights; economically, he had even less. Custom dictated that he should do this or that, though practice demanded that his labor should be subject to the call of the lord at all times. It mattered little how much the serf had to do on his own holding as long as the lord's work was done. It was of no concern to the lord that a tenant's hay might be ruined by a storm, provided the lord's hay had been protected. Bracton, a famous English jurist of this period, has vividly described the serf as one who did not "know in the evening what he will have to do on the morrow." The deadening effect of this insecurity must have gone far towards restricting the initiative of the serf. Nor could he have been overcareful of his work on the lord's demesne. In addition he was subject to a number of petty and burdensome feudal taxes and exactions of which the *merchet* and *heriot* were probably the most severe. The *merchet* was the fee paid by the serf for the right of marrying his daughter to someone outside the manor. The *heriot* permitted the lord to claim, upon the death of his tenant, "the dead man's best beast or best moveable possession while the priest commonly took the second best as a 'mortuary.'" Frequently the *heriot* was paid in money.

Servile Uprisings

Generally speaking, a lay lord was more considerate of his villeins than an ecclesiastic, although the difference between the two was exceedingly small. Conspicuous exceptions might be noted. For example, Bishop Lyndwood is reported to have said, "It would be very rigorous that no beast should be left to the wife and children of the defunct, especially when they are poor and needy." In the main, however, church lords exacted all that was due them from the *heriot, merchet,* tithes and other ecclesiastical assessments. Small wonder was it, therefore, that the serf profoundly disliked the well-fed, well-dressed lord who exercised control over his material and spiritual well-being. Conscious as the villein was of his political and economic insecurity, he did not hesitate at times to rise against his master, whose sleep, like that of Henry I, must have been disturbed by visions of servile revolts. John of Worcester records that Henry's slumbers once were ruffled by rough serfs who "gnashed upon him with their teeth and demanded I know not what debt of him." Later in 1229 at Dunstable and then again in 1280 at Mickleover, the villeins rose in rebellion against their lords only to be beaten down by the superior military and legal weapons of their lords. Miserable as was the lot of the English medieval serf, it was much

better than that of the continental serf. English law protected the serf from murder and bodily mutilation, but, as
Professor Coulton has aptly stated in his *Medieval Village,* it
was on utilitarian rather than on moral grounds that these
safeguards were accorded the villein.

Manorial Economy

The serf's economic status may also be illustrated by glanc-
ing at his home, family life, food, and clothing. His home
usually consisted of a miserable one-story thatched hovel approximately twenty feet in length and twelve in breadth.
Frequently this hut was divided into two rooms, one of which
served as a living room and the other as a stable, in the event
the serf had no barn or outhouse. The walls, loosely held together by the crudest of beams, were pierced to make open
spaces which served as doors and windows. To keep out the
rain, wind or snow the poor tenant had to depend upon miserable wooden makeshifts or skins and hides that were filthy with
dirt and age. An open fireplace, usually in the center of the
room, served both as kitchen and furnace, while the smoke
found its way out through a hole in the roof. Within these
four walls lived the serf, his wife, and his children. Infant
mortality must have been excessive while life itself was much
shorter than the biblical "three score years and ten." Sanitation could not exist amid surroundings characterized by dirt
floors, the debris of meals, and the constant visitations of the
goose, pig, hen, or cow. The manorial rolls are crowded
with references to filth and dirt, while a contemporary poet,
in speaking of the serf, wrote, "At his bed's feete feeden his
stalled teme; His swine beneathe, his pullen ore the beame."
And yet in such a home all the ordinary and intimate family
relations took place.

For clothing, the average serf must have satisfied his wants
in the simplest manner. Occasionally one reads of linen being

used, but surely this must have been exceptional. In general, the coarsest of cloth served for dress, coat, apron, or hose, while leather shoes, too cumbersome for comfort, were worn at various times. Probably the serf went barefooted whenever the weather permitted. Some of his clothing was obtained from his stock, which also provided him with food. Geese, ducks, and other fowl were important for their eggs and feathers as well as for food. Cattle, sheep, rabbits, and pigeons were also eaten, while pigs furnished an opportunity for feasting at Christmas and other special days. Milk, butter, and cheese were common foods, and honey was employed for sweetening. Bread, which usually was baked for a sum at the lord's oven, was made from the coarser grains like barley and rye; wheat was consumed only by the better classes. Finally, it should be noted that the serf washed his food down with a potent ale which had an additional value in that it permitted him to drown his sorrows in drunkenness.

In the hands of the serfs, cotters, and freemen rested the task of cultivating the land. The methods used during the period under consideration improved as time went on, though at the beginning they were far from efficient. Agricultural economy, as followed by the Teutons in Europe, employed either the simple open-field or one-field system of farming. Under the former method new and uncultivated soil was used each year. As one season followed another, a virgin tract was brought under the plough; after harvest, therefore, the tribe moved to untilled land. Tacitus refers to this when he states "they change the ploughed fields annually and there is land to spare." On the other hand, the one-field system called for the continual use of the same land. Both of these methods were employed by the Teuton when he invaded and conquered England. Here, except for the Celtic villages where the open and one-field systems prevailed, another method was in use, commonly known as the three-field system. It had been employed by the Romans in England and was far more scientific in that it permitted crop rotation. Moreover, a part of the land was left uncultivated each year, and this tended to decrease soil exhaustion. Sensing the evident advantages of the Roman procedure and finding England too small for yearly migrations, the Saxon invaders slowly adopted their economy to the three-field system. At first they seem to have followed a plan which permitted the cultivation of but one part of the arable land and left the other section fallow, or untilled. Each year the process was reversed, allowing the soil to regain its former vitality. The two-field system had much in its favor, and, like the one-field system, was used in England long after the medieval period. Even as late as the nineteenth century, farmers in Yorkshire followed the two-field arrangement. Long before, English farmers generally had adopted the three-field plan. It was the method used on most medieval manors. Under this scheme the arable land was broken into three sections, one of which was planted with wheat, another with barley, and the third was allowed to lie fallow. Each year the order was changed, so that within three years each field had a period of rest. It is clear that by the use of three instead of two fields more land could be cultivated. On the other hand a smaller area was left idle and in this way soil exhaustion proceeded more rapidly than under the two-field arrangement. Improved methods of farming, plus a better scheme of rotation, removed this defect in the course of time.

Under either arrangement a mixed method of cultivation was followed. Each farmer held strips of land in different parts of the manor, and the size of these strips constantly varied. In one instance it might be two hundred yards in length and twenty-two yards in width, or the equivalent of about an acre. In other cases, the strip might be only a half- or quarter-acre. Each strip was set off from the others by a *balk* or an unploughed bit of land. In earlier days these strips seem to have been allotted annually to the cultivators so as to promote greater equality in holding. In time, however, owing to the rise of individual economic and political power, it became the practice for a person to retain his strips over an indefinite period.

Medieval farming gave small chance for individual effort. The entire scheme of manorial economy was one which subordinated the individual to the well-being of the manor. The underlying purpose of the manor was to provide an economic base for a political superstructure. The rules and techniques of farming, moreover, tended to force the laborer to do certain things in ways which had been found profitable in the past. Traditional conservatism frowned upon any extensive changes. Checked by these principles and practices, the cultivator fell into bad and slovenly habits. The industrious farmer must have complained bitterly about his neighbor who allowed his land to yield both weeds and grain. Although the strips were separated by *balks,* it was almost impossible to keep one's neighbor from tramping across land which was not his own. Many ambitious farmers must have bemoaned the time spent and effort involved in going from one strip to another. Finally, it should be noted that it was the lord and not the farmer who determined what should be planted and how it should be cultivated. In short, every detail of husbandry rested upon the decision of the lord, who based his actions upon past practices and not upon the wish of a tenant.

Bad as the picture may seem, the tenant at least knew that his family had a place to live, clothing to wear, wood to burn, food to eat, and at times merry-making with his fellow-workers. Legally, as has been pointed out, his position was uncertain, but ejection seldom took place. Paternalism, tinged with capitalistic characteristics, was the order of the day. Unlike his successor of the modern age, when individualism became triumphant, the medieval farmer was not driven from his holdings because of some pressing mortgage or debt. Though the medieval laborer was weighed down by many inequalities, he had at least some degree of economic security.

On the other hand, he probably had little leisure time, as most of his waking hours were utilized in a score of different ways. Cultivating his own strips and those of the lord was but a part of the usual work. There was also the task of caring for the meadows, and here the principle of mixed ownership held true as in the case of the arable land. Generally, the extent of meadowland was limited; manorial economy, therefore, gave much thought to its use. The yearly crop of hay was highly prized, as it provided a valuable source of food for the livestock. From February to August, the meadows were closed by crude and temporary fences. At the end of this period, the grass was cut, dried, and distributed to those entitled to a share. Once the hay was removed, the fences were taken down and the land was thrown open for pasture. The meadows, therefore, gave to the tenants both hay and pasture.

Other parts of the manor were used for pasture the year around. Pastureland might be found not only on the meadows but also in the woods and at times on arable land. More often, the pasture was placed in the wasteland, which was not suitable for farming and, though temporarily fenced, was known as the commons. No attempt was made to allot this land to the tenants; each person was allowed to let his cattle and sheep roam about in search of food. Swine might also be pastured, but then an area was fenced off to keep the animals from running wild over the manor. By the early part of the thirteenth century, sheep raising had become so profitable that manorial lords sought to restrict the rights of their tenants to the pasture. The common way of doing this was to set up permanent fences and to reserve the land so enclosed for the lord's own herds. This method of enclosing was entirely one-sided in its benefits, as the tenants were forced to find less-desirable grazing land for their own stock. Needless to say the tenants protested in no uncertain terms, but in general their complaints fell upon deaf ears. Furthermore, the right of a noble to enclose the commons, subject to certain restrictions, was written into the law of the land by the Statute of Merton in 1235.

The custom of using cattle for both food and labor did not result in the breeding of a high grade of stock. Further, the manorial order had no satisfactory way of caring for the animals during the winter. The use of carrots and other roots was not known, and the supply of hay or grain for feed purposes often was not enough to keep the entire herd alive until the spring. During the fall, therefore, many of the cattle were slaughtered, salted down, and used for food by the tenants. Again, the common pasturing of the cattle permitted loose breeding and the easy spread of disease. A full-grown cow, therefore, seldom exceeded in size an average calf of today. Common pasturing brought about undersized sheep. Horses were relatively poor and because of their having to be shod could not be used satisfactorily for husbandry. The horse, moreover, was a necessary part of the lord's equipment when called upon to do military duty, but was too expensive for the ordinary tenant, who often found it quite hard to keep a few fowl, ducks, and a yoke of oxen.

The crops raised on the manor were not numerous or varied. Wheat, which was sown in the fall, provided food for the well-to-do, while the average tenant was quite content to eat bread made of wheat and rye, or of rye alone. Oats were also used, as were peas and beans, though the latter two were often given to the stock. Barley was grown chiefly for the ale which was made from it. Uncultivated grapes yielded a sour wine. In the raising of these various articles, manorial economy used very crude methods. The wasteful rules of farming which grew out of the practice of strip cultivation have already been mentioned. A limited scheme of crop rotation was another serious defect. The use of roots was unknown and only hoeing and ploughing helped to keep the soil fresh. The use of fertilizer seems to have been understood and was managed by allowing the stock to graze over the arable land after harvesting was over. On some of the better farms the lords mixed a thick soapy-like soil, known as marl, into their fields to check soil exhaustion. Soil exhaustion was a factor which was always being fought; but with crude ploughs and hoes, a limited knowledge of husbandry, and an uncertain labor supply, the outcome must have been largely unsatisfactory. Further, a lord usually viewed his manor as a means of permitting him to fulfill his feudal duties. Such a policy worked against the prosperity and well-being of the tenants.

The average tenant seldom left his lord's estate. Only on rare occasions was he asked to do military duty and then only as a member of the militia. A few freemen or able serfs may have followed their lords to war or attended them at a fair or a meeting of the Great Council. Again, some of the inhabitants carried supplies to neighboring estates, villages, and boroughs, and returned with articles not raised or produced on the manor. Iron, manufactured goods, salt, medical supplies, spices for seasoning and preserving, and some bolts of silk, lace, or other luxuries constituted the bulk of this import. Some of these goods were also brought by traveling merchants, traders, wandering bands of singers and entertainers who told of the doings of the outside world. Royal officers, like the sheriff, the coroner, and the itinerant justice also visited the manor.

Generally speaking the manor was an isolated affair. Since it could produce most of the goods needed to sustain life, intercourse with the outside world was slight. Greater mobility would have followed had the manor been conceived on other than a subsistence basis. As a result neither local nor national governments were much concerned about maintaining suitable roads or highways. The chief arteries of trade and travel were those that had been laid by the skilled engineers of the Roman period. These highways were badly in need of repair and, though classed as "king's ways," were seldom improved by either local or royal authorities. Nor was there anything definite as to who was responsible for their proper maintenance. When a road was impassable, the traveler was allowed to detour as he saw fit, even if it took him over the arable land or pasture of a manor. The secondary roads of England, lacking the stone foundation of the main arteries, meandered and followed the contour of the country, and frequently were little more than tracks through swamps and forests. Moreover, robbers infested these areas and preyed upon those who, of necessity, had to travel. Transportation was by foot, horse or ox, the latter two often drawing cumbersome carts and waggons. When possible, the traveler availed himself of the navigable streams and rivers, but even these had their disadvantages. In spite of the dangers and difficulties attending travel, a goodly number of people moved back and forth across the realm, breaking down provincial feelings and attitudes, and laying the basis for national life.

The government of the manor was lodged in the hands of the lord who exercised this power through a manorial court which included all of his tenants, bond or free. The manorial court kept a record of its activities and from this roll one may gain much of the information presented above. In addition the manorial rolls illustrate the type of justice and law which was rendered. Fundamentally, the manorial court was a private jurisdiction and concerned itself with infractions of local feudal law or manorial economy. When a serf failed to render proper service or allowed his cattle to roam over cultivated land, he was summoned before his lord to show reason why he should not be fined or punished. The lord's court also legislated in the sense that it laid down rules for husbandry. It also held assizes for determining the quality and quantity of flour which should go into a loaf of bread. Violations of the latter resulted in fines, evidences of which abound in the manorial rolls. The manor was also an integral part of the hundred and, as such, certain judicial actions were settled in the hundred court.

The manor also played an important rôle in ecclesiastical affairs. The local priest possessed status and privilege which often proved burdensome to the serfs. At the same time he was prominent in the social life of the village. He opened the church and the churchyard for public meetings, allowed traders to display their wares, and permitted entertainment of certain types within his holding. The village priest also cared for the spiritual and physical well-being of the tenants. He was often the good Samaritan who healed the sick. Moreover, he provided whatever was available in the way of education.

SELECTED BIBLIOGRAPHY

M. M. Knight's *Economic History of Europe* (New York, 1926); N. S. B. Gras' *Introduction to Economic History* (New York, 1922), and N. Neilson's *Medieval Agrarian Economy* (New York, 1936) furnish general material as to the origin, structure and purpose of the manor. More detailed information may be found in F. Seebohm's *English Village Community* (London, 1913), and H. L. Gray's *English Field System* (London, 1915). Seebohm stresses the Roman origin of the manor; Gray reviews the Celtic and Germanic influences.

Most of these references may be used for an examination of manorial economy and agricultural methods. In addition there are N. S. B. Gras' *History of Agriculture in Europe and America* (New York, 1925); W. J. Ashley's *Economic Organization of England* (New York, 1920), and F. G. Davenport's *Economic Development of a Norfolk Manor* (Cambridge, 1906). Highways, roads and bridges are treated in J. J. Jusserand's *English Wayfaring Life in the Middle Ages* (London, 1889); J. F. Willard's "Inland Transportation in England" in *Speculum* I: 361–365; L. F. Salzman's *English Trade in the Middle Ages* (Oxford, 1931), and G. G. Coulton's *Social Life in Britain* (Cambridge, 1919) and his *Medieval Village* (Cambridge, 1931).

CHAPTER VIII

The Medieval Town

Early Mining Activities

ALTHOUGH medieval England was fundamentally a country of manors, considerable attention was paid to commercial and industrial activities. Most of the commercial and a large share of the industrial life of the nation centered in the towns. On the other hand, the more significant extractive industries were located in the rural areas of England. The mining of coal, for example, was a rural rather than an urban enterprise though the distribution of this commodity was largely in the hands of burgesses. The Romans knew of this mineral and gained a supply sufficient for their needs. Even this limited use was terminated by the ravages of the Saxon, and it was not until the twelfth century that coal was used again. Actual mining of coal did not take place for another century, when it would appear "that practically all the English coal-fields were being worked to some extent." Most of these fields were worked from the surface. Owing to a dearth of scientific knowledge no extensive tunneling or sinking of deep shafts could be undertaken; nor was there any demand for coal which these surface mines could not fill. Had English homes been adapted to the use of coal for heating purposes more coal would have had to be mined. As it was, the greater share of the coal mined was utilized by the iron and lime industries.

Iron seems to have been used for a long time, and during the Roman age attracted the attention of a number of people. The Saxons largely ignored the mining and refining of this metal, and it was not until the Norman period that a revived activity took place in this trade. During the twelfth and thirteenth centuries, forges and furnaces appeared in various parts of rural England. Most of this activity centered in Sussex and Kent, where forests provided ample fuel for the working of iron. Charcoal rather than coal was commonly used in the smelting of this ore. Iron was used for ornament in the homes of the nobles and in the building trades, though most of it was fashioned into hardware and weapons of war. Sussex alone on one occasion provided Henry III with thirty-two thousand horseshoes and twice as many nails. Iron tools were used to some extent on the manors, and iron bells appeared in the better and larger churches. How many people were engaged directly or indirectly in the mining and refining of iron, and in the manufacture of iron goods, is not known. It is certain that thousands, however, were dependent upon this industry for their living. Most of the hard manual work was done by men although women were employed to break the ore and handle the bellows. Manual power seems to have been used entirely, except in the washing process where water power was employed to some extent.

Water power was also used in the lead and silver industries, which had existed during the Roman period. The Saxon did little to develop these enterprises, but with the coming of the Norman definite progress took place. By John's reign the output of the lead mines had increased considerably. The lead mines centered chiefly around Alston Moor, the Mendips, and the county of Derby. Even as early as the time of Henry II, the rents arising from the mines of Alston Moor amounted to one hundred pounds a year, which was quite a sum for that age. The fields of Derbyshire were far more important, though those of Devonshire enjoyed a temporary superiority in the late thirteenth century. Devonshire also held a high place in the mining of tin, an activity which antedated the arrival of the Romans. Devonshire continued to hold this leadership until the days of Henry III, when the Cornish mines yielded larger and more profitable quantities of ore. The value of these mines and the use to which tin was put is attested by the large income which the crown received in the form of tolls and fees. The crown was also interested in the quarrying of stone and marble, products that were of prime importance in the building of castles and churches. Saxon architecture was characterized by the use of wood; that of the Normans, by stone. Quarries were scattered throughout the realm, though those close to some stream were favored, as carriage by water was cheaper and easier than by land. The massive walls of the Norman Keep at Canterbury or of the Tower of London illustrate how extensively block stone was used, while the roofs of many buildings were topped by thin slabs. Marble, while seldom used for external purposes, was common within the palaces and cathedrals. Purbeck, in Dorset, was the chief center of the marble industry; and many a cathedral, like that at Lincoln or Chichester, contains marble pillars, columns, and figures which date from this period. Chalk and alabaster were of minor importance, and at no time during the period now under discussion was there mining of gold or copper.

Last among the extractive industries, but by no means least in value, was fishing. As early as the Domesday Survey the herring trade of Suffolk and Sussex assumed some importance, while the cod fisheries at Grimsby and Scarborough were well known by the middle of the thirteenth century. Oysters, mussels, shrimps and whelk were also used as staple articles of food, especially within the towns. The burgess of John's reign, according to one authority, literally ate everything the sea had to offer from shrimps and eels to whales, though the latter were valued chiefly for their oils and fats. In general most fish were caught by net or trap and if marketed were kept alive in barrels or specially constructed wells. When transported by land, the fish merchants packed their catch in salt which was usually made by evaporating sea water.

Industrial Life

In addition to fishing and the other extractive industries, many Englishmen were employed in the building, metalwork-

Courtesy Assoc. British and Irish Railways, Inc.

WEST FAÇADE, YORK MINSTER. The largest English medieval cathedral. The great window and sculptured portal are of special significance.

ing, brewing, pottery, glass, clothing, and leather trades. Skilled and unskilled labor was employed in these enterprises, subject to the direction of master mechanics, engineers, and architects. William de Sens, Ailnoth, Elias de Derham, and Walter de Colchester are outstanding examples of the genius and ability of the men who conceived and ordered the construction of the buildings of the twelfth and thirteenth centuries. Wells, Lincoln, Salisbury, Westminster, and Canterbury cathedrals all attest the importance of the building trades, to say nothing of the numerous castles and towers which were erected throughout the island. Today one speaks about the building industry and if one contemplates the construction of a home, store, factory, or apartment, he consults first of all an architect. Often the latter undertakes the actual construction or it may be turned over to a contractor who arranges for the purchase of materials, labor, and equipment. In the medieval age there was no contractor, and the future owner of a castle or church bought the needed materials and equipment and paid the labor himself. In this manner the costs of construction were materially reduced, a factor which helps to explain why so many extensive and lofty buildings were reared. Although the manual labor of men and women was the primary source of power with which these edifices were constructed, it is of interest to note that cranes, derricks, and wheels together with scaffolds and piles transported or lifted huge stones, tiles, and sculptured figures. Masons and carpenters usually coöperated in this work, though the latter alone generally handled the construction of the many wooden buildings which characterized the English town.

The skill and expert craftsmanship shown by these artisans in the building industry were matched by those who worked in metal. Gold and silversmiths, merely mentioned in Saxon sources, became more common during the Norman and Angevin period. Silver and gold plate, elaborately and artistically designed, adorned the tables of the wealthier classes, while rich and beautiful vases, candlesticks, and sacramental vessels were used by the churches and monasteries. Most of the gold and silver of the age was utilized for these purposes rather than for commercial or banking activities. It is not surprising, therefore, to read that when John was in need of gold he often raided the religious houses of the Church. There were also pewterers, bellmakers, and foundry workers.

Many a vessel fashioned by a goldsmith was used as a drinking cup for ale or wine, beverages consumed by all classes. Beer was not generally used until the close of the fourteenth century, and cider was not common until after the Conquest. Both wine and cider were imported from France in large quantities, for there was little domestic manufacturing of these products until the thirteenth century. Ale was an Englishman's drink and practically every manor and borough had its brewery. The Canterbury, Ely, and Shoreham breweries were particularly well known. Most of the work in the breweries was performed by women who also labored in the baking trade. Important as these activities were, they did not equal the manufacture of woolen cloth which employed a large number of hands: men, women, and children. London, Stamford, Nottingham, Oxford, Lincoln, and Winchester are but a few of the more important centers of this trade. Much of the cloth was made into sheets, spreads, and blankets, was cheap in quality, and probably was used chiefly by the poorer classes. Better grades, however, were produced and were in demand by the wealthier and noble ranks. The brilliant scarlets, russets and blues of Beverley and Stamford figured in an export trade to Lübeck, Milan, and Venice. So extensive was this industry and so large were the returns which accrued to its owners that the weavers were quite willing to pay heavy fees to the Crown. In return for this income the Crown forbade other domestic merchants to engage in this trade. In spite of the importance of the woolen trade and its effects upon manorial economy, the greater share of the woolen goods consumed in England were either made on the manors themselves or imported from the Lowlands.

Each industry referred to was subject to regulations imposed by the Crown, by a local authority, or by the workers themselves. Most of the royal and local rules were conceived for revenue purposes, while those laid down by the workers concerned the quality, quantity, and cost of the goods as well as the hours, wages, and conditions of work. The lot and fortune of the laborers varied in respect to the work rendered. The wages paid to the ordinary male worker were relatively low, but those earned by women and children were still less. In the lead industry the laborer received, in addition to his meager pay, an occasional allowance for needed supplies plus certain tools which were the property of the operator. Moreover, it is of interest to note that the basis for wages in many a medieval industry rested upon piece work as well as upon hours of employment. Skilled labor received slightly higher returns while those who owned or directed a trade earned profits in the form of prices, fees, interest, and rents. Manufacturing and mining, therefore, rested upon a capitalistic base with the greater benefits falling into the hands of a small privileged group. Coal, iron, and lead mines as well as the quarries were, in many instances, operated directly by the owners, whose vested rights were protected by royal or local charters. Often, however, the owner leased his property to others who paid rent in kind or money. The presence of wealthy traders and merchants in the cloth industry also raises the presumption of a capitalistic base, which is strengthened by a knowledge of how profits were made and allocated during the medieval period. The student should not conclude that capitalism as it existed in the Tudor and Stuart period or, as it functions today, was present in the same form during the twelfth and thirteenth centuries. The reader should understand, however, that capitalistic forces were at work laying the foundations for a future social and economic order.

An examination of the medieval crafts and gilds will serve to make these observations clear and at the same time will present a picture of industrial organization. Gilds seem to have existed as early as the Saxon age and while it may be true that a few of these were engaged in manufacturing, probably the greater share were little more than organizations or associations of men and women for social and religious objectives. Fraternal organizations of this type continued to function throughout the medieval period and well into later years. The fraternal aspect, moreover, existed in other associations which were built on the basis of trade and labor. The affiliation of individual workers along this latter line ultimately gave rise to the so-called merchant gild. In general, a merchant gild included skilled and unskilled laborers, masters, operators, and owners. At first glance it might appear that the merchant gild was essentially a democratic device in which the conduct of trade and labor was regulated in the interest of all. A closer examination, however, reveals that beneath this outer structure there existed an inner group, small in number, but ever so effective in determining the policies of the association. Vitally interested in profits, these leaders regulated the economic and political life of the gild. Moreover, because of their prominence, they were often able to dictate the government of the borough. Private capitalism and local politics, therefore, were frequently but one and the same thing. At times it is almost impossible to divorce the two. On the other hand an effort was made in some localities to keep the members of the merchant gild out of municipal offices, where they were prone to abuse government for their own ends. Profits, hours of work, quantity and quality of production, in fact almost everything which concerned the manufacture, sale, and distribution of a product was lodged in the hands of the wealthier and governing classes. As a result the merchant gild was often given a virtual monoply of the industrial life of a borough. Every activity of importance,

whether clothmaking, brewing, building, or baking, was included within the jurisdiction of the merchant gild. Minor
enterprises were left alone and seem to have functioned on
an individual basis. Not all of the labor and industry of a
borough, therefore, was included within the scope of the merchant gild though the greater share was governed by its
authority.

The merchant gild had a different form of government from
the borough. Each had its own organization, laws, and courts.
When differences developed among the gild members, they
were usually settled by the gild court. If the gildsman was
dissatisfied with the decision, he might have his case reviewed
by the borough court, which also had original jurisdiction in
all ordinary civil and criminal disputes.

The Medieval Borough

A statement of the general privileges and powers enjoyed
by the merchant gild and borough was outlined in the town's
charter, which was issued by the corporation's overlord, king,
baron, or ecclesiastic. Those granted by the Crown were far
more liberal than those allowed by the barons, while those
issued by the ecclesiastics were generally more restrictive.
The Crown's interest in a borough was but one of many interests, while that of a baron or prelate was more personal and
vital. The king had neither the time nor inclination to dominate the petty affairs of the burgesses. He was concerned with
larger and more important matters, and was willing to leave
his boroughs alone provided they rendered their dues and services. Such a policy relieved him of the task of appointing
and supervising a multitude of minor officers. He proved an
"easy master" and had no desire to play the rôle of a "local
tyrant." Royal boroughs appreciated their good fortune and
generally did the king's bidding in return for concessions that
brought good business and profit. Baronial towns were less

fortunate. Constant interference on the part of the lord led to many bitter and prolonged contests. As long as the feudal noble insisted upon prying into the activities of his borough and upon using it for selfish purposes there could be no thriving trade or prosperity. The financial needs of the baron, however, were such as to force him to grant concessions which, in time, brought greater advantages to the borough. Those connected with the Church suffered even more. Here and there some liberally minded abbot granted a charter which accorded considerable freedom. In general, most ecclesiastics dictated every move and activity of the borough. They appointed the local officers, assessed burdensome taxes, and sometimes treated their vassals most shamefully. At times the burgesses rose in rebellion against their lords. The disaffection of the towns also played an important rôle in the servile uprisings of the fourteenth century. Not until the Reformation, however, were the ecclesiastical boroughs able to throw off the tyranny of their lords.

When a charter was granted to a borough, certain definite rights and privileges were bestowed upon the burgesses. The borough itself became a corporation and as such could determine its governmental life. In addition, it was allowed to manage in a general way local trade and industry, and to handle the collection of taxes without the interference of an officer of the feudal overlord. Domestic and alien merchants were forbidden to distribute within the borough any products which might compete with local goods. They were permitted to sell produce and manufactured articles which the borough needed and which were not made by the members of the merchant gild. In return for these privileges the outsider paid heavy fees or tolls. The maintenance of local markets and fairs was also included in the terms of the charter. Many of these boroughs eventually gained a voice in the determination of national affairs through their right of sending representatives to the meetings of parliament.

Merchant and Craft Gilds

In an age which was characterized by no extensive national control over industry, the merchant gild rendered decided benefits to its members and to the borough at large. The individual worker or trader was protected against all interlopers, a home market was secured, and the quality and quantity of manufactured goods were kept at a standard of which the town might often be proud. A community interest was fostered which found expression in elaborate dinners and feastings in which all of the gild members participated. The members were also active in church work and helped to stage many of the religious pageants for which the medieval period is known. At stated times the gild held formal meetings at which regulations were debated and adopted relative to the conduct of trade. Provision was also made for charitable and humane work. Widows and orphans were taken care of as well as the sick and poor.

The economy of the merchant gild was useful for its time. Its merits, however, have blinded some students to its defects. The theory of gild management did not always coincide with practice. Frequently the gild set a price on a given commodity that injured the producer. To illustrate, importers of leather goods often found that the price offered by a member of the gild precluded sale at any other price or to any other prospective buyer. Shoddy goods were shown in the markets and many a purchaser was robbed. Hats to withstand rain proved to be sieves, and woolen cloth a yard long measured less after having been washed. Old skins and furs were dressed to appear as new, and imported wine turned out to be a sour domestic brand. Professor Coulton is of the opinion that gild economy was not favorable to invention and cites the fact that "though Marco Polo described the Chinese printed banknotes before 1300, at least 120 years passed before men began, in Europe, even so elementary an imitation as to print little figures of saints on paper." Theoretically, the gild merchant was supposed to fine and punish all who violated the trading regulations. In practice the gild often remitted fines and allowed infractions to continue unnoticed.

The merchant gild, like the modern industrial union, included all trade activities within related fields. Within the clothmaking trade, for example, there were spinners and weavers. The spinning of yarn or thread, therefore, was a specialized trade. The spinner did not sell his yarn to the general public; rather did he sell it to the weaver who used it to make cloth. Although subject in a general way to the merchant gild, the spinner had his own problems and interests and naturally sought to protect himself against the domination of the weavers. To gain this end, groups of spinners formed loose associations which, by the end of the twelfth century, had developed into craft gilds. Craft gilds became numerous during the course of the next century and gradually emancipated themselves from the merchant gild.

Within each craft were found all the workers engaged in that activity, and no one was allowed to practice his trade within the borough unless he was a member of the craft and observed its rules. Admittance rested upon the vote of the active members, provided the candidate had passed successfully a number of different tests. In the first place the worker was required to serve as an apprentice for a number of years, usually seven, during which period he was taught the arts of the craft. While an apprentice, the laborer worked at the home of a master who provided his pupil with food, clothing, and lodging. In return for these services the master was entitled to whatever goods the apprentice produced. At the end of the seven-year period the apprentice might, if possessed of funds, work independently as a journeyman or continue as a wage earner in the shop of his master. Later he became a master and enjoyed all the social, economic, and political privileges of that class. Craft policy was handled by the masters, whose wealth and influence tended to create a gap between themselves and the workers.

Neither the crafts nor the merchant gild should be confused with modern trade unions, although in their fraternal and social life they have some things in common. Unlike the present day organizations, the medieval associations were not predicated upon the assumption of an existing conflict between labor and capital. Not a single craft existed which had to bargain as to hours of work, wages, piece work, accident insurance, and the like. Nor does any reference appear as to strikes, lockouts, picketing, or arbitration. Not that complaints and grievances did not arise, but matters which today cause so much grief to producer, laborer, and consumer were then handled by the craft, supposedly in the interests of all concerned. Today a workman is interested in his job primarily for the remuneration he receives. During the medieval period the laborer was also interested in his pay, but he was equally concerned as to the quality of his work. Quality, moreover, was determined by the gild or craft, while at present it is fixed either by the manufacturer or by a governmental agency, national or local.

Not all of the medieval industries were affected by the gild or craft associations. This does not imply the absence of organization. Among the miners of tin, silver, iron, and coal, societies existed whose purpose and structure were somewhat different, while in the fishing industry there seems to have been no organization at all. Usually in the mining industries either the owner worked the field himself or leased it to some operator; in either case the actual labor, except where the owner did the physical work, was performed by wage earners who had nothing to say as to the conduct of the industry. Among the owners and operators of a local area, however, an association existed which sought in some way to define the mining law. Notable in this respect were the tin miners who, through their association known as the Stannaries, had far-reaching authority and influence. Even here the power was lodged chiefly with those who held the better mines or who possessed the greater capital. The lot of the small independent tinner was not much better than that of the average day laborer of the borough. Often he was compelled to pledge his tin in advance to "the adventurers and tin-dealers" who traded in tin and did not mine themselves. In the words of Salzman, "while the economic position of the small tinners must have been little, if at all, superior to that of ordinary laborers, their political position was remarkable. They constituted a state within a state; the free miner paid taxes not as an Englishman, but as a miner. His law was not the law of the realm, but that of his mine. . . . His courts were the mine courts, his parliament the mine parliament."

Town Life

Probably in the last analysis the lot of the town laborer or miner was about the same as that of the manorial serf. In some respects he was at a disadvantage, particularly as regards economic security. His earnings, which were chiefly in the form of wages, afforded but a scant basis for the maintenance of family life and were upset easily by a business depression. His home, which was built of wood and covered with thatch, constructed so that the outside walls touched the home of his neighbor, was a fire hazard of the worst type. Moreover, when one recalls that none of these houses had chimneys and that a spark from an open fire in the center of the room found its way out through a hole in the ceiling, one can readily understand why fires were common occurrences in a medieval town. Twice during the early part of the twelfth century, London was partially destroyed by fire. Once a building caught on fire the object was not to put the flames out but to keep them from spreading to an adjacent structure. This was accomplished by pulling roofs off with specially prepared hooks and ropes. Water was seldom used, largely because of the absence of any pressure system.

A few of the larger towns, like London, seem to have piped water for drinking and cooking purposes from nearby springs or streams; but in every case the pressure depended upon the force of gravity. Bathing was probably unknown among most classes, a fact that doubtless did much to spread disease. Anything like an adequate drainage system existed only in the monasteries or private homes of the more fortunate. As a result, garbage, waste, and filth were freely thrown into the streets, where it usually remained unless washed away by a severe rain storm. Most of the houses and stores, cramped by the confines of the town's walls, were built close to the narrow and irregular streets from which filthy odors and dust arose. Within these homes little sanitation existed and, like the huts of the serf, they were not built for comfort or health. The average residence had a very narrow frontage. Moreover, in view of the limited area encompassed by the town's walls, buildings were constructed vertically rather than horizontally. The first floor was practically a basement and was covered by two and sometimes three additional stories. Daylight was admitted by windows in the front and rear of the house. Greater radiation existed in the homes of the wealthier classes whose domiciles served as both residences and places of business. Shops were uniformly placed on the second floor, which generally was level with the street. Above the shop were the living quarters of the merchant's family and servants.

Sleeping accommodations were generally inadequate and night clothes do not seem to have been used to any extent until the sixteenth century. In spite of these evident disadvantages the average inhabitant did not live amid conditions generally worse than those in most large American cities or towns. Tenements surrounded by squalor and gaunt poverty did not exist, nor was the population by any means as dense or diverse. Children were not forced to play in crowded streets at risk of life or limb. Beyond the walls, inviting fields were accessible to all. Many artisans had their own garden plots or farms near-by, and there were inhabitants who gained their entire livelihood from agrarian activities. The average merchant or shopkeeper enjoyed many social contacts. He was a member of the gild and, as such, had caste and dignity, and could attend the feasts and meetings which were held in the gild hall. The gild hall, like the town hall, rivaled the church in architectural beauty and was the center of much activity. Few of us would care to have lived in "Merry Old England," yet there were some compensations for its evident shortcomings.

SELECTED BIBLIOGRAPHY

The works by Stephenson and Tait are of prime importance for a study of borough life and organization. C. Gross' *Gild Merchant* (Oxford, 1890) is an excellent treatment of trading associations as is G. Unwin's *Gilds and Companies of London* (London, 1908). F. W. Maitland's *Township and Borough* (Cambridge, 1898), and S. Kramer's *English Craft Gilds and the Government* (New York, 1905) are also of value. The following works are of value for a study of the individual industries and trades, as well as for a knowledge of urban living conditions: E. L. Cutts' *Scenes and Characters of the Middle Ages* (London, 1926); L. F. Salzman's *English Trade in the Middle Ages* (Oxford, 1923); D. Knoop and G. P. Jones' *The Medieval Mason* (Manchester, 1933); G. G. Coulton's *Social Life in Britain from the Conquest to the Reformation* (Cambridge, 1919); L. F. Salzman's *English Life in the Middle Ages* (Oxford, 1927); G. G. Coulton's *The Medieval Scene* (Cambridge, 1930), and E. Power's *Medieval People* (London, 1924).

CHAPTER IX

Commerce, Thought, and Science

Money, Economy, and Credit Devices

COMMERCE in its broadest sense may be defined as the exchange of goods and services. Accordingly when a serf or gildsman bartered with some passing pedlar for a trinket or bolt of cloth, commerce may be said to have taken place. Similarly, the transactions may be described which occurred between the merchants of London and Bristol or between Englishmen and aliens. Any discussion of these activities demands at the outset, a summary of the tools of trade. Concerning the first, barter, little need be said beyond noting that while historically the oldest, it nevertheless continued to meet the needs of most medieval Englishmen. However, conditions arose as early as the Celtic age when the exchange of goods was facilitated by the use of money. The practice was followed in some cases by the Romans and Saxons, but it was the Normans who made this method more or less common throughout England.

Following Continental and Saxon practices, the Norman kings held that the coinage of money was a royal right. Exceptions were made in favor of the bishops of Durham, whose duties as wardens of a frontier county necessitated far-reaching powers. Otherwise, save for the stormy years of Stephen, no coins were issued except those struck off at the royal mints. Prior to 1180, these coins varied as to size and shape, but after that date a medium was established which remained much the same during the twelfth and thirteenth centuries. For purposes of accounting, this medium, bimetallic in nature, consisted of pounds, shillings, and pence. A pound, except of the alloy, amounted to a pound of silver, one-twentieth of which made a shilling, while one-twelfth of a shilling made a penny. Needless to say, traders and governmental officials used other terms in speaking of these coins or multiples of the same. For example, the penny was often called a "sterling," while four of these were known as a "groat." Again, when referring to one hundred and sixty pence the word "mark" was used. Yet the only coins minted were the penny, groat, half-penny, and farthing, the last three of which were not employed until the late thirteenth century. The penny, therefore, was the chief medium used; and, except for a period during the reign of Henry III when gold was tried, it was made of silver.

Although the Normans and Angevins prevented others from minting coins, they had no end of trouble in respect to mutilation. In spite of many laws and severe punishments, and in the face of technical devices conceived to prevent defacement, many a coin was clipped or filed. To illustrate, early in the reign of Edward I, royal agents found that coins held by certain Jewish traders had lost, through mutilation, seventeen per cent of their original value. Flemish merchants were also found guilty of this crime, which greatly hampered fiscal dealings with Europe. Moreover, a debased currency tended to drive good money out of the realm, and this in turn upset the bimetallic basis. It was in the hope of retaining gold and silver at home that the government late in the thirteenth century laid restrictions on the export of the precious metals. Nevertheless, no satisfactory solution of this problem was arrived at during the period now under study.

In addition to these uncertainties, merchants were annoyed over the absence of coins suitable for large transactions. The good housewife had no trouble in buying "one a penny, two a penny, hot cross buns," but the London wine importer frowned upon his Yorkist client's paying him a fifty-pound debt in pennies. Such a transaction required strong arms and stout boxes; the heavy load overburdened porter or horse and the presence of so much cash always invited attack or robbery. Seeking to avoid these difficulties, the trader used existing credit devices, of which the tally, as employed by the Court of Exchequer, has already been mentioned. This court used tallies both as recognitions of payments to the Crown and as promises to pay. Accordingly, the Yorkist purchaser of wine, instead of sending fifty pounds in pennies to the London importer, merely forwarded a tally which the latter accepted. In time the tally, like a check of today, appeared in the hands of a local Yorkist merchant who presented the same to its original owner for settlement. Transactions of this type, however, were relatively few in number.

Letters of credit were also used in medieval England. To illustrate, a Bristol merchant wishing to buy foreign goods in the London market, or desiring to arrange for the expenses of himself, family, or agent while at parliament or fair, wrote to a fellow trader in London asking him to provide the needed money. This letter was a promise to pay which through ordinary business routine was finally honored in Bristol. Like these letters of credit were bills of exchange drawn between merchants engaged in foreign trade. Doubtless some charge was made for the service rendered. Discounting, in other words, was practiced by those who might be called the bankers of that time. Discounting, moreover, became a device by means of which interest was exacted and this continued in the face of church and state law to the contrary. Indeed both church and state officials availed themselves of this method to levy interest. Open and public usury was frowned upon by good Christians, but discounting was not viewed as a violation of the word of God. Jews, on the other hand, whose souls according to Christian ideals, were damned, might engage in loaning money. This was done at exorbitant rates of interest. Christians also exacted interest in another way. A merchant in need of cash often gave a promissory note to repay a loan, the amount of the note being in excess of the sum borrowed. The rising wealth of the Jews was soon tapped by the Crown in the form of taxes. To meet these levies, the Jews had to sell the securities which their debtors could not meet. The latter condemned the Jews, and spread an intense anti-Jewish feeling over England. By the reign of Edward I the economic fortunes of the Jews were at a low ebb; they could no longer meet royal taxes, and Edward courted popular favor by expelling the Jews from the kingdom in 1290.

In keeping royal accounts or in ordinary business transactions the simplest of methods were used. Practically all who engaged in such activities computed their assets and liabilities by means of a counting board more or less like the one used by the Court of Exchequer. These sums were then entered in a book made of parchment. Anything like a modern system of entries was entirely lacking, and it is the opinion of those who have studied this problem that medieval bookkeeping was careless even for that age. Arabic numerals, while known, were not commonly used until the sixteenth century.

English medieval commerce consisted of foreign and domestic trade subject to central and local regulation. Imports were liable to dues and fees, the greater share of which was levied and collected by local rather than national officers. Indeed the first known royal tariff was an *ad valorem* tax of 1203. This duty lasted only a few years and it was not until the second half of the same century that further assessments were made. The bulk of these imports came from France, particularly from those sections which were feudal holdings of the English kings. Woolen goods, salt, and wine constituted a large share of this trade although these commodities

also entered from the Lowlands. The Baltic states shipped
cargoes of oil, timber and masts, while high-grade woolens and
velvets came from Spain and Italy. Iron, skins, hides, and
Cordova leather were entered from Spain. Spain and Italy
also shipped silks and satins, as well as large quantities of rice,
figs, almonds, dates, raisins, sugar and spices. Judging from
the royal household accounts of 1287, nearly twenty thousand
pounds of almonds were purchased in that year alone. Very
little sugar was imported until late in the same century, honey
having served as sweetening before that date. Fruit was
seldom used except by the greater nobility. Many of these
commodities bulked large in the import trade only after the
Crusades had introduced England to what was almost a different world.

The Influence of the Crusades

Although England took a major part in the Third Crusade
only, she was influenced by these expeditions from the first.
Actuated by various religious motives and appeals, stimulated
by visions of free land which would enhance the feudal system, and impelled by a love for adventure, Englishmen enthu-
siastically cast their lot in this great enterprise. Estates were
mortgaged, debts contracted, and future earnings promised so
that military equipment and transportation might be obtained.
Then after having been fleeced by local money changers and
having risked the storms of the sea and attacks by infidel and
Christian pirates, they finally landed at some Near Eastern
port, unless perchance they had cut their way overland through
Catholic lands whose rulers and peoples often acted as enemies
rather than as friends. Battle and murder followed, and after
having spent life and treasure, those who survived trailed home
much the worse for the effort. Honor was showered upon
these Knights of the Cross, poets sang of their deeds (the
great and virtuous ones), and at death they were given signal

ceremonies and distinctions. Visitors today still stand hushed before the tomb of some forgotten crusader. On the other hand, an inquiry into the lot of the popular hero after his return from the Holy Land will show that many a knight was forced to adjust himself to lower standards by reason of unpaid debts. Lands and feudal rights changed quickly; much of the wealth passed from the noble to the merchant who had kept the home fires burning by making personal profit while the crusader was away. Feudalism, in short, received a severe blow as a result of the Crusades.

Many a crusader, moreover, was fundamentally changed by his contacts and experiences in the Near East. He had walked on paved streets, had worn garments of a quality beyond his dreams, had seen streets lighted at night, had looked upon houses that were not tinder-boxes, had watched fire departments in action, had drunk cool and pure water and had eaten food which was quite strange. Small wonder, therefore, that he found his English fare, his coarse woolens, his dark muddy streets strangely uninviting and in consequence was led to alter his former wants and standards. A demand now arose for newer goods and commodities, a demand which in turn stimulated trade and industry.

England, in order to pay for these articles, was forced to exert greater efforts in her export trade, which prior to the Conquest had been small. Since Hastings, however, an increase had taken place, especially to those parts of France held by the English kings. Tin, corn, fish, cheese, leather, hides, salt, wool and woolen goods were the more important exports. The bulk of both export and import trade was carried in foreign ships whose owners and merchants had been favored by English monarchs from the first. This was due to the relatively few domestic ships and merchants engaged in foreign commerce rather than to any partiality on the part of the Norman kings. Moreover, the government promoted alien activity by a number of regulations. Henry II, for example,

in 1157 granted to the merchants of Cologne rights which included having a gild hall in London.   Later, a treaty with the
Empire gave special consideration to the traders of that state.
Magna Carta also recognized the value of these activities by
allowing alien traders to come and go from the realm in safety
and freedom.   Finally, by the close of the thirteenth century
one encounters the famous Statute of Merchants, which provided legal procedure for the collection of debts owed these
foreigners.   By this time, Italian, French, Scandinavian, German, and Flemish traders were much in evidence.   The latter
two had gained considerable importance and were known as
the Hanse merchants.   By the first of the new century, the
Flemish Hanse disappeared, leaving the field to its rivals, the
Teutons, who were grouped in the so-called Hanseatic League,
a combination of several German cities which had merged
their interests and which dominated England's north European trade for a century or more.

Export and Import Trade

In the meantime, English interests had asserted themselves,
especially in the woolen trade to the Lowlands.   By the middle
of the thirteenth century, this influence had grown so large
that its merchants were known as the Merchants of the Staple.
These traders gained many rights for themselves abroad and,
by the close of that century, were exporting over one-third of
the total wool which cleared from England.   Recent investigation, moreover, has revealed the presence of English settlers
at Genoa as early as the late twelfth century.   Partnerships
were formed and an active trade was promoted in trade and
groceries.   In the Mediterranean trade, most of the ships were
larger than those used elsewhere.   The vessels were long and
low with steep sterns and bows, and were propelled by sails
and oars.   Those of the Mediterranean often had two masts;
large paddles fastened to the starboard side of the stern guided

these clumsy ships of which the average was not much over one hundred tons. Rudders were not used until the middle of the thirteenth century when the magnetic needle also was first employed. Since none of these ships had real decks or holds, the cargo was stored in the open, unprotected from rains or storms.

On account of the small size of these ships, foreigners were able to sail up the Ouse, Trent, and Thames to compete with local merchants. Most of the inland trade, however, was in the hands of Englishmen. Few of these streams were kept open by dredging, a factor which added to the difficulties of navigation. In addition, tolls were levied by feudal lords and boroughs, while mills and fishing nets were a constant source of annoyance. So numerous were the latter that Magna Carta contained a provision which called for their removal, but no actual change took place for some time. Those who traded by land, already handicapped by poor roads and numerous robberies, were further irritated by tolls. The small itinerant trader, known as a pedlar or chapman, bore the brunt of these difficulties and yet seems to have enjoyed a profitable business. Often he carried his wares upon his own back though the use of animals was common. Carts were also employed, especially by the wealthier traders and those who dealt with the towns and monasteries rather than with the rural areas.

Urban trade centered chiefly in the hands of the gildsmen, who had special rights accorded them by charters. None of the Saxon towns was characterized by much industrial or commercial life. Under the Norman kings a pronounced change took place. Thoroughly familiar with borough life and aware of its commercial advantages, these monarchs aided in the development of old towns and in the founding of new ones on the European pattern. So significant was this factor in English economic life that historians have often described the thirteenth century as the age of town growth and development. Although these centers were sometimes arbitrarily located,

geographic forces were usually of great importance. Cross
roads, a forded stream (Oxford), a deep or sheltered port—
these, and many other factors, explain the location of many an
English town of today. It should be noted, moreover, that
the thirteenth-century town was quite different from that of
the Norman or Saxon age. Then the borough was characterized by governmental, military or agrarian affairs. In contrast
the thirteenth-century town, while often possessing these features, was clearly an industrial and commercial center.

The conduct of trade and industry within these boroughs
rested on a charter which likewise determined the form of
government. Borough council courts and local officers were
provided for as well as the *firma burgi,* a yearly tax paid by
the town to its lord. The right of collecting this tax was one
of the powers which towns struggled for over a long period
of time in order to prevent the lord's agents from interfering
in town affairs to the detriment of the citizens. Left to themselves the local officers arranged affairs of trade and industry
except as restricted by the town's charter, the rights of foreigners (those from other parts of the realm), and those of
aliens (nationals of other states).

Markets and Fairs

Practically every known phase of control was exercised,
either by the town council or by the local gild or craft. Hours
of work, prices, quantity and quality of goods were regulated.
Even the location of the trades within the town was stipulated. Zoning regulations kept the corn dealers within a certain area, the principal street of which became known as Corn
Lane. Many an English city or town of today has lanes or
streets, like Milk Lane or Bread Street, reminiscent of medieval life. In addition to the regular shops most boroughs had
markets where goods were traded between the townspeople
and those of the neighboring areas. As often as not these

markets were held on Sunday and frequently were located within the churchyard. Enterprising merchants openly displayed their wares on tombstones and counted their sales within the shadow of the cross. Although opinion frowned upon these practices, no puritan blue law or "sabbatical sanctity" existed. Indeed the local ecclesiastic welcomed the market because of the tolls it yielded, and he was among the last to favor a change.

Interesting as these markets must have been, they were of less importance than the fairs which took place at certain periods throughout the year. The right to have a fair was zealously contended for as the financial return was large, and not every borough had a fair. Usually the fair was held outside the town and necessitated the erection of temporary buildings and stalls. Merchants and traders from all parts of the realm rubbed shoulders at these gatherings with local producers. Surplus farm goods, cloth, leather, and other town products were bought or exchanged for commodities raised or made elsewhere in England or Europe. Some of these, such as the Sturbridge fair, gained provincial importance and occasionally rose to international fame. In view of the fact that fairs were short in duration and were attended by foreigners, and because disputes arose which demanded immediate settlement, temporary courts were set up whose law and procedure were known as the Law Merchant. International in nature, except in respect to local factors, the Law Merchant was well conceived to render its peculiar type of justice. In England, its courts were known as the Courts of Pie Power, which was the English way of pronouncing *pied poudre*. The term itself was applied as descriptive of the right of a claimant to rush into court with "dusty feet" and have his case settled at once.

Many colorful descriptions of these fairs and town activities exist in the literary remains of the age. Ample insight is given as to the habits and thought of the time. Honesty and virtue, thrift and sobriety, as well as fraud, immorality, and vice are skillfully depicted. To illustrate, the *Chronicles of Old London* record in 1272 that "throughout all this year no punishment was inflicted upon the bakers; but they made loaves at their own will, so much so that each loaf was deficient one-third in weight, or one-fourth at least." Then again, one Reginald, a monk of Durham, has left a fascinating account of the life of *St. Godric* in which the customs of the itinerant traders are well shown. These sources are also of value in that they reflect the literary life of the period.

Literature and Scholasticism

It will be recalled that prior to the Conquest, Saxon literature had been quite varied as to form and content. With the arrival of the Norman, a great change occurred. The language itself was enriched by a facile Roman vocabulary permitting many shades of meaning which the Saxon had been unable to express. At the same time many words were eliminated. Methods of expression were changed, forms and endings were altered, and all of this helped to extend Norman ideas and thoughts. European scholars, who taught the youth what might be called a new learning, were brought to England. Finally, it should be noted that native students visited the Continent in greater numbers than before, and on their return they greatly improved English intellectual activities.

Literary pursuits still remained, as in the Saxon age, chiefly in the hands of the Church and, as a result, reflected religious interests. An examination of the writings and libraries of a Lanfranc, an Anselm, or a Stephen Langton reveals the truth of this statement. Similar evidence appears in the church homilies, which are rich in contemporary material as to the routine life of priest, trader, soldier, farmer, and housewife. Special attention was paid in these homilies to Mary "Queen of Heaven." By the thirteenth century, references to the

Mother of Christ abounded in hymns, orisons, and sermons. In part this was caused by an intense religious devotion. It may also represent, as a recent scholar has pointed out, an attempt by the Church to offset the immense popularity of the secular love themes sung by wandering poets and singers.

Equally important are the Latin chronicles which continued the work started by Alfred but became more numerous and valuable. The high tide for these writings was in the reign of Henry II, whose patronage of literature did much to stimulate students and writers. Closely akin to these chronicles were the poetical and historical works. What impresses the reader is the fact that many of the authors were men not high merely in church circles but also prominent in affairs of state. Roger of Hoveden, one of the better known chroniclers, at one time followed Henry II to France and was raised by that monarch to many public offices. Walter Map, the author of *De Nugis Curialium* and many other works of prose and poetry, had studied in Paris, had been an itinerant justice, and in 1197 became Archdeacon of Oxford. Peter of Blois, Gilbert Foliot, both prominent clergymen, and John of Salisbury, whose education was chiefly received at Paris and Chartres, may serve as other examples. Probably none rose higher in literary work than John of Salisbury, most of whose creative writing was done while a member of the cathedral staff of Canterbury, during a period when he was also employed as a royal secretary and diplomat. John of Salisbury was a writer of great force and ability, as may be seen by an examination of his lives of Becket and Anselm, his letters, and many other writings. His volumes reveal the skill and influence of a royal adviser, the keen satire of a penetrating mind, and the careful pen of an historian. Small wonder that John of Salisbury is often acclaimed as the leading man of letters not only of England but of all Europe during the last half of the twelfth century.

Other writers of this period were also interested in historical work. Reference should be made to Geoffrey of Monmouth, Matthew of Paris, William of Malmesbury, Eadmer and Giraldus Cambrensis. Mention should also be made of the efforts of Michael Scot, Alexander of Hales and Roger Bacon, all of whom are well known for their contributions to philosophy and science. Adelard of Bath and Alexander Neckam contributed to the field of scientific writing, while Glanville and Bracton made reputations in legal compilations and books. Others, like Robert Grosseteste, Henry of Huntington, Nigel Wireker, and Ordericus Vitalis are well known to students of medieval thought and letters.

In all these writings and others too numerous to mention, the religious theme predominated, though attention was paid to satire, history, science, and law. Much was written in Latin and Norman-French, though by the thirteenth century many a work appeared in English. An example of the latter may be found in the *Brut,* written by one Layamon, a priest of Ernley on the Severn. The *Brut* is of interest not only for its careful reflection of the spoken English of the time but also because it became the vehicle by means of which the Arthurian Legend was introduced into English literature. The *Brut* likewise shows the growing tendencies of the thirteenth-century writers to revolt against the standardized religious subjects of the past. Similar to the *Brut,* in this respect, is the *Owl and the Nightingale,* the authorship of which is in much dispute. Other vernacular works appeared, in which satirical ballads, humorous stories, myths and historical tales are presented. Questionable as some of the more boisterous stories may have been, they seem to have enjoyed as much popularity as the more elegant narratives of the Arthurian verse or the "hell and damnation" themes which appeared in the *Poema Morale* and *Be Domes Daege.* In all these works stock characters and stereotyped ideas seem to have been much in vogue. In spite of this, however, a distinct note of a new order was sounded in literary pursuits and the way was cleared for the greater gains of the next two centuries. When one studies these later volumes the indebtedness of a Chaucer to the writers of the twelfth and thirteenth centuries is clearly revealed.

England's broadening intellectual horizon, as shown by the literary activities already cited, was but a part of a general renaissance which swept over Europe in the twelfth century. This movement was continental in origin, but its influence was felt in Britain from the first. This was due in part to the infiltration of a new learning through the channels of the Conquest. It was also due to the temporary exodus of English students to Europe, who upon their return did much to stimulate intellectual growth in Britain. The field of interest and effort which tied these scholars to this renaissance is commonly known as scholasticism, a mode of inquiry and thinking which dominated thought for several centuries.

Scholasticism had its genesis in the endeavors of the churchmen to iron out the existing conflicts between man's experiences and the Roman faith. On the one hand the Church, through its doctrines and sacraments, taught that man, if he would have eternal life, should follow the patterns of faith and habits laid down by Peter and his followers. Yet as man battled with himself, his enemies, and nature, he often departed from the precepts of Rome. Reason, in other words, clashed with faith. Conscious of this fact, the teachers and philosophers of Rome sought to find a way out of this intellectual impasse. One of the first to offer a solution was Anselm, who declared in no uncertain terms that science or knowledge was of no value unless it was in accord with the teachings of Christ and Rome. Man, so to speak, had been placed by God in a world surrounded by living walls of faith and creed. Within this closed area free inquiry and speculation might be pursued without restraint. Reason thus became the handmaid of authority. As Anselm said, "I believe in order that I may know." In sharp contrast came the reply of a contemporary, Roscellinus, "Seeing is believing." This was

also the position held by Abelard, one of the greatest of medieval thinkers.   Abelard held that a faith not built upon reason
and logic was a denial of truth and that truth was God.   In
his epoch-making work, *Sic et Non,* Abelard cleverly expounded his views by submitting the cherished quotations of
the church to a most exacting inquiry.   He passed no judgment, but by presenting both sides left the reader bewildered
as to whether faith or reason should be followed.   Naturally,
those who accepted the teachings of Abelard were led away
from the scholastics of Rome and, like Abelard, were believed
guilty of heresy.

Abelard's influence was offset somewhat by the more orthodox writings of Peter Lombard, who in his *Sentences* directed
thought along the path of ecclesiastical authority.   Scholasticism, therefore, became the accepted philosophy and discipline
of the Church and its devoted schoolmen.   In and out of season, these teachers avowed the necessity of obeying the faith,
doctrine, and morals of the "powers-that-be."   Individualism
was frowned upon unless it was content to speculate within the
closed walls of the "City of God."   Here and there some adventurous soul, like Roger Bacon, pushed his researches beyond the confines of Rome; but in the main, most writers
blindly accepted the scholastic philosophy of the day.

Early Medieval Education, Science, and Art

Most of the faculties of English universities followed the
realistic teachings of the fundamentalists.   These institutions
had been built upon the efforts of the cathedral and monastic
schoolmen and upon the experiences of European universities.
Saxon England had its church schools whose quality had been
improved by the new learning brought in by the Conquest.   A
brief statement of the more salient features of education from
1066 to 1300 will illustrate how far English education had
advanced since the days of Alfred.

The lowest or most elementary schools were the song schools where young boys were taught to sing the chants of the Church. As these verses were in Latin, some instruction in that tongue was offered. Next in order were the monastic schools for prospective monks. It is the opinion of those who have studied the records of these schools that the enrollment was small and that the training afforded was of the meanest type. What seemed important was that the novice should become thoroughly regimented to monastic life. One writer has described the monastic schools as places where the pupils "were treated . . . not as boys at school . . . but like rogues in a reformatory." What these schools lacked, however, the grammar schools provided, and it is no exaggeration to assert that worth-while education centered in these institutions. Their chief objective was the teaching of Latin grammar, which included reading and writing as well as logic and rhetoric (public speaking). These subjects constituted the *trivium* and were offered chiefly to the younger students. For the more advanced the *quadrivium* (arithmetic, geometry, music, and astronomy) was given. Most of the pupils were from ten to seventeen years old and were under the direction of secular priests in most cases. Some of these grammar schools were really preparatory schools for the universities and often were associated, both as to location and faculty, with a university. Others were affiliated with monasteries and churches. While most of the waking hours of each day were devoted to study and church services, plenty of opportunity was given for games of various kinds which, at certain times of the year, became exceedingly boisterous if not actually brutal.

From the grammar school the medieval student went to a university. Universities first made their appearance in Europe during the twelfth century. Oxford was founded during the reign of Henry II, and Cambridge got its start early in the next century. By 1225 England had two institutions of high standing. Their faculties included some of the best minds of

Europe, and instruction, though chiefly along religious lines, was good. The curriculum included an extended *trivium* and *quadrivium* to which were added law, theology, and philosophy. All classwork and reading were in Latin, though the latter was restricted by reason of the limited number of manuscripts in the libraries. Textbooks did not exist; hence the student had to lean chiefly upon the lectures of the faculty. Memory became the prop upon which the pupil relied to pass examinations. Class attendance, though not required, was viewed as a privilege and not as a duty. Six to seven hours were usually spent in this manner, while the rest of the day was given to study, sleep, and recreation. The latter consisted of rough unorganized play, drinking, hazing, and feasting, subject to some degree of administrative control. There were no fraternities, student activities, or athletic contests. On the other hand the students, if they found an instructor a bore, might voice their feelings to bring about a change either in the conduct of the instructor or of the teacher himself. In general, however, it is the opinion of scholars that student life was not much different from that of today.

Instruction in the natural sciences, as that term is now understood, did not exist; yet much more was actually accomplished than is commonly supposed. Part of the existing scientific knowledge was based upon earlier Latin treatises but much more was added by direct contact with the Greek and Saracen teachers and writings. A number of English students delved deeply into these foreign sources and brought the fruit of their studies back home. The use of Arabic numerals was introduced; lunar months and eclipses of the sun and moon were calculated; the magnetic needle was placed at the disposal of sailors; gunpowder was discovered; lenses, chimney flues and scores of other practical applications of scientific principles were made known. Indeed some hardy and keen minds boldly admitted that the earth was spherical in shape. In spite of these advances, further progress was checked by scholastic reasoning and by a willingness to accept idle tales, myths, and hearsay as scientific data. Medieval science was a strange assortment of good and bad. Doctors frequently prescribed heavy doses of foul-tasting purgatives mingled with the scales of snakes or parts of mice, and bled their patients unto death. Astrology and alchemy were as much in vogue as the Arabic numerals. Dismal as the picture may seem, many a bright light was cast by the experimental methods of men like Adelard of Bath and Roger Bacon.

In sharp contrast to the inefficiency of medieval science towered the great cathedrals of the Church. Here no creed or dogma cramped the architects or the wealthy who liberally patronized the construction of these temples. Massive columns supporting lofty stone vaults, a multiplicity of arches, ponderous and thick walls, and richly carved capitals and doors, recessed orders and an amazing consistency in style and decoration characterized the churches which the Norman generously scattered throughout the realm. Such heaviness and massiveness made it impossible for the masons to pierce the walls for many windows, so that the interior was dark. By the twelfth century, however, this Norman adaptation of the Romanesque began to be softened. Gothic influences already at work on the Continent gradually penetrated the island with the result that greater lightness, ease, and height were obtained. Man reached higher and higher in his desire to obtain "eternal grace."

Similar architectural growth appeared in the monasteries and the homes and castles of the Norman lords. Anyone who has walked through the Tower of London, Colchester Castle, the Keep at Canterbury, the cathedrals at Ely, St. Albans, and Westminster cannot avoid seeing how stoutly the Normans built their homes and churches. Even the monasteries reflected the same characteristics. Monastic life, following the Cluniac model, blossomed in England under the protecting hand of the Norman kings. Several hundred new monasteries were constructed, generously endowed and enriched by wealthy nobles, while the older homes were remodeled. For a time religious fervor kept pace with material prosperity, but by the reign of Henry I definite signs of internal rot appeared in the ranks of the regular clergy. Lip-service was still paid to the Cluniac ideal, but there was much wealth, property, and loose living. Often the sacraments of the Church were sold and considerable income was secured through the use of relics. Miraculous cures and resurrections from the grave were attributed to these relics. Practically every religious house or church had its relic, the authenticity of which was not disputed. The monks of Durham claimed to have portions of Moses' rod, of John the Baptist's cloak, of Mary's raiment, and of the tree under which Abraham sat. At times different monasteries boasted of relics which other religious houses stated had been stolen from them, and when occasion warranted, relics were manufactured. The acquisition of wealth led to immoral practices. Monks no longer slept in the common dormitory but had separate quarters where they received and entertained guests. Even the rise of the more rigid Cistercian order during the first half of the twelfth century did little more than check this downward movement. And while it would be unfair to state that the monasteries no longer fed the hungry, cared for the sick, widows, and orphans, and instructed the youth, the fact remains that the older ideals were giving way under the constant pressure of wealth and comfort.

Public opinion soon transferred its support to the humble friars of the thirteenth century. The earliest orders were the Dominicans and Franciscans, who took their names from their founders, the keen-minded St. Dominic and the saintly St. Francis. Both men were conscious of the existing worldliness of the monasteries and of the cancerous condition of the Church at large. It was St. Dominic's purpose to combat heresy, cleanse the temples of God, and elevate the soul to ultimate salvation by appealing to man through thoughtful and purposeful preaching. St. Francis, on the other hand, sought these same objectives by going out into the highways and byways, healing the sick, comforting the oppressed, and living a life weighed down by poverty and misery. Such success followed the earlier endeavors of these reformers that by the first quarter of the thirteenth century, papal endorsement paved the way for the founding of the Dominican and Franciscan orders. Both groups adhered to an organization which demanded of their members strict observance of vows and rigid obedience to Church law. The Dominicans entered England in 1220, while the Franciscans came in 1224. Everywhere the spiritual influence of these orders was to be seen, within the academic circles of Oxford, the lofty cathedrals of the metropolitan areas, the humble parishes of rural England, or out on the roads and highways. Rich and poor, schoolman and shopkeeper, noble and serf, all paid increasing respect and homage to the friars who did so much to lift England out of the moral decay into which it had fallen.

SELECTED BIBLIOGRAPHY

In addition to the references for the previous chapter, the student will find the following works of value for a study of economic development: C. Gross' *Select Cases concerning the Law Merchant* (London, 1908); W. Mitchell's *Early History of the Law Merchant* (Cambridge, 1904), and A. M. Hymanson's *A History of the Jews in England* (London, 1908). T. A. Archer and C. L. Kingsford's *The Crusades* (New York, 1895) and W. B. Stevenson's *The Crusaders in the East* (Cambridge, 1907) are standard works.

Scholasticism, education, architecture, science, letters and religion are treated in A. F. Leach's *The Schools of Medieval England* (London, 1916); M. Gibbs and J. Lang's *Bishops and Reform* (Oxford, 1934); A. Mansbridge's *Older Universities of England* (Boston, 1923); C. H. Moore's *Medieval Architecture* (New York, 1912); E. Power's *Medieval English Nunneries* (Cambridge, 1922); C. H. Haskins' *Studies in the History of Medieval Science* (Cambridge, 1924); L. Thorndike's *A History of Magic and Experimental Science* (New York, 1923); A. Jessop's *Coming of the Friars* (London, 1895); E. Hutton's *The Franciscans in England* (London, 1927); M. Creighton's *Historical Lectures and Addresses* (London, 1903), and G. G. Coulton's *Five Centuries of Religion*, Vol. III (London, 1936).

CHAPTER X

Foreign, Domestic, and Religious Discord

The Conquest of Wales

LATE in the reign of Henry III the government turned its attention toward Wales, the greater part of which was nominally subject to the English. During the thirteenth century, however, the native rulers of North Wales, resenting this alien domination, initiated a movement for independence. Partial success crowned these efforts, with the result that in 1267 Prince Llewelyn was recognized by Henry as feudal lord over a vastly enlarged domain. And yet, by reason of Llewelyn's oath of homage and fealty, England technically remained in control. Upon Henry's death in 1272, Edward I asked for a renewal of this oath, but Llewelyn, misjudging the new king, refused to do homage. Thereupon Edward led an army into Wales and after some bitter fighting, overcame the raw Welsh levies. The victor then proceeded to parcel out most of Llewelyn's estates among his own English vassals, leaving to that prince a much reduced domain in North Wales which he held in homage to the English King. Edward also imposed English law and administration upon the conquered areas.

Smarting under the sting of defeat and irritated by alien officials who brutally displayed their authority, the Celtic provinces became a hotbed of dissension and revolt. Overtures were made by the disgruntled Celts to Llewelyn, who hastened to champion their cause. By 1282 most of Wales was in open rebellion. Once again, Edward marched westward and during the course of the next two years waged a relentless war. In the end Llewelyn was killed, and a new peace was imposed at the point of the sword. English troops, moreover, were stationed throughout the land to keep the Welsh subdued and to protect the English colonists who were brought in to make the conquest more complete. As a climax to these arrangements came the Statute of Rhuddlan (1284), providing for

Courtesy Assoc. British and Irish Railways, Inc.

CASTLE SQUARE, CARNARVON, WALES. One of the imposing medieval fortresses in Europe. A late thirteenth-century structure.

the annexation of Wales to England and for an extension of the shire system of government. English law was enforced except in those areas held by the Lords of the Marches, but even here English custom and influence forged ahead. To all intents and purposes, Wales became an integral part of England in spite of Celtic opposition, which weakened itself in a futile uprising in 1294. From then on the Welsh made no serious bid to regain independence. It was during the course of these wars that Edward I gave to his son, who had been born at Carnarvon, the name of the Prince of Wales, which ever since has been the title of the male heir apparent to the English throne. Edward's Welsh policies, though marked by much brutality, remained practically unchanged until the sixteenth century.

Scottish Troubles

In the meantime Edward was having trouble with his neighbors to the north, as a result of the death of the last member of the reigning family of Scotland. Had the Scottish nobles refrained from factional disputes and had they centered their loyalties upon one of the collateral lines, it is doubtful if Edward would have been embroiled in the affair. In 1291, however, Edward forced himself into the controversy by summoning the barons of Scotland to meet him for the purpose of settling the disputed election. Edward based his right to arbitrate, upon the rather questionable feudal overlordship which English kings claimed over Scotland. Edward's decision was challenged, but there were few bold enough to draw the sword in defense of Scottish rights. Accordingly, having gained from the aspirants to the throne a promise to abide by his decision, Edward bestowed the office upon John Balliol, who showed his gratitude by taking an oath of homage to the English king. Balliol's power, therefore, from the first, rested on the armed support of Edward, who constantly interfered in the affairs of that kingdom. The Scots were irritated to the point of rebellion, and when Edward ordered Scottish troops for the French war, Balliol yielded to his barons and flatly refused to support the English. Hoping to ward off the consequence of this act, Balliol made an alliance with France. Although this embarrassed Edward, he was able in 1296 to invade Scotland and scatter the opposition. Balliol abdicated and Scotland became subject to England.

English domination was resented, however, by most of the

Scots, who finally rose in rebellion under the banner of Wil-
lam Wallace, whose recent killing of an English officer had
made him the hero of Scotland. English troops were driven
out and Wallace assumed control. It was not long, however, before Edward thundered north with a large army before which Wallace's government collapsed. The Scots kept
up the uneven contest until the capture and execution of their
leader in 1305. Wallace's death and the stupid conduct of
English officials led to a renewal of the conflict under Robert
Bruce, a distant relative of the last reigning Scottish king.
During 1306 and 1307 the tide of victory went first one way
and then another, but with the death of Edward I in 1307, the
cause of Scottish independence gained ground. Owing to the
ineffectiveness of Edward II, who had none of the virility of
his father, and to the smashing defeat Bruce inflicted upon
the English at Bannockburn in 1314, England retired from
Scotland. In 1328 Edward III formally acknowledged Scottish independence.

The Hundred Years' War

Throughout these Scottish wars the English had been at a
disadvantage by reason of their difficulties with France. It
will be recalled that in 1205 Philip Augustus had driven the
English out of France, except for the duchy of Aquitaine. At
the time neither party accepted the status as being definitive,
and both continued to advance their claims on every occasion. During the rest of the thirteenth century the two nations were frequently at war over this dispute, with the French
generally on the winning side. By the accession of Edward III
in 1327, the English held only a small strip of Gascony,
recognition of which was exceedingly distasteful to the French.
The situation was satisfactory to neither party, and numerous
disputes arose over feudal rights and administration. By 1337
Edward III had come to the conclusion that war was the only

available method to end the ancient feud between the two
states. Accordingly, he informed parliament and the nation
that France had not only rejected his peace proposals but was
actually preparing to invade England. While it is true that
Philip had rebuffed Edward's diplomacy there is not the slightest ground for believing the cry of impending invasion.
Edward's ambition, however, was blind to truth, and England
was flooded with effective war propaganda. The fleet was put
on a war basis, seaports were fortified and the militia was made
ready for an attack. Parliament and the clergy voted supplies. Edward's agents abroad, moreover, were busy forming alliances with the Empire, Bavaria, and a number of Flemish towns. Having effected these ends, Edward in 1337 proclaimed a war against France.

In seeking to evaluate the antecedents of this contest, known
as the Hundred Years' War, consideration should be given to
the dynastic aspirations of Edward III. In 1328 Charles IV of
France died without male issue, and while the nobility of that
kingdom were debating the succession, Isabella, Queen of England and mother of Edward, claimed the French throne for
her son. She based her rights upon the fact that she was a
sister of Charles, a claim which she considered as good as that
of Marie, daughter of Charles. The barony of France, however, gave scant attention to this plea and elevated to the throne
Philip, son of Charles Valois and uncle of the past three kings.
Although Isabella and Edward protested against this award,
formal recognition of Philip's title was made by Edward in
1329 and again in 1331. On the basis of available evidence it
seems quite likely that Edward never reconciled himself to the
loss, and in 1337 he boldly claimed the throne of France.
Surely the French had something to say as to who might be
their ruler, and had the situation been reversed, one can well
imagine how the air would have rung in England over alien
pretensions. But Edward was determined to start a war, cost
what it might to England. Personal ambition was of far

greater importance than the lives and fortunes of his subjects. On Edward's decision, therefore, must rest much of the responsibility for the Hundred Years' War.

Dynastic reasons for this conflict were reinforced by imperialistic considerations. For nearly two centuries Gascony had been under English control. The basis for this attachment was fundamentally economic and existed in the valuable wine trade between the two peoples. In addition, English capital had been invested in Gascony, and this in turn had led to a migration of some Englishmen to that province. The English government, moreover, reflected these activities by introducing extensive political agencies in Gascony, which served as a training school for future officers and administrators at home. With but one exception all the mayors of Bordeaux during the reign of Edward III were well known and distinguished Englishmen. Gascony, in brief, was a colonial possession as dear to the crown in the fourteenth century as India is today. To retain this valuable holding became a prime objective of the English governing and business classes. To destroy this connection, however, was the aim and purpose of the French kings. To the latter, the presence of a foreigner upon French soil was intolerable, and there was no logical reason why French capital should not have its share of the wine trade.

Closely allied to the Gascon problem was one concerning Flanders, the industrial hub of Europe and the center of an important woolen trade. England exported large quantities of raw wool to Flanders and thus provided employment for thousands in the agricultural and shipping life of the island. But Flanders was a fief of the French king, who for some time had been trying to absorb this county as an integral part of the royal domain. Once again, therefore, nationally minded Frenchmen were seeking a way to deprive English traders, farmers, and capitalists of a profitable connection. Let the Count of Flanders, upon order of Philip of France, place an embargo upon English shipping and the docks of English seaport towns would be piled high with raw wool, and the mills of Flanders would lie idle. Naturally, therefore, the Flemish were willing to accept Edward's offer of alliance and thus were drawn into the war.

With France constantly interfering in the Flemish and Gascon trades it was certain that there would be numerous clashes between the sailors engaged in this exchange of goods. There was also the Franco-Scottish alliance. As long as England sought to control the kingdom to the north, Scotland would seek French aid. France willingly supported Scotland so as to keep England busy at home. Edward realized, therefore, that a definite settlement of the Scottish problem could be obtained only upon the battlefields of France. Whether the Scottish or naval disputes would in themselves have led to war no one knows, though they were contributing factors of significance in bringing about this conflict. The primary antecedents for the contest, however, existed in the clash between two growing and expanding nations, in the valuable capitalistic interests involved, and in the personal ambition of Edward III.

Although the war began in 1337 and did not end until a century later, it would be quite wrong to assume that there was a hundred years of constant fighting. Indeed the conflict was repeatedly stopped by treaties, by utter exhaustion, and by the ravages of the Black Death. By 1396 England had lost heavily in life and treasure, and retained, besides Calais, only a strip of Gascony running from Bordeaux to Bayonne. Twenty-four years later, the situation was reversed owing largely to internal dissensions within France and the unusual ability shown by the Lancastrian generals and kings. In that year Charles VI of France concluded the Treaty of Troyes, whereby most of northern France was handed over to Henry V, King of England, who became Charles' son-in-law by marrying the French princess, Katherine. Charles' own son and heir was ignored and the future of France was entrusted to Henry, who was to become King of France upon the death of Charles. Henry did not live to govern his expanded kingdom, though his rights were claimed by the English upon the death of Charles in 1422. At this point France rallied behind Charles VII to oppose the forces of the English pretender, the infant Henry VI, which were under the command of the Duke of Bedford. Bedford proved to be more than a match for the French and might probably have won the contest but for the timely assistance rendered by Joan of Arc. Declaring that heaven had commissioned her to protect Charles and save France from English control, Joan so electrified French nationalism as to force the English back to the Loire. The siege of Orleans was raised and Bedford was compelled to give further ground. Even though Joan was captured by the English and put to death on the charge of being a witch, her spirit continued to dominate the situation. Bedford's death in 1435 weakened the English defense. Maine was ceded to France in 1446, and in 1450 Normandy was captured by the troops of the French king. Three years later the English tried to regain Gascony. The English were defeated and the Hundred Years' War came to an end. With the exception of Calais and the Channel Isles, England had lost the extensive empire she once had governed.

For over a century England kings had striven to impose an alien domination upon France. During the greater half of the contest an intense display of English nationalism had swept to one side the armies of France. Most of the important battles had been won by the English. Yet when the war was over, France was master of her own territory. In accounting for this crushing defeat one must credit as the most important factor, the rise of French nationalism under Joan of Arc. Even then the conflict might have been prolonged had it not been for the waning interest of the English. England was not less nationalistic than she had been, but her people were growing tired of a war which seemed to have no end. The levies of men and money had become excessive, and with the loss of Gascony in 1451 all hope of retaining an economic or political foothold in France disappeared.

English pride, moreover, had been touched to the quick by the success of the French; and as is often the case, the blame for defeat was placed upon the shoulders of Henry VI. Actually, Henry had played a minor rôle in the war. From 1422, the time of his father's death, to 1437, Henry was a minor, and his uncles, the Dukes of Bedford and Gloucester, had governed English interests at home and abroad. Their task was rendered doubly difficult by reason of the French war and by a spirited opposition on the part of some of the English nobles. With Bedford's death in 1435, the opposition found that Gloucester was not the equal of his brother and that Henry, upon taking the throne in his own name, was little more than a puppet. Quick to sense the possibilities of the situation these disgruntled nobles poured forth abuse and ridicule upon the royal ministers who had allowed dissension to develop in England and the enemy to win the day in France. Henry's gestures in behalf of his councillors became the signal for an outburst of popular disapproval which culminated in Cade's rebellion.

Civil Disturbances

Cade's uprising was not only an economic protest on the part of the peasants who participated in it, but a political demonstration in which men of property and means joined in hoping to bring to an end the mismanagement of government. Cade's troops actually entered London but were driven out by the citizens. Shortly thereafter the rebellion was put down, though the government was still annoyed by bands of soldiers returning from France, who rioted throughout the kingdom. Henry, utterly bewildered, blundered time after time as he followed the suggestions of those who contended against his rule or those who supported his administration. The latter group were known as the Lancastrians, while the former were called the Yorkists after their leader Richard, Duke of York. Actually, neither party cared much for Henry. Lancastrians and Yorkists alike were concerned in advancing only their own personal and political desires. Henry's position and prestige declined, in spite of the Herculean efforts of his wife, Margaret of France. To cap the climax, Henry became insane and thus precipitated a wild scramble among the nobles for the regency. Richard, Duke of York, gained this position. The ascendency of the Yorkists, however, was cut short by Henry's recovering his health and by the birth of an heir to the throne. Before this event Richard had been next in line and the Yorkists fully believed that their leader would shortly become king. With the reversal of events, however, the Lancastrians lorded it over their rivals, who struck back by appealing to the sword. The Yorkists took as their badge the white rose, while the Lancastrians at a much later date took a red rose, as a result of which the contest has been known as the War of the Roses.

Little need be said of this dynastic contest (1455–1485), which in the main was a conflict between the two houses of York and Lancaster with the crown as the stake. The tide of victory went first one way and then another. In 1461 the Lancastrians had been swept out of power and the Yorkists had placed Edward, son of Richard, Duke of York, on the throne. Edward IV, however, had to fight for his title and it was not until 1471, with Henry VI dead, that Edward's position was secure.

Edward IV reigned until 1483, when the affairs of state and the well-being of his sons, Edward V and Richard, were entrusted to Richard, Duke of Gloucester, brother of Edward IV. Richard's character had already been soiled by his actions during the past twenty years, a fact which may help to explain why the Woodville family, in whose keeping the princes were before Edward's death, proceeded to take steps against Gloucester. Not waiting, however, for his enemies to strike, Richard seized his nephews and locked up a number of the Woodville faction. Determined to become king, Richard circulated wild rumors about the illegitimacy of the princes, whose birthright was denied by a hand-picked parliament in 1483. Aware that their presence endangered the throne, which in the meantime he had seized as Richard III, the new King arranged for their murder in the Tower.

Public opinion, which had never been favorable to Richard, flared up in violent opposition. Even the Yorkists had little to say in behalf of their leader, who now had to face the possibility of a Lancastrian revolt championed by Henry Tudor, a cousin of Henry VI and a distant relative of Edward III. Numerous communications passed back and forth between Henry Tudor and the disgruntled group at home. Finally in October, 1485, Henry, supported by the French king and assured of assistance in England, landed and hurried to meet his rival in battle. At Bosworth Field the contest was waged, with the result that Richard lost both his life and crown while Henry marched on to London where parliament proclaimed him Henry VII, King of England.

The War of the Roses, although it dragged over a number of years, was an affair which concerned chiefly the nobility. Total casualties were low in number, while the ravaging which took place did not materially affect the nation. Both Thorold Rogers and Charles C. Kingsford, who studied the social consequences of the war, conclude that there was little disturbance to everyday life. Politically, the contest checked the drift towards a limited monarchy and made possible the strong-arm methods employed by the Tudor dynasty.

Ecclesiastical Disputes

During the course of these domestic squabbles and the French war, England had become involved in a religious upheaval which helped to prepare the ground for the reformation of the sixteenth century. Ever since the days of Anselm, Rome had sought to advance its interests in England. Against this movement Norman and Angevin monarchs had contended somewhat successfully though Henry III allowed these gains to be partially lost. Benefit of clergy and other rights were enjoyed at the expense of the central government. Rome, moreover, emphasized its claim of superiority over kings in all matters, spiritual or temporal. Finally in 1296 Boniface VIII, in the bull *Clericis Laicos,* denied the right of any prince to tax clerics without papal approval. To this challenge, Edward I, who took his religion seriously, made no direct answer. But when the English clergy refused to vote a subsidy on the ground that it violated papal orders, Edward in no uncertain terms informed them that they would have to choose between paying the tax or being placed beyond the protection of royal justice. Anxious to escape a sentence of outlawry, many of the clergy sent in their share of the subsidy, while those who did not, suffered a confiscation of their property. When Boniface heard what had happened and learned also of the stiff opposition which his bull had encountered in France, he modified his policy and within a year completely nullified *Clericis Laicos.* Moreover, Boniface and his successor, Clement V, outdid themselves in granting Edward special favors, and in return the King allowed Rome to levy annates, a fee which a clergyman paid the Pope upon his installation to a benefice, and which had never before been used in England. The assessment of this tax raised a storm of protest from the clergy who but a short time before had been most emphatic in expressions of loyalty to Rome. Realizing the futility of appealing to Edward, the clergy joined hands with

the barons and commonalty at Carlisle in requesting the Crown
to stop this tax as well as other papal exactions which had irritated the laity. Very judiciously Edward allowed parliament
to pass an act to this effect and then proceeded to set aside
those sections which touched annates. With this exception,
however, Edward rigorously enforced the Statute of Carlisle.
More significant than this action was the fact that England
had taken a bold stand against papal interference in domestic
affairs.

Edward's Roman policy was not altered until 1343 when a
situation arose which revived the old feud between the two
authorities. It will be recalled that when Boniface issued his
bull, sharp protests arose in France and the Pope hastened to
retract the offending measure. Hardly had this quarrel been
settled when another issue arose with the seizure and trial by
Philip IV of France of a papal legate on the charge of treason
and heresy. Boniface answered this attack by issuing the bull
Unam Sanctam, which proclaimed that man's salvation depended upon complete allegiance to Rome in all matters.
Philip replied by sending officers to Rome with instructions to
bring the Pope to France for trial before a general church
council. Boniface refused to be intimidated, and though a
prisoner of the French, checked their attempts to carry him
to France. Shortly thereafter Boniface died and was followed
by Benedict XI who during the few months of his reign was
rather friendly towards Philip. Philip's fortune rose to greater
heights when his friend the Archbishop of Bordeaux became
Clement V in 1305. Clement immediately showed his hand
by being crowned at Lyons and by moving his capital to Avi-
gnon in 1309. From then on until 1377, the papacy remained
in France, subject to the will of that state.

Although France was highly pleased with existing conditions, other nations, including England, resented French
domination over ecclesiastical affairs. England, moreover, was
at war with France at the time and felt that the papacy was

using its influence against her. English feeling against the papacy was well expressed by the following comment, current in Europe at the time: "Now the Pope has become French and Jesus has become English; now it will be seen who can do more, the Pope or Jesus." Further ill will was created by the Pope, who announced in 1343 that the Church intended to push the practice of "provisions." Provisions were papal documents which had the effect of taking the appointment to ecclesiastical holdings out of the hands of the local clergy and of placing it at the disposal of Rome. England protested against these provisions chiefly because they invaded what had been considered a domestic affair and because many of the appointees were aliens. Parliament echoed these sentiments by passing the celebrated Statute of Provisors which forbade the further use of these documents in England. And when Rome sought to evade this measure by having disputes relative to it transferred to the papal court for settlement, parliament replied with the Statute of Praemunire (1353) which denied appeals to foreign courts of all cases affecting royal justice. Pope Urban V considered this act equivalent to a declaration of war and tried to force an issue over the arrears of papal rents which John had promised more than a century before. Edward III and parliament informed the Pope that John's promise amounted to nothing. It was also proposed in parliament that Peter's Pence be withheld and that if Rome sought to collect John's debts England would resist to the utmost. Needless to say Rome could do nothing, and with that the dispute came to an end. The temper of the English government was significantly shown in the case of the Bishop of Ely, who had become involved in a lawsuit with one of the royal family. An acute situation arose when the Bishop's chamberlain slew one of the servants of the King's household. The Bishop was brought to trial on the charge of abetting murder. He was refused trial by his peers and found guilty by a jury of common people. And when

Innocent VI championed his cause, the English government excluded papal bulls excommunicating royal justices on pain of outlawry.

Anti-clericalism was also shown by the desire on the part of the Commons to shift the burden of taxation to the shoulders of the English clergy who claimed that they were not subject to parliament in matters of taxation. At the same time Edward quarreled with the clergy over their refusal to attend meetings of parliament. Their actions tended only to increase the strong anti-clerical feeling which was present in England. It would be wrong, however, to assume that this sentiment created a definite break between England and Rome or that the Statutes of Provisors and Praemunire brought to an end either the use of provisions or of appeals to Rome. Edward frequently found it to his advantage to forget these measures. In the last analysis these acts should be judged not so much by their degree of enforcement but rather by their content and purpose. In this sense they reflect the growing anti-papal and anti-clerical feeling in England.

Wycliffe Breaks with Rome

The parliament which outlawed John's debts witnessed the appearance of John Wycliffe (c.1330–1384), whose name ever since has been connected with the anti-papal movement. Of Wycliffe's early life little is known. He was educated at Oxford, took holy orders, and in 1360 became master of Balliol College, Oxford. Here he expounded scholastic philosophy and began his investigations of ecclesiastical life and thought. During this period, moreover, he became an outspoken critic of his Church. What irritated the man most of all was not the presence of abuses within the Church but rather the failure of Rome to remove them. Wycliffe admitted that French domination had done little to improve the standing of the Church, and together with thousands of others must have applauded Gregory XI's flight from France to Rome in 1377. The accumulative effects, however, of the long sojourn in

France (1309–1377) precipitated a crisis in Church government which resulted in a serious schism; one faction remained at Rome under Urban VI, the other returned to France under Robert of Geneva, who assumed papal authority as Clement VII. Thus, there were two popes, each with his own college of cardinals, while Christians everywhere were called upon to decide which of the two was the lawful successor of St. Peter. The net result of these events gave Wycliffe much to think about.

Wycliffe had already become prominent in English political and intellectual circles by the time of the Great Schism. His deep-seated disgust of clerical abuses had caused him to advocate disendowment of Church property by the state on the ground that those who were in mortal sin could hold neither office nor property. Sovereignty in such matters, he proclaimed, lay with the state and what the state had given could be taken back. A pronouncement of this type speedily attracted the attention of those who had been criticizing the Church for the manner in which it had administered its offices and sacraments. The spoliation of the Church became "a reasoned and deliberate policy" of the government. Foremost in this group was John of Gaunt, a son of Edward III and an uncle to the future Richard II. Gaunt befriended Wycliffe and protected him from the attacks of the ecclesiastics as long as Wycliffe confined his complaints to the temporal aspects of the Church. When Wycliffe, however, assaulted the theological tenets of Rome, Gaunt withdrew his support and gave the Church an opportunity to silence its enemy. In 1382 at Blackfriars, London, the clerical party condemned many of Wycliffe's statements. Shortly thereafter Oxford was purged of heretical teachers and teaching, while Wycliffe was forced to retire to Lutterworth, where he spent the two remaining years of his life.

Wycliffe's influence transcended his own life and country. In his writings, notably the *Civil Dominion* and the *Divine Dominion,* queries were raised which did much to pave the way for the reformation both in England and on the Continent. The abuses within the Church, which Wycliffe so effectively displayed, were patent to all. Immorality, ignorance, corruption in administration, oppressive judicial action—these and many other shortcomings were as clear to the laity and clergy as they were to Wycliffe. He wished to expose these evils as a true friend of the Church. Rome had experienced similar attacks before but, according to Wycliffe, had done little to improve conditions. The Great Schism, moreover, challenged the thought of all and as Rome seemed unable to find an escape from the impasse, Wycliffe thundered forth his views in no uncertain terms.

Wycliffe maintained that the Bible rather than the Pope was the sole and final authority in all matters of faith and doctrine. Salvation, moreover, depended more upon one's mode of life than upon a group of sacraments, many of which Wycliffe denounced. He questioned the spiritual powers of the priests and denied the doctrine of transubstantiation. That a priest, whose hands in many cases were stained with earthly sins, could by the recitation of certain words change ordinary bread and wine into the actual body and blood of Christ was utterly incomprehensible to Wycliffe. Biblical authority, he asserted, provided no basis for such a doctrine, and as the holy Word of God was more reliable than the dictates of princes and popes, Wycliffe rejected the current theological interpretation of the Lord's Supper. The espousal of what contemporary opinion deemed heretical cost Wycliffe caste and his position at Oxford. He retained his views, however, and laid the foundations for what was known as Lollardism. The Lollards were humble missionaries who, armed with Wycliffe's English translation of the Bible, went about the realm propagandizing in favor of a new ecclesiastical order. Wycliffe's views, moreover, gained converts on the Continent and in time led John Huss of Bohemia to raise the standard of revolt in that locality. What Huss taught and died for, Luther substantially accepted and successfully advanced in the sixteenth century.

Though Wycliffe never suffered complete condemnation or death, the lot of his followers was less fortunate. The strong arm of the government came down upon the Lollards, many of whom paid with their lives for what they believed and taught. Parliament endorsed these repressive measures and in 1401 provided for the burning of heretics. In 1414 an attempt at rebellion led by Sir John Oldcastle, a follower of Wycliffe, was effectively quelled and Lollardism was driven to cover. Little more is heard of the movement, though it is the opinion of several scholars that Lollardism smoldered on in the hearts and minds of hundreds of Englishmen until the days of Henry VIII, when it reappeared and helped to make the English reformation a success. Wycliffe's equalitarianism, his denunci- ation of papal and clerical abuses, his condemnation of war, his insistency that Christ, the Prince of Peace, ruled man by the Word of God as revealed in the Scriptures, and his rejection of man-made doctrines and creeds were far in advance of his age. Nationally minded, objective and critical in his re- searches, Wycliffe fanned a flame which burst forth in the English reformation.

GENEALOGICAL GUIDE FOR THE FOURTEENTH AND FIFTEENTH CENTURIES

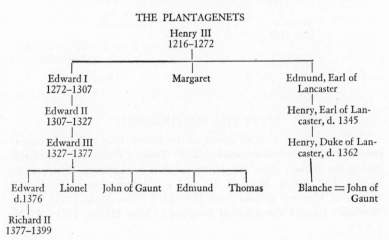

THE PLANTAGENETS

Henry III
1216–1272

Edward I
1272–1307

Margaret

Edmund, Earl of Lancaster

Edward II
1307–1327

Henry, Earl of Lan-
caster, d. 1345

Edward III
1327–1377

Henry, Duke of Lan-
caster, d. 1362

Edward   Lionel   John of Gaunt   Edmund   Thomas
d.1376

Blanche = John of
Gaunt

Richard II
1377–1399

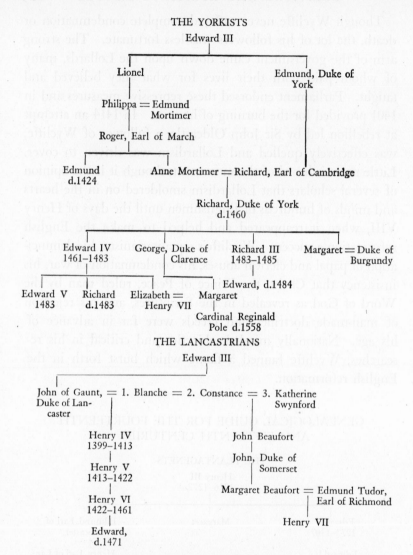

THE YORKISTS

Edward III

Lionel

Edmund, Duke of York

Philippa = Edmund Mortimer

Roger, Earl of March

Edmund d.1424

Anne Mortimer = Richard, Earl of Cambridge

Richard, Duke of York d.1460

Edward IV 1461–1483

George, Duke of Clarence

Richard III 1483–1485

Margaret = Duke of Burgundy

Edward V 1483

Richard d.1483

Elizabeth = Henry VII

Margaret

Edward, d.1484

Cardinal Reginald Pole d.1558

THE LANCASTRIANS

Edward III

John of Gaunt, = 1. Blanche = 2. Constance = 3. Katherine
Duke of Lan-   Swynford
caster

Henry IV 1399–1413

John Beaufort

Henry V 1413–1422

John, Duke of Somerset

Henry VI 1422–1461

Margaret Beaufort = Edmund Tudor, Earl of Richmond

Edward, d.1471

Henry VII

SELECTED BIBLIOGRAPHY

The extension of English power in the British Isles and in France is presented in the following works: T. F. Tout's "Wales and the March during the Baron's War" in *Historical Essays* (London, 1902); J. E. Morris' *The Welsh Wars of Edward I* (Oxford, 1901); E. Curtis' *History of Medieval Ireland from 1110–1513* (New York, 1924); R. A. Newhall's *English Conquest of Burgundy* (New Haven, 1924); L. V.

D. Owen's *Connection between England and Burgundy* (Oxford, 1909); E. Lavisse's *Histoire de France*; Vols. III and IV (Paris, 1911), and E. C. Lodge's *Gascony under English Rule* (London, 1926).

W. Longman's *History of the Life and Times of Edward III* (London, 1869); J. H. Ramsay's *Lancaster and York* (London, 1913); J. Mackinnon's *History of Edward III* (London, 1900); J. H. Wylie's *History of England under Henry the Fourth* (1884–1898) and *Reign of Henry V* (Cambridge, 1914–1929); J. Gairdner's *History of the Life and Reign of Richard III* (Cambridge, 1898), and C. L. Scofield's *Life and Reign of Edward Fourth* (London, 1923) are general histories which reflect England's imperial growth. They are also of value for the narrative history from 1300–1485. The War of the Roses is reviewed in R. B. Mowat's *War of the Roses* (London, 1914); J. E. Thorold Rogers' *History of Agriculture and Prices in England* (Oxford, 1886–1902), and C. L. Kingsford's *Prejudice and Promise in XVth Century England* (Oxford, 1925). C. L. Kingsford's *Henry V* (New York, 1901); R. B. Mowat's *Henry V* (Boston, 1919); M. E. Christie's *Henry VI*; C. Oman's *Warwick the Kingmaker* (London, 1891); A. G. Bradley's *Owen Glyndwr* (New York, 1901), and S. Armitag-Smith's *John of Gaunt* (Westminster, 1904) are standard biographies.

Most of the above-mentioned works are rich in ecclesiastical affairs. In addition there are G. M. Trevelyan's *England in the Age of Wycliffe* (London, 1925); J. Gairdner's *Lollardy and the Reformation* (London, 1908); J. F. Willard's *The English Church and the Lay Taxes of the Fourteenth Century* (University of Colorado Studies, 1907), and H. B. Workman's *John Wyclif* (Oxford, 1926).

CHAPTER XI

Constitutional Growth

The Genesis of Parliament

FROM the time of John's death in 1216 to that of Richard III in 1485, the English constitution underwent far-reaching alterations. Several factors contributed to these changes: first, the influence of Magna Carta and its reissues; second, the inherent strength and virility of the central government; third, baronial opposition to the crown; fourth, the growth of new administrative and legislative devices; fifth, the infiltration of a new economic order; and sixth, the personalities of men like Henry III, Simon de Montfort, Edward I, and Richard II. At the opening of this period the King possessed considerable power; at the close he was subject to a number of restrictive influences. The purpose of this chapter is to trace the transition from an absolute to a limited monarchy.

Probably the most effective agency in producing this result was the rise and development of parliament. It will be recalled that John, while engaged in his contest with the barons, had hit upon the idea of having representatives of the county juries meet him in conjunction with the Great Council. John's experiments were of little value except as they pointed the way for his successor, Henry III. Throughout the latter's reign (1216–1272), representatives of the shires met in conjunction with the Great Council for the purpose of reporting upon local conditions, of voting taxes and of discussing affairs of the realm. At one of these gatherings, that of 1265, representatives of selected boroughs were also present because of the influence exerted upon the King by Simon de Montfort. De Montfort's parliament, as this meeting has been called, is of decided interest. Not that it may be described as a parliament in a precise sense, but it contained all the elements necessary for future development in so far as election and representation were concerned.

De Montfort's experiments, as well as those of Henry III, were not forgotten by Edward I upon his accession to the throne in 1272. Edward, aware of the value of these past assemblies, frequently summoned knights, burgesses, and representatives of the lesser clergy to meet with the Great Council for governmental purposes. The net result was a gathering in 1295 which has been known as the "Model Parliament." This body consisted of members of the Great Council, the lesser clergy, knights of the shire, and burgesses from selected towns and cities. The last two elements were elected by the local units. In other words, parliament, like similar bodies on the Continent, was simply a medieval assembly formed of the three social and political classes (estates) of the realm. There was, therefore, little in the English experiment to distinguish it from similar activities in Europe. Moreover, the parliament of 1295 was a unicameral body like the States General of the French; and in the light of contemporary evidence, it might well have gone the way of the French assembly, which became a harmless gathering under royal control. The parliament of 1295 hardly deserves the title of "Model" in so far as structure, organization, or purpose are concerned. And yet it was a pattern in the sense that it stood as the fruition of past experience and progress.

Although Edward I and Edward II recognized the value of an assembly of the estates, it was baronial opposition to the crown which made these gatherings significant. The king's interest centered chiefly in the question of finance, and to gain

approval to taxes, he summoned no less than thirty-two parliaments between 1307 and 1322. Knights met regularly with
the Great Council from 1311, though burgesses were called
at other times. Clerical consent to taxation was gained
through Convocation, the assembly of the clergy. But did the
king contemplate a union of all estates into a single parliament? The evidence is scanty but seems to point to a negative answer. A union, however, did take place but it was
the barons and not the king who forced this action. The
Commons in parliament could be used by the barons as allies
against royal absolutism. On the other hand, the barons had
no interest in advancing the position and power of the Commons and expected to use them for selfish purposes. The insistency on the part of the barons on popular representation
ultimately led to the predominance of these popular elements.
It was also agreed by all parties that in great matters, legal
and political, "the final decision must be in parliament." This
concept appeared in the Statute of York (1322) which stated
that "matters . . . for the estates of the realm and of the people,
shall be treated, accorded and established in Parliament, by our
lord the king, and by the consent of the prelates, earls and
barons, and the *commonalty* of the realm." (Italics are the
author's.)

The Appearance of the House of Commons

Today at Westminster there assembles a body composed of
two houses, Lords and Commons, neither of which existed in
1295. At that time the three estates (the greater clergy, the
greater lords, and the representatives of the counties, lesser
clergy and selected boroughs) gathered in one large room at
one end of which was the king or his representative. Here
they listened to the crown and here they endorsed what their
ruler requested. Indeed the crown was not required to ask for
their opinion or assent to this plan. Experience, however, con-

vinced Edward I that it was far easier to gain desired ends
by securing their views and consent to taxation than by ignoring them.   Parliament, in brief, was but a royal device for promoting the king's wishes.   It was not conceived by anyone
as a democratic body.   Furthermore, it may well be conjec-
tured whether the lesser clergy, knights and burgesses had
much interest in coming to parliament, voting financial grants,
or rubber-stamping what the king ordered.   Spiritual duties,
the management of manors and the handling of business were
of far greater concern to these elements.   Hence it was to their
advantage to approve of royal requests as quickly as possible
and to hurry home to what really interested them.   Representation was a burden, rather than a privilege.

Among those who felt out of place in parliament were the
lesser clergy, who but recently had assisted in the establishment of Convocation.   Here they played a rôle which pleased
them and here they voted taxes for ecclesiastical purposes.
The tradition of separatism between the Church and state,
and the constant pronouncements of papal supremacy in temporal affairs had made the clergy class conscious.   Accordingly, they resented their inclusion in the parliaments of Edward I and Edward II.   They realized that their independence
was slipping from their hands.   As a result they often
quarreled with the crown over the form of summons and
the legality of taxes voted by parliament and imposed upon
them.   These difficulties induced the crown to allow the lesser
clergy to absent themselves from parliament on the understanding that they would vote taxes in Convocation for royal
needs.   Beginning with 1322, the lesser clergy no longer appear on the rolls of parliament.   Writs summoning these persons to attend parliament, however, were issued as a matter
of form throughout the fourteenth century.   It is important
to remember, however, that political thinkers of the medieval period held that the authority of the kingdom was "expressed concurrently in Convocation and in Parliament."

From the reign of Edward I, these two bodies together "gave a double, yet unequal rhythm to English public life." The fact that the Convocation's consent to taxation was sought throughout the fourteenth century illustrates the truth of this comment.

In the meantime the attitudes of the knights and burgesses had changed. Although the former were allied by blood and contract to the greater barons, they came to realize that they had more in common with the representatives of the towns. Fundamentally, the knight was but the manager of a business enterprise, the manor, and as such he found the burgess much like himself. Realization of this fact was brought sharply to the front as the Hundred Years' War forced both elements to meet unprecedented taxes. Moreover, the knight and burgess had considerable interest in preventing a servile uprising; the former because his chief income came from the labor of these dependent cultivators, the latter because of his increasing investments in rural property. Once this union of ideas and purposes became known, it was not long before both groups voiced their feelings on the floor of parliament.

But how could they accomplish much in an assembly which favored the greater clergy and nobility? Believing that they needed greater freedom in debate, knight and burgess joined hands in seeking a gathering place of their own. Finally, some time around 1340 a separation between these groups and the Great Council was effected, probably with the knowledge and consent of the King. A bicameral legislature had come into being, though the modern terms of a House of Lords and a House of Commons may not be applied to these bodies from a legal point of view, until the fifteenth century.

With the establishment of a two-chambered assembly the ground was prepared for an extension of parliamentary power, especially in respect to the lower house. The key to the situation was the general question of taxation. Magna Carta had asserted the principle that all extraordinary feudal dues were to be approved by the barons. Although this particular section of the charter did not appear in any of the reissues, the principle involved became an essential part of feudal law and was more obeyed than some of the provisions which remained within the charter. Evasions, however, did take place. At the same time, Edward I placed heavy burdens upon the woolen merchants and irritated the agriculturists by excessive requisitions of salt and grain. No matter how loudly Edward might shout about the need for these actions, citing foreign wars by way of justification, the barons insisted that time-honored rights had been ignored. Driven to desperation, the barons presented in 1297 a formal statement of their complaints coupled with a petition which begged Edward to rule in accordance with law. Anxious to pursue his wars and fearful of baronial opposition, Edward yielded in what is known as the *Confirmation of the Charters*. Among other things, Edward promised not to levy any extraordinary charge without his tenants' approval. Although the language was feudal, the evident intent was that the Confirmation should cover non-feudal taxes as well; and in spite of Edward's later evasions the formulation of a new principle was never forgotten. Legally, therefore, the Crown was dependent upon parliament for any additional revenue beyond the established customs and wool tariffs.

The Confirmation, however, did not provide any definite way of gaining parliamentary consent, and this omission gave Edward and his successors ample room for action. Repeated evasions, chiefly on the part of Edward III, evoked many sharp protests which centered about the matter of custom dues. Edward claimed rightly that the law allowed him to increase these assessments by private agreements with alien merchants. When he insisted that he could raise customs with the sole consent of native traders, he was on less tenable ground. At first the Commons were greatly puzzled by the King's action and were uncertain as to what the existing law actually covered. Taking advantage of their doubts Edward drove many a profitable arrangement with alien and native merchants and thus was able, in part, to finance the French wars without asking for parliamentary grants.

Touched to the quick by these practices the Commons realized that if an assembly of merchants could vote taxes, parliament's rôle might be reduced to practically nothing. Protest followed; but Edward continued the wool tax, which, because of its abuse, earned for itself the name of *maltote* or evil toll. In spite of the *maltote* and the usual parliamentary grants, Edward experienced great difficulty in 1340 in financing his wars. He was forced, therefore, to listen to the complaints of his subjects and, in return for a subsidy, yielded to parliament the right to levy charges or duties. Moreover, all doubt as to the legality of taxation by an assembly of woolen merchants was removed. In the future, parliament was to control a large measure of taxation. Although Edward III ignored this act on several occasions, parliament always reminded him by passing the measure anew. And when Edward sought to evade the issue, parliament withheld supplies until the King had redressed their grievances.

With the control of the purse lodged more and more in parliament, or to be precise, in the Commons, further gains in governmental powers were made. Subsidies were voted for definite purposes, subject to an auditing committee of the Commons. As a final check over royal finances, parliament impeached those ministers who violated law. With the possible exception of a brief period during the reign of Richard II (1377–1399), these gains became accumulative in their effects and were held in high respect by the king during the first half of the fifteenth century. On the other hand, parliament was not able to prevent the king from resorting to forced loans. Henry IV and Henry V, in particular, often extracted sums from unwilling merchants who had every reason to believe that they would never receive payment. Finally, it should be noticed that in 1407 the Commons gained the sole power of initiating money bills.

The introduction of money measures in the lower house was an integral part of a movement to acquire a voice in the making of law. Prior to 1300 little attention had been paid to this problem, since practically all law was made by the king in the form of ordinances. Even the statutes of this age were the pronouncements of the monarch. At the same time the Crown allowed parliament to act as a clearing house for the petitions which came from all parts of the realm. By the time of Edward III, parliament had transferred most of this work, which involved judicial action, to some appropriate court. However, petitions which were general in nature were reserved for parliament's consideration. The procedure which was followed provided that the petition, having secured parliament's approval, was submitted to the Crown which might or might not issue the same in the form of an ordinance. To overcome this veto, parliament merely refused to vote taxes until the king had granted the petitioner's request. In this manner some degree of legislative authority was gained. There was nothing, however, to prevent the king from altering the terminology of the petition or to dispense with its operation for an individual or to suspend it entirely. By the reign of Henry V, the Crown had been forced to modify this practice, while in the reign of his son, petitions might be introduced as ordinary bills. Upon passing parliament and upon receiving royal consent these bills then became laws. The power to dispense or suspend legislation, however, was not taken from the King until the latter part of the seventeenth century.

Gains in parliamentary power were matched during the early half of the fifteenth century by the acquisition of privilege. Heretofore the Commons had found it extremely difficult to present their views to the king, who often gained false impressions or advance information which in turn hampered the work of the lower house. The Lords, on the contrary, as members of the Council, were always able to approach the king on any matter. To eliminate this difficulty, the Commons utilized the office of speaker, which had been established by the close of the fourteenth century, as the means whereby the Crown and the lower house should communicate with each other. At first the Crown was reluctant to accept this practice, but by Henry V's reign the Commons had won this most cherished right.

Freedom of access to the monarch was followed by freedom of speech. Commons believed that unless it could debate freely on all matters, there was little reason for its existence. Edward III had yielded much ground in this respect though Richard II sharply contested the issue with parliament. In 1397, for example, Thomas Haxey was convicted of treason for having spoken against Richard from the floor of the Commons. Although Haxey received a royal pardon from Richard and later a repeal of the sentence by Henry IV, the Commons still believed its position to be none too secure. In the reign of Henry IV, the Commons twice withheld supply, and in this way forced the King to admit the principle of free speech. However, in 1451 and 1453, the Crown successfully interposed its authority and jailed a commoner who had criticized the government. From then until the advent of the Tudors little discussion took place relative to this problem. Possibly the Commons felt reluctant about pushing the issue in an age which witnessed considerable respect for the office of king. As Bishop Stubbs has put it in his monumental work, the various episodes referred to would hardly "be worth recording . . . were it not that these earlier notions . . . were to be used by the protagonists of privilege at a later date."

The incident of 1453 also involved the right of the king to arrest members of the Commons. Here was a matter which deeply concerned the welfare of that body, and one is not surprised to note sharp remonstrances against this royal practice.

Throughout the Lancastrian age (1399–1461), the Commons strove to protect its members against arrest and by 1485 had won the point at issue. As finally agreed to, this privilege, while not extended to treason or felony, secured from arrest all members of parliament for a stated period before, during, and after a session of that body. Closely allied to this privilege was the contention on the part of the Commons that it alone could discipline its members for disorderly conduct.

Victories in respect to privilege were equaled by gains in other fields, one of which concerned the general question of franchise and qualification for membership in Commons. During the thirteenth century the shire representatives were chiefly knights. Reluctance on the part of these nobles to assume parliamentary duties forced the Crown to admit those of lower rank. Moreover, the Crown was not averse to having lawyers and merchants present in view of the diversity of problems which arose during the fourteenth century. Illustrations of these practices may be found in a number of measures of which the act of 1445 is the most significant. According to this law, county representatives were to be chosen from the knightly class, but when these were not available, gentlemen "as shall be able to be knights" were to be elected. No serious modification of this scheme took place during the period now under discussion.

In the meantime, far-reaching changes had taken place in respect to the franchise. During the earlier years of parliament, anyone who was a qualified suitor in the shire court was eligible to participate in an election to the lower house. Little interest was shown by the electors until the Hundred Years' War, when heavy taxation incident to this conflict and the internal discord engendered by peasant revolts made these elections spirited affairs. With property rights at stake, individuals vied for the right of going to parliament and did all in their power to get out the entire voting population. Many persons, moreover, who were not qualified voters were added to the electorate. In order to rectify this abuse and to produce some degree of uniformity, parliament in 1430 passed an act which restricted the franchise to those whose net incomes amounted to forty shillings from a freehold or tenement. By this measure, which remained unchanged until 1832, the right of voting was limited to those of property, who alone might stand for election.

Property rights also played a decisive part in determining borough representation. Age, sex, and residence were common prerequisites, as were other requirements local in nature. The explanation for the variations rests in part upon town charters and upon the absence of any parliamentary measure dealing with borough franchise. Hence, what entitled a person to vote in one borough might not qualify another having the same standing in a different community. Only a small number of towns and cities possessed representation, and these were distinguished from the others by the title of "Parliamentary Boroughs." Actual voting was done in the town court under the direction of a local officer. Practically no change in these organic provisions took place until the early nineteenth century. Generally, both borough and county units were each allowed two delegates who, for a time, received compensation for their services from the central government. Other than the wish of the King, there was no uniform practice as to when a parliament might be summoned or dissolved, though for a few years in the fifteenth century an attempt was made to provide for annual elections. England of the fourteenth and fifteenth centuries was far from being a democratic country. With the landed and wealthy classes safely entrenched in both houses there was practically no opportunity given to the other social elements to share in government. In spite of this defect important gains had been made by parliament, especially by the Commons, and these gains in many instances were extended to all Englishmen.

Membership in the upper house rested primarily upon the feudal duty of a king's vassal to attend the Great Council. Custom soon dictated that this duty depended upon the receipt of a personal summons issued at the king's command. At first the powers of this group were relatively large and included the right to advise the king in the making of law, of dispensing justice and of elevating the king to the throne. In respect to its judicial power it should be noted that this function was divided between the Great and Little Council but at no time in its history, either as the Great Council or later as the House of Lords, did it ever lose this judicial aspect. Even today it stands as the highest court of the realm, and the Book of Common Prayer of the English Church still contains a prayer for the High Court of Parliament.

The amount of work done by the upper house, while relatively heavy in the fourteenth century, had become lighter by 1400, owing in part to the breakup of feudalism, which lessened the political importance of the barons. More important, however, was the growing efficiency of the various governmental bureaus and the rise of the Commons, which during the fifteenth century became economically independent of the Lords. Commons, moreover, encroached considerably upon the activities of the Council membership. By 1450 the Council depended primarily upon the wishes of the lower house, which also stipulated the salary of each councillor. On the other hand both houses kept their hands off the common law courts and chancery, giving these bodies a splendid opportunity for continuing the good work that had been started two centuries before.

Parliament Deposes the King

Everything which parliament had accomplished had been done at the expense of royal power. Other factors, however, had aided, such as the continued efficiency of the departments of government (Chancery, King's Bench, and Common Pleas by way of illustration), the power of the Church, and the growing importance of the towns. More significant were the limitation imposed by the coronation oath, the terms of the feudal contract, the rise of common law, the power of electing and deposing the monarch, and the practice of placing the Crown in commission. It will be recalled that when William I gained the throne, the ancient Saxon principle of election was exercised by the Witan. This power was acquired and used by the Great Council, which in turn passed it on to parliament. Throughout the period from 1066–1327, no serious conflict arose over the exercise of this right. In 1327, however, owing to the vacillating, extravagant, and frivolous policies of Edward II, steps were taken to rid England of the King. The Queen, the Great Council, and the authorities of London joined hands in creating a nation-wide sentiment in favor of deposition. Archbishop Reynold's sermon, "The voice of the people is the voice of God," illustrates the type of propaganda which was employed. Parliament was summoned, and with the approval of both Lords and Commoners the throne was given to the King's son, Edward III. Here, then, is an illustration of the exercise of the power of election; but what is more important, it was resorted to before the reigning monarch had been deposed. Edward II was formally deposed by parliament five days after his son had been named king. Heretofore kings had been elevated to the throne, but at no time had one been deposed. The significance of this show of constitutional power was even more dramatically revealed in 1399, when an assembly of nobles, prelates, knights and townspeople unseated Richard II and put in his place Henry, Duke of Lancaster. In Henry's case, however, it is important to note that the throne was not given to the next in line, Edmund, Earl of March, but to another heir who had championed the cause of parliament.

Parliament Places the Crown in Commission

Richard's deposition, as well as that of Edward II, was resorted to only after every other attempt had been made to curtail the absolutism of the King. In their endeavors, parliament and the nobility had been guided by Magna Carta which, it will be recalled, had created a baronial committee to govern England in John's name. John's subsequent conduct and the jealousies of the barons had nullified this attempt, though the principle involved was not forgotten by de Montfort in 1258. At that time the nobility, aroused to action by the repeated insults of Henry III, by unheard-of taxes and by severe economic depression, cornered the King at Oxford and wrung from him the appointment of a baronial committee of twenty-four. This body presented to parliament a series of propositions which were enacted into law and which have been known as the Provisions of Oxford. According to these regulations, the Crown was to govern subject to the approval of a standing committee of the barons responsible in turn to the Great Council. Even though the success of the scheme was halted by internal squabbles among the barons, the principle of limitation by commission was not discarded. Nor did the failure argue against another trial in 1311 when a number of acts created the Lords Ordainers, who were to govern in Edward II's name. Each of these illustrations of a baronial commission contains no reference to the Commons. For this reason these commissions may be viewed as attempts at aristocratic monopoly in government. A final illustration of this practice came in 1387 in the person of the Lords Appellant, but this time it was parliament and not the Great Council which sought to restrict Richard II. Even though this attempt, like earlier ones, was actuated by a selfish barony, the fact remains that an important device in the interest of constitutional government had been tried and found sound in principle.

Parliamentary development, the practice of election and deposition, and the principle of placing the Crown in commission may be viewed as positive invasions upon royal power from the outside. At the same time forces were at work in the same direction from within. In evaluating these internal factors, one is impressed by the influence exerted by the Crown itself, notably by Edward I. Not that this monarch introduced much that was new, but he quietly cultivated the work of his ancestors in a manner which bore definite fruit in time to come. Edward fashioned the central government into a more efficient agency that in turn checked the inroads which feudalism had been making upon the monarchy. Other kings had sensed the disintegrating tendencies of feudalism and had introduced innovations which Edward now improved. Seignorial courts, accordingly, were restricted by the imposition of drastic prohibitions and by an extension of the royal courts and justices. Edward also forbade further subinfeudation and forced his tenants to fulfill their obligations to him. Nor was the King unmindful of the military strength of the barons who in theory constituted the King's police and army. Practically, however, they frequently ignored their monarch's summons when their interests clashed with those of the King. To meet this difficulty Edward reorganized the local militia, armed them with a new weapon, the long-bow, and placed them under his control. Further, he forced all property-owners with incomes of twenty pounds or more to accept knighthood, and bound them to answer his call for service regardless of their obligations to their immediate lord.

Edward, the English Justinian

In undertaking these measures Edward could not see that their future development was going to place the monarchy in an embarrassing situation. Each of these devices, though conceived as an aid to the King, actually placed military and political power in the hands of his subjects. His governmental and judicial reforms served as a splendid training school for local and national self-government. Unconscious, however, of these broad undercurrents, Edward forged ahead with the determination of making the royal power supreme. So successful was he that subsequent ages have styled him the "State-maker" and the "English Justinian."

Like the great Roman emperor, Edward sensed the absence of uniformity in existing law. Common law had been growing, but no statement of these gains had appeared in the statutes of the realm. Believing that the time had come for codification of these newer principles, Edward provided for their enactment into law. Each of these statutes, though they can hardly be so described if by statute is meant legislative action, amounted to a clear statement of past law as pronounced by the common-law justices. Many of these measures, such as Westminster I and II, related to feudal matters; others, like Acton Burnell, provided regulation for commercial and industrial activities. There was also the Statute of Mortmain, which forbade all future alienation of land to the Church except by royal license. In the framing of these acts, as well as in their enforcement, Edward leaned heavily upon his clerks and departmental chiefs. Most of these, recruited from the middle class, had been in the service of the state for some time and had come to identify their success with that of the monarchy. Their interest in feudal matters, however, was small; and for this reason Edward advanced them to offices of trust and confidence. At the same time their promotion removed from government the self-seeking noble whose purpose in statecraft was opposed to that of the King. As a result there developed a body of trained experts aware of their value to the state and knit together by an *esprit de corps* which aided the growth of orderly government. Many of these men were members of the courts which at the time were making definite inroads on private and local jurisdictions. Finally, it should be noticed that out of the residual power of the Council there developed the practice of referring cases involving equity to the Chancellor's office. Out of this procedure arose in time the celebrated Court of Chancery.

The Lancastrian Constitution

Edward's achievements helped to lay the foundation for the limited monarchy which characterized government during the greater part of the fifteenth century. So pronounced was the drift away from absolutism that the age of Henry IV, V, and VI (1399–1461) has been described by the name of the Lancastrian constitution. England had no written document in the American sense of the word, but these kings were forced to rule in accordance with fundamental and organic law. Historical evidence endorses this interpretation and points convincingly to a long line of causation beginning with the deposition of Richard II. In selecting a new ruler, the revolutionists of 1399 had successfully championed the cause of their leader, Henry IV, though in so doing they passed over the claims of Edmund, Earl of March, who was a direct descendant of Lionel, the second son of Edward III. Military success rather than inheritance made it impossible to choose any other person. As in the case of William I, when the Witan faced the victor of Hastings and immediately proclaimed him king, so the notables and commonalty in 1399, having witnessed the triumphal march of the Duke of Lancaster, hailed him as their new ruler. While it is probably true that no constitutionally called parliament elected Henry to the throne, it is none the less clear that none beyond the followers of the Earl of March questioned the legality of Henry's succession.

Henry's success in defending his title was due in no small way to his skill in practical politics and in the art of government. Not that he added much to royal power, but in an age of political upheaval and discord he managed to hold the reins of government so tight as to prevent the spread of feudal anarchy. At the same time, he defeated several abortive attempts at rebellion by the friends of the late King and the followers of the Earl of March. Although these strong-arm measures increased Henry's hold on the throne, there still remained uppermost in his mind and in that of the barons the fact that Henry's right to rule rested upon popular consent rather than upon inheritance. Richard's reign had fairly echoed with flagrant violations of political gains made by parliament during the reign of Edward III. It was against this tyranny and not in favor of Henry that the opposition had struggled in 1399. Quite naturally, therefore, those who had risked all in the late revolution were unwilling to hand over government to a new king without first binding him to respect the rights of the people. Nothing in the nature of a written agreement was entered into, but both parties knew precisely what was in the mind of the other. Henry, in particular, realized that circumstances had made him King and that the legality of his reign rested upon popular consent. The new King also knew that he and his heirs could retain the throne only as long as they did nothing which might rob the revolutionists of the fruits of their victory.

Compelled to respect the views and rights of those who had made him King, Henry's reign was void of any strong assertions of personal power. Upon his death in 1413, Henry V elected to follow the same middle-of-the-road policy. The third of the Lancastrian Kings, Henry VI (1422–1461), was lacking in ability and permitted the steady encroachment upon royal power. As stated earlier in this chapter, parliament acquired during these reigns, power and authority in finance and legislation and protected these gains by insisting upon parliamentary privilege. Moreover, this period witnessed parliament's control of the Council and of the inroads made by the Commons upon the Lords. In general, therefore, it may be concluded that during the reigns of the Lancastrians dis-

tinct progress had been made towards a constitutional monarchy. Nothing like the absolutism of the Norman rulers or
early Plantagenet kings existed.

The Lancastrian constitution represented the embodiment
of past political experience. On the other hand there is good
reason for believing that its principles were in advance of the
age. Relatively, a limited monarchy had come into being;
the king had been forced to recognize the will of the Lords
and the Commons. At the same time the opinion of the
nobility was not entirely in sympathy with the existing situation. Although they were willing to hamper the royal
power, these men lost all sense of values when they plunged
the country into the unhappy War of the Roses, which developed in the middle of the fifteenth century. The action of
the nobility was thoroughly in keeping with the spirit of the
age and reveals most admirably the inherent prematurity of
the Lancastrian constitution.

On top of this disaster to orderly government came the
reigns of Edward IV (1461–1483) and Richard III (1483–
1485). Both lacked political experience, and faced by the task
of defending their titles against their enemies, the Lancastrians,
both rulers resorted to many high-handed acts. The activities of the common-law courts were interfered with by the
forcing of decisions favorable to the Crown and by the corrupting of local officials and juries. In one instance, Edward IV
went so far as to remove a judge who had resisted the will of
the King. Edward is also credited with having introduced the
use of torture in England. Even in his relations with the
Council, Edward acted in an arbitrary way by selecting ministers who were content to draw salaries from their benefactor.
At the same time he weakened the control parliament had held
over that body and extended the Council's jurisdiction in ways
that helped the monarchy. Edward's reorganization of the
Council was due as much to the weakness of parliament as it
was to his own energy. Indeed parliament played a very un-

important rôle throughout his reign and that of Richard III. Relatively few parliaments were summoned and none of these was given either the time or opportunity to advance its power. Elections were frequently tampered with and the Commons were forced to elect a speaker favorable to the King. Moreover, Edward was often relieved of the necessity of asking parliament for money because of the use of forced loans and by sums which he received from the King of France. In a war with Scotland, for example, Edward was able to finance an army of twenty thousand men without a single penny from parliament.

The net result of the War of the Roses and of the virility of Edward and Richard was to retard the growth of parliamentary power and to hasten the return of strong monarchy. By 1485 much that had been struggled for during the past two centuries was pushed to one side. Parliament and the forms of government were kept intact and continued to be used, not in the sense of the Lancastrian constitution, but rather as the monarchy wished.

SELECTED BIBLIOGRAPHY

The references mentioned at the close of the previous chapter have suggestive material on the constitutional growth of England. Special treatment is given in T. F. Tout's *Chapters in the Administrative History of Medieval England* (Manchester, 1920); W. A. Morris' *Medieval English Sheriff* (London, 1927); T. F. Tout's *Edward the First* (London, 1893); E. Jenk's *Edward Plantagenet* (New York, 1902); J. C. Davies' *The Baronial Opposition to Edward II* (Cambridge, 1918); T. F. Tout's *Place of the Reign of Edward II in English History* (Manchester, 1914), and F. W. Maitland's *Constitutional History of England* (Cambridge, 1911). Recently G. Lapsley has reviewed the election of Henry IV in "Parliamentary Title of Henry IV" in *English Historical Review,* July and October, 1934. Miss M. V. Clarke's *Medieval Representation and Consent* (London, 1936) is a timely résumé of research in parliament's history.

C. H. McIlwain's *High Court of Parliament* (New Haven, 1910) is a stimulating volume as is A. F. Pollard's *Evolution of Parliament* (London, 1920), which is based largely upon McIlwain's researches.

D. Pasquet's *Essay on the Origin of the House of Commons* (Cambridge, 1925) and C. Wittke's *The History of English Parliamentary Privilege* (Columbus, 1921) are valuable contributions. L. O. Pike's *Constitutional History of the House of Lords* (London, 1894) and T. F. Plucknett's "Place of the Council in the Fifteenth Century" in *Transactions of the Royal Historical Society* (London, 1918) are of value.

CHAPTER XII

An Economic Revolution

THE fourteenth and fifteenth centuries witnessed the decay and disintegration of an economic order and the rise of a system which is strikingly like present-day life. Kings and queens, nobles and prelates, still played the leading rôles in the current dramas of that age, though every now and then some understudy like a Wycliffe, a Wat Tyler, or a capitalist like William de la Pole stole the stage and won the applause of the galleries. In general, however, older scenes and time-honored customs prevailed. Externals were much the same. No better example exists than the agricultural economy of that period. Fundamentally, England's agricultural and economic life was still molded along approved manorial lines. Land was still held rather than owned. Serfs continued as before to perform manual services to lords whose rights over the lives and fortunes of their tenants crowd the manorial records. To the careless observer then and now, the feudal and manorial systems would appear more deeply entrenched than ever. Actually, these arrangements were little more than shells which encompassed a seething mass of discordant elements, shells so thin and brittle that they finally cracked and burst apart under the pressure of an expanding capitalism and the growing demand of the serf for the right to live and not merely to exist.

The Intellectual Background for Revolt

Vocal protests on the part of the serf were common during the twelfth century; and in the thirteenth, actual revolts appeared. The philosophy which underlay these disturbances and those which followed in the reign of Richard II is a most interesting subject for investigation. Throughout the medieval period, the Church had taught by sacrament and sermon the concept of man's equality in the life hereafter. God, however, so the argument ran, arbitrarily placed man during his earthly sojourn into one of four airtight compartments. First and most important were the clergy who cared for man's soul and directed it towards eternal salvation. Protecting the Church from worldly forces were kings and nobles, who also governed man in accordance with the word of God and Rome. Thirdly, there were the citizens and merchants, who contributed to the material greatness and splendor of life. Finally, there was the humble laborer, who supported the entire structure by his toil. Every individual, therefore, had a rôle to play; and if perchance the serf bemoaned his poverty, he was immediately informed of the nobleness of labor and of Adam's curse. Proper articulation of labor with the other servants of God was vital, moreover, for the well-being of all. Time after time these views were set forth with telling effect from the pulpit and public meeting places like St. Paul's, London. And yet no one, least of all the clergy, denied that the divine order did not function properly. Society, instead of being in tune with God, was forever giving homage to Satan. In conjunction, therefore, with their appeal for a better political and social order, the clergy were engaged in an impassioned attack upon the frailties of man.

Satire and ridicule were hurled by these preachers upon all four classes. The husbandman was charged with having neglected his duties to God and Caesar. Prayers and supplications were drowned by the boisterous cry of the drunkard and adulterer. At the same time the unethical practices of the shrewd merchant who exacted interest or sold inferior goods were fiercely condemned along with the sabotage of the industrial laborer. Nobles, high and low, were asked to explain why they mistreated their serfs, why they accumulated wealth and power and did not give freely to the poor. Even the women fell under the ban of the clergy for living loose lives and for decorating themselves with silks and satins, rouge and powder. Perhaps the most interesting of these clerical attacks were those which were leveled at their own order. A single extract from the sermon of the Archbishop of Armagh will illustrate. "For there are," so the preacher asserted, "in the church of God those bearing the name of prelate—the greater and the lesser alike—who are fornicators . . . to the manifest scandal of our status. There are others . . . who one or more each day are inebriated with such drunkenness and give vent to such filthy and scandalous scurrilities, that those sharing a common life . . . abhor their society. Alas! alas! alas! . . . do such dare to handle the spotless sacraments of the Church. . . . Others there are . . . who are always exercising the cry 'Shear, Shear, Shear, Raise, Raise' and never fulfil the command 'Feed, Feed!' "

These and many other condemnations fell upon the ear of the serf and produced a strange reaction. At first he hung his head with shame as he listened to his own shortcomings; later he squared his shoulders and concluded that if the clergy who knew God's will and law could seek carnal pleasures, then he could also. No less a person than William de Rymyngton, the head of Oxford and a severe critic of Wycliffe, proclaimed that there was little hope of redeeming the ordinary man if the clergy would not practice what they preached. In other words, while the clergy were busy trying to reconcile the habits of man with the word of the Master, they were unconsciously preaching the gospel of discontent. Those who squirmed under the oppression of feudal and manorial lords or obediently watched the Church reap where it had not sown now awoke under the sermons of the clergy and found a religious justification for armed revolt. The intellectual background of the Great Revolt of 1381 had been ably prepared by those who had sought reformation but had inadvertently propagated revolution.

Commutation and the Alienation of the Demesne

In the meantime a change had silently been taking place within the manorial system itself. During the earlier medieval age, the manorial lord had advocated serfdom as the means of gaining labor for the cultivation of his holdings. Subsistence farming, in other words, encouraged a system of dependent cultivators. At least as early as the reign of Henry I, there were estates where this principle was partially discontinued. Instead of exploiting labor, the custom of allowing the serfs to commute their services gradually developed. Manorial lords had adopted this device because of the expensiveness of serfdom. Court records contain many references to serfs who shirked their duties, and it must be admitted that the latter had little interest in promoting profits for their masters. Heavy fines and penalties utterly failed to correct the indifference of the serf to the lord's property or rights. Quite naturally, therefore, the lord changed his tactics and paid for work done on the demesne, a procedure which brought greater returns to himself and a different attitude on the part of the serfs. As the new scheme functioned better than the older methods, the system was extended by allowing the serfs to meet their obligations by money payments rather than by customary services. The income so derived permitted the lord to hire additional labor, which was recruited from the poor cottagers or villeins, many of whom had fled from their ancestral holdings. If the lord profited by this arrangement, so did the serf, who could now devote more time to his own strips and thus produce a greater income for himself. Commutation of servile duties, therefore, did much to break the iron nexus which heretofore had bound the serf to his lord.

Keen-minded lords also recognized, by the opening of the fourteenth century, that the profit to be gained as the manager of an estate was less than what could be earned by renting the demesne. The farmer made way for the landlord. Rents in the form of money were much more desirable than unwilling and costly services from villeins. Accordingly, many a lord parcelled the demesne among his serfs as renters or else deeded it to capitalists who proceeded to engage wage earners. Investments of this type were not infrequent during the fourteenth century. Relieved of his duties as farmer, the lord turned his attention to political and social activities. Alienation of the demesne and commutation of services, therefore, worked hand-in-hand in causing a disintegration of the manorial system. At the same time they tended to make the serf more class conscious and equipped him materially for a determined stand against abuses in government and in the economic system.

The transition from a natural economy to a money economy had already begun when England was visited by the Black Death. Having originated in the East, this plague reached Western Europe and England through commercial and military channels. It first made its appearance in England in 1348 and spread rapidly throughout the British Isles. A second and third epidemic occurred in 1360 and 1369; a fourth attack appeared in 1379. The destruction which followed in the wake of this disease was enormous. Rich and poor, prelate and monk, old and young alike were struck down with little or no warning. A lack of medical knowledge, coupled with the usual amount of filth and ignorance characteristic of the age, permitted the disease to run its course. When the epidemic had subsided, the total population of England had been lowered by at least one third. The excessive mortality did much to shake the existing social and economic foundations.

It created extreme religious scepticism on the part of some who seemed determined to make the most of their earthly existence without giving much thought to the life hereafter. Others hastened to order their conduct as though the end of the world were in sight. Then again there were some, like the Flagellants, who abused and mortified the flesh to the point of fanaticism. Everywhere accepted moral standards were loosened, and a decimated clergy were unable to stem this disintegration or to administer properly their accustomed services. As monastic life slackened, hospitalization and education lagged and fell below normal standards. With the government taking little or no interest in such matters, the physical and mental well-being of the nation was seriously impaired.

Judged by present-day knowledge these social consequences were the most important results of the Black Death, though for the time being the economic effects appeared to be more significant. Indeed the impact of the plague temporarily wrought great havoc in all business activities. The woolen industry suffered greatly; sheep roamed the fields subject to little watch or care; yearly shearing declined, and the export of raw material fell below the normal rate. Tin, which had been an important item in English industry, did not recover its former position until the close of the medieval period. The building, metalworking and pottery trades also suffered severe losses. Greater devastation, however, took place in agriculture, which normally employed more people and in which considerable capital had been invested. Not that there was less arable land, but there were fewer hands available for work. Of necessity, therefore, the lord had either to increase wages or allow his land to stand idle. As he could not afford to lose his original investment he was forced to double, and in some cases triple, his labor costs. Nor was the serf blind to the possibilities of the situation. Amid rising wages and prices, the serf migrated from one manor to another in accordance with the supply and demand of labor. Migrations of this type, though not uncommon before the plague, were greatly increased by the effects of the Black Death.

The Great Revolt of 1381

One should not suppose, however, that manorial lords everywhere yielded to the demands of labor. In many instances concessions were made only as a last resort, while in others the tenants were forced to adhere to the older standards. With wages rising nearly fifty per cent, landlords sought to protect themselves by parliamentary legislation. The famous Statute of Laborers (1351) represents an attempt on the part of the landed class to protect their interests against the aspirations of the serf and artisan, for the industrial trades were also affected by a scarcity of labor. According to this law all able-bodied men and women, regardless of their servile status, who were without means of gaining a living were to labor at the older wage rate. The government not only passed this measure but also took steps to provide for its enforcement. Considerable diversity of opinion has existed as to the results of this legislation. The most tenable conclusion, however, is that these measures checked a further rise in wages for the time being, permitted the lords to check servile attempts to escape from service, and increased the ill will of the villeins towards their masters and government. It should also be noted in passing that the law represents one of the earliest instances on the part of government to regulate labor.

Chafing under the restrictions imposed by this statute and inflamed by the fiery speeches of John Ball, one of Wycliffe's more radical followers, and determined to make the most of the opportunities furnished by the plague, commutation of services, and alienation of the demesne, the serfs rose in rebellion. The immediate antecedent for this uprising, however, was political and was connected with the government's poll taxes of 1377, 1379 and 1380. Originally, this assessment was not intended to burden the lower classes. However, owing to clumsy methods of collection many a serf was called upon to pay more than he was able. As a result payments were not forthcoming; and when the King's officers tried to collect the sums due, forcible resistance appeared. This was particularly true in Essex and Kent. From there the movement spread as far north as York and as far west as Somerset.

Led by Wat Tyler, who may have had experience in the French wars, and John Ball, the men of the southeastern counties marched on London in the early summer of 1381. As they proceeded, they blazed a trail by firing manorial houses and court records. With their entrance into the capital, the government was at the mercy of the peasants. Through their leaders, the King was informed of what the rioters wanted, namely the abolition of personal servitude and the commutation of their duties. Not being in a position to resist, the Crown granted these demands. Charters were issued accordingly, and as fast as these were distributed, bands of serfs withdrew from London and started homeward. In the meantime rioting had broken out in the city. Property was destroyed, and in a few cases royal officers were slain. The combined effect of these disturbances and the withdrawal of some of the serfs weakened the position of Tyler, who was now called upon to face resistance on the part of the citizens of London. In the course of the conferences which took place, Tyler was incited to make a personal attack upon the King. This led in turn to a brush-at-arms in which Tyler was killed and the peasants scattered and routed. Immediately thereafter, Richard's government revoked its concessions and sent troops throughout the country to quell the rebellion. By the early fall of 1381 the insurrection was over.

Richard's victory foreshadowed a definite attempt on the part of the government and the landed classes to push the lower elements back into their old servile status, and for the time success crowned these efforts. Throughout the remainder of the fourteenth century and during all of the fifteenth, villeinage continued with the complete sanction of the law. On the other hand, opposition on the part of the serfs, organized even to the point of forming what might be termed unions, and actual revolt occurred well down into the Tudor period. Legislative attempts to preserve existing privilege were hotly contested by those who followed in the wake of a new economic order. Commutation of duties and alienation of the demesne continued to progress in spite of all that the manorial lords might do in or out of parliament. By the opening of the sixteenth century, there were fewer villeins than there had been when Wat Tyler's band was driven from London.

Agricultural, Commercial, and Industrial Growth

The economic activities of the serf, landlord, and manorial manager had as their chief objective the raising of crops and stock for local sustenance and sale. At the beginning of the fourteenth century, manorial economy was chiefly concerned with subsistence farming. By the close of the fifteenth, foreign and alien markets were important, and an agrarian revolution was under way. The reorganization of agricultural economy was precipitated by the same basic factors which had ushered in the Great Revolt. Their inception may be traced to a previous century. The age of greatest progress, however, came after the peasant uprisings and was characterized by an enclosure movement, a rise in rents, a consolidation of holdings, and an increased use of marginal lands. In each of these activities one may see the rapid extension of a capitalistic structure, the urge for distant markets, and an increase in the purchasing power of the consumer in town and country. Communication and transportation were speeded up, and this, together with the other forces mentioned, helped to unite the English people into a nation.

Consolidation of holdings resulted in the creation of larger

estates in the hands of a landlord class. An examination of the
land transfers of this period establishes this beyond any shadow
of a doubt. Land was bought and sold like any other article,
much to the profit of those who traded, though the results to
the actual cultivator proved, in the long run, to be disadvan-
tageous. For the time being, however, agricultural laborers
benefited by higher wages and a lessening of servile obligations. Even among the laborers themselves, there was a definite drift towards a concentration of their strips. Furthermore, the combined effects of increased holdings by laborer
and landlord did much to improve the quality of husbandry.
A cultivator did not have to walk hither and yonder to reach
his strips, nor did the inefficiency of his neighbor affect him as
it had the farmer of two hundred years before. Agricultural
knowledge, however, did not keep pace with these advances;
nor was there much done to improve farm equipment or to
increase the yield or quality of the crops. Wheat, oats, peas,
barley, and rye continued to be the chief products grown, with
little attention given to roots or other vegetables.

Definite gains, however, were made in the raising of sheep
for food and wool. The importance of wool in English economic life has already been noted by reference to the *maltote*
and the market in Flanders. Merchants and traders who
handled this commodity, as well as industrialists from other
fields, came to view sheep raising as a profitable form of investment. As long as the old manorial system functioned,
little stimulus had existed for releasing capital savings, but
with the breakup of that structure, capital rushed into agriculture. Not only did it encourage the sale of land as a commodity, but it also made for larger pasturelands. Through the
acquisition of land which heretofore had been used for agrarian
purposes, the needed space was gained for larger flocks of
sheep. In order to protect this pastureland from encroachment
by the growers of grain, fences were constructed and the land
thereby was enclosed. Although many a customary tenant be-

came a hired shepherd, the greater number either drifted into the towns to be employed in the building and shipping trades, or else roamed about the country as vagrants. The displacement of this rural population was gradual, and the full effects were not to be seen until a much later date.

England's rising prosperity in agriculture was matched by similar gains in industry. The progress in clothmaking was one of the most important. Prior to the second quarter of the fourteenth century the bulk of English raw wool was shipped to Flanders for manufacture. Domestic clothmaking, however, was greatly stimulated by the policies of the Plantagenets and Lancastrians. Alien craftsmen were brought into England during Edward III's reign and were given unusual opportunities to advance their earnings. At the same time domestic weavers were encouraged; and while often at odds with their foreign competitors, they nevertheless produced an increasing quantity of cloth. The export and import trade, moreover, in wool and woolen goods was frequently adjusted to the advantage of the home producers. The government showed a paternalistic attitude by passing measures which regulated the quality and size of cloth. The net result of this protective policy was an increase in the domestic consumption of woolen goods and a corresponding decline in the export of both wool and cloth. Nor should one forget the stimulus which this activity exerted upon sheep raising. By the advent of the War of the Roses, however, a slump took place in the woolen trade; and it was not until the days of the Tudors that the production of woolen cloth regained its former position. In addition to woolen goods, there was some manufacture of linens.

Metalworking, such as the making of bells for churches and monasteries as well as for military purposes, employed an increasing number of hands during the two centuries under discussion. Pottery, glass, tiles, and bricks were also used in greater quantities than before, and leather goods found an ever-increasing market. Ale and cider continued to satisfy the thirst of most Englishmen, though during the fifteenth century domestic beer grew in popularity. English wine, on the other hand, never was consumed to a great extent because of the inherent superiority of the French vineyards. Among the extractive industries fishing continued to prosper, as did the mining of iron and tin and the quarrying of stone and marble. Little progress, however, took place in the coal trade. This commodity was used chiefly by the smiths, ironmongers, and lime burners. When used as fuel it was burned largely by the poorer classes who could not afford to buy wood. Even then its use was limited to those areas near the mines.

Shipments of coal for both domestic and foreign ports, probably never exceeded seven thousand tons in a given year. Moreover, most of this coal, which cleared from the Tyne, served as ballast and could be bought for as low as two shillings a ton. Tin, lead, hides, and iron were also exported in small quantities, chiefly to France and Italy. Corn, except during years of unusual productivity, was seldom shipped to foreign parts. Gascony alone seems to have received the bulk of this export, which in 1334 amounted to 416,000 bushels. Gascony also took the greater share of the shipments of fish, while France and the Lowlands consumed most of the butter and cheese which left England. Practically all of these exports were carried in foreign ships though the conduct of the trade itself was in the hands of both domestic and alien merchants.

In sharp contrast to the limited export of these commodities was the trade in wool. During the first quarter of the fourteenth century, approximately 30,000 sacks (364 pounds a sack) of wool left England each year. The outbreak of the French wars cut into this trade, but it was not until the close of the century that any considerable drop took place. From then on, a marked decrease was registered throughout the fifteenth century. The total export for any given year was probably from thirty to sixty per cent less than it had been in the reign of Edward II. This decline was brought about chiefly by the rise of English-made woolen goods, a restriction in the acreage devoted to the raising of sheep, and the effects of the French wars and civil disturbances. During the years 1459 to 1462, when Yorkists and Lancastrians were struggling for power, the average export was down to 5,000 sacks though it rose some 3,000 sacks during the stability of the reign of Edward IV. During the fourteenth and fifteenth centuries most of the export, both as to quantity and value, was in domestic hands, with the Hanseatic and Italian merchants sharing the balance.

The importance of the wool trade is attested by the government's use of it in foreign affairs and as a source of revenue. It is difficult to see how Edward III could have financed the French wars without the customs arising from wool. The rapid rise of a wealthy mercantile and trading class also reflected the growing value of this commodity. The organization of the Staplers developed largely out of the export of wool. The Staplers was a trade association of wool merchants and shippers who, from early days, had concentrated their European activities at some focal point. Aided by the Crown and later by parliament, these efforts were organized under the name of the Fellowship of the Merchants of the Staple. This body enjoyed extensive legislative, administrative, and judicial rights, privileges which no government of today would think of extending to any industry. Endowed with these far-reaching powers the Staplers dominated the wool trade and were able to have the Crown establish, in 1363, Calais as the Staple town in Europe. With but two exceptions, therefore, all wool which cleared from England had to be shipped to Calais. Italian merchants were allowed some concessions, as were other aliens and denizens who might export wool to Italy and the Lowlands. Even though these exceptions accounted for only a small share of the trade, considerable ill will developed between the aliens and the Staplers. In addition to this grievance the Staplers frequently found fault with the Crown for having licensed trade in conflict with their rights. The king, however, was always in need of money and paid scant attention to the complaints of these merchants. Finally, the Staplers were robbed of their just returns by the inability of the government to prevent smuggling.

Another group which frequently suffered by infractions of the law was the Merchant Adventurers, a name loosely applied to all traders who trafficked in non-staples. Many of these merchants centered their activities in the export of woolen cloth, as did the Hanseatic traders to a great extent. Because English merchants lacked the proper facilities for handling commercial transactions abroad during the twelfth and thirteenth centuries, the way had been opened for more capable organizations such as the Bardi Society of Florence, the Lucca Society, and the Hanseatic League. As corporate groups they acquired from the king valuable administrative and judicial powers, the right to own property, and exemption from some of the royal tariffs. At the opening of the fifteenth century, for example, the Hanse paid lower rates than domestic exporters of woolen cloth. Concessions were also granted to other aliens. All this produced bitter opposition on the part of the Merchant Adventurers. It was not, however, until the reign of Henry VII that the privileges of these aliens were seriously curtailed.

Throughout the fourteenth century the shipments of cloth gradually increased in quantity and value. During Richard II's reign they rose to 43,000 pieces of cloth, and by the middle of the next century the export was over 50,000 pieces. The renewal of the French wars and the outbreak of civil disturbances at home tended to decrease the volume of this trade. Moreover, the constant quarrels between denizens and Hansards brought about a temporary loss of North Baltic markets. No appreciable improvement was witnessed until after 1476.

It is of interest, however, to note that throughout the period now under discussion most of the export of woolen cloth was in the hands of denizens, particularly the Merchant Adventurers. This latter group also outdistanced their rivals, by the close of Edward IV's reign, in respect to commodities imported. Their exports were now worth two and one-half times those of the Hansards; the value of their imports was five times as great.

A valuable export and import trade also existed between England and Iceland, Scandinavia, Spain and the Mediterranean. Much of this activity as well as that with France and the Lowlands was actually carried in alien ships in spite of the navigation act of Richard II, which sought to limit the Gascon trade to English ships. Among the many commodities which entered England were fish, fruit, nuts, groceries, oil, vegetables, corn, copper, iron, military stores, naval and medical supplies, linen, woolen goods, silks, and articles of luxury. By far the most important commodity imported, with the exception of woolen cloth, was wine from Gascony. The wine trade, however, suffered severely during the latter half of the Hundred Years' War.

The distribution of these imports rested first of all in the hands of the trader, sea captain, or business concern, who frequently lost both ship and cargo by storm or by the attack of pirates who infested the Channel in large numbers. Those who were able to pay the relatively high insurance rates or who could turn their vessels into a man-of-war suffered no serious loss. Once a cargo had reached the port of destination and had paid the customs, local distributors relayed the goods to the consumer by land or by water. Coastwise traffic as well as traffic via navigable streams like the Thames, Severn, and Trent transported a large share of both foreign and domestic produce. Roads were employed, of course, though the quality and quantity of these highways, not to mention bridges or fords, were exceedingly poor. Imagine the plight of a merchant who, having safely escaped the ever-present robber, found himself facing a huge hole in the road, recently dug by some farmer in need of clay or marl. In spite of these difficulties, chapmen and traders, great and small, journeyed over these roads on foot or in carts, bringing to the consumer some article which may have come originally from faraway Venice or Danzig.

During the first quarter of the fourteenth century, most of England's trade was domestic in nature and was characterized by an exchange of goods and services. Natural economy, however, slowly gave way to money economy; and as this developed, trading at a distance became increasingly common. The rapid rise of towns during the thirteenth century and the increasing purchasing power of the serf and artisan account for much of this change. The government, as well as prosperous merchants and traders, helped by developing a more elaborate system of trade and finance. Gold coins, especially the penny and the florin, appeared by Edward III's reign to supplement the silver penny in use since the Conquest. Finally, Henry VII issued a new coin, the sovereign, which was equal in value to twenty shillings. The government passed frequent measures providing for the retention of silver and gold bullion within the kingdom, for establishing central places for exchange, and for preventing the mutilation of the coinage. Standardization of weights and measures was also effected, while the tallies, bills of exchange, and letters of credit common to the Norman and Angevin periods, were used on a much larger scale. Domestic and international trade was stimulated by the continued development of business and maritime law. Finally, it should be noted that both the government and the merchants facilitated commercial transactions by a rapid extension of a credit system, by loans, and by the use of interest.

Illustrations of the new economic order appeared in every avenue of life. Towering cathedrals and enlarged parish churches built and endowed by pious and well-to-do merchants, as well as more pretentious domestic structures, inns, and crosses were the external features of a more prosperous England. Increased custom tariffs, an agrarian revolution, the rapid growth of towns and cities with their numerous gilds and trading associations, the expansion of domestic trade, the penetration of European markets, the rise in wages and purchasing power—these and other factors too numerous to mention bespeak the presence of private capitalism. Surplus earnings and savings were invested in ever-increasing amounts in

Courtesy Assoc. British and Irish Railways, Inc.

St. David's Cathedral, Pembrokeshire. Showing entrance to ruins of Bishop's Palace, built by Bishop Gower about 1347.

land, in the manufacture of woolen goods and in a hundred or more trading and mercantile adventures. Losses were sustained to be sure, especially by those who had profited in wine and wool, while England held control over Gascony and Calais. Generally speaking, however, in spite of war and civil commotion greater wealth and prosperity appeared on every hand. Without a capitalistic base this advance could not have taken place. Nor could Edward III have secured the loan of £76,180 in 1339 from William de la Pole unless the latter had immense reserves of capital.

The workshop, so to speak, of the medieval capitalist was the town. Here, living in relative comfort, were the industrialist, the banker, and trader. At the opening of the fourteenth century most of these individuals identified their activities with the local merchant gild, which generally controlled both the economic and political life of the town. The expansion of commerce, national and international, gradually gave greater power to the trader, who in turn forced many a small shopkeeper or merchant out of the gild into one of the growing craft organizations. With subsequent economic developments favoring specialization of industry, the gild merchant slowly yielded control to the borough council. By the close of the fifteenth century, the merchant gild functioned chiefly as a social or religious group. During this period of decline, however, the individual crafts grew in size and importance. Within these groups were centered the apprentices, the journeymen and the master workmen, all of whom were subject to the regulations of the gilds and of the borough government. Each gild was controlled by an assembly composed of the craftsmen, and by an executive body known as the wardens; occasionally, there was also a common council. These agencies dictated the policy of the gild in respect to hours of work, wages, quality and quantity of production, and settled any disputes that might arise among the members. In addition, they articulated the work of the gild with similar organizations and the borough itself. Between the various gilds there were frequent clashes as to where one activity ended and another began. Who, for example, might sell new shoes; the gild which made shoes or the gild which repaired shoes? Again, the gilds during their earlier days often quarreled with the merchant gild, while throughout their life they were often at odds with the town. In other words, was the craft to be subject to the overlordship of the town or was it to be allowed to function in a free manner? In some cases municipal control was all but complete, and in practically every instance considerable restriction was imposed by the town. Ultimately, town authorities recognized the futility of too much control and delegated to the crafts a semi-legal position. In the last analysis, however, the town retained the final voice and frequently interposed its authority in the way of electing gild officers, in determining hours of work, and in protecting the individual worker and citizen.

Municipal control tended throughout the fifteenth century to weaken the strength of the gilds, which by this time were suffering from too much exclusiveness, monopoly, and power. Apprentices found it exceedingly difficult to advance, while many a journeyman was blocked from becoming a master by reason of economic and social jealousy on the part of the masters. As a result a number of journeymen withdrew from the gild and set up organizations of their own, much to the annoyance of the superior craftsmen. The subsequent clashes which took place between the two groups ultimately forced the town to intervene and restore order, frequently in favor of the journeymen. Craft gilds, however, continued to play an important rôle in industrial life long before the advent of the Tudors. Socially, the crafts presented a most picturesque feature of the late medieval period. In every religious or humanitarian activity or pageant, the gildsmen were conspicuous. Their prosperity and prominence were shown by their ornate dress, their commodious homes, and their willingness to aid in the construction of churches and cathedrals. Conscious of their importance and possessed of an *esprit de corps,* the more important members of each gild provided themselves with fine suits of livery.

Government Taxes and Finance

Finally, in this treatment of the economic and social life of the fourteenth and fifteenth centuries, attention should be paid to the financial policies of the English kings. Feudal assessments, such as aids and scutage, together with manorial rents, court fees and fines, treasure trove and tallage, while sufficient for Norman and Angevin monarchs, were quite inadequate for the needs of the Plantagenets and Lancastrians. This was due in part to the decline in feudal income which attended the disintegration of the feudal and manorial systems. It may also be explained by the increased cost of government which followed in the wake of Henry II and Edward I. Finally, it should be remembered that the later middle ages were crowded with numerous and very expensive wars which demanded new forms of taxes. Following the Conquest, the earliest additional levy that is known was a royal assessment on exports, called *Lastage,* a term which probably was borrowed from the "last" which was a unit of measure equal to eighty bushels of wheat. Imports, on the other hand, paid upon entry a *Scavage,* a word which implied "showing." Early in the thirteenth century, a definite tax amounting to one fifteenth of the value of the goods was placed upon all imports. Late in the same century came the customs on wools and hides, and in 1303 there appeared the "new custom" on these commodities as well as on wine, cloth, wax, and all other merchandise. The new custom concerned both export and import, a tariff arrangement which was continued during the fourteenth and fifteenth centuries.

Although the volume of English trade rose during this

period, the total income derived was not sufficient to meet the expenses of government. Agreements with foreign and domestic traders as well as forced loans were of some help. To augment their incomes English kings resorted to other taxes, of which the oldest was a duty on movable property. Levied for the first time by Henry II, this tax fell upon grain and livestock in the rural areas and upon household goods and merchandise in the towns. By the reign of Edward III, this levy had become an accustomed source of income and was graduated upon evaluations which amounted to one fifteenth in the country districts and one tenth in the towns. At the same time the clerics contributed a tenth on the movables of their tenants. For nearly a century after 1334, the total yield of this subsidy equaled about £37,000. It will readily be seen that the burden of this tax fell upon the lower classes and not upon the landed estates, in respect to their total income.

In an attempt to rectify this unequitable arrangement as well as to provide Henry IV with revenue, parliament in 1404 authorized a tax on incomes. In 1411 and again in 1431 and 1435, this form of assessment was tried with beneficial results. So successful had these levies been that in 1436 an extensive income tax was adopted, which assessed all incomes arising from lands, rents, offices, and annuities. The minimum tax amounted to six pence on every pound over five and up to one hundred. Incomes over a hundred pounds were graduated upwards, so that those of four hundred or more paid ten per cent. It is of interest to note that the returns showed taxable incomes which netted £191,000, of which £45,000 came from the greater barons. On the other hand over ninety per cent of the returns came from the lesser nobility, gentry, and well-to-do merchants. From a constitutional point of view the difference between baronial and nonbaronial returns indicates a definite economic independence, on the part of the latter, in parliament. Indeed there is reason for believing that the Commons were moved to adopt this tax for the simple purpose of forcing those classes, which had escaped the burden of the tenths and fifteenths, to meet the expenses incident to war.

SELECTED BIBLIOGRAPHY

The agrarian changes and the servile uprisings of the fourteenth century are treated in E. Powell's *The Rising in East Anglia in 1381* (Cambridge, 1896); C. Oman's *The Great Revolt of 1381* (Oxford, 1906), and G. M. Trevelyan's *England in the Age of Wycliffe* (London, 1909). The studies by Prothero and Gray are standard works of value. G. R. Owst, in his *Literature and Pulpit in Medieval England* (Cambridge, 1933), presents the intellectual background of the peasant uprisings. G. G. Coulton's *Medieval Village* (Cambridge, 1931) has pertinent material on the revolts of this age. W. H. R. Curtler's *The Enclosure and Redistribution of Land* (Oxford, 1920) and B. H. Putnam's *Enforcement of the Statutes of Labourers* (Columbia University Studies, 1908) are of value. Mention should also be made of T. W. Page's *The End of Villeinage in England* (New York, 1900).

Industrial and commercial activities are splendidly treated in the works of Salzman. E. Power and M. E. Postan's *English Trade in the Middle Ages* (Oxford, 1931); G. Unwin's *Finance and Trade in the Fifteenth Century* (New York, 1933); A. Bearwood's *Alien Merchants in England, 1350 to 1377* (Cambridge, 1931); D. G. Barnes' *A History of the English Corn Laws* (New York, 1930); Mrs. J. R. Green's *Town Life in the Fifteenth Century* (New York, 1894), and J. F. Willard's *Parliamentary Taxes on Personal Property* (Cambridge, 1934) are studies of merit and insight.

CHAPTER XIII

National Consciousness, Art, and Science

THE wealth and splendor of the London Livery Companies reflects in no small way the existence of an English nationality. Where their progenitors had been content to view themselves as citizens of London and all other Englishmen as foreigners, there had developed by the time of the Yorkist kings a sense of solidarity between these metropolitan traders and those of Bristol and York. Local barriers had broken down. Subsistence farming and industry gave way to an everexpanding market which was national in scope and purpose. And what was true of internal activity was even more apparent in international trade. The significance, however, of this commercial and industrial growth lies not so much in its economic effects but rather in its influences upon the mind of the English trader. He became aware that he was a member of a community which was accomplishing something worthwhile; he gloried in the achievements of other Englishmen; he became proud of the country of which he was a part.

The Rise of English Nationalism

In promoting a national concept, the foreign policy of the government also was a significant factor. Welsh, Scottish, and French wars brought Englishmen together in a common cause, as did the repeated clashes between Rome and England. Alien domination was strongly resented. In constitutional matters national awakening was evident at every turn. Government had grown from an absolute to a limited monarchy and with this had come the development of a degree of uniformity in law and opinion.

Possibly no better evidence of the presence of national consciousness may be found than that in the educational and literary activities of the age now under discussion. At the opening of the period, scarcely a person existed who could write or teach English, at least among those who directed government and Church. Norman-French and Latin were the approved mediums for all such efforts. Furthermore, all acts of government, legal as well as administrative, were couched in one or both of these tongues. Within the Church, Latin was used regularly for song and prayer. On the other hand it was a physical impossibility for the humble priest to minister to his flock without using English. His followers might be awed to respect the elaborate ritual and ceremony, but to indoctrinate them with the precepts of truth, honesty and virtue, English had to be employed. Again, unless the sheriff resorted to English, royal decrees and court actions would have been so much mystery. And when representatives of shires and towns entered parliament or when they undertook extensive mercantile activities, the door was opened for a wider use of the vernacular. During the reign of Edward III, for example, suitors were permitted to plead in their own tongue, and by the time of Richard II, English was being taught in most of the grammar schools. Later in the Lancastrian age English was used in the House of Commons and in the meetings of the Council. A reading public, therefore, was practically secured for those writers who wished to use the native language. John Trevisa, a Cornishman, recognized this fact and published a number of translations of popular European works. At the same time, there appeared an English edition of the *Travels of Sir John Mandeville,* which was one of the most widely read books of this period.

Equally significant was Wycliffe's translation of the Bible. Heretofore certain books of the Bible had appeared in English, especially in the north and midland areas where French and Latin were generally less used than in the south. Wycliffe's version rapidly superseded these isolated translations and became immensely popular with the middle classes. It is to the credit of the Roman Church that no attempt was made to check the spread of this volume until it became identified with Lollardism. Even then it was not the reformer's translation which was condemned but rather those editions which contained commentaries hostile to the papacy. Both Wycliffe's version and those employed by the Lollards seem to have been used rather extensively, and while it is probably true that too much emphasis has been placed upon their influence on the growth of English, the ultimate effects were none the less important. Wycliffe's Bible was the first complete English translation and through its wide adoption did much to advance the growth of a unified language for all England. Additional stimulus, in this respect, was provided by Reginald Peacock, head of a London college, who published a number of semireligious tracts in English. Notice should also be taken of the various satires, tracts, and sermons delivered and published in English, such as the works of John Ball and Thomas Wimbledon. Finally, late in the fifteenth century there appeared the translations by Caxton, and Malory's *Morte d'Arthur*.

Turning from prose to poetry one encounters in the fourteenth century the brilliant work in English done by John Gower, Geoffrey Chaucer, and the author or authors of *Piers Plowman*. Who actually drafted *Piers Plowman* has never been completely established. Some have attributed it to William Langland, though this view has fewer advocates than formerly. Whoever composed this captivating literary satire must have been exceedingly well educated and informed of the many crosscurrents in the political, religious, and social thought of the times. Moreover, the author clearly intended to depict life as he found it and to stimulate his readers to a proper appreciation of existing abuses. What better medium existed, therefore, than the language of the average merchant, husbandman, or artisan? Not that the latter two groups were able to read, but the content of the poem was spread by word of mouth by those who could read and understand. Gower, on the other hand, while not unwilling to disclose social and political characteristics, utilized his talents for stylistic and literary ends. Moreover, he preferred using French or Latin and it was not until late in life that he employed English in his writings. In his *Speculum Meditantis,* which was in French, Gower treated of the vices and virtues inherent in man and the ways whereby the "sinner" might return to God. His Latin work, *Vox Clamantis,* recorded the author's opinion of the misfortunes which attended the reign of Richard II and the hope which the Lancastrians placed in the new monarch, Henry IV. Gower's English is best expressed in the *Confessio Amantis,* which concerned chiefly man's interest in love. In a simple storytelling manner Gower recounted a number of popular tales taken boldly from the writings of Ovid and other classical and early medieval sources.

Gower seems to have known Chaucer and it may well be that this contact explains the former's use of English, which Chaucer employed with remarkable and lasting success. Chaucer was well schooled in Latin, French, English, and possibly Italian, and possessed as well the skill to depict in a learned and often humorous manner the various subjects which interested him. His *Canterbury Tales,* well known wherever English is understood, are aglow with brilliant satirical passages. A penetrating objectivity is still another characteristic, which must have annoyed some of his contemporary readers although it wins applause today. These essential features appear in his other writings, notably the *House of Fame, Troilus and Criseyde,* and the *Parliament of Fowls.* Although Chaucer wrote primarily for the middle and upper classes, the fact remains that he did much to popularize the use of English. More important than this, however, was the ultimate effect achieved, the shaping of a local dialect into a medium which in time served as the basis for the English of today. In his wake there followed a number of authors, many of whom patterned their writings on the theme and style of Chaucer, who helped to advance the use of English both in prose and poetry.

William Caxton and the Printing Press

Literary activities of the fifteenth century, however, fell short of the heights reached by Gower and Chaucer. It was not until the last quarter of this century that anything like a renewed interest manifested itself. This quickening was stimulated, in part, by the invention of the printing press, a device which William Caxton promoted in England. In the course of his literary and business life on the Continent, Caxton became acquainted with the publishers and printers who had been plying their trade for some thirty years before he set up his press at Westminster in 1476. To Caxton, therefore, should be given the credit not only for having introduced the printing machine into England but also for having published the greater share of the three hundred and fifty books which were printed in the kingdom before the sixteenth century. Other presses were also established before 1480 at St. Albans, London, and Oxford. Although the actual progress of printing in England was slow, and in productivity much below that of the European presses, it is important to note that books could now be produced at a much lower cost than ever before. Cheapness widened their use and with this expansion a larger reading public was secured. Although a number of these volumes were in English, the greater share were still composed in either French or Latin, as were the manuscript efforts of this period. Anything else would have been entirely foreign to medieval culture. On the other hand, the increased use of English was an important indication of the quickening of a national consciousness.

Educational Activities

The development of educational activities during the late medieval period reflects the growth of nationality. The influence of the Church and the general rise of economic standards did much to further the spread of learning. During the fourteenth century a number of new colleges were founded at Cambridge and Oxford, and to these institutions came an ever-increasing number of students and teachers. The universities attracted the best minds of England, and from their classrooms flowed a steady stream of men whose reputations spread throughout Europe. Duns Scotus, William of Ockham, Henry Beaufort, Bishop of Bradwardine, and Thomas Wycliffe are but the greater lights in the educational galaxy of this century. Nor should it be forgotten that some of the leaders in political affairs owed their success to the splendid training received at the universities. Further progress would have been made but for the ravages of the Black Death, which decimated the ranks of the faculties and retarded increases in enrollment. Again, the conservative reaction which swept through the educational world following the liberal teachings of men like Wycliffe did much to stultify intellectual growth. In the last half of the century a few new colleges were founded, notably New College, Oxford; but these failed to show any inclination to espouse the older humanitarian equalitarianism. Fewer students matriculated and the faculties contained men whose scholastic standing was decidedly provincial. Even during the fifteenth century no appreciable improvement took place until the reign of Henry VII.

In the meantime important gains had been made along other educational lines, chiefly in the founding of a large number of grammar schools, choristers' schools and so-called colleges. Many of these started during the fourteenth century, an age which one authority has described as the "Era of School Statutes." Numerous regulations relative to matters of curriculum, faculty control, and student life appeared. In most schools, for example, all instruction was given either in French or Latin well down into the fourteenth century, when English became the common medium of expression. The subjects taught still consisted of the *trivium* and *quadrivium* though there was a noticeable drift towards a more liberal curriculum. True learning was encouraged also by a generous amount of "tanning," while students were at all times forbidden to engage in gambling, drinking, and boisterous games. The endless procession of rules concerning misconduct is in itself convincing evidence that student irregularities taxed the time and patience of faculties then as today. Nor were the parents of that age unfamiliar with letters from their sons begging for additional spending money.

The advent of the Black Death did much to check the growth of secondary schools though a decided improvement took place during the Lancastrian period. Henry VI, in particular, devoted much energy and money to the promotion of grammar schools, of which Eton is perhaps the best known. And while Henry's schools, like those modeled upon them, distinctly reflected orthodox religious views and concepts, definite anti-sacerdotal tendencies appeared in other institutions. Sevenoaks, London, for example, used laymen rather than clerics as teachers. Moreover, while most of the schools were either totally or partially endowed by pious souls, there were others like that at Maxfield, Cheshire, where instruction was entirely free. A number of schools charged tuition. In every case, however, the financial backing of these enterprises rested in the Church, King, and nobility, or some well-to-do merchant like Michael de la Pole, a descendant of William de la Pole, the great capitalist of Edward III's reign. In general, most of the students who attended the universities and grammar schools were recruited from the landed gentry and merchant princes of the towns. The nobility still preferred to educate their sons at home under the guidance of a tutor. Intellectual and educational activities, therefore, were attracting a more diversified group than ever before. The day was passing when English education was largely in the hands of the Church, which sought primarily to train men for the ministry.

An examination of the literary and philosophical writings of the period reveals the growth and extension of academic activities. During the fourteenth century there was a strange mingling of the older and newer concepts. On the one hand scholastic reasoning predominated, as may be seen from the works of Wycliffe, Ockham, and Duns Scotus. Of these writers, Duns Scotus probably represented the past far better than the other two. Ockham and Wycliffe, though they used scholastic methods, broke sharply with the established order. Both denounced orthodox theology and paved the way for individual self-expression in research and thought. Excommunication, religious and political disapproval, and death drove these rugged men and their followers from the halls of learning and for a time gave the victory to the conservative forces. Stagnation and sterility of thought followed. Humanistic inquiry, however, slowly reshaped and reasserted itself, particularly by the middle of the fifteenth century. Thanks to the efforts of certain men like Humphrey of Gloucester, Italian scholars were brought into the kingdom, and with them came the first signs of a new learning known as the Renaissance. Cornelio Vitelli introduced Greek at New College, a departure which was copied by Magdalen, Eton, and Winchester. Stimulated by the introduction of the classics, many Englishmen visited Italy for further research and study. William Grocyn, Thomas Linacre, and William Selling may be mentioned as examples of Englishmen who profited by Continental contacts. On their return home these scholars hastened to spread the Renaissance by writing and teaching. And while the results of these activities were manifested chiefly during the Tudor period, it is significant to note that their inception took place in the last half of the fifteenth century.

Scientific Growth

In sharp contrast with the strides which had been made in literary and academic circles was the poverty of scientific knowledge. Much that was ancient and tinged with quackery pervaded the medical fields, as may be evidenced by the frightful mortality which attended the ravages of the Black Death. Actual experimentation and observation were none too common, but every now and then one encounters sound practice, as in the work of John Gaddesden, a famous fourteenth-century doctor. In general medicine was weighed down by humbug, fraud, and meaningless mystery. Religion, moreover, was none too kindly disposed towards experimenting with established ideas and precepts as to the human body or man's purpose in life. Charms and symbols played an important part in the medieval doctor's bag of tricks. A certain knight of Chesterfield, for example, was seized by a sudden spasm and was saved from death only by the timely placing of a charm, written on a parchment, on the back of his neck. Scrofula, to use one more illustration, was usually treated by having the King "touch" the sufferer. Doctors leaned heavily upon astrology for effecting cures, as the position of the planets was thought to have a profound influence over the health and life of man. The fact that most practitioners were known as Surgeon-Barbers reflects the medical standard and knowledge of that day.

In the field of mathematics and astronomy very little improvement seems to have taken place. Only in physics was an advance made, and even then solely as this science was related to architecture. Trial and error, plus constant experimentation with towering vaults and massive walls, made for a greater knowledge of the principles relative to stress and volume. The absence of a laboratory science, however, did not prevent the construction of imposing cathedrals, elaborate

Courtesy Assoc. British and Irish Railways, Inc.

WEST FAÇADE, LINCOLN CATHEDRAL.

parish churches and monasteries or even of more pretentious domestic buildings. Norman architecture, which predominated during the first half of the medieval period, vested its Romanesque base, by the close of the thirteenth century, with characteristics which have been called Early Gothic. Round arches were supplanted by pointed ones, and intersecting curves replaced what had been a full half-circle. Windows, while still narrow, were heightened into a shape known as the lancet. These features became common and increasingly complex in the Plantagenet period. During this age the chancel, which had already begun to be lengthened, was thrown wide open to the communicants in the nave. A more frequent use of aisles also characterized the fourteenth-century church, which was being remarkably altered by the influence of the friars. These humble clerics, bound by the strictest vows of poverty and educated primarily to preach the gospel of Christ, naturally gravitated to the towns where larger congregations could be reached. In return for their worth-while efforts, the

Courtesy Assoc. British and Irish Railways, Inc.

WELLS CATHEDRAL, SOMERSET, FROM WEST ENTRANCE. A splendid example of early English Gothic architecture of the thirteenth century. Note the inverted arches, built in 1338, to prop up central tower.

laity, rich and poor alike, showered upon them gifts of money and land with which the friars reared large and elaborate churches. Within these edifices the architectural design was drawn to meet the needs of the preacher. Wide aisles, lofty arches set on light stone columns, walls pierced for broader and higher windows are but a few of the many changes introduced by the masons to satisfy the needs of the clergy. Since windows were particularly necessary, the architects took the lancet type and developed windows beautiful for their tracery. Although many of these features appeared in the cathedrals, they were far more common among the parish churches which arose in increasing number during this period. In both types elaborate ornamentations and moldings were employed. Externally, the churches were marked by massive buttresses which foreshadowed greater changes for the future.

Gild houses, manor homes and barns, and even the simple home of the artisan and husbandman reflected an expanding order. Chimney flues, which had been introduced during the thirteenth century, now became more common. Additional rooms were added in the form of wings or annexes attached to the original four-walled structure. The larger share of these buildings were of wood, which accounts for their disappearance in the course of time. Many of the gild halls were bountifully decorated with rich, delicate, and complex carvings, which also appeared in the panels, arches, pews, altars, and fronts of the churches. Marble and alabaster as well as metal were employed with great effectiveness by the architects of this period. Painting, never reaching the heights attained on the Continent, was nevertheless ably represented by murals depicting biblical and allegorical scenes. Colored glass likewise helped to make the churches a fit dwelling place for the King of Kings. Within the monasteries many of these features were used by the monks, who showed great skill and art in laboriously copying and decorating manuscripts. Psalters, song and service books frequently had their margins crowded with colored designs and pictures, many of which had their inspiration in the daily work and play of man. It must have been quite refreshing to a chorister to see before his eyes, as he chanted some noble song of the Church, a merry throng of children dancing or spinning tops.

Medieval Music

From very early times singing had played an important rôle in church services. Primitive organs with bellows worked by hand or foot had been common in the Saxon period, and the song schools of York and Rochester had trained choir boys and clerics to sing the Gregorian chants, which even today are featured by Roman and Protestant communions. Throughout the medieval period the Church devoted considerable thought to this aspect of ritual and ceremony. Secular composition, of which the "Song of Spring" is probably the best known, began in the thirteenth century. Other efforts followed, though it was not until the close of the fourteenth century that England produced a musician whose skill and knowledge "almost amounted to the discovery of a new art." John Dunstable's work was contemporary with the compositions of Lionel Power. Carols and songs, sacred and secular, appeared in greater number during the early Lancastrian period. One recounted with stirring nationalistic fervor Henry's victory over the French at Agincourt. Beginning with the War of the Roses, a decline in original productions seems to have taken place.

Most of the songs and chants of the medieval period were written for one, two, four, and even six voices. Frequently musical instruments accompanied these songs, and separate instrumental renditions without the voice were not unknown. The variety of instruments used added much to the pleasing qualities of the song. Harps of different types, brasses, drums, and stringed instruments were constantly employed by the musicians of this age. Bagpipes, hurdy-gurdies, and cymbals were also used. The wandering minstrel, who was a singer, musician, and news-vender all in one, likewise illustrates the appeal which music made to all classes. Whether the minstrel was singing from an elaborate gallery, as in Exeter Cathedral, from a balcony overlooking the Great Hall of some noble, or from the doorsteps of the village church, the audience was attentive and appreciative.

For his theme, the minstrel used some epic verse recounting the deeds of a famed warrior or traveler, or some satirical poem or ballad which possessed a popular appeal. Often he employed his skill to point out human frailties; at other times he openly propagandized in favor of some social or political reform. Many of his songs were traditional folk lays, the origins of which have long been forgotten, but which were none the less most effective. Women, in particular, were singled out as the object of satirical verses of which the following may serve as an example:

> For tell a woman all your counsel
> And she can keep it wonderfully well
> She had rather go quick to hell
> Than to her neighbor she would it tell
> *Cuius contrarium verum est.*

Drinking songs were also much in vogue and one can well imagine the boisterous college boy of this era, well in his cups, singing some racy or convivial verse. Love songs depicting the grace and charm of an attractive maiden were also sung by the frequenter of an alehouse or by some passing minstrel. On the other hand, religious themes were widely used, and each season of the Christian year had its own special words and airs. The Christmas and Easter carols which are popular today are but samples of the many songs which delighted the heart and fired the imagination of the medievalist. And where is there greater or more emotional music than in that quaint old Welsh tune, "All Through the Night"?

Medieval Wayfaring

The wandering minstrel was in one sense a wayfarer whose arrival in town or manor was a cause for much merry-making and celebration. The entire population hurried to listen to his songs and to hear the latest news of foreign happenings. On other occasions jugglers and acrobats won hearty applause. Performing monkeys, horses, and bears also thrilled young and old alike. At other times miracle plays were staged by traveling bands of actors or by the members of the local medieval gilds. Usually these plays depicted in a rather rough fashion some scene borrowed from well-known biblical themes. Entertainment of this type seems to have been rather common. Dancing also seems to have been freely engaged in by both the professional entertainer and the audience. Medieval wayfarers must have enjoyed these pleasures after a hard day's travel. Those who were minstrels, traders, friars, or pilgrims were always certain to receive a cordial welcome. On the other hand, strangers were viewed with great suspicion. Nor is this to be wondered at when one recalls the relative provincialism of the period. The majority of the population seldom went beyond the limits of town or manor. As a result the appearance of a foreigner was an event which might bring dire misfortune to a community. "Hark, Hark, the dogs do bark," was a warning which no good housewife failed to observe.

In spite of these hazards there probably was more moving about during the middle ages than is actually recorded. The presence of shrines, chantries and crosses at fords, bridges or crossroads attests to a desire on the part of the locality to provide shelter and rest for the tired traveler. Monasteries and manor houses afforded sleeping and eating accommodations for many, especially the greater nobles and clergy. Inns, on the other hand, were frequented chiefly by pilgrims, merchants, and actors. If no inn was available the ever-conspicuous alehouse could always be used. Food and lodging, though lack-

Courtesy Assoc. British and Irish Railways, Inc.

MARKET CROSS AND STOCKS, RIPLEY, YORKSHIRE.

ing much in comfort and sanitation, were sufficient for that day. Most people traveled either by foot or on horseback. Freight was usually carried in the same way. Ladies of high rank and, occasionally, nobles were borne by horse litters or in carriages not unlike the covered wagon used by American pioneers.

Medieval Costuming

Litters and carriages were extravagantly built and were richly decorated within and without, in proper keeping with the dignity and dress of the traveler. The costuming of the later medieval period reflects quite well the general rise in economic standards since the days of Henry II and Henry III. One should guard, however, against interpreting the illustrations, the ornate statuaries or even the satirical verse of poets and preachers as being true delineations of what men and women then wore. A judicious use of these sources and an examination of available household accounts will yield a picture which is fairly precise. Among the titled and well-to-do classes there was a distinct tendency throughout the fourteenth and fifteenth centuries to accentuate one's dress by extravagance and foppery. Some of this may be explained by native practices, but foreign influences played a far more important part. A well-dressed man of this period probably wore an outer garment in the form of a long, full robe which had enormous sleeves and which was tied or fastened at the front of the neck by an elaborate bow or some sparkling pin. His shoes were snouted and bent upward at the toe a full finger's length, while his many-colored hose of cloth or velvet extended from his feet to his coat. In some instances the hose was pulled up over the breeches or might even serve in place of the latter. The headgear, however, was the *pièce de résistance* and usually consisted of an elaborate hood fashioned like the cap worn by the hero of present day "Spearmint" copy. Caps of various shapes and cloths were also worn; though by the reign of Richard II, turbans became more common. At times the cap was worn over the hood or turban. During the Lancastrian period caps alone were used, though the hood, now extending down the back, was often pulled up over the cap. The body garment consisted of a tightly fitted coat, buttoned in front, which usually extended down to the waist. Over this cloth there often appeared a stomacher and over that nothing less than a heavy silk or velvet petticoat. On approaching one of these gentlemen from the rear, one would find it extremely difficult to tell whether the person was a man or a woman unless robe and petticoat were raised to avoid being dragged through muddy streets or over dirty floors.

Women likewise wore a snug-fitting coat which varied in length. Multi-colored hose was worn and over both coat and hose appeared a petticoat or two, covered in turn by the full-sleeved robe. The simple silk or cloth wrapping which covered the head of the thirteenth-century lady had given way to a towering fantastic mass which often extended on one side. A little later the entire gear was dropped down on both sides so that it touched the shoulders. By Edward IV's time, fashion dictated a return to greater simplicity and the head was covered by a small rounded cap with flaps which touched both cheeks and neck. During the same period the coat was trimmed at the top so as to allow the front of the neck to appear. Women's shoes were like those worn by the men. Both were modified in the interest of simplicity in the days of Richard III. Men and women of the merchant and trading classes patterned their costumes after the fashion of the court, though there was much less show of wealth. Artisans and serfs seem to have contented themselves with clothes that were extremely simple. A coarse, loose-fitting garment topped at times by an outer coat or skirt constituted about all that could be afforded. Shoes were worn, though going barefooted was exceedingly common, as were cloth hose wound about the legs much like the service leggings used by American soldiers in the World War. Hoods or caps, when used at all, covered the head.

Moralists and satirists frequently taunted the upper classes for wearing such costly costumes. Even the clergy were attacked for the extravagance displayed in their dress. Men were condemned for their skirts and petticoats while women were ridiculed for their tight-fitting body garments, which in the eyes of the moralists constituted indecent exposure. One writer styled them "the daughters of Babilone," while another described them as having "gay heddes sett up on hyse and horned as an unreasonabyl best." Chaucer's Wife of Bath is pictured as a woman "with here hedes y-horned, schort clokes unnethe to the hupes with bendels [scarfs], chapellettes and frontelles y-set above the heued y-lyche to a wylde beste that hath no resoun." Many of these complaints arose from the clergy, whose attitude towards women was sadly twisted by memory of what Eve had done to Adam. And while it must be admitted that the sources often show women to have been overbold in dress and in their deportment towards men, there is little cause for believing them to have been as worldly as their fathers or husbands. Religious attitudes and public opinion generally consigned women to a life of unending love and service towards man. It was her humble duty to watch over the children, keep the house, cook the meals and listen quietly to her mate's scoldings or victories at the tournament, bowling green, or gambling table. Strict attention to man's needs was forever uppermost in a woman's mind nor was she to find any fault in her husband's conduct. In all classes of society, it was generally held that man might administer physical punishment to his wife whenever desired. On the other hand, there were women who refused to be tied to their husband's petticoat, and occasionally one reads of a wife's "tanning" her gift from heaven.

The picture which has been drawn of fourteenth- and fifteenth-century England stands in rather sharp contrast to the preceding period. Definite improvement had taken place in government and law, while economic and social standards had taken a turn towards the better. Even in the field of art and science a change had taken place. England, in other words, had grown in wisdom and stature. The way had been paved, through a quickening of national consciousness, for the appearance of the aggressive nationalism which is so aptly manifested by a Henry VIII, an Elizabeth, a Drake, and a William Shakespeare.

SELECTED BIBLIOGRAPHY

The references at the close of Chapter IX may be used for a study of social and intellectual conditions during the fourteenth and fifteenth centuries. In addition the following will be of help: G. L. Kittredge's *Chaucer and his Poetry* (Cambridge, 1915); G. G. Coulton's *Chaucer and His England* (London, 1921); R. K. Root's *Poetry of Chaucer* (Boston, 1922); A. Abram's *English Life and Manners in the Later Middle Ages* (London, 1913); W. Denton's *England in the Fifteenth Century* (London, 1888); H. S. Bennett's *The Pastons and Their England* (Cambridge, 1922); D. Chadwick's *Social Life in the Days of Piers Plowman* (Cambridge, 1922); F. M. Kelly and R. Schwabe's *Historic Costume* (New York, 1929), and Trail's *Social England*, Vol. II.

CHAPTER XIV

Renaissance and Reformation

RICHARD'S defeat and death at Bosworth Field paved the way for the domination of the Tudor dynasty from 1485 to 1603. Significant as were the unusual accomplishments of this family in government and industry, the success of the Tudor kings and queens rested fundamentally upon the spirit and life of the sixteenth century. No one will deny that these monarchs were endowed with strong personalities nor that they were skilled in the art of government. England, indeed, owes much to a Henry VIII and an Elizabeth for having guided the nation through an age crowded with pitfalls and uncertainties. On the other hand, it is equally true that these rulers were but products of their age. It was the driving force of this period rather than the ability of the monarchs which accounts for their success and for the expansion of the kingdom from an England to a Great Britain.

The Advent of the Renaissance

During the Tudor era, England experienced a profound spiritual and material awakening. Elsewhere in Europe this quickening impulse, commonly called the Renaissance, had been operating for some little time. English educational and literary activities had been stirred by this movement during the late fifteenth century, though it was not until the advent of the Tudors that the full impact affected all parts and classes of the kingdom. So extensive were the influences which attended the Renaissance that contemporary opinion then and for several centuries afterward interpreted the movement as a "re-birth" of culture. To these writers, the medieval days had been extremely dismal and they were responsible for the term "the Dark Ages." More recent historical investigation has shown how inaccurate this description was, and how brightly burned the lights of intellectual activity during the medieval period. One has only to examine the literary accomplishments of England during the eighth and ninth centuries, or those of France during the days of Charlemagne, to be convinced that there were no Dark Ages. A more precise definition would characterize the Renaissance as a vitalizing force which impelled man to build a more glorious social order. In sharp contrast to scholasticism, which had dogmatically asserted man to be but a cog in a world church or state, the Renaissance boldly proclaimed the enthronement of the individual. Heretofore man blindly and in good faith had followed where his king had led, or through the medium of the priest had gained eternal salvation. The new order, however, stressed the individual's inherent right to think and pray objectively. Scientific methodology, rather than scholastic authority, was insisted upon by the ardent disciples of the Renaissance.

Able champions of the new humanistic movement appeared throughout Western Europe. Dante, Petrarch, and Boccaccio have often been referred to as the advance guard of an unnumbered band which sought to elevate man to a proper appreciation of his abilities and rights. Most diligently did these scholars search for forgotten masterpieces of art and literature. Most earnestly did they submit their findings to investigation and most zealous were they in their devotion to new canons of scientific method. As a result man thought and talked in terms of established truths rather than upon unreasonable authority. A world of beauty, which before had been shunned because of its alleged connection with the forces of evil, was opened for man to explore and revel in to his heart's content. *Earth's but a desert drear, He'ven is my Home,* though still sung in churches today, was a striking reflection of what man believed to be the purpose of life. The fruit of humanism, however, changed all this. Drab, color-less, and flat paintings, drawn chiefly from religious experi-ences, were supplanted by a brilliancy and perspective worthy of their creators—Fra Angelico, Botticelli, Leonardo da Vinci, Michelangelo, Van Eyck, and Raphael. Sculpturing reflected the newer order, as is attested by the work of Donatello and Giotto, and architectural changes were introduced by the great builders of Florence and Venice. Expansion in science was demonstrated by the discoveries of Prince Henry the Navigator, Diaz, and Columbus, and by the astronomical findings of Copernicus and Galileo. Finally, the invention of the printing press did much to spread the results of the Renaissance.

The effect of these activities upon England was enormous. Literary pursuits were encouraged by the study of Greek, by an increased use of the vernacular, and by the writings of men like Sir Thomas More. Artistically, the Renaissance showed its influence in the rapid development of Gothic architecture and by what may be called English schools of painting, carv-ing and music. In the field of science, the voyages of the fishermen of Bristol and of Cabot, Drake and Frobisher were matched by the medical accomplishments of Harvey. Impor-tant as each of these movements was, their chief result was a change in the mental attitude of Englishmen. Heretofore England had been largely outside the center of European life. Its national position, while not negligible, was much lower than that of the Empire, France, or the Papacy. Economi-cally, it counted for less, as all major trade routes and indus-trial activities were Continental in scope and influence. On the other hand England had acquired a strong political organization and had established an economic foundation which foreshadowed definite gains in the future. The discovery of America revolutionized the trading life of Europe. England was now thrown into the very heart of a new commercial world. Her hands stretched forth and touched both America and Europe. Her merchants traveled to faraway Russia, the Levant, India, the Gold Coast, Virginia, and the Caribbean. In the wake of these pioneers came colonization and wealth. English nationalism became a living thing and England's position in the councils of Europe rose to that of a first-rate power.

Henry VII's Governmental Policies

England's position, however, demanded toleration, moderation, and capable leadership. A hasty and impetuous prince might easily wreck the fortunes of his subjects upon the shoals of dynastic controversies or upon the shifting sands of European diplomacy. Clearly, England had had its share of civil and foreign wars. The time had come for rehabilitation and growth. Peace at home and abroad was vital if economic and social foundations were to be made secure. But were these essentials a part of the program of Henry Tudor? No one knew the man sufficiently well to answer yes or no. In the light of his past record and the lean years which his party had enjoyed, it might be expected that the new King would rule with an iron hand in the interests of the Lancastrians. If so, there would be a continuance of the War of the Roses and further disaster. Fortunately for England, Henry realized the longings and needs of his subjects and from the first gave indications that he intended to rule in the interests of all. At the same time Henry was aware that his title to the throne was none too good and that were he to proclaim himself king by right of conquest, the future might be none too secure for himself and his dynasty. Anxious to protect himself and his heirs, Henry wisely refrained from any extensive proscription of Yorkist life and property. Moreover, by his marriage to Elizabeth of York, the outstanding Yorkist claimant to the throne, he removed all just cause for jealousy on the part of his rivals. Public opinion generally applauded Henry's actions and rallied wholeheartedly to his side when certain Yorkist malcontents raised the standard of revolt. Financed by Margaret, sister of Richard III and wife of the Duke of Burgundy, Yorkist forces were thrown into England under the nominal leadership of one Lambert Simnel, who was represented as none other than one of the princes whom Richard had destroyed in the Tower. Henry met the attack by defeating the enemy in June, 1487, at Stoke, and returning home with the impostor a prisoner, who spent the remainder of his life as a servant in the King's kitchen.

A few years later the Yorkists repeated their efforts to unseat Henry by sponsoring an invasion led by one Perkin Warbeck, who was said to be a Prince of the House of York. Aided by foreign support and by internal dissatisfaction arising out of excessive taxation, Perkin kept annoying Henry from 1491 to 1497, when he was finally captured. Although Lambert and Perkin might have made considerable trouble for Henry, the throne was made secure more by the loyalties of his subjects than by military victories. Harsh as was the rule of the first Tudor, Englishmen preferred it to the uncertainties of civil war. A single illustration, taken from the correspondence of the Spanish ambassador, will show how even the ordinary folk resented these Yorkist uprisings. "Friday the 3rd of July," so DePuebla wrote to Ferdinand of Spain, "the so-called Duke of York came to England. . . . A portion of his troops disembarked but the people rose in arms against them without the intervention of a single soldier of the King. The peasants . . . made great havoc of the troops and if the vessels had not been at hand, not a single man of them would have escaped alive."

Foreign and Commercial Affairs

Meanwhile Henry had gained reputation and recognition abroad. Anxious to strengthen his hold upon the throne, Henry cast about for European alliances. France was ignored for the time being, while overtures of friendship were addressed to Spain, which had but recently established its birthright by defeating the Moors and by uniting its people under the standards of Castile and Aragon. Spain, moreover, was more than willing to listen to Henry's invitation, provided the latter would join in an armed attack upon France. Henry was well aware that neither his treasury nor his people would stand a prolonged war. On the other hand an alliance with Spain could not be had for the mere asking, and the war itself might be conveniently short. Accordingly, in 1489 a treaty was signed between the two states binding England to assist Spain in a French war. In return Spain expressed confidence and friendship in England, and sanctified the arrangement by a marriage between Katherine, daughter of Ferdinand and Isabella, and Arthur, Henry's eldest son. The pecuniary advantages, coming in the form of a handsome dowry, were not overlooked by Henry. Indeed upon Arthur's death in 1502, Henry hastened to save both dowry and alliance by a treaty, signed in 1503, which provided for the marriage of Katherine to Prince Henry.

In the meantime England had dispatched troops to assist Brittany and Burgundy, who were resisting Charles of France while Spanish troops attacked from the south. Suddenly, however, Henry's enemies made peace with Charles, who, bent upon undertaking an Italian campaign, agreed to pay England a large sum for the withdrawal of its army. Henry accepted the offer and retired from France, while his ally Ferdinand won from Charles title to certain contested areas in the eastern Pyrenees. Spain had gained her objective, and England had lived up to her promise in a matter which netted

Henry a financial profit and an increased reputation as a clever diplomat. A little later, in 1496, Henry's position was enhanced by an arrangement with the European powers who were contesting French aggression in Italy. By the terms of this treaty, England was to support the allies by agreeing not to assist France. In the same year a Scottish invasion was repelled. This was followed in 1502 by a compact between England and Scotland which provided, among other things, for the marriage of Henry's daughter Margaret to James IV of Scotland.

In economic matters Henry was as successful as he had been in the field of diplomacy. Conscious that his kingdom needed material prosperity, Henry arranged for a number of treaties with foreign states providing for the promotion of trade and commerce. At the same time he encouraged the passage of several acts which increased the shipbuilding, corn, and woolen industries. Pressure, moreover, was placed upon foreign merchants in England. Without depriving them of their right to trade, Henry made it extremely difficult for them to hold their former preëminence. Manufacturing and agriculture were also aided by the adoption of a paternalistic policy by the government. England, in other words, was given exactly what she needed—peace and prosperity—and while this was attended by a show of absolutism on Henry's part, the nation generally approved of his actions. Disorder was stamped out, livery and maintenance were sharply curtailed by the arbitrary decisions of the Court of Star Chamber, while Henry's justices wrecked the aspirations of many a criminal. In literary and educational matters Henry encouraged the progress of humanistic inquiry and turned Englishmen's eyes westward by aiding Cabot and others in their voyages and explorations.

From a political point of view Henry's conduct of government was a distinct success. At no time did he destroy any of the existing features of the constitution, yet his use of it did much towards the establishment of Tudor absolutism. Probably one of the best illustrations of his policy may be drawn from the handling of finance. Ordinary revenue arising from feudal assessments, customs dues, and the like were not sufficient to satisfy the King's needs. Additional revenue might be gained from parliament, as indeed it was, but a continuance of this method would lead inevitably to parliament's control of the Crown. To prevent such an event Henry resorted to forced loans; and thanks to the continued efforts of his agents, a goodly sum was gained. He handled foreign affairs in a manner which entailed the lowest possible expense with the greatest possible profit. Through his rearrangement of trade and industry, further income was secured in the form of higher customs dues. The net result of this technique was to be seen in the number of times parliament was in session. Seven parliaments met during the twenty-four years he reigned, and of these, all but one met before March, 1497. None of them actually sat for more than a few months at a time, and the total sessions probably did not exceed the equivalent of two years. Financial independence, evidently, had been secured; and so full were his moneybags that Henry did not have to call parliament during the last four years of his reign. Finally, it should be noted that Henry was one of the most penurious kings England has ever had.

Henry VIII

In the Venetian Calendar relative to English affairs, there is an entry in which Henry VII is described as having been a "very great miser," who was supposed to have accumulated more gold "than well nigh all the other kings of Christendom." All this stood his son in good stead when he ascended the throne in late April, 1509. Henry VIII in all probability would never have ruled but for the sudden death of his brother Arthur in 1502. From that time on, however, his life was shaped and schooled for the office of king. His marriage to Katherine was an affair of state, and was but a passing episode in the life of a Prince who, at the time, was three days short of being twelve years old. Prior to this epoch-making event, Henry seems to have been tutored for service in the government. At least there is no reason for believing that his appointments to the Wardenship of the Cinque Ports, and Lord Lieutenancy of Ireland, and the office of Earl Marshal indicated a desire on the part of his father to have his son enter the Church, as later writers stated. Altogether too young to assume the duties of these positions, Henry was allowed plenty of freedom for play and physical development. Here, then, were laid the foundations which enabled the Prince at a later date to withstand the strain of council work, long hours in the saddle, strenuous games in the tournaments, and feastings and excesses which would have killed anyone less prepared. Henry was tall and handsome, so the sources report, and had a genial and winning personality. Mental growth kept pace with physical development. Even as a boy Henry displayed unusual ability. His tutors were wisely selected, and from them he gained skill in Greek, Latin, French, Italian, and mathematics, as well as a thorough understanding of contemporary philosophy and theology. Later, as an author, he confounded his rivals by penning the *Defense of the Seven Sacraments,* which ably stated the Roman case against Luther. In return for his zeal, the Pope bestowed upon Henry the title of the Defender of the Faith.

Into the hands, therefore, of this precocious youth, known to history as Henry VIII, fell the destinies of England in 1509. Thundering applause greeted him when he graciously pardoned a score of political offenders, while his order for the execution of certain offensive governmental officials made him a favorite with his subjects. The consummation of his marriage to Katherine was hailed as a continuance of the Spanish alliance. At the same time he bewildered his court and the nation by a continual round of revels and games which, though dangerously expensive, made him a monarch beloved of all. Occasionally he dashed into the council chamber to show that he was not unmindful of government. In the main, however, he allowed the Council a free hand during the first two years of his reign and followed where they and his chief adviser, Ferdinand of Spain, led. It was largely as the result of the latter's influence that Henry plunged the country into a European war which was then being waged between France, on the one hand, and the Empire, Spain, and the Papacy on the other. These latter states had allied themselves in what was called the Holy League, and Henry believed that England should be congratulated upon joining so respectable a company. The King imagined that military success would enhance his personal position, and that a liberal slice of French territory would serve to remind Englishmen of the country's former greatness. Bitter disappointment, however, attended the entire affair. His allies, especially Ferdinand, left him in the lurch after they had gained their objectives, and Henry was forced to a separate treaty with France. Thanks to the splendid work done by his chief minister, Thomas Wolsey, England withdrew without too much loss of pride or caste. One of the more dramatic phases of this peace concerned the marriage between Mary, Henry's sister, and the aged French king, Louis XII.

National prestige was somewhat gratified by an overwhelming victory gained against the Scots at Flodden Field in 1513 and by the continued success which crowned the brilliant diplomacy of Wolsey. Although a member of the clergy, Wolsey devoted most of his energies to affairs of state, and he was able to lead England during the next fifteen years from one height to another. More than the equal of his European rivals in statecraft, Wolsey managed to outguess them on many an occasion and to force them to realize England's key position in the balance of power. As might be expected, this policy called for war, and war in turn necessitated unusual expenditures. To meet these, Wolsey was forced to exact from parliament very heavy subsidies, and when these were not enough, he compelled the wealthy to contribute benevolences, which was but another word for forced loans. Although the English enjoyed the ever-mounting position of the state in European affairs, they groaned and complained bitterly when payment for the show was demanded. In 1525 domestic disturbances broke out and both Henry and Wolsey were compelled to stop benevolences. The nation had effectively rebuffed Henry, who immediately attempted to salvage the situation by a reorganization of foreign affairs. Peace was made with France, and a war was instituted against the Empire. Before any overt act had taken place, however, Henry was forced to modify his entire program as a result of an estrangement which had grown up between him and his queen, Katherine.

Henry Seeks a Separation from Katherine

Henry's domestic relations with Katherine had been rather happy for a number of years, during the course of which she bore him several children of whom only one, Mary, survived. Mary's birth came in 1516, approximately two years after Henry had expressed dissatisfaction with Katherine. This was due in part to misfortunes which had attended the alliance with Spain, an arrangement which Henry was all but ready to discard in August, 1514. Before the next year, however, Henry and Ferdinand were drawn more closely together as a result of an irritation which had developed between France and England. Shortly thereafter Katherine presented Henry with the Princess Mary, a fact which cheered him to believe that a son might still be born. By 1519 it was evident that his hope would never be realized. From this time on Henry became more and more concerned with the question of a royal heir. Possibly, he argued, he had sinned against God in having married his dead brother's wife, a conjecture which had arisen in the mind of Henry VII in 1503. A papal dispensation at the time had removed the canonical difficulties but had not eliminated all doubt in the mind of Pope Julius II, who had reluctantly given his consent to the marriage. Small wonder, therefore, for so penetrating a theologian as Henry to reason that God had punished him for having violated the sacrament of marriage. Even then it is quite likely that Henry would not have been disturbed if Mary had been a boy. The prospect of bequeathing the throne to a woman was as displeasing to the nation as it was to Henry. No woman as yet had been Queen of England, and were Mary to be the first there would, in all probability, have been disorder if not civil war. Political considerations, therefore, argued most convincingly for a male heir and this seemed to demand another marriage. Conscientious motives, however, became the screen behind which the King concealed his real desires. It was decidedly unfair to Henry to insist that his passion for Anne Boleyn was the determining factor, as kings before Henry's time had been known to keep mistresses, and Anne had been all of that for the past two years. Fundamentally, the future of the Tudor dynasty rested upon a legitimate heir and not upon an unlawful child which Henry might have of Anne, or upon the Duke of Richmond, the son of Henry VIII and Elizabeth Blount.

Convinced of the justice of his case, Henry let it be known in April, 1527, that he intended to ask Rome for a separation on the technical ground of having erred in marrying his dead brother's wife. If Clement VII could be made to accept this view, a decree of separation was all that was needed to satisfy Henry's desires. Clement's hands, however, were tied by the recent victory won by Katherine's nephew Charles, the ruler of the Holy Roman Empire. With Clement a virtual prisoner of Charles, the efforts of the English agents at Rome were practically nullified. What Clement might have done if conditions had been different, no one knows; though in the light of a recent papal dispensation permitting the Duke of Suffolk to separate from his wife on grounds much like those of Henry, it is likely that the King would have gained his ends. Marriage ties in those days were not so binding that political or personal considerations could not weigh more than the canons of the Church. Regardless of what might have happened, Clement, faced by Imperial troops, could only permit an investigation of the case to take place. Accordingly, Cardinals Campeggio and Wolsey were commissioned to hold court in England. Acting under secret instructions Campeggio delayed proceedings and finally transferred the case to Rome for final settlement. To Henry this amounted to defeat. Believing Wolsey to be the responsible party, he proceeded to wreck the subsequent life of his great minister. Charges of having violated the Statute of Praemunire were presented against the Cardinal; and in spite of the latter's contention that what he had done had been undertaken at the King's request, Wolsey had his property confiscated. Moreover, he was dismissed from royal service.

Henry Breaks with Rome

Having failed to gain a separation through diplomatic channels, Henry now instituted economic and religious pressure upon Rome in the hope of forcing Clement to yield. Parliament, summoned in 1529, immediately passed measures affecting the position of Rome. Non-residence of clergy was forbidden, as was the practice of allowing ecclesiastics to violate the canons of the Church through papal dispensations. Parliament likewise empowered Henry to withhold all future payments of annates, and Henry believed this would bring Clement to his senses. In the meantime the clergy of England had been compelled in convocation to admit that the King was the supreme head of the Church in England so far as the law of Christ allowed. While this qualifying phrase may have soothed the injured feelings of the clerics, few, if any, doubted that Henry would interpret the Master's laws as he saw fit. Although disturbed over these actions, Clement refused to be coerced and Henry came to realize that only through his own actions might he win his objective. Accordingly, he determined to have the affair settled in England; and having gained the appointment of his friend Cranmer to the vacant see of Canterbury, Henry commissioned the Archbishop to begin trial. Personal considerations then forced him to marry Anne secretly in January, 1533; and in May of the same year Katherine's marriage was pronounced null and void by Cranmer. When news of these proceedings reached Rome, the Pope hastened to declare Henry excommunicated, though it was not until 1538 that the bull was formally published.

Henry's separation from Rome, commonly called a divorce, has attracted far more attention than it should. The event has been interpreted by many as the sole cause for the break between the Catholic church in England and that of Rome. To others, it has appeared only as an important antecedent. An impartial examination of the evidence at hand shows that the divorce was but a minor episode and that the appearance of the Church of England depended on far more important considerations. Powerful as Henry was, no fundamental change could have taken place unless the minds and attitudes of his subjects were ready for a change.

The Antecedents of the Reformation

Of the forces which paved the way for the Reformation, probably the most important was the development of English nationalism. This force revealed itself in two ways. First, it may be seen in the growth of opposition to Rome as a foreign state which was seeking to impose its authority over purely domestic affairs. The fourteenth-century anti-papal legislation, the popular support of Wycliffe and Lollardism, and the hostility against absentee clerics who drew ample incomes from English holdings may be advanced as proof of this contention. Nor should one overlook the natural stiffening of Englishmen against all outsiders as they became conscious of their own national life. The Church in England from the earliest times had been extremely provincial in its relation to Rome, and while it always considered itself a part of the universal Church, it was nevertheless strongly saturated with local independence. Not that its laity or priests wished to depart from the creed or faith of Rome, but they aimed at self-government in all things which were distinctly English.

Closely akin to nationalism as a factor in producing the religious upheaval in England was the failure of Rome to democratize its government. Throughout the late thirteenth century and the two which followed, governments everywhere were experimenting with liberal ideas. In France had appeared the States General; in Germany, the Diet; in England, Parliament; in Spain, the future Cortes; and even in Italy itself, local assemblies known as the *parlimento* had arisen. Manifestations of this tendency cropped out within the Church in what is commonly called the Conciliar Movement. The endeavor to substitute a church council for the Pope as the supreme authority in ecclesiastical matters reached its height in the Councils of Pisa and Constance. However, those who favored domination by a single head, the Pope, successfully combated this movement. In consequence there was enthroned at St. Peters a conservative philosophy which was none too kindly disposed toward those who wished to have a voice in the determination of policy. Had there been an international council in control of the Church in the sixteenth century, it is quite possible that there would have been no violent Reformation.

Most certainly there would have been a reform in respect to existing abuses. A more pristine tone among the clerics would have been insisted upon, while the sale of church offices and sacraments would have been checked if not abolished. Frauds in the widespread use of relics and the temporal domination of the priest over his parish would have been eliminated. Greater attention would have been paid to religious and secular instruction, and the social gospel of Christ would have been preached and practiced. All these results were ultimately realized by Rome and surely would have been attained much earlier if the humanistic ideas of the Renaissance had been given a free hand. The spirit of humanism with its unflinching devotion to scientific methodology would have rectified error without having destroyed the universal organization or creed of the Church. Many of the finest minds among the Renaissance leaders never broke with Rome. Of these, Erasmus and Sir Thomas More might be cited as examples, yet these men honestly desired a purification of the Church.

On the other hand humanism did lead many to challenge doctrine. Possessing themselves of the original sources, students critically examined the Bible, the writings of the Church Fathers and the early pronouncements of Rome. As a result they not only pointed to the abuses in Church government and doctrine but also cast definite doubt upon the validity of both. Where, they asked, was there any authority for the temporal power of the Church? Had not Christ stated "Render . . . unto Caesar the things which are Caesar's and unto God the things that are God's"? Had not the astronomical findings of Galileo and Copernicus established a concept of the genesis of the universe, the world, and man different from that depicted in the Old Testament? By what interpretation could an individual cling to the belief of the corporeal presence of Christ in the Lord's Supper or of the sacredness of a priestly caste? Europeans in large numbers, as well as Englishmen, were raising these questions and giving to them their own answers. Wycliffe had pointed the way in the fourteenth century, and the effects of Lollardism had smoldered long after the heretic burnings of Henry IV and V had been forgotten.

On the Continent, John Huss had spread unrest by his teachings; and Martin Luther of Germany had set his country on fire by his contest with Rome. In England, Lutheran ideas were advanced privately and publicly. Tracts and discourses flooded the land faster than the hangman or fires could eliminate them. Bishop after bishop was annoyed by unorthodox utterances on the part of laity and cleric, and no amount of admonishment or punishment could stop the growth of these heretical views. Henry himself sought to check the movement by his memorable volume in defense of the sacraments. Yet he and his minister Wolsey, together with stout defenders like Gardiner and Foxe, were unable to undo the change which had affected many of the people. The seeds planted by the Renaissance, by nationalism, and by an aversion to the worldly practices of Rome had prepared the minds of Englishmen for a new order. The Reformation, in short, was an accomplished fact long before Henry became concerned over the future of his dynasty or before he ever set eyes on Anne Boleyn. If one judges this monarch correctly, the conclusion is borne home most convincingly that Henry could never have led his people away from Rome unless they were ready for the move and unless he knew of their desires. Seldom, indeed, did Henry or any of the Tudors force upon their subjects anything for which they had not shown a decided inclination in advance.

The English Reformation under Henry VIII

Bolstered by public opinion, Henry in 1534 persuaded parliament to end papal authority in England and to declare him the supreme head of the Church within the realm. Another act stopped all money payments to Rome, and another established the heirs of Henry and Anne as the only lawful successors to the throne. All statements as to the King's being a heretic, infidel, or usurper were declared treasonable. In the meantime royal agents had been exacting an oath of submission to the recent acts of succession and supremacy. Many subscribed to this requirement, though there were some, notably Sir Thomas More and Bishop Fisher, who would not. Neither of these two men questioned the right of parliament to pass these measures or their being the law of the land. On the other hand both strongly objected to the oath, for by subscribing to it, they would have denied the spiritual headship of the Pope, and this their consciences would not allow. Acts of attainder were accordingly passed by parliament against these men who shortly thereafter were executed for having disobeyed the laws of England. Neither of the men had been convicted of treason by a court. An act of attainder merely declared them to be traitors; and as treason was punishable by death, they met their fate. Others were also put to death for the same reason.

Determined to stamp out all vestiges of papal power, Henry in 1536 and again in 1539 secured parliamentary authority for the suppression of both the greater and lesser monasteries. A recent investigation of these houses by Wolsey and later by Cromwell, who had risen to the office of chancellor by reason of his loyalty to Henry, revealed that many an institution had fallen into moral and physical decay. On the other hand this was not true of the great majority, and a series of remedial measures could have rectified existing abuses. Henry, however, was in dire need of money, and had undertaken the examination for fiscal purposes as well as to destroy this center of papal sympathy. As a result of these acts several thousand inmates were driven from their holdings and an even greater number of dependents were ejected from their former occupations. A few of these unfortunates were compensated from the funds gained from confiscation. Henry himself retained only a small part for himself; the bulk he distributed in the form of land to the nobility, who, by accepting it, identified themselves with the future success of the King's program. The destruction of the monasteries had two other results.   In

Courtesy Assoc. British and Irish Railways, Inc.

THE WEST FRONT, ABBEY CHURCH, BATH. One of the last pre-Reformation churches. Note the magnificent window, flanked by turrets, on which are carved ladders with angels ascending.

northern England, an armed revolt commonly called the Pilgrimage of Grace may be traced to Henry's act. In the House of Lords the number of clerical seats available was reduced, for all priors and abbots were deprived of membership. Henry also destroyed a number of shrines, notably that of Thomas Becket at Canterbury, since as long as they existed they would be a constant reminder of Rome. At the same time their abolition brought Henry a goodly income.

With the authority of the Pope expelled, with the monasteries in ruins, and with a generous number executed, Henry's position was made relatively secure. On the other hand considerable misgivings had arisen as to doctrinal matters as well as to individual beliefs in respect to the King's morality. Henry, it seems, had become disappointed in Anne, owing to her inability to produce a son though she had blessed him with a daughter, Elizabeth. Once more, therefore, conscientious scruples were advanced to conceal his real desire to have a male heir. Accordingly, Anne was convicted of infidelity and was beheaded in May, 1536. In the same month Henry married Jane Seymour, while parliament proceeded to declare Elizabeth illegitimate, as had been done earlier in respect to Mary. A year later, Edward VI was born. The combined effects of these marriages and of the repressive acts of parliament argued strongly for a settlement of doctrinal matters. To meet this need Henry gained from convocation the Ten Articles, the tenor of which was clearly orthodox Catholicism. Luther's idea of justification by faith, however, was accorded a place, while several Roman practices, like prayers for the dead, were modified. Moderate Romanists and Protestants might accept these articles without mental reservations. All in all Henry had acted wisely. He had not offended the religious convictions of most of his subjects, and he had kept faith with his own theological views. In 1539 appeared further doctrinal changes known as the Six Articles, which reaffirmed the catholicity of the English Church. Transubstantiation, for example, was decidedly stressed, and denial of the doctrine was punishable by death. Shortly thereafter appeared an

English translation of the Bible which together with a new service book, likewise in English and known as the King's Primer, was to be used by all the clergy. These later pronouncements showed clearly how loyal Henry was to the faith and creed of his birth and how lightly he intended to tread in Protestant fields. Protestant adherents, however much they found fault with the Six Articles, were clearly outnumbered by the great majority who applauded Henry's religious settlement.

In the meantime Jane Seymour had died, and Cromwell, anxious to promote a foreign alliance with the Protestant princes of Germany, suggested that Henry marry Anne of Cleves. Always interested in the beauty of his consorts, Henry looked upon an oil painting done by the master Holbein and then nodded approval to Cromwell. After certain slight modifications in doctrinal matters had been arranged, Anne arrived in England. Then came the big disappointment. Anne turned out to be much unlike her portrait; and although Henry went through with the marriage, he hastened to secure a separation on the thin ground that she had already been engaged. Poor Cromwell was then brought to trial for having favored Protestantism and for having encroached upon royal authority. A verdict of guilty was pronounced and Cromwell suffered death. A little later Henry married Catherine Howard but hurried her to the block in 1542 on charges of conduct unbecoming a queen. The next year he married Catherine Parr, who so mothered the King that he could find no possible flaw in her conduct. This was Henry's last matrimonial adventure.

With Cromwell out of the way, Henry tried to govern England himself. With a strong arm the King firmly checked all attempts of Rome and its followers to regain control; at the same time he remained loyal to the historical catholicity of the English Church. It should be noticed, however, that Protestantism was slowly gaining ground, thanks to the efforts of Cranmer and other prominent divines. Had Henry been younger, it is likely that he would have sensed the danger of these extreme anti-papal movements. As it was, he had grown somewhat sluggish. His former trim and athletic figure was now covered with excessive weight and his entire system was undermined by labor and disease. By the fall of 1546 he had to take to his bed, where he died January 28, 1547. Henry's life had been extremely strenuous. His indomitable courage and his keen sense of what the nation desired had carried him through many a storm. Rome had been ejected and the Church of England had been made subject to the Crown. On the other hand the Church was certainly not Protestant, and Henry today would rise from his grave to wreak vengeance upon anyone who dared say that he had founded the Church of England. To him that Church was distinctly Catholic.

GENEALOGICAL TABLES OF THE TUDORS
AND ALLIED FAMILIES

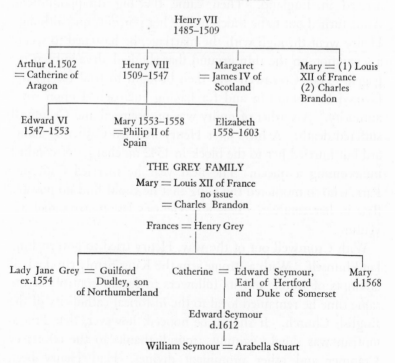

Henry VII
1485–1509

Arthur d.1502
= Catherine of
Aragon

Henry VIII
1509–1547

Margaret
= James IV of
Scotland

Mary = (1) Louis
XII of France
(2) Charles
Brandon

Edward VI
1547–1553

Mary 1553–1558
=Philip II of
Spain

Elizabeth
1558–1603

THE GREY FAMILY

Mary = Louis XII of France
no issue
= Charles Brandon

Frances = Henry Grey

Lady Jane Grey = Guilford
ex.1554   Dudley, son
of Northumberland

Catherine = Edward Seymour,
Earl of Hertford
and Duke of Somerset

Mary
d.1568

Edward Seymour
d.1612

William Seymour = Arabella Stuart

THE STUART DYNASTY

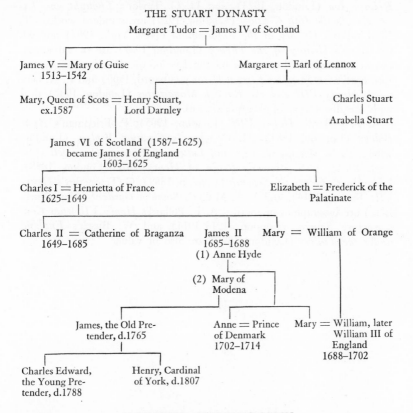

Margaret Tudor = James IV of Scotland

James V = Mary of Guise
1513–1542

Margaret = Earl of Lennox

Mary, Queen of Scots = Henry Stuart,
ex.1587   Lord Darnley

Charles Stuart

Arabella Stuart

James VI of Scotland (1587–1625)
became James I of England
1603–1625

Charles I = Henrietta of France
1625–1649

Elizabeth = Frederick of the
Palatinate

Charles II = Catherine of Braganza
1649–1685

James II   Mary = William of Orange
1685–1688
(1) Anne Hyde

(2) Mary of
Modena

James, the Old Pre-
tender, d.1765

Anne = Prince
of Denmark
1702–1714

Mary = William, later
William III of
England
1688–1702

Charles Edward,
the Young Pre-
tender, d.1788

Henry, Cardinal
of York, d.1807

SELECTED BIBLIOGRAPHY

For an appreciation of the Renaissance J. Burckardt's *Civilization of the Period of the Renaissance in Italy* (London, 1878) is of considerable value. J. A. Symond's *Renaissance in Italy* (New York, 1878–1888); A. Hyma's *Christian Renaissance* (Grand Rapids, 1924); F. Seebohm's *Oxford Reformers* (London, 1914); L. Einstein's *Italian Renaissance in England* (New York, 1902); W. H. Hutton's *Sir Thomas More* (London, 1895); J. H. Lupton's *Life of John Colet* (London, 1887); P. S. Allen's *Age of Erasmus* (Oxford, 1914), and P. Smith's *Erasmus* (London, 1923) stress the intellectual and social aspects of the Renaissance.

Some of the above-mentioned works have pertinent material on the Reformation. In addition F. J. C. Hearnshaw's *Social and Political Ideas of . . . the Renaissance and Reformation* (London, 1925); F. A. Gasquet's *Eve of the Reformation* (London, 1913); P. Smith's *Age of the Reformation* (London, 1920); R. S. Arrowsmith's *Prelude to the*

Reformation (London, 1923), and H. O. Taylor's *Thought and Expression in the 16th Century* (London, 1920) are standard works. T. M. Lindsay's *History of the Reformation* (New York, 1907) and M. Creighton's *History of the Papacy* (London, 1901) are of value. A. Savine's "English Monasteries on the Eve of the Dissolution" in *Oxford Studies in Social and Legal History* (Oxford, 1909) and F. A. Gasquet's *Henry VIII and the English Monasteries* (London, 1902) deal with the dissolution of the monasteries.

A. F. Pollard's *Henry VIII* (London, 1905); P. Friedman's *Anne Boleyn* (London, 1884); M. Creighton's *Cardinal Wolsey* (London, 1888); R. B. Merriman's *Life and Letters of Thomas Cromwell* (Oxford, 1902); J. S. Brewer's *Reign of Henry VIII* (London, 1888); J. Gairdner's *Henry the Seventh* (London, 1889); G. Temperley's *Henry VII* (Boston, 1914), and J. A. Muller's *Stephen Gardner* (New York, 1926) are biographies of merit. A. F. Pollard's *Henry VII from Contemporary Sources* (London, 1913–1914) and W. Busch's *England under the Tudors* (London, 1895) are also of value.

CHAPTER XV

The Religious Settlement

Protestantism Gains Ground

THE government of England, upon the death of Henry VIII, passed to a Council of Regency headed by Edward Seymour, Earl of Hertford, and later, Duke of Somerset. Had Edward VI been of age, this arrangement would not have been necessary; but sensing the difficulties involved Henry had entrusted affairs to a hand-picked council which was to rule England during the minority of his son. Fate was exceedingly unkind to the young King, as he died in 1553 at the early age of sixteen. During his short life he displayed a keen mind and frequently confounded his advisers by his knowledge and grasp of government. What the future might have brought England had this promising prince lived, no one knows, though it is well established that his youth permitted Somerset and later Northumberland to lead the realm into no end of trouble. This was due in part to the individual eccentricities of these leaders, to a lack of vision on their part, and to the appearance of disturbances in the economic structure of the nation. Personal ambition helped to complicate the situation, though the religious attitude of Englishmen during this age was probably the greatest single factor contributing to the difficulties.

When Henry died in 1547, the religious complexion of the realm did not differ much from what it had been at the opening of the century. With the notable exception of the repudiation of papal authority and one or two other matters such as the destruction of the monasteries, the appearance of the King's Primer, and the modified prayers for the dead, the doctrine of the English Church was predominantly Catholic. To those who remained loyal to Rome, the repudiation of the Pope, of course, amounted to a complete denial of Catholic doctrine. The Henrician settlement was acceptable to the great majority of the English people though it was not in accordance with the wishes of either the orthodox papists or the followers of Protestantism. Here, then, was a problem which called for the most careful handling; and the first acts of the new government seemingly indicated that caution would be used. The Six Articles were repealed, as were the old heresy laws of the fifteenth century, while much that constituted treason under Henry VIII was removed. Catholic and Protestant alike benefited by these changes, though neither was particularly pleased with the gains made by the other.

It was evident, however, to those who had accepted the Henrician settlement that Somerset and his followers were bent on making the English Church more Protestant than Catholic, and in this they were not mistaken. Gardiner, Bishop of Winchester, may be cited as one who was greatly disturbed over the action of the Council. The well-known attitudes of Cranmer, Bishop Latimer, and other divines convinced the supporters of Henry's policies that the repeal of the Six Articles only foreshadowed an influx of radical views. In addition, a steady stream of aliens, all heavily saturated with Lutheranism, Calvinism, and Zwinglianism poured into the kingdom to seek refuge from religious persecution on the Continent. The government not only extended to them a cordial welcome but proceeded to advance their cause during the summer of 1547 by advocating a simpler ritual, by a further desecration of shrines, by completing the destruction of chantries, and by forbidding such practices as the use of Holy water, candles, and the like. Considerable consternation followed in the wake of these actions. Moreover, when Gardiner and Bonner, Bishop of London, protested, Somerset sought to silence them by assigning them quarters in the Tower.

"THE TOWER" AND TOWER BRIDGE. A grim fortress, which has been in continuous use since William the Conqueror had it built to control the London citizenry.

Further evidence as to what might be expected came in January, 1549, in the appearance of an Act of Uniformity, which forced upon all the clergy the use of a Book of Common Prayer. Public opinion did not take kindly to this innovation, which clearly revealed the Protestant hand of Cranmer. The reaction which followed coincided, moreover, with certain economic upheavals and led to an armed rebellion during the summer of the same year. Although Somerset sympathized with the rioters on economic grounds, he was compelled to put them down by force. Somerset's attitude in time led to a rift with Northumberland, who championed the cause of the landed class. In addition a quarrel was provoked in the Council over Somerset's conduct of foreign affairs. As a result Somerset was ousted and lodged for safekeeping in the Tower. Later, in 1552, he was executed.

With Somerset out of the way, Northumberland at once indicated that a more liberal religious program was to be followed. Coöperating closely with Cranmer, Northumberland persuaded parliament in 1552 to pass a second Act of Uniformity, which imposed upon the laity as well as the clergy a revised Book of Common Prayer. In drafting this volume Cranmer had communicated with Gardiner, who stoutly defended the Catholicism of Henry's days. Cranmer, however, refused to adhere to the position which he had championed during the life of his benefactor and threw his influence largely to the cause of Protestantism. As a result, practically every item in the first prayer book which Gardiner had approved as historically sound in doctrine was left out of the Second Book of Common Prayer. To illustrate, the earlier volume had asserted that the whole body of Christ was present in each piece of bread while the new book contained the very significant words "Take and eat this, in remembrance that Christ died for thee." The memorial aspect of the Lord's Supper had supplanted the sacrificial feature of the sacrament. The words "altar" and "priest," moreover, were changed to "table" and "minister," while the prayer of Humble Access, so important to English Catholics, was placed before the consecration. Shocking as these innovations were to those who resisted the swing toward radicalism, what annoyed them more were the severe penalties imposed for nonobservance of the Prayer Book. Additional definition as to the faith of the Church appeared in June, 1553, in the form of the Forty-two Articles, which incidentally never received parliamentary approval.

Lady Jane Grey

Fortunately for Gardiner and those like him, Northumberland's power did not last much longer. This was due in part to a steady wave of discontent which had spread over England against the arrogance of the government. At the same time it was evident to many that Edward's days were numbered. The King, while growing in mind, was steadily declining in physical strength. No one knew this better than Northumberland, who, anxious to perpetuate his own authority, forced the Council to vest the succession to the throne in the person of Lady Jane Grey, a distant niece of Henry VIII. In doing this the Council set aside the line of succession as prescribed by the former King. According to Henry's wishes the throne was to go, in the event of Edward's dying without issue, to Mary; and were she to leave no descendants, her half-sister Elizabeth was to reign. To Northumberland and the entire Protestant group the prospect of Mary, a devoted Roman Catholic, as their ruler, conjured up in their minds visions of papal domination and worst of all, persecution and death. Northumberland, moreover, had no desire to step to one side and allow his former enemies, like Gardiner, to govern in the Council. Accordingly, having gained from that body recognition of Lady Jane Grey, he proceeded to marry her to his son Guilford Dudley. In this manner England would be spared a Catholic reaction, his own power would be kept intact, and his issue would reign one day over England. Everything was now in readiness for the expected death of Edward.

On July 6, 1553, that "godly and virtuous imp yielded up the ghost." A few days before, however, having heard of her brother's impending death and anticipating Northumberland's plan to lodge her in the Tower, Mary fled from London. Mary's escape proved to be Northumberland's undoing, though for the time being he believed that he could overcome the effects of her flight. First of all he had Lady Jane Grey proclaimed queen, though this evoked little enthusiasm from the citizens of London. Disappointed over the reception his plans had received, Northumberland marched forth to meet the Marian forces which had gathered in Suffolk and Norfolk. With the Protector out of London, courage returned to the citizens; and as reports kept pouring in of Mary's increasing strength, vocal protests were made against Lady Jane Grey. The Council, under the direction of Suffolk, father of the innocent Lady Jane Grey, sensed the inevitable, and, amid the joyful applause and illuminations of the populace of London, announced Mary as queen. Meanwhile Northumberland witnessed wholesale desertion among his troops and finally, on July 20, came out in favor of Mary. Early in the next month Mary entered London "all the streets by the way . . . standing so full of people shouting and crying 'Jesus save her Grace' with weeping eyes for joy, that like was never seen before."

Mary Restores Catholicism

Immediately Gardiner, Norfolk, and others faithful to Henry's policies were released from prison, while their places were taken by Northumberland, Lady Jane Grey, and those who had risked all on the success of the recent *coup d'etat*. Later Gardiner was made Chancellor and the government settled down to the problem of restoring order and sanity. Few monarchs ever faced so critical a task as that which confronted the daughter of Henry and Katherine. Economic conditions were none too pleasing, and there was widespread discontent among all classes. The question of a religious settlement was most pressing. Inexperienced in government,

Mary turned to her Council only to find that it was sadly divided on all questions. As a result, she frequently was forced to decide matters for herself or else follow the advice offered by Renard, the astute agent of the Emperor Charles. Had the Queen been free to do what she wished, there is no doubt that she would have restored papal authority at once and have silenced the sturdy Protestant opposition by imprisonment and persecution. However, with Cranmer deeply entrenched at Canterbury, she had to curb her desires and content herself with a parliamentary act which returned the Church to the position established by her father.

Although conservative opinion applauded this step and listened most respectfully to a solemn requiem mass by Gardiner in behalf of the dead Edward, the citizens of London in general filled the air with cries of "papist" whenever the mass was celebrated in the parish churches. Tracts and pamphlets denouncing the drift towards Rome were scattered throughout the city and kingdom. In certain sections, moreover, distinct opposition appeared; and in a few cases priests were actually convicted for having resorted to popish practices. Yet amid this show of disapproval Mary plunged the nation into great turmoil by intimating her intention to marry in the near future. No one objected to the Queen's marrying, indeed there was general sentiment in that direction. But whom would she marry? If she were to choose an Englishman of her own faith, public opinion in the main would support her decision. If on the other hand she were to pick an alien, and rumor had it that she was more than friendly towards Philip of Spain, then England was ready to protest. English nationalism violently rebelled against the idea of being tied to the cart wheel of an alien power which might lead the country into no end of trouble. Representations of these views were made to Mary by Gardiner, although he was unable to overcome the influence exerted by Renard. As a result Mary announced her determination to marry Philip and commissioned her ministers to draft a treaty to that effect. Thanks to the efforts of Gardiner, the negotiations were carried through in a way which protected English interest, but which did not remove from the mind of Mary's subjects their opposition to a foreign marriage. This feeling was clearly shown when the boys of London showered snowballs upon the Spanish ambassador on his arrival in the city, in January, 1554. Further ill will was shown by the desertion of Sir Peter Carew, a prominent member of the nobility, from London and by the news that he and others, notably Suffolk and Sir Thomas Wyatt, were about ready to raise the standard of revolt.

English Opposition to Mary's Foreign Policy

Of these men only Wyatt made any headway, and by February 6, 1554, he was actually within London. Fortunately for Mary, the city refused to support Wyatt; and finding himself trapped by the royal forces, he surrendered. Wyatt, without ignoring religious issues, had built his hopes upon the opposition to the Queen's foreign policy. The fact that he all but succeeded in unseating Mary is convincing proof that the nation strongly resented her Spanish alliance. Nor did the public execution of Wyatt and some fifty others implicated in the late rebellion do much to quiet the existing unrest. Lady Jane Grey and her group of conspirators suffered death at the same time, while a determined effort to remove Elizabeth failed only because the latter had cleverly refused to be a partner to Wyatt's revolt.

Further signs of discontent were registered upon Philip's arrival in England and upon the restoration of papal authority in November, 1554. At that time Cardinal Pole, a relative of Mary, formally received England back into the fold of the Roman Church. Parliament obediently repealed all measures which had been passed against the papacy and reëstablished, in January, 1555, the laws against heresy. It seems reasonable to assume, therefore, that national opinion was more concerned in 1554 and 1555 with Mary's foreign policy than with her religious program. It should be noted, however, that the Pope's request for the restoration of confiscated church property, particularly in respect to the monasteries, occasioned strong opposition. Mary endeavored to carry out the papal program but found that even the Roman Catholic lords, who had profited by the destruction of the monasteries and chantries, refused to return this property. Loyal as these lords were to Mary and Rome, they were quite unwilling to restore what they had received from Henry VIII.

Although England was not inclined to rebel against the restoration of papal authority, there was an active minority who were determined to resist Rome to the utmost. Keenly aware of the consequences, this group launched its attack. Thanks to the key positions held by their leaders, Cranmer, Ridley, and Latimer (to mention but a few), they believed that something might be accomplished. In any event, even though they might suffer death, they permitted no doubt to exist in the minds of the English people as to the sincerity of their motives. Accordingly, abuse and ridicule was hurled by these Protestants on every occasion. They expected to receive no quarter and were equally unwilling to offer any to their foes. Toleration, religious or political, had no place in their program so far as it concerned the followers of Rome.

The Marian Persecution

To Mary, this position was quite understandable. Heresy, to her, was not only treason to the state but was an unpardonable crime in the eyes of the Church and God. Accordingly, she girded herself for a holy war against these Protestants and asked for no favors or consideration. She, too, did not know the meaning of the word "toleration." Religious motives alone, however, do not explain the dreadful persecutions which followed. Had reason alone dictated, she might have been more lenient; but her heart also was wrapped up in the entire affair. To her great sorrow and shame, Philip proved to be the most neglectful of husbands. He had visited England in the summer of 1554 to become Mary's husband; but after several months, during which he witnessed constant rioting in London between his attendants and the citizens, he returned to the Continent. His desertion, plus the fact that her fondest hopes of having a child never materialized, preyed upon her mind day and night. Finally she came to believe that Philip's prolonged absence and the lack of an heir was nothing short of a punishment inflicted upon her by God for not having stamped out heresy in England. None of her advisers were willing to go so far as she wished, since their idea was to pursue a mild program of persecution in the hope of convincing others either to be quiet or else to leave the realm. Mary, however, would not harken to earthly counsel and frequently upbraided them for their reluctance to follow her plans.

The Marian persecutions respected neither rank, wealth, nor birth. Humble individuals in town and country bravely faced trial and death, as did nobles and ecclesiastics. Probably the most important of her victims were Bishops Latimer and Ridley and the aged primate, Cranmer. Fearful of the consequences if their trial were held in London, Mary had them transferred to Oxford. Here they were tried; and on October 16, 1555, Latimer and Ridley were publicly burned. Although the following quotation has appeared many times, its significance warrants repetition: "Be of good comfort, Master Ridley," cried Latimer as the flames mounted high, "we shall this day light such a candle by God's grace in England as, I trust, shall never be put out." Several months later Cranmer was brought to the stake. During the course of his trial and confinement Cranmer's mind became distinctly shaken by reason of his infirmity and his fear of execution. Accordingly, he often signed recantations in an effort to save himself, but at the last moment he boldly repudiated these statements and walked bravely to his death.

Mary's religious program was doomed to failure. It was manifestly impossible to carry on persecution forever, as sooner or later England was bound to turn against the Queen. Equally disastrous was her foreign policy. For this she had to thank her unreliable husband, who in the spring of 1557 paid England a fleeting visit. Before his departure, however, he had persuaded his wife to forget the terms of the marriage agreement and to join with him in a war against France. Public opinion frankly resented this violation of the law of the land and held Mary responsible for the French capture of Calais in January, 1558. This was the last Continental holding of England; its loss was a severe blow to English pride and was keenly felt by Mary. On top of this came the news that France and Scotland had formed an alliance through the marriage of Mary Stuart and Francis, the Dauphin. Worn out by repeated disasters, by the neglect of her husband, and by her inability to stamp out heresy, Mary contracted a malignant fever, which was sweeping England, and died November 17, 1588. Mary's cardinal sin was not born of her fanatical devotion to Rome but rather of her ill-fated alliance with Philip of Spain. Had she followed Gardiner's advice and married an English Romanist, it seems likely that her reign would have been far less troublesome. As it was, she accepted the counsel of a foreigner who was concerned solely in advancing the fortunes of his Empire. Her decision to marry Philip led directly to Wyatt's rebellion, to an unhappy domestic life, and to a failure in foreign affairs. Had she lived longer no one knows what might have happened, but her death certainly was received by most Englishmen as a blessing and not a misfortune.

Finally, it should be noted that during the Marian regime a large number of Englishmen, lay and ecclesiastic alike, had fled to Switzerland for safety. Here they came in contact with Calvinism, which was an extreme form of Protestantism. Upon Mary's death these exiles flocked back home, bringing with them religious concepts which account in part for many of the domestic problems which afflicted the nation during the course of the next one hundred years. Elizabeth herself had to deal with these extremists after she ascended the throne, though the early part of her reign was concerned chiefly with undoing her sister's Roman program.

Elizabeth's Early Life

Prior to 1558, Elizabeth's life had been crowded with many misfortunes. To begin with, her birth had not pleased her father, who had risked all for the sake of a male heir. Shortly thereafter her mother was beheaded, while she herself was exiled from the court and publicly proclaimed illegitimate. During the remainder of her father's life and that of her brother, Elizabeth was placed in the hands of near relatives who saw to it that she received a liberal education. Thanks to her tutors, who were carefully selected, Elizabeth soon became proficient in Greek, Latin, French, and Italian. At the age of eleven, her skill was shown in an Italian letter written to Catherine Parr and in an English translation of a book written by Margaret of France. She also acquired a keen knowledge of both Catholic and Protestant creeds and became something of an artist on the flute and violin. About this time she became exposed to the rather degrading court life which had followed in the wake of Henry's matrimonial ventures. As a result she had a most unfortunate experience with Thomas Seymour, brother of Somerset. Much of the coarseness which characterized Elizabeth's later speech and mannerisms may be credited to the unhappy experiences of her youth.

Upon Mary's accession to the throne in 1553, Elizabeth was summoned to Court, where she was given an opportunity of identifying herself with the Catholic program of her sister. To have refused to comply with Mary's request for a frank espousal of the Roman faith would have brought down upon the Princess exile and persecution. Elizabeth therefore proceeded with great caution. While appearing with Mary at mass, she did so in a manner which revealed that her endorsement was not of her own free will. Although she was disappointed over this action, Mary could find no fault with Elizabeth's outward conformity. She was more than pleased to allow her more attractive sister and heir to leave Court in 1553. The following year the two women were thrown violently together as a result of Wyatt's rebellion, which had as an objective the seating of Elizabeth on the throne. This fact was clearly established during the course of Wyatt's trial, but when confronted with this evidence Elizabeth refused to admit that she had been a partner to the conspiracy. Nor were the secret-service men of Mary able in any way to present proof to the contrary. Unable to convict her sister, Mary allowed her to retire to the country, where, except for a forced visit in 1555, Elizabeth remained until the Queen's death in November, 1558.

The Elizabethan Religious Settlement

Among the many problems which faced Elizabeth as she took over the reins of government, probably the most pressing was that relating to religion. As might be expected, the daughter of Anne Boleyn aimed at the expulsion of the Roman Church and at the restoration of the English Church to the position it enjoyed under her father. Measures to this end were introduced in her first parliament, which sat from late January to early May of 1559. On the basis of the acts then passed, the government of the Church was lodged in the Queen as the supreme governor. The term "supreme head," which had been used by her father, was thus modified in a way which appeased the English Romanists. The Act of Supremacy, however, revived a number of Henry's laws, among which was one that expressly stated the "royal majesty is and hath always been by the Word of God, Supreme Head on earth of the Church of England." Thus the obnoxious word "head" was retained, thereby giving Elizabeth power as complete as that which her father had enjoyed. Elizabeth, however, never paraded this act or title. The Act of Supremacy provided also that the laity were to receive both the bread and wine at communion. This was distinctly opposed to the Roman practice of limiting the laity to the bread.

Public worship was defined by an Act of Uniformity which provided for the use of a revised edition of the Second Prayer Book of Edward VI. The tone of this volume was exceedingly moderate, as its author, who was chiefly Elizabeth, aimed at conciliation rather than irritation. In no way was this better illustrated than in the passages devoted to the Lord's Supper. In Edward's prayer book the minister had been required to say in giving the bread, "Take and eat this, in remembrance that Christ died for thee," and in presenting the wine to say, "Drink this in remembrance that Christ's blood was shed for thee." Elizabeth's prayers, however, enjoined the use of the following: "The Body of our Lord Jesus Christ, which was given for thee. . . . Take and eat this in remembrance that Christ died for thee," and "The Blood of our Lord Jesus Christ which was shed for thee." The interpretations which were put upon these new words were at least three in number. First of all, the Protestants claimed that the memorial aspect predominated, while the English Romanists added that the real presence of Christ was established by the opening words "The Body" and "The Blood" of the Saviour. Clearly Elizabeth had drafted a formula which offended neither group; and if asked as to its meaning, she could have answered "Christ was the word that spake it, He took the bread and brake it; and what his words did make it, That I believe and take it."

Less ambiguity existed in the provisions relating to vestments, for here Elizabeth showed a decided preference for Protestant practices. She forbade the elaborate costuming typical of Mary's days; and in general the greater clergy were limited to the use of a rochet, occasionally a cope, while the lesser clergy seldom went beyond a simple surplice. Moderation had been Elizabeth's prime motive. She wished to offend no one and at the same time establish a church which could demand and secure the loyalty of her subjects. Later, in 1563, convocation adopted the Thirty-Nine Articles which became the law of the land by parliamentary sanction eight years after. In these articles the same middle course was sought. Protestants favored them because of the rejection of papal rites and for the acceptance of certain ideas like predestination. Catholics likewise found them worth while for their retention of historical practices and ceremonies and for the insistence upon a sacerdotal hierarchy. The Elizabethan settlement, by way of summary, provided first, for the entire repudiation of papal authority; second, for the establishment of the Crown as the supreme authority over the Church; third, for the transfer of ecclesiastical legislation from convocation to the Crown; fourth, for the setting up of a body known as the Court of High Commission, which was to have jurisdiction over all ecclesiastical offenses; fifth, for the use of one prayer book which clearly denied to Catholics and extreme Protestants freedom of public worship; and sixth, for excessive fines and penalties for nonattendance at church or for violation of the various laws.

The Elizabethan settlement did not of course please everybody. Extreme Romanists and Protestants found fault time after time, and upon these the government visited persecution and punishment. Elizabeth, however, resorted to the latter only when other ways had failed. She frankly admitted that scores and scores of honest people would differ as to items, great and small, and from these she sought only outward conformity. She had no desire to pry open the windows of her subjects and see what was going on within. As one writer has put it, "She wished no one to be molested who did not go out of his way to invite it." The justification of her policy and wisdom was to be seen centuries later when the Church of England had become not merely the state church but the church of most Englishmen. During her reign, however, a large number of the greater clergymen and a much smaller percentage of the local priests resigned their charges rather than desert Rome. Vacancies were speedily filled. The papal bull of excommunication, which was found nailed to the door of the residence of the Bishop of London in 1570, evoked no uprising which seriously endangered either Elizabeth or England. Zealous Romanists who sought to stir up domestic strife were confronted by a fresh batch of parliamentary acts which nullified their endeavors. Persecution and death were meted out to a few, like Campion; but these and all others who felt the weight of Elizabeth's strong arm had to thank only the Pope for what befell them. In self-defense England was bound to retaliate against Rome and her Jesuit priests, and if a few suffered death it was due to those who had ordered them to treasonable attacks against the state.

Towards the extreme Protestants Elizabeth was never so harsh as she was to the followers of Rome. Had the latter refrained from their unwarranted interference in English affairs, it may be that the lot of the former would have been less happy. Protestant and Anglican alike could unite against Rome, and as long as there was danger from Rome less attention was necessary for Calvinists or Presbyterians. When the Armada of 1588 had spent its strength and the Catholic peril was over, the government was called upon to deal with the Protestants. Most of the latter believed that Henry and Elizabeth had not gone far enough in the reformation of the Church. Anything that smacked of Romanism, especially as to ritual, ornamentation, or vestments, was contrary to the ideas of these extremists. In general they were known as Puritans, though it should be borne in mind that at no time was there a Puritan Church. Puritanism was nothing more than a state of mind on the part of a goodly number of people who wished the Church of England to be purified of Roman practices. There was also the Calvinist group, which religiously sought to insist upon the tenets of John Calvin even to the point of withdrawing from the Anglican Church. For this reason they were known as Separatists. They were staunch believers in the doctrines of predestination and of the complete equality of man in all avenues of life. Their scheme of church organization was essentially democratic in that the choice of ministers rested with the congregations, while all government centered in a series of assemblies graduated from the local parish to larger units. In striking contrast to this group were those Puritans who did not wish to leave the English Church, but who did desire a more simple service.

To meet the attack of the Separatists and of the milder Puritans, Elizabeth instructed her government to enforce the Act of Uniformity; and when this failed, parliament obediently passed several measures forbidding Protestants to assemble in what were called conventicles. Persecution and death were meted out to the violators of the law, though it is to the credit of Elizabeth that her policy of oppression was much less severe than that of Mary. Fundamentally, the persecution which had existed in England since the days of Henry VII rested upon the time-honored assumption that religious dissent was treasonable. This had been the basis upon which the Roman Church had operated during the medieval period; hence it became part of the historical heritage of Protestantism. Freedom to believe as one wished had no place in the religious philosophy of Rome. Toleration, in other words, did not exist. Elizabeth's attitude, however, differed in that it respected the individual's conscience. Public exercise of dissenting views, on the other hand, was strictly forbidden, as nothing but the Established Church was to function. A limited form of toleration, therefore, existed under the Elizabethan settlement. Further progress could not be made as long as Protestant and Catholic aimed at the destruction of the state church. Not until the central government felt itself strong enough in popular esteem to ignore the religious practices of minority groups could anything like toleration be granted. Secular considerations rather than religious motives underlay Elizabeth's policies towards Protestant and Catholic. Man's spiritual salvation actually depended upon himself, and Elizabeth forced her subjects to follow where she led only because in her own mind the future welfare of the state was bound up with uniformity. Nevertheless, she had taken a step in the direction of toleration when she admitted freedom of conscience. Several centuries later when religious fears were calmed, the bans against dissenters were removed. To the Reformation, therefore, and to its leaders must go the credit for present-day concepts as to toleration, political and spiritual, in religious affairs.

SELECTED BIBLIOGRAPHY

A. F. Pollard's *History of England from the Accession of Edward VI to the Death of Elizabeth* (London, 1910) and his *England under Protector Somerset* (London, 1900) are volumes of decided merit. The Roman Catholic point of view is presented in L. Lingard's *History of England,* Vol. VII (London, 1823). F. A. Gasquet and E. Bishop's *Edward VI and the Book of Common Prayer* (London, 1891) should be read in conjunction with W. H. Frere's *New History of the Book of Common Prayer* (London, 1910). H. Gee's *Elizabethan Clergy and the Settlement of Religion* (Oxford, 1898); H. N. Birt's *Elizabethan Religious Settlement* (London, 1907); W. K. Jordan's *The Development of Religious Toleration in England* (Cambridge, 1932); R. G. Usher's *The Rise and Fall of the High Commission* (Oxford, 1913), and J. H. Pollen's *The English Catholics in the Reign of Queen Elizabeth* (London, 1920) are standard works on the English Reformation. Consult bibliographies for chapters XIII and XVIII for further material.

R. Davey's *The Nine Days' Queen, Lady Jane Grey* (London, 1909) elaborates on one of the most dramatic episodes in English history. C. H. Smyth's *Cranmer and the Reformation under Edward VI* (Cambridge, 1926) is a valuable reference.

CHAPTER XVI

Elizabeth, the Queen

ELIZABETH, at the time of Mary's death, was living at Hatfield House some twenty-five miles from London. Here she remained for nearly two weeks before going on to London, receiving visitors from the Council, listening to various reports and weighing the problems of state. England itself was in the throes of a depression. Famine hung over the land, industry was at a standstill, and the port towns were crowded with idle shipping. Unemployment was increasing and in its wake came widespread disorder and rioting. These disturbances had been caused in part by the discovery of America. The gold of the Incas had flooded European markets and had skyrocketed prices. War also had contributed its usual misfortunes, and in the case of England the ill-effects had been enormous. For this the young Queen had to thank her sister, who in keeping faith with her shifty husband had all but bankrupted the government. The national debt was colossal and rested upon a credit structure which had been undermined by a debased currency and by expenses far in excess of England's immediate ability to pay. Dismal as the outlook was, Elizabeth was far more concerned with the existing attitudes of her subjects. What did they think of her? One queen had all but ruined the nation, would Elizabeth now destroy the little that was left? What was her view as to religion? Did she favor Romanism and would she illuminate public squares with burnings? More significant than these problems was the question as to whether Elizabeth would be Queen of England or a puppet of Catholic Spain.

Fortunately, the "young lass," as the Spanish Ambassador de Feria called her, was keenly aware that her people needed peace. Above all she was proud that she was English. A new broom sweeps clean, yet one often finds in the rubbish valuable household effects. Accordingly, Elizabeth wisely decided to use Mary's broom for a brief period, while her people had time to fashion one which would fit her own needs. Her religious settlement, outlined in a former chapter, was not completed until May, 1559. Meanwhile she retained the good will of Romanists at home and abroad. In affairs of state, her first council contained a majority of Mary's advisers. Of these, none was more valuable than Cecil, whose service in government dated from the days of Henry VIII. In appointing Cecil to the Council, Elizabeth spoke to him in the following terms: "This judgment I have of you, that you will not be corrupted by any manner of gift, and that you will be faithful to the state; and that, without respect to my private will, you will give me that counsel which you think best, and if you shall know anything necessary to be declared to me of secrecy, you should show it to myself only, and assure yourself I will not fail to keep taciturnity therein, and therefore herewith I charge you." Cecil accepted the arrangement and the understanding was kept inviolable until his death.

Elizabeth and Philip of Spain

It was with some assurance of success, therefore, that de Feria faced the task of guiding Elizabeth to benefit his master Philip II of Spain. Both de Feria and Philip interpreted Elizabeth's early acts as indicating a friendly policy toward Rome and Spain. Uppermost in the mind of Philip was the thought that the English alliance must be retained; for were

Elizabeth to join with France, Hapsburg domination in Europe might be overthrown. The recent war, to be sure, was practically over; but there was plenty of time for Elizabeth to upset Philip's plans. Keenly aware of the uncertainties which attended the entrance of heretical Elizabeth into world affairs, for Philip knew his sister-in-law all too well, the Spanish King sought to disarm her by offering his hand in marriage. Religiously, Philip shrank from any compact which might endanger his beloved Church. Secular motives, however, predominated; though the King believed that as Elizabeth's husband he might soften her attitude towards Rome.

Not for one minute did the Queen misunderstand her rival and suitor. Flattered by the proposal, she still declined the honor in a manner which did not irritate Philip or endanger the Spanish alliance. As a result she was able to conclude with the French the Treaty of Cateau-Cambresis which brought peace to her distracted realm. At the same time Philip made peace with France. Had Philip coöperated with Elizabeth, England might have retained Calais, the last English stronghold on the Continent. But Elizabeth's refusal to marry had stiffened Philip's attitude against his sister-in-law, and he would do nothing to prevent the removal of the inscription over the gates of Calais which read, "Then shall the Frenchmen Calais win, when iron and lead like cork shall swim." And so the English flag was hauled down from the battlements of Calais over which it had flown for two centuries. The loss of Calais, however, was more than compensated for by the establishment of peace. The economic security of Elizabeth's government was threatened by a continuation of the war.

Elizabeth Quarrels with Mary Stuart

Hardly had the Queen settled her differences with France when she became involved in a dispute with Scotland. Scotland's queen, Mary Stuart, was not only next in line to the English throne but was also the wife of Francis II of France. Both Mary and her husband were devoted Catholics and had, moreover, the will to advance Mary's position in England. They were also determined to maintain the Franco-Scottish alliance and dispatched French troops into the Northern Kingdom for that purpose. Their hostility to Elizabeth was shown by placing the English and Irish coats of arms on the French insignia, thereby intimating that Mary was Elizabeth's heir apparent. Elizabeth sensed the seriousness of the situation and feared what might happen if Philip were to join Scotland and France in a holy war to unseat her and restore Catholicism. At this juncture occurred several events which gave to England a temporary advantage. In the first place Spain informed England that she would remain neutral in the event of a Scottish war. Then, Scotland broke up into two hostile camps, one headed by the followers of Mary, the other by John Knox, the stout defender of Protestantism and nationalism. The former group enlisted French aid, while the latter invited Elizabeth to join in a war against the Catholics. Before France could do much to defend her position in Scotland, English troops scattered the Marian forces and wrung from the latter a treaty, which obligated Mary to refrain from any further use of the English and Irish coat of arms. Mary promptly disavowed the treaty only to find her hands tied by the death of her husband and by the Scottish parliament's espousal of Presbyterianism, which was the form Calvinism took in that realm. Not wishing to stay in France, Mary eluded a watchful English fleet and landed safely in Scotland.

Mary, Darnley, and Bothwell

Nodding her approval of Presbyterianism and gaining thereby the good will of most of her subjects, Mary waited for Elizabeth to act. Elizabeth's popularity in Scotland had waned since Mary's return. Nor had her refusal to marry the Scottish Earl of Arran done much to enhance her prestige. Elizabeth demanded that Mary ratify the recent treaty as the price of English friendship. But Mary would not sacrifice her claim to the English throne and was delighted to find her people behind her. In the course of the next two years, the two women sought to outwit each other. Mary's position was distinctly the stronger of the two. Not only had she weakened English influence in Scotland, but she continued to make the most of her claims to the English throne. In order to promote her advantage, Mary, in 1565, married somewhat against Elizabeth's wish, Lord Darnley, a Roman Catholic and a great grandson of Henry VII through Henry's daughter Margaret. Whatever affection Mary had ever had for Darnley rapidly waned as his despicable character revealed itself. Moreover, he offended his wife by questioning her relations with her Italian secretary and adviser, Rizzio. Finding others who disliked the foreigner, Darnley framed a plot which ended in Rizzio's death. Instead of bringing a penitent Mary to her knees, however, Darnley soon discovered that he had lost her completely. Events then moved forward with striking consequences. Mary threw herself into the arms of Bothwell, a handsome lover but a blustering and blundering fellow. Mary followed his counsels and probably encouraged him and several others of her ministry to cause Darnley's death at Kirk O'Field. Soon after the two were married. Darnley's murder shocked public opinion, but the effect was negligible in contrast with that which followed Mary's acceptance of Bothwell as her husband and chief adviser. The Protestants rallied their forces and opened war against the royal pair. One misfortune after another befell Mary. Her troops were defeated, Bothwell was driven into the Highlands and oblivion, and she was made a prisoner. Forced to resign her throne in behalf of her infant son, James VI, Mary risked all in another uprising. She escaped from prison, but was defeated in battle. Thoroughly discouraged, Mary thought for a time of fleeing to France, but for reasons which are not altogether clear decided to enter England. This she did in May, 1568.

Elizabeth was now placed in a most difficult position. She could not endorse the action of Mary's subjects in taking up arms against their ruler, for to do so would have weakened her own position at home. Had she approved of the right of rebellion, she would have encouraged revolt in England. Furthermore, Elizabeth was exceedingly sensitive about the rights of monarchs. On the other hand, Mary's religion was a disturbing element. A goodly number of Englishmen, especially in northern England, were still loyal to Rome and viewed Mary's presence as a golden opportunity for the advancement of their cause. Elizabeth knew this and the danger Mary offered to the throne, yet she hesitated to allow Mary to leave the realm. Conscious that a detention of her cousin might lead to grave consequences, Elizabeth decided to take the risk and keep Mary where she might be watched. Accordingly, after a farcical trial as to Mary's complicity in Darnley's death, which closed with no decision one way or the other, Elizabeth moved her royal prisoner southward, away from the Catholic lords of the North.

Mary, a Prisoner in England

For a prisoner, Mary was treated with great consideration. Elizabeth's kindness, however, was forced by reason of the strong political influence Mary had abroad and in England. Both Spain and France had religious interests in Mary's welfare, while Spain of late had become alarmed over the penetration of her colonial trade by English sailors and merchants. In evaluating these factors Elizabeth discovered that internal dissension in France lessened the danger from that country. As for Spain, the Queen recognized the need of proceeding with great caution. Recently, a general assembly of Catholic prelates at Trent had reaffirmed the doctrinal position of the Church and had ordered the deposition of all Protestant rulers. Would Philip seek to carry out this program in the face of Moorish insurrections at home, a threatened Turkish invasion, and an armed revolt by his Dutch subjects? Elizabeth concluded in the negative but was far from certain as to what her Catholic lords might do. Among these malcontents was the powerful Duke of Norfolk who wished to restore Catholicism, remove Cecil from the Council, return Mary to her Scottish throne and force Elizabeth to recognize Mary as her successor. To enhance his own position, he asked Mary to marry him. She accepted the offer and waited for Norfolk to convince Elizabeth that the match should be consummated. In September, 1569, the English Queen forbade the alliance and ordered Norfolk to appear at Court. His refusal was followed by his arrest, whereupon Mary's northern friends raised the standards of revolt. In haste Mary was brought farther south, while a royal army marched against the rebels. Robbed of their leader and denied any foreign aid, the Catholic lords dashed into Scotland and the insurrection collapsed. As for Scotland, a recent uprising gave Elizabeth an opportunity to invade that country and establish as regent the Earl of Lennox who at the time was pro-English. Her attempt, however, to settle the Scottish problem by offering to restore Mary to the Scottish throne, provided Mary would renounce her claim to the English throne and place her son, James, in Elizabeth's care, failed because the Scottish lords did not want Mary back in Scotland.

Catholic Plots Against Elizabeth

The following year, 1570, the Pope formally excommunicated Elizabeth; and through his secret agent, an Italian banker Ridolfi, incited the Catholics to plot against the Queen. Once again the plan called for Norfolk's marriage to Mary and the unseating of Elizabeth. Thanks to the splendid secret service employed by Walsingham, one of the Queen's chief ministers, the plot was discovered. Ridolfi saved his life by guarded confessions, but Norfolk and several other nobles lost their heads. The Spanish Ambassador, moreover, was sent home because of his connections with the affair. And what of Mary? If Walsingham and his followers had had their way she would have shared Norfolk's fate. Elizabeth, however, in spite of all evidence to the contrary, spared her cousin's life. Clearly, Mary and Philip were the Queen's chief enemies. Repeated insurrections in the Spanish Lowlands prevented Philip's open espousal of Mary's cause. No matter how anxious Rome and Mary were to have Philip invade England, nothing could be done until the Netherlands were made secure. Consequently, Elizabeth secretly aided the Dutch and kept inciting France to embarrass Spain. Although English opinion had violently reacted against the massacre of the French Huguenots, on St. Bartholomew's Eve, 1572, Elizabeth held fast to her policy of peace with France. Moreover, she sought to make the alliance more effective by suggesting that she might marry one of the King's brothers. The marriage arrangements ultimately fell through as she intended they should, though for the time they were instrumental in keeping the peace and in forcing France to challenge Spanish domination in the Netherlands.

By 1575, Elizabeth's tortuous foreign policy was bringing its rewards. The avoidance of costly wars and the maintenance of friendly relations with Spain and France had materially reduced the national debt. Elizabeth's credit rose high in financial circles and English trade and industry rose to new levels. The depression which had begun in Mary's reign had vanished, and the cause of Rome in England was all but lost. Greater prosperity and security depended upon two factors. First, there was the question of what to do with Mary Stuart. Should she or should she not be executed? Elizabeth refused to face the issue and allowed time to take its natural course.

Second, there was the problem of the Netherlands. Elizabeth was kindly disposed towards the Dutch Protestants but was aware that their cause conflicted with the imperial program and rights of Philip, who was determined to reëstablish his authority and Romanism in these areas. Could Elizabeth check Philip's designs? Unless this was accomplished, English trade through Antwerp would suffer, and Spain, once in control of the Lowlands, might undertake an invasion of England. Her alliance with France was in her favor, but she questioned whether she could persuade Philip to grant political and civil liberty to the Dutch. Nevertheless she approached the Spanish King with this proposition and assured him that if he accepted, she would recognize his sovereignty in the Netherlands and allow him to restore the Roman Church. It was a hopeless cause, for neither the Dutch nor Philip would consider such an arrangement. For several years, however, she engineered negotiations so as to prevent a renewal of Spanish attack in the Lowlands.

In 1579, however, her policy was upset by the secession of the southern half of the Netherlands and the subsequent organization of a pro-Catholic Spanish government in that area. Close upon the heels of this event came a determined attack by Philip against William of Orange, the leader of the Protestant half of the Netherlands. French opposition to Spain weakened at this point, and in spite of Elizabethan gold and English adventurers the Dutch slowly gave ground to the Spanish infantry and the Inquisition. In 1584 William of Orange was assassinated. His death alarmed Elizabeth and her Council. Ample reason existed for the panicky feeling which swept the government and country. Recently Campion and Parsons, Jesuit priests, had been caught spreading religious discontent and political dissension, and a number of plots against the Queen's life had been frustrated only by the skill of Walsingham's agents. Rome also had caused trouble by sponsoring an expedition against the English in Ireland, by encouraging Jesuits to plot in England, and by assuring others that the assassination of Elizabeth would not be an unpardonable sin.

Trial and Execution of Mary Stuart

Behind all these enterprises lurked the figure of Mary Stuart, and against her Walsingham thundered with all the force of a patriot. Almost a decade before he had stated in respect to Mary, "So long as that devilish woman lives, neither her Majesty must make account to continue in quiet possession of her crown nor her faithful subjects assure themselves of the safety of their lives." Since then Walsingham had grown more bitter, and though he had succeeded in impressing Elizabeth with the seriousness of the situation, he had failed to wring from her permission to bring Mary to trial. Convinced that the Queen was loath to proceed against her rival and realizing that further plots would follow, a number of young noblemen, friends of Walsingham, formed an association pledged to protect the person of Elizabeth. Their action came none too soon, for in 1586 Walsingham became aware of a clever scheme known as Babington's plot. According to the arrangements, Elizabeth was to be killed, Mary made queen, and England restored to Rome. The conspirators worked with utmost secrecy. Ambiguous and ciphered letters passed back and forth between Babington, Mary, and influential friends at Rome, Paris, and Madrid. Practically every one of these communications fell into Walsingham's hands, and at the right time Babington and his group were brought to trial.

As the evidence of their guilt unfolded, Elizabeth realized that the archcriminal was Mary Stuart. The Queen hastened Babington and his friends to death in September, 1586; but against Mary, Elizabeth refused to act. Further evidence was gained against Mary, but even then all that Walsingham could wring from Elizabeth was an order summoning her cousin to

stand trial and authorizing parliament to vote condemnation
if Mary were found guilty. A special commission soon established indisputable evidence against Mary, and late in October
of the same year, parliament petitioned the Queen for "the
speedy execution of Mary." To Elizabeth the idea of ordering
a cousin's death was bad enough, but the execution of a queen
raised implications she did not care to face. The sanctity of
queens and kings was dear to Elizabeth, and she did not desire to set an example which might be used against her at a
later date. Parliament, the Council, and most of her subjects,
however, were insistent that the public enemy be removed at
once. Yielding to this pressure, the Queen publicly proclaimed sentence against her lifelong rival. She refused, however, to set a date for the execution until February, 1587. Even
then she tried to persuade Mary's keeper to put his prisoner
out of the way. An emphatic and blunt refusal was the answer she received. In the meantime the Council had taken
things into its own hands and on February 8, Mary's head
toppled forward into the basket. Sackcloth and ashes, reprisals
against some of her ministers, and tearful letters of innocency
abroad failed to remove the impression that Elizabeth was
fundamentally responsible for Mary's death. England paid
little attention to the Queen's sighs and tears. Mary Stuart
was dead. The job had been well done, and now, on to the
fray with Philip of Spain!

The War with Spain

One of Mary's last acts had been to implore Philip to lead a
holy war against England as though he needed an excuse to
attack that kingdom. His cup was overflowing with sour
wine which Elizabeth had been pouring in, drop by drop,
ever since her accession to the throne. He detested England
and its ruler for holding heretical views, and the steady progress of events served only to assure him that God and Rome

would march behind his standards into London. No one should question the sincerity of Philip's faith. He was strongly of the opinion that it was his religious duty to draw the avenging sword in behalf of Christ. Heretofore the Turk, the Moor, the French and above all, the Dutch had prevented action, but now in 1587 things were different. A large and victorious army was encamped in the Lowlands ready to be transported across the Channel. Orders were issued to speed up naval preparations begun the year before to sweep the seas of English pirates and to convoy the army to Britain.

Other considerations besides religion led Philip to war. Ever since Sir John Hawkins had penetrated the colonial markets with a cargo of slaves, Spanish control had been weakened. In vain did His Majesty invoke papal sanction for Spain's closed empire, and without effect did he remind Elizabeth that Spanish law forbade interlopers. Repeatedly the Queen apologized for her sailors' actions, but with each expression of regret went a commission to these men to carry on. Foremost among those who boldly sailed across the papal line of demarcation and out into forbidden waters was Sir Francis Drake. Sanctioned by Elizabeth this man steered a little fleet into Spanish America, destroyed property right and left, passed through the Straits of Magellan, sailed up the Pacific coast and finally, after a three-year absence, docked in England with an untold treasure of Spanish gold and silver. When Spain protested, Elizabeth publicly announced her regrets. Turning her back, however, she faced Drake and asked for a share of the booty and urged him on to new depredations. Spanish capitalists, therefore, were solidly behind Philip in demanding that England either observe the law of Rome and Spain or face the consequences of war. Who, they asked, could hope for victory over an armada and the best infantry Europe had seen since the days of Caesar?

Spanish nationalism had been touched to the quick by English intervention in the Lowlands. What possible justification existed for Elizabeth's actions Spaniards failed to see. The Dutch insurrection was a purely domestic affair in which English Protestantism and capitalism had no rights. England, on the other hand, argued that Spain had shown no regard for English feelings relative to religion and had actually been a partner to the plots against Elizabeth's life. Spain's answer was that heretics deserved no consideration. England replied that as heretics they might do as they wished at home, on the high seas or in the Netherlands. From Philip's angle, however, the presence of English troops in the Lowlands was not the act of a neutral. It connoted war. Moreover, by what right did Elizabeth assume to police the channel, to interfere with the shipping of supplies, and above all to "borrow" the pay for the Spanish troops in the Netherlands, which had been blown by storm into English harbors? England's reply failed to satisfy Spain and when Elizabeth's sea dogs were forced into Spanish harbors, persecution and the Inquisition were used to save souls and strike terror into the hearts of Englishmen.

A policy of frightfulness, heavily tinged with religious feeling, served only to quicken reprisals on the part of English seamen. In 1587, Drake, at Elizabeth's command, dashed into Cadiz and destroyed a large share of the fleet which Philip intended to use against England. Drake was anxious to renew his visit, but Elizabeth hoped Spain would avoid an open war. Philip, however, had made his decision, and with Mary's death he exerted all his strength for the impending conflict. Judging by standards of that age as well as those of today one must conclude that Spain had ample ground for drawing the sword. On the other hand, English nationalism had been challenged by Spain and Catholicism. No actual declaration of war was made, as a state of hostility had existed since 1585, when Elizabeth had thrown armed forces into the Netherlands.

The Armada left Spain in the summer of 1588 with plans which called for clearing the Channel of English men-of-war and convoying the Spanish army to England. To resist the powerful thrust of Spain's fleet, which included some sixty first-rate ships, the English concentrated off Plymouth harbor a larger force, less heavily manned and of smaller tonnage. Had the Spanish bottled up the forces under Drake, Hawkins, and Lord Howard, or had they forced an engagement, the odds might have been in their favor. As it was they ignored the English fleet and sailed on up the Channel with Drake sniping away successfully at the stragglers. This running battle had continued for three days when the Armada dropped anchor off the Dutch coast. Lord Howard then thrust forward a number of fire ships which spread such consternation that the Spanish cut their cables and took to the open sea. A pitched battle followed, with no decisive result either way; but an opportune storm swept down upon the Armada and drove it northward toward Scotland. By this time the Spanish command realized that the objectives had been lost; and making the most of a bad situation, retreated home by way of Scotland and Ireland. The Armada had failed.

Flushed with victory, Drake sought to carry the war into Spanish waters. Elizabeth's Council wished to leave well enough alone, but the Queen sent Drake on his way. The expedition which followed, known as the Counter-Armada, was a source of annoyance to Philip, but did not achieve so much as it should have because Elizabeth had been stingy with supplies and money. From 1589 to 1596, however, the English kept up the attack on Spanish ports and shipping in a manner which checked all Philip's plans for another invasion. What might have happened to the raw English levies if the Armada had won the day is a question that needs no answer. Drake's superior strategy had brushed this danger aside. More significant than this result was the effect upon England itself. In the first place the essential elements of the Elizabethan settlement were made secure for all time. The English Reformation was a complete success. Secondly, Drake's victory marked the rise of England's naval power. Thirdly, it opened untold opportunities for overseas expansion and trade. Finally, it stood as the living embodiment of a virile English nationalism.

Irish Troubles

During the remainder of her reign, Elizabeth was not called upon to meet any serious attack from Spain. However, she continued to send men and supplies into the Netherlands and used her good offices to embarrass Philip in his relations with France. When France was in the throes of a civil and religious war, she generously aided the Protestant forces and was partly responsible for making Henry of Navarre, Henry IV of France. Towards Scotland she maintained a policy which kept James VI, the son of Mary Stuart, safely surrounded by her Protestant allies in that kingdom. Success, however, did not attend her ventures in Ireland, over which England had claimed control since the close of the twelfth century. England had been much too concerned with other affairs to give much attention to Ireland, and it was not until the days of the Tudors that an attempt was made to extend English power. Henry VII and his son had sent several expeditions to Ireland and had been able to institute favorable legal changes. Later, during the reign of Edward VI, colonists had been planted with a view to creating a closer alliance between the two states.

In the main, Elizabeth sought to keep Ireland subject to English control and free from foreign domination. However, excessive taxation on the part of her agents caused the Irish to welcome the military and spiritual support which Rome and Spain poured into the island. Consequently, English troops were sent into Ireland to undertake the task of restoring royal authority. Civil war actually continued long after Elizabeth's death, and at no time during her reign could it be said that she had achieved her objectives. This was due in part to the incompetency of the English leaders, in part to the unwillingness of the Queen to provide them with adequate supplies, but above all it was attributed to the rise of Irish nationalism.

The Irish problem paved the way for the last uprising against Elizabeth in England. Oddly enough, this lost cause was championed by no less a man than the Earl of Essex, a nephew of Elizabeth's old friend, possibly her sweetheart, the Earl of Leicester. Essex represented a group of young noblemen, including Sir Walter Raleigh, who stood for an aggressive foreign policy. According to their ideas, Elizabeth had always lacked determination; and with Spain's rapid decline in power, they called for measures which would bring to England economic and political strength in the form of a world empire. The Spanish holdings in the New World, so they argued, could be had for the taking; and they urged Elizabeth to undertake the task. Against this scheme stood Cecil and Walsingham, heads older in government, who believed that England should make good its recent victories before seeking advancement abroad. Elizabeth listened to the voice of young England, especially as it was championed by so attractive a man as Essex. Essex soon rose to power. His well-chosen words, his pleasing manners, and his repeated avowals of affection captivated the woman now well advanced in years. Her old failing once more demonstrated itself. Long ago she had determined that England alone would be her husband, though she never hesitated to offer her hand in marriage as a device to outwit her foreign rivals. Each time she finally found some flaw in the candidate or discovered good reasons for withdrawing her offer. Yet her heart always throbbed and her face invariably flushed, surrounded as it was by the best of silk, satin, and cosmetic art, whenever some gallant spoke of her beauty or charm.

Elizabeth and Essex

Susceptible as Elizabeth was to flattery, she none the less always managed to keep her head. This probably explains why she accepted Cecil's advice and appointed his son, Robert, Secretary of State, a promotion which did much to check the designs of the Essex faction. However, when the time came to select a command for an Irish invasion in 1598, Essex was her choice. Essex might have returned a conquering hero if the campaign had called for something dramatic. As it was, the Irish wore down the English troops, avoided major engagements, and allowed sickness to decimate Essex's forces. In the end Essex accepted a treaty which Elizabeth promptly disavowed. Thereupon, the Earl left his post and rushed madly to England, hoping to save all by an outburst of love and loyalty. Elizabeth listened to his pleas but her better judgment told her that Essex had blundered and should therefore be punished. A special commission examined the evidence and found him guilty of having left his command without orders. He was deprived of his office and for a time kept a prisoner in his own home. From then on the Earl played a tortuous game. On the one hand he showered the Queen with affectionate letters and sought in all ways to ingratiate himself. On the other he toyed with the idea of rebellion. His plan called for an insurrection which would unseat Elizabeth and place James of Scotland on the throne. Early in January, 1601, the government heard of what was going on and forced the Earl's hand. With a small band of followers he dashed into London hoping to arouse the city and compel Elizabeth to meet his demands. London refused to be moved, and Essex on returning home found a formidable force besieging him. In the end he surrendered, and after a trial, was beheaded for treason.

During the remaining years of her life, Elizabeth enjoyed comparative peace. She died on March 24, 1603. Elizabeth's reign had been long and troublesome. Spain, France, Scotland, and Rome had sought by every means to destroy her power. At times her life had been threatened. To protect herself and her kingdom, she followed a policy which was crowded with grave dangers and which worried her ministers to the point of distraction. Clearly she had been an opportunist, and when occasion called for action, her vacillations often brought the country to the brink of disaster. Supported by a virile nationalism and by an economic foundation which was to become the marvel of Europe, Elizabeth successfully defied Rome, humbled Scotland, executed dangerous rivals, kept peace with France, and crushed the power of haughty Spain. Probably the key to her immense popularity and ultimate success is to be found in her unending faith in the desires and aspirations of her people. She sensed their needs, refused to squander their earnings, and protected them in the hour of danger. Ample appreciation was shown for her Herculean efforts; and while scores of voices arose against her brutal executions of humble souls who had followed political leaders, many of whom received no punishment worthy of the name, England correctly evaluated Her Majesty. Few monarchs have ever done so much for their subjects. To sixteenth-century Englishmen there never had been so able a ruler as Elizabeth, the Queen.

SELECTED BIBLIOGRAPHY

E. P. Cheyney's *History of England from the Defeat of the Armada* (New York, 1914–1926) is indispensable for a study of Elizabethan England and supplements the earlier narratives by Froude, Innes and Pollard. C. Read's *Mr. Secretary Walsingham* (Oxford, 1925) and his *The Tudors* (New York, 1936) are important contributions. The biographies of Elizabeth by Beesly and Creighton, though out of date, are still of value. M. A. S. Hume has exploited the Spanish sources in his *Two English Queens and Philip* (London, 1908); *The Courtships of Queen Elizabeth* (New York, 1898), and *Treason and Plot* (New York, 1901). W. L. Mathieson's *Politics and Religion* (Glasgow, 1902); J. E. Neale's *Queen Elizabeth* (New York, 1934); S.

Zweig's *Mary, Queen of Scotland* (New York, 1935); R. Bagwell's *Ireland under the Tudors* (London, 1885–1890); M. A. S. Hume's *Philip II* (London, 1897); T. F. Henderson's *Mary, Queen of Scots* (London, 1905); S. Cowen's *Mary Queen of Scots* (London, 1901), and J. B. Black's *The Reign of Elizabeth* (Oxford, 1936) are stimulating and helpful narratives.

CHAPTER XVII

Tudor England

The Commercial Revolution

PRIOR to the Tudor period England had not played a major rôle in European affairs. In contrast to France, the Empire, and the Italian city-states, England's position was distinctly inferior. The day came, however, when an Italian, sailing under the Spanish flag, discovered the New World and when another of the same race, sponsored by an English king, made known the existence of North America. As a result of these and other epoch-making voyages, Europe turned its face from the Mediterranean and looked out on the broad Atlantic. A new order was in the making. Trading at a distance became the characteristic maritime activity. Overseas colonies were founded, empires were established, and new markets with valuable raw materials came into being. The "Commercial Revolution" was in process. The Atlantic seaboard nations rose to prominence and soon gained the ascendency in all European undertakings. Although England was slow to take advantage of this mighty upheaval, the realities of the situation could not be denied, once her people had settled their religious differences, and England had been made secure from foreign attack.

In the meantime England set her economic house in order. Thanks to the gradual development of trade, industry, and finance during the medieval period, a firm foundation had

been established for later growth. The early Tudors, moreover, did much towards enhancing England's position. Basically their policy had been what students have termed mercantilism, which may be described as the economic side of
state-making. Power, according to the mercantilists, rested
upon plenty; and that nation which commanded the largest
supply of gold and silver would be great in Europe. To obtain this end, governments should direct economic life by
stimulating exports and by restricting imports. Force the
alien, so the argument ran, to pay in cash for English goods,
and compel Englishmen to buy as little as possible abroad.
Subsidies and bounties encouraged domestic production, tariff
walls protected the home market, overseas trade was limited
as far as possible to English-built and -manned ships. Mercantilism, therefore, aimed at national self-sufficiency.

Henry VII and his son did much in this direction. Treaties
with foreign states, notably the *Intercursus Magnus* with the
Netherlands in 1496, opened new markets for English goods,
which in some instances were given advantages over similar
foreign commodities. These endeavors, moreover, inflicted
injury upon the Hanse traders, who found their supremacy
in the Lowlands and the Baltic challenged by English merchants and traders. Domestic shipping profited by these arrangements as well as by navigation acts, which sought to
confine trade between Gascony and England to ships owned
and manned by Englishmen. Henry's activities carried his
subjects' exports and shipping to Iceland, to the Baltic ports,
and to Pisa, where an English consulate was established in
1486. Nor was Henry blind to the opportunities presented by
Bartholomew Columbus in the interest of his brother Christopher. Henry invited the latter to come to England, and had
it not been for Ferdinand and Isabella it is likely that the
English flag would have been planted at San Salvador in 1492.
As it was, Henry encouraged John Cabot to undertake his
voyages of discovery and exploration as well as a number of

Bristol seamen, who followed in the wake of Cabot. Henry VIII continued this work; but what is equally important, he reorganized the royal navy, placed it under a separate department of state, and laid the foundations for future maritime supremacy. Little naval progress was made during the reign of Edward VI. Mary, on the other hand, supported the enterprises of Richard Chancellor and Hugh Willoughby, who, after a perilous voyage to Archangel, opened trade with Russia.

Elizabeth continued the work of her sister. English merchants tramped throughout the kingdom of Ivan the Terrible, tapped the markets of the Caspian sea and penetrated into northern Persia. The activities of the Muscovy Company, as the merchants who traded with Russia were known, were matched by the Eastland, Levant, Venetian, Barbary, and East India companies, all of whom received royal charters between 1555 and 1600. In addition to these commercial enterprises, English initiative was displayed by the voyages of Drake, Frobisher, Hawkins, and Raleigh and by colonization efforts at Roanoke, Virginia. The significance of these activities is threefold: first, they provided opportunity for the investment of capital in overseas trade; second, they laid the foundations for imperial growth in the seventeenth century; and third, these companies, patterned after the medieval association of the Merchant Adventurers, became the model for the trading and colonizing organizations of the Stuart period. All the Tudor companies depended upon the central government for subsidy and protection, in return for which the monarchy exacted an expanding trade, the payment of imposts and the loaning of money, a supply of naval stores, an increase in shipbuilding, and a definite interest in colonization.

Mercantilist theories were also advanced by governmental regulation of the grain trade. During the medieval period the bulk of this activity was internal in nature and chiefly regulated by local laws conceived primarily in the interests of the consumer. Later the export and import trade was subjected to regulations known as "corn laws," which favored the consumer and provided the state with revenue. The producer received less attention, though the acts of 1563 and 1571 aimed at encouraging domestic production for export and for the increase of the "Navye and Marioners of this Realme."

Agricultural Growth

The interest shown by the paternalistic Tudors, in the conduct of the corn trade, reflects the importance of English agricultural life. A gradual increase both in grain exports and in food prices also illustrates the significance of farming in the sixteenth century. Externally, the countryside was much as it had been three hundred years before. Without noticing any marked change, a Wat Tyler, a John Ball, or a Piers Plowman reborn in the age of Mary or Elizabeth might still have wandered over open fields which produced about the same yield in quantity and quality per acre. In reality, however, a basic transformation had taken place. First, there was a definite increase in the number of independent farmers and wage earners whose connection with a manorial system was only nominal. Subsistence farming had dwindled, and in its place production for a metropolitan market or foreign markets had appeared. Second, there was a tendency on the part of some farmers to enclose their holdings, to make secure the raising of a staple commodity, or to protect their land against roaming cattle. In the third place, there was a shifting of population from one rural area to another as well as to the towns. This migration in keeping with the economic changes which had taken place was speeded by the destruction of the monasteries under Henry VIII. Contemporary opinion viewed this movement of population with much concern and believed that the country was overpopulated. It is true that tramps and vagrants wandered more freely than before, and that the cities were growing in size. On the other hand, the growth of population in the urban centers is explained by the withdrawal of laborers from the farms and not by a marked increase in the birth rate. The transposition of labor, however, does point to basic agricultural changes. A satisfied farming class would hardly have left their ancestral holdings unless they hoped to improve their conditions.

Industrial and commercial progress probably attracted a number from the farms, but the bulk of those who left were forced to go because of insecurity of tenure. Few freeholders actually gave up their estates, which indicates that small-scale farming was still profitable. Others, however, were driven out by capitalists who wished to introduce larger holdings and a more progressive agricultural regime either for agrarian purposes or for pasture farming. Pasture farming called for the enclosure of arable land which would provide for the raising of sheep. A movement in this direction had begun in the late medieval period, though it was not until the age of the Tudors that it reached real significance. The low price of corn, the high price of wool, and currency fluctuation, which was caused by the gold mines of America and the debasement policies of Henry VIII, probably account for the continued development of the sheep industry. Here and there some land was enclosed for agrarian purposes, but the greater part enclosed was for pasture farming. Actually, the amount enclosed was small in contrast to that set aside during the eighteenth and nineteenth centuries. The effect upon labor and agriculture was nonetheless decisive. Manorial authorities, with but scant consideration for those engaged in farming, simply invoked local power and law whenever they wished to enclose land.

Sharp protests were raised by the husbandmen of England against these practices, which time after time were declared illegal by parliamentary enactments. Enforcement of these laws was not an easy matter for a government weighed down by political and religious problems of greater significance to the state. Having failed to secure a protection from the monarchy, many of the peasants revolted in 1536 and again in 1548 to 1550. Although religious opinion played a rôle in these uprisings the fundamental grievance was economic. Upon the banners of the Lincolnshire men, for example, was shown a ploughshare, while "laggards were spurred forward with the cry 'What will ye do? Shall we go home and keep sheep.'" Sympathetic as the government was towards these unfortunates, it could not tolerate rebellion. Consequently the government used its strength in the interest of the landed gentry. From the point of view of the state the financial and political support of the latter was more important than the good will of the peasants. Statutes against enclosure, decisions of the courts, and royal edicts somewhat softened the rigors of enclosure but did little in the long run to protect the helpless farmer. Evictions, moreover, could be checked only by giving legal security to the tenants. This the government could not do in the face of landed opposition.

Industrial Development

For the same general reasons, the government was equally concerned with industrial activities. Foremost among these was the woolen industry, which was highly capitalistic in nature and was under the control of a number of important clothiers. John Winchcombe, William Stumpe, John Vane, and Thomas Spring may serve as examples of capitalists who gathered within their halls and buildings a number of laborers who were little more than wage earners. Ownership of the raw material, the buildings, the looms, and the capital was lodged in the hands of these industrialists in a manner which is strikingly like the factory system of today. Nor was piece work unknown as may be seen by an examination of the various grades of spinners, weavers, and dyers connected with the woolen industry. Labor protested against its exploitation, and many of the corporate towns passed regulations favoring the smaller independent merchants. The state itself frowned upon the factory system because it afforded an opportunity for the concentration of a discontented class which might riot and rebel. Statutes were passed to check capitalistic development and to protect the smaller woolen merchants. Some improvement did take place, but in the main the government was unable to retard the growth of industrial capitalism. Only by adopting a strong program of regulation and control could the Tudors have forced big business to withhold its oppressive hand from the independent weaver and wage earner. To have embarked upon such a policy would have alienated the capitalist group, and without their support foreign and religious policies would have been endangered.

The Increased Use of Coal

The expansion of the woolen industry was matched by the rapid increase in the use of coal. For three and a half centuries prior to Elizabeth's accession, the annual yield of the mines of England, Wales, and Scotland seldom exceeded 200,000 tons. During her reign the output was greatly increased. Most of this came from the fields of Durham, Northumberland, and the Midland counties, with Newcastle as the chief port of shipment and London as the center of import. Clearances to other English towns as well as to foreign markets attest the growing importance of this activity. Why the rich veins of England were not tapped before may be explained by the absence of any appreciable demand for coal and by the difficulties which capital met in securing title or lease to these fields. As long as England had an available timber supply and as long as the Church, in whose hands rested most of the coal fields, was reluctant to lease or sell its holdings, little demand existed for coal. By Elizabeth's day, however, timber was becoming scarcer and more costly, while a larger share of the houses were being equipped with chimney flues, a device which encouraged the use of coal. At the same time the dissolution of the monasteries and the confiscation of the property of the religious gilds in 1547 had brought into the hands of the state and nobility a large part of the nation's mining properties. Capital at once rushed into the coal industry and, thanks to an increasing demand for coal, received large returns.

The development of the coal industry, coinciding as it did with a timber shortage, reacted in a favorable manner upon other trades. The shipping industry was stimulated, and by the close of the sixteenth century practically all of the coastwise and foreign trade was in British hands. The production of iron likewise increased during the Elizabethan period, as did the salt, glass, soap, gunpowder, building, and textile industries. Although it would be wrong to assume that this expansion would not have taken place without coal, it is nonetheless true that the industrial revolution of the sixteenth century would hardly have reached the heights it did without coal. An examination of the increasing production of these and other industries clearly reveals the extensive changes which had taken place in England's economic life. It was nothing less than a revolution which was in progress, and in accounting for this tremendous transformation, the coal industry deserves special recognition.

Tudor Capitalism, and Unemployment

Behind this activity, as well as behind the expansion which occurred in the woolen, commercial, and agricultural industries, was the driving force of capitalism. Capitalist production permeated the entire nation and under the guiding hand of the Tudors was greatly encouraged. The medieval day of subsistence farming, of short overseas trading, and of small-shop production was slowly giving way to large-scale methods and techniques in commerce, industry, and agriculture. An early industrial revolution signified that in economic life England was entering the modern period. This is patent when one examines the change which had taken place in the gild organizations. During the late medieval age, craft gilds had replaced the worn-out merchant gilds. It now became the turn of the crafts to yield to capitalistic influences. These organizations still existed, but their activity was lessened by their own internal squabbles and by big business which, favored by the state, introduced newer methods of production, management, and distribution at the expense of the gilds. The domestic system of manufacturing, wherein production was carried on in the homes of small masters assisted by journeymen and apprentices, still prevailed and continued to characterize the industry of the sixteenth century. On the other hand, something like the factory system was in the making, while capitalistic production was to be seen in all manufactures and trades.

Aiding in this development was a paternalistic government. Not only did it encroach upon the favored position held by the Hanse and other foreign merchants in English trade at home and abroad, not only did it foster English shipping, pasture farming, mining and the like, but under Elizabeth it restored the currency to its old standards. In 1571, moreover, the government legalized the exaction of interest on loans and investments. It granted monopolies to a number of industries. The Hanse merchants forfeited their privileges in 1578 and gradually retired from England altogether. The Venetian fleets, which heretofore had brought Mediterranean goods to England, came less often and, after 1587, disappeared entirely from English ports.

Considerable confusion and distress attended the revolutionary changes which characterized the Tudor period. The ejection of farmers from their holdings, the growth of urban centers, the exploitation of the coal fields, and the suppression

of the monasteries and religious gilds had produced many social problems of significance. Poverty, which had been common enough in the medieval period, multiplied during the
sixteenth century. To meet the situation a number of laws
were passed of which that of 1601 was the most notable. According to this measure the property holders in every parish
were taxed by "overseers" to provide funds for the care of the
poor. Those who were able to work received relief in the
form of employment, while the shiftless and physically unfit
were lodged in houses of correction. Cumbersome and inadequate as modern critics have found this measure to be, it is
of interest to note that no radical change took place in the
poor law of England until 1834. Practically nothing worthy
of recognition was done to improve the sanitary, fire, or police
conditions of the towns.

The Tudors also showed a strong hand in dealing with
labor problems. Although the government often bemoaned
the increasing hardships which capitalistic production was in-
flicting upon labor, it really did little to improve conditions.
As an illustration there is the famous Statute of Apprentices
passed in 1563, which remained the law of England until
1813. According to this measure, which reënacted the essential features of the Statute of Laborers, gainful employment
was made compulsory. Wages were to be standardized
yearly by local officers, and a working day of twelve hours
was prescribed for all but the winter months. Finally, all
relations between the apprentice, journeyman, and master
were subject to national regulation.

Tudor Architecture

Mercantilism and paternalism were twin forces which did
much to improve England's economic position. Most of the
benefits which arose from the new order favored the landed
and industrial classes. The rising fortunes of these groups

were reflected by broad estates and pretentious residences. The government built numerous fortifications and palaces such as St. James, Whitehall, and Hampton Court. Brick and stone characterized these structures as well as the ornate homes of the nobility. Somerset House, Loseley Hall, and Hatfield House illustrate the building activities of the latter

HAMPTON COURT PALACE. Built in 1514 by Cardinal Wolsey; reconstructed by Sir Christopher Wren in 1695. A royal residence from Henry VIII's day to 1737.

group, and present-day England is still adorned by the attractive manor houses constructed by the lesser gentry. Cambridge and Oxford prospered by the donations of the nobility and wealthy merchants; and an architectural style, the "collegiate," was created. The style has been copied by numerous American universities. Tudor building was more restrained than that which preceded it and did not manifest itself in towering cathedrals of the Gothic type, but acquired a domestic quality which was simple and pleasing. The Tudor masons retained many of the essential features of the past but utilized their skill and art in a manner which foreshadowed the classical tendencies of the seventeenth century. The classical motives were imported from France or Italy and were copied with meticulous precision. Nothing of the flamboyant was present. License was replaced by strictness in structural lines though the flying buttress and perpendicular lines reflect the influence of the past.

Timber was used generously both within and without. Richly ornamented and decorated panelled walls and ceilings characterized the interior, and open beams, surrounded by brick or stone, the exterior of many homes. The pointed arch was softened, its curves lowered until it appeared almost square. To the eye it was complete and peculiarly restful. Windows appeared in greater number; crowstepped gables and brick chimneys adorned many a roof. Although these palaces and buildings were significant indexes of material prosperity, they were not the abodes of the average Englishman. Rows upon rows of miserable wooden structures, tightly jammed within the town walls, housed the artisan and his family. Few of these homes had any sanitary devices and many of them constituted fire hazards. In the rural areas, except for the manor houses, conditions were not much better. The typical home, while somewhat larger than that of the medieval period, was none too inviting; nor could it be otherwise in the face of such an uneven distribution of wealth.

Living and Sanitary Conditions

Artisan and husbandman lived in a manner which was not conducive to health or long life. On the other hand wealth did little to protect those of the upper strata. They were sometimes able to escape plagues and fevers by fleeing to their rural homes or by frequenting the baths. Buxton Wells and the spa at Bath were already well known by Elizabeth's day. Many of the nobility, like Cecil and Mary Stuart, enjoyed these waters for physical and social purposes. The presence of a "greate number of pore and dyseased people," however, annoyed the elite, who were able to prevent the former from using the baths. Probably most of the poor viewed bodily cleanliness as neither a virtue nor a necessity. Those who cared to keep clean usually bathed in streams or ponds, though Cambridge University forbade its students and faculty from bathing within the waters of the county. Those who did were placed in stocks, whipped, fined, or expelled. These punishments and others were generously inflicted for crimes and misdemeanors, many of which were punishable by death.

Visitors at Bath, or any other town, put up at a local inn or at an alehouse, which frequently served as a makeshift hotel. Except for the larger hostelries, accommodations were meager and unsanitary, in spite of numerous state and local regulations. Wandering bands of minstrels, actors, and wayfarers visited these places and provided entertainment. Drinking was indulged in to an extent which evoked sharp criticism from the Puritans, while the government viewed with suspicion those who frequented the bar or gambling table. In general the food served was none too good. Quantity, however, made up for quality. In the homes of the upper classes considerable attention was given to eating. Here cooking became an art; and staples, pastries, and food luxuries burdened their tables. The amount of food consumed by these people was enormous. When Elizabeth, for example, visited Lord North in 1577, 140 bushels of wheat, 67 sheep, 34 pigs, 1200 chickens, 2500 eggs, and 400 pounds of butter were used in three days, to say nothing of a cartload of oysters and many other articles. Among the lower classes, rye and barley were the basic cereals; mutton, beef, and pork were the chief meats; cheese, milk, ale, and an occasional pudding also were used. Vegetables were practically unknown, except among the laboring classes, while fruit seldom appeared save upon the tables of the rich.

Tudor Costuming

Dame Fashion was as changeable, as exacting, and as fascinating to men and women alike in the sixteenth century as in the twentieth. Clothes made the man, even then, and the rich or noble Englishman was careful to dress for the part he played in the social or economic world. Today the New York stores are proudly featuring something new and different in lingerie styles and fabrics, especially underwear of handkerchief linen. The Tudor gentlemen knew about that three hundred years ago. A waistcoat was an important, not to say essential part of the well-dressed man's outfit. Prior to the middle of the sixteenth century, the fashionable silhouette demanded a short, close-fitting waistcoat with a low-cut neckline and long, tight sleeves. Tight-fitting hose extended from waist to feet. Over his waistcoat, the man wore a loose jacket with sleeves and skirt of varying length. For ceremonial or social occasions, he covered the jacket with a full, flowing gown that extended to his calves. This was richly decorated and had a standing collar and short, billowing sleeves. Over the gown, was worn a cloak draped or slung from the shoulder. The head gear varied from a low, rounded hat to a bonnet, a toque, or a sweeping sombrero. Shoes ranged from heelless, duck-billed slippers to footwear that featured a high front and narrow sides tied with a small, colored bow. In Henry VII's time hair was long and bobbed.

After the middle of the sixteenth century Fashion decreed certain changes. The low-cut neckline of the waistcoat became a bombastic collar, and the waistcoat itself resembled a tight-fitting corset with a stuffed hump overhanging the girdle. Sleeves became full and heavily padded. The loose jacket became smooth-fitting, and its skirts were decidedly shorter. After Mary's reign, hose were changed in style so that the upper half appeared to be a separate pair of breeches, though in reality the hose were still in one piece. By Elizabeth's day, men wore their hair shorter; and mustaches and beards became increasingly popular. All garments were richly decorated. A favorite device was the slash in the sleeve which allowed linen underwear to stand out in contrasting effects. Although the lower classes were unable to wear the rich silks and woolens of their social and economic superiors, they copied the costumes as closely as possible.

Fullness and length characterized the body garments of the well-to-do women. Gowns at first were low-necked and décolleté. Broad shoulder-collars and sweeping trains were attached to this habit, which also had upper and under sleeves of a monkish type. Ladies of high birth wore long mantles over their gowns. Beneath these garments there were a full petticoat and linen underwear. By Elizabeth's day the gown had become two practically separate pieces, a long-waisted, corset-form bodice and a bulging funnel-like skirt. Petticoat and underwear were altered accordingly. The skirt was frequently bustled and hooped, while the bodice had a generous décolleté neck or a full laced collar. A gable-hood hat with flowing lappets was popular until about 1550; afterward it became a curved linen cap with or without a veil behind. The latter style allowed the hair to show more prominently than before. The hose throughout the Tudor age were long stockings gathered about the knees; while the shoes, which usually were concealed by the skirt, were the type worn by the men. Ladies of rank used richly decorated and ornamented cloth and silk; those of humble birth employed cheaper materials and often fewer clothes.

The trains and sweeping gowns of the women must have been ideal dust and dirt collectors. Fortunately, these ladies were transported either on horses or in elegant carriages as they toured over the miserable roads of England. The wives of the farmers or townspeople usually remained at home and tramped over dusty or muddy roads. Even within the towns these roads were narrow and seldom paved. Standing pools of water or piles of debris were common sights, and these, together with the dangers of travel, drove both men and women to use the Thames whenever they wished to go from Westminster to London. Rivers, indeed, were often spoken of as highroads. Transportation, even at its best, was none too pleasant; and considerable time was used in going from one place to another. In spite of these difficulties, however, there was considerable traveling, especially since economic and social factors were breaking down the provincial attitudes of a former age.

Scientific Achievements

The Tudor age, moreover, witnessed an increase in scientific knowledge. Evidence of this progress appeared in architecture, navigation, printing, and map-making. In the field of medicine less was accomplished, though the contributions of European savants were known in England. On the other hand Englishmen like John Keys, professor at Cambridge, assisted materially in administering to the victims of scurvy, influenza, and pleurisy, which seem to have exacted a heavy toll at that time. Materia medica was seriously handicapped by quackery and humbug. Astrology was still viewed as an important factor in determining man's health. The barber-surgeons and physicians were not all doctors in the real sense of the word. William Gilbert, though a fellow of St. John's, Cambridge, and President of the College of Physicians, is better known for his experiments in electricity and magnetism and is usually credited as being the founder of these sciences. John Dee, Elizabeth's favorite astrologer, was far better as a mathematician, while Leonard Digges, Cuthbert Tonstall, and Robert Recorde were also known for their activities in this science. Recorde was the author of several books dealing with mathematics and was probably the first to use the symbols $+$ and $=$. "No 2 thynges," he stated, "can be moare equalle" than two parallel lines. Recorde's volumes as well as an English edition of Euclid were printed in England and were referred to in the first published catalogue of English books edited by Andrew Maunsell in 1595. Printing made such great progress during the Tudor period that the government took definite steps to regulate the industry and censor all publications. Licensed presses were set up at London and one or two other places, and all books, tracts, or pamphlets were to be registered at the Stationers' Office. Music also continued to receive attention, as may be seen from a study of the compositions by Robert Fayrfax and his contemporaries. The first printed score appeared in 1530.

Literary Activities

The invention of the printing press and the rapid extension of educational facilities created a reading public which the Tudor writers did not ignore. The theological discourses of Cranmer, Parker, Foxe, and Gardiner found an honored place in the libraries of the nobility and the well-to-do. Stowe, Camden, and Harrison fired the imagination of these groups with stimulating descriptions of England and its history. Attention was also paid to chroniclers like Hall and Holinshed who strangely mixed truth, myth, and idle rumor. Mention should also be made of Hakluyt's volumes depicting the voyages and discoveries of the Elizabethan seamen, of Lyly's *Euphues,* Sydney's *Apology for Poetry,* Bacon's *Essays,* More's *Utopia,* Spenser's *Faerie Queene,* and the dramatic compositions of Christopher Marlowe. Few of these writers, however, deeply stirred the minds of the middle class who formed the bulk of the reading public. On the other hand, hundreds of authors, seldom mentioned in the courses on English literature, supplied this group with books of various descriptions. Handbooks for the improvement of table manners, dress and conversation like Francis Seagus' *The School of Virtue* and William Fiston's *The School of Good Manners* were in great demand. Instruction also was furnished in other works as to thrift, godliness, education, and domestic happiness. Travel, science, drama, and history had readers, and many a writer amused others with humorous sketches which often bordered on the obscene. Particularly successful were those authors who wrote about woman's moral and social position. Abraham Vale's *The Deceit of Women* and C. Pyrvye's *The Praise and Dispraise of Women* were enjoyed by both men and women.

Sharp protest was voiced by the Puritans against these productions which used language and action in a free and frank manner. Nor did the literati approve of penny volumes written in an abominable style and filled with ignoble themes. In spite of these complaints, the demand for popular works steadily increased. English nationalism, the backbone of which was the middle class, found abundant opportunity for action and reflection in the literary productions of the Tudor age. Manifestations of this national quickening had appeared before, but it remained for the sixteenth century to reveal the full significance of the movement. Henry VIII and Elizabeth were English rulers in a sense that no other monarch had been, while the voyages of a Drake and the intense patriotism of a Raleigh or Essex illustrate how conscious Englishmen had become of their country.

SELECTED BIBLIOGRAPHY

Many of the references for the preceding four chapters have pertinent economic and social material. Valuable source material may be found in R. H. Tawney and E. Power's *Tudor Economic Documents* (London, 1924); R. H. Tawney's *Agrarian Problem in the Sixteenth Century* (London, 1912); E. F. Gay's "Inclosures in England in the Sixteenth Century" in *Quarterly Journal of Economics,* Vol. XVII: 576–597; G. Unwin's *Industrial Organization in the Sixteenth and Seventeenth Centuries* (Oxford, 1904); J. U. Nef's *The Rise of the British Coal Industry* (London, 1932); H. Heaton's *The Yorkshire Woollen and Worsted Industries* (Oxford, 1920); E. Lipson's *History of the Woollen and Worsted Industries* (New York, 1921), and N. S. B. Gras' *The Evolution of the English Corn-market* (Cambridge, 1915) are scholarly studies. England's foreign trade, voyages, and discoveries are treated in N. R. Deardorff's *English Trade in the Baltic during the Reign of Elizabeth* (Philadelphia, 1912); W. G. Gosling's *The Life of Sir Humphrey Gilbert* (London, 1911); J. S. Corbett's *Drake and the Tudor Navy* (London, 1899); R. Hakluyt's *Principal Navigations* (Glasgow, 1903–1905); M. Epstein's *Early History of the Levant Company* (London, 1908), and A. L. Rowland and G. B. Manhart's *Studies in Commerce and Exploration in the Reign of Elizabeth* (Philadelphia, 1924).

Literature, thought, and science are treated by E. K. Chambers' *The Elizabethan Stage* (Oxford, 1923) and *William Shakespeare* (Oxford, 1930); G. E. B. Saintsbury's *History of Elizabethan Literature* (London, 1887); S. Lee's *Great Englishmen of the Sixteenth Century* (New York, 1904); A. R. M. Stowe's *English Grammar Schools in the Reign of Queen Elizabeth* (New York, 1908); C. E. Mallet's *History of the University of Oxford* (London, 1927); P. Smith's *History of Modern Culture* (New York, 1930); A. Wolf's *A History of Science, Technology, and Philosophy in the 16th and 17th Centuries* (New York, 1935); C. Singer's *A Short History of Medicine* (New York, 1928); F. Cajori's *History of Physics* (New York, 1899), and W. R. Ball's *Short Account of the History of Mathematics* (New York, 1912).

Architecture, music and the arts are treated in P. C. Buck's *Tudor Church Music* (Oxford, 1923–1930); C. H. C. Baker and W. G. Constable's *English Painting of the Sixteenth and Seventeenth Centuries* (New York, 1930); L. F. Salzman's *England in Tudor Times* (London, 1926); H. T. Stephenson's *Elizabethan People* (London, 1910), and W. H. Godfrey's *The Story of Architecture in England* (New York, 1928).

CHAPTER XVIII

Tudor Government

THE age of the Tudors has often been described as one of royal absolutism. Government, in other words, was ordered and directed by monarchs who imposed their will upon the English people. _ It was Henry VII who fashioned and bound his subjects, so it is said, to absolutism. Later, his son quarreled with Rome and stamped his wishes into law by the Act of Supremacy. It was Elizabeth who forced the nation into a Spanish war and risked all by insisting upon a dangerous policy with her cousin, Mary Stuart. Through their hand-picked ministry these rulers influenced parliament in a manner that practically destroyed its former independence. A contemporary poet, John Skelton, in an abusive verse ranted against the arrogance of Wolsey, Henry VIII's great minister, as follows:

> He is set so hye
> In his ierarchy
> Of frantycke frensy
> And folysshe fantasy
> That in the Chambre of Starres
> All maters there he marres
> Clappying his rod on the borde
> No man dare speke a worde
> For he hathe all the sayenge
> Without any renayenge

That the Tudors were powerful and dynamic rulers, capable of achieving their ends, must be admitted. Moreover, their advent to the throne followed the stormy days of the Lancastrians and Yorkists who had paved the way for absolute power. The parliamentary gains of the fourteenth and fifteenth centuries had been pushed aside by Warwick, the king-maker, and by Edward, Duke of York. The Lancastrian Constitution, an embodiment of past political experience, was torn to shreds by the War of the Roses. The Tudors, therefore, found everything ready for strong personal government and quite easily bent English law and custom to their liking. The wonder is that they did not destroy parliament, as they might have done. They elected, however, to rule with the help of this body. Absolutism, therefore, was clothed in parliamentary activity and consent. The English constitution, though not destroyed, was suspended for almost a century and a quarter. But were the organic laws suspended in the sense that they became inoperative? An analysis of Tudor ways of government provides the answer.

The Structure of Government

The central government of England from 1485 to 1603 consisted of an executive, the King, a Privy Council, a legislature in the form of parliament, and a judicial system of courts ranging from the sessions of the three Common-Law Courts to the quarterly visitations of the itinerant justices. Local government, moreover, was subjected to royal will through these agencies and such officials as the sheriff and justice of the peace. Theoretically, the Crown was all-powerful. Every act of state was in the name of the King whether it was a decision of a court, an order in council, or a law of parliament. War and peace, the conduct of trade and commerce, the regulation of poor relief and the summoning of parliament depended upon the will of the Crown.

Absolute as the Tudor was in theory and practice, he was forced to depend upon others to carry out his wishes. Assisting the Crown was the Privy Council, which was the title given by the sixteenth-century writers to the *Curia Regis*. In general this body was composed of lay and ecclesiastical members such as Archbishop Cranmer, Cardinal Wolsey, Lord Burleigh, and Sir Francis Walsingham. In addition there were a large number of non-noble members who served in various capacities. Omitting the latter, who acted as clerks or assistants, the Privy Council did not number over twenty, many of whom followed the monarch about the realm while others were permanently located at London. So enormous were the duties which fell to this body that the practice developed of allocating much of the ordinary business to certain standing committees. Chief among the members were the Lord Chancellor, the Treasurer, the Chancellor of the Exchequer, and the Lord High Admiral. The last named officer as well as the President of the Privy Council and Secretary of State were recent creations. The genesis of the Secretary of State goes back to the thirteenth century, but it was not until the Tudor period that this officer acquired any great significance. The office was filled by men of power, influence and ability who had charge of a number of duties of which foreign affairs were the most important. The Council, though clothed with extensive jurisdiction, was always subject to the King and should in no wise be viewed as a cabinet or responsible ministry. Indeed the Crown was not required to consult with this body unless it so desired. A wise monarch, and the Tudors were particularly gifted with wisdom, usually sought the advice and coöperation of the council. Several notable exceptions to this policy took place. In 1527, for example, when Henry VIII was feverishly working for a separation from Katherine, he dispatched Knight to Rome without informing his chief minister, Wolsey, to whom this delicate problem had been entrusted. Later, Mary overrode

the advice of her council by insisting upon marriage with
Philip II of Spain.

The Privy Council functioned in a number of ways. Some
of the members were to be found in both houses of parliament, where they initiated royal legislation, checked any opposition that might arise, and through their personal influence
and pressure controlled many votes. As administrators, they
had charge of the various departments of state, acted as diplomats, enforced the laws, and possessed a secret service which
was a constant annoyance to those who sought to evade royal
commands. They supervised the persecution of recusants and
non-conformists, handled questions of piracy and coinage,
and controlled the conduct of the bishops and justices of the
peace. Their orders and proclamations, moreover, possessed
the validity of law. Probably the greatest duty rendered by
the council was in the field of justice. Some of the members were permanently attached to the common-law courts,
the Court of Chancery, and the special jurisdictions such as
the Court of High Commission. In this way the will of the
Crown found ample room for action. The Council, moreover, came to possess the residuum of all judicial power not
definitely conferred upon the other royal courts. It possessed
both original and appellate jurisdiction, as may be seen from
an examination of the *Acts of the Privy Council*. Civil and
criminal cases were brought before it whether they concerned
the security of the state or the well-being of a subject. In
some matters it shared power with the House of Lords, which
still retained judicial control over certain cases. The distinction, however, between the two courts was not clearly defined, and this permitted a rapid extension of authority on the
part of the Privy Council. The interests of absolute government, moreover, were definitely promoted by this situation,
and the Tudor monarchs saw very little reason for disturbing
an arrangement to which there was no opposition and which
was favorable to them.

The Court of Star Chamber

The precise difference between the Privy Council and the extra-judicial bodies like the Court of Star Chamber is difficult to define. Some authorities have contended that the Council was a child of Star Chamber, which in turn was a development of the *Curia Regis*. It is evident that the guiding personnel in each of these courts was much the same and that their jurisdictions frequently overlapped. In general, Star Chamber had its own field of action, and, unlike the Council, sat at stated intervals during the year, while the Council was always in attendance upon the Crown. Star Chamber took its name from a room decorated with stars in Westminster Palace, in which it held its meetings. These gatherings appear to have taken place before 1485 and were concerned chiefly with livery and maintenance, or the practice followed by the nobility in arming and clothing the military, and protecting them from local and national law. During the War of the Roses the *Curia Regis* frequently assembled in Star Chamber and exercised judicial power over livery and maintenance, riots and disorders. Henry VII recognized the value of this judicial power when he came to the throne in 1485. Availing himself of the residual power of the Council, Henry strengthened the *Curia Regis* by the addition of two chief justices. Later, in 1487, he gained from parliament an act which gave this court special jurisdiction in all cases involving livery and maintenance, riots and disorders. And from this time on the court was known as the Court of Star Chamber.

The peculiar significance of Star Chamber rested upon the fact that its officers were royal appointees acting under the king's orders, and that its procedure was not in accordance with common law. Star Chamber had control over all cases which involved a breach of public order. Riots and assaults as well as actions concerning forgery and libel were within its jurisdiction. Perjury, contempt of royal proclamations,

duels, frauds, and other offenses were included in the powers
of this court. A riot, according to Tudor interpretation, constituted not solely a public disorder, but likewise private conflicts between quarreling housewives and personal attack.
Libel included both direct and indirect statement of facts.
Moreover, one might be brought to trial for having read a
libelous tract. Professor Cheyney has furnished a splendid
illustration of the scope of Star Chamber when he relates
the incident when Justice Shallow saw Falstaff assaulting his
men and kissing the keeper's daughter. "I will make a star
chamber matter of it," exclaimed Justice Shallow, "if he were
twenty Sir John Falstaffs he shall not abuse Robert Shallow,
Esquire. . . . The council shall hear of it; it is a riot."

The procedure followed by Star Chamber was even more
extensive than its jurisdiction It did not have to follow common law or common-law jurisdiction and might adopt methods which were certain to bring conviction. There was no
jury. All witnesses and evidence were reviewed privately by
the court in the absence of the defendant who, while entitled
to see and answer the charges, was examined without counsel.
Moreover, the prisoner was forced to sign his name to the questions put by the court. Star Chamber might also use torture
to obtain evidence or confession. It might be said that in
one sense the court used equity jurisdiction in criminal cases.
Arbitrary as was Star Chamber and open as it was to abuse
by influential individuals, the court must be judged in the
light of that time and not according to present-day standards.
The existing common-law courts of the late fifteenth and sixteenth centuries were unable to stem the anarchy which followed in the wake of the War of the Roses and the disturbances which attended the Reformation. Local magnates openly
scoffed at the jury system, which they found to be impotent
and sometimes dishonest. Determined to restore law and
order, the Tudors resorted to the arbitrary methods of Star
Chamber, whose justices tried cases which the ordinary courts

did not dare to handle. Its punishments, which included imprisonment, fine, public humiliation, and physical suffering, were not more severe than those imposed by the common-law courts. It had few friends among the nobility and was frowned upon by the legal profession, which resented Star Chamber's interference in established legal practices and procedures. To the average Englishman, however, Star Chamber was, on occasion, a tower of strength and justice against feudal anarchy.

In addition to judicial work, Star Chamber exercised legislative power. The basis for this authority rested upon the residual prerogatives of the Crown in council. Law, in other words, might be made by both the Privy Council and Star Chamber as well as by parliament. Today every order of the Privy Council rests upon an act of parliament and has the same effect as though it had been promulgated by the legislature. During the Tudor age, however, parliament's control over the Council was quite limited. As a result, numerous orders were issued relative to trade, industry, dueling, and the like. In general these measures did not encroach upon the organic law of the nation but regulated affairs not covered by existing legislation. Nevertheless, the power of the Crown to make law through either the Council or Star Chamber was a definite threat to the legislative independence of parliament.

Parliament During the Tudor Period

The Tudors were keenly aware of their legislative power; and while anxious to make the most of their opportunities were careful to avoid definite conflict. Many a time these rulers waited patiently for parliament to pass a measure rather than to resort to their own residual rights. On other occasions, the Crown announced by proclamation or order what the law was, regardless of parliament, the courts, or common law. In certain matters, foreign affairs for example, the Crown argued that parliament had no jurisdiction. This position was not seriously questioned by the Tudor parliaments. On the other hand, parliament claimed certain legislative powers which the Crown could overcome only by interfering with the conduct of that body. The presence of ministers in parliament was often sufficient to gain this result. Other devices, as will appear later, were also employed. Critics of the Tudors, moreover, point to the *Lex Regia* (1539) as convincing proof of royal absolutism in legislation. According to this measure, parliament enacted that royal proclamations were to have the force of statutes. Today such a delegation of authority would be equal to a surrender by parliament of its legislative power. Henry VIII, however, never interpreted this measure in that light, and there is little evidence to prove that he ever used the power given him by the *Lex Regia*. In Henry's mind there was a valid reason for the act. The government, it will be recalled, had broken with Rome, which claimed supreme authority over all Christendom. Anxious to deny papal power in England and to convince his subjects that he was master in his realm, Henry persuaded parliament to enact the *Lex Regia*. Following the Acts of Supremacy of 1534 and 1535 and conceived largely as a weapon to be used in the contest with Rome, the significance of the *Lex Regia* should not be overemphasized. Furthermore, the measure itself was repealed in the reign of Edward VI.

Tudor authority rested in part upon the income enjoyed by these monarchs. The finances of the government were at a low ebb when Henry VII ascended the throne in 1485. A political scientist of that age would have said that the king could meet his normal requirements from the rents or sales of his own land, the fees and fines exacted by the courts, and the established customs dues and what might arise from feudal aids and incidents. The gross income from all of these sources, however, was not sufficient to meet the ordinary demands of the Crown. In order to supplement his revenue for these and extraordinary needs, such as war, the Crown was supposed to gain the consent of parliament. But the Tudors were not beggars nor did they care to risk parliamentary opposition. History revealed that the chief weakness of the fourteenth- and fifteenth-century kings had been their dependence upon the financial help of parliament. The Tudor rulers, therefore, had to increase their income without irritating the tight-fisted middle class which dominated the Commons. To gain this end, Henry VII and his successors extracted large sums by confiscating the property of political offenders, abolishing the monasteries and chantries, by benevolences and forced loans, and by increasing the valuations placed upon imported goods and commodities. When war required additional sums, the Tudors either gained subsidies from parliament or by clever diplomacy managed to shift part of these expenses to their allies. Frugality on Elizabeth's part and a more efficient treasury also provided extra income. In spite of these endeavors and the sales of monopolies, the indebtedness of the central government rose steadily from Henry VIII's time. In general, however, the Tudors managed to avoid parliamentary squabbles over finance and maintained an independence which fostered royal power.

At the opening of the Tudor period, parliament included seventy-eight peers and two hundred and ninety-four commoners. Membership in the upper house rested upon holding a barony of the Crown either through inheritance or by creation of peerage by letters patent. The lords spiritual, who held their seats by virtue of being tenants of the Crown, numbered forty-nine of whom the great majority were heads of religious houses. The ecclesiastics, therefore, outnumbered the lay lords. The upper house enjoyed legislative and judicial powers. It might initiate any measure other than a money bill and reject or pass any bill, money or otherwise, which came from the Commons. As a court it might try cases referred to it by the Crown and exercise jurisdiction over all impeachment charges preferred by the Commons. Membership in the lower house rested upon property qualifications and upon a franchise, which was determined by the forty-shilling freehold act of 1430 or by a municipal charter. In 1485 there were two hundred and twenty members from incorporated cities and boroughs and seventy-four knights of the shire. Commons possessed the power to initiate money bills and all other measures whatsoever. Through its control over finance, it was in a position to limit governmental policy and institute impeachment proceedings against the Crown's ministers. Moreover, it claimed to have the rights of free speech, freedom from arrest, and access to the Crown through the speaker. On the other hand, it should be noted that parliament could meet only on call of the Crown, and might be prorogued or dissolved at royal pleasure. "It is in me and my power," Elizabeth said in 1593, "to call parliaments: it is in my power to end and determine the same."

Theoretically, parliament was in a position to check the Crown as it had done through the Lancastrian age. Actually, none of the Tudors was ever seriously restricted by parliament. This was due in part to the use these monarchs made of parliament. By the dissolution of the monasteries, the spiritual members were reduced in number. Those who retained office were bound securely to the Crown by the consequences of the Reformation. On the other hand the lay lords increased in number. The forty-nine who existed by the close of Elizabeth's reign, however, were subject to royal order as a result of favors, gifts, and offices which the Crown had given them. In respect to the Commons there was no alteration in suffrage or qualification for office, though there was a decided increase in numbers. The incorporation of Wales in 1535 and the granting of representation to a number of unenfranchised boroughs swelled the total number to over four hundred and fifty members by 1603. In theory, both houses held the same powers and rights as in 1485. Actually, the changes in personnel had created a body which did not function as it had two centuries before.

When Elizabeth said "It is in me . . . to call parliaments" she was but expressing the established procedure in respect to the summoning of that body. During the entire period from 1485 to 1603 there were thirty-three general elections or one for every four years. In contrast to present-day requirements, which call for a general election every five years, the Tudor record was good, but the advantage is lost upon examining the duration of these gatherings. No uniformity existed during the Tudor age as to the length of parliament. In Edward's reign one parliament lasted but one month; under Elizabeth one parliament lasted all of seven years. Today, parliament must be in session every year and usually sits for several months. It should be noted, however, that continuity of personnel was advanced by the practice, which developed after Henry VIII, of having sessions of parliament. The Tudors were in a position, therefore, to use parliament as they wished and as long as that body was of any value to the Crown. Moreover, these monarchs protected their interests by interfering with the conduct of elections. This was accomplished in part by creating new parliamentary boroughs. It was also managed by requiring election boards to return suitable or approved candidates. Expressed recommendation of particular individuals also helped. Elizabeth, for example, used this latter method to secure a seat in the Commons for one of her chief secretaries of state. The government further regulated the conduct of parliament through those members who were also of the Privy Council.

Particularly significant was the control exercised by the Crown over the Commons through the office of speaker. Through this officer, royal wishes were issued as commands that were seldom questioned. Prior to Elizabeth's reign, the Commons lacked fire and showed an unwillingness to insist upon their rights. Probably they recognized the overpowering strength of the monarch; though in the case of Richard Strode in 1512, the Commons denied the Court of Stannaries any jurisdiction over the speeches of its members even if these utterances were hostile to the interests of the tinners. In respect to the Crown, however, the Commons was meek and seemed to be slow to advance its rights. There was little occasion to force an issue or to insist upon the exercise of this privilege. With the Commons taking no stand, Henry VIII could boast that the discussions in parliament "are free and unrestricted." However, when a member attacked Cranmer, Henry was quick to act. "Tell that varlet that if he does not acknowledge his fault. . . I will . . . punish him to the example of others." The Commons showed more life and often irritated Elizabeth by commenting on her actions, her repeated granting of monopolies, and her refusal to marry. Sharp commands to cease such practices followed. While the Commons usually respected the Queen's wishes it was able on occasion to wring from her a few concessions. During the last parliament of Elizabeth's reign, considerable hostility was shown toward the Queen. The debates were turbulent and physical force was used to prevent members from voting. Moreover, when Elizabeth addressed parliament in October, 1601, there were few of the Commons who "greeted her with the customary 'God save your Majesty.'" Thanks to the courage of several members, notably Paul and Peter Wentworth, the Commons gave considerable attention to Elizabeth's interference with its privilege of free speech. "Free speech and conscience in this place," said Peter Wentworth, "are granted by a special law. . . . It is a dangerous thing in a prince [sic] to oppose or bend herself against her nobility and people."

Generally speaking, the Tudor parliaments allowed the Crown to have its way. They permitted Henry VIII to determine the succession to the throne and paid his debts in 1527, 1529, and 1543. On the other hand parliament's submission does not imply that the Tudors were despotic nor that the forms and customs of the English constitution were discarded or suspended. Every important power held by that body in the Lancastrian age was exercised during the Tudor period. Even the determination of succession to the throne was stipulated by parliamentary procedure in accordance with the Crown's wish. The letter of the constitution was complied with, though the spirit was bent to meet royal desires. In spite of the bullying tactics of Henry VIII or the pointed commands of Elizabeth, these monarchs never overstepped public opinion. When Henry VIII exacted a forced loan, he received a sharp rebuff and was required to beat a hasty retreat. When Mary insisted upon marrying Philip, she faced a formidable uprising led by Wyatt. And when Elizabeth carried her grants of monopolies too far she was compelled by parliament to alter her program. Moreover, many of the important accomplishments of the Crown reflected the wishes of parliament and the nation. The progress of the Reformation illustrates this fact as does the passage of the Poor Law. Recent investigation has established that local regulations relative to poor relief existed before the passage of the national law and actually motivated the enactment of the latter statute. The dissolution of the monasteries was highly pleasing to the reformers as well as to those who reaped financial profit by their destruction. The woolen interests applauded the enclosure measures, and the mercantilist policies of the Crown echoed the desires of the commercial and industrial classes. Nor should it be forgotten that Elizabeth's anti-Spanish program afforded English nationalism the opportunity it wanted for self-expression and expansion.

At the same time it must be admitted that the Tudors regulated government in a way that laid the foundations for Stuart absolutism. The activity of Star Chamber illustrates this fact as well as the Court of High Commission. These courts, like the Council of the North, the Court of Admiralty, the Council of Wales, and the Court of Requests, disregarded common law and dispensed a justice which was exceedingly arbitrary. All were products of the Privy Council and frequently were subject to its general jurisdiction. Sharp protest was made by the common-law lawyers at these invasions of their jurisdictions but in general the Tudors had their way. At no time, however, did these rulers utilize these agencies as instruments of oppression to the degree that James and Charles did during the first half of the seventeenth century.

Local Government During the Tudor Period

The Tudors were equally cautious about interfering with the local governments. Indeed it may be said that the central state prospered because of the inherent vitality of county and municipal institutions. Much of the strength of local government rested upon the achievements of the past. To this heritage the Tudors added features of importance. During the medieval period the vill or manor had served to some extent as the agency of the Crown. By the sixteenth century these units had become more or less obsolete and had been superseded by the parish. Once the Church was placed under the control of the state, the central government used the parish as a medium for royal power. Mary and Elizabeth in particular employed the parish authorities in a number of ways. Through them local relief was administered and the maintenance of highways controlled. Other duties were assigned to the parish so that by the opening of the seventeenth century this unit had become an important agency for law and order. The parish officers, though popularly elected, were subject to the justices of the peace. These justices had existed before 1485, but to them the Tudors granted additional powers. In their hands rested the enforcement of law. Justice was dispensed by these officers, who were recruited from the local gentry. In one sense they became the mirror by means of which the Crown gained the reflection of local opinion and desires. When the king advocated some measure which these gentlemen desired or to which they were not opposed, there was little difficulty in securing legislative or judicial sanction. Four times a year, the justices of the peace for every county gathered in what was known as the Quarter Sessions. Here they displayed considerable skill in handling a variety of duties. Their jurisdiction covered local criminal offenses such as murder, theft, and violations of the laws against the Church. They had no civil powers though they frequently assisted in such matters. In addition they determined the conduct of the grain trade, supervised poor relief, licensed inns, and handled the repair of the highways. Through them and the lords' lieutenants, local military officers created in Edward VI's reign, the central government secured valuable information regarding local attitudes and conditions. Reference should also be made to the sheriff who served as a channel of governmental communication, exercised certain financial duties, and was an important member of the county court.

Centrally and locally, the Tudors exercised wide powers and ruled far more despotically than their Yorkist and Lancastrian predecessors. The English constitution, while not destroyed, was bent in spirit more than in form. Additions were made, such as the extra-procedural courts; parliament was often ignored; and revenue was frequently gained by means that were unlawful as judged by later standards. But in spite of numerous evasions of the law the Tudors apparently did what they did with the consent of the governed. This may be explained in part by the fact that the Tudors wanted what the nation wanted. Mere coincidence of purpose or objective is not the whole explanation for the success of these capable monarchs.

When Henry Tudor defeated Richard III at Bosworth Field, the nation witnessed but another of the many battles which had been waged between the Yorkists and Lancastrians. These encounters had followed the nerve-racking and treas-

ure-exhausting experiences of the Hundred Years' War. Foreign and civil conflicts had done little to advance the prosperity or culture of England. Life and fortune had been
squandered. Education and spiritual values had been allowed
to decline. The monarchy was being eclipsed by a feudal
nobility which thought only in terms of its own material gains.
Townspeople and husbandmen bemoaned the absence of orderly government. What England wanted was peace so as
to set her foundations anew, and it is precisely this that the
Tudors brought to England. Law and order, despotic as it
was, proved not an unmixed blessing to the middle class. An
opportunity for investment was offered to surplus capital.
Englishmen were encouraged to sail the high seas in search
of treasure and empire, while at home domestic industry and
trade expanded at the expense of foreigners who ultimately
were forced to leave the realm. Henry VII and Henry VIII
gained the good will of their subjects and utilized their support on many occasions. Had it not been for this fact and
that England detested the alien domination of Rome, the Reformation might not have gone the way it did. Many questions were raised concerning Henry's repeated marriages, and
these might have been dangerous for a government which
lacked the confidence of its subjects. Once Rome had been
expelled, the nation slowly began to manifest an interest in
government. Some indication of the strength of this movement was felt by Mary, but it remained for Elizabeth to experience the full impact of this change of opinion. Her strong
arm and mind, however, wrought so many good things for
her people and she so endeared herself to the nation that no
direct attack upon her power was made during her lifetime.
After her death, the protest against arbitrary government burst

upon the House of Stuart with devastating results that would have confounded even Henry VIII and his daughter Elizabeth, had they still been alive.

SELECTED BIBLIOGRAPHY

Consult the references given for the previous chapters beginning with Chapter XIV.

CHAPTER XIX

A Divine Monarchy

A FEW hours after Elizabeth's death, Robert Carey, a cousin of the Queen, rode north to hail James VI of Scotland as the new ruler of England. James's title to the English throne had already been recognized by Elizabeth's councillors. The nation at large, moreover, was kindly disposed towards the Scottish king. Had the English been able to see into the future, however, it is likely that the Crown would have gone, as Henry VIII's will provided, to Edward Seymour, a great grandson of Henry's sister Mary. Not gifted with foresight, the Council acted in accordance with Elizabeth's guarded suggestions and proclaimed James, king of England.

James VI of Scotland

James's early life had been crowded with difficulties. He had been elevated to the Scottish throne after his mother's marriage to Bothwell. Surrounded by the Lords of the Congregation, he had witnessed their silent approval of Elizabeth's treatment of his mother and had been reared in the Presbyterianism of John Knox. At the same time his tutors had indoctrinated him with the idea of absolute monarchy and he had become a firm believer in the theory that kings govern as divinely appointed agents of God. Monarchs, according to

this theory, were responsible to no one but God and might
rule with or without parliament. Every subject was in duty
bound to obey the dictates of a divine right king, even though
the latter might violate the commands of God. Resistance to
the royal will was treason before the law and sinful in the
sight of God. So convinced was James of the truth of these
views that while yet in Scotland he incorporated them in a
volume entitled *True Law of Free Monarchies.* In this work
as well as in many of his speeches to parliament, James proclaimed that kings are the "breathing images of God" and
that the "State of Monarchy is the supremest thing upon earth;
for kings are not only God's lieutenants upon earth and sit
upon God's throne, but even by God himself they are called
gods."

Such a philosophical foundation was bound to make its
arch exponent sure of himself and quite intolerant towards
those who questioned his thesis. James surrounded himself,
therefore, with advisers who believed as he did; and while
some of his councillors had ability, the great majority were
of little consequence. George Villiers, for example, won
James's friendship and a dukedom by his personal charm and
clever tongue. His influence, particularly after he had been
created Duke of Buckingham, became so extensive that it almost eclipsed that of the entire council. James, moreover,
failed to grasp the spirit of the English constitution and was
unwilling to listen to the wishes of his subjects. When it
pleased him to bully he did so, regardless of consequences.
When stern opposition appeared in his path he resorted to
arbitrary means. At no time did he display skill or tact in
dealing with a stubborn and sensitive House of Commons.
Where the Tudors would have hesitated to tread, James
marched in with supreme confidence. Upon his opponents
he hurled ridicule, abuse and contempt. Monarchy took on
the complexion of a poorly run school; James was the all-wise
master and dictator who frowned upon dissent. James, how-

ever, was an intellectual giant so far as academic questions of government or religion were concerned. He could hold his own in debate with the keenest theologians, and frequently he confounded his councillors by his penetrating observations. In private circles he was kind and generous and never disgraced himself by intemperance. Probably he merited the characterization given him by one of his contemporaries who called him the "wisest fool in Christendom."

Puritanism

In 1603 England needed a wise and tolerant monarch. The day for arbitrary government was rapidly passing. Spain and Rome had been humbled and the Anglican Church had intrenched itself in the hearts of the English. England had set its economic house in order. Public opinion demanded that government should rule in accordance with the will and needs of the people and not in the interests of a king or dynasty. Manifestations of this feeling had appeared during Elizabeth's later days and upon her death crystallized into what might be termed the Puritan-Parliamentary group. In religious matters this bloc proclaimed the right of the individual to free himself from episcopal domination. Man, moreover, had been emancipated from authority by the Renaissance and Reformation and was free to approach God without the intercession of a priest. The English Church, so this group declared, had done well to break with Rome but still was in need of further purification. The services must be simplified; there should be more singing and preaching and less ritual and ceremony. Anything that smacked of Rome should be removed. The historic Anglican Church was not to be destroyed but was to be saved from self-destruction. Although these views represented the attitude of most Puritans there were some among them who wished to go further and establish an ecclesiastical order similar to Presbyterianism. John Calvin's concept of the inherent equality of those predestined for salvation appealed strongly to the latter faction, many of whom evidenced their feelings by withdrawing from the Anglican communion and setting up their own religious organization.

Politically, the Puritan-Parliamentary group held that the Crown should govern through the elected representatives of the people and not through a hand-picked council. Sovereignty rested with the people and not with a king. Firm believers in this theory of government, the Puritans stoutly denied James's theories and eagerly accepted his challenge. There was little in the annals of England to 1603 to sustain the ideal of national or parliamentary sovereignty. Final authority, according to law, actually rested in the hands of the king, in spite of the gains which had been made during the struggles of the fifteenth century. These gains, moreover, had been materially reduced during the period of the War of the Roses and the Tudor monarchs. It became the avowed objective of the parliamentarians, however, to reëstablish what they claimed to be their former powers and rights. If history endorsed the position taken by James it did not deny the existence of an evolutionary force which was working for the establishment of a new order.

The Hampton Court Conference

Shortly after his arrival in England, James was waited upon by a group of Puritans at Hampton Court, one of the royal palaces. At this gathering the Puritan attitude toward religion was presented in what was known as the Millenary Petition because of its alleged thousand endorsers. Although the petitioners had avoided suggesting any change in church government, it was evident to all that the question of the episcopacy was the very heart of the controversy. James knew this as well as the Puritans, and when one of them carelessly referred to the "presbytery," the Scotch system of church gov-

ernment, the entire issue was brought before the conference.
James broke up the meeting by exclaiming, a "Scotch Presbytery . . . agreeth as well with a monarchy as God and the
Devil. Then Jack and Tom . . . shall meet and at their
pleasure censure me. . . . Stay, I pray you for one seven years
. . . and if then you find me pursy and fat and my wind-pipes
stuffed, I will perhaps harken unto you."

The Anglican clergy and the royalists in general applauded
the King's position, which so eloquently endorsed divine right
monarchy and the rule by bishops. Scottish Presbyterianism,
which called for a democratic arrangement of church life,
represented the exact opposite. Puritanism meant to James
the abolition of both the episcopacy and monarchy. The Puritans had ample reason, therefore, to be alarmed over the results of the Hampton Court Conference in spite of a few
concessions which the Crown allowed, notably the famous
King James's version of the Bible. James, moreover, rigorously enforced the use of the Book of Common Prayer even
though some three hundred of the clergy forsook their livings
rather than subscribe to this liturgy. During the rest of
his reign (1603–1625), the Puritans gained little ground in
their religious opposition to the King, though their constant
running attack caused him no end of trouble. He did not
"harry" them out of the realm as he had threatened at Hampton Court; and those who set up their own churches or withdrew to Holland and later to the New World did so of their
own choice and not because of any severe persecution on
James's part.

The Gunpowder Plot

In advocating Puritanism, the Protestant element was aware
of James's sentimental devotion to Rome. His mother had
suffered death partly because of her staunch Catholicism.
Gossip harped upon this fact and intimated that James was

an ardent Romanist. Evidence of James's desire to espouse Catholicism, so it was claimed, existed in his lax enforcement of the penal laws against the Catholics. More convincing, however, was the attitude of the Romanists themselves. Why should they be showing their true colors or why should they be talking so openly about their faith unless they had reason to think that James intended to reëstablish Catholicism in England? Many Anglicans agreed with the Puritans in the latter's judgment of James's actions. But James had no desire to restore Roman authority. He realized the inherent strength of the Anglican Church and was willing to conform to its creed for political reasons. Divine right monarchy, moreover, and papal power agreed as well as "God and the Devil." James was and always would be an Anglican.

Hoping to silence the opposition and correct their views, James ordered stricter enforcement of the penal laws. The Catholic element interpreted this as a challenge that could not be ignored. James as well as parliament was responsible for this anti-Roman policy. Accordingly, a number of misguided Catholics risked all in a foolish attempt to blow up the parliament buildings in what was known as the Gunpowder Plot. The timely discovery of the plot frustrated the attempt, which if successful might have caused the death of many Lords and Commoners as well as James, who was in attendance at parliament at that time. A fresh batch of anti-Catholic laws and the execution of the ringleaders in the plot, followed. Later in his reign, James relaxed these measures, thereby arousing Protestant and Anglican fears of Rome.

James and Parliament

Puritan sentiment was present in every major political issue that arose during James's reign. A controversy was precipitated as early as March, 1604. In issuing writs for a general election, James had informed the voters that they were not to return bankrupts or outlaws. Bucks County, however, elected an outlaw. When James heard of this he declared the election null and void. The House of Commons interpreted James's action as a violation of its rights and informed the King that it alone was the judge of elections. Although a compromise was effected, the Commons expressed their views on this and other constitutional matters in the famous *Apology* of 1604. Though never presented to James, these resolutions may be viewed as the platform of the parliamentarians for the next forty years. "The privileges of the subject," so it was stated, "are for the most part at an everlasting stand." The Commons did not intend that the King's prerogatives should override the liberties of Englishmen. James did not ignore the challenge. In haughty terms he berated them for their presumptuous conduct and closed their mouths by dissolving parliament.

Parliamentary protests appeared in later meetings of the Commons. Few indeed were the occasions when the Crown and parliament were in accord. Unable to work harmoniously with this body, James at times endeavored to rule without their assistance. His success in this respect rested primarily upon the absolute devices which he had inherited from the Tudors. Thanks to his control over the personnel of the common-law courts he was able to gain decisions favorable to the royal prerogative. To illustrate, for some time parliament had refused to provide for a political union of the kingdoms of England and Scotland. James had hoped for the passage of such a measure and never could understand why Englishmen allowed ancient enmities to overshadow the advantages which would follow from a consolidation of the two states. His justices, however, were more conciliatory, and in *Calvin's Case* ruled that a Scot born after James's accession to the English throne became a subject of the king of England. While this decision did not create a political union, it did grant a legal status to Scotchmen. About the same time this ruling was announced, the Court of the Exchequer in the *Bates Case* stated that the Crown might levy impositions (additional customs dues) without parliamentary authority. Historically, the right of the Crown to increase these rates was sound and legal. The Tudors had done this and there was no law which invalidated a continuance of this practice by James. Even the parliamentarians admitted this, though they were determined not to sanction it through fear of consequences.

James Humbles the Courts

James's good fortune in these two cases, as well as his faith in divine right monarchy, led him to pose as a Solon or Solomon before his courts. But when James asserted that he was empowered to hear and settle any point of law, bitter opposition appeared. Led by Chief Justice Coke the united bench forced James to beat a hasty retreat. And when James by proclamation created offenses unknown to existing law, Coke and his fellows frankly told the King that he had erred, as the "king hath no prerogative but that which the law of the land allows him." A little later the situation was reversed in the celebrated case of *Commendams*. The issue involved concerned the right of appointing an individual to a church holding or living. Bishop Neale of the diocese of Litchfield had received from James the grant of a living to be held *"in commendam,"* that is, in conjunction with his bishopric. As the legal head of the Church, James claimed the right of making appointments *in commendam*. The plaintiffs, Colt and Glover, however, held that past practices accorded them this right. Hearing that Coke and his colleagues favored the plaintiffs, James asked the bench to withhold their decision until he had spoken to them. The judges replied that their duty forbade any delay. Whereupon the King summoned them and sharply reprimanded them for their action. The entire bench was so overawed that it begged for pardon. Shortly thereafter Coke and the other justices were asked to reverse their views on royal power and abide by the King's wishes in the future. A refusal implied an abandonment of any future professional advancement. All yielded to James except Coke, who reiterated his opinion that the King's request for delay was a violation of law and that he would act in the future as befitted a justice of England. For his bold stand, Coke was dismissed from the bench. Later, he appeared in the House of Commons as a determined foe of James. Royal influence of this type was not new, though never before had a judge been dismissed for having opposed the Crown in a matter that was primarily political in nature.

Financial and Foreign Affairs

Independence of parliament was also sought by James in financial affairs. The *Bates Case* had netted over $350,000 a year. The sale of crown lands and peerages brought in additional sums as did loans and friendly benevolences. These, as well as the amounts which came from ordinary sources, were most acceptable to James, who had inherited a heavy national debt from Elizabeth. In justice to James it should be noted that the total revenue was below the cost of government and, even had the King pruned his budget drastically, a deficit would have remained. Government had grown more complicated since the Tudors had taken office, and to meet the extra cost additional revenue was needed. Irish disturbances, a legacy of Elizabeth to James, called for further outlay. Nor should it be forgotten that the discovery of gold in America had skyrocketed prices throughout Europe. At the same time many of the sources of revenue, which had been so profitable in medieval times, either had totally disappeared or had dwindled to almost nothing. The Puritans knew this but were unwilling to help, though they accused the Crown of maintaining an extravagant and immoral court.

Unable to meet his bills, James reluctantly summoned parliament. Limited subsidies were voted but never enough to satisfy the King. Tampering with elections failed to bring the desired results. No better illustration of James's relation to parliament may be cited than his experience with his third parliament, which sat from January, 1620 to January, 1622 inclusive. Financial needs, prompted in part by James's entrance into the Thirty Years War in defense of his daughter's husband, the Elector Palatine of Germany, had necessitated the calling of parliament. James believed that parliament would come to his support and it might have, had it not been for the announcement on his part that he was negotiating an alliance with Spain. Charles, James's heir, was to marry the Infanta of Spain. In return for this alliance, Spain was to exert pressure on Germany in favor of the Elector. Unfortunately, James thoroughly misunderstood English opinion toward Spain. The mere suggestion of an alliance with Catholic Spain created consternation throughout the realm. The House of Commons was openly hostile and discussed foreign affairs in a manner that irritated the King. James ordered it not to meddle in his affairs, but the Commons replied by asserting both jurisdiction and freedom of speech. James scolded it for its impudence. The Commons answered by the celebrated Protestation of December, 1621. In this document the Commons affirmed its historic right to debate freely all matters of government. Nor could any member be imprisoned or harmed for what he had said, except at the command of the Commons. James, in his anger, asked for the Journals of the House and with his own hands tore out the Protestation. After this he dissolved parliament (January, 1622).

In the meantime Charles, accompanied by his friend, the Duke of Buckingham, had gone to Spain. Nothing came of this courtship, for Charles found the Infanta unattractive and the Spanish court rather cold and disrespectful. James informed parliament of these facts when it assembled in the early spring of 1624. Parliament was anxious to promote a Spanish war and would have voted supplies had James but asked for them. The King, however, did not want a war with Spain. His plan called for a continuation of hostilities in Germany. For a time parliament and James were at loggerheads. A compromise was finally reached whereby limited sums were voted for increasing the navy and for subsidizing the Dutch, who were fighting the Catholic princes on the Continent. It is of significance that the supplies were granted for an express purpose, thus reviving the practice, followed during the Lancastrian period, of stipulating the object of appropriations. Beyond this, James's last parliament did nothing except to impeach the Earl of Middlesex, one of James's ministers. Three years earlier Francis Bacon, then Lord Chancellor, had been removed from office on the charge of bribery. In both cases, the Commons had revived an ancient practice. Whereas the Tudor monarchs had held that their ministers were responsible to the Crown, the Commons was informing the Stuarts that ministers were the agents of parliament. Clearly a new order was in the making. But James died in March, 1625 and the storm burst over the monarchy in the reign of his son, Charles I.

Charles Becomes King of England

Charles was as stout a defender of divine right monarchy as his father. Moreover, in spite of a genial disposition and an athletic figure, he made himself decidedly unpopular. His intense religious feelings were distrusted because of his well-known devotion to Rome. His marriage to Henrietta, sister of Louis XIII of France, filled England with alarm. France, though less distasteful than Spain, was Catholic and thoroughly under the domination of Cardinal Richelieu, an outstanding foe of the Protestant princes of Germany. The marriage alliance, moreover, called for a relaxation of the penal laws. In addition, Charles openly flirted with Arminianism, the views of the Dutch theologian Arminius who was fundamentally opposed to Calvinism. The Puritans condemned Arminianism not only because it rejected Calvinism, but also because it stressed a creed too much like that of hated Rome.

Parliament Attacks Charles and Buckingham

Charles's religious policy, therefore, was subjected to criticism by his first parliament which met in June, 1625. The Commons also opposed the continuance of the Continental war. But Charles was determined to carry on this conflict and brusquely asked parliament for additional supplies. Although the Commons respected the King and was chastened by his request, it refused to vote adequate appropriations. What was more significant, it refused to grant tonnage and poundage for life as every preceding parliament had done at the accession of a new monarch. The Commons was willing to vote this supply for one year pending an investigation of the question of impositions, but neither the Lords nor Charles would accept the offer. As a result, tonnage and poundage was not granted, though Charles levied this tax on the ground that the Commons had no right to withhold this supply. Shortly thereafter the lower house heard of Buckingham's use of the navy, in conjunction with the French fleet, against the Huguenots of Rochelle. To the Puritans this was positive proof of Charles's Roman tendencies and they flatly refused further supply until the King agreed to select as ministers individuals in whom they had confidence. Charles recognized this as an attack upon his prerogatives and his friend Buckingham and met the challenge by dissolving parliament.

Limited in funds but overendowed with folly, Charles then allowed Buckingham to undertake a naval attack against Cadiz, for a war with Spain had been declared in the meantime. The expedition was miserably handled and proved a complete failure. Puritan opposition rose to new heights and when Charles met parliament in February, 1626, he and Buckingham were subjected to fierce criticism. Moreover, the Commons introduced impeachment charges against Buckingham. Hoping to cripple the opposition, Charles forbade such an attack on his friend and told the Commons to hasten his request for funds for the Spanish war, "or else it will be worse for yourselves; for if any ill happen, I think I will be the last that shall feel it." The Commons resented this as an attack upon its freedom of speech and was convinced that Charles was its foe when he imprisoned Sir Dudley Digges and Sir John Eliot. It refused to vote a penny or continue business until these men were released. Charles yielded but when the Commons renewed the assault on Buckingham, the King had to choose between retaining his minister or securing supplies. He decided in favor of Buckingham and proceeded to dissolve parliament. Driven to desperation, he threw discretion to the winds and imposed a forced loan. Soldiers were sent throughout the realm, quartered among the civilians and at the point of the sword they collected over a million dollars. Stout resistance to the legality of this loan led Charles to dismiss Chief Justice Crew, who had refused to sanction the law, and to imprison a number of citizens, who had refused to pay the tax. Among those placed in custody were five knights who sought to test the legality of the tax and their arrest by suing for a writ of *habeas corpus*. Charles's lawyers replied by showing that these men had been jailed by order of the King. The court decided that this was good and sufficient reason for detention and remanded the knights to custody. No definite charge had been named by Charles in arresting these men and, as matters stood, he might im-

prison anyone without assigning cause, a procedure which cut
boldly across the principles of common law. Technically, the
King could have named no other charge than the refusal to
meet the forced loan, the legality of which he himself doubted.

The Petition of Right

In the meantime Buckingham had sought to recoup his
fallen fortunes by influencing Charles to precipitate a war
with France. Hoping to return a national hero, Buckingham
led a naval attack against the French island of Rhè. The enterprise was an utter failure, and Charles, hard pressed for
funds, was forced to summon parliament. Brushing aside the
royal plea for subsidy, parliament opened a determined attack
upon the Crown. It denied the legality of the forced loan,
found fault with the quartering of troops and the use of martial law, and challenged the King's arbitrary methods of imprisonment. These opinions were finally put into a bill which
passed both houses. Realizing that he could gain no money
unless he accepted the measure, Charles reluctantly gave his
consent to what is known as the Petition of Right (1628).
The Commons showed its appreciation by voting several subsidies. Sentiment was also strong for granting tonnage and
poundage for life. But when a petition was presented to
Charles asking for Buckingham's dismissal, the King replied
by proroguing parliament. Before that body reconvened,
Buckingham was dead, struck down by an assassin.

Eliot's Resolutions

Buckingham's death might have helped Charles had he not
continued to alienate his subjects by arbitrary government.
In open violation of the Petition of Right, which had stated
that no "gift, loan, benevolence, tax, or such-like charge" could
be made except by act of parliament, Charles had levied ton-

nage and poundage. Moreover, the King and his Archbishop, Laud, had been promoting Arminianism in a manner which evoked sharp protest from the Protestants. Small wonder, therefore, that the Commons ignored the King's pleas for funds when it assembled in January, 1629. Instead it undertook a searching inquiry into the conduct of government. When Charles heard of these proceedings he instructed the speaker to adjourn Commons. As the speaker was about to rise, signifying an adjournment, two robust members pinned him to his seat while Eliot proposed several resolutions condemning the action of the King. The speaker refused to put these resolutions and Eliot, confounded by what had happened, cast them into the fireplace. Charles, informed of these proceedings, sent a peremptory command to the Commons to adjourn and, while this order was being brought to the house, the Commons passed by acclamation Eliot's Resolutions, which one Holles repeated from memory. Then the speaker was released and the Commons adjourned, only to be formally dissolved in March of the same year.

Eliot's Resolutions never became law though they represented a statement of opinion by the Commons to the entire nation as to Charles's recent actions. Anyone, so these resolves ran, who sought directly or indirectly to extend or introduce Popery or Arminianism was to be regarded as a capital enemy of the state. Moreover, anyone who advised the levying of tonnage and poundage or who paid it when not voted by parliament was declared a traitor to the liberties of England. Charles showed his disdain for these views by governing the realm without parliament for the next eleven years.

Charles Rules without Parliament

During this interval the Crown's ministers provided Charles with funds sufficient to maintain government. Tonnage and

poundage was imposed and enforced by arrest and imprisonment. Monopolies were also granted in large numbers and
the royalties netted Charles a handsome sum. Obsolete laws
were revived like that requiring knighthood of all property
owners, whose estates were valued at £40 a year. More important than these was "ship-money." This tax was of ancient
origin and provided for the building and equipping, in time
of war, of a ship for naval purposes. Only the maritime
counties and towns, however, were liable for this tax which
during the course of time had been commuted from ships
to money. In 1634 Charles announced that "ship-money"
would be levied in view of recent depredations upon English
trade by pirates. In spite of the flimsiness of this excuse, a
goodly sum was secured. The following year the tax was
repeated but this time it was imposed upon the inland as
well as the maritime counties. This clearly was an infraction of the letter and spirit of the tax and evoked sharp protest.
Charles, however, was so gratified with the returns that in
1636 he issued orders for another levy, thus revealing that
financial needs rather than danger from an enemy were his
real motives.

Among those who refused to pay "ship-money" was John
Hampden, a Puritan and country gentleman of some wealth.
Hampden carried his case to the courts. By a division of
seven to five, the judges upheld the legality of the tax. The
bench ruled that when the Crown deemed the country to be
in danger such taxes might be assessed. The reaction of the
Puritan-Parliamentary group to this decision was one of dis-
may. The way had been opened for further taxation which
in the absence of parliament could be met only by armed
protest. The decision also demonstrated how dependent the
judiciary was upon the king. In the future, the rights of
Englishmen were to be denied any legal protection.

Flushed by this success, Charles continued to levy "ship-
money." Financial independence had been secured. Let

Charles live within his income and embark upon no foreign war, and there would be no need for summoning parliament. One of the King's ministers in speaking of the decision said, "Let him [Charles] only abstain from a war a few years, that he may habituate his subjects to the payment of this tax, and in the end, he will find himself more powerful and respected than any of his predecessors." Unfortunately for the cause of divine right monarchy, Charles allowed himself to be drawn into a conflict with Scotland over religious matters.

The Laudian Policy in England and Scotland

Ever since the death of his father, Charles and Archbishop Laud had attacked Puritanism and Calvinism within the Anglican Church. Dissenting clerics were removed from office, and staunch believers in Arminianism filled their places. Elaborate rites and ceremonies were introduced into the ritual. To the Puritans, Laud's program foreshadowed an early return to Rome, though in justice it should be said that the prelate never harbored such an idea. Having purged England of undesirables and having forced the Book of Common Prayer upon the clergy, Laud turned his attention toward Scotland. Scotland, however, rejected Laud's innovations; and when one loyal cleric at Edinburgh tried to use the royal service book, a riot followed. All over the northern kingdom meetings were held and under able leadership there appeared a National Covenant which obligated its thousands of signers to defend the "true religion." Taken aback by this show of resistance, Charles compromised for a time; but in 1639 he dispatched an army against the "Puritan crew of the Scotch Covenant." The royal troops, many of whom had been impressed into service were no match for the well-drilled forces under Alexander Leslie, an officer tutored by no less a master than Gustavus Adolphus, King of Sweden. No actual engagement ever took place and the First Bishops' War, as the event has been called, came to an end. Once again, Charles proceeded to compromise, allowing the Scots to reëstablish the Presbyterian system.

In the meantime Charles had girded himself for a renewal of the conflict. From Ireland, he recalled Thomas Wentworth, whose success in advancing the royal cause over the turbulent Irish marked him as the proper man to deal with the Scots. Shortly after his return he was made Earl of Strafford and, as a member of the King's Council, dominated events for the next few years. Strafford advised Charles to summon parliament and ask that body to support a Scottish war, and if it refused, to resort to arbitrary government. The Crown accepted this counsel and on April 13, 1640, he outlined to parliament the Scottish situation and asked for a subsidy to put down the rebellion in the northern kingdom. Parliament, while none too friendly to Scotland, was determined that the King should redress grievances before a penny was voted. Sentiment ran high against Charles's use of Star Chamber and High Commission, his illegal fiscal policies and his disdain of parliament. Charles's interference with the privileges of that body and his arbitrary imprisonment of its members led to provocative speeches in which the King's conduct was fiercely attacked. Moreover, some of the leaders negotiated with the Scots in the hope of bringing pressure against the King from that direction. When this became known to the King and when he became convinced that the Commons would not vote a supply, Charles dissolved parliament. Later, because of the shortness of its session, this parliament was known as the Short Parliament.

The Summoning of the Long Parliament

Following its dissolution, Charles resorted to various devices to raise money and an army. Advised by Strafford, the King exacted taxes and loans wherever he could, only to encounter bitter opposition or refusal. Strafford's influence was evident everywhere; his violence and despotism knew no bounds. In the end Charles gained but little income. On the other hand he reaped considerable hostility. Blind to the realities of the situation, Charles hurried north with a motley army which the Scots easily defeated. Durham and Northumberland were then occupied by the enemy, and the Second Bishops' War ended in a greater failure than the first. In desperation, Charles summoned the Great Council which had not met as such since the days of Edward III, but obtained little help from this body which distrusted him as much as he did the council. Negotiations with the Scots also were undertaken. While these were in process, writs were issued for a meeting of parliament. Considerable effort and some money was expended in an attempt to influence the elections so as to secure a majority favorable to the Crown. The Puritans, however, conducted a counter campaign and the victory lay with them and not with Charles. On November 3, 1640, Charles formally opened the Long Parliament, so-called because it continued to sit until legally dissolved in April, 1660.

SELECTED BIBLIOGRAPHY

S. R. Gardiner's *History of England, 1603–1642* (London, 1901) is by far the most complete study available for this period. F. H. Relf's *Petition of Right* (Minneapolis, 1917); J. F. Figgis' *Divine Right of Kings* (Cambridge, 1914); C. H. McIllwain's *Political Works of James I* (Cambridge, 1917); G. P. Gooch's *History of Democratic Ideas* (Cambridge, 1898); W. H. Hutton's *William Laud* (Boston, 1897), and H. H. Henderson's *Puritanism in England* (London, 1912) are of considerable interest and value. J. E. Tanner's *English Constitutional Conflicts of the Seventeenth Century* (Cambridge, 1928) presents the legal and constitutional aspects of the reigns of James and Charles. Source material may be found in G. W. Prothero's *Select Statutes and other Constitutional Documents* (Oxford, 1913) and S. R. Gardiner's *Constitutional Documents of the Puritan Revolution* (Oxford, 1906). For additional material consult the references at the close of the next chapter.

CHAPTER XX

Republican England

HAD Elizabeth been alive in 1640, she would hardly have recognized the parliament which faced Charles. Structurally, it was much the same except for a marked increase in the number of peers. She would have wondered, however, at the wealth and political influence of the commoners and at their independence of thought and action. Deep respect for the monarch's skill in statecraft had given way to profound disgust as a result of Charles's repeated blunders. Mysteries of state had become matters of common knowledge. The Commons, moreover, had little to fear from Charles. He was practically bankrupt and, without its financial support, could not rid England of the Scottish army. Conscious of their strength and knowing that the King could not dissolve parliament and keep faith with the Scots at the same time, the Commons opened a determined attack upon royal privilege.

Parliament Reorganizes Government

From November, 1640, to August, 1642, the House of Commons undertook to purge the realm of absolutism. In the first place it introduced impeachment charges against the Crown's ministers, many of whom immediately fled to the Continent. Laud and Strafford, however, faced their accusers. Strafford was charged with treason in that he had advised Charles to use force to destroy English liberties and had sought the assistance of Romanists. But was the Earl guilty? Everything that he had done had been done at the request of the King. Actually, therefore, it was Charles rather than his minister who had violated the law. Treason, moreover, as then defined by law, constituted an offense against the King. Conscious of the weakness of their position and knowing that the House of Lords would not return a verdict of guilty against Strafford, the Puritan opposition altered its tactics. The impeachment charges were dropped and a bill of attainder was introduced. A bill of attainder was a simple statement of guilt and required no judicial action or trial. Like any other bill, all that was needed to pass this measure was a majority vote of both houses. Charles, on hearing of the Commons' action, denounced the latter in emphatic terms and proclaimed the inviolability of his minister's life. But the Commons would not be deterred; and when the Lords intimated their unwillingness to approve of the bill, the Puritan leaders called upon their friends in London for help. Noisy demonstrations by an unruly mob from the City so disturbed the peace of the Lords that many became "indisposed" and absented themselves from the Upper House. As a result of these tactics, a majority was obtained in the Lords for Strafford's attainder. At first Charles refused to sign the bill. Repeated deputations from parliament and street demonstrations before Whitehall Palace, however, forced the King to give his assent. Strafford was executed May 12, 1641 while Laud, against whom a similar bill was introduced, suffered death four years later.

In the meantime the lower house forged ahead with parliamentary reform. The extra-procedural courts, which the Stuarts had used as engines of oppression, were swept out of existence. The entire question of taxation was declared a parliamentary and not a royal power. The Triennial Bill provided that parliament should be in session every three years, though nothing was said as to the frequency of general elections. Parliament also enacted that it could not be dissolved except by its own consent. Attention was also given to the religious question. General hostility existed toward Anglicanism, but when the Commons tried to substitute something in its place they found so many differences of opinion that nothing could be accomplished. A "Root and Branch Bill," which aimed at the complete extermination of the episcopacy, failed to pass the Commons.

The debate over this measure had opened the Puritan ranks to attack, and Charles lost no time in taking advantage of the situation. A wiser monarch would have counseled moderation and would have supported those in parliament who had resisted Puritan tendencies. Instead, he yielded to the advice of his wife and friends and went north to raise an army of loyalists. Charles hoped to gain the armed support of the Scots. He disguised his departure from London by stating that he merely wished to negotiate with the enemy who was about to evacuate the northern counties and return home. Parliament concluded that Charles intended to use the Scottish troops against the liberties of the English people. Steps were taken to defend the kingdom against this attack. In the meantime Charles found the Scots unwilling to give assistance. In the end the King returned home without accomplishing a thing except the increasing of parliament's suspicions. On top of this came the news of an Irish rebellion. Parliament, unbalanced by recent events and believing that Charles intended to use force, argued that the King and Rome had instigated the Irish uprising. On the other hand, English hostility against the Irish demanded that the latter be punished. Fearful, however, of what Charles might do, parliament proposed to raise an army but insisted that it be placed under parliament's control. Charles considered this a direct attack upon his constitutional powers and refused to approve of the plan on the ground that the command of the military was vested in the Crown. Legally, he was right, but parliament had no intention of raising an army which, under Charles's control, might be turned against the English people. This difference of opinion led to further misunderstanding, allowed the Irish to go unpunished, and resulted in the Grand Remonstrance of November 22, 1641.

The Grand Remonstrance

The Grand Remonstrance was a direct appeal by parliament to the English people. It outlined the evils of Charles's administration, it pointed to the constructive achievements of the Long Parliament, and indicated what remained to be accomplished if liberty were to exist in England. The Remonstrance also directly challenged the political power of the House of Lords and struck a fierce blow at the episcopal system of church government. The passage of this measure had been attended by much confusion and had been carried by the slim majority of but eleven votes. Its sponsors, however, believed themselves strong enough to print and circulate the Remonstrance throughout the realm. In taking this step the Puritans realized that they were calling upon the nation to decide whether the King or parliament was to govern England. While the English people were deliberating upon this bid for support against the Crown, Charles had an opportunity to determine his own course of action. Two choices presented themselves. He might accept the situation and endeavor to regain lost ground by a wise use of royal power. This plan called for the cultivation of royalist sentiment, which was fairly vocal throughout the realm, and for the abandonment of absolutism. Such a policy would restore the standing and prestige of the Crown without offending the attitudes and aims of the Puritan-Parliamentary group. On the other hand, Charles might follow the counsel of his wife and close friends and stake all upon a civil war. By the close of 1641, the King gave signs of favoring the first procedure. At the same time, however, he openly flirted with the idea of using force. In January, 1642, for example, the King asked the Lords to arrest and impeach certain members of parliament on the charge of high treason. The Lords realized that they had no constitutional power to impeach a commoner, as the lower house was the sole judge of the conduct of its members. Moreover, the only way by which Charles could sue a commoner for treason was by a jury trial. Accordingly, the Lords refused to grant Charles's request. More significant was the appointment of a committee to inquire into the legality of the request.

Charles Uses Force and Causes a Civil War

On hearing of the action of the Lords, Charles dispatched a messenger to the Commons to arrest Pym, Hampden, Holles, and two others. The House refused to yield on the ground of privilege. Thereupon the King marched upon the Commons with several hundred soldiers. With the military pushing into the chamber, Charles walked over to the speaker and asked him to point out the offending members. The speaker fell on his knees and said, "May it please your Majesty, I have neither eyes to see nor tongue to speak in this place but as this House is pleased to direct." Charles then tried to find the culprits himself but found, as he said, that the "birds had flown." As he left the room he was greeted by the cry of "privilege, privilege." Although the Commons had defied the King, none expected this to be the end of the matter. Some feared that Charles might dissolve parliament at the point of the sword. Hoping to prevent this the House adjourned so as to meet again in London under the protecton of that city's militia. In the meantime Charles had returned to Whitehall Palace and made arrangements for leaving the capital. The King left January 10, 1642 and, after spending several months at Hampton Court and Windsor, went to Nottingham where he unfurled the royal standard and summoned all

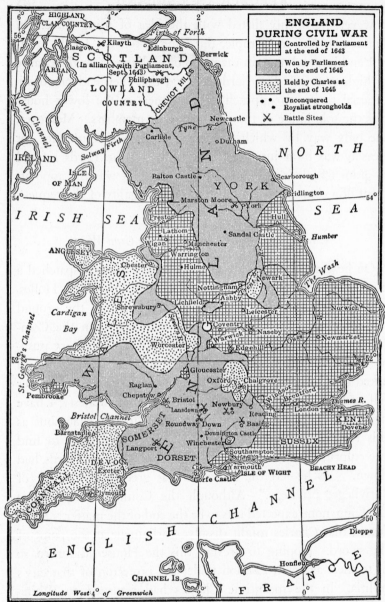

ENGLAND DURING CIVIL WAR

Controlled by Parliament at the end of 1643

Won by Parliament to the end of 1645

Held by Charles at the end of 1645

• • Unconquered Royalist strongholds

✕ Battle Sites

HIGHLAND CLAN COUNTRY

Firth of Forth

Glasgow ✕ Kilsyth ○ Edinburgh

S C O T L A N D
(In alliance with Parliament, Sept. 1643)

Berwick

ARRAN

Philiphaugh ✕

L O W L A N D
C O U N T R Y

CHEVIOT HILLS

North Channel

IRELAND

Solway Firth

ISLE OF MAN

Tyne R.

Newcastle

Carlisle

○ Durham

N O R T H

Balton Castle

Scarborough

Bridlington

Marston Moore ✕

✕ York

Y O R K

S E A

I R I S H   S E A

Preston

Lathom

Wigan

Manchester

Warrington

Chester

Hulme

Sandal Castle

R. Humber

Hull

The Wash

Newark

E N G L A N D

Nottingham

Ashby

Lichfield

Shrewsbury

Leicester

Norwich

Cardigan Bay

Coventry

Warwick

Naseby

Newmarket

Worcester

Edgehill

R. Ouse

St. George's Channel

W A L E S

Gloucester

Oxford

Chalgrove

Raglan

Chepstow

Bristol

Newbury

Windsor

Brentford

London

Thames R.

Pembrooke

Lansdown

Reading

KENT

Dover

Bristol Channel

Roundway Down

Basing

Barnstaple

SOMERSET

Donnington Castle

Winchester

SUSSEX

Langport

Southampton

DORSET

Yarmouth

ISLE OF WIGHT

BEACHY HEAD

D E V O N

Exeter

Corfe Castle

C O R N W A L L

Plymouth

E N G L I S H   C H A N N E L

Dieppe

Honfleur

CHANNEL IS.

F R A N C E

Longitude West 4° of Greenwich

loyal Englishmen to aid him in purging the kingdom of the Puritan scourge. The Civil War had begun.

For the next four years Charles supported by the Established Church and the Royalists, contended against the forces of parliament. In general, the western, southwestern and north central sections of England remained loyal to the King. Parliament, however, had the advantage because it held the wealthier and more prosperous parts of the kingdom. The supporters of parliament also controlled the areas north and northwest of London in a manner which split the royalist section into two parts. From a military angle this was a distinct asset to the Puritans who also had command of the sea. As long as the navy remained loyal to parliament, Charles's chances of gaining any help from France were exceedingly slim. Finally, parliament enlisted the help of the Scots in 1643 by the Solemn League and Covenant. According to this treaty the Scots agreed to furnish an army and to coöperate for the preservation of the rights of parliament and "liberties of the Kingdoms." Parliament was to meet the cost of maintaining the Scottish troops and to admit into their sessions representatives of the northern kingdom. The integrity of the Scottish Presbyterian Church was guaranteed, and a joint committee of both states was established to unify the religious beliefs and practices of the English and Scotch. In this manner, Anglicanism, Arminianism, and Romanism might be extirpated from England and Scotland.

Parliament had paid a high price for Scottish assistance, but without it Charles might not have been defeated. As it was, the royal forces at first defeated the poorly trained and captained troops of parliament. No one was more aware of the inefficiency of the Puritan armies than Oliver Cromwell, who finally convinced parliament of the need of reorganizing the military. Largely as a result of his own efforts, there had been raised in the eastern counties a troop of cavalry known as the "Ironsides." In recruiting these men Cromwell was not concerned as to a soldier's religion so long as he was God-fearing and opposed to Rome. He did insist upon bodily strength and intense loyalty to the cause of parliament. As a result of this policy and a strong arm, Cromwell succeeded in creating an army of great value. Parliament accepted Cromwell's proposal to mold a new army upon the pattern of his "Ironsides" and forced the resignation of incompetent commanders. In 1645 the New Model Army took the field and, in conjunction with the Scots, defeated the Royalists in a number of engagements.

Charles Sues for Peace

By the spring of 1646 Charles's cause was hopeless. Fortunately for him he was not forced to sue for peace, as the Scots interposed between the King and parliament with an offer of mediation. Charles grasped at the chance and early in May entered the Scottish camp at Newark. The rest of the year was spent in fruitless negotiations between the Scots, the Army, the Long Parliament, and the King. Each had its own axe to grind and none seemed willing to make concessions. For some time parliament had been anxious to part company with the Army which, as a result of its victories, had come to control government. Anxious to rid itself of the Army, parliament was ready to treat with Charles provided he would surrender his constitutional rights over the army and navy, to avoid possible repetition of the events of 1642. With parliament in command of the military, Charles's power over that body would be destroyed, and with Charles ruling as the agent of parliament the New Model Army would be forced to disband. Scotland, equally concerned over the growing influence of the Army, asked the King to accept parliament's terms and accord religious toleration to the northern kingdom. But Charles was not in a mood to listen to these overtures. Though defeated in battle, he still claimed

Courtesy Assoc. British and Irish Railways, Inc.

PHOENIX TOWER, CHESTER. Charles I stood on this tower, in 1645, and saw his troops defeated at Rowton Moor.

to be king of England and was unwilling to yield his power over the military. Charles's refusal led the Scots to hand over their royal prisoner to parliament which now expected the King to accept its terms and disband the Army.

The Army was not unwilling to disband provided certain fundamentals were secured, but these parliament refused to consider. Accordingly, Cromwell seized Charles and kept him a prisoner at Newmarket. Not only was the Army in a key position because of its armed strength, but because of its democratic political organization it was united in its opposition to the Long Parliament and Presbyterianism. Shortly after the inception of the New Model Army, a graduated series of soldier's councils had been established which permitted freedom of debate and opinion on practically all matters. By means of this device the Army, in July 1647, had sketched a rough constitution for the future government of England. In this document, known as the Heads of Proposals, parliament was to have control over the King but was not to have a free hand in government. Social and political reforms were outlined to secure the retention of the episcopacy and to accord a limited form of religious toleration. Presbyterianism, therefore, was not to be the state creed. This was a direct slap at both parliament and the Scots who had agreed in the Solemn League and Covenant to establish the Presbyterian system. Indeed, a committee known as the Westminster Assembly had been at work on the problem of establishing Presbyterianism in England. The Heads of Proposals completely nullified the labor of this Assembly and produced considerable discord among the Scots and the members of parliament. Finally, it should be noted that the Heads of Proposals suggested far-reaching changes in suffrage and representation.

Had parliament been willing to accept these fundamentals it is likely that the Army would have disbanded. Parliament, however, rejected these suggestions as did Charles. Had the King approved of them the Army might have forced its terms upon parliament and the Scots. Charles reasoned that by refusing to accept the proposals, he could promote the three-cornered fight which existed between his enemies. Continued discord of this type might lead to his advantage. Cromwell and the Army leaders sensed the King's scheme and determined upon deposition. At this juncture Charles escaped and

fled to the Isle of Wight. By December, 1647, he had strengthened his position by a treaty with the Scots. In return for
their armed support, Charles recognized the Presbyterian system for three years, following which a definite religious settlement was to be reached by him and parliament. Bolstered
by this agreement Charles renewed the war in the spring of
1648 hoping that parliament would not ally itself with the
Army. The contrary happened and Cromwell marched
against the King determined "to call Charles Stuart, that man
of blood, to an account for the blood he had shed and the
mischief he had done to his utmost against the Lord's cause
and the people in these poor nations." Cromwell smashed
the Royalists in battle and then turned upon parliament, which
was up to its old game of forcing the Army to disband. Colonel Pride was sent to parliament with orders to purge that
body of its Presbyterian element, a task which the Colonel
did in true military style. Those who remained, known
henceforth as the Rump, were ready to do the Army's bidding.

The Rump Parliament

Elected in 1640, the Rump was but the sad remnant of the
Long Parliament. When Charles had gone to Nottingham in
1642 he had taken with him one hundred and seventy-five
commoners and all but thirty of the peers. These individuals
served as a parliament for Charles, but their authority was
not recognized by those who remained at Westminster. On
the other hand Charles contended that the parliament at Westminster was not a legal body so long as it refused to accept
his rights and prerogatives. Moreover the Long Parliament
had become an unrepresentative body because of the withdrawal of so many of its members. Further withdrawals followed during the war. Pride's Purge had reduced the Commons to less than eighty members. Nevertheless, the Rump
declared itself qualified to deal with Charles and established

a tribunal to try him for treason. The King refused to recognize the legality of this court and declared himself innocent of the charge. There was no law or precedent, he insisted, that permitted Commons to sit as a court. Existing law, he affirmed, defined treason as a crime against the king and, as he was king, how could he have taken up arms against himself? Cromwell and the Army ignored these technicalities and proceeded with the trial. The court found Charles guilty, and on January 30, 1649 he was beheaded. The execution and the action of the court was unlawful as neither the court, Cromwell, nor the Rump possessed power to declare Charles a traitor under the existing constitution. In the last analysis the extreme Puritan group rested its case upon the right of revolution. To them treason constituted an act against the state and not against the Crown, a concept which, while conflicting with established law, was thoroughly in keeping with the changing ideas of sovereignty. Sovereignty, according to the Rump and the Army, rested with the people and not with Charles. As long as Charles lived, divine right monarchy endangered the liberties of the English people, and to protect these the Army had gone to extremes. It is doubtful whether the majority of the English approved of the trial and execution, but their desires did not interest Cromwell. Militarism was in control.

Eight days after Charles's death, the Rump abolished monarchy and the House of Lords. A little later a Council of State was created, and on May 19, 1649 England was declared a "Commonwealth and Free State." England remained a commonwealth until December, 1653. During these years political power rapidly passed from the Rump to the Council which was dominated by Cromwell. Cromwell quarreled with the Rump as much as Charles had with parliament. On the other hand the Rump found fault with the Army, refused to vote supplies and generally made itself disagreeable. Even the public criticized the Rump for its arbitrary measures restricting games and amusements and for insisting upon a sabbatical sanctity seven days a week. Finally on April 20, 1653, Cromwell, surrounded by a military detachment, went to parliament, cleared the room of its members, locked the doors and declared the Rump dissolved.

The dissolution of the Rump was followed by the abolition of the Council of State and the creation of an executive committee chosen by the Army. After some deliberation this committee proceeded to select, from a list of names submitted by the Puritan clergy, a new parliament, sometimes known as the Nominated or Barebones Parliament. During the latter half of 1653 Cromwell earnestly tried to govern England through this parliament but found it as quarrelsome as the Rump. Shortly before Christmas, Cromwell dissolved the Nominated Parliament, and with its disappearance the Commonwealth came to an end.

Cromwell Becomes Lord Protector

In its place the Army substituted a Protectorate whose powers were defined by a written constitution known as the Instrument of Government. This document marks an important milestone in English history. Never before had England been subject to a written constitution, though it should not be supposed that the English were unprepared for this novel experience. The historical antecedents for this new form of government were deeply rooted in the past. The coronation oath, the feudal contract, the charter idea, and the growth of parliament and legal custom had created a body of organic law which had functioned as a constitution until the War of the Roses. This conflict plus the strong hand of the Tudors brought this development to a close. Later, Protestantism had reasserted these ideas anew. The Presbyterians and the extreme Puritans had established within their religious organizations, formal documents for the conduct of their churches and lives. Many of these extremists were in the Long Parliament and the Army and frequently supported the demand for a written constitution. Accordingly, when the Long Parliament was negotiating with Charles after his withdrawal to Nottingham, they drafted their terms in a form which, if accepted, would have served as a constitution for the realm. Later, the Army submitted to Charles several similar proposals which also should be viewed as experiments in constitution making. The Instrument of Government represents the culmination of this movement, which was thoroughly in keeping with the constitutional development of the medieval period and the political aspects of seventeenth-century Protestantism.

An analysis of the Instrument of Government shows that its authors were not thinking in terms of modern democracy. It is true that they talked about a "Commonwealth" and clothed parliament with far-reaching legislative and financial powers. It is also true that they extended the franchise and redistributed the units of representation in a manner which foreshadowed the reforms of the nineteenth century. On the other hand a "government of the people and by the people" was not desired. Cromwell and his followers had had considerable trouble with so-called popular assemblies. On more than one occasion the government had been hampered by the turbulent agitations of a Rump or Nominated Parliament. But this was exactly what James and Charles had argued, and against this royal plea the Puritan-Parliamentary group had contended. Cromwell was well aware of his changed position but insisted that wisdom and expediency demanded such a course. Sovereignty, he admitted, was lodged in the hands of the people but this was curtailed by certain provisions in the new organic law which left authority with the middle class and the Army. As indicative of this philosophy, the Instrument of Government provided that while a unicameral legislative body was to hold office for a definite period of time, the Council and the Lord Protector were to hold office for life.

Furthermore the representatives of Ireland and Scotland were selected by the Protector. They were not elected as was the case in England. It should not be supposed, however, that Cromwell, who was named Protector in the Instrument of Government, ruled England alone with an iron hand. All of his important acts had to be approved by the Council, which jealously insisted upon exercising its powers. Gardiner, the great authority on the Stuart period, concluded that Cromwell, during the early years of the Protectorate, was not a despot and that the Council checked him on several notable occasions. Finally, it should be noted that the kingdoms of England, Scotland and Ireland were all included under the government of the Protectorate, anticipating, thereby, the United Kingdom of Great Britain and Ireland of the nineteenth century.

Although the Instrument of Government was adopted in December, 1653, parliament was not in session until September of the following year. During this interval a number of ordinances were issued by Cromwell and the Council, most of which parliament approved when it assembled. In general these laws sought to modify the social habits of the nation. Cock-fighting, swearing, drunkenness, dueling, and horse-racing were prohibited, while the Book of Common Prayer was declared a "blasphemous volume." Other ordinances concerned the appointment of church officers, and in this respect Cromwell followed a liberal policy. Presbyterians, Baptists, and Independents alike were given preferment so long as they professed faith "in God by Jesus Christ." In adopting this program Cromwell was acting in accordance with the provisions of the Instrument of Government, which had proclaimed religious liberty for all except believers in Popery or Prelacy. Rome and the Church of England, therefore, were not to exist in England.

Parliament, when it assembled, gave little attention to the religious policies of the Protector. It was far more concerned with political matters and was in no mood to give Cromwell a free hand. It questioned his right to govern and openly challenged the legality of the Instrument of Government. By what right had Cromwell and a group of the Army drafted this document and imposed it upon the nation? Parliament and parliament alone, acting for the English people, was empowered to determine the organic law of the land. In the face of this stern opposition Cromwell very wisely allowed parliament to amend the constitution but he was most careful about retaining his own power. Bitter controversy followed, with Cromwell's feelings rising day after day. Finally, in January, 1655, Cromwell showed his hand by dissolving parliament.

From that time until his death in September, 1658, Cromwell was master of the realm. Increased financial difficulties due to a series of royalist revolts and a Spanish war caused the Protector no end of trouble. In addition to these distractions Cromwell had to contend with the bitter attack of the Levellers and Fifth Monarchy Men. The former, under the leadership of John Lilburne, argued for a republican form of government as opposed to the military dictatorship of Cromwell. The Fifth Monarchy Men, however, challenged the Protector on religious grounds. According to their ideas the second coming of Christ, as promised by Jesus, might be expected any minute. England, therefore, should abandon its futile discussion about king, parliament, and protector and prepare for the coming of the King of Kings. And who could do this better than the "Saints" of the church? To meet these attacks Cromwell was forced to imprison some of his enemies and to censure the activities of others. He was also compelled to summon parliament. Anticipating opposition from this body he sought to influence the elections, and when this failed he boldly purged this assembly of troublemakers. Although permitted to do this by the constitution, his act clearly violated the wishes of the electorate.

Those who supported Cromwell argued that greater power should be given to the Protector and warmly endorsed the establishment of a monarchy with Oliver as king. Cromwell realized the steady drift toward the restoration of monarchy. He knew that the abolition of the Rump, the inception of the Protectorate and the vast powers which had been assigned to him had reëstablished the monarchical idea in government. He also knew that the English people were more sympathetically disposed towards monarchy than republicanism. Cromwell gave the proposition much thought. Gossip reported that he was seen one day in the act of placing the crown upon his head. In the end he refused the offer but did permit a thorough revision of the Instrument of Government through the adoption of the Humble Petition and Advice. According to this document, Cromwell was to name his successor and to govern the country as though it were his kingdom. The Council was reduced in size and relegated to a subordinate position. More important than this in showing the drift back towards monarchy was the creation of an "Other House." Membership in this upper house depended upon Oliver's appointment, subject to the approval of the lower house which was to be elected in much the same manner as provided by the Instrument of Government. It should also be noted that the Humble Petition and Advice largely reaffirmed the religious complexion of England. The endowed church, Puritan in nature, was to be continued.

In governing England under this new arrangement, Cromwell made good use of the Army. The system of major-generalships, begun under the Commonwealth, was continued and England was divided into a number of military districts. Over each of these was placed an officer, directly responsible to

Cromwell, who enforced the law in a despotic manner. Bitter opposition arose against this military regime, particularly in the lower house, which recently had become anti-Cromwell by reason of the removal of many of the Protector's friends to the "Other House." Conscious of their power and realizing the hostile feeling toward Cromwell throughout the country, these republicans opened a determined attack. Negotiations were undertaken with a number of Cromwell's enemies. On hearing this, Cromwell stalked into the lower house, scolded that body for its conduct, then proceeded to dissolve parliament saying "I think it high time that an end be put to your sitting. . . . And let God be Judge between you and me." In taking this step Cromwell was aware that he was cutting himself off from further financial support which he needed badly, for the government was heavily in debt and the Army had not been paid for months. He believed that he could weather the storm until a fresh parliament had been elected. Before this took place, Cromwell was dead.

From the day Cromwell assumed command of the New Model Army until his death, he had followed a policy strikingly like that pursued by Charles and for which the latter had been executed. Cromwell owed his authority to his strong personality and leadership, and to the loyal support which he received from the Army. Thus he was able to dissolve parliament, influence its election, interfere with its actions and impose a form of government as despotic as Charles might have, had the latter possessed an army. He collected taxes at the point of the sword and fostered social legislation which was as irritating to some as that by Charles had been to the Puritans. Both rulers seem to have been equally despotic. This much may be said for Cromwell: he believed he was acting for and not against the liberties of the English people. Charles also believed the same, but behind his policies was the might of divine right monarchy which conflicted with the privileges of the subject.

The Return of the Stuarts

Richard, Oliver's son, became Protector upon his father's death, and for a few months he endeavored to govern as Cromwell would have done. Richard, however, was fundamentally a civilian and had been reared to be a gentleman. He had neither the ability nor the inclination to rule, and allowed the dissatisfied elements to air their grievances. The Army, irritated because it had not been paid and fearful less the Protectorate would be overthrown, openly agitated against Richard. The republicans also were aroused, as were the royalists who believed the time was ripe for a return of the Stuarts. England, in brief, was sickening of the iron rule of the Protector. Cromwell and the Army never had had the united support of the nation, and the arbitrary military and financial methods of Cromwell had served to strengthen this opposition. Even among the army leaders the conviction had grown that England could be saved only by a restoration of the Stuart monarchy. Against this drift of opinion Richard threw himself, only to find that he was removed from office by the Army. The Rump Parliament was recalled but it failed to do as the Army wished and was sent home.

At this juncture, George Monck, Major-General of Scotland, arrived in London. Within a short time Monck sensed the need of bringing back the Stuarts. The Rump was recalled, including those living members of the Long Parliament who had been excluded by Pride's Purge. Acting upon Monck's advice and urged by the financial interests of London, the Rump ordered a general election on the basis of 1642, and then formally dissolved itself. With this action the way was cleared for a restoration of the Stuarts. The new parliament, known as the Convention Parliament, because it had not been summoned by royal writ, gathered at Westminster in 1660. Under its direction, Monck and several others approached Charles Stuart, the son of Charles I, who was then living in the Dutch town of Breda, as to his return to England. Charles listened to their proposals, and in the same year landed in England as Charles II, King of England.

SELECTED BIBLIOGRAPHY

Samuel Gardiner in his three studies, *History of England from Accession of James I to the Outbreak of the Civil War*; *History of the Great Civil War*, (London, 1901) and *History of the Commonwealth and Protectorate* (London, 1903), has presented a brilliant narrative of which but few lines "need to be erased." Supplementing these volumes is C. H. Firth's *Last Years of the Protectorate* (London, 1909) and *Oliver Cromwell* (London, 1900). Other standard biographies are *Oliver Cromwell and His Times* (London, 1912) by H. Johnstone, and F. Harrison's *Oliver Cromwell* (London, 1912). Thomas Carlyle's *Letters and Speeches of Oliver Cromwell* (London, 1904) is also of interest. Leopold von Ranke's *History of England* (Oxford, 1875) should also be consulted. David Ogg's *England in the Reign of Charles II* (New York, 1934) has interesting material relative to the closing years of the Protectorate.

The constitutional and political aspects are summarized by L. Jenk's *Constitutional Experiments, 1649-1660* (Cambridge, 1890) and F. A. Inderwick's *The Interregnum* (London, 1891). Special treatment is given in L. F. Brown's *Political Activities of the Baptists and Fifth Monarchy Men* (Washington, 1912) and in T. C. Pease's *Leveller Movement* (Washington, 1916). John Forster's *The Arrest of the Five Members* (London, 1860) and H. L. Schoolcraft's *The Genesis of the Grand Remonstrance* (Urbana, 1902) are good studies. W. A. Shaw's *English Church during the Civil Wars and under the Commonwealth* (London, 1900) and G. B. Tatham's *The Puritans in Power* (Cambridge, 1913) are of value for ecclesiastical affairs.

CHAPTER XXI

Restoration and Revolution

Charles and the Declaration of Breda

CHARLES II was thirty years old when he entered London in May, 1660. The reception which he received was most gratifying and helped to erase the bitter memories of his continental exile. To the populace, which had thronged the highways from Dover to London, Charles appeared as a gracious and handsome monarch. In stature, he was somewhat taller than most of his contemporaries. His grave face was offset by sparkling eyes and thick ringlets of black hair, which he had inherited from his mother, Henrietta of France. His motions were easy and graceful and his voice was gentle and pleasing. The sharp contrast between Charles and the stern military face and figure of Cromwell was quite apparent to the inhabitants of London, whose cheers showed how happy they were that Charles was back home. But what was behind the genial countenance of the new king or what his intentions were no one knew or particularly cared to know. The reign of the Puritan Saints was over. The Stuarts had returned. What more could England desire?

From Charles's point of view the arrangement was quite satisfactory. For nearly twenty years he had wandered throughout France and the Lowlands, living at times more like a peasant than a prince. Cost what it might to the theory of divine right monarchy, Charles would not follow in the footsteps of his father. England was his home and here he intended to live and die. Lazy as he was, bored by governmental duties, forever seeking pleasure and avoiding responsibility, Charles nevertheless kept the office of king secure. Royal rights were strengthened and the domination of parliament was delayed for nearly fifty years. At Breda, in consultation with the English agents as to the terms of his return, Charles so handled himself as to secure his return as a sovereign and not as a paid agent of parliament. The discussions at Breda had centered about the questions of the arrears due the army, the status of land transfers under the Interregnum, the fate of those who had brought Charles I to death, and the future religious organization of England. Charles promised to settle these difficulties as parliament wished. Beyond these conditions the Breda agreement did not go. It said nothing of the actual powers of either the Crown or parliament. On paper, therefore, the restoration was to be accomplished at no great cost to the monarchy.

Charles kept his word by assenting to bills providing for the payment of arrears due the soldiers, offering an amnesty to all except a few of the culprits of 1649 and promising the return of confiscated land to the Crown, Church, and nobility. Those royalists, however, who had lost property through forced sales received no compensation. Contracts, in short, entered into by an illegal government, the Commonwealth and Protectorate, were null and void, though those between individuals were held binding on the basis of common law. Charles also approved of the demobilization of the army, except for a few regiments, and of the abolition of many feudal dues. An understanding also was reached in respect to finance. Charles was given the revenue arising from customs and excise and such grants as parliament might make from time to time. The Convention Parliament honestly believed that it had made ample provision for royal needs and had left the question of extraordinary supply for ministers and politicians to wrangle over. Actually, Charles's income was below his needs. Mismanagement and high interest rates added to the Crown's embarrassment and forced the King to be more dependent upon parliament than was originally intended. Before the close of Charles's reign, however, the excise and customs receipts, plus gifts from friends abroad, made the King practically independent of parliament.

The Clarendon Code

The Convention Parliament failed to settle the religious problem. Willing as the Anglican members were to accept a system which included a modified Presbyterian doctrine and discipline, no formula could be found capable of commanding a majority vote. The inability of the Protestant group to accept a modified and restricted episcopacy made possible the passage of the "odious acts" of the Cavalier Parliament which met in May, 1661. Opposition to non-conformity by this Anglican parliament was not the only motive which inspired the Clarendon Code, so-called because the Earl of Clarendon was supposed to have fostered this legislation; nor were the Anglicans thinking solely in terms of their own faith and rights. A series of incipient rebellions by non-conformists and disgruntled Cromwellian soldiers substantiated the rumors, which had been circulating since the summer of 1660, of an insurrection against the Stuarts. An hysterical fear swept over the country as one plot after another was uncovered and smashed. Had these demonstrations appeared at another time they would have caused much less alarm. Now, however, parliament connected these disturbances with the religious question and enacted the Clarendon Code in the interest of law and order.

By the Act of Uniformity, the use of the Book of Common Prayer was prescribed for all churches, schools, and universities, while freedom of worship outside a church was forbidden except for family services. Private devotionals, however, were not to include more than five persons beyond the number of the family. Protestant clergy who rejected the use of the prayer book were not to come within five miles of a corporate town. Finally, all town officials were to worship as Anglicans and to take an oath supporting the Crown. Toleration, in short, ceased to exist, while all teaching and governing positions were placed in Anglican hands. Charles had favored a more liberal policy. His later devotion to Rome has been explained on political grounds or because he wished to please those who were his closest friends. Probably, he was not a religious person and as such stood for a wider toleration than Anglican thought would tolerate. He was forced, however, to accept the dictates of parliament or else run the risk of losing the latter's financial support. Possibly this may explain why Charles winked at the many evasions of the Code. In general, however, these laws were so well enforced as to secure an Anglican supremacy for years to come.

The passage of the Clarendon Code was the work of an Anglican parliament. Loyal as this body was to the King, it never allowed divine right monarchy to assert itself as in the days of his father and grandfather. Nor did the House of Lords ever regain the power it had enjoyed prior to the Civil War. Costly as this contest had been, sovereignty passed from the crown in council to the crown in parliament, which by the close of the seventeenth century came to mean the House of Commons. The Restoration, therefore, while it reëstablished the Anglican Church, the House of Lords, and a Stuart monarchy, never erased the constitutional gains made by the Long Parliament. Monarchy might seem to be more deeply entrenched but royal absolutism was ended. Parliament, while it gave the King a freer hand in the Restoration problems of Scotland and Ireland, retained its key position.

Charles's Foreign Policy

Charles II never forgot his father's death nor allowed his ambition to overpower his reason. On several occasions, however, he tried to exalt the royal power, particularly in foreign and religious affairs. That Charles would cultivate the friendship of Louis XIV of France was a foregone conclusion. His mother had been a daughter of a former French king and during the late war and Interregnum the Stuarts had found a home in France. Moreover, Cromwell's foreign policy had resulted in a French alliance against Catholic Spain. Both England and France also had grievances against the Dutch, while Charles's marriage with Catherine of Braganza of the royal Portuguese house had the additional value of enlisting another ally against Spain. Finally, Charles gained the good will of Louis by selling him the port of Dunkirk captured by the English in the Spanish war of 1658. Before Charles and Louis could agree upon an alliance, however, England was drawn into a naval and commercial war with the Dutch. The contest came to an end in July, 1667. According to the treaty of peace, the Dutch ceded to England their North American province, the New Netherlands, which James, Duke of York, had captured in the war. In honor of his achievement the colony was named New York.

Within a month after this peace, Charles lost the advice of his old friend, the Earl of Clarendon. Clarendon had become the object of attack from many quarters. Catholics and non-conformists blamed him for the religious settlement, while others intimated that Clarendon was responsible for the inadequate financial arrangements made in Charles's favor by the Convention Parliament. The Earl was also accused of having thwarted the just claims of the royalists who had suffered during the Civil War, and public opinion in general blamed him for the sale of Dunkirk, the retention of which was dear to English nationalists. The Commons reflected these attitudes by introducing impeachment proceedings which the Earl avoided by fleeing to Europe, where he died in 1674. The significance of the incident does not rest in the attack upon Clarendon but rather in the fact that Charles could not retain as minister one who had lost the confidence of parliament. The King, however, sought to make capital out of the situation by seeking to conduct affairs himself. Accordingly, he bent his energies toward a French alliance and as the latter necessitated the return of Rome to England, Charles worked for the restoration of Romanism.

Louis prevented the immediate realization of this program by attacking the Dutch. The latter, fearful of losing their independence, sought Protestant allies who were alarmed over the pretensions of Catholic and imperial France. Sweden joined hands with the Netherlands in 1668 as did Charles, who saw distinct advantages in the situation. At home he could pose as a defender of Protestantism and thus disguise his Catholic plans. His action, moreover, pleased the English trading classes, who had come to view France rather than the Netherlands as their chief rival. At the same time Charles could bring pressure to bear upon Louis for a speedy settlement of their mutual objectives. Louis sensed the situation and proceeded to detach England from the Allies by the Treaty of Dover (1670). According to this treaty, which was not made public, Louis promised Charles a yearly pension so as to relieve the latter from financial dependence upon parliament. Louis also agreed to furnish troops whenever Charles believed he could force Catholicism upon England. In return, Charles promised to aid the French against the Dutch. Both parties had bargained well and Charles was particularly pleased by the prospect of establishing Catholicism and royal authority in England.

A Catholic Peril

Hoping to conceal his plans still further, Charles announced his French alliance against the Dutch but said nothing as to the other commitments. Anxious, however, to help Rome, Charles issued in 1672 a Declaration of Indulgence which swept aside the existing penal laws. The nation was dumb-founded by the King's foreign and religious policies and talked loudly of a Catholic peril. Parliament, which met in February, 1673, echoed these sentiments and forced the King, who was in need of funds, to annul the Declaration. Flushed with victory and determined to strike hard at Catholicism, parliament then passed the Test Act. Briefly, this measure excluded from all offices and places of trust under the Crown every person who refused to take the oaths of supremacy and allegiance and to commune according to the rites of the Anglican Church. Though non-conformists were included within the scope of this law, many took the required oaths without injury to their religious convictions. Devout Catholics, however, could not compromise so easily. As a result, practically all Romanists were denied participation in government.

The Test Act illustrates the position of parliament. The Crown had been forced to withdraw a program which aimed at exalting the royal prerogative. It also shows how dependent the King was upon parliamentary supply, and that, in spite of French gold. Parliament followed these gains by attacking the King's ministers. For some time Charles had been ignoring the Privy Council and had been conducting the government by means of an inner group known as the Cabal. Knowing that the Cabal had aided the King in his Catholic plans, the opposition attacked and destroyed that body. And while many were concerned over the marriage of James, heir to the throne, to Mary of Modena, a Catholic, it was hoped that Charles would mend his ways and rule with parliament. The opposition, moreover, believed that it had curbed Charles by bringing the unpopular Dutch war to an end. Charles realized his defeat and although he continued to accept Louis' pension, he knew that he could not make England Catholic. Accordingly, he dropped this scheme and selected as his chief minister Thomas Osborne, the future Earl of Danby. Danby, though a firm believer in royal prerogatives, was opposed to Rome and to French domination in English affairs. Around Danby, Charles gathered a ministry which was willing to support the royal power against the dominance of parliament.

Charles's political experiments resulted in the appearance of the modern party system. Blocs and groups had existed before, but at no time had there been an organization possessed of political leaders and a common platform. Moreover, the late seventeenth-century factions adopted the techniques and devices used by party bosses of today. Danby and his followers were known as the Court Party, the ancestor of the modern Tory, or Conservative Party. In opposition to this group was Shaftesbury's Country Party, later to be known as the Whig and Liberal Party. Shaftesbury sought to restrict the royal power and for a time had his way. The King was forced to consent to a marriage between Mary, daughter of his brother James by his first marriage with Anne Hyde, and the Protestant prince, William of Orange. The Country Party knew that James, a devout Catholic, would succeed his brother to the throne. The fear, however, that James would saddle Catholicism upon England was lessened by the knowledge that after his death, Mary, a Protestant, would be queen.

The success of the Country Party was made more effective by the events of 1678. In that year England was swept by a Catholic peril precipitated by the loose and lying tongue of Titus Oates. Although Oates was probably seeking only notoriety, he succeeded in alarming the nation. Catholic arms and money, so he declared, were ready for a civil war.

Charles was to be dethroned, a true Catholic placed in control, and Rome was to dominate England. Oates's disclosures attracted so much attention that the ministry was forced to take action. A copy of Oates's charges was placed in the hands of Sir Edmund Godfrey, a justice of the peace, for investigation. Godfrey's mysterious death in October, 1678, convinced the nation that Oates's stories were well founded. This opinion was reflected by parliament which unanimously passed a resolution to the effect "that there hath been, and still is, a damnable and hellish Plot, contrived and carried on by the Popish recusants, for the assassinating and murdering the King, and for subverting the government, and rooting out and destroying the Protestant religion."

Fundamentally, Oates's disclosures were of significance because they marked the climax of discontent which had been brewing since the days of the Clarendon Code. Charles's reluctance to enforce these laws, the Catholic implications of the French alliance, and the Declaration of Indulgence were the basic factors which produced the Catholic terror of 1678. Oates merely fanned a fire into a raging conflagration. Parliament was swept along with the tide and passed a second test act which excluded Catholics from both houses. Further repressive legislation might have followed but for Oates's insane charge that the Queen had tried to poison the King. Sober judgment then asserted itself. Oates and his followers were tried and found guilty of perjury. With that the Catholic peril subsided.

Charles Versus the Whigs

In the meantime the Country Party, now known as the Whigs, had strengthened their position. At Shaftesbury's suggestion, impeachment proceedings were begun against Danby. The basis for this action was a letter which Danby at one time had written Louis of France in which Charles promised to maintain friendly relations with France provided Louis would pay him an additional sum of money. The French king, annoyed by Charles's foreign policy, had placed this letter in Shaftesbury's hands. Danby pled royal protection on the ground that he had written the letter at Charles's request, but parliament refused to listen. Hoping to save his minister, the King dissolved parliament and issued writs for a new election. Parliament met again in March, 1679, with the Whigs in control. The attack against Danby was immediately renewed. A bill of attainder was passed and the Earl was placed in the Tower. Five years later he was released but by that time his influence in government was a thing of the past. Danby's case is important in that it reëstablished the principle of impeachment. In the same year, parliament passed the Habeas Corpus Act, compelling a jailor upon a writ of any justice to show cause why an individual was in custody.

Having disposed of Danby, the Whig Party attacked the royal brother James by introducing a bill excluding Catholics from the throne. Although Charles was in need of money, he dissolved parliament to protect his brother. A second exclusion bill, however, was introduced by a new parliament in the fall of 1680. Dissolution once again saved James. By this time considerable opposition had developed against the Whigs. Anti-Roman sentiment had subsided and in its place there appeared the fear that the Whigs were going to force a civil war over the question of succession. The memory of the Cromwellian period was still vivid. Shaftesbury, moreover, alienated the support of others by openly advancing the claims of the Duke of Monmouth, an illegitimate son of Charles II.

The King welcomed this shift in public opinion and summoned parliament to meet him at Oxford, a royalist center. The Whigs, who were in a majority, came to this meeting protected by an armed band and demanded the passage of a measure excluding the Duke of York from the throne. Charles met the attack by dissolving parliament. This act met nation-wide approval. Shaftesbury had played into Charles's hand and was brought before a grand jury on the charge of treason. Although a bill of indictment was not returned, Shaftesbury was forced to flee to Europe. Two other prominent Whigs, however, were found guilty and executed, while the Duke of Monmouth was exiled to the Netherlands.

In the meantime Charles had instituted legal proceedings against some seventy boroughs, strongholds of the Whig Party. By the writ *quo warranto* these towns were asked to prove their right to seats in parliament. Charles claimed that they had forfeited their charters and thus were not entitled to representation. The issue was argued before the King's Bench, loyalist throughout, and one after another of these boroughs lost their charters and representation in the House of Commons. Charles granted new charters to the majority of these towns but rearranged the suffrage to insure a Tory return at the next general election. The King never summoned another parliament. French gold plus an expanding income from excise and customs dues provided Charles with ample funds. He did not, however, disturb his good fortune by reviving his Catholic schemes. He left the conduct of government to his Tory ministers and buried himself in a life of pleasure and dissipation. Charles had never been temperate in moral affairs and his weakened body could not stand this last debauch. In February, 1685, he died of apoplexy. Before his death, he publicly announced his belief in the Roman faith.

James II and Parliament

The new king, James II, was over fifty years old when he came to the throne. During the Interregnum he had soldiered under Louis XIV, and as a naval officer had won fame in the

Dutch Wars. Later, as Lord High Admiral, he had demonstrated skill as an administrator. Nor was he handicapped, as Charles had been, by intemperance and loose living. On the other hand he was a typical Stuart. He believed firmly in the absolutism of the Crown and refused to defer to public opinion. The terrible ordeal of the Civil War, the execution of his father and the parliamentary contests of his brother made no impression on James. The English people, however, did not believe that James would raise the question of divine right monarchy. His first acts, moreover, convinced many that he intended to rule as a parliamentary king. He was punctilious in attending to his duties, and the suppression of a rebellion in Scotland and western England was generally applauded. Even his espousal of the Roman faith alarmed only the extremists. The bulk of the nation believed that James intended to keep his religious practices a personal affair.

Parliament, stacked with Tory members as a result of Charles's *quo warranto* proceedings, showed its faith in James by voting him a handsome subsidy. It refused, however, to pass a measure removing the test acts. Disappointed by this show of resistance, James allowed parliament to adjourn; and although he did not dissolve it until the summer of 1687, it never met again. James had committed himself to the blundering policy of making England Catholic. He failed to see that Elizabeth's religious program and the events of the Civil War had made England Protestant. Catholicism, under James, was a lost cause. A wiser and less stubborn king would never have raised the issue.

Fearful as the nation was of James's religious policy, it refused to support Monmouth, who appeared in southwestern England as a pretender to the throne. James suppressed this rebellion as well as one in Scotland under the Earl of Argyle. Both Monmouth and Argyle paid with their lives for their actions. Public opinion, however, was antagonized by the brutal methods employed by James's agents in western England. Here Judge Jeffries, acting on royal order, imposed such severe punishments as to alarm the nation. Nor were the English blind to the fact that the King continued to receive financial assistance from France. Any connection with that kingdom was generally interpreted as a renewal of the Dutch Wars and a revival of the Catholic peril. Rumor had it that James was about to use his army for a religious war in England and the presence of some ten thousand soldiers near London seemed to be proof of his intentions. As parliament had refused to repeal the test acts, James actually began to use force. Backed by the military, the royal courts in 1686 sustained the King's power of dispensing with the test acts. Catholics were appointed to a number of offices in the government. In order to compel obedience to his wishes, James defied the nation by reëstablishing under the name of the Court of Ecclesiastical Commission, the Court of High Commission, which the Long Parliament had abolished. Flushed with victory, James then made a bid for non-conformist support by issuing in 1687 a Declaration of Indulgence which suspended the operation of the test acts and penal laws.

Non-conformity, however, preferred the discrimination of these measures to the supremacy of Rome and allied itself with the Whig Party which reappeared at this time. James received a clear indication of the nation's attitude in the trial of seven bishops who had refused to read from their pulpits the Declaration of Indulgence. Though the judges instructed the jury to bring in a verdict of guilty, the prisoners were pronounced innocent. James was dumbfounded, but the nation hailed the verdict as the beginning of a new order. In London the populace showed their feelings by parades and bonfires and by burning the Pope in effigy. The tide against James rose to greater heights on the birth of a son to the King. The prospect of a line of Catholic kings did not appeal to the English people, who warmly supported the overtures made by prominent Whigs and Tories to William of Orange. William was invited to come to England and rid the land of its Catholic dynasty. William accepted the offer and landed with a Dutch army in November, 1688. James marched to meet his foe, but before an engagement was fought, the bulk of the royal forces had deserted. Realizing that his cause was hopeless, James fled to France. James had failed in spite of the largest standing army England had seen since the days of Cromwell. Nor had the loyalty of his courts protected him in the hour of need. An aroused nation swept these justices aside and convinced the King's soldiers of James's intent to subject Englishmen to absolutism and Romanism. Had James possessed the political sagacity of his brother and had he not surrounded himself with Jesuit advisers, it is likely that he might have weathered the storm. Loyalty to Rome and the principle of divine right monarchy cost James his throne.

The Glorious Revolution

William moved on to London, after James's flight, and met in council such members of Charles's last parliament as could be gathered. These men advised him to assume the office of king pending a general election. William possessed no constitutional power to call a parliament but accepted the advice and issued writs for an election. The parliament, therefore, which met in January, 1689, had no legal basis. Expediency and revolution alone justified its existence. Whig and Tory alike recognized the realities of the situation, however, and united in offering the throne to William and Mary. The royal pair accepted the offer and set forth their views as to government in a declaration, which later was embodied in the famous Bill of Rights, passed by parliament in October of the same year. This measure vested the throne in the persons of William and Mary, provided for the succession of

Anne, Mary's sister, in the event the new monarchs left no issue, enumerated the grievances under which the country had suffered and declared them illegal. The Bill of Rights also declared standing armies illegal except as voted by parliament, and provided for frequent and free elections to parliament. The sovereignty of parliament was restored and the power to suspend or dispense with law was denied the Crown. Moreover, no Roman Catholic was to rule in England. Finally, it provided that excessive bail should not be required.

There was little that was new in the Bill of Rights. The enumeration of past wrongs and the statement of guaranties against royal absolutism constituted but a restatement of past constitutional principles. The day of absolutism as practiced by the Tudors and Stuarts was over. The authority of the English people as represented in parliament was made supreme. Monarchy was preserved but its powers was curtailed by the sovereignty of parliament. The political experiences of the English people begun in the medieval period had evolved a constitutional basis which protected life and liberty. Truly, the events of 1688 and 1689 constituted a glorious revolution, void of bloodshed. James had been deposed and a new king had been proclaimed pledged to rule in accordance with the will of parliament.

Parliament reflected the spirit and aims of the new order by passing a number of measures which supplemented the Bill of Rights. By the Mutiny Act the control over the army was vested in parliament. The renewal of this act, which was limited in life to less than a year, became an annual duty of parliament. In this manner annual sessions of parliament were provided, a procedure which has been followed from that day to this. Later, in 1694, the Triennial Act was passed which provided that parliament could not sit for more than three years. The following year parliament removed most of the strict censorship laws against the press and in 1696 provided a clearer definition of what constituted treason, and what procedure was to be followed in such trials. The question of revenue was settled by a measure passed in 1690. According to this act the Crown was voted a sum known as the Civil List. The amount of this grant was large enough for the king to meet his household expenses and the cost of maintaining the ordinary civil and military branches of government. Extraordinary grants for the army and navy were to be voted as occasion warranted. Finally, parliament passed the Toleration Act of 1689 which accorded to non-conformists the right of public worship provided they took the oaths of allegiance and supremacy and affirmed their disbelief in transubstantiation.

The passage of these measures was not always in keeping with William's wishes. He was forced, however, to accept them because of the implications of the Glorious Revolution and the expanding power of the party system. Although William in 1689 had accepted Whig ministers as the only way of checking the pretensions of the followers of James, known as Jacobites, he did so with much misgiving. Had he been master of the situation, he probably would have chosen Tories who were friendly to the idea of royal power. For a while, William tried to please both groups, but as the orderly conduct of government depended upon the support of the majority in the Commons, William, by 1693, accepted the principle of choosing his ministers from the majority party, which at the time was Whig. Parliament, through the party system, sought to determine the choice of the ministry and established thereby what might be called the first party ministry. At this time the ministry was known as the Whig Junto, which like the Cabal of Charles II, should be viewed as the ancestor of the modern cabinet. The Junto, however, did not function as the cabinet does, for it did not resign after the defeat of the Whig Party in the election of 1698. The fact that it remained in office for nearly a year after the election shows that the idea of a responsible ministry had not been accepted as a permanent feature of the constitution.

Both Whig and Tory coöperated in 1701 in passing the Act of Settlement. William, who had been a widower since Mary's death in 1694, was childless, as was Anne, his sister-in-law and heir apparent. In order to forestall any Jacobite movement in favor of James's son, parliament provided that, upon Anne's death, the throne should go to the Protestant Electress of Hanover, Sophia, a granddaughter of James I. The Act also stipulated that every monarch was to be an Anglican and that England was not bound to protect the foreign possessions of its ruler. In the future, moreover, the king was not to leave the realm without parliament's consent. Membership in the House of Commons was denied to all officers and pensioners of the king. Finally, the act provided that judges were to hold office during good behavior and could be removed upon address of both houses of parliament and that no royal pardon could be pleaded against a bill of impeachment. The Act of Settlement together with the Habeas Corpus Act, the Bill of Rights, the Triennial Act, and other measures passed since 1679 provided a firm bulwark in the interests of democracy against the pretensions of absolutism.

Foreign Affairs

The Act of Settlement was caused in part by William's conduct of foreign affairs. Shortly after his succession to the throne, William was forced to take up arms against the Irish, who had risen in behalf of the exiled James. Elizabeth, it will be recalled, had had her share of trouble in Ireland and had left a troublesome heritage to James I. The blood and iron policy of Wentworth had quieted the turbulent Celts but had not solved the problem of English control. During the Cromwellian period, English authority had been maintained at the point of the sword. The Roman faith had been outlawed and Celtic landowners in Munster, Ulster and Leinster had been driven into the distant and unproductive area of Connaught. Loyal Irishmen and soldiers of Cromwell were then settled in the evacuated areas. During the reigns of Charles II and James II the Irish remained quiet, but upon the overthrow of the Stuarts in 1688, they rose in revolt. James appeared in Ireland and for a time gained control of the Irish parliament. English troops were beaten in several engagements while a hostile French fleet patrolled the Channel. The combined Dutch and English squadrons attempted to defeat the French but were overcome at Beachy Head in June, 1690. In the meantime, William landed in Ireland; and at Boyne, July 1, 1690, he routed the Jacobite forces. James fled to France while William's soldiers resisted a French invasion. The last remnants of James's army surrendered at Limerick the following summer. A military peace, known as the Treaty of Limerick, was then imposed. Among other things, it accorded a limited degree of toleration to the Irish Roman Catholics. The English parliament, however, refused to accept this treaty and passed a statute which excluded Romanists from offices or seats in the Irish government. The Irish parliament, which included only Protestants, followed with a religious code which prevented Romanists from teaching, and in 1697 exiled all the higher Catholic ecclesiastics. From the Irish point of view, this legislation was considered as an infraction of the Treaty of Limerick, and England was labeled as a country that had not kept its word.

Stuart followers also forced William to send an army into Scotland. Although the Scottish parliament had accepted William and Mary, considerable sentiment existed in favor of James. Most of the Stuart sympathizers were Highlanders, who were despised by the Lowlanders for the former's repeated ravagings and border warfare. To protect southern

Scotland from the attack of the Highlanders as well as to stamp out the Stuart cause, English troops were sent north. Victory followed, but the Scots never forgot the brutal massacre of the Macdonald Clan at Glencoe.

Several years before the Glencoe Massacre, William succeeded in forming an alliance against France. The Holy Roman Empire, Spain, and the Netherlands joined with England in an attempt to check the imperial domination of Louis XIV of France. Internal strife among the allies, however, weakened William's endeavors. A naval victory at La Hogue in 1692 was more than offset by French victories at Namur and Steenkerke in the same year. Later the French crushed the allies at Neerwinden and frustrated an English expedition to Brest. During 1694 the English fleet managed to regain control of the Mediterranean. Repercussions of the European war arose in America where the English colonists contested with the French in what is known as King William's War. The conflict dragged on in Europe and the New World for two more years and in 1697 was terminated by the Treaty of Ryswick. Louis agreed to stop supporting James and acknowledged William as King of England. All territory conquered during the war was restored except for certain border towns, which Louis had taken from the Dutch. Although the allies had not won a clear victory, Louis had received his first major rebuff.

Hardly had peace been established when a new threat of war arose over the succession to the Spanish throne. Charles II, King of Spain, was childless, and because of ill health was expected to die at any time. Several claimants appeared. Louis XIV, through his marriage with Charles's sister, pressed his rights, as did Leopold I, ruler of the Holy Roman Empire, who also had married a sister of the Spanish King. A third candidate appeared in Joseph Ferdinand of Bavaria. If the Spanish throne, which governed a far-flung empire in Europe and the New World, were to go to any of these nations, the balance of power in Europe would be destroyed and a general war would follow. William viewed the situation with concern and proceeded to engineer a series of European conferences in the interest of peace. In the agreements which followed, known as the Partition Treaties, the Spanish domain was parceled out in a manner which, it was hoped, would preserve the peace of Europe. Charles II, however, disliked the way his heirs had divided his empire; and under the influence of Louis XIV, he drafted a will in October, 1700, giving the empire to Philip, a grandson of Louis. A month later Charles died. Louis at once deserted the allies, and the War of the Spanish Succession followed.

Although dynastic reasons helped to bring on this contest, which extended to all parts of the world, economic considerations were far more important. The colonial and commercial power of England and the Netherlands was endangered by the prospect of a French and Spanish combination. Determined, therefore, to retain his valuable commercial advantages in India, the Far East, and North America and to maintain the European balance of power, William formed the Grand Alliance of Holland, England, and the Empire. In March, 1702, William died, leaving the settlement of the war and the government of England to his heir, Anne.

SELECTED BIBLIOGRAPHY

Many of the works cited for the previous chapter have material pertinent to the Restoration and Revolution. T. B. Macaulay's *History of England from the Accession of James II* (London, 1913–1915) is a brilliant study for the years 1685 to 1697. David Ogg's *England in the Reign of Charles II* (New York, 1934) is by far the most complete and valuable volume for the reign of Charles II. Keith Feiling's *History of the Tory Party, 1640–1714* (Oxford, 1924) and W. Wood's *History of the Tory Party* (London, 1924) are of value for party activities. R. L. Schuyler's revision of Adams' *Constitutional History* furnishes a good account of the constitutional issues.

Foreign affairs are well handled by J. R. Seeley's *Growth of British Policy* (Cambridge, 1897) and his *Expansion of England* (Boston,

1883). J. S. Corbett's *England in the Mediterranean* (London, 1904); W. L. Clowes' *Royal Navy* (London, 1897–1903), and A. T. Mahan's *Influence of Sea Power upon History* (Boston, 1891) are of value for military and naval affairs. P. H. Brown's *History of Scotland* and W. E. H. Lecky's *History of England in the Eighteenth Century* (New York, 1887) are valuable for Scottish and Irish history. R. H. Murray's *Revolutionary Ireland and its Settlement* (London, 1911) is helpful.

J. Corbett's *Monk* (London, 1889); H. D. Traill's *Shaftesbury* (London, 1888); O. Airy's *Charles II* (London, 1901), and T. H. Lister's *Life and Administration of Edward, Earl of Clarendon* (London, 1837–1838) are good biographies. G. Burnet's *History of His Own Times* (Oxford, 1833); Pepys' *Diary* (New York, 1893–1899), and John Evelyn's *Diary* (London, 1906) depict the narrative history of this period in an interesting and personal manner. J. S. Clarke's *Life of James II* (London, 1816) is of questionable value. For ecclesiastical history see below, p. 449.

CHAPTER XXII

Economic Aspects of the Seventeenth Century

ENGLAND'S foreign trade was world-wide in scope and character when James I succeeded to the throne in 1603. Trading posts and factories were established in Asia, Africa, Europe, and America, while the English flag was carried to all parts of the world by hardy and nationally minded Englishmen. An intensive anti-Spanish feeling had nourished a national spirit which Elizabeth's age had exalted to great heights. Glorification of England and the desire to extend dominion over land and sea had led Drake, Hawkins, and Raleigh to sail the high seas and build new trade connections. Private capitalists were quick to sense the advantages opened by these seamen and invested heavily in numerous enterprises. Colonies were planted at strategic points and were protected by a royal navy which became the pride of English imperialists.

The Regulated and Joint-Stock Companies

The conduct of England's overseas trade at the opening of the seventeenth century was in the hands of the Merchant Adventurers and the Merchant Staplers. Medieval in origin and structure, the Merchant Adventurers became the model upon which the great Stuart trading companies were founded. In general, two types of companies developed—the regulated and joint-stock. In a regulated company, each member conducted his trading on the basis of his own capital and the regulations of his fellowship. There was no pooling of capital and no sharing of profits or losses. One writer has likened their activities to the modern stock exchange. Only members may trade on the stock exchange, subject to general regulations, but each member keeps his own capital, profits, and losses. The Merchant Adventurers, the Eastland, Russia, and Levant companies are examples of the regulated enterprise. In a joint-stock company, each trader trafficked in a corporate capacity and divided profits and losses with his fellows. The East India and Hudson's Bay companies were important joint-stock companies. Throughout the period now under discussion, the Merchant Adventurers largely controlled England's trade to and from the Continent. For a time the Hansards, their ancient rivals, contested with the Adventurers for control of this trade, but ultimately they were driven from England. Fresh opposition came from the Dutch, who were experts in navigation and business transactions. As a result of the seventeenth-century wars and a series of parliamentary enactments, the Dutch were forced to relinquish their hold on the trade to and from England though they retained control over most of the carrying trade of Europe. The Adventurers, moreover, met stubborn resistance at home on the part of independent merchants who wished to destroy the monopoly enjoyed by this fellowship. Most of the opposition centered in southwest England. Determined to free themselves from the domination of London capitalists, the merchants and traders of Bristol and Plymouth charged the Adventurers with unfair practices and excessive financial exactions. So effective was this propaganda that by the reign of Queen Anne, parliament had granted important concessions to these rivals. The Adventurers, however, continued to exist as late as the opening of the nineteenth century.

Similar opposition was encountered by the East India Company. England's superior resources finally forced the Dutch to yield ground in the Far East. The supremacy of the East India Company was then challenged by the Levant merchants and independent traders. As a result the East India Company's century-old monopoly was broken, and its legal status was more clearly defined by the Privy Council and parliament. A large share of the India trade was opened to the independent merchants and to another group known as the New East India Company. Thanks, however, to the strength of the older company in India, where factories had been planted and important privileges had been gained from native princes, the East India Company successfully met the attack of its rivals.

In the hands of these traders as well as those of other companies rested most of England's foreign trade. In the export trade woolen goods continued to bulk large. Linen, lead, and tin were exported. Grain, flour, fish, hides, beer, cheese, groceries, and coal were sent to Europe, India, Africa, and the New World. In return, England imported wine, groceries, iron, timber, naval stores, fruits, soap, rugs, tapestries, and many other articles. At the opening of the seventeenth century, the ships which carried these goods were constructed much like those of the medieval period. They were small in size and were built primarily for short hauls. The discovery of America and the quickening of interest in the Far East led to the building of larger ships to withstand the rigors of overseas navigation. Ships, moreover, were built to meet the attack of foreign men-of-war. These structural changes benefited England's trade to distant parts but worked to a disadvantage in the shorter voyages to Europe. The Dutch, more expert in such matters, constructed lighter and faster ships for European waters and were able to sail and fight where the English could not.

The Navigation System

The superior skill of the Dutch in shipbuilding and navigation led to their success in gaining a large share of the carrying trade of Europe. Nationally minded Englishmen viewed with shame the presence of these foreigners in their ports and demanded legislation which would allocate most of this trade to their own merchants. Scottish ships also frequented English ports too often. At the same time English shipbuilders and insurance companies clamored for greater advantages and the defenders of the royal navy declared that national security demanded a larger fleet and merchant marine. Representatives of these various interests pressed their views so effectively that in 1651 the Commonwealth parliament passed the first of a series of navigation acts.

Under this navigation policy, England's trade was divided into several categories. These divisions are revealed by an analysis of the acts of 1651, 1660 and 1663. First in importance was the European field, heretofore largely dominated by the Dutch. By the new legislation, all European imports, with but few exceptions, were to be carried to England in English ships (built and owned by Englishmen and manned by a crew three fourths of whom were English) or in vessels of the country that produced or manufactured these commodities. French wines, for example, were to enter in either English or French ships. Imports from Asia, Africa, and America were likewise restricted. A similar arrangement existed in the export and import trade of the Colonies. European exports to the plantations first had to land in England, pay duty, and then be reshipped in English or Colonial bottoms. The bulk of Colonial exports was also restricted as to carriers, and had to clear either to England or another plantation. A cargo of Virginia tobacco, therefore, might be shipped to Massachusetts, Bermuda, or England but not to France or Germany. Only by reëxportation from the Mother Country could these goods reach a foreign market.

Mercantilism, which may be defined as the economic side of state-making, was the cornerstone upon which the navigations acts rested. The Mother Country was placed in a most advantageous position. Its trade with foreign states was guarded so as to throw increasing profits to English merchants and traders, while the plantations were viewed as markets for the sale of domestic goods and manufacturers. Non-English commodities could reach the Colonies only by way of England and then were subject to customs and carriage in English bottoms. At the same time the raw materials of the plantations were to be brought first to England or another English colony. English merchants, traders and artisans profited by this arrangement, and the government was assured of an increased revenue.

Anticipating the difficulties relative to the enforcement of these laws, complicated export and import taxes and bonding devices were enacted. Failure to comply with the law resulted in the forfeiture of the bond. So extensive was the trade involved, and so inadequately prepared were the agents of enforcement that violations were numerous. Americans often shipped goods directly to Europe and returned home with commodities which should have cleared through England. The English government, moreover, found it necessary to allow the import of European goods contrary to the acts. Although steps were taken in an effort to correct these abuses, the seventeenth century closed without any great improvement.

It would be wrong, however, to assume that the Navigation Acts accomplished nothing. Important results followed, though most of these were not apparent until the eighteenth century. In the first place a political and economic unity was established between the plantations and England. The acts, moreover, shifted English interest from the European trade to that of the New World and India and stimulated the commercial life of western towns like Plymouth and Bristol. Owing to the expulsion of foreign capital from the Colonial trade and to the absence of alien competition, greater profits were reaped by English and Colonial shippers. In the European trade, however, the foreigner was as active as before. Contemporary opinion as expressed by Sir Josiah Child and Roger Coke, staunch protagonists of the Navigation Acts, contended that the Dutch prospered in spite of these laws. Finally, it should be observed that the Navigation Acts led to international disputes and wars.

England Acquires a Colonial Empire

England's entrance into the colonial world had been retarded by the religious and political upheavals of the sixteenth century. Catholic Spain had never been troubled with a Protestant revolt as had England. Spanish imperialists and traders experienced none of the severe internal discord and strife which hampered the overseas expansion of Englishmen. Once these were settled England directed her efforts toward the founding of colonies. The motives behind this movement were numerous. First, there existed a large supply of surplus capital seeking opportunities for investment. Well-to-do merchants, landlords, and manufacturers recognized the possibilities of Colonial expansion and eagerly provided funds which transported thousands of Englishmen to the New World. Companies were formed, like the London and Virginia enterprises, to foster Colonial growth and trade for financial profit. Often the promoters of one company were heavy investors in another. Interlocking of capital and personnel was frequent. A comparison of the lists of members of the Virginia and East India Companies will show a similarity of a hundred names. Sir Thomas Smith, treasurer of the Virginia Company, was also governor of the Muscovy and East India Companies and a prominent member of the Levant Company.

The New World, moreover, was thought to be a land of milk and honey with gold and silver available in great quantities. Hundreds of individuals and scores of capitalists migrated to America in the hope of getting rich quickly. During the first months of the Jamestown settlement most of the colonists spent their time panning the waters of the James River for gold. Financially embarrassed feudal lords saw in America a chance to replenish their fortunes, while younger sons pictured the New World as a place for the establishment of feudal domains. Public opinion, moreover, viewed England as overpopulated and encouraged the exodus of thousands to relieve congestion at home. Actually, the kingdom was not overcrowded but, because of economic changes during the sixteenth century, a migration had taken place from the farms to the towns. The crowded highways and congested cities convinced Englishmen that the country suffered from overpopulation. Humanitarian motives also entered into the colonization movement and many a person was shipped to America as a means of releasing him from sordid conditions at home. The absolutism of the early Stuarts also drove Puritans in large numbers to New England, while the rigors of the Cromwellian era stimulated Cavalier migration to Virginia. Finally, many came to America to escape religious persecution at home. Political and economic forces, however, were more important.

Agricultural Development

Colonial and commercial development was matched by an expansion in agriculture. Throughout the seventeenth century the character of rural economy was much like that of the Tudor period. On the other hand, owing to the disappearance of the manor as a political unit and the rapid decline of feudalism, the Stuart age became transitional in nature. Medieval forms of tenure still existed, as did medieval methods of farming. Among the changes which were taking place none was more important than that of enclosure. Enterprising farmers and landlords who bemoaned the ancient methods of cultivation eagerly sought to fence in the open fields for more intensified and profitable farming. In some quarters violent opposition arose, leading at times to revolt on the part of the farm laborers and small landowners. The central government, while forced to quell these disturbances, generally tried to restrict extensive enclosure until after the Restoration, when the benefits of large-scale production became apparent. Though protests were registered against enclosure during the reign of William and Mary, the hostility was less pronounced and the way was paved for the great enclosures of the eighteenth century.

Elizabethan defenders of enclosure had argued that their program would result in larger and better crops and would stimulate improved methods of farming and scientific investigation. In general these results were realized. Turnips, which had been grown during the sixteenth century as a garden plant, as well as clover, sainfoin, and other plants were cultivated in greater abundance. Arable and pastureland was enriched by this process and larger yields per acre resulted. During the Tudor period the average yield of wheat per acre had been from eight to ten bushels, while during the seventeenth century it ranged from ten to twelve bushels. The cultivation of roots, moreover, removed the necessity of keeping one third of the land fallow and provided food for cattle during the winter months. No longer did the farmer, as winter approached, have to kill most of his stock through fear of being unable to provide them with fodder. Greater attention was given to the breeding of cows with the result that larger and better milch and beef cattle were raised. Increased pasture and arable land was secured by an intensive program of land drainage, particularly in the Great Fen district, an area of four hundred thousand acres watered by the Stour, Ouse, Welland, and Witham Rivers. The work of reclaiming this land was begun by private capitalists and encouraged by government subsidies and land grants. The Earl of Bedford, for example, spent over £100,000 in this undertaking.

Various mechanical devices were employed by the more alert farmers. Information concerning these, like the Norfolk plough and Plattes' sowing machine, appeared in a number of tracts and pamphlets. Of these, Houghton's *Collections,* Stevenson's *Twelve Months,* Markham's *The English Husbandman,* and the "Enquiries" of the Royal Society of London were the best known. In spite of these publications and the support which the government gave to agriculture, only the more progressive farmers accepted the newer devices and methods. The greater share preferred to follow the customary divisions and treatment of land that characterized the medieval age.

The interest shown by the central government in agriculture was quite logical. For centuries farming had been the cornerstone of England's economic order. Immense sums of capital had been invested in agrarian activities, from which the greater share of the population gained a living. At the close of the seventeenth century England had a population of over five and one-half million people, four millions of whom lived on the farms or in small agricultural centers. Most of the rural population was engaged in raising grain for domestic and foreign consumption. So important had this activity become that the government enacted various regulations of which the Corn Laws were the most important. These laws covered every conceivable phase of the domestic and foreign traffic in grain.

Before the Restoration the export trade in grain had attracted less attention owing to the fact that most of the grain raised was consumed at home. Laws had been passed relative to both the export and import of grain, but nothing in the way of a coördinated policy had developed. After 1660 the government's attitude underwent a definite change. Probably this was owing to an appreciation on the part of the Restoration parliaments of the economic strides the country had made since the days of James I. Accordingly, laws were enacted in great number. Of these the acts of 1670, 1673, and 1689 were the most important. The producer was encouraged by low export duties and bounties to raise grain for foreign markets. The encouragement of tillage was considered vital to agriculture, and at the same time it was the surest means of promoting shipping. A pronounced mercantilistic philosophy was evident. The stimulus given to the export trade is shown by a comparison of the exports before and after the bounty act of 1673. During the years 1660 to 1672, no one port shipped more than 16,000 bushels of wheat a year. But from 1675 to 1677, the yearly average from London alone was over 680,000 bushels. This increase was caused in part by the unusual demand for grain in the Netherlands. The decline, however, which set in after the bounty act lapsed in 1681 and lasted until the act was reëstablished in 1689, shows how the bounty had promoted export. By furthering increased production for export, the government had also assured the domestic consumer of a steady supply. This end was gained by permitting export as long as the domestic price of grain did not exceed a limit fixed by law. The act of 1663, for example, forbade the export of wheat when the domestic price was above six shillings a bushel. If perchance the domestic price was six shillings a bushel, foreign importation was encouraged by removing the existing import tax of eight pence a bushel. Normally, the import tax tended to exclude foreign wheat, thereby giving a monopoly over the domestic market to the local producer.

Both before and after the Restoration, the government gave considerable attention to the domestic trade in grain. Numerous acts were passed regulating the purchase, sale, and marketing of grain, while severe penalties were imposed on those who tampered with the quantity, quality, or price of grain. Government regulation of business was a characteristic feature of the Stuart age. The rapid growth of London had created a metropolitan area which forced the Crown to articulate the demand and supply of grain. Numerous offices were created for handling this problem in London and the other urban centers. Moreover, by the Assize of Bread, the weight and content of a loaf of bread were definitely established. The consumer, in short, was protected against inferior quality and weight. The government took its task seriously and generally enforced these various laws.

The Domestic System of Manufacture

A paternalistic policy was followed by the government in respect to industry. Before the Tudor period the prevailing form of industry was the gild system, remains of which existed as late as the nineteenth century. The gild system gave way during the seventeenth century to what is known as the domestic system, which in turn was supplanted by the modern factory. All three forms of manufacturing existed during the Stuart age, though the domestic system was most common. Under the domestic system, the ownership of raw materials and, to a certain extent, the machines and tools used by the workers was lodged in the hands of a capitalistic group of producers who directed production. The demands and nature of a national and international market necessitated this arrangement. The gild system, partly capitalistic in nature, was not able to meet the situation, because of its adherence to medieval methods of production and control. Hence there arose the domestic system, in which the manufacturer, entrepreneur, and stockholder functioned as agents of a capital-

ist order. In many instances those who supplied the capital
had no technical knowledge of the trade involved. They were
not manufacturers in the medieval sense of being able to
make a finished article by the labor of their own hands; nor
were they manufacturers in the modern sense of directing the
processes of work. Concerned solely with profits, these persons employed others to manage and control production. In
brief, they were what one might call trading or commercial
capitalists. The joint- or semijoint-stock company was the
favorite form of organization, though there were enterprises
in the hands of individual capitalists.

The amount of capital required to undertake production
varied in respect to the size and nature of the industry. In
the woolen industry, the capitalist invested large sums of
money to buy raw materials, pay wages, and distribute the
finished article. This capital may be called circulating capital,
in contrast to that furnished by labor in the form of tools,
machines, and place of manufacture. These latter items are
known as fixed capital. In the final process of finishing the
woolen cloth for the market, the capitalist usually provided
the shop and tools. On occasion, he provided the worker with
looms and spare parts such as gears. In the coal industry, the
owner generally provided both the fixed and circulating capital. The greater the amount of capital involved, the larger
the industry became. Large-scale production increased during the Stuart period and, in some instances, labor actually
worked in the employer's shops. The factory system, therefore, may be said to have appeared this early in England.
Present-day methods of production were clearly anticipated by
the specialization of labor. In the watch industry, for example, one workman made the wheels, another the spring, a
third the case, a fourth the dial and so on, until the parts were
assembled and the finished product made ready for sale.
Combers, spinners, weavers, dyers, and finishers assisted in
making cloth. Bladesmiths, hafters, and sheathers worked in

the knife industry. Piece work, to use a modern term, was a common feature of industry. Most of the labor was performed within the homes of the artisans, the entrepreneur, or capitalist furnishing the raw materials. This method of production, commonly known as the domestic system, was also described as a "putting out" system. In return for his labor, the workman received wages based both upon piece and time work.

Labor had little voice in the determination of policy and, like today, was under a system of wages which caused constant conflict with capital. Disputes arose as to wages, hours of work, and the right of labor to organize for collective action. As the national government was suspicious of all organizations, and as management controlled labor by a wage system, disputes often gave rise to industrial warfare. Sabotage and dishonest workmanship often characterized the attitude of labor. Unemployment also added to the laborer's difficulties, for he seldom had any financial reserve to tide him over periods of idleness. The picture usually presented of the contented and self-sufficient woolen worker is far from true. The laborer had a home, such as it was, but no garden plot, chickens, pigs, or cows. Exceptions may be noted in Yorkshire, but elsewhere the artisan depended for his living upon the wages which he and his family might earn, for women and children were employed under the domestic system. The woolen worker was skilled in only one trade and during periods of unemployment found it difficult to obtain a job. Agricultural labor was hazardous as it injured his hands and made him unfit to resume his accustomed work at the loom. This factor tended to keep the woolen worker off the farm in order to avoid endangering his earning capacity. Wages were none too high even when employment was constant. Weavers earned about twelve cents a day and spinners about the same, while the wool combers received only a trifle more.

Coal miners earned about a dollar a week, while those employed in the linen, silk, hosiery, and glass industries received less. Even though these sums should be multiplied from seven to eight times to express their value in accordance with modern standards, wages were unquestionably low. It is not to be wondered at, therefore, that labor resented the conditions of employment and frequently resorted to sabotage and strife to improve its lot.

The Rise of a Coal Industry

A detailed discussion of the management and productivity of these and other enterprises would fill a large volume. An examination of the coal industry, however, will furnish insight into this problem and show how England's economic life had progressed since the advent of the Tudors. Coal mining expanded rapidly during the reign of Elizabeth. Natural advantages in mining and the wide distribution of England's coal fields help to explain this industrial development. The almost universal use of the chimney flue was another important factor. Heretofore most homes were constructed with the fireplace in the center of the house, the smoke finding its way out through a hole in the roof. Coal could not be used under these conditions. The introduction of the chimney flue solved this problem, but it was not until the Elizabethan age that its use became common enough to influence the mining of coal. More significant than these factors was the effect of private capitalism. Before the dissolution of the monasteries the majority of the coal fields of England were in the hands of the Church. Wealthy as the Church was reputed to be, individual ecclesiastics were not prepared to invest heavily in mining, and the leases which they offered to private speculators were not always attractive. The Church, moreover, was neither disposed to accept the economic and political philosophy of the industrial and commercial classes nor willing to assist these groups by throwing its fields open to the public. The social and economic changes which attended the Reformation altered the entire situation. Property on a large scale was transferred from the Church to the Crown and in turn to private capitalists who opened new mines with astonishing rapidity. Capital was needed to undertake the expenses of deeper mining. The Church had been unable and unwilling to meet the demand which was now filled by entrepreneurs and capitalists.

Added stimulus to the coal industry arose from an acute timber shortage. The depletion of England's limited forests had continued steadily throughout the medieval period. The demand for wood, moreover, had increased as the population rose and as new uses for timber appeared. Wood prices rose accordingly. The poor were not able to meet the increased costs and began to use coal. For the same reason manufacturers also turned to the use of coal. Metallurgical improvements also made it easier to use coal in industry. The net result of these forces was an economic revolution.

For nearly four hundred years prior to 1560, the annual output of the mines of England, Wales, and Scotland seldom exceeded two hundred thousand tons. During the one hundred and fifty years which followed, the yearly output rose to nearly three million tons. Nef, in his recent study of the coal industry states, "Even to the modern automobile or oil magnate, accustomed as he has been to treble or quadruple his turnover every decade, this early expansion in the coal trade . . . cannot seem insignificant." To the Englishman of the seventeenth century this growth was little short of a miracle. Small wonder that a contemporary poet wrote, "England's a perfect world; has Indies too. Correct your Maps; Newcastle is Peru."

At the middle of the sixteenth century about fifty per cent of the coal mined found a market on the Continent. By the end of the next century, foreign markets absorbed about twenty per cent, the remainder being used chiefly in eastern and southeastern England. The increased productivity of the coal industry assisted in an improvement in the shipbuilding, salt, and glass enterprises. As the demand for coal rose, there was a corresponding demand for more ships to transport the product of the mines. English shipbuilders profited, and the bulk of the trade, foreign and domestic, soon fell into English hands. The manufacture of salt and glass was rendered easier and more efficient as a result of inventions and improvements in the use of coal by these industries. More and more English architects allowed greater space for windows made of glass. So extensive did glass windows become that the government ultimately utilized them as a basis for taxation. The use of coal, moreover, permitted a rise in the manufacturing of saltpeter, gunpowder, soap, and beer. Some authorities contend that coal also aided the textile production of the seventeenth century. Regardless of this, any economic survey of this century reveals that an unprecedented expansion had taken place in many industries. Without coal an expansion would have come, but with coal it rose to much greater heights. England experienced an early industrial revolution.

Coal was used generally by the producers of iron wares, particularly in the cutlery trades. No satisfactory method, however, had been discovered for making pig and bar iron with coal. Numerous patents had been granted by the government since Elizabeth's reign, but it was not until the eighteenth century that a suitable method was found for making iron with coal. Pig and bar iron producers used charcoal, which tended to become scarcer and more expensive as a timber shortage developed. In spite of this handicap, the total output of iron goods rose during the Stuart period. The iron industry, like the coal and woolen trades, was organized upon a capitalist basis and was subject to a number of national laws which directed the general conduct of this activity.

The Establishment of the Bank of England

The great change which had attended the expansion of trade, industry, and agriculture resulted in the founding of the Bank of England in 1694. Before this date a number of goldsmiths, woolen traders, and merchants had functioned as bankers. Most of these had a limited amount of ready currency and were not able to extend the credit necessary for the large undertaking which an expanding industrial order demanded. The central government, moreover, found it difficult to finance itself and engage in war on the basis of its revenue or loans secured from the goldsmiths. Many of these loans became fixed interest charges against the central government and furnished the basis for a national debt. One authority has estimated that the cost of wars from 1688 to 1697 amounted to nearly $1,000,000,000, of which over $670,000,000 was borne by later generations in the form of a national debt. In order to facilitate the floating of loans for domestic and foreign purposes, the government invited a group of wealthy merchants to establish a bank with a capital of over a million pounds. The offer was accepted and the government straightway borrowed most of this sum, subject to interest charges which netted the Bank of England one hundred thousand pounds a year. The directors of the bank also were allowed to receive deposits and make loans to private individuals, and to issue paper currency. The net result of the establishment of the Bank of England was to increase the use of credit and paper money. Investment and production were greatly stimulated by these devices. Money economy, the characteristic feature of the late medieval period, was being supplemented by a credit system of economy.

The government's chartering of the Bank of England was in keeping with its paternalistic policy. Before the Restoration the government sought to stimulate industry, trade and agriculture by means which would enhance the royal power.

In the colonial and commercial fields, for example, charters were issued granting extensive privileges. In practically every case, however, the final authority was lodged in the Crown. The state did not fail to grasp the financial benefits which these undertakings afforded. Parliament assisted by the passage of acts, but in the main it was the executive and not the legislature which determined policy. Industry and agriculture were also encouraged by charters and concessions subject to government supervision, chiefly that of the Privy Council. After 1660 the government sought to check the evils of monopoly which had developed in many of these activities. It also improved the national well-being by stimulating the growth of regulated companies. It is important to notice, however, that it was parliament and not the Crown which conceived and directed this movement. Navigation acts, enclosure measures, corn laws, and charters to industrial, commercial, and banking companies illustrate the procedure followed. Regulation of poverty, the care of the aged, and the status of labor were also considered by parliament. Fundamentally the entire policy rested upon the theory of mercantilism. At times protests were raised against these national protective devices and arguments in favor of free trade and a minimum of state supervision were advanced. The Stuart period, however, remained loyal to the older economic theories and through them sought to advance the welfare of the kingdom.

SELECTED BIBLIOGRAPHY

No better general discussion of economic development may be found than in E. Lipson's *Economic History of England* (London, 1931). W. E. Lingelbach's *Merchant Adventurers* (Philadelphia, 1902); C. P. Lucas' *Beginnings of English Overseas Enterprise* (Oxford, 1917), and W. R. Scott's *Constitution and Finance of English, Scottish and Irish Joint-Stock Companies* (Cambridge, 1910–1912) are of special value. Thomas Mun's *England's Treasure* (New York, 1895) and Josiah Child's *A New Discourse on Trade* (London, 1694) are splendid expositions of the mercantilistic theory. S. A. Khan's *The East India*

Trade in the Seventeenth Century (Oxford, 1923) and W. A. S. Hewin's *English Trade and Finance chiefly in the Seventeenth Century* (London, 1892) have pertinent material. The *Economic History Review,* organ of the Economic History Society of England, and the discontinued *Journal of Business and Economic History,* published by the Harvard University Press, have many articles of significance for this period. M. P. Ashley's *Financial and Commercial Policy under the Cromwellian Protectorate* (London, 1934) is of value. The general political histories referred to in the previous chapters contain pertinent material. For colonial activities see below, p. 74.

J. U. Nef's *The Rise of the British Coal Industry* (London, 1932) is a valuable contribution and shows the influence of private capitalism. H. Hamilton's *The English Brass and Copper Industries to 1800* (New York, 1926); T. Ashton's *Iron and Steel in the Industrial Revolution* (New York, 1924); E. Lipson's *History of the English Woolen and Worsted Industries* (Oxford, 1920), and H. Heaton's *Yorkshire Woolen and Worsted Industries* (Oxford, 1920) are stimulating accounts of industrial growth and organization. Banking and finance are presented by A. Andreades' *History of the Bank of England* (London, 1924); R. D. Richard's *The Early History of Banking of England* (London, 1919), and A. E. Feaveryear's *The Pound Sterling* (Oxford, 1931). R. E. Prothero's *English Farming, Past and Present* (London, 1912); D. G. Barnes' *History of the English Corn Laws* (New York, 1930); J. S. Nicholson's *History of the English Corn Laws* (London, 1904); E. C. K. Gonner's *Common Land and Enclosure* (London, 1912), and N. S. B. Gras' *Evolution of the English Corn Market* (Cambridge, 1915) are of value for a study of agriculture.

CHAPTER XXIII

Social Aspects of Stuart England

THE political and economic transformations of the seventeenth century profoundly altered the social life of the English people. Medieval nomenclature and classifications remained, but their original meaning was forgotten. Crown, noble, and prelate still displayed the insignia of a privileged order and received homage and respect from merchant and cultivator. The rise of nationalism, the aftermath of the Reformation and Civil War, the growth of empire, and the penetrating influence of private capitalism, however, had created a new social alignment, the basis of which was wealth and not blood. Feudalism and the manor were gone. Title to land rested upon ownership and not upon tenure. Land was bought and sold for speculation, for investment, and for the development of extensive estates. Landlords and realtors reaped a profit in rents and sales. The close contact which had existed between lord and vassal was replaced by an impersonal relation between landlord and tenant.

Social Classes of the Seventeenth Century

Actual occupancy of land was divided among the gentry or squire class, the small independent farmers or yeomen, and the more numerous tenant farmers and wage earners. Before the Civil War the gentry had lived in relative comfort and luxury on estates which ranged in value from hundreds to thousands of dollars. Their homes, constructed in the Elizabethan manner, glowed with hospitality and entertainment. Their libraries were stocked with serious books to look at and admire and popular works to read and enjoy. They took a keen delight in the well-being of their tenants and adopted a paternalistic attitude like that of the Southern gentleman towards his slaves. Good food and plenty of it, to be washed down by English ale, adorned the table, which often gleamed with fine silver and linen. In local and national politics the squire played a dominant rôle. The Civil War altered these conditions. Most of the gentry continued to live on their estates, cramped by debts contracted in the service of Charles I. But the genial atmosphere of the earlier period was gone. Even the architecture of the home was changed. The great hall, which had characterized the medieval manor house, no longer served as dining room and sleeping quarters. Its ceiling was lowered and bedrooms appeared above, reached by stairways which were often highly decorated. Paneling, wall paintings, and tapestries were common features as were the heavy and somewhat cumbersome oak chairs and tables. Politically, however, the squire retained his former position.

Somewhat like the squire was the yeoman or small independent cultivator. Thrifty and hard working, the yeoman clung tenaciously to traditional methods of farming and was none too friendly to the enclosure movement. Many were non-conformists though probably most of them remained loyal to the Crown and the Church of England. Economically, the yeoman was better off than the tenant farmer who rented land of the yeoman or squire class. The number of tenant farmers increased during the seventeenth century, as did the body of wage earners. Private capitalism had cut deeply into the independence of the small cultivator and had forced his economic status downward. Neither the tenant farmer nor wage earner enjoyed a comfortable living. His home was a timber and plaster cottage of not more than two stories. On the other hand it harmonized with the picturesque country which surrounded it. The lower floor of his home, divided into living and kitchen rooms, was connected with the second story by diagonal wedge-shaped treads which gave the appearance of a spiral staircase. Ceilings were low and windows none too numerous until late in the century. Some attempt at decoration was made, particularly about the fireplace, which generally was at one end of the room. Food was simple but wholesome, and dress modest and practical. The yeoman's lot was somewhat better. He dressed more like the squire, while his table was more abundantly supplied than that of the tenant farmer. The yeoman's home, built often of brick and stone, was more of a house than a cottage, and was more elaborately decorated and furnished than that of either the wage earner or tenant farmer.

Urban Growth and Life

Social distinctions were sharply drawn in the urban centers. With the exception of London, which had about a million people, there were few towns of over ten thousand. Prior to 1666, London was a city of narrow and crooked streets. Row upon row of densely packed wooden houses faced cobbled thoroughfares which were stingily illuminated on winter nights by lanterns and linkboys, who for a penny would carry a torch before the weary traveler or gay young blood. Most of these houses served as shop, store, and home. Well-to-do merchants had homes of wood, brick, or stone, surrounded by walls and small gardens. The greater nobles had palaces of some size and distinction. Except for these favored few, most Londoners saw little sunshine. Beyond the city walls lay the slums, through which the traveler had to pass unless he possessed the means of going by boat on the Thames. Although London was but a few miles from Westminster, most people of rank preferred the Thames to the dirt roads, which in wet weather were almost impassable. Even after the great fire of 1666, travelers used the Thames. London, however, was a changed city after this conflagration had wiped out a third of the city, including the cathedral, the city hall, and a score of churches. The extensive building program which followed gave Christopher Wren ample opportunity for the display of his architectural talents. Brick and stone houses, greater in size and more comfortable in equipment, arose upon the old foundations and in the gardens that had been deserted. Shopkeepers sought new market stalls beyond the walls and shoved the slum area westward. The nobility withdrew to what is now the West End of modern London. Within the new city and the developed sections beyond, arose numerous shops, coffee houses, taverns, and restaurants, like the Dolphin frequented by Pepys. The fire, however, did not materially improve the winding cobbled streets. The paving was poorly done and frequently left unrepaired. Lumbering wagons and fine carriages bumped along splashing the pedestrian with water and refuse of unspeakable age.

Bristol and Southampton were similar to London except that they had experienced no mixed blessing in the form of a fire. In all the cities and boroughs of England poverty rubbed shoulders with wealth. Paupers, beggars, and criminals, miserably housed in hovels, formed a class which society generally condemned but did little to improve. The Elizabethan poor laws, as amended by the Cavalier Parliament, sought to provide work for the able, relief for the infirm, and punishment for those who refused to labor. The activities of the legislatures and parishes to establish almshouses and workshops amounted to little. Adequate relief involved increased taxation, and this the property classes tried to avoid. Each parish, moreover, intent upon keeping its rates down, eagerly enforced the law which permitted deportation of paupers who had come from another settlement. Here and there, private philanthropy manifested itself, as in the activities of the London merchant, Thomas Firmin, who employed the needy at clothmaking and opened schools for the children of the poor. Exceptions of this type were few and far between.

The majority of the town's population consisted of humble artisans who found employment in the shops and stores of the traders and manufacturers. Most laborers were wage earners, possessing few political privileges and having little voice in the determination of governmental or economic policy. Dissatisfied with their conditions, they were usually at odds with the wealthier classes and found Anglicanism of little comfort. Though not enfranchised, they threw their strength behind the Puritan in the Civil War and supported the Whig Party at a later date. Above the wage earner was the merchant, whose activities covered every conceivable form of trade. Some were simple bakers or shopkeepers, others owned and directed business establishments, while others were capitalists and entrepreneurs. Many of the latter were prominent in imperial expansion and sat as directors in the meetings of the great trading companies. Sir Josiah Child, governor of the East India Company, is said to have had a fortune of over $5,000,-000. In politics these men exercised considerable power and were largely responsible for the acts promoting trade and domestic manufacturing. Finally, it should be noted that they were chiefly of the Anglican faith.

The Anglican Church

The clergy of the Church of England represent one of the most interesting elements of English society. Before the Puritan revolution the majority were devoted Anglicans and firm believers in the cause of monarchy. Non-conformist views were held by some, but because of the thorough policy pursued by Charles and Archbishop Laud most of these were silenced or driven from the Church. During the interregnum, Puritanism penetrated deeply into the ranks of the clergy and profoundly affected ritual and doctrine. Although the Restoration caused many Puritans to leave the Church, a number remained, who by outward conformity retained their livings. The continued presence of Puritan opinion in the Established Church served as an obstacle to the "indoctrination of clergy and laity with the principles of the high churchmen of the Caroline school." A tradition of friendliness towards nonconformity was maintained by the Puritan clerics within the Church. Puritanism also was present in the Church through the laity, many of whom were Anglicans only in name. The continued existence of Puritanism within the Church was paralleled by a growing broad-mindedness on the part of those clergymen who were called latitudinarians. Though willing to accept the idea of the episcopate and use the Book of Common Prayer, they were more concerned with virtue than with abstract doctrine. They were, moreover, kindly disposed toward non-conformists and the Puritan element in the Church, and they worked quietly for a modification of existing religious laws. Their sermons sought to aid man to live a Christlike life and not necessarily to understand the mysteries of the Holy Communion.

In opposition to the latitudinarians were the high churchmen, who were as Laudian in their catholicity as the great archbishop himself. To them the Anglican Church was an apostolic institution clothed with peculiar powers and rights which were exercised by a sacerdotal hierarchy. They refused to admit that the Church of England was less Catholic than Rome and sought zealously to combat Romanism and Protestantism. Their sermons echoed with pointed references to these rivals and to the catholicity of the Established Church.

Among the leaders of the Church there was considerable wealth and learning. Gwatkin, one of the ablest students of this period and no particular friend of the Church, concludes that the "episcopate never stood higher than in the time of Charles II." In spite of the practice of pluralism (whereby an ecclesiastic held more than one church office), rapid promotion, and the accumulation of personal wealth, the Anglican clergy maintained the highest standards. Their scholarship and learning were profound and rivaled their piety and loyal churchmanship. Among the lesser clergy, particularly the country parson, a different situation existed. Salaries were too low to attract the better students of Oxford and Cambridge. Moreover, in the rural areas a large share of a cleric's income was in the form of tithes received from the laity. Very often these tithes were paid in kind rather than in money. A natural dependency developed between the local cleric and his parishioners. This was especially true in the case of the squire who influenced the conduct and attitude of the parson in many ways. The squire was thoroughly wedded to the political philosophy of the Tory Party and was able to have his party tenets expounded from the pulpit. Toryism and Anglicanism became willing partners. Few of the lesser clergy showed any great interest in intellectual matters. Nor were they always careful as to the conduct of their lives. Macaulay's brilliant passage as to the condition of the Anglican clergy in 1660 has much in it that is true, though he probably overstated their shortcomings and underestimated their virtues.

Non-conformity and Catholicism also had their clergy, though they were unlicensed and not supposed to exist until after the passage of the Toleration Act of 1689. The benefits of this measure, however, did not apply to Roman priests or to those who sought to advance the teachings of William Penn. Quakers had few friends and generally were subject to much abuse and ridicule. At times they were deported like criminals, and during the severe winter of 1683–1684 many suffered in the miserable prisons of that day. The humble tenets of the Friends together with the influence of the nonconformists and the tolerance of the latitudinarians, however, paved the way for a change in religious matters during the course of the next two hundred years. In political affairs the

Protestant also had to wait until a later date to effect any great changes. During the seventeenth century, Anglicanism was identified with the monarchy. The clergy constantly preached the doctrine of passive obedience to hereditary rights, and the sinfulness of rebellion. After the Restoration these concepts slowly disappeared but the connection between state and church remained as fixed as before. Whig and Tory alike felt it necessary to continue the Established Church and contested fiercely for the control of ecclesiastical patronage.

Englishmen at Play

Parson and politician had ample time during this century for amusement and recreation. For centuries hunting had been a national pastime enjoyed by all. During the Stuart period, however, numerous game laws tended to exclude the rural population from this sport. Poaching followed, and with it came legislation which inflicted severe punishment for violation of the preserves. Horse racing attracted the attention of many, and hundreds of Londoners flocked to Epsom to witness the horse races. Charles II was an enthusiastic horseman and maintained an elaborate stable at Newmarket for his Arabian steeds. The cockpit drew large crowds of spectators, as did bearbaiting. Bowling, tennis, various forms of football, and something suggesting modern baseball were played by men and boys throughout England. Dancing, dominoes, dice-throwing and the like were common sports though cards were by far the most popular of these indoor amusements. Frequently the cards were decorated with rough sketches of public figures. After the Restoration, for example, the Jack of Spades bore a crude likeness of Oliver Cromwell while the face of Charles II adorned the King of Hearts. All of these games encouraged excessive drinking and gambling which often led to dueling and fighting.

In London, Vauxhall Gardens was a favorite amusement

resort. Here one could find public stalls or secluded arbors where food and drink were served in abundance. Gambling and dancing topped these pleasures and attracted many rough and boisterous characters. The elite of London spurned the plebeian atmosphere of Vauxhall Gardens except when some genial host staged a "slumming" party. They preferred the re-fined surroundings which characterized Bath, Buxton, Tun-bridge, Epsom, or any of the many spas which were prominent in the seventeenth century. During the reign of James I most people visited these places to improve their health, but by the time of his grandsons they came for pleasure and entertainment. The moral tone was considerably lower than it had been. John Aston, writing in 1700, stated that "all the wanton dalliances imaginable" were present at Bath. "Celebrated beauties . . . languishing eyes, darting glances . . . attended by soft music . . . ladies with their floating Japan bowles, freighted with confectionery, knick-knacks, essences and perfumes, wade about like Neptune's courtiers, suppling their industrious joints." Additional diversion was to be had at the cake houses, inns, and coffee shops where gambling, smoking, and drinking continued well into the night.

Drinking was freely indulged in by all classes. Ale and cider, supplemented by imported and domestic beer, satisfied most Englishmen, though wines and brandies were popular among the wealthier classes. Drunkenness was common and that in spite of Puritanism. God-fearing men and women frowned upon drinking and all sports in general and sought to mold society according to their views. A sabbatical sanctity permeated their lives. Sunday was the Lord's day and on it "thou shalt do no manner of work." During the reign of James I and Charles I, the Puritans found fault repeatedly with the moral attitudes and practices of both Church and state. James's approval of dancing, "either of men or women, archery . . . leaping, vaulting or any other such harmless recreation . . . after the end of divine service" was viewed as a violation of God's commandment. Not until the Civil War had destroyed divine right monarchy were the Puritans in a position to impose their blue laws upon the nation. The Cromwellian period witnessed a suppression of games, drinking, dancing, and theater-going. Stocks and whipping posts were much in evidence. Puritan soldiers quartered themselves in St. Pauls, converted the nave of St. Asaph into a stable and amused themselves by throwing stones at the beautiful stained-glass windows.

After the Restoration many of the older pleasures were reestablished. Card playing, gambling, and excessive drinking on the Lord's day increased. Puritanism, however, had entrenched itself too deeply to allow these evils to go unnoticed. Pepys might take excursions into the country on Sunday and spend his time in entertainment and love-making, the Privy Council might meet on the Sabbath, and Charles might amuse himself with charming Nell Gwyn, but these and other excesses were publicly condemned by the non-conformists. Anglicans joined in the crusade. Oxford University forbade the opening of coffeehouses or the drinking of coffee within one's home on Sunday. Numerous societies for the reformation of morals were founded, especially in the larger cities and towns. The net result of these various forces was to be seen in municipal legislation against defaming the Lord's day as well as against drunkenness and gambling. Gentlemen and women still frequented Vauxhall Gardens or rushed from divine service to the gambling tables at Bath, but the free and abandoned atmosphere of the Restoration was disappearing.

The Blue Laws of the Puritan

It has been common for many writers to refer to the Puritan as a stiff-laced and austere individual. While there is some truth in this statement, the fact of the matter is that the Puritan was not much different from his contemporaries. He enjoyed good food and was not ashamed to drink ale or beer. He disliked excess but did not disapprove of a temperate life.   History has been unkind to the Puritan and has often pictured him as a ridiculous, narrow-minded reformer.   Many were of this type. Recent investigation, however, has established the presence of organs, flutes, violins, and other musical instruments in the homes of many Puritans.   Their children were taught the latest and proper dancing steps while several of the more im-portant musical composers were of the Puritan faith.   Nor was the Puritan necessarily stiff and prim in his dress.   Pictures of everyday seventeenth-century life reveal that Puritan and non-Puritan dressed much alike, and that both wore their hair long or short.   Biblical and non-conformist names were bestowed upon Puritan children in great abundance.   Faith, Hope, Char-ity, Prudence, Samuel, Peter, Saul, and the like were the Chris-tian names of many a Puritan.   But Anglicans used the same names while many a Puritan employed the more simple, John, Henry, or Will.   The Puritan, however, did not inflict upon his children such names as Fly-Debate Roberts, More-Fruit Fowler, Redeemed Compton, or Faint-Not Hewit.   It is true that one of Cromwell's friends was named Praise-God Barebones, but it is not established that his brother bore the title of "If-Christ-Had-Not-Died-Thou-Hadst-Been-Damned Barebones."

An analysis of the daily life of the Puritan shows that he was much like other Englishmen.   Distinctions as to dress, deport-ment, or carriage rested more upon wealth and rank than upon creed.   This is apparent when one investigates the diet of sev-enteenth-century England.   Meat was consumed in large quan-tities by all classes, though those of birth and wealth enjoyed choicer cuts and greater variety.   Henri Mission, a Frenchman, who visited England in William's reign, records that a sub-stantial gentleman dined on roast beef, boiled beef, mutton, pork, fowl, or game garnished with "heaps of cabbage, carrots, turnips, or some other herbs or roots."   For dessert there was an elaborate pudding.   White or dark bread was served as well as wines, brandies, or ale.   Salads, fish, pastries, and cheese were also eaten.   The artisan and rural laborer had less variety but seems to have fared well. Fruit appeared upon the tables of only the rich. Honey was still used for sweetening, particularly among the agricultural workers who rose early, partook of a light breakfast, dined at noon, supped toward sundown, and then retired at an early hour. Much the same schedule was followed by the town laborer, though the gentry and wealthy class often did without breakfast. At the opening of the century, the upper classes had their chief meal about eleven in the morning, followed by a light repast in the late afternoon, and a heavy supper in the evening. By William's reign a definite drift toward a noonday meal became apparent. Numerous exceptions existed, especially among the rich who dined most extravagantly and at unusual hours. Pepys' *Diary* is crowded with information concerning meals and mealtimes. Among other things he notes that the arrangement of the meal was in courses, "one dish after another, but a dish at a time."

Cooking had become an art during the Tudor period. It remained for the later Stuart age to make eating a source of pleasure. The time spent at the table was lengthened and the meal was interspersed with conversation and entertainment. Singing and dancing often accompanied these meals. Hotels and inns, anxious to cater to the tastes of their wealthy guests, adopted these devices. Moralists and lawmakers frowned upon this aspect of hotel management, believing that the sole object of these houses was to provide simple food and lodging for the traveler. Licenses were granted and elaborate provisions were issued for the conduct of the hostelries. In spite of these regulations, the traveler often found accommodations unsatisfactory, particularly if he lodged at one of the smaller inns or was journeying off the main highways.

Transportation

Transportation, either by land or water, was not much better than it had been during the Tudor period. Traveling was difficult, dangerous, and slow. Those who went by coach or horse often lost their way or were mired. It took two days of thirteen hours each to go from Oxford to London, a distance of less than sixty miles. Some improvement took place towards the close of the century, when "flying coaches" covered between thirty and fifty miles a day depending upon the season and condition of the roads. Water transportation was much safer, though it was quite unsatisfactory for the movement of goods and produce. Some attempt was made in Charles II's reign to improve the river systems, and several patents were issued for linking the streams by canals. A lack of capital plus an unwillingness on the part of the mill owners to permit these changes retarded any great development. Communication by letter was stimulated when the government assumed responsibility for the postal service at the opening of the century. Regular service was maintained, the cost being met by a charge paid on delivery, based upon the numbers of sheets used and the distance covered. In London, after 1680, a penny rate was established; but the rest of the country was subject to a higher charge. Franking was common and influential persons unconnected with the government were given this privilege. The practice of dated postmarks, introduced by a private speculator, became a monopoly of the state in William's reign.

Scientific Achievements

The seventeenth century witnessed a remarkable development in scientific knowledge. The researches of Galileo, Copernicus, and Descartes had opened a new world in a more astonishing way than had Columbus. England aided in this movement through the efforts of individual scientists, the cooperative work of learned societies, and the universities. Oxford and Cambridge graduated many scholars who acquired international fame, though the average alumnus was but a mediocre student. Better results could not be expected as long as these institutions adhered to antiquated teaching methods. Content information was acquired but it was about the same as when Wolsey or Colet attended college. Strict adherence to a semischolastic manner of thought and a knowledge of Greek and Latin turned out men who were clever in debate and who could read Plato and Cicero with ease and understanding. These graduates, however, had little appreciation of the scientific discoveries which were being made. During the Commonwealth, an attempt had been made to restate the aims of education and to enlarge the curricula. The Restoration checked this tendency and throughout the eighteenth century, Oxford and Cambridge remained the passive agents of the Anglican Church. Among the secondary schools, which had graduated many of the notables of the Tudor period, conditions were even more depressing. A decrease in endowments and the exclusion of non-Anglicans cramped the usefulness of these institutions. In the final analysis, an educational institution is evaluated not by a learned faculty and a few outstanding alumni, but by the intellectual stature of its average graduate. In this respect the colleges and universities of Stuart England were deficient.

In sharp contrast to Oxford and Cambridge was the Royal Society whose origins may be traced to 1645, though it was not incorporated until 1662. Scientists, thinkers, and men of letters were members of this organization which sought to establish truth on the basis of experimentation and observation. The society published *Transactions* of its investigations and activities. An examination of this publication reveals articles on the atomic nature of matter, the sting of an insect, some recent astronomical discovery, the process of tin mining, and an improved device for farming. By these articles the reading public was acquainted with the latest scientific information. Many illustrations could be given of contributors whose researches are remembered today. Robert Boyle in the field of chemistry, William Harvey, Thomas Sydenham, Robert Glisson, and Richard Wiseman in medicine, and above all Sir Isaac Newton in physics and mathematics may serve as outstanding examples. Newton was born on Christmas day, 1642, the posthumous son of a farmer. He entered Trinity College in 1661, receiving his Bachelor's degree four years later. During the course of the next two years he discovered the binomial theorem, experimented with fluxions, analyzed the nature of color and laid the foundation for his later discovery of gravitation. Optics, telescopes, and theoretical mechanics also interested him, and in 1687 he published his famous *Principia*. At his death, in 1727, he was honored by the British government by a public burial in Westminster Abbey.

Newton's work in mathematics represents only a part of the progress made by English mathematicians. William Oughtred introduced the symbol x for multiplication and invented the slide rule. John Napier discovered the principle of logarithms which was rapidly advanced by Henry Briggs, Gresham Professor of Geometry. Mention should be made also of John Walles who devised a method of effecting the quadrature of a curve and of Isaac Barrow whose application of a tangent at a given curve influenced Newton to develop the principle of fluxions.

The sciences of mechanics, light, sound, and meteorology were advanced. Notable improvements were made in chemistry by Robert Boyle, Robert Hooke, Richard Lower, and John Mayow. The numerous discoveries of these scientists did much to improve mechanical engineering. Ventilating shafts, deeper adits, and suction pumps driven by water were employed in mining. Power-driven pumps provided London and Ware with a dependable water supply, those at London being used as late as 1822. Steam, though known, was not commonly used. Reference, however, should be made to the many patents and machines produced by Edward Somerset in the latter half of the seventeenth century. Definite progress was made also in medicine. In spite of these gains the health of the English people was not greatly improved over what it had been in

Elizabeth's day. Superstitious practices prevailed, and mid-wives and barbers operated where skilled surgeons were needed. The heavy mortality which attended the plague of 1665, seventy thousand dying in London alone, illustrates how little was actually known of the science of medicine. "With a high death rate and the usual practice of child-bearing every year few households were long without funerals."

Literature, Drama, and Art

The publications of the Royal Society and of individual scholars form but a small part of the literature of the seventeenth century. In an age when religious and political controversies predominated, the bulk of the writing was within these fields. Jeremy Taylor's *Liberty of Prophesying,* Thomas Fuller's *Worthies of England,* and Bunyan's *Pilgrim's Progress* are examples of the better-known religious tracts. More popular were the works which flooded the country on baptism, predestination, and sabbath-breaking. King James's *Book of Sports,* Dr. John Prideaux's *Doctrine of the Sabbath,* and Alexander Leighton's *Sion's Plea against Prelacy* are typical of the latter group. Political works were of equal interest to the average reader. Beginning with King James's *True Law of Free Monarchies,* the press turned out an astonishing quantity of political writing. Many were popular in nature, like Dr. Gauden's *Eikon Basilike,* John Lilbourne's *England New Chains Discovered,* and John Rushworth's *The Trial of Thomas, Earl of Strafford.*

More serious and destined to affect subsequent political thought were the works of Thomas Hobbes, John Locke, and Robert Filmer. Hobbes had studied at Oxford and during the course of his foreign travels had met many foreign scholars like Galileo and Descartes. His best known volume, the *Leviathan,* was published in 1645. Hobbes was a stout defender of the royal prerogative, but he did not vindicate the

Crown on the thesis of divine right monarchy. According to
Hobbes the king was the constant embodiment of the sovereign will of the English people. Hobbes held that the state
had originated in a contract entered into by men who were
naturally free. Each partner to this contract conceded some
segment of his private rights. These concessions were made
to a sovereign who exacted absolute obedience from the subjects. They and their children were forever bound by this
contract to obey the sovereign in all matters. The power of
a king was to be unquestioned and the absolute form of government was to be enforced as the best means of promoting
law and order. Locke accepted Hobbes' contract idea but
fashioned it to mean an agreement between the people and
the sovereign. This bilateral contract was binding upon both
parties and could be broken by either provided the other had
violated his duties and obligations. Locke published his views
in 1690 in the *Essay Concerning Human Understanding.*
The Whig Party of that date immediately seized upon it as
the philosophical basis for their revolt against James II.

Economic writings also appeared in the Stuart period. Sir
Josiah Child's *A New Discourse of Trade,* William Petty's
Treatise on Taxes, and Thomas Mun's *England's Treasure by
Foreign Trade* influenced the conduct of business and estab-
lished the supremacy of mercantilism in national economy.
Closely allied were the works of the explorers and colonists,
like George Percy's "A Discourse of the Plantations of the
Southern Colonies in Virginia," published in Purchas' *Pil-
grims,* and the several writings by Captain John Smith. His-
torical studies also appeared. Of these, Bacon's *Henry VII,*
Clarendon's *History of the Rebellion,* and Burnet's *History of
His Own Times* may be cited. Better known are the literary
writings of Robert Burton, Isaac Walton, Thomas Brown, and
Francis Bacon, whose philosophical and scientific works fill
several stout volumes.

Poetry had many disciples like John Donne, George Herbert,

and Robert Herrick. More important were John Milton and John Dryden. Milton's *Paradise Lost* and Dryden's *Hind and the Panther* are classics in the history of English literature. In the field of drama the age was enriched by Dryden, Crowne, Otway, Congreve, Etherege, and by the greatest of all playwrights, William Shakespeare. Although Shakespeare is usually classed as an Elizabethan playwright, he composed some of his best known plays in James I's reign. Dramatic productions had been sharply curtailed by the Puritans, who closed the theatres in 1642. After the Restoration the stage regained its position and attracted people in large numbers. Charles II patronized the theatre and influenced it along Continental lines. Practically every gentleman of birth at one time or another in his life wrote some comedy or drama and thrilled to the applause of the pit. So numerous were these productions that few of them ever ran for more than two weeks. French influences may also be seen in the many essays which were published. Those by Dryden and Bacon are the best known.

In sharp contrast to these learned works were the tracts read by the servants in the kitchens and the visitors to the inns and coffeehouses of that day. Prose and poetry alike were used by the authors to depict murder, rape, fire, ghosts, travel, and hell. The sensational life of Titus Oates served as a model for numerous stories of rogues and villains. No attempt was made to tell the truth; the more impossible the narrative the better, though the authors affirmed the authenticity of the characters and took pains to draw a moral from a life of crime. Others tried to appeal to the frailties of their readers by depicting, in coarse and obscene words, the life of a scarlet woman or faithless husband. Many of these verses and tracts were read and seemingly enjoyed by the wealthier classes, who found a living example for looseness in Charles II and his court. Literary activities and conviviality were factors which assisted in the establishment of clubs. Prior to the Civil War several organizations of this type existed, notably the Apollo Club, which probably had its meetings at the Devil Tavern in Fleet Street. During the Interregnum the trend of political events and the appearance of the coffeehouses did much to encourage the growth of these societies. The Rota, which often gathered at Miles's coffeehouse, was by far the more important and served as a model for others which appeared after the Restoration, notably the Green-Ribbon Club.

It is quite likely that Shaftesbury and the Whigs, who constituted the membership of the Green-Ribbon Club, read at their meetings the current issue of the *London Gazette,* which had been established at Oxford in 1665. Older than this were the *Mercurius Politicus,* the *Public Intelligencer,* and the *Parliamentary Intelligencer.* Later, there appeared the *Observator* which, like the others, interspersed governmental activities with local news items and advertisements. In 1675 there appeared the *City Mercury,* designed for traders and merchants. All these papers were small in size and circulation, but they prepared the way for the greater newspapers of the eighteenth century.

SELECTED BIBLIOGRAPHY

The references for the previous chapter will be found of value for this topic. W. C. Sydney's *Social Life in England from the Restoration to the Revolution* (New York, 1892), and M. Coate's *Social Life in Stuart England* (New York, 1925) are standard surveys. Arthur Bryant's *The England of Charles II* (New York, 1935) is exceedingly well written though it should be used with caution. Chapter three in Macaulay's *History of England* is worth reading. E. Trotter's *Seventeenth Century Life in the Country Parish* (Cambridge, 1919) and H. M. Gwatkin's *Church and State in England to the Death of Anne* (New York, 1917) are of interest for religious affairs. R. J. Allen's *The Clubs of Augustan London* (Cambridge, 1933); Joan Parkes' *Travel in XVIIth-Century England* (Oxford, 1925) and *Englishmen at Rest and Play,* by members of Wadham College (Oxford, 1931) furnish valuable information relative to travel, inns, games, and spas.

The Oxford History of Music (New York, 1902–1932); P. A. Scoles' *Puritan and Music* (London, 1934); M. A. Nutting and L. L. Dock's

History of Nursing (New York, 1909); W. C. D. Dampier-Whetham's *History of Science* (New York, 1929), and A. Wolf's *A History of Science, Technology, and Philosophy in the 16th and 17th Centuries* are of value. S. Morison's *The English Newspaper* (New York, 1932); J. B. Williams' *A History of English Journalism* (New York, 1908); B. Wendell's *Temper of the Seventeenth Century in English Literature,* and L. Stephen's *Literature and Society in the Eighteenth Century* (New York, 1904) are of help for an understanding of literary movements.

CHAPTER XXIV

Domestic and Foreign Affairs
1702-1783

Tory Versus Whig

QUEEN ANNE, the last of the Stuarts, reigned from 1702 to 1714. During these years she valiantly tried to preserve the waning power of the Crown against the encroachments of party government. She claimed to have no party affiliation, but her devotion to the Established Church and her hatred of the Whigs, led her to seek ministers from the Tories, staunch defenders of Anglicanism. One of her first acts was to ignore the Whig majority in the Commons by dismissing the Whig ministers of William. In their place she appointed a ministry which ostensibly was Tory. Her chief adviser was John Churchill, Earl of Marlborough, whose mild partisanship irritated the leaders of the Tory Party. They disliked the arrangement and criticized him for having admitted to the ministry members of the Whig opposition. But Churchill had no other choice as long as the Whigs retained control of the Commons; nor were the Whigs satisfied with the situation. Their dominance in Commons argued for control of government and patronage. Although included within the ministry and willing to accept such "spoils" as Churchill might grant, they tried to undermine the latter's position. Marlborough's influence with Anne alone prevented his immediate downfall. Anne liked Marlborough but might have dismissed him had she not been under the thumb of her chief lady-in-waiting, Sarah Jennings, the wife of Churchill. So intimate was the relationship between the two women that ordinary conventions and court etiquette were forgotten. Anne addressed her confidante as Mrs. Freeman, who in turn called the Queen Mrs. Morley. For several years Anne obediently followed the advice of her friend, and Marlborough weathered the attacks of his enemies.

The first general election in Anne's reign came in 1702 and returned a Tory majority. Three years later the Whigs gained control of the Commons and demanded a greater voice in government. Marlborough recognized the strength of their position and openly coöperated with that party. Anne resented this and proceeded to turn a deaf ear to Mrs. Freeman who became a violent Whig partisan. In 1708, Anne replaced Marlborough's wife by a new favorite, Mrs. Masham, a Tory of pronounced convictions. In the meantime, the ministry's conduct of the Spanish War, that Anne had inherited from William, had alienated public opinion, which was tired of financing a conflict over the disposition of the Spanish domain. Marlborough tried to salvage the situation by suggesting to Anne that he be made "Captain-General." Through this office Marlborough hoped to free himself from party conflicts. The plan had merit, but it opened him to attack on the ground that he was seeking to be a second Cromwell. At this juncture, an incident arose which swept Marlborough and the Whigs out of office.

Dr. Sacheverell, an extreme Anglican divine, had touched the Whigs to the quick by a series of caustic sermons extolling the monarchy and damning the revolutionists of 1688. In an attempt to silence the preacher, the Whigs resorted to impeachment. Sacheverell at once became the object of Tory sympathy, particularly after the Commons had tried and convicted him. Public opinion condemned the verdict and the ministry did not dare to impose a severe punishment. Leniency was interpreted by the opposition as a sign of ministerial weakness and bitter attacks followed on the part of Anne and her Tory friends. The ministry's position became so unstable that most of them resigned, their places being filled by Tories friendly to Anne. The Queen's new councillors entrenched themselves by patronage and by bitter denunciations of Marlborough's conduct of the war. These factors together with the Sacheverell episode largely explain why the Tory Party won the general election in September, 1710. For the remainder of Anne's reign the Tories remained in control of government.

Scottish and Foreign Affairs

During this period of party strife, the realms of England and Scotland were united into the Kingdom of Great Britain. Since 1603, when James VI of Scotland became James I of England, both states had been ruled by the same king. Each kingdom, however, retained its own parliament and law. Personal unity through a common monarch as well as the implications which developed from *Calvin's Case* strongly argued for political unification. More important was the growing realization among the merchants and industrialists that greater gains might result from political coöperation and unity. The ill-fated Darien Company illustrated this quite well. The Darien Company was a Scottish enterprise which sought to promote trading activities between Scotland, Africa, and the Indies. Capitalist interests in London were opposed to this venture, and Spain declared the company's station in Panama an infringement of Spanish rights. The directors of the Darien Company were unable to withstand this joint attack and had to give up the entire affair. Scottish merchants, therefore, became staunch advocates of political unification. Nothing, they argued, could be accomplished without the aid of England. The net result of the various forces was the passage of the Act of Union (1707). According to the terms of this measure, the trade of both nations was open to all the citizens of Great Britain. Scotland, moreover, was to have representation in the English parliament, retain its own laws, legal procedure, and the Presbyterian Church.

Anne viewed the union as a victory. She was also pleased when the European war was brought to a close by the Treaties of Utrecht (1713). By this peace, Philip, the grandson of Louis XIV, was recognized as King of Spain with the understanding that France and Spain never should be united under a single head. France agreed to recognize Anne as queen and to stop supporting the Stuart pretender. Austria, Savoy, and the Netherlands received territory in various parts of Europe. Britain received Gibraltar, the Hudson's Bay area, Minorca, Nova Scotia, and St. Kitts. Finally, by a separate agreement with Spain, known as the Asiento, England was allowed to engage in the slave trade to the Spanish-American possessions for thirty years. She was also given the privilege of sending a single shipment of English goods to the Spanish colonies once a year.

The remainder of Anne's life was spent in an attempt to check a Whig return to power and to keep the Tories from quarreling among themselves. She succeeded in keeping the Whigs out of office but could not quiet her Tory supporters who divided their support between Harley, Earl of Oxford, and St. John, Viscount Bolingbroke. Hoping to oust Harley, Bolingbroke secured the passage of the Schism Act (1714), which closed the teaching profession to all but Anglicans. Bolingbroke cared little for the Established Church or for any creed. He knew Anne was passionately devoted to Anglicanism and detested non-conformity as much as Romanism. He capitalized on her sentiments and gained royal favor. Oxford was dismissed on July 27, 1714. Bolingbroke's triumph was short, for on August 1, Anne died, leaving the throne to her distant relative, George, Elector of Hanover.

Many of the Tories were willing to support the Stuart pretender, but the majority would not unless he renounced Catholicism, and this he would not do. Accordingly, the Tory Party joined with the Whigs in elevating George to the throne in accordance with the Act of Settlement of 1701. Personal eccentricities and his refusal to learn English made George unpopular. Moreover, he was indifferent to the affairs of state and was inclined to allow his ministers a free hand in government. These ministers were Whigs, having been appointed by George before his arrival in England. Parliament, however, remained Tory until the election of 1715 when a Whig majority was returned. Several of the Tory leaders were forced to flee to France, where they openly plotted with the Stuart pretender for the overthrow of George I and the Whigs. The Scottish Earl of Mar was approached, and in 1715 the Stuart standards were flown in the Highlands. The English government promptly squelched the uprising, and the Tory Party, which had expressed Stuart sympathy, was consigned to comparative oblivion for the next forty-five years.

The South Sea Bubble

Throughout the reigns of George I and George II (1714–1760), the Whigs retained control of the government. Tory opinion did not count and the Whigs were free to squabble among themselves for power and patronage. One serious crisis arose, however, which the Tories might have capitalized but for the brilliancy of Robert Walpole and the fact that their hands were stained by the uprising of 1715. Three years before Anne's death, there had been organized the South Sea Company, the object of which was to promote English trading interests in South America. Fortune attended this effort, and by 1720 it had become the leading financial and trading company in England. Stimulated by this success a number of other organizations were formed, many of which had no legitimate reason for existence. The unparalleled prosperity, which the country was then enjoying, blinded many investors and paved the way for considerable speculation. Industry and trade expanded by leaps and bounds, and money could be had for as low as four per cent. Fortunes were made so rapidly, however, that many investors failed to distinguish between honest and dishonest enterprises.

Those in control of government were influenced by this wave of prosperity. Why, they asked, should the government pay six and eight per cent on its indebtedness, when private undertakings paid less? Moreover, was there any valid reason why the national debt should not be reduced? The ministry agreed that the debt should be reduced and lower interest rates secured. But would the government creditors accept a lower rate or a payment of their loans, which in many instances were for a long period of time? The government, of course, could not break existing contracts, but it could alter the form of its indebtedness. Accordingly, it proposed to the directors of the South Sea Company that they should assume the national debt. The government creditors were to receive shares of the company in lieu of their claims upon the government. As the market value of these shares was exceedingly high, no actual loss would be sustained by this transaction. Moreover, the creditor might sell his shares and net for himself a handsome profit. At the same time the Company was to receive about four per cent from the government on its acceptance of the national debt. As the Company was anxious to increase its capital and as it was assured of a steady and secure income from the government, the ministry's offer was accepted. Actually, the deal proved to be a misfortune for the Company which, by stimulating the sale of its stock, increased the wildest forms of speculation by other companies less well established. For a time everyone was pleased, especially those who sold out at a profit. Finally, the mania ran its course. Sales of stock declined, leaving many with worthless paper. Other companies also failed in large numbers.

Public opinion blamed the ministry for the crash, alleging that some of its members had promoted the sales of stock and had made handsome profits. The Whig Party was in a delicate situation, as several of its leaders had been active in the councils of the South Sea Company. Most of these hastened to resign their government positions and allowed the party to reorganize. Robert Walpole, whose financial skill had been shown in Anne's reign and who, in 1721, had become a member of the ministry, set to work to restore the government's credit. Thanks to his ability, the liabilities of the Company were settled and its remaining assets were apportioned among the directors. To the investor who had lost all or part of his savings, Walpole's success was poor solace.

Walpole's Ministry and Foreign Wars

From 1721 to 1742 Walpole retained the post of chief minister. An expert politician and judge of men, Walpole healed many an internal party conflict and led the nation forward to firmer economic foundations. To gain his ends, he did not hesitate to bargain with friend or foe, nor was he opposed to intimidating or bribing the electorate. His skill as an orator convinced many that what was apparently unsound was nevertheless expedient. Seats in the Commons were bought and sold and that body was thoroughly corrupted to advance the designs of Walpole and his Whig friends. On occasion, as for example his tax reforms of 1733, when he discovered the extent of popular disapproval, he beat a hasty retreat rather than risk defeat in a general election. On the other hand he was able to facilitate trade by lowering export and import duties. He also reduced the land tax and lowered the rate of government loans from eight to four per cent. Toward the close of his political life he encountered opposition from certain Whigs like George Grenville and William Pitt, the future Earl of Chatham. Walpole belittled their sniping but gradually lost ground to those who wished him out of office.

Walpole's downfall came as a result of his conduct of foreign affairs. Ever since the Asiento, England's relations with Spain had been strained. Instead of abiding by the terms of this agreement, English traders smuggled slaves and goods into Spanish colonial ports. Spanish imperialists resented this and severely punished those caught violating the Asiento. Sharp protests from Madrid were pigeonholed by London, and the government saw no reason for interfering with the illegal methods of English traders. The English government, however, countered by questioning Spain's practice of searching English ships and of punishing English violators of the treaty. A diplomatic crisis was reached in 1738 when one Captain Jenkins told of his experiences in the Spanish trade. Time after time, before excited crowds, Jenkins related how cruelly he had been mistreated. Coming as it did when the air was filled with the wildest tales of Spanish atrocity, Jenkins became a popular hero and martyr. He was brought before the Commons and asked to recount his story. When requested to furnish proof of bodily injury, he produced an ear, carefully wrapped, which he claimed had been sliced off his head by a Spanish captain. Gossip magnified the incident by reporting that when Jenkins was asked as to what he did when attacked, he replied, "I commended my soul to God and my cause to my country." Parliament and the nation were swept into a patriotic frenzy over Jenkin's ear and clamored for war. Walpole tried to stem the tide, claiming that England should continue to seek economic stability and stay out of war. His views received scant consideration and in October, 1739, parliament voted for war. Walpole's reluctance to support this conflict gave his rivals a chance of attacking him. Belated concessions on his part failed to appease his enemies, and in

February, 1742, he resigned in favor of Henry Pelham, brother of the powerful Whig boss, the Duke of Newcastle.

In the meantime, England had been drawn into the War of the Austrian Succession. The origins of this conflict centered about Maria Theresa, the eldest daughter of the Emperor, Charles VI. Charles had no male heir, and sensing the difficulties that would face his daughter on his death, tried to prevent them by a series of European treaties known as the Pragmatic Sanction. England as well as the other powers had solemnly promised to accept Maria and her husband Francis as the future rulers of the Austrian Empire. After Charles's death in 1740 several claimants to the throne appeared and were immediately befriended by Prussia and France, both of whom desired to upset Austria's predominant position in Europe. War followed, with Spain, Bavaria, and Saxony joining France and Prussia. What England might have done if Spain, which recently had allied itself to France in the War of Jenkin's Ear, had remained neutral, no one knows. Attacked, however, by these two powers, English statesmen sought Austrian assistance. Although England publicly explained her entrance into the Austrian war on the basis of the Pragmatic Sanction, the fundamental reason existed in her quarrel with France and Spain. Parliament voted Maria a generous subsidy and raised a force to fight the French in the Netherlands.

The war dragged on until 1748. During this period the fighting was extended to the colonial world. New England soldiers, aided by a British fleet, captured Louisburg on Cape Breton Island. On the Continent, battles were fought and won by both contestants. England's efforts might have been greater but for a Scottish uprising in 1745 in behalf of Charles, the Stuart pretender. Charles gained an initial victory and invaded England in October of the same year. By the close of the year, Charles had been driven back into Scotland and at Culloden, in April, 1746, was thoroughly defeated. Charles fled to Europe. This was the last serious attempt by the

PRINCE CHARLES'S MONUMENT, LOCH SHIEL, SCOTLAND. Charles raised his standard here, August 19, 1745.

Stuarts to regain the English throne. Charles died in 1788, while his brother Henry, cardinal in the Roman Church, lived until 1807. With his death, the direct male line of the Stuarts became extinct.

The withdrawal of English troops from the Continent to meet the Scottish uprising had weakened the position of the allies. By 1746, the situation was reversed owing to the retirement of Bavaria and Prussia from the war. As a result the remaining contestants met at Aix-la-Chapelle in 1748 to patch up their differences. With the exception of Silesia, which Frederick of Prussia had captured, there was a mutual restoration of all conquered territory. Maria's husband was recognized as Emperor and England was given a four-year extension of the Asiento. Except for this concession, the results of the war were negligible. The fundamental grievances with Spain were left unsolved, and the struggle with France for empire loomed as a cause for future conflict. Austria and Prussia remained at swords' points over Silesia. In the last analysis the recent war had accomplished nothing beyond paving the way for another conflict. Cost what the conflict had in life and treasure, imperialists, capitalists, and monarchists were certain that propaganda and some trivial incident like Jenkin's ear would arouse the people to make greater sacrifices in the future. To achieve this end, the Austrian foreign office sought an alliance with France. Austrian diplomacy bombarded Louis XV with presents and pretty women, and finally convinced the King that Austria was France's natural ally. When English statesmen heard of this alliance, they forgot the Pragmatic Sanction and joined hands with Prussia. Russia, which heretofore had largely kept out of European entanglements, now allied herself with Austria.

Hostilities opened in 1756 and rapidly spread to all parts of the world. In India, where Robert Clive had been defending English interests against the French under Dupleix, war broke out afresh. English colonists in the New World contested with the French for the Ohio Valley and Canada. On the high seas the British fleet won several victories, but on the Continent Prussia found herself in a critical condition. Much of the success which attended the British was due to the leadership of William Pitt. Realizing the importance of the conflict, Pitt had reorganized the army and navy, had sent Wolfe to Canada, had liberally subsidized Frederick, and had kept parliament and the nation on his side. Pitt, who had promised to help Frederick to the end, then turned his energies toward gaining a smashing victory on the Continent. Public opinion questioned the expediency of this policy and refused to believe that England's interests necessitated a Prussian triumph in Europe. Pitt believed that England's gains could be made secure only by a Prussian victory over France and Austria.

George III Attacks the Whig Party

At this juncture (1760), George II died and was succeeded by his son, George III, who took his duties as king most seriously. From childhood he had been tutored to believe that a monarch should rule in his own name and not through a group of ministers. The entire system of ministerial government was challenged by the new monarch. Pitt's position was endangered by the rise of Lord Bute, personal friend and adviser to George. The theory of "the king's constitutional duty to accept and continue the ministers of his predecessor was held by no one in 1760, not even by the ministers themselves." On the other hand, unless George should accept Pitt, the future of the Whig Party and the conduct of the war would be uncertain. Pitt, Newcastle, and the older Whigs immediately tried to bargain with George and Bute so as to remain in office and continue the war. George's determination to be king in his own name, and the inability of the Whig Party to unite on a common program frustrated Pitt's schemes. Pitt re-

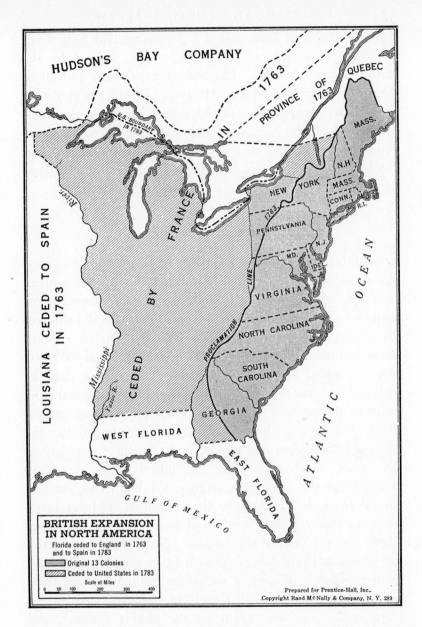

HUDSON'S BAY COMPANY

IN 1763

QUEBEC

PROVINCE OF 1763

U.S. BOUNDARY IN 1763

MASS.

N.H.

FRANCE

NEW YORK

MASS.

CONN.

R.I.

1783

PENNSYLVANIA

N.J.

River

LOUISIANA CEDED TO SPAIN IN 1763

MD.

DEL.

CEDED

BY

LINE

VIRGINIA

PROCLAMATION

NORTH CAROLINA

Mississippi

Yazoo R.

SOUTH CAROLINA

OCEAN

GEORGIA

WEST FLORIDA

EAST FLORIDA

ATLANTIC

GULF OF MEXICO

BRITISH EXPANSION
IN NORTH AMERICA

Florida ceded to England in 1763
and to Spain in 1783

Original 13 Colonies

Ceded to United States in 1783

Scale of Miles

0   50   100   200   300   400

Prepared for Prentice-Hall, Inc.
Copyright Rand Mc Nally & Company, N. Y. 289

463

signed in favor of Bute, and the election of 1761 returned a
parliament favorable to peace. Peace was secured by the
Treaty of Paris in 1763. England gained Canada and all of
North America east of the Mississippi. France was driven
from India though she retained several islands in the West
Indies and off the Newfoundland coast. Spain, who had entered the war in 1762 on France's side, ceded Florida to England. In return she gained Louisiana from her ally. England
also received land in Africa, and Prussia kept Silesia.

Colonial Problems

English imperialists and capitalists had won a great victory.
An abundance of undeveloped land, rich in natural resources,
was opened for settlement and exploitation. Industrialists
acquired a market worldwide in scope. But what did this cost
the average Englishman? Since 1702 the English government had spent over $900,000,000 on war, of which $555,000,-
000 was added to the national debt. It is evident that the
national revenues did not equal the expense of these wars, the
ultimate payment for which was passed on to future generations. Government, in other words, in order to promote the
aims of industrialists and traders conducted these wars largely
on credit. And who paid the interest and principal?
Throughout the eighteenth century, the burden of taxation
passed from the landlord to the consumer. Indirect taxes,
such as window, stamp, hearth, and excise taxes, provided over
eighty-five per cent of the revenue. No definite figures can
be secured as to the loss of life, but for that age it must have
been enormous. Finally, it should be pointed out that these
wars stimulated the old theory of colonial government,
namely, that colonies existed for the Mother Country, and
paved the way for the American Revolution.

Extensive as had been the gains by England in the Seven
Years War, public opinion condemned Bute for not having

secured more. So bitter did this feeling become that Bute, in order to silence the criticism against George, resigned in favor of George Grenville, who remained in office from 1763 to 1765. During this brief period, Grenville initiated a colonial policy which ultimately led to the American Revolution. At the close of the Seven Years War England found itself facing the problem of governing and protecting an extensive empire. Historically, England had had but little experience in colonial administration, and its entire policy of colonial government had developed around the idea of trade and commerce. The commercial value of the colonies was uppermost in the minds of English statesmen. They appreciated that much of England's balance of trade depended upon colonial markets, especially those in the British West Indies. Jamaica, for example, during the years 1739 to 1748, was by far the most important. Professor Gipson, in a recent study, states that during this decade Jamaica purchased from England almost as much as Virginia and Maryland combined, and more than all of New England. In view of these facts it is not surprising to find that Englishmen were better informed of the West Indies than they were of New York, Virginia, or Massachusetts. Britain's colonial policy, therefore, was largely shaped upon economic considerations. Political questions, while important, received less thought and attention. Moreover, in 1760 English opinion had not reached a level where the idea of a federation of self-governing colonies or dominions could possibly function. Until a body of well-organized governmental opinion had developed, British statesmen were bound to follow the mercantilistic philosophy of the old colonial system.

Heretofore the chief agencies of colonial control had been the Board of Trade, created in 1696, and the Secretary of State for the Southern Department, which included colonial affairs, the Privy Council, the customs officers, and the governors. The colonial agents, stationed at London, were also of significance. Of these agencies the most important was the Board

of Trade, which had extensive powers of investigation and recommendation but little voice in determining or executing
policy. Early in its history the Board did splendid work, but
after 1714 its efficiency gradually declined. Increased vitality
was shown in the 1750's, but in 1761 a reorganization of the
Board resulted in further inefficiency. During most of the
century the English government was concerned with other
problems and in general became rather ignorant of the colonial world. Outside of a few Americans who had taken up
residence in England, retired West India merchants, navy,
army, and revenue officers who had seen service in North
America, and a small group of English industrialists, there
were none in parliament who knew much about or were interested in the political life of the colonies. American dispatches seldom were examined as they should have been, and
violations of the Navigation Acts were generally unpunished
or not noticed.

The Antecedents of the American Revolution

One writer has described the eighteenth century as a period
of "salutary neglect." England's indifference proved to be a
golden opportunity for colonial self-expression. Year after
year colonial assemblies met and passed measures which an
alert British government should have reviewed most carefully.
Politically, the colonies became largely self-governing units.
Indian problems, like King Philip's War of the seventeenth
century, had been handled by the colonists and had led to the
formation of the New England Confederacy, which functioned feebly long after the close of this conflict. The eighteenth century wars, moreover, taught the colonists valuable
lessons in the need for coöperative military and political activities. At Albany in 1690 and again at the same place in 1754,
delegates from many of the colonies gathered to discuss action
against the French and to devise plans for an American union.

With the defeat of the French in 1763, the colonies found themselves no longer in need of British military and naval assistance. A colonial concept of self-sufficiency in political matters had been established.

The non-enforcement of the Navigation Acts added materially to the independence of the colonist. He was given an opportunity to develop his own resources and to conduct an illegal trade with foreigners. Grenville's proposal to reduce but enforce the old Molasses Act of 1733, which laid prohibitory duties on foreign rum, sugar, and molasses but which had been generally evaded, evoked sharp protest from the colonists, who had become accustomed to comparative freedom in trade matters. Although Grenville's measure, which passed parliament in 1764, provided for a fifty per cent decrease in duties and was declared a revenue and not a discriminatory measure, a wave of resentment swept the plantations. Had the American been subject to stricter control in the past, he would have viewed this act as a blessing rather than a curse.

A year later Grenville announced a plan for quartering troops in America for defense against the Indians and possible foreign enemies. Americans declared that they could take care of themselves though an uprising of Indians in the Northwest, known as Pontiac's Conspiracy (1763) revealed how ill-prepared the colonies were to meet a serious emergency. What irritated the American was the fact that he was to pay a share of the expense through a stamp tax. Before levying this tax, Grenville gave the colonies time to offer a better device, but this they were unable to do. Accordingly in 1765, the Stamp Tax became law. America replied by a colonial congress which condemned the measure and petitioned parliament for its repeal. Boycotting of English goods followed, while in several sections mobs prevented the collection of the tax. At this juncture Grenville was forced out of office in favor of Rockingham, who, supported by Pitt, Burke, the

English exporters to America, and the West India merchants, repealed the obnoxious measure. Internal dissensions among the Whigs led to Rockingham's retirement in 1766. The new ministry, headed by Grafton and Pitt, unfortunately became a sponsor for the proposal of Charles Townshend, the leader in Commons, to tax glass, paint, tea, and paper imported in the colonies. Townshend's plan was not conceived as a colonial measure, but rather as a way of balancing the government's budget. Although Townshend did not live to see the results of his measure, the bitter protest which followed in America, forced his successor, Lord North, to repeal all except a three-penny tax on tea.

To the colonist, the tax was a trivial matter. Actually it was cheaper for him to buy tea so taxed than to pay for tea illegally imported. He resented the tax because it granted a monopoly to tea agents of the East India Company in America. The Americans refused to pay the tax and formed non-intercourse agreements against the use of English goods. Inflammatory speeches and tracts appeared, while brushes with the English military followed. The Boston Massacre had occurred earlier. In 1773 came the Boston Tea Party. The British ministry was forced to combat this show of resistance and in 1774 the so-called Intolerable Acts passed parliament. These measures closed the port of Boston, forbade town meetings, amended the Massachusetts charter, provided for the transfer of criminal cases from that colony to Nova Scotia, and arranged for further quartering of troops. Later in the same year came the Quebec Act, which extended the boundary of Canada to the Ohio and gave religious toleration to the Romanists in Canada. Americans resented these measures as an invasion of their political rights, stormed at the idea of Catholicism being brought so close to their portals, and questioned the legality of the act, which cut squarely across their claims to western lands.

These sentiments were echoed by the First Continental Congress which met in Philadelphia in September, 1774. Congress denounced the acts, formulated a statement of rights, agreed to non-intercourse measures, petitioned for redress, and endorsed a resolution which intimated the possibility of armed resistance. When news of this reached London, Pitt, North, Burke, and others were for conciliation, but George III would approve only a measure which provided for taxation and maintenance of royal authority in the colonies. It is of interest to note in passing that the English exporters who had supported the repeal of the Stamp Tax did not follow Pitt in this matter. This was probably due to the rapid increase which had taken place in domestic consumption of domestic goods. Producers were less dependent upon the American market. Many of the merchants actually presented petitions in favor of the colonies but voted to support George III. William Lee, writing from London in March, 1775, to Thomas Adams stated: "The ministry knew well enough the merchants, except two or three of us were not at all serious. . . . The Glasgow merchants played the same game . . . they sent a strong petition . . . in favor of America, but at the same time gave Lord North to understand . . . that they did not mean any opposition, but to gain credit in America, and thereby more easily collect their debts." Before the new measure of 1775 reached America, conflict had broken out at Lexington and Concord. The Second Continental Congress convened and placed George Washington in command of the forces to be raised against the British. The battle of Bunker Hill followed, and on July 4, 1776 the Congress enacted the Declaration of Independence.

In reviewing the factors which led to this step, one is impressed by the influence of George III. That he honestly tried to maintain royal and parliamentary rights at home and in the colonies cannot be questioned. To lay the entire blame on his shoulders, however, is unfair. Throughout the eighteenth century the colonies had grown politically and economically. Through their legislatures they governed themselves and by their own efforts had achieved a measure of economic independence. The determination of the ministry to enforce the Navigation Acts and promote a more efficient measure of colonial control irritated America and served to convince the colonies of their political and economic independence. Had Britain been willing to concede dominion status, the Revolution might not have taken place. But British opinion was not educated to this method of imperial control and was, moreover, thoroughly wedded to the old colonial system.

"No Taxation Without Representation"

As to the right of parliament to tax the colonists there can be no doubt. Parliament had exercised this right to tax territory beyond the island before 1660, and what powers the crown had before that date had passed to parliament by the Civil War and the Glorious Revolution. Legally, the American was subject to parliament; and the distinction drawn between external and internal taxes, while justified on the basis of colonial practice, was not valid from the point of English law. The American position in respect to taxation was affected fundamentally by colonial ideas of representation. In the colonies there had developed a system of actual representation whereby an individual was responsible to the unit which had elected him. The representative did not act as a delegate for the colony as a whole. In England, actual representation was not practiced. The commoner viewed himself as a delegate of the unit which elected him, as well as of England, and the Empire. Virtual representation, therefore, existed in England. America rejected this concept, claiming that of necessity the great majority of the commoners were unfamiliar with and uninterested in colonial problems. On the other hand the American did not want representation in parliament. He knew only too well that distance would handicap the effectiveness of his agents and that these representatives would be outnumbered by those of Britain. The Stamp Act Congress voiced this sentiment when it voted, "That the people of these Colonies are not, and from their local circumstances, cannot be, represented in the House of Commons." The phrase "no taxation without representation," therefore, implied simply that the American wanted nothing short of local self-government, and to achieve this end, many of the colonists were ready to fight.

The Thirteen Colonies Acquire Independence

Had the telegraph, radio, or steam and oil-burning vessel been in existence it is likely that the Revolution would have been prevented. As it was, considerable time was lost in communicating back and forth. Often when redress of colonial grievances reached the New World, they were not suitable because of new circumstances which had arisen in the meantime. Nor should one forget the influence of the frontier in developing political and economic independence which would tolerate no interference even though the latter might be valid from the point of view of British law. Again, it should be noted that many of the colonial leaders had economic interests which were endangered by the new British policy. The skill with which these men inflamed public opinion went far toward creating a situation that was solved only by an appeal to arms. Finally, it should be observed that American and British political attitudes and philosophies were incompatible even though they had evolved from the same common source. Political divergence plus economic and geographic forces probably explain the Revolution, though they do not account entirely for the fact that the West Indies, Canada, Nova Scotia, and Newfoundland did not revolt. These possessions were subject to the same general policies as were the thirteen continental colonies. Personal direction on the part of a Hancock, a Henry, or a Samuel Adams determined to a great extent the attitude of the thirteen colonies. A more conservative leadership, aided by peculiar economic considerations in the case of Nova Scotia, saved the other North American plantations for the British Crown.

During the course of the hostilities which followed Lexington and continued until Yorktown in 1781, the British were handicapped in a number of ways. Their troops, many of whom were mercenaries with little interest in the war, had to be transported from distant points. The majority of the officers knew less of the military problems involved than they should have, and were often at a loss as to how to deal with the American methods of warfare. Disturbances in Ireland helped to weaken the British, and they were compelled to devote to that problem time and energy, which could have been used with profit against the colonies. Again, France and Spain, anxious to avenge the defeat of 1763, helped the rebellious colonies and the conflict became a world war. French gunpowder, troops, money, and men-of-war gave the colonists advantages over their enemy. England also encountered difficulty over trade matters in the Baltic, where a number of states formed the Armed Neutrality League in an attempt to break British domination on the high seas. Finally, it should be noted that there was a growing opposition to the war in England. The accumulative effects of these factors made possible American independence. Treaties of peace were consummated at Paris in 1783. According to these agreements, America was accorded independence and title to all the land east of the Mississippi except for the Floridas, which went to Spain. The northern boundary of the United States was marked by a line drawn through the Great Lakes and along the St. Lawrence, which led to decades of boundary disputes. America was accorded fishing rights off the Newfoundland banks, while both states were to have equal privileges in the Mississippi. England promised to give up her forts in the Middle West and Congress agreed to urge the states to compensate the loyalists in America for losses in the war. France received several West India islands.

England emerged from the conflict with its empire rent asunder, and its reputation badly injured. A general apathy developed toward the idea of empire, while British merchants and traders became concerned over trade relations with the United States. They resigned themselves to the loss of debts contracted before the war, but what success would they have in supplying the American market now that trade was thrown open to all countries? George III's plans for the restoration of royal power, moreover, had received a severe setback, though the liberal views as held by certain wings of the Whig Party were not yet in control of government.

SELECTED BIBLIOGRAPHY

W. H. Lecky's *History of England in the Eighteenth Century* (New York, 1882–1890) is a standard work of considerable merit. Military and naval affairs are treated by A. T. Mahan in his *Influence of Sea Power upon History* (Boston, 1891); J. S. Corbett in his *England in the Mediterranean* (London, 1904); G. N. Clark in his *Dutch Alliance and the War against French Trade* (Manchester, 1923), and J. W. Fortescue in his *History of the British Army* (London, 1899). W. M. Coxe's *Memoirs of Sir Robert Walpole* (London, 1899) and N. A. Brisco's *The Economic Policy of Robert Walpole* (New York, 1907) are of value. W. S. Churchill's *Marlborough: His Life and Times* (New York, 1933–1935) is a brilliant account of Anne's famous minister. A. Andreades' *History of the Bank of England* (London, 1909) and W. T. Laprade's *Public Opinion in Eighteenth-Century England* (New York, 1936) should be noted.

The wars with France and Spain are treated in R. Lodge's *Great Britain and Prussia in the Eighteenth Century* (Oxford, 1923); H. W. V. Temperley's "Causes of the War of Jenkin's Ear" in *Transactions of the Royal Historical Society,* 3rd series, Vol. III; G. B. Hertz's *British Imperialism in the Eighteenth Century* (London, 1908); G. Forrest's *Life of Lord Clive* (London, 1918); J. R. Seeley's *Expansion of England* (London, 1895); R. G. Albion's *Forests and Sea Power* (Cambridge, 1926), and R. G. Thwaites' *France in America* (New York, 1905).

The story of the American Revolution is treated in H. L. Osgood's *American Colonies in the Eighteenth Century* (New York, 1924–1925); G. L. Beer's *Old Colonial System, 1660–1754* (New York, 1912) and *British Colonial Policy, 1754–1765* (New York, 1907); S. G. Fisher's *Struggle for American Independence* (Philadelphia, 1908); C. H. Van Tyne's *History of the Founding of the American Republic* (Boston, 1922–1929); C. W. Alvord's *Mississippi Valley in British Politics* (Cleveland, 1917); C. M. Andrews' *The Colonial Background of the American Revolution* (New Haven, 1924) and *The Colonial Period of American History* (New Haven, 1934); L. H. Gipson's *The British Empire Before the American Revolution* (Caldwell, Idaho, 1936), and C. H. McIlwain's *The American Revolution* (New York, 1923). The British point of view is expressed by G. O. Trevelyan's *American Revolution* (New York, 1905–1912); W. H. Lecky's *American Revolution* (New York, 1898), and H. E. Egerton's *Short History of British Colonial Policy* (London, 1913). W. T. Root's *Relations of Pennsylvania with the British Government* (New York, 1912), and A. H. Basye's *The Lords Commissioners of Trade and Plantation* (New York, 1925) are specialized studies.

CHAPTER XXV

Eighteenth-Century Politics

DURING most of the eighteenth century the government of England was in the hands of the Whigs. The political philosophy of this party was based upon the ideals and accomplishments of the Glorious Revolution. Parliament, dominated by the Whig aristocracy, rather than the king, was to be supreme in England. Sidney and Locke developed this concept in their political writings and provided the sources from which Walpole, Pelham, Newcastle, Pitt, and Fox formulated a definite system of domestic and foreign policy. Royal prerogatives were transferred from the Crown in council to the Crown in parliament. In achieving this end the Whigs, without the enactment of a single statute, evolved the cabinet system of government. The personal peculiarities of George I and George II, their indifference to duty, and their refusal to learn the English language gave the Whig leaders an opportunity to control patronage and gain a majority in the Commons. Although the devices employed by the Whig oligarchy were often corrupt, the fact remains that these methods helped to make possible a system of responsible government.

The Growth of the Cabinet System of Government

Under this system the Crown selected its ministers from the party which controlled the House of Commons. Any attempt to do otherwise would lead to an impasse between the Crown and parliament and bring orderly administration to an end. Much of the difficulty which existed between Queen Anne and parliament was caused by her refusal to accept this principle. But the idea of a responsible ministry was not completely understood by either her ministers or parliament. During the reign of her successors, however, the principle became more established though it was not until the nineteenth century that the cabinet system became the rule of government.

With but few exceptions, eighteenth-century ministries remained in office as long as they retained the confidence of the Commons or until there was a general election. When the ministry was defeated on an important issue in the lower house, it lost the confidence of that body and usually either resigned in favor of the opposition, which immediately formed a new ministry, or appealed to the electorate for support in a general election. A ministry, however, did not stay in office indefinitely as parliament was dissolved at stated times by statutory provision. During the eighteenth century, a new parliament was elected every seven years in accordance with the Septennial Act of 1716. By this arrangement the ministry or cabinet, as it is also called, was made responsible to the party which controlled the House of Commons. At times, votes were so evenly divided in that body that no one party had a majority. In this case, a cabinet was formed from enough blocs or parties to insure a working majority. Such a cabinet was known as a coalition ministry. All cabinet members were members of the ministry. The latter, however, included certain departmental heads who did not have a seat in the cabinet. All acts of the cabinet were performed in the name of the Privy Council, which consisted of the members of both cabinet and ministry. The Privy Council, however, did not function as an executive body. During the Tudor and Stuart periods the Privy Council, appointed by and solely responsible to the Crown, served a useful purpose. After the Restoration, the Council became unwieldy and gradually gave way to the smaller and more effective body, the cabinet, which was responsible to parliament. As the Council tended to include all past and present cabinet ministers, regardless of party affiliation, and many others, it could not be considered as the responsible agent of the Commons. For this reason only those of the Council, who, at a given time, represented the Commons as the king's ministers, sat and functioned as the Privy Council. Certain members of the cabinet had seats in the House of Lords, and during the eighteenth century the prime minister was often a member of the upper house.

The more one examines the conduct of the Whig Party in the eighteenth century, the more one marvels that so democratic a device as the cabinet evolved. Political morality was at a low ebb and otherwise high-minded men saw nothing wrong in corrupting the electorate or in misusing public funds. Public opinion viewed the British constitution as the epitome of political wisdom and refused to admit that any improvement was necessary or could take place. An examination, however, reveals that the constitution was far from being democratic and that vital changes would have to be made if the nation were to live up to the praise heaped upon it by foreign admirers.

Parliament in the Eighteenth Century

The chief feature of the eighteenth-century constitution was parliament. Membership in the upper house rested upon hereditary and elected rights. The first class included the lay and ecclesiastical lords, the latter being present by virtue of their episcopal office. Since appointments to the episcopacy were made by the Crown at the request of the ministry in power, the holders of these offices became political appointees. Most of the clerical lords of the eighteenth century, therefore, were members of the Whig Party. The lay lords secured their seats by means of what has already been described as letters patent. Most of the medieval creations had become extinct by the close of the eighteenth century. The great majority of the lay peers, therefore, owed their office to creations which had been made since Elizabeth's reign. During most of the Georgian period new creations were made in the interest of the Whig Party. According to the Act of Union (1707), the peers of Scotland were to choose, at each general election, sixteen of their number to seats in the House of Lords. These represented the elected peers. The upper house, therefore, represented vested interests and privileges and was in no sense a body chosen by the English people.

The House of Commons, on the other hand, was an elected body. In the eighteenth century it numbered about five hundred and fifty-eight members, of whom almost eighty-eight per cent came from England, the remainder being elected from Wales and Scotland. Each county was entitled to two representatives, possessed of property which yielded £600 in rent. These representatives were elected by those who held freeholds, the annual income of which amounted to forty shillings. This qualification, it will be remembered, had been in existence since 1430. Between that date and the eighteenth century, England had grown. What had been a logical qualification in the fifteenth century had become an anachronism by the reign of George III. Freeholds had decreased in number and many individuals owning titles, the income of which amounted to many times more than forty shillings, were not enfranchised. One authority has estimated that the total county electorate amounted to about 160,000 and that most of these exercised their right to vote in a perfunctory manner. Many were easily influenced by propaganda. Others were so completely under the economic domination of the squire or local magnate that they had to vote as directed. Finally, votes were bought and sold in large numbers. So effective were these controls that probably not more than five per cent of the electorate ever voted in a free manner. As a result, political rights and powers were largely in the hands of party bosses, who manipulated elections as they wished. As the costs of an election were met by the candidates for office and as the expense involved usually amounted to a high figure, there was a decided inclination on the part of the bosses to avoid a spirited contest. Assured of their dominance in many counties, campaign managers avoided contests whenever possible. Whig strongholds, therefore, were seldom contested by the Tories. Rarely, in the eighteenth century, did the county elections assume great importance. Moreover, a share of the seats were, out of courtesy, allocated to the sons of peers. In the election of 1761, for example, sixteen of the eighty county representatives elected were sons of peers. Similar conditions existed in Wales and Scotland.

Borough representation varied greatly throughout the realm. The distribution of parliamentary boroughs, moreover, favored the south and southwest portions of England. Approximately one half of the House of Commons was elected from these sections of the kingdom. As a result there were many towns, particularly in the central and northern parts, which had no representatives. Others, like Old Sarum, were overrepresented, and in some cases underrepresentation existed. London, for example, with a population equalling one tenth of the entire country, had but ten seats, though it should have had over fifty. Probably not more than ten per cent of the boroughs had an electorate of over one thousand while about the same number had less than a thousand. Moreover, as the determination of franchise rested upon the borough's charter, and as these had been granted at various times in the past no uniform qualifications beyond age and the possession of property existed. What might qualify one to vote in a particular borough did not necessarily entitle another possessed of the same qualifications to vote in a different borough. In some of the boroughs, spirited elections were held by those who took their responsibilities seriously. In general, however, the electorate was open to bribery and intimidation, and frequently was completely under the control of the government, a powerful lord or a group of interested politicians. Bountiful supplies of liquor were distributed by the local bosses, who were instructed to keep the voters "sober till they have voted." Many a voter, however, staggered as he mounted the platform to cast his vote. Strong-arm methods were resorted to, and it was not an uncommon sight to see voters escorted to the polls by a bodyguard. At times, rioting took place, heads were smashed, and lives taken.

In both county and borough elections, voting was done in the open, each elector verbally declaring his choice of the candidates. The expenses attending these elections were heavy. Although the cost of erecting the polls, paying the salaries of the officials, and the like was large, the greater expense arose from wining, dining, bribing, intimidating, and kidnapping the voters. Lord William Seymour, in 1754, offered an alderman of Totnes over three thousand dollars for his vote, while the usual cost of winning a borough election ran from ten to twenty-five thousand dollars. Clever politicians visited the borough days before the election and spent much time and money in meeting the electors and their families. Robert Maxwell in 1754 informed Lord Sackville from London, "I arrived here last night from Taunton after a great deal of smoking, some drinking and kissing some hundred of women; but it was to good purpose . . . I may venture to say that I have now near 150 majority." As a result of these tactics many a seat in the Commons was directly controlled by the government, a peer, or by some powerful commoner. By controlling the representation from Cornwall, Wiltshire, Yorkshire, Devonshire, Hampshire, Dorsetshire,

Sussex, Somersetshire, and Suffolk, nine counties in all, it was possible to gain a majority of the votes in the House of Commons.

George III and the Whig Opposition

Before 1760 the Whigs encountered no serious opposition from the Tories in contesting these elections. The latter party had lost caste by reason of its espousal of the Stuarts in the uprising of 1715. The advent of George III profoundly altered the situation. George intended to free himself from parliamentary control and restore the power and dignity of the Crown. The Whigs rushed to meet the attack which, if successful, would undo all the Glorious Revolution had accomplished. With consummate skill George played one Whig leader off against another, gained control of key positions in parliament, bribed the electorate, and forced his opponents to take opposite sides on important social issues. The Whigs became hopelessly split over the colonial question, the Irish problem, and the issue of parliamentary reform. Although one faction might hold office through its acceptance of the King's policies in respect to the American Revolution, the other blocs formed a disjointed opposition in the Commons.

A similar situation developed over the Crown's persecution of John Wilkes, a member of the Commons and publisher of the paper, *North Briton*. Wilkes thoroughly disliked George and Lord Bute for their conduct of the peace negotiations of 1763 and printed a bitter denunciation in number forty-five of his paper. George interpreted this as a personal attack and persuaded the cabinet to prosecute Wilkes. Wilkes's position was rendered more difficult by reason of his obscene poem, "Essay on Women." Wilkes had written this for private consumption but one of his friends betrayed him by showing it to certain members of the House of Lords. Public feeling ran high. In the Lords, the poem was declared to be a "scan-

dalous, obscene and impious libel." Wilkes's home was illegally raided and searched for further evidence. Popular
demonstrations, however, favored Wilkes, who was viewed as
hero and martyr. Ultimately, George's power became too
much for Wilkes, who fled to France for safety. In his absence, Commons expelled him, and the Court of the King's
Bench declared him guilty of an unjust attack on the King,
and of obscenity in the "Essay on Women." Wilkes returned
to England in 1768 and after serving a jail sentence was
elected to the House of Commons from Middlesex. George
induced the Commons to expel Wilkes. When he was re-
elected, the House declared him ineligible for membership in
that body. The Whig Party should have rallied to Wilkes's
defense but it was so rent by internal squabbles and its sensibilities had been so shocked by the "Essay on Women" that
it overlooked the illegal methods used by the King against
Wilkes. More important, it lost sight completely of George's
attack upon the supremacy of parliament.

George paid dearly for his victory over Wilkes as it became
the basis for a searching inquiry into the structure and nature
of the House of Commons. The episode showed how corrupt
and unrepresentative this assembly had become. The question of parliamentary reform, though brought before the public by the Wilkes's case, had been agitated earlier by non-
conformist writers. Debarred from parliament by reason of
their religious opinions, these men exposed the corruption of
that body and advocated an extension of the franchise. Foremost among these writers were Dr. Richard Price, Joseph
Priestley, and James Burgh. Bribery, they argued, should be
eliminated from elections and the Crown's influence over the
Commons brought to an end. They also insisted upon more
frequent elections so as to convince the members of the Commons that they were responsible to the electorate and not to
the Crown. Although these writers had a limited audience,

there is no doubt that they helped to promote a critical attitude toward the existing structure of parliament.

Parliamentary Reform

Greater credit, however, should go to the several reforming societies founded after 1769. Among these societies the most important were the Supporters of the Bill of Rights, the Society for Constitutional Information, and the Yorkshire Association. In their meetings and publications, one encounters men like Christopher Wyvill, Major Cartwright, John Wilkes, Horne Tooke, and Thomas Hardy. In general the reforming groups were relatively conservative. Most of them reflected their social heritage by insisting that political power (voting) should be based upon property rights. Burgh, Wilkes, and Cartwright rejected this limitation and stood for universal manhood suffrage. Continued agitation and publication, supported by county meetings and petitions to parliament, finally won friends among the Whig leaders. In 1780, the Duke of Richmond introduced a reform bill drafted along lines suggested by Cartwright's *Take Your Choice*. Cartwright advocated annual elections, equal constituencies, payment of members in the House of Commons, and universal suffrage. Richmond endorsed these proposals with the single exception of universal suffrage. Richmond considered this too radical but he did argue for a lowering of existing property qualifications. Nothing came of this measure, though it cleared the way for another bill introduced by Pitt, the son of the Earl of Chatham. During the course of the election of 1784, Pitt had stressed the need of reforming parliament and had won the support of men like Cartwright and Burgh. They believed that he would introduce a reform measure. Pitt's bill (1785) provided for an extension of the franchise and for the abolition of some thirty-six boroughs.

Pitt was none too enthusiastic about the measure. "These boroughs," he had said in 1783, corrupt as they are, "must be considered as the natural infirmity of the constitution" and should be borne with patience. Fox agreed with Pitt. As a result the bill received scant support in the Commons and was decisively defeated when brought to a vote. Two years later, Grey, whose name will be forever associated with parliamentary reform, introduced a bill, but this also was snowed-under by the conservative members of both houses.

Shortly thereafter the English had their attention turned toward France, which at that time was entering the early stages of the French Revolution. The English reformers and many prominent politicians viewed this movement with interest and applauded the achievements of the French in restricting the absolutism of the Bourbon government. From 1790 to 1793, the Society for Constitutional Information and similar organizations passed numerous resolutions endorsing the French activities. They entered into communications with the French revolutionary societies and published a number of tracts, notably Thomas Paine's *Rights of Man*. Conservative British opinion frowned upon these efforts and became alarmed when many of the local organizations promoted the establishment of the London Corresponding Society which sought to unite under one general head all reforming groups throughout England. Late in 1792 the British government had its attention drawn toward the London Society which had informed the French National Convention that English opinion would not tolerate the use of force against the French. Vested and conservative interests were touched to the quick by this communication and urged the ministry to proceed against the reforming societies. Burke employed his best oratorical arts to condemn the reformers and belittled Sheridan and others in parliament who mildly approved of the course of the French Revolution.

The tactics followed by some of the English groups also

served to convince the ministry that French revolutionary principles were gaining ground in England. How startled George III must have been when he heard that Thomas Paine was feted by the students of Hackney College and while some sang "God save the King," others broke forth in *"Ca Ira,"* a popular revolutionary song of France. An examination of the papers of the Home Office, a department which concerned itself with domestic disturbances, reveals how panicky the government became. Tricolors, it seems, were waved at Sheffield by a "determined set of villains" upon receipt of the news of the French victory at Valmy. Every local gathering was viewed as seditious, and local officers were instructed to report most minutely any demonstrations that might take place. Further governmental persecution followed upon the outbreak of war between France and England in February, 1793. Private letters were opened and spies were employed to ferret out those engaged in treasonable practices. Parliament reflected the hysteria by passing a series of repressive measures. In 1794 the Habeas Corpus Act was suspended, in 1795 the Treason, and Seditious Meetings Acts were passed, and in 1799 there appeared the Corresponding Societies Act. The effect of these laws was to be seen in the strangulation of the reforming societies, and the persecution of the important ringleaders. Jail sentences were freely given, while men like John Frost stood for hours in the public pillory exposed to insult and humiliation. Others, like Thomas Muir, Thomas Palmer, Joseph Gerrald, and Maurice Margarot were transported as criminals to New South Wales.

Popular demonstrations in favor of parliamentary reform and social improvement were stifled by these repressive measures. Conservative opinion, however, was not able to silence those Whigs, who within parliament did what they could in the interests of liberal reform. Grey's measure of 1797 for triennial parliaments (that is, a general election at least every three years), for the abolition of the rotten boroughs and the practice of allowing a voter to vote in more than one constituency, the extension of the franchise, and the creation of single-member constituencies, though befriended by Fox, Sheridan, and some ninety others was defeated by the two hundred or more who followed the leadership of William Pitt. Grey and his group were discouraged and could see little value in attending a parliament which they believed did not represent the best interests of the English people. Further indication of the strength of conservative opinion was given when the King's party refused to pass measures designed to improve the lot of agricultural workers and chimney-sweeps, to repeal the Test and Corporation Acts, to revise the penal code, and to modify the laws affecting lunacy. Although the defeat of these measures may be explained on the ground of vested interests, the reformers would have gained more support but for the French Revolution. Many an English liberal, stampeded by the excesses of the French revolutionists, refused to champion reforms which he would have endorsed a decade earlier.

The Reforms of William Pitt

In the meantime William Pitt had undertaken a number of reforms in administration and imperial affairs. At the close of the American Revolution, British finances were in a deplorable state. The national debt had been increased by over $250,000,000, which was an enormous sum for that day. At the same time the government's income was decreased by the loss of the customs revenue which had accrued from the American colonies. The excessive expenditures incident to the American war had impaired the government's credit, which already had been weakened by maladministration, graft, and corruption. Nor was the Crown receiving all it should have from the English customs which had become hopelessly entangled by numerous charges and rates. To illustrate, in determining how much an importer of wheat should pay, the revenue officer assessed the cargo first upon the basis of an early eighteenth-century act, then upon one of a decade later and so on until the date of import. The various sums were then added and the total amount constituted the amount which should have been paid. A timely bribe or some pressure from the outside often resulted in a lower assessment. Other articles of import were subject to different duties and special assessments. In order to meet the interest charges on the national debt, for example, no less than fourteen distinct rates were levied. Plenty of opportunity existed for error and corruption. This complicated and expensive system plus the well-known avarice of the revenue collectors forced many an importer to adopt illegal ways of avoiding these charges. Bribery became rampant, but what robbed the treasury most of all was the wholesale practice of smuggling goods into the realm.

Tobacco, rum, brandy, tea, and other dutiable articles were smuggled in large quantities. Along the Sussex shore and on the Isle of Man smuggling was conducted almost in the open. Professor Gipson also cites a case where a group of smugglers used a hearse and four horses to convey tea, gold, and French lace from Shoreham. Over one and one-quarter million pounds of smuggled tobacco was seized between 1732 and 1750. Most of these violations could have been avoided had the government possessed an honest revenue and customs service. The latter often winked at infractions of the law, accepted bribes, and frequently allowed violators to escape fine and imprisonment. Others who were sent to jail were released before their term of service was over.

Pitt was determined to correct these abuses and to increase the government's income. He struck an effective blow at smuggling when he secured the passage of the Hovering Act which provided for the capture of suspicious ships found within twelve miles of the coast. At the same time he made smuggling less profitable by lowering many of the duties and removing officers who were known to have received bribes. Pitt also introduced more accurate accounting of public funds by forcing the fiscal agents of every department to present yearly reports which were to be scrutinized by expert auditors. More important was Pitt's Customs Act of 1787. According to this measure many of the existing duties were abolished, and in their place there was substituted a single charge which was easily understood and collected. The consolidation of the customs was a boon to both the importer and the government, and Pitt's reputation was greatly enhanced as a result.

More important were Pitt's attempts to reduce the national debt. In 1786, the government's income exceeded expenses by about four and one-half million dollars. Rather than spend this and any future surplus, Pitt proposed that these sums be used as a sinking fund to retire the national debt. All surpluses were to be invested and, together with accumulated interest, kept intact until an amount had been secured which would wipe out existing indebtedness. Parliament accepted the idea and for several years the plan worked remarkably well. In 1792, however, there was no surplus and Pitt, in order to maintain the sinking fund, was obliged to borrow. Had the country remained at peace, it is likely that further borrowing would have been unnecessary. As it was, the Revolutionary and Napoleonic Wars (1793–1815) upset the scheme and when finally abolished in 1823, the sinking fund had cost the country around a hundred million dollars.

Indian and Canadian Affairs

Pitt also sought to bring about a settlement of Indian affairs. Prior to the Seven Years War (1756–1763), the British government had been concerned chiefly with maintaining the commercial and trading rights of the East India Company. The results of this war brought about a change in policy. Under the leadership of Robert Clive, the resident governor of the Company in India, English influence was rapidly extended throughout Bengal and into the province of Oudh. Clive used his power to advance the fortunes of the directors of the Company, and, incidentally, of himself. Little or no regard was shown for the rights of the Indians nor was any thought given to the stockholders of the Company who were interested in profitable trade connections with India. India was bled and exploited so that a privileged few might amass enormous fortunes. Clive's abuse of power and the rapid decline of East India stock forced the government to inquire into the conduct of the company. Although Clive was exonerated of the charges that had been made against him, the fortunes of the East India Company were not improved. Hoping to salvage the situation, the Company's directors appealed to the government for aid. It was stated that unless a loan of a million dollars was made, the Company would have to retire from India. Lord North, who was then prime minister, accorded the Company some relief when he gave it a monopoly of the tea trade to the American colonies. In return, the Company accepted the Regulatory Act of 1773 which reorganized the Company so as to bring it partially under parliament's control. The new governor Warren Hastings, appointed under this act, brought order out of chaos. His success, however, was impaired by his cruel treatment of the natives, who resented the exploitation of their country's resources by the English. Numerous complaints as to Hasting's conduct reached England and finally led to a government investigation. Hastings was ordered home and in 1786 he was brought to trial. It was not until 1788, however, that the trial got under way, and it was not until 1795 that a decision, favorable to Hastings, was given.

In the meantime two distinct attempts were made to rectify conditions in India. In 1783, Charles James Fox introduced an India bill which aimed at placing the East India Company completely under control of parliament. The bill passed the Commons but was defeated in the Lords as a result of George III's personal interference. The King informed the Lords, through a letter addressed to one of his friends, that he would consider whoever voted for the bill as his enemy. The Commons resented this attack and passed a resolution which severely condemned the use of the King's name or opinion in respect to any measure before parliament. Such an act was viewed as a "high crime and misdemeanour, derogatory to the honour of the crown, a breach of the fundamental privileges of parliament, and subversive of the constitution." On the same day that this resolution passed, the Lords rejected Fox's India Bill. Shortly thereafter George III dismissed the Fox ministry and entrusted the conduct of government to William Pitt, the Younger.

Pitt's youth (he was not yet twenty-five) was against him. His critics admitted that he had established an enviable reputation as Chancellor of the Exchequer in 1782 under Lord Shelburne, but questioned whether he was experienced enough to assume the office of prime minister. Others openly declared that Pitt would take orders from the King and that the English constitution had been endangered by his appointment. More significant was the fact that his rival, Fox, commanded a majority in the Commons. Such a situation could not exist today, but in 1783 the Cabinet System of government was not so well established. In spite of public disapproval and repeated defeats in the Commons, Pitt refused to resign. Nor did Fox want him to resign. Fox hoped to continue a running attack until March, 1784, when the Mutiny Bill would come up for renewal. Fox believed that he could defeat the passage of this measure and thus force George III to restore him to power. Pitt's cool indifference to Fox's parliamentary attacks and his splendid display of leadership won support and when the Mutiny Bill was introduced it was Fox rather than Pitt who was defeated.

Having secured himself in Commons, Pitt proceeded to attack the Indian problem. Pitt proposed that the Crown should appoint a governing board which was to have complete control over the government of India, but that patronage was to remain in the hands of the East India Company. Parliament accepted this bill in 1784, and from that date India ceased to be the possession of a private trading organization. Pitt's India Bill, though modified at a later date, served as the basis for Indian administration until 1858, when the East India Company was formally abolished.

Pitt's interest in imperial affairs was also shown by his colonial policy. Between 1783 and 1791, Canada was governed according to the terms of the Quebec Act of 1774. This arrangement, however, was not satisfactory, as the English loyalists, who had left the American colonies because of the Revolution, to begin life anew in Canada, clamored for a greater voice in government. Pitt was favorably disposed and in 1791 secured the passage of the Canadian Constitutional Act, which divided the country into two areas known as Upper and Lower Canada. Lower Canada included the older and more densely settled part inhabited chiefly by French-speaking peoples. Upper Canada included the newer and less developed area to the west. In each province there was to be a governor and council, appointed for life by the Crown, and an assembly elected every four years. Although Pitt's measure left many matters unsolved, local self-government was initiated in a manner which reflected the experience of the American Revolution.

Union with Ireland

About the same time the English government had its attention turned toward Ireland. Economically, that island was in a deplorable condition. Irish trade enjoyed none of the advantages of the British Navigation System and existed solely for the profit of the Mother Country. Heavy taxes burdened a peasantry which chafed under an abominable system of land tenure. Most of the landlords were Englishmen who remained comfortably at home enjoying the revenue which their agents brutally exacted from the poor Irish tenants. Excessive rents left the cultivator in a state that approached extreme poverty. Most of the Irish, moreover, were Romanists and were denied religious freedom, the right of holding public office, and the right of practicing law. England governed Ireland as a conquered dependency and afforded the Irish no representation in the parliament at Westminster.

Ireland resented English overlordship and domination. Failing to secure any consideration or redress through ordinary channels, Irish agitators resorted to violence. Secret organizations were formed to defy English authority, and houses of Protestants were burned. Matters reached a crisis during the American Revolution, and the English government was forced to make a number of concessions. Most of these were of no great significance, though the Irish leaders, notably Gratton and Flood, viewed the establishment of an independent Irish parliament in 1782 with favor. Membership in this body was denied the Catholics. Elections, moreover, were completely under the control of English landlords and politicians. Accordingly, little was done to improve the situation, and the Irish continued to press their demands for reform by a policy of frightfulness.

Added incentive was afforded the Irish by the disturbances in France. The spread of French revolutionary doctrine and the success of the French assembly in curtailing Bourbon absolutism served as a model for Ireland. In 1791 Wolfe Tone, a Dublin lawyer, sought to unite the various Irish groups. Many Irish Catholics refused to join because of Wolfe's connections with the radical French societies which had opened a frontal attack upon Rome. In spite of this, Tone was able to found the Society of United Irishmen. Hoping to weaken this movement, the English government relaxed the penal laws and permitted Romanists to vote in elections for the Irish parliament. Pitt, who had sponsored this measure, hoped that Ireland would accept this concession and cease its agitations against the Crown. What the outcome might have been no one knows, but Pitt's expectations were blasted by the unexpected policy introduced by the Lord Lieutenant, the representative of the Crown in Dublin. This officer believed that he was acting in accordance with Pitt's wishes when he proposed that a bill be introduced in the Irish parliament admitting Catholics to membership in that body. Gratton and the Irish leaders were delighted but a howl of protest on the part of the English and Protestant interests forced Pitt to take sides. While disposed to treat the Irish Romanists with fairness, Pitt had never suggested giving them seats in the Irish parliament. Worried by the outbreak of war with France in 1793 and pestered by George III, who was fanatically anti-Roman, Pitt recalled the Lord Lieutenant and blocked the passage of the bill.

Tone and his followers immediately opened war upon the English. France was asked to help, and several expeditions to Ireland were undertaken. England replied by suspending the Habeas Corpus Act in Ireland and by proclaiming martial law. Civil war continued to 1799, when Pitt proposed to bring matters to a close by uniting the Irish and British parliaments. Many of the Irish, who by this time were demanding complete independence, rejected the proposal. Pitt's supporters, enforced by a campaign fund that exceeded five million dollars, bought enough votes in the Irish parliament to secure the passage of an act of union. In the British parliament less opposition was encountered, and on August 1, 1800, George III gave his assent to the bill which created the United Kingdom of Great Britain and Ireland.

According to this measure, the Irish peers were allowed to elect twenty-eight of their number to life membership in the House of Lords while four Irish bishops of the Established Anglican Church in Ireland were raised to the peerage. Ireland was also given one hundred seats in the House of Commons. Free trade was established between the two islands. Pitt hoped that the union would bring peace to both countries. He had failed, however, to make any provision for the Irish Roman Catholics. Accordingly, in a cabinet meeting, Pitt raised the question of Catholic relief. George III, on hearing of this, became intensely angry and informed Pitt that if he continued he would incur royal disapproval. Not wanting to oppose the King, Pitt resigned his office in February, 1801. Within a month he was back in office, first having assured George that he would never raise the Catholic question again as long as the King lived. The failure to settle this vexatious affair paved the way, in part, for future disturbances in the nineteenth century. Irish opinion was touched to the quick by Pitt's failure to initiate legislation which would have removed the Catholic question from politics. Indeed, many had supported the Act of Union on the general understanding that Catholic emancipation would follow. Although Pitt had never given any promise, he had done nothing to counteract the favorable hopes which his agents in Ireland had circulated. Had Pitt been made of sterner stuff he might have challenged George III's right to dictate policies of government. Pitt, however, had a profound respect for the office of king. Moreover, he honestly believed that the Whig Party, torn as it was by internal strife and factions, could never manage to remain in office without his support. And he feared what might happen if the Tories were to come into power. Pitt, and Pitt alone, stood between orderly and disorderly government.

SELECTED BIBLIOGRAPHY

J. H. Rose has produced two works of standard value and favorable to William Pitt, *William Pitt and the National Revival* (London, 1911) and *William Pitt and the Great War* (London, 1911). John Morley's *Edmund Burke* (London, 1867) and *Burke* (London, 1879); A. Rosebery's *Lord Chatham* (London, 1910); B. William's *Life of William Pitt, Earl of Chatham* (London, 1913), and E. G. Fitzmaurice's *Life of William, Earl of Shelburne* (London, 1927–1928) are standard biographies. D. A. Winstanley's *Personal and Party Government* (Cambridge, 1910); H. W. C. Davis' *The Age of Grey and Peel* (Oxford, 1929), and W. T. Laprade's *England and the French Revolution* (Baltimore, 1909) are specialized studies of merit.

CHAPTER XXVI

The French Revolution and Napoleonic Era

The Antecedents of the French Revolution

DURING the eighteenth century a number of Europeans visited England. Some were but tourists who roamed through the Tower, Canterbury, and Westminster Abbey and frequented the coffeeshops and show places of London and Bath. Others, more seriously inclined, came to study England, and were the guests of English statesmen, nobles, and men of letters. Among this latter group were many prominent Frenchmen, notably Voltaire, Montesquieu, and Rousseau, who marveled at England's economic condition and carefully examined existing social and political institutions. Voltaire, for example, lived in England from 1726 to 1729 and became the friend of men like Bolingbroke. Through their kindness he was introduced to such writers as Pope, Clarke, and Swift, to the King, and a number of men and women prominent in society, government, and business. He buried himself in the works of Milton, Shakespeare, Hobbes, and Locke and became aware of the tremendous cultural heritage of England. Voltaire was astonished at the freedom of speech that existed and the liberty accorded the press. England, he said, was a country "where people think freely and nobly, unrestrained by servile fear." It was his privilege, moreover, to attend the funeral of Newton and witness the national honor bestowed upon the great scientist. All this was in marked contrast to his own country. On his return home, Voltaire never ceased to tell of his English experiences; and he incorporated his admiration for England in his many plays, essays, and histories. What Voltaire did, Montesquieu and Rousseau did also; and France was introduced to a country which became its model in many respects.

Voltaire and his two associates were but the greatest lights in France's galaxy of writers, philosophers, and thinkers. Most critically did these men examine French society, government, industry, and church. Proud as they were of their country's accomplishments, they were not blind to existing evils and inequalities. The medieval absolutism of French government was exposed, the corrupt and immoral practices of statesmen and nobles were revealed, and the unparalleled privileges enjoyed by the Roman clergy were depicted in graphic terms. Voltaire, for example, in his *Epistle to Uranie* ridiculed an ecclesiastical system and creed which extolled a God who drowned the fathers and then later died for the children. Again, in his play, *Don Pedro,* he declared in respect to monarchy, "A king is but a man with name august; first subject of the law and by the law just." Montesquieu, moreover, believed that liberty did not and could not exist in France until his country adopted a governmental system like that of England. Rousseau, in language that the French peasant understood, proclaimed that man was born free and endowed by nature with the inalienable right of revolution. Finally, there were the French economists, like Diderot and Turgot, who advocated the abolition of feudal dues, services, and tariffs as a means for economic development.

In general these writers sought a thorough reorganization of French society, government, church, and industry. Not one of them suggested that France should become a republic; rather did they seek to establish a limited monarchy where privilege would be supplanted by equality. Liberty, Equality, and Fraternity became the watchwords and battle cry which echoed from the stage, salon, and press on many occasions. The middle class, keen to see the advantages offered them by this scheme, became ardent disciples, and the village priests, zealously guarding their own copies of this revolutionary philosophy, poured it out to their flocks by sermons and conversations. Bit by bit the writings of the French philosophers trickled down to the peasant and artisan. These humble toilers did not understand the fine distinctions drawn between monarchical and republican forms of governments or the restraints which liberty imposed upon the citizens. To them this philosophy meant little. What they did see was the inequality which existed, and to achieve freedom they risked all in revolution.

The philosophers furnished the text and idea for revolution, but it remained for the peasant and artisan to translate them into action. History is replete with evidence as to the justice of their cause. Heavy taxes, which the rich and noble classes managed to avoid, fell upon the lower orders, who could ill afford to maintain a corrupt and inefficient government. In addition, the serf was required to meet an unnumbered assortment of feudal dues and services. Severe fines and punishments were imposed for violation of these duties, while the military needs of the state requisitioned man power and money with deadening regularity. A brighter picture is revealed by contrasting the lot of the average Frenchman with that of his fellow European. With the exception of England, no country had progressed so rapidly as France; and contrary to usual belief, serfdom was on the decline. Moreover, in spite of the handicaps which existed in trade, commerce, and transportation, private initiative had developed a colonial empire, overseas trade, and the beginnings of an industrial revolution. In one sense, therefore, the French Revolution was precipitated by improved rather than by depressed conditions. Man became conscious of the medieval chains which restrained freedom of action and thought, and demanded that monarchy reorganize itself and the nation. Had the French monarchy been solvent, it is possible that a peaceful revolution might have taken place. As it was, the monarchy was hopelessly in debt, and after several vain attempts to balance its budget, was forced to summon a national assembly to consider means of forestalling national bankruptcy.

In May, 1789, there assembled at Versailles a gathering of the States General, a body which had not met since 1614 and concerning which no one was well informed. It was medieval in origin and structure, possessed no power like parliament's, and represented chiefly the privileged classes of France. The situation favored the monarchy, and but for the lack of wise leadership on the part of Louis XVI and his ministers, a different story might be told. Blunder and mismanagement, however, resulted in the conversion of the States General into a National Assembly pledged not to dissolve until a constitution and a limited monarchy had been established. By 1791 this was accomplished, and a so-called Legislative Assembly, elected on a broad franchise, took over the task of restoring order to a chaotic nation.

British Opinion Towards the French Revolution

During the interval between the meeting of the States General and the Legislative Assembly, a series of constructive reforms had been enacted which evoked considerable applause in England. Fox eulogized the French in their endeavors to gain liberty. Wordsworth, one of England's greatest poets, exclaimed in his enthusiasm for the movement, "Bliss was it in that dawn to be alive, but to be young was very heaven." On the other hand Burke and the conservative forces frowned upon the Revolution and pointed out the dangers implied in the destruction of the Bastille, the growth of republican principles, and revolutionary societies. Liberty, they declared, had become a disguise behind which sinister forces had perpetrated excess and destruction. More important, Burke maintained, was the effect these disturbances were having upon England. Dangerous radical societies, he claimed, were being formed at London and elsewhere. European kings were alarmed over the treatment the French had given Louis XVI, for they saw in the movement a direct attack upon the sacred institution of monarchy. One of these rulers, the Austrian Emperor, prepared to take action. In 1791 he carelessly addressed a pompous and irritating remonstrance to the French, calling, in short, for the restoration of the old order. Louis XVI, who anxiously awaited armed assistance from European kings, was placed in a difficult situation by the Emperor's action. In the end, Louis mismanaged affairs and was forced by the Legislative Assembly to declare war upon Austria in April, 1792. Austria was immediately joined by Prussia.

The French were ill-prepared for war, and by September, 1792, it appeared that Paris might fall before the Prussians under the aged Duke of Brunswick. Dumouriez's stand at Valmy, however, forced the Duke to retreat; and in November, 1792, the French won a decisive victory over the Austrians at Jemappes. At the same time other French troops had routed the enemy in Savoy, and captured Speyer, Mainz, and Frankfort, while Dumouriez's columns occupied Antwerp, Liége, and Brussels. Flushed with victory and determined to extend dominion, the French government issued in November the following revolutionary decree: "The National Convention declares . . . it will bring fraternity and aid to all peoples that wish to recover their liberty." Shortly thereafter, Savoy was annexed to France, while Belgium was made into a satellite state. Another decree opened the river Scheldt to all navigation, in defiance of international agreements, a British guaranty of 1788, and a French treaty of 1785.

English opinion was stunned by the rapid progress of events. Trade connections with the Continent were upset, and the opening of the Scheldt promised to ruin English commercial interests in that quarter. Simultaneous with these signs of French expansion came the news of the confiscation of royalist and church property in France, and the massacre and execution of many of the nobility. The trial and execution of Louis XVI in January, 1793, was the climax. England, together with the rest of Europe, came to realize that an aggressive policy of conquest "rationalized in terms of a universal crusade to liberate all oppressed people" plus the revolutionary enactments and excesses in France was a danger to the established order. "To crush the menace of the armed doctrine of the French Revolution became a matter of life and death to all legitimate governments." On January 24, 1793, the French agent at London received his passport; and on February 1, the French replied by a declaration of war upon England.

England Declares War

The English ministry, under the leadership of Pitt, girded itself for action. A series of repressive measures destroyed the revolutionary societies at home and effectively silenced those who otherwise would have criticized the government. Legislation was enacted to safeguard English industry, trade, and agriculture and to prevent the neutral from engaging in the colonial trade of the enemy. The Traitorous Correspondence Act of 1793, for example, strictly forbade all trading and communication with the enemy except as licensed by the Crown. The enforcement of the time-honored Navigation System and the Corn Laws, moreover, was relaxed by numerous orders of the privy council. Steps were taken to protect the financial structure of the government, and a series of new taxes were imposed to meet the cost of the war. Drastic as these measures were, Pitt did not believe further action necessary, for he questioned France's ability to wage a long war. Pitt expected a speedy victory, and to achieve this he entered into a series of European alliances commonly known as the First Coalition. Bountiful subsidies were paid by Pitt to Austria, Prussia, Sardinia, and Spain, while Portugal, the Empire, Naples, and Russia agreed to coöperate on the high seas. The British navy and allied fleets effectively blockaded the enemy's coasts, and European armies successfully invaded France.

A French nation in arms met the attack. An intense nationalism swept over the country. The allies were driven from France and the war carried into their territories. Internal jealousies tended to weaken the coalition, while England wasted its energies in a number of small expeditions which generally were unsuccessful. By 1795 the Netherlands had been captured by the French, and Prussia had withdrawn from the war. Shortly thereafter Spain made peace with France, which was thus freed to concentrate its efforts on Austria and Sardinia. Enthusiastic troops, drilled and equipped by Carnot, "the organizer of victory" and captained by men like Moreau and Bonaparte, carried the French standards along the Rhine and into Italy. By 1797 Austria was willing to make peace. Austria ceded territory in the Netherlands to France and recognized a number of Italian republics, founded by Bonaparte as satellite states of France. As a result of these victories, France was enabled to direct its entire attention toward England, the only significant remaining member of the First Coalition.

For a time the French government thought of invading England, but the superior naval resources of the latter made such an enterprise impossible. Might not France, however, attack and destroy Britain's power in India by landing a force in Egypt and marching from there to India? Bonaparte favored the idea; and the French government, anxious to remove so popular a hero from France, commissioned Napoleon to undertake the expedition. Although Bonaparte won a number of important victories, the destruction of the French fleet by Nelson in Aboukir Bay (August, 1798) cut Napoleon's communications with France. Stunned but not discouraged, Bonaparte moved his forces into Syria. The Moslem ruler of this area, Achmed Pasha, assisted by a British fleet, stopped the French at Acre and forced Napoleon back into Egypt. The expedition had failed, and Bonaparte, so the English thought, was bottled up in Egypt. Pitt seized the opportunity of forming a second coalition, and early in 1799, Russian and Austrian armies spread defeat among the French in Italy and on the Rhine. The French government, honeycombed by dishonesty and inefficiency, was in desperate straits when suddenly Bonaparte, leaving his army in Egypt, appeared in France. Public opinion rallied to the side of this popular hero, and Napoleon, taking advantage of the situation, overturned the existing government and established what is known as the Consulate, with himself as chief executive.

Having reorganized affairs at home, Bonaparte departed for the front. With lightning rapidity and in defiance of accepted practices of war, Napoleon smashed the Austrian forces in Italy while Moreau inflicted similar defeats upon the enemy along the Rhine. In the meantime Russia had withdrawn its forces. Austria was not able to continue the conflict, and early in 1801 accepted a military peace imposed by Napoleon. Once again, in spite of England's victories on the sea and Pitt's diplomacy, France had emerged triumphant. Pitt's dream of an easy victory had vanished, while England itself was in the throes of an industrial and agricultural depression. A series of harvest failures had caused an unprecedented rise in prices and had led to rioting. At Bath a poster announced, "Peace and Large Bread or a King without a Head," while at London another proclaimed, "Bread or Blood. . . . Have not Frenchmen shown you a pattern to fight for liberty?" Throughout the country the glare of burning stacks and bakehouses threw a vivid color over an exhausted nation. The accumulative effects of these disturbances plus French victories on the Continent forced Pitt out of office. Addington, the new minister, brought the war to an end by the Treaty of Amiens, ratified early in 1802. By this treaty France agreed to withdraw from Egypt and relinquish some of her Italian possessions. Britain promised to restore the conquered colonial possessions except for Ceylon and Trinidad and to give Malta an independent status under general European protection.

The Peace of Amiens

In spite of the public demonstrations and parades in London and Paris in honor of peace, neither the English nor French governments viewed the treaty as more than a truce. Both needed a breathing spell and accepted the treaty only as a means to permit intensive preparations for a definitive conflict. The desires of the ordinary citizen had no place in the councils of the statesmen. England's commercial interests frowned upon French domination in the Netherlands and supported the ministry, which refused to yield Malta until Bonaparte ceased his policy of annexation on the Continent. Most of Italy had become dotted with new governments directly or indirectly under Napoleon's control. Switzerland had been formed into the Swiss Confederation as the military ally of France. Southern Germany, though remaining technically independent, became subject to French control. The enormous expansion of Napoleon's power in Europe was a challenge to England. At the same time Napoleon's naval program was viewed with alarm, while his attempt to reëstablish an empire in the New World, through the acquisition of Louisiana from Spain and the conquest of Santo Domingo from the native blacks, was interpreted as a direct attack upon England's colonial possessions. The situation was quite different from that of 1793. No longer did England talk of preserving monarchy and property against revolutionary philosophy. It was now a struggle for self-preservation; and in May, 1803, England declared war.

The Renewal of War

For over a year neither party aggressively attacked the other. In England, Addington was replaced by Pitt, who, before the close of 1805, had formed alliances with Russia and Austria in what was known as the Third Coalition. During this interval Bonaparte was engaged in establishing his power in France and its dependencies and in converting the Consulate into an Empire. A large French army had been assembled at Boulogne ostensibly for an invasion of Britain. The failure of the French admirals to clear the Channel of the English fleet and convoy the Grand Army across into England frustrated the contemplated invasion. Nelson's decisive victory at Trafalgar (October, 1805) over a combined French and Spanish fleet had saved England. Before this engagement had been fought, however, Bonaparte, already despairing of any help from his navy, had broken camp and by forced marches had captured an Austrian army at Ulm. In December of the same year, he won a brilliant victory over the Russians and Austrians at Austerlitz. Immediately, Austria accepted peace while Russia withdrew its crippled forces to prepare for another campaign. In executing these military manoeuvres Bonaparte had violated Prussian neutrality by marching a division of his army across the Prussian state of Ansbach. Further encroachments upon Prussia followed during the spring of 1806. Driven to desperation, Prussia declared war upon Napoleon, who brushed aside the Prussian troops at Jena and Auerstadt and in November, 1806, entered Berlin.

Frederick William III, the Prussian King, retreated into East Prussia and effected a junction with the Russian troops. In spite of this arrangement, Bonaparte won the battles of

Ewing Galloway.

TRAFALGAR SQUARE WITH NELSON COLUMN, LONDON.

Eylau and Friedland and in July, 1807, dictated the celebrated Treaty of Tilsit. According to this treaty, Russia and
Prussia were to join with Bonaparte in the war against England and to exert pressure upon other European states to
enter the alliance. During the course of the next two years,
Napoleon extended his power over most of Europe. Satellite
states were set up and several kingdoms were founded over
which he placed his brothers, marshals, and near relatives.
Chafing under the rigors of military despotism, the Spanish
people rose in revolt, while Austria in 1810 joined hands once
more with England. Bonaparte's troops never successfully put
down the Spanish opposition, which was supported by English
armies, though he humbled Austria most decisively and de-
tached it from the British alliance by marrying Marie Louise,
daughter of the Austrian emperor. By this time, Alexander,
Czar of Russia, was ready once more to cross swords with
Bonaparte; and in 1811 and 1812 Bonaparte marched into
Russia and withdrew without defeating his enemy. This was
the signal for an uprising all over Europe. Napoleon met the
attack in a series of brilliant campaigns in 1813 and 1814, but
when Austria joined his enemies he was forced back into
France and was compelled to sue for peace. Not having tasted
victory for many years, the allies demanded and secured the
abdication of the emperor. In return Napoleon was given the
island of Elba, in the Mediterranean, with full sovereignty
and all the rights and titles of an emperor.

On May 4, 1814, Bonaparte landed on his island kingdom
while the allied statesmen gathered at Vienna to rearrange
the map of Europe. Elaborate festivities and conferences
were held. Napoleon, established at Elba, cast longing eyes
on Europe. Encouraged by reports from France, Napoleon
at last risked returning to the Continent. The Congress of
Vienna broke up and Europe hastened to meet the imperial
troops under Bonaparte. In the face of almost insuperable
odds, Napoleon won several important victories; but at

Waterloo, June 18, 1815, his dreams of empire were blasted by a combined Prussian-English army under the Duke of Wellington and General Blücher. Napoleon was forced to sue for peace, but this time the allies treated their foe as a public enemy. Accordingly, Napoleon was exiled to St. Helena, where he died in 1821.

Napoleon's defeat may be explained by the rise of nationalism throughout Europe, the spendid efficiency of the British navy, the inherent economic strength of England, and the combined military forces of Europe. More significant than any of these factors was the so-called Continental System developed by Bonaparte and upon which his great empire was founded. Antecedents of this system existed in the enactments of the French revolutionary assemblies, but it remained for Napoleon to give these life and form in the famous Berlin and Milan decrees of 1806 and 1807. In substance these measures provided for a blockade of the British Isles and for the interdiction of all trade by friend, enemy, and neutral between Britain and the Napoleonic Empire. England met the attack by a series of orders in council which closed enemies' ports, forbade direct trade in contraband between the neutral and the enemy, and forced such trade as existed to clear through the British Isles. Steps in this direction were taken shortly after the outbreak of war in 1793 and at once precipitated trouble between the United States and England which ultimately resulted in the War of 1812.

The War of 1812

Shortly after war had been declared in 1793, France found trade with her West Indian possessions seriously impaired by the superiority of the British navy. Heretofore, France had closed this trade to all but her own nationals, but upon their inability to continue it, she opened this commerce to neutrals. American shippers and merchants reaped splendid profits,

until England forbade them on the ground that a trade which
had been closed to them in times of peace could not be legally
opened to them in times of war. America protested but England stood firm. Americans, however, soon found a way
around this difficulty by importing French colonial goods to
the United States and then reshipping them direct to France.
The United States claimed that by importation, these goods
had become American property and unless declared contraband could be shipped to France. At first England accepted
this interpretation and allowed the neutral to provide the
enemy with valuable supplies. The Tory ministry, however,
soon yielded to the demands of English shippers, who resented the rapid growth of American trade and shipping, and
declared the practice illegal. The British claimed that the
shipment of French colonial goods to the United States and
thence to France was a continuous voyage, and since France
had closed this trade to the neutral before 1793, it could not
now be engaged in by Americans.

Ever since 1783 the American government had been en-
deavoring to arrange a satisfactory commercial treaty with
England. Independence had deprived the Americans of their
former favored position within the British economic empire
and had closed, moreover, the valuable trade which had existed between the colonies and the British West Indies. In
1795 the Jay Treaty had been accepted by both parties; but
this arrangement, while permitting trade between the United
States and England, had not opened the West Indian ports.
Anxious to revise this arrangement and at the same time to
solve the problems which had arisen as a result of the French
Revolutionary wars, Jefferson sent Monroe to England. During 1805 Monroe received scant consideration from the Tory
ministers, but with the advent of the Fox ministry in 1806, a
change for the better appeared. Fox honestly wished to settle
these American differences but found his hands tied by the
rapid growth of French power under Bonaparte.

Engaged in a life and death struggle, England was forced to resort to a number of questionable practices which complicated the American negotiations. First, the Americans argued that Britain's blockade of French ports was illegal, as the English were not in a position to prevent trade along a coast which extended from Spain to North Germany. This area had been blockaded by orders in council; but as the British could actually close but a limited number of ports, America claimed the arrangement was but a paper blockade and hence was illegal. England refused to accept this contention. Second, England in her desire to man her ships and maintain mastery of the seas resorted to impressment. By impressment was meant the seizure of Englishmen in the employ of neutral traders and shippers. The United States did not question this right as applied to English deserters, but vigorously protested when American citizens were seized on the ground of former English citizenship. Although Britain was able to show that American naturalization laws were loosely drawn and enforced, the United States claimed the right of regulating her own affairs and would not listen to the English argument, once an Englishman always an Englishman. Again, America resented interference in the trade between the United States and France and repeatedly found fault with Britain's expanding list of contraband. Finally, the United States protested against the English practice of stopping American ships on the high seas and visiting and searching these for escaped Britishers or contraband.

Day after day Monroe and his assistants tried to unravel these disputes; but the Whigs, in spite of the best of intentions, would not yield. Finally, Monroe cast aside his instructions and agreed to a treaty which he must have known President Jefferson would not accept. Just before submitting the treaty to Monroe for signature, the British ministers added an additional clause which they claimed was necessary in view of the Berlin Decree (November, 1806). According to this clause,

America, in order to avail itself of the treaty, was to agree to resist Bonaparte's measure, while England promised to undertake no act which might injure the neutral until the United States had approved or rejected the treaty. Monroe signed the treaty; but before Jefferson could take any action, the British issued the Order in Council of January, 1807, which retaliated against the Berlin Decree by forbidding Americans to engage in the coastwise trade of France. Shortly thereafter the Whig ministry fell and was succeeded by a conservative Tory government, which proceeded to treat America as of no concern.

The celebrated Orders in Council of November, 1807, which followed, practically closed all trade to the Continent except that which the British might license. To avail himself of this privilege the neutral had to stop at an English port, purchase a license, and then sail to a port designated in the license. Since Bonaparte, however, considered all neutrals who respected the British orders as enemies, the American was forced into an impossible situation. In an attempt to overcome this difficulty, the American bought French licenses which Napoleon was willing to sell owing to the needs of his Empire for certain raw and manufactured articles. Both French and British licenses were bought and sold in large numbers, thus contravening the purpose of both orders and decrees. Neither belligerent, however, could exist without some trade, so each proceeded to trade with the other by means of the neutral. England imported in this way valuable cargoes of food stuffs, wines, and articles of luxury from France, while Bonaparte's troops marched in English boots and English made woolens.

In spite of the opportunities afforded the neutral by the license system, the total volume of American trade dwindled, while seizure of American goods and citizens continued. Hoping to avoid war and at the same time to force both belligerents to modify their decrees and orders, Jefferson secured the passage of the Embargo Act of 1808. By this and several supplementary measures, all export from the United States was forbidden, except for coastwise purposes. Although these acts were rigorously enforced and exports to England declined over ninety per cent, neither belligerent altered its program. Jefferson had overestimated European dependency upon American supplies, and in 1809 the Embargo was replaced by a Non-Intercourse measure. Trade with both France and England was suspended, though the president was empowered to retract the act for whichever of the two nations should first abandon its restrictions. For a year no change was effected, and American trade was all but driven from the high seas. In May, 1810, a new president, James Madison, secured the passage of the Macon Bill No. 2, which repealed all former measures but allowed the president to renew them against one belligerent when the other had adopted a policy favorable to American trade.

In the meantime, American men-of-war had been attacked by British ships and impressment continued with increased severity. At this juncture Bonaparte cleverly convinced Madison that the French decrees no longer affected the United States. Straightway, Madison invoked the power granted him by the Macon Bill and declared non-intercourse with Britain. Actually, Bonaparte had not modified his decrees, but Madison was made to believe the opposite. In America there seemed to be little hope of avoiding a war with England. British orders, her interference with American trade, and her policy of impressment had created a situation which offered little basis for believing that peaceful relations might be maintained. In addition, the British government had supported the activities of English fur traders in the West and had influenced the Indians to attack American settlements. Although the war group within the United States talked loudly about neutral rights, it was evident that the sentiment for war was strongest in those areas least affected by British policy on the high seas. Recent investigation has shown that the southern and western representatives at Washington had visions not only of driving British fur interests from the West but of conquering Canada. Economic and imperial motives were uppermost in the minds of those who kept urging Madison to declare war. The President was urged into action and on June 18, 1812, the United States declared war.

Two days before, the British ministers yielded to the requests of her commercial and manufacturing classes, who wished renewed trade with the United States, and repealed the obnoxious orders in council. Had America heard of this action in time, Congress might not have declared war. But the day of the radio was far distant and not knowing what had transpired in London, Washington declared war. Madison, however, had the opportunity of postponing hostilities and reopening negotiations. As a matter of fact, the president did make a feeble attempt to patch up differences but his demands were too stiff for England to accept while American opinion supported prompt military action now that war had been declared. Although individual American ships won important engagements, the superior resources of the enemy finally captured, sank, or drove American vessels into port. A British army was landed, Washington was captured, and America was all but defeated. By this time, Bonaparte was on the island of Elba, and the causes which had led to the War of 1812 were largely removed. Accordingly, both parties agreed to make peace by accepting the Treaty of Ghent of 1815.

The Cost of War

At the opening of the French war in 1793, the national debt of England was almost 238 million pounds sterling which would equal approximately $1,190,000,000. By 1815 the debt had risen to 860 million pounds or about $4,300,000,000. With the British Isles having a population of about nineteen to twenty millions this represented a debt of $215 a head. It is evident, therefore, that the cost of the French and American wars had not been met by taxation, even though England raised greater sums than ever before in its history. In spite of rising trade and manufacturing, and extensive agricultural improvements, the British government had to tax almost everything and borrow sums at exorbitant rates of interest. Some of these taxes were direct, such as a ten per cent income tax which netted nearly fifteen million pounds in 1815. Legacy duties on personal property gained one and one-quarter million pounds in 1815. Both of these assessments were new for that age, having been imposed for the first time in 1799 and 1796 respectively. Approximately 63 per cent of the total amount raised by taxation, however, was indirect, and was levied upon articles of common use. While it is true that the wealthy classes contributed large sums, the burden fell chiefly upon the lower classes, whose sons and fathers were in the army and navy. About one third of the average laborer's annual income was appropriated by the government. Although the well-to-do paid heavy assessments, their net income continued to provide comfort and advancement for themselves and families. Their financial reserves, moreover, permitted patriotic subscriptions to government loans which netted handsome interest returns. The laborer, on the other hand, enjoyed none of these advantages and could do little more than exist. England had defeated Napoleon but had done so at a tremendous cost in life and treasure.

SELECTED BIBLIOGRAPHY

The majority of the works cited for the previous chapter may be used here. In addition F. E. Melvin's *Napoleon's Navigation System* (Philadelphia, 1909); W. F. Galpin's *Grain Supply of England during the Napoleonic Period* (New York, 1925); H. Adams' *The History of the United States* (New York, 1889–1891); A Cunningham's *British Credit in the Last Napoleonic War* (Cambridge, 1910); E. F. Heckscher's *The Continental System* (Oxford, 1922); J. H. Rose's *The Life of Napoleon* (New York, 1910); S. F. Bemis' *A Diplomatic History of*

the United States (New York, 1936), and W. A. Phillips and Arthur
H. Reede's *Neutrality, The Napoleonic Period* (New York, 1936) are
specialized studies of value. C. Oman's *History of the Peninsular War*
(Oxford, 1902–1914); L. Gershoy's *The French Revolution and Napoleon* (New York, 1933), and A. T. Mahan's *Influence of Sea Power
upon the French Revolution and Empire* (Boston, 1898) and his *Sea
Power in its relation to the War of 1812* (Boston, 1915) are of help.

CHAPTER XXVII

Social and Economic Factors, 1700-1815

Basic Considerations

ENGLAND'S victory over France may be attributed in part to the soundness of her economic structure. Not once during that contest had English manufacturers, agriculturists, or distributors failed to produce and deliver the sinews of war; nor were British bankers and capitalists tardy in furnishing subsidy and credit. The unparalleled economic expansion which took place during the French wars, however, had not been caused by the demands of war. In the final analysis, it was due to the industrial and agricultural development which, beginning in the medieval period, had progressed by mighty strides during the Tudor and Stuart eras. One should not forget, either, the significant contributions made by the scientists in chemistry, physics, astronomy, and mathematics. Without their help it is hard to picture English capitalists and engineers digging so deeply for coal and iron, transporting such quantities of bulky goods, or constructing buildings to withstand the weight and stress of huge machines. The work of these scientists, encouraged by government and business, continued throughout the eighteenth and nineteenth centuries, and, together with managerial genius and the skill of English laborers, transformed Britain into the leading industrial state of Europe.

An Agrarian Revolution

Equally significant were the changes in agriculture. At the opening of the eighteenth century, English agriculture was fundamentally medieval. The one-, two-, and three-field systems of cultivation prevailed, and most farmers continued to grow and harvest the same crops their ancestors had raised. Here and there some enterprising cultivator planted roots like the turnip or used the light Norfolk plow. But even these were handicapped by the inertia of the average farmer and the inadequate methods of transportation. Insecurity of tenure, which checked experimentation or investment in undertakings that necessitated years before profit could be made was another obstacle; nor could winter crops be grown where pasturing was permitted from August to February.

In spite of these obstacles certain pioneers appeared who ultimately succeeded in revolutionizing agriculture. Foremost among these men was Jethro Tull, who perfected a drill for sowing wheat, and who plowed his land often enough to permit, with the aid of fertilizers, larger and more frequent crops. Charles Townshend also should be remembered for his experiments in crop rotation. So successful were his efforts that he abandoned the three-field system, which annually kept one third of a farm fallow, and utilized all of his land the entire year through. The example set by these men was followed in time by others, so that by 1815 most of England was farmed as Tull and Townshend had done. New machines like the drill, reaper, mower, and thresher appeared. Stock breeding was advanced by men like Robert Bakewell. Larger and better cattle were bred, while sheep were raised for food as well as for wool. The diet of the nation was changed by these improvements as well as by the common use of turnips and other roots. Little variation took place among the cereals; and although Indian corn was raised for fodder, the bulk of the nation continued to eat rye bread and oat meal.

The total production of grain, however, mounted steadily from 1700 to 1815. In the first place, an increase in population and the rise of urban centers necessitated a greater supply of food. By 1760 England had at least six million people, while the first general census of 1801 showed about nine million. Then again the effects of the French Wars and the conflict with the United States cut off England from its accustomed foreign supplies and stimulated domestic production. High prices also encouraged greater production and investment in farm lands. So important did domestic production for local consumption become that an export trade in grain practically disappeared after 1756 and a partial dependency developed upon American and North German supplies. During the years 1800 to 1814 inclusive, a total of 169 million bushels of grain was imported from foreign sources. The absence of an export trade, the rapid expansion of an import trade, and the exigencies of the European war rendered the Corn Laws of little importance during these years.

More important than any of these factors in explaining increased production was the enclosure system. The fencing-in of land for agrarian purposes had begun during the seventeenth century. Public opinion, however, clung stubbornly to medieval methods and blocked the advocates of enclosure. Deep-rooted inertia continued to operate as late as 1750, and probably no more than 350,000 acres were enclosed during the first half of the century. After 1750, however, an increase in enclosure followed, owing to the evident advantages of large-scale farming, to the extensive publicity given it by local agricultural societies, the press and private individuals, to the rising demand for larger food supplies, and to a number of harvest failures. The unprecedented shortage of the harvests of 1799 and 1800, plus the high price of wheat, and heavy foreign importations caused the government to pass the General Enclosure Act of 1801.

Heretofore considerable delay and expense attended the introduction and passage of an enclosure bill. Each particular measure had to contain a number of diverse facts such as the apportionment of expenses and the rules for the construction of ditches. During the course of the eighteenth century these regulations had become standardized but had to be inserted within each enclosure bill. The Act of 1801 recited these various rules and provided that in the future they should automatically be inserted in every enclosure bill by merely reciting the clauses of the Act of 1801. Beyond standardizing the law of enclosure, the Act of 1801 had less influence upon enclosure than its framers anticipated. The Act of 1801, moreover, dealt chiefly with common lands; open fields were not touched until the reign of William IV (1830–1837). In spite of this restriction no less than 300,413 acres were brought into cultivation in one year. Before the close of the Napoleonic era, a total of 1,483 acts had enclosed about a million acres.

The effect of these enclosures and scientific discoveries upon production was enormous. The yield of wheat per acre rose from 12 bushels in 1714 to 15 in 1750, and by 1815, it had climbed to 20 bushels. By the middle of the eighteenth century the total production of wheat, as estimated by Charles Smith, a prominent student of agriculture, was approximately 32 million bushels, while a parliamentary committee of 1814 calculated the yield at 83 million bushels. Had this increase not taken place it is difficult to see how England could have fed its rising population in the face of the Continental System, Jefferson's Embargo, and the War of 1812. Equally important was the fact that the newer methods of farming advocated by Tull, Townshend, Arthur Young, the Royal Agricultural Society, and numerous other agencies could not have progressed without enclosure. The latter was a necessary preliminary to the former. The enclosures also brought about a rapid rise in rents and land values. Fewer hands were needed to farm the enclosed areas. This decreased the costs of production. Landlords, investors, large farmers, and lawyers grew wealthy and prosperous as a result of enclosure. On the other hand the small tenant farmer was squeezed off his holdings, while the cottage tenant became a proletarian.

Social Consequences

Contemporary sources of the late eighteenth and early nineteenth centuries bristle with evidences of protest on the part of the agricultural laborers. The Journals of the House of Commons and the papers of the Privy Council are crowded with petitions and complaints. Even Arthur Young, one of the staunchest defenders of enclosure, was not blind to existing evils and abuses. Man's memory of misfortune, however, is exceedingly short; and historians in general have overlooked the destruction wrought upon England by enclosure. It has been assumed that the losses of one group were more than compensated by the gains made by the state and society. The independence of the rural community, however, was destroyed. Time-honored rights and privileges were tossed aside in the name of progress and in the interest of those who profited from rents and bumper crops. A painful and distressing exodus of ejected tenants took place from the country to the city, and today the scars inflicted redden when examined by an impartial student. Possibly the poet Goldsmith had a glimpse of the future when he wrote, "A bold peasantry, their country's pride, when once destroyed, can never be supplied." Again, Gray may have had the last stand of the common cultivator in mind when he wrote, "Some village Hampden that with dauntless breast, the little tyrant of his fields withstood." The contest, however, was one-sided. Thousands were driven from their ancestral homes, losing "Estate and House . . . and all their sheep."

Not all of the ejected tenants migrated to the factory towns. Many preferred to stay on the farms and eke out a living as

Courtesy Assoc. British and Irish Railways, Inc.

GRAY'S MONUMENT, STOKE POGES.

wage earners. A barren existence confronted this group. Local or national relief was imperative if this class were to be saved from a lot which was far more degrading than medieval

serfdom. Poverty and hunger, moreover, are the handmaids
of revolution, and the property classes of England had sufficient reasons for not wanting that to take place. Accordingly, an attempt was made to alter the diet of the laborer in
a manner which would decrease the latter's expenses. "Con-
sume less wheaten bread and be content to eat oatmeal without milk," was the advice given these unfortunates. Labor
scorned such suggestions, refused to eat Indian corn, "the
fodder for cows," or potatoes that might not "poisson tha'
pigs" on the ground that it needed a more solid diet to meet
the rigorous life on the farm. If the city population would
not employ these substitutes, why should the farmer be asked
to forego his daily bread and meat? Dieting, as a device,
failed to ameliorate the lot of the dependent farmer. Might
not a minimum wage be fixed which would guarantee life
and not mere existence? Samuel Whitbread, James Fox, the
future Earl Grey, and a number of liberally minded Whigs
supported this view but failed in 1795 and 1800 to carry such
a measure through parliament. Pitt and the great majority
declared that the bill was revolutionary in nature, that the
sufferings of the poor were overdrawn and that conditions, if
left alone, would adjust themselves by natural laws and principles.

Other suggestions were offered, a few of which were
adopted, such as making it easier for labor to migrate from
one parish to another in search of better conditions. More
important, however, was the so-called Speenhamland System
adopted by the General Quarter Sessions for Berkshire, May
6, 1795. This was adopted in time by almost all the counties
of England. In substance, this system assumed that each laborer needed for bodily sustenance a prescribed number of
loaves of bread each week with an additional supply in case
he were married and had a family. When the price of bread
rose above a certain rate, the laborer was to receive either a

proportionate increase in his wages or an allowance from the poor rates. Wages, it was argued, would keep pace with rising prices. The fallacy in this contention was that wages to begin with were not sufficient to maintain a respectable standard of living. Only by a drastic increase in wages could the lot of the dependent farmer be improved, but this the well-to-do refused to accept although many voices were raised in support of labor's case. The wealthier classes, in short, did not want labor to expect a larger share of profits, but in order to appease their discontent adopted a system which kept the poor from becoming poorer. Labor disliked the arrangement but it had no way of voicing its sentiments. It was illegal to organize for relief and as yet no representative of this class sat in parliament. Otherwise one may be sure that the government would have been severely criticized for spending some seven million dollars in pensions and sinecures while not one penny was appropriated for directly improving the lot of the dejected farmer. The general prosperity of the country from Speenhamland to Waterloo clouded the real situation, and it was not until 1816 that labor determined to gain its end by threatening revolution.

Changes in Industry and Commerce

The agrarian revolution of the eighteenth century was not characterized by the application of motive power to production and distribution. New techniques and machines were introduced, but in every instance horses, oxen, or men furnished the necessary motive power. The exact opposite, however, took place in industry, where water and steam were used extensively. During the seventeenth century, water power was employed on a small scale in the woolen and mining industries. Cloth was fulled, water pumped from mines, and ventilation obtained in the shafts by engines propelled by

INDUSTRIAL ENGLAND

▨ Important Manufacturing Districts

Scale of Miles
0   10   25   50   75   100

SCOTLAND

Lead   Coalfields
       Pottery
Iron
              Iron

Iron

Woolens

Cotton   Iron
    Woolens
    Pottery
Ships   Coalfields
   Machinery
Salt   Cutlery

Slate   Salt

Slate   Iron   Lace
          Pottery Iron
          Coalfields
     Pottery   Iron
       Hardware

WALES

Woolens

Coalfields
Pottery
     Iron   Iron; Steel, and
Coalfields   Shipbuilding

          Ships

Tin
Granite

Copper   Ships   CHANNEL

ENGLISH

Prepared for Prentice-Hall, Inc.
Copyright Rand McNally & Company, N. Y. 289

water. By the end of that century, English miners, as they dug deeper into the earth, were in need of more adequate devices. Thomas Savery met the problem by patenting and selling a steam engine. Savery's engine was improved by

Newcomen in 1712 and by James Watt in 1769 and 1782. As a result of these inventions the mining of coal and iron became a simpler process. Greater economy and production were secured and seams were tapped lower than before. During the years 1681 to 1690, the annual output of the English, Scotch, and Welsh coal mines equaled nearly three million tons, while from 1781 to 1790 it amounted to over ten million tons. A similar expansion took place in the mining of iron. Without the invention of the steam engine, however, both industries would have been seriously cramped. By the nineteenth century, steam was also a factor of importance in the woolen and cotton trades.

Steam, however, would have been of little value in the textile trades had it not been for a series of mechanical inventions that appeared, beginning with Kay's flying shuttle in 1733. By this device the weaver was able to double his output, and the demand for thread and yarn was similarly increased. The spinners, however, could not meet this demand, and until Hargreaves, in 1764, perfected the spinning jenny, no progress was effected. The spinning jenny did away with many of the laborious tasks heretofore done entirely by hand. A little later, Arkwright invented a water frame, a carding device, and several other machines, while Compton's mule (1779), so-called because it employed the features of the jenny and water frame, produced stronger and finer thread than before. In a short time the quantity of spun yarn was greater than the weaver could use. To overcome this difficulty Edmund Cartwright invented a power loom in 1785, which increased the productivity of the weavers. Cartwright's invention, however, was not generally used in the woolen industry until the second quarter of the nineteenth century, though by 1810 it was commonly employed by the cotton producers.

Cotton cloth had been manufactured in the seventeenth

century. Not until the opening of the cotton fields of North
America, however, did any considerable activity take place.
Further expansion was handicapped by the primitive hand
methods used in separating the cotton from the fibre. In
spite of this difficulty the value of English cotton goods grew
from £23,000 at the opening of the century to £200,000 by
1764. Additional stimulus was given in 1793 by Eli Whitney's
cotton gin, which did away with the laborious and expensive
hand process of preparing cotton for the market.

The distribution of cotton and other raw materials and the
marketing of the finished product was seriously hampered by
inadequate transportation facilities in 1700. Primary and secondary highways had fallen into a deplorable condition.
Local authorities, in whose hands rested the responsibility of
maintaining roads, were reluctant and apathetic about making
improvements. Not until 1773 did parliament pass an act
which required proper road maintenance. Prior to this measure, the traveler and merchant journeyed at their own risk.
Carriages and carts frequently sank in mud to the axles, while
an impassable road delayed progress for days at a time. It
took hours to travel short distances. Conditions within the
cities were not much better. Winding roads, poorly paved,
made transit dangerous and tedious. The latter half of the
eighteenth century, however, witnessed vast improvement.
Traveling became more common and the transportation of
goods easier. Waterways were improved and an extensive
program of canal building swept the country. The first canal
was opened in 1761. Others followed in rapid succession, the
most notable being the Leeds-Liverpool Canal, which was
completed in 1810.

Similar progress took place in the construction of ships and
docks. It was not, however, until after 1760 that any notable
change occurred. Before that date the average trading vessel
was about three hundred tons burden, though the East India
traders used ships three times as large. Docking facilities

were also limited. The American Revolution and the French wars stimulated the building of ships both as to size and number. By 1815 vessels of three thousand tons were quite common, while a number of elaborate docks were built at Glasgow and London. The West India Dock at London was an enormous affair covering twelve acres of water, with adequate slips and warehouses. Practically all of the sea-borne trade was carried by sailing vessels. In 1802 the first steamship appeared on the Clyde, but it was not until 1815 that any great progress took place in steam navigation.

Urban Conditions and Social Reforms

The results of the industrial revolution, however, were not limited to greater productivity in manufacture or new facilities for transportation. A definite increase in population followed, particularly within the towns and cities. London expanded and contained within its limits approximately a million people. With this increase came a number of social and economic problems which even today have not been solved. Nothing in the way of adequate housing conditions existed; sanitation was conspicuous by its absence, fire hazards were enormous, and the local police often found it impossible to preserve law and order. Crime was rampant; and though the death penalty was generously imposed, little improvement took place. In the case of felony (and most crimes were felonies), the defendant had no counsel to speak in his behalf. The prisoner's lawyer was allowed only to cross-examine witnesses. Making a false entry in a marriage register or picking a pocket to the value of twelve pennies was a capital offense. Prisoners were hanged, women were publicly flogged, and the pillory was in common use. An execution was usually witnessed by scores of spectators. At Leicester, for example, in 1817, hundreds gathered as early as six in the morning to witness the hanging of six rioters. The execution did not take place until some time later. In the interim the crowd was entertained by the speeches and songs of the condemned and then thrilled by the physical agony of death. "We lament to say," so wrote a reporter, "that most of the misguided men, in the bloom of life, have left widows and more than thirty children to add to the miseries of the present truly calamitous times." With the government approving these spectacles and with the public feasting its eyes on them, it is not to be wondered at that many youths regarded the victims as heroes and sought to follow their lives of crime.

Some attempt was made to improve these abominable conditions. Interested individuals were recruited largely from the wealthy, educated, and leisure classes. Others were members of the governing class, all of whom had nothing to gain personally from the reforms they advanced. Among these reformers was the "Clapham Sect," so-called because the members held their meetings in Clapham, southwest of London. All of them were devout communicants of the Church of England, but were interested in the humanitarianism of Christ rather than in the doctrine of the Lord's Supper. Tinged with an evangelical attitude, they were called by their critics the "Saints of the Clapham Sect." Another group, almost atheistic in religious matters, was known as the "Utilitarians" or "Benthamites," because they followed the view of Jeremy Bentham, who declared for "the greatest happiness of the greatest number." Another center of reform was at 16 Charing Cross, London, the home and shop of Francis Place. Place was a retired tailor, having risen from dire poverty to comparative wealth. He was a radical reformer whose shop was a circulating library of extreme literature and a rendezvous for reformers of all types. The propaganda and efforts of these men showed results in the formation of a number of humanitarian societies. In 1787 there was formed the Society for the Abolition of the Slave Trade. Other groups were organized for bettering the condition of the poor, for the suppression of vice, for propagating the Bible, for improving the lot of orphaned children, for prison reform and the like. Organization was followed by petitioning parliament for remedial legislation.

Among the members in parliament who sponsored this movement was Sir Samuel Romilly, a London lawyer and close friend of Bentham. In 1808 he had the good fortune of advancing through parliament a bill which reduced the penalty for pocket-picking from death to transportation. Two years later he introduced three other measures designed to lessen the number of cases for the death penalty, but he was defeated by a majority vote. The House of Lords, whose members represented church and property, was adamantine to reform. Severity in law, so it was argued, checked crime; and capital punishment was necessary if private property were to exist. Some relief was obtained between 1813 and 1815 when death was no longer a punishment for breaking machines and when disemboweling and quartering were prohibited. Attempts were made also to improve prison conditions, though only a few measures succeeded in clearing the religious and property hurdles in the House of Lords. Another reform centered about the abolition of the slave trade, the profits from which had made many men wealthy. William Wilberforce, a Claphamite, became sponsor for this movement as early as 1789; but it was not until 1807 that he was able to overcome prejudice and self-interest and secure the adoption of his measure. In achieving this success, Wilberforce and his fellow-reformers owed much to the untiring efforts of the Friends who were sponsors of many reforms and worked diligently for the abolition of war. Condemnation of war had been voiced in the fourteenth century by Wycliffe and had been advanced by George Fox, the founder of the Society of Friends, in 1660. William Penn's *Plan for the Permanent Peace of Europe* (1693) was distributed in

England by the Quakers, especially by John Bellers of Gloucester. Tracts and pamphlets extolling peace appeared throughout the eighteenth century and prepared the way for the definite organization of peace societies. Thanks to the efforts of Dr. David Bogue and William Allen, there was finally founded, June 14, 1816, the "Society for the Promotion of Permanent and Universal Peace."

Labor Revolts

Another significant result of the industrial revolution was the development of the factory system, in which the tools of production were owned largely by an industrial capitalist, and where the work was performed under one roof, likewise the property of the employer. Wages were low, and women and children were employed under most deplorable conditions. Mill workers at Glasgow, for example, received about $5.00 a week. Women operators earned from $1.25 to $3.00 per week, while children received much less. From this wage, labor had to buy food, lodging, and clothing at prices which left little if anything for health or advancement. Doubling these figures, to approximate money values of today, one is startled at the difference which often existed between income and prices. Probably it cost less to live in England in 1800 than in America today, but it should be remembered that wages were lower than now. Living conditions were abominable, while hours of work generally were from sunrise to sunset. Bad as the condition was, it was aggravated by the rapid mechanization of industry, which swelled an already existing army of unemployed. Labor demonstrated its feelings by smashing machines and burning mills and factories. Added misfortune arose in harvest failures and an increase in food prices. A drastic food shortage arose in 1799 and 1800 and led to considerable rioting. Although the great majority of the rioters were English, the presence of a few French agents gave the affair a more significant aspect.   From Wilford, near Nottingham, the news reached the Home Office that "the persons who meet together are rank Jacobins and the scarcity of grain is merely a pretext.   They cry out for a Revolution, and after the French fashion date their days of liberty from the commencement of these riots."

Similar disturbances arose in 1810 and 1811 and probably were caused more by the high price of bread than by the industrial system then in vogue.   Riots broke forth in various parts of the realm.   At Bristol, Carlisle, and Glasgow these grew to an alarming size.   The following notice, taken from the Home Office Papers, shows the seriousness of the situation.   It was addressed to a Mr. Douglass who owned a mill near Manchester:

If you do not advance the wages of your workmen . . . you shall have all your mills burnt to the ground immediately.   It is harder upon us here than upon those who receive parish relief.   We are starving by inches by reason of our small wages and provisions so high.   The Poor cry aloud for bread, Prince Regent shall lose his head, and the rich who oppress the poor in a little time shall be no more.

These disturbances have been known as the Luddite Riots, so-called because labor's demands were signed by one Ned Ludd.   Who Ludd was no one knows, though his followers obeyed his orders by destroying factories and machines in large quantities.   The government quelled the revolt by armed force, by putting a number to death, and by exiling others to Australian penal settlements.   On the other hand some attempt was made to improve the lot of the factory worker.   At the opening of the century the care of the poor, indigent, and unemployed rested upon the Elizabethan Poor Law, hopelessly out of date.   Particularly inadequate were those provisions which related to pauper children and orphans.   Manufacturers and mine owners employed these unfortunates at very low wages and exposed them to brutal managers and foremen.

No opportunity existed for education or leisure. They worked from sunrise to sunset and often late into the night. The first attempt to remedy these conditions came in 1785, when the city of Manchester refused to apprentice pauper children to the mill owners. In 1802, parliament passed the first Factory Act, according to which all factories were to be whitewashed once a year and to have proper ventilation. Apprentices were to work but twelve hours a day, were to be educated and were to go to church at least once a month. Boys and girls were to sleep apart, and no more than two were to occupy the same bed. Unfortunately, the measure lacked adequate machinery for enforcement, and although some improvement took place, evasions were numerous and frequent. Practically nothing, however, was done in respect to labor conditions in the mines.

A large number of the factories, which developed as a result of the industrial revolution, were in the vicinity of the coal and iron fields of central England. The proximity of Liverpool to the American trade routes and the moist atmosphere of the Mersey valley, which kept the yarn pliable and not brittle, were factors of importance. The growth of industry in these areas resulted in a rapid rise of the local population. This was due in part to an increased birth rate, though the migration of thousands of laborers from southeastern England was of greater significance. The value of this abundant labor supply to the capitalists was as high as the ready supplies of coal and iron. Bent on making the most of their opportunities, the factory owners exploited labor as freely as natural resources. Some of the industrialists, like Boulton and Wedgwood, were men of good judgment who sought to improve the lot of labor. The greater share, however, were hard-headed business men who commonly sacrificed human values for material gains. In support of their policy, they could cite the rapid expansion of England, the growth of trade and industry, and the multiplication of the necessities and conveniences of life. The absence of any body of governmental law which might have restricted their efforts, moreover, gave a legal sanction to their program. There also arose a school of economists who exalted individual rights, the spirit of free competition, and a minimum of governmental regulation.

The Rôle of the Economists

Foremost among those who advocated the new freedom was Adam Smith (1723–1790). Although Smith published his monumental study, *The Wealth of Nations* (1776), before much of the industrial upheaval had taken place, he was in agreement with contemporary thought, which believed that the day of mercantilism was over and that the older governmental restrictions were handicaps to economic development. Smith asserted that while commerce had its advantages, the national wealth would be increased by the production of consumers' goods. Triple the output, Smith declared, and England would find extensive markets at home and abroad. Government, he insisted, should leave the direction of industry to business. History, moreover, was replete with evidence to show that state interference had always led to confusion and loss. Follow natural laws and allow business to grow under free initiative and competition, and the results would benefit all. This, in brief, was the economic theory of *laissez faire* (let alone), which has ever been associated with the work of Adam Smith. Smith believed that an enlightened industrial group would protect itself against attack by giving labor a larger wage scale and by curtailing excess profits.

The rapid accumulation of capital in the hands of a few, however, together with the resulting degradation of labor, illustrates how industrialists rejected Smith's restrictions upon their operations. They favored his concept of *laissez faire* but refused to accept its limitations. On the other hand they welcomed the views of Thomas Malthus (1766–1834), who contended that neither the state nor private individuals had any responsibility for the lot of the wage earner. Malthus held that a country's population increased by a geometrical progress (2, 4, 6, and so on), while the food supply advanced by an arithmetical rate (1, 2, 3, and so on). Nature, he argued, had imposed this rigid law and had created misery, poverty, war, starvation, and death as labor's best friends. In a later edition of his work on population Malthus modified his views, but the governing and wealthy classes ignored these and cited his earlier views as justification for their actions. Later generations, however, demonstrated that education and birth control were better alternatives than poverty and early death.

Conservative opinion viewed with concern the extension of coöperative societies, trade-unionism, and socialism. Its philosophy, already well established by the teachings of Adam Smith and Malthus, received additional stimulus by the findings of David Ricardo (1772–1823). Ricardo, the son of a Jewish stockbroker, accepted the *laissez-faire* views of Smith and the population theory of Malthus. On the basis of the latter, Ricardo propounded a law of wages which accorded the worker sufficient compensation to subsist and perpetuate his kind. If wages were to increase, population would increase, and the former equilibrium would be restored. If wages, however, were to decline, then labor would starve and industry would decline. Manufacturers and industrialists endorsed this law and used it as an argument against labor's demands for higher wages. They did not, however, take so kindly to his doctrines of free trade or that the results of the law of wages would lead to a decline in profits. Ricardo insisted that if wages, expressed in terms of foodstuffs, remained constant, the amount of wages would have to increase since the cost of producing food inevitably would rise as marginal lands were cultivated to take care of the needs of a natural increase in population. Labor, therefore, would be receiving relatively the same wage as before and the increased costs of production would have to be borne by capital, which meant decreasing profits. On the other hand the landlords would receive greater rents and thus grow wealthier.

Changes in Architecture and Costuming

Comparatively little, therefore, was done to improve the evil conditions of labor in the factory or on the farm. As long as those who profited from *laissez faire* were in control of government, no redress was possible. On the other hand the social conditions of the more fortunate elements tended to become better. During the reigns of Anne and the first two Georges, material prosperity generally corrupted the standards and morals of the upper classes. Coarseness and vulgarity characterized the balls and banquets of the wealthy, who flaunted their wealth by building pretentious homes. The architectural designs of the Georgian and Anne periods provided for a sedate and restful exterior, flanked by peaceful gardens, and ornamented by fences and walls well screened by iron or lead grilles. Ease and dignity characterized the interior of these dwellings, whose stairways were built with spiral balustrade, fluted columns, or brackets. The furnishings carried out the same restful motive, but to build and maintain these homes required a large fortune. Even the homes of the middle class were relatively expensive. Christopher Wren and Robert Adam were the architects who initiated this building, remains of which are to be seen in practically every modern English town or city.

The owner of one of these homes usually wore a wig that was tied, braided, or plaited in the rear and raised somewhat like a pompadour. Beneath the wig, which was always powdered for elaborate functions but generally not for street attire, the head was shaven or cut close except for a curl in front and at the nape. His hat was a three-cornered, slightly cocked affair until 1770, when style dictated the front peak to point upwards. Wide, Quakerish hats and the forerunner of the top hat were worn on less formal occasions and for sport. Shoes with broad, square toes were worn, though boots, extending at times to the knees, were more common. Stockings, clocked with gold and silver, showed above the boots. The breeches were generally tight to the thigh but full and gathered in the seat. Above the breeches came a handsome linen shirt covered by a waistcoat which, before 1750, usually reached to the knees. After that date the waistcoat became shorter. Over this came a full coat which, as the century progressed, became shorter and more ornate. Swords, canes, watches, and snuff boxes added to the gentleman's dress. Women followed the same tendency toward richness and display. Before 1760 the hair was kept close to the head with a few curls at the side and a "bun" at the back. After that date the hair was dressed higher to proportions that were astonishing. For formal events powder was invariably used. This elaborate coiffure called for towering hats, bonnets, and hoods, though earlier in the century simpler gears were worn. Shoes were generally high until the French Revolution, when lower heels came into style. Coats, jackets, and petticoats were worn on various occasions and in great variety, while elaborate gowns and cloaks presented a pleasing picture. Custom dictated the use of bustles and hoops, the latter extending sideways as much as sixteen inches. The neck, which during the earlier part of the century was generously displayed, became more daring as time progressed.

These were the men and women who frequented the spas, the theaters, balls, and parties so freely indulged in by the upper classes. Gambling, drinking, and swearing characterized these gatherings, which often were masquerades to allow greater freedom and license. During the daytime, which began rather late in the morning, it was the proper thing to "swing" through the park. After this parade the men gathered at the coffeehouses to read the papers, discuss politics, play games, or swap stories of various colors. During the first quarter of the century, clubs such as the Mohocks, the Robin Hood Society, and the Hell-Fire Club still flourished in large numbers. Though these groups lost their popularity as the century progressed, they continued to be a center of attraction down into the nineteenth century.

Deism and Methodism

In the center of this world of fashion stood the historic Church of England, unmindful of what was going on about it. Many of the clergy tripped along with their wealthy parishioners in one round of pleasure, blind to the misery and poverty of the lower classes. Others, members of the House of Lords, devoted much time to politics and to the defense of the rights of the Church. Clerical preferment depended too often upon one's political and social connections. A premium, in brief, was not always placed upon piety and learning. On the other hand there were prelates who took their spiritual duties seriously. Recent investigation shows that in spite of these extraneous duties and the difficulties attending travel, the bishops visited their parishes with considerable regularity. Humble priests, moreover, labored without thought of worldly gain or promotion. Many serious works were published, some of which rank high in the field of English literature. The content of these writings is of interest insofar as it reveals how the clergy met the attack of their opponents, the deists. Religious skepticism abounded among the upper classes, who accepted the scientific and mechanical discoveries of the century as a denial of dogma and faith. The deists argued that it was old-fashioned to believe in the supernatural. Religion, they declared, was vital for man but should be built upon logic and reason.

It is to the credit of the Church that its clergy met the attack in a creditable manner and refused to supplant faith with reason. Rationalism, however, did invade the sanctuaries; and many a cleric, particularly of the lower orders, found fault with a church that ignored the rôle of the Good Samaritan and refused to stir the emotions of the laity by religious revivals. Among these were John and Charles Wesley, graduates of Oxford, who sought to bring to the laity spiritual inspiration and comfort. Their work began while they were students at Oxford and was greeted by their Anglican friends with abuse and ridicule. Their opponents dubbed them "Methodists," but this aspersion failed to dampen the ardor of the Wesleyan group. Into the highways went this band, preaching and stimulating by prayer and song. In this movement the Wesley brothers were aided by the oratory of George Whitefield, whose sermons regenerated many a listener. Whitefield, moreover, argued that the Methodist group should sever itself from the Church of England and establish a communion of its own. John Wesley opposed this, and not until after his death (1791) did Methodism become a separate faith.

It was easy for the Church of England to criticize this movement. Too often had the Methodists resorted to extravagant utterances, assumed an overrighteous attitude and by preaching hell-fire had won converts through fear. On the other hand, like the modern Salvation Army, they brought the gospel to the masses. They invaded the factory towns, administered to the poor and did not shut their eyes to the suffering about them. The Anglican Church did not do this, and lost, thereby, thousands who avowed membership in Methodism. Ultimately the Wesleyan movement aroused the Church from its apathy and stimulated the existing Protestant sects to greater activity. Finally, much of the social and philanthropic activity that followed, especially in the nineteenth century, may be traced to Methodism.

SELECTED BIBLIOGRAPHY

Specialized studies exist in large numbers. In respect to agriculture, R. E. Prothero's *English Farming, Past and Present*; R. Curtler's *Enclo-*

sure and Redistribution of our Land; D. G. Barnes' *A History of the English Corn Laws,* and E. C. K. Gonner's *Common Land and Enclosure,* all cited elsewhere in this text, are of value. J. L. and B. Hammond's *Village Labourer* (London, 1920) depicts in sombre colors the lot of the small farmer. A. M. W. Stirling's *Coke of Norfolk* (London, 1912) describes the work of a prominent reformer in agriculture. G. Slater's *The English Peasantry* (London, 1907) is useful for a study of the enclosure of common fields. J. H. Clapham's *Economic History of Modern Britain* (Cambridge, 1927) is also of value.

The following will be of help in respect to industrial changes and commercial activities: J. L. and B. Hammond's *Town Labourer* and *Skilled Labourer* (London, 1917 and 1919); Paul Mantoux's *La Révolution Industrielle au XVIII Siècle* (Paris, 1906); J. L. and B. Hammond's *The Rise of Modern Industry* (New York, 1925); L. C. A. Knowles' *The Industrial and Commercial Revolution in Great Britain* (New York, 1926); W. Bowden's *Industrial Society in England towards the End of the Eighteenth Century* (New York, 1925); G. W. Daniel's *The Early English Cotton Industry* (Manchester, 1920); T. S. Ashton's *Iron and Steel in the Industrial Revolution* (Manchester, 1924); J. Lord's *Capital and Steam Power* (London, 1923); J. U. Nef's *The Rise of the British Coal Industry* (London, 1932); Ivy Pinchbeck's *Women Workers and the Industrial Revolution* (London, 1930), and F. O. Darvell's *Popular Disturbances and Public Order* (New York, 1934) are of value. A convenient bibliography for both agrarian and industrial changes is found in the *Industrial Revolution* by E. Power (London, 1927).

For social legislation and reform see E. P. Cheyney's *Modern English Reform* (Philadelphia, 1931); Mr. and Mrs. S. Webb's *English Poor Law History* (London, 1927); B. L. Hutchins and A. Harrison's *History of Factory Legislation* (London, 1911), and J. C. Clapham's *Economic History of Modern Britain.* The new political economy may be found in Adam Smith's *The Wealth of Nations,* edited by E. Cannan (New York, 1904); T. R. Malthus' *Essay on the Principle of Population* (see the 1798 edition published by Macmillan, 1926); J. Bonar's *Malthus and his Work* (New York, 1924); E. Cannan's *A History of the Theories of Production and Distribution* (London, 1917), and H. Peck's *Economic Thought* (London, 1935).

J. H. Overton and F. Relton's *History of the English Church, 1714–1800* (London, 1906); C. T. Winchester's *Life of John Wesley* (New York, 1906), and N. Sykes' *Church and State in England in the XVIIIth Century* (Cambridge, 1934) are of value for ecclesiastical affairs. R. J. Allen's *The Clubs of Augustan London* (Cambridge, Mass., 1933) is of interest.

CHAPTER XXVIII

Cultural Aspects, 1700-1815

ENGLISH literature reflected the effects of the industrial and agrarian revolutions. Reference has already been made to the writings of Adam Smith, Thomas Malthus, David Ricardo, Charles Smith, and Arthur Young in the field of economics and agriculture. Hundreds of other books and tracts were published dealing with corn laws, navigation acts, harvest failures, mechanical improvements, and inventions. Most of these were highly technical or controversial in nature and were read by a small select group. Philosophical and religious writings also appeared from men like the third Earl of Shaftesbury, Bishops Berkeley, Hoadley, and Watson, and a score of other divines, Anglican and non-conformist. Political writings abound during this period. Jeremy Bentham's *Introduction to the Principles of Morals and Legislation* (1788) represented a philosophical approach to a study of political science. Thomas Spence, the author of the *Rights of Infants* and the periodical *Pig's Meat,* William Oglivie, Thomas Paine, William Godwin, and Charles Hall were outstanding contributors to socialistic literature. Few of these writers attracted much attention. Their popularity is not to be compared to that which greeted the writings of David Hume, who probably was the most profound Englishman of the eighteenth century. His *Treatise of the Human Understanding* furthered a scientific approach to a study of human conduct and knowledge, and helped to develop a skeptical attitude toward organized religion.

Hume, moreover, was a historian, and has left us a brilliant *History of England* which tended to shape historical opinion for more than a century. Greater than Hume in the field of history was Edward Gibbon, whose monumental *Decline and Fall of the Roman Empire* has gone through many editions and is held in high esteem today. John Oldmixen, Gilbert Burnet, and William Robertson were also historians of note. In contrast to the historians of the past, these men discarded the old annalistic approach. They sought to present, in a finished literary style, conclusions which were based upon a study of original sources and documents. Their efforts, moreover, revealed the influence of rationalism as advocated by Locke, and illustrated the growing tendency to explain man's actions by scientific methods.

The Press and Publishing Houses

Hume's *History of England* first appeared in 1762 and became so popular that a new edition was published in 1763. Other editions appeared in 1773 and 1788. The profits arising from the sale of this book produced a decided boom to the publishers. Printing and publishing had become an important industry by the close of the eighteenth century. This was due in part to the repeal, in 1695, of the licensing acts of 1662 and 1685, which had placed the entire control of printing in the hands of the government. The freedom of the press was still restricted by a law of libel which was rather strictly enforced during the reign of Anne. Greater toleration was granted by the governments of George I and II. George III attempted to restrict the press, but during most of his reign there was a gradual increase in the liberty of expression. The advent of the French Revolution checked this movement, and it was not until after 1832 that the freedom of the press was firmly established. During most of the eighteenth century, however, considerable latitude existed, and the way was cleared for greater newspaper and publishing activity. Jacob Tonson and Bernard Lintot had founded publishing houses shortly after the Glorious Revolution, and in 1724 the London firm of Longmans appeared. Others followed in rapid succession. The houses of Elliot, and Constable and Murray were the most important. At first the various publishers adopted a noncompetitive arrangement which usually provided for the publication of a book by a number of firms. By the close of the century free competition had developed. This resulted in the closure of many small firms which could not stand price-cutting or the high prices paid to certain popular authors. Cheap editions and reprints also shut out the smaller publishers; and the practice, introduced by Harrison in 1799, of printing by installments in periodicals like the *Novelists' Magazine* was a blow to the lesser competitors.

Important works on science, religion, and travel netted the authors as high as $5,000. Poets, dramatists, and fiction writers earned more. In 1807, for example, Scott received more than $5,000 in advance for *Marmion,* and Longmans, in 1814, paid Thomas Moore $15,000 for a poem still unwritten. Constable and Murray willingly parted with large sums for books and articles which appeared in the *Quarterly* and *Edinburgh Reviews.* Other periodicals, like the *Agricultural Magazine,* the *Annual Register,* the *Anti-Jacobin Review* and Flower's *Political Review* appeared, devoted to scientific and political matters. The *Literary Panorama* reviewed current literature, while the *Repository of Arts* provided drawings and sketches of interest to men and women. Newspapers multiplied. Dublin was the first city to have a daily paper, *Pue's Occurrences,* founded in 1700. Three years later the London *Daily Courant* appeared. Others followed, notably the *Daily Courier, Morning Chronicle,* and the *Times.* Many of the provincial cities and boroughs had daily or weekly papers. Often the publisher of one was the owner of others. John Nicholson, for example, edited the *London Evening Post, The British*

Spy, and several others.   Parliamentary debates, official papers, foreign news, commercial intelligence, and crime filled most of the columns.   In contrast to newspapers of today, advertising was less important and usually appeared on the front page. The circulation of these papers was limited not only by the law of libel but by a stamp tax and by a duty on all advertisements.   The first Stamp Tax Act was passed in 1712 and netted the government such a neat sum that it was continued and increased until it reached eight cents on each paper printed.   The government also taxed advertisements at the rate of about eighty-five cents.   These duties plus the cost of paper, raised the price of newspapers to twelve and fourteen cents.   The working classes, therefore, could not afford to buy these papers and their sale was restricted generally to the well-to-do.   In spite of these difficulties, which incidentally tended to stifle criticism against the government, the newspaper became an important device for spreading news.   One writer has estimated that the aggregate number of copies of newspapers sold in Britain, in 1753, equaled nearly seven and one-half million.

Essayists, Novelists, and Poets

Most of the several hundred volumes which were published annually during the last decade of the eighteenth century were literary works.   During the age of Queen Anne, English prose writers adhered rather closely to classical forms, depicting their ideas with meticulous precision as to construction and approved conventions.   The artificiality which resulted has been severely criticized at times.   In spite of this defect, these writings have a peculiar sincerity and beauty, illustrated by the essayists of the period.   Among these, none were more important than Joseph Addison and Richard Steele, whose joint work in the *Tatler* and *Spectator* attracted considerable attention.   A sparkling sense of humor pervades their writing and the creation of Sir Roger de Coverley revealed the hand of a genius. Many imitators, encouraged by the success of Addison and Steele, arose to help popularize the essay. Some of these writers were political propagandists, such as Jonathan Swift, one-time Dean of St. Patrick's, Dublin. Swift's independence of thought was shown by his satirical attacks on Whig and Tory and by his slashing comments on current religious dissensions. His most notable writings include *The Tale of a Tub, Journal to Stella,* and the immortal *Gulliver's Travels.* The latter, because of its appeal to children and its criticism of war and private capitalism, has been translated into many tongues. Recently the Soviet government of Russia made it the subject of a fascinating motion picture.

Equally desirous of displaying the sham and cant in society was the journalist and school teacher, Dr. Samuel Johnson. Like many an author, Johnson often had to resort to hackwriting in order to make ends meet. In spite of these difficulties he was known as a great writer. This judgment later generations have corroborated. His *Dictionary* was a remarkable effort, though his *Lives of the Poets* was by far his greatest work. Much of Johnson's prestige is due to his biographer, James Boswell, who carefully recorded the daily routine and sayings of his hero and patron. Among Johnson's contemporaries was Daniel Defoe, who is often called the founder of the modern realistic novel. Defoe had difficulty in establishing himself and not until late in life did he gain any great attention. In 1719, however, he produced *Robinson Crusoe,* which adults and children enjoy today. Possibly his *Moll Flanders* is rated better by critics who appreciate the author's searching delineations of existing social and moral attitudes. Frequently Defoe used strong and coarse language, but it must be remembered that most of his readers as well as his characters spoke in this manner.

Defoe's success encouraged others, of whom Samuel Richardson, Henry Fielding, Tobias Smollett, and Laurence Sterne are the most important. *Clarissa Harlowe, Joseph Andrews, Tom Jones, Roderick Random,* and *Tristram Shandy* were representative novels of these authors. Originality, vividness, and careful delineation of character and scene were outstanding features of these writers. Moral improvement was often an aim of these authors, as it was with Fanny Burney, whose *Evelina* is fairly well known. Realism also appears in the *Vicar of Wakefield* written by Goldsmith. Shortly thereafter, Horace Walpole's *Castle of Otranto* was published. Walpole sought to jar English complacency by creating a reaction against realism and classical traditions. As one critic has said, "It was a stupid novel," but it marked a revolt against existing tendencies and opened greater possibilities to future novelists. Romance, stark-fear, and terror pervade his works and those of his imitators, Clara Reeve, Mrs. Radcliffe, and Mrs. Roche. "I have been reading," wrote Lady Holland in 1800, "multitudes of novels . . . abounding with the general taste for spectres, hobgoblins, castles, and so forth."

By the opening of the nineteenth century the vogue of terror novels had run its course. In its place there reappeared the realistic work minus the vulgarity and coarseness of Smollett or Fielding. Feminism pervaded the new novel, the authors of which in many instances were women. Hannah More, Miss Austin, Miss Edgeworth, and Mrs. Sherwood exalted virtue, honesty, and sobriety in lieu of dark chambers, dripping daggers, and secret passageways. Middle-class respectability, with its constant round of church-going, modest parties, and quiet evenings at home was appealed to. Toward the close of the period now under consideration there appeared the first noteworthy historical novel, *Waverley,* by Sir Walter Scott. Reference should also be made to Mary Wollstonecraft's *Vindication of the Rights of Women,* which, although not a novel, illustrates the rôle played by women in the literature of this period.

English poetry paralleled the growth of the novel. At the

opening of the eighteenth century, classicism prevailed, as is shown by the writings of Alexander Pope. Pope was a master of versification and inspired others to compose poems perfect in style but rather stilted from a modern point of view. Pope made a profound impression upon his age and influenced poetical writing until the second half of the eighteenth century. A romantic and nature-loving movement was introduced by James Thomson, the author of the *Seasons,* and by Thomas Gray's *Elegy Written in a Country Churchyard.* Samuel Coleridge's *Ancient Mariner, Kubla Khan,* and *Christabel,* all written before 1815, reveal the influence of the romantic movement. William Wordsworth and Lord Byron, famous bards of the "Lake School," depict the same characteristics in the *Lyrical Ballads, English Bards and Scotch Reviewers,* the *Prelude,* and the *Excursion.* In recognition of the achievements of their poets, the British government, in 1690, established by letters patent the post of poet laureate. This office had existed since the age of Chaucer but it was not given official standing until the reign of William and Mary, Dryden being the first to hold the post. Since that date the government has always had in readiness the services of an outstanding poet to recount a military victory or the birth of a royal heir.

Playwrights and Musicians

In contrast to the encouragement given by government to poets were the restrictions imposed upon the playwrights. By an act of 1737 all dramatic productions had to receive the approval of a state officer, and no theater could operate without a royal license. New theaters could be established only by act of parliament. Even if a producer could pass these hurdles, he still had to overcome the prejudice of the nonconformists, who frowned upon questionable scenes and favored a delineation of evangelical attitudes and themes. Greater latitude was afforded by an act of 1788, which granted to local magistrates the power of establishing theaters and of determining what plays should be shown. This concession, however, did not extend to London, which could boast of but twelve show houses in 1815. Drury Lane and Covent Garden alone enjoyed a freedom which was denied to others. These two theaters had been licensed by Charles II and were not subject to the restrictions imposed elsewhere. The net result of these narrowing ideas and limitations was a dearth of good productions. Drama hardly existed; and though Goldsmith and Sheridan had enlivened the stage by comedies in the 1760's and 1770's, little of consequence appeared thereafter. On the other hand Shakespeare was revived, and the great actors of the late eighteenth century, Garrick and Kemble, thrilled their audiences by their delineations of Hamlet, Shylock, and Richard III.

Meantime, the theater-going public also gave homage to the musical productions of Handel. Though of German birth, Handel made England his home in 1712 and devoted his talents to the composition of choral masterpieces like the *Messiah* and *Joshua*. In general, however, music was more stagnant than the stage. This could not have been due to Puritanism, which, as indicated in an earlier chapter, was not unfriendly to song and dance. No satisfactory explanation has been made for the few musical offerings of this age. Charles Wesley composed a number of hymns; the Anglican Church stimulated instrumental music, notably the organ, and professional choirs appeared toward the close of the century. Beyond this and the usual number of semipopular songs, little advance took place.

Art and Education

During the first half of the eighteenth century little interest was shown in painting. William Hogarth was the first to attract attention by his satirical drawings of existing social practices. Hogarth rejected the standards of his immediate predecessors, who had sketched fantastic and unrealistic scenes. In a forcible manner, Hogarth painted pathos, comedy, drama, and poverty, as may be seen by an examination of his *Taste of the Town* and the *Rake's Progress*. Hogarth was followed by Thomas Gainsborough, Joshua Reynolds, and George Romney, who introduced what is known as the "Golden Age" in English painting. Features, dress, pose, and character were delineated by these artists with a skill that few have equaled. Reynolds' landscapes also reflect the renaissance in English painting. Reynolds, moreover, was the first president of the Royal Academy of Art, founded in 1768 for the purpose of promoting painting, sculpture, and architecture. Mention should be made of Thomas West, who ranks as one of England's greatest historical painters.

Educational tendencies of the eighteenth century ranged from the accomplishments of Oxford and Cambridge to the Sunday schools of the industrial towns. Elementary education, at the opening of this era, was in a deplorable condition. A number of endowed or charity schools existed. Here poor children received a minimum of training, plus, sometimes, board and room. Spinsters and widows also gave instruction in the so-called Dame's Schools, which seem to have existed more for the teachers than the pupils. Pauper children were taught simple facts and vocational training in the industrial schools. None of these systems received any aid from the government; and when Pitt in 1796 and Wilberforce in 1806 argued for greater educational opportunities, conservative opinion refused to admit either the need or the wisdom of such measures. Where the state failed, private initiative succeeded. In 1780, Robert Raikes opened a Sunday school at Gloucester where the children of the parish were given elementary instruction. Raikes' experiments were tried in other cities, and in 1785 a London Society for the Establishment of Sunday Schools was founded. Early in the next century the various local units were centralized under the direction of the Sunday School Union.

Non-conformist and evangelical opinion endorsed the Sunday schools and encouraged the efforts of educationalists like Hannah More and Joseph Lancaster. Conservative groups, however, frowned upon the movement, declaring the curriculum to be too liberal. As long as the reformers restricted their teaching to simple arithmetic, reading, and writing, no fault was found; but when Methodism was taught in the schools of Hannah More, she was charged with heresy and treason. Communism was then unknown, but contemporary opinion viewed Jacobinism in the same manner, and accused Miss More of furthering revolutionary ideas. Lancaster was subject to stronger condemnation for his refusal to teach religion beyond reading from the Bible. Lancaster was called a deist and an emissary of Satan, while no less a man than Coleridge compared these schools to jails and prisons. Fearing the inroads of the Lancastrian schools, which multiplied in number, the Church of England, in 1811, founded the National Society for the Education of the Poor in accordance with the ideals of the Established Church. Persecution and competition, however, failed to arrest the progress of the Sunday schools and those founded by Lancaster. Elementary education prospered; and while the number of illiterates remained appalling for a country which boasted of its cultural standing, the situation was far better than before.

The genesis of secondary schools is found in the boarding-schools, originally medieval religious institutions, where poor children might receive, free of charge, a minimum of training. Paying students were admitted by some, and so lucrative did this policy become that a number of the boarding schools finally closed their doors to dependent pupils. Eton, Winchester, Rugby, and Harrow became flourishing schools of this type and recruited their pupils from the lower noble and middle classes. The curriculum, moreover, attracted attention in that these schools sought to foster a knowledge of literature and the classics. Little time was given to science or mathematics. The brilliant student was one who could recount the glories of England and recite or compose Latin and Greek verse. An aristocratic school system developed, a system which aimed at cultural appreciation and prepared boys to enter Oxford or Cambridge.

The average student, on entering one of these universities, was about eighteen years of age and was bent on securing an education which would equip him for a career in parliament or the Church. The subjects taught, therefore, while more advanced than those at Eton or Rugby, were fundamentally cultural in nature. Individualized training, however, was fostered by a tutorial system whereby the student came in direct contact with his teacher. Oxford was more conservative than Cambridge; and while it advertised its colleges of law and medicine and its chairs of history, mathematics, and political economy, very little training was actually secured. Cambridge devoted more attention to these practical disciplines, and established lectures in physics, chemistry, and anatomy. Friendlier relations, moreover, existed between teacher and student. In general, however, an aristocratic system developed in both institutions. Scientific knowledge was considered beneath the dignity of a true Englishman. Virgil, Ovid, and the Bible became the accepted textbooks. One has only to read the speeches in parliament to see how well schooled these men were in cultural subjects but how ill-informed they were of the real world about them. Those who were interested in science, medicine, or law matriculated at the Royal College of Physicians, the Inns of Court, and other specialized institutions. The Inns of Court, founded in the medieval period, are still in existence. Many American tourists and Continental visitors find these Inns interesting because of their architectural design.

Scientific Achievements

In spite of existing educational restrictions, English interest in science was enormous during the eighteenth century. In an age which was demanding better methods of transportation, the construction of factories, and the invention of new machines, improvement was bound to take place. This advance was fostered not only by the captains of industry but by the various scientific societies. Public lending libraries were established and a number of technical books and periodicals appeared. Among the societies that were founded, reference should be made to the Literary and Philosophical Society of Manchester (1781), the Pneumatic Institute of Bristol (1792), and the Royal Institution founded by Benjamin Thompson in 1799. Thompson was an American who left the colonies and after spending some time in Bavaria, where he acquired the title of Count Rumford, came to England. The work accomplished by these societies and private individuals rested fundamentally upon the scientific contributions of Copernicus, Kepler, Galileo, Brahe, and the Englishman, Sir Isaac Newton. It is to the credit of these seventeenth-century men that medieval notions were discarded. Their researches revealed that the world was but a small segment of the physical universe, and that this universe was subject "to the same law of gravitation and the same laws of motion so that all physical objects or events in one part of the universe exercise some influence upon all others and thus constitute one cosmic system of interconnected parts."

Eighteenth-century English mathematicians were slow in understanding the achievements of their fellow countryman, Newton. Many, like John Ward, were totally uninformed. Ward, indeed, thought he had discovered the binomial theorem, although Newton and Wallis had established it a quarter of a century before. Other illustrations might be given to show that English mathematicians were out of touch with each other and often were ignorant of current discoveries. Students, moreover, generally recognized no distinction between algebra and arithmetic, while at Cambridge there was no disposition to employ the negative in algebraic formulas. Progress, however, took place. A number of textbooks were published. Ward's *Young Mathematician's Guide* went through twelve editions by 1771 and was adopted by the faculties of Yale, Dartmouth, and Harvard. Elementary handbooks like the *Gentleman's Diary* had a wide circulation. The government, moreover, reflected these advances by promoting a much-needed reform in weights and measures, while business introduced better accounting methods. Thomas Simpson made trigonometry easier by using abbreviations for various functions, and Brook Taylor made improvements in calculus. Other names, like James Sterling and Nicholas Saunderson, might be added. Saunderson added little that was new; but the enthusiasm which he showed, in spite of blindness, stimulated others to greater efforts.

The debt of the other sciences to mathematics was enormous, for without it, little research and progress could have been made. In the field of physics this was particularly true. Correct notions as to matter and mass involved a broad knowledge of mathematics. In reviewing the progress of physics and chemistry in the eighteenth century, one is impressed by the influence of Newton and Boyle. At the beginning of this era it was generally believed that substances burned because of an inherent property or fire element known as phlogiston. The first to explode this concept was Joseph Black of Edinburgh, who by experiments demonstrated the existence of a gas or "fixed air" as he called it. Joseph Priestley investigated the nature of this gas and provided findings which helped to discredit the theory of phlogiston. More significant were the discoveries of Henry Cavendish who carefully and scientifically disproved the older concept and established the principle of gas in a burning susbtance. Cavendish visited and communicated his ideas to Antoine Lavoisier of France, who seized upon this knowledge and destroyed the theory of phlogiston. In all cases, he argued, substances burned because of the combination of the gas or air (he called it oxygen) with the substance itself.

Similar progress was made in respect to the theory of matter. Among others who studied this problem was John Dalton, who revived the Greek theory of the atomic nature of matter (the varying properties of matter are due to the differences in size and nature of atoms) and rejected the Aristotelian concept that matter was continuous in structure regardless of size or form. Dalton, moreover, probably with the help of a Manchester physician, Dr. Henry, determined the laws governing the liquefaction of gases and their related combinations. Professor Thomas Thompson of Edinburgh University also did work on gases and the nature of matter. Theories of light and sound were altered by the researches of Thomas Young and David Brewster, while Joseph Black made some notable discoveries in respect to heat and thermodynamics. Achromatic lenses and telescopes were perfected by Dollond. Particularly significant were the advances made in magnetism and electricity. Stephen Gray, Sir Humphry Davy, and others, like Wall, Wheeler, and Watson interested themselves in this work. Finally, reference should be made to the studies of James Hutton and William Smith in respect to geology. Hutton's *Theory of the Earth* (1778) was a notable work in its day, while both Smith and Hutton made discoveries as to fossils and erosion.

Medical progress was characterized chiefly by a consolidation of past investigations and by improvements in teaching and technique. The contributions made by Boerhaave and Haller on the Continent in the field of clinical teaching were made known to Englishmen through foreign and domestic publications. Several of Boerhaave's students were instrumental in founding the Edinburgh Medical School, which rates today as one of the best in the world. Among those who benefited by this training was the Scotch surgeon, Sir Charles Bell, who in 1811 established the motor and sensory nature of the nervous system. The experiments of Joseph Black, Henry Cavendish, and Joseph Priestley in the field of air and biology did much to promote medicine, while Matthew Baillie and William Hunter contributed through their post-mortem examinations. The profession of medicine was also advanced by John Floyer's "pulse watch." Floyer's watch, though not widely used, permitted the physician to count the heart beat by the introduction of a second hand to the ordinary watch. In the field of surgery and obstetrics few new principles were introduced, though the application of past discoveries brought improvement in technical operations. Only in the field of venereal diseases and in the treatment of labor were any advances registered. English doctors advocated the use of mercury and obstetrical forceps.

Others who benefited by the teachings of Boerhaave were John Pringle and James Lind, who advocated preventive medicine and examined the nature of typhoid fever and scurvy. The work of these men was confined to the British army and navy, in which they held commands, but Thomas Percival of Manchester introduced their methods to civilians. Others applied the same knowledge to hospitals and prisons. This in turn influenced the efforts of John Howard and Elizabeth Fry in prison reform. Hygienic conditions improved throughout the country. Parliament assisted by passing measures which allowed London, Manchester, Birmingham, and other provincial towns and cities to rid their streets of open streams which had served as drains, to build sewers, to construct water supplies, and to pave streets. Although conditions were far below modern standards, definite progress took place. During the latter half of the century, moreover, a number of medieval hospitals like St. Bartholomew's were rebuilt, while several new institutions were founded. Dispensary service was also provided, and the quality of nursing was greatly improved. The effect of these advances was shown in the decline of child mortality. One authority has estimated that before 1750, about seventy-five per cent of the children died before their fifth year. By 1800, it is believed that the death rate had fallen to forty-one per cent.

Part of this decline was due to the attention the government gave to epidemic diseases. Strict quarantine regulations at the ports of entry halted the progress of communicable diseases, among which smallpox was the most prevalent. Private initiative helped to check the ravages of this disease. It was discovered that the death rate among those who had had smallpox was much lower than those who had not, and this led men to think about the possibility of developing some form of immunity. Mary Montagu and Richard Mead advocated and practiced inoculation. It remained, however, for Edward Jenner to further the theory of inoculation by his experiments in cowpox, a disease among cattle. Jenner found that individuals who contracted cowpox were immune to smallpox, and on the basis of this fact, he developed a vaccine to combat the latter.

Moral Standards

In reviewing the cultural aspects of the eighteenth and early nineteenth centuries one is impressed by the coarseness of that age. On one hand there are visible signs of material wealth and prosperity; on the other, gaunt poverty and ignorance. The imperial growth and the mechanization of society which characterized the Georgian period probably account for much of this sordidness. Morality was at a low ebb in spite of the restraining influences exerted by Anne, George III, and the Established Church. National standards were set by the royal family whose court parties and balls were characterized by looseness in dress and language, and in gambling and drinking. The middle class, except for the non-conformists, imitated their social betters, and the lower orders tried to drown their misfortunes and sorrows by similar activities. One of the most pernicious pastimes of this period was that of masquerades. These nightly gatherings rapidly degenerated into drunken brawls where men and women of ill-fame displayed "scandalous licentiousness." Josiah Tucker declared in 1749 "that the greatest rakes that all Europe can produce, when they arrive in England, and come to London, are quite shocked and scandalized at the unparalleled lewdness and debauchery reigning among us, so far beyond any thing they could have imagined." Similar conditions are reported in respect to home gatherings. Few of these intimate parties were considered a success unless they were turned into a drinking or gambling bout. Virtue and honesty were not stressed. Statesmen and party leaders, like Walpole, the Prince of Wales, and Wilkes, saw no harm in self-indulgence or in graft and dishonesty. Votes were bought and sold, and pensions were showered upon men and women for political and social favors.

It would be wrong to assume that the average laborer or trader spent his time in such an atmosphere. There were hundreds of thousands who had neither the time, money nor inclination to indulge in such practices. And yet one can not help concluding that the Georgian period was characterized by low standards of morality. Better notions and practices are to be found among the non-conformists, especially the Methodists and Friends. Deprived of political rights in many instances and thoroughly discredited by conservative and Anglican opinion, these men and women furthered scientific development and social reforms of significance. Joseph Priestley, John Dalton, Elizabeth Fry, Joseph Lancaster, and John and Charles Wesley are examples of the humanitarian and scholarly evangelists. Many of the important changes which were consummated in education, hospitalization, prisons, peace, temperance, and slavery were furthered by these Protestants.   England owed much to non-conformist opinion which paved the way for greater accomplishments in the nineteenth and twentieth centuries.

SELECTED BIBLIOGRAPHY

Many of the works cited for the previous chapter have pertinent material on the cultural aspects of eighteenth-century England. Although E. Halévy's *History of the English People* (New York, 1924) centers about the year 1815, there are splendid résumés of eighteenth-century life, as, for example, in his Book III.   Volumes XI and XII of the *Cambridge History of English Literature* present general accounts of literary development.   Edmund Gosse's *History of Eighteenth-Century Literature* (London, 1889), and Oliver Elton's *Survey of English Literature, 1780–1830* (London, 1912) are of value.   Valuable bibliographies are to be found in most of these works which will introduce the student to detailed studies of men like Wordsworth, Byron, and Coleridge.   Thomas Rees' *Reminiscences of Literary London* (London, 1896) is important for a study of publishers and booksellers. Ernest Ford's *Short History of English Music* (London, 1912) and the *Oxford History of Music* (London, 1929–1932) are of value. E. A. Chesneau's *English School of Painting* (London, 1895) is a standard work.

Educational activities are treated in Leslie Stephen's *History of English Thought in the Eighteenth Century* (New York, 1902); Charles E. Mallet's *History of the University of Oxford* (London, 1927); A. E. Dobb's *Education and Social Movements, 1700–1815* (London, 1919), and D. A. Winstanley's *University of Cambridge in the Eighteenth Century* (Cambridge, 1922).   Lecky's *History of England in the 18th Century* (London, 1913); Traill's *Social England*; J. B. Botsford's *English Society in the Eighteenth Century* (New York, 1924), and the biographies of William Allen, Wilberforce, Wesley, and other reformers devote attention to educational matters.   J. B. Black's *The Art of History* (New York, 1926) treats of the historical works of Gibbon, Hume, and Robertson.   A. S. Turberville's *Johnson's England* (Oxford, 1933) is of value.

H. Buckley's *A Short History of Physics* (New York, 1927) is a convenient handbook of general information.   Edward Thorpe's *Essays in Historical Chemistry* (London, 1931) presents an account of the work of Joseph Priestley and Henry Cavendish.

CHAPTER XXIX

Reaction and Reform

ENGLAND'S political and economic foundations were strengthened by the victory over Bonaparte. A formidable rival had been swept aside, new colonies and naval bases had been won, and the way was cleared for a tremendous expansion in trade and industry. The industrial and agrarian revolutions, moreover, had made Britain the foremost nation of the world. Her national debt, it is true, was of staggering proportions; but in the face of unparalleled productivity, no cause for alarm existed. Science, moreover, had made remarkable discoveries which foreshadowed an age of steam, iron, electricity, and oil. Luxury and material comfort for many existed as never before, while expanding metropolitan centers were matched by increased acreage of cultivated land in the rural areas. Englishmen had ample reason to be proud of their country's mastery on land and sea. Pride, however, bred self-satisfaction and overconfidence. Burke had likened the English constitution to the sturdy native oak which had carried Britannia's navy and ship of state through many troubled waters. What better government could Englishmen want? No people, Burke declared, could "produce anything better adapted to preserve a rational and manly freedom than the course that we have pursued." Wellington expressed the same thought when he said that England's representative system enjoyed the "full and entire confidence of the country," while Sydney Smith, in reviewing Bentham's philosophy, concluded that "it looks well in theory but it won't do in practice." Education, Tory opinion held, was no cure for poverty and vice. A reading knowledge of the Bible and Prayer Book was enough for manual laborers.

Burke, Wellington, and Smith spoke as individuals possessing full political and economic rights in a land of milk and honey. There were others, however, in a world of poverty and abuse, who differed with these gentlemen and who claimed that economic progress had outdistanced constitutional growth. John Bull, they argued, had grown in stature and girth but was dressed in a constitutional suit that scarcely covered his huge frame.

Conservative Opinion Blocks Reform

Several notable attempts had been made in the late eighteenth century to amend the existing organic law. Conservative opinion plus the hysteria which attended the Revolutionary wars had checked this movement. Conditions after Waterloo, however, were far different from those at the time Priestley, Cartwright, Price, and Fox had argued for parliamentary reform. In 1790, liberal views were held generally by disgruntled Whigs and disenfranchised non-conformists. English labor, moreover, though disturbed by enclosure and machine production, had turned a deaf ear to the impassioned appeal of the reformers. Eighteen-fifteen, however, was not seventeen-ninety; and the devastation of the village communities and the rise of congested factory towns had made liberals and radicals of force and understanding. England's vaunted economic structure, it was declared, was built upon the broken backs of labor. Toiling women and children in the factories and mines, orphaned chimney-sweeps, impoverished rural workers, and impressed soldiers and seamen constituted an England which Wellington failed or refused to see. The priests of St. Paul's or Westminster did not appreciate the situation either. Congregations might thrill to the biblical story of the Good Samaritan but preferred to follow the *laissez-faire* philosophy of Adam Smith. Poverty, so Malthus had reasoned, was to be deplored but in the face of immutable natural laws could not be avoided. The Elizabethan Poor Law and the Speenhamland System were about all that the Church and State could offer by way of relief.

In the meantime, Methodism had brought about an evangelical awakening. Non-conformist leaders were arguing for parliamentary reform. Hannah More, Joseph Lancaster, and others had founded a new educational system, and the Clapham Sect and the utilitarian followers of Bentham had agitated for a new social order. One should not forget the liberal group which gathered at Francis Place's shop in Charing Cross or the persecution which had attended the Luddite Riots. Clearly, the Anglican Church, the Tory Party, and vested interests had ample warning of an impending revolution. Self-satisfaction and nationalism, however, blinded them to realities. Though the slave trade had been abolished and a factory act passed, few believed that further changes were needed.

The English government, at the close of the Napoleonic era, was lodged securely in the Tory Party, whose leaders were Lord Liverpool, Viscount Castlereagh, and Lord Eldon. Thoroughly wedded to their party's creed and apt pupils of Smith and Malthus, these gentlemen and their parliamentary majorities embarked upon a conservative program which cast gloom over all England. An indication of what might be expected appeared as early as March, 1813, when a Commons' committee was appointed to inquire into the corn trade of the realm. For nearly a decade the agrarian interests had conducted their business without the aid of the time-honored corn laws and navigation acts. The exigencies of war had suspended these measures, but by 1813 a demand arose for a revision of the corn laws in the interest of English agriculture. Investigation showed that while agriculture was fairly prosperous, dark days were ahead if prices were to decline; and the prospect of a general peace made this more or less inevitable. Investors had little difficulty in proving that existing prices must be maintained if compensation were to be had for the heavy capital outlay which had attended the enclosure movement. Manufacturers, on the other hand, pointed out that high food prices caused high wages, a cost which might be lessened, while labor clamored for cheap bread even if made from German or American flour. Neither of the latter two groups, however, had any adequate representation in parliament, and the landed classes easily carried the corn laws of 1814 and 1815.

According to these acts, grain and flour might be exported at all times without duty or bounty, while foreign supplies were restricted by heavy tariffs. Wheat, for example, could be imported free of duty only when the domestic price was ten shillings a bushel. The net result of this legislation was to keep prices high in the interests of a landed agricultural class. Although it is true that the new acts did not maintain the high prices which existed from 1800 to 1813, when war and harvest failures combined to create unusual prices, they did prevent the decline which should have followed the bountiful harvest of 1813 and the peace of 1815. The consumer, in short, was taxed to protect the investments of a privileged group. Greater misery, however, was in store for English labor. The harvests of 1816 and 1817 failed, and food prices soared. American grain was rushed into the markets but failed to reduce prices materially. At the same time manufacturers lost heavily, because of foreign competition and tariffs and the inability of the English to purchase needed supplies. Industry and agriculture were in the throes of an unprecedented depression. Government orders for military supplies, so lucrative a short time before, had disappeared. Thousands of ex-service men walked the streets in search of work. Unable to find employment, many of these men joined with the underpaid factory hands and resorted to violence. In the rural areas workers vented their feelings by burning barns and breaking down fences.

The government met these demonstrations by repressive measures. The right of assembly was denied, the *habeas corpus* act was suspended and a censorship imposed upon the press. At the same time the income tax, which the property and salaried classes had been paying, was repealed, and steps were taken to deflate the currency. Troops were sent into the manufacturing centers to quell the rioters. Secret agents, like "Oliver the Spy," were ordered to mingle among the masses to gain legal evidence against the latter. Comparatively few convictions, however, were obtained, because of the influence exerted by labor upon the juries and local magistrates. Conditions improved by 1818 because of a bountiful harvest, but a crop failure in the fall of 1819 brought another series of riots. Many of the rioters of 1819 believed that if representation were given them in parliament, their miseries would vanish. In Manchester, for example, several thousand people gathered at St. Peter's Fields in defiance of the law against free assembly and agitated for parliamentary reform. Unfortunately, the local officers became panicky, and in a desire to enforce the law, ordered the military to fire upon the crowd. Only a small number were injured by this attack, known later as the Peterloo Massacre, which the government proceeded to justify by passing repressive measures known as the Six Acts. Most of this legislation was but a continuation of the laws of 1816, and in general was not vigorously enforced. For the return of order, however, the ministry was indebted to nature, which showered the land with bumper crops in 1820. Cheaper food lulled the discontented and allowed the Tory Party to escape a proletarian uprising. Conservative forces, moreover, were more deeply entrenched than ever by the Tory victory in the election of 1820, which had been caused by the death of George III and the accession of George IV (1820–1830).

Shortly after George IV's accession to the throne the gossips of England were delighted to hear that a divorce was pending between George and his wife, Caroline. Their marriage in 1795 had been a matter of state and convenience. Neither seem to have taken their vows seriously and after a year lived apart. In 1818, George took steps to obtain a divorce. Caroline, incensed by his action and irritated because her name was left out of a new edition of the Prayer Book, appealed to the nation for help. She asked that her name be inserted in the Prayer Book and that she be recognized as queen. George's reply came in the form of a bill, introduced by Liverpool, which aimed at the elimination of her title and the granting of a divorce. Public opinion supported Caroline and forced Liverpool to change his tactics. The following year (1821), the Queen ruined her cause by seeking to force herself into the coronation services. A month later she died, and with her death the affair terminated.

A Liberal Tory Government

The significance of this episode rests chiefly in the support which the middle class had given the Queen. A bold stand had been made against the Tory ministry and a demand had arisen for a more liberal government. Time had erased much of the hysteria which had once attended any suggestion of reform. The constant agitation of labor and the non-conformist groups was beginning to have effect. Liverpool recognized the situation and in 1822 allowed Peel, Huskisson, and Canning, liberal Tories, a place in the cabinet. At once this leaven began to work. Commercial and manufacturing classes had for some time been chafing under existing trade restrictions. Adam Smith's *laissez-faire* policy, moreover, had undermined the old mercantilistic theory of government regulation. In 1820 the London merchants had petitioned parliament for a tariff for revenue only. This demand, which bordered upon free trade, received scant consideration from the older Tories. With Huskisson as President of the Board of Trade, however, a hearing was granted and a searching inquiry instituted as to the effects of the tariff upon trade and industry. Privileged groups opposed the investigation, but Huskisson was able to introduce measure after measure which gradually reduced most of the important duties. The navigation system also was modified by a more liberal policy in the colonial trade. Free ports in some of the colonies had existed since the late eighteenth century. Huskisson extended this system and threw open to foreigners much of the colonial trade. Preferential duties still protected the domestic trader, but in the colonial fields equality for all was established. In spite of the criticism, these reforms resulted in better foreign relations and friendlier feelings between England and the colonies.

Huskisson's liberality was also shown by his attitude toward labor. Earlier in this volume, reference was made to the craft gilds. Medieval in origin and affording advantages chiefly to the master workmen, these groups had declined in importance. In their place there had arisen, by the end of the seventeenth century, associations of workers somewhat like the modern union. The rapid extension of private capitalism and the factory system in the following century increased the number of these organizations. Class warfare between labor and capital followed, as was evidenced by the Luddite Riots. In every instance the industrialist gained the victory and proceeded to make the most of his advantages. Labor sought protection under the Elizabethan Statute of Apprentices and other laws which provided employment for skilled workers and empowered the local magistrates to determine wages. Capital, well schooled in the doctrine of *laissez faire,* denounced these measures and with justification argued that skilled artisans were not needed to operate the factory machines. Accordingly, women, children, and inexperienced men were hired at low wages in violation of the law. The next step came in 1813 and 1814, when parliament repealed these restrictions at the request of capital. The government, moreover, refused to interfere when employers resorted to unfair practices and violated trade agreements. To illustrate, in 1810, there was a strike among the mine workers for steadier employment. Their demand for nine days' work every two weeks was rejected at first by the owners, on the ground that accident and nature often forced mines to close. Labor admitted this and agreed to suspend its demand when a mine could not be operated. The workers, however, were to receive daily two and a half shillings after a mine had been closed for three days. The owners used this arrangement in slack time by working a mine a day and then closing it for three. Although the owners were justified in protecting themselves against accident or nature, it is evident that their interpretation of the agreement in idle periods was an apparent subterfuge.

More annoying than fraud or the refusal of the government to protect labor were the Combination Acts passed in 1799 and 1800 as a result of the food riots of those years, and the hysteria which followed the French Revolution. According to these acts, labor groups seeking to improve working conditions or wages were illegal. Any attempt to organize or strike constituted a violation of the law. Although these acts were intended also to prevent trade agreements among the manufacturers, numerous infractions occurred and the government did not prosecute. On the other hand, labor was punished severely even when, at the request of an employer, meetings had been held to discuss wages or hours of work. As long as the Combination Acts were maintained as the law of the land, labor was of necessity at a distinct disadvantage.

In the meantime Francis Place of Charing Cross had been working for a repeal of these measures. Gaining the support of certain friends, he was able to interest Huskisson in the matter. In 1823 a parliamentary committee proceeded to investigate the operation of the Combination Acts. The committee's findings resulted in the introduction of a measure which, when passed in 1825, repealed the obnoxious legislation. Trade unions immediately sprang up in all parts of the realm, and before the close of the year had precipitated many strikes in favor of higher wages. Conservative opinion pointed to these disturbances as proof of labor's insincerity and forced a modification of the act of 1825. Certain types of meetings were forbidden, while the local magistrates were empowered to deal severely with either an employer or an employee who resorted to intimidation. In spite of these restrictions and a business depression in 1829, labor unions continued to function. During that year manufacturers generally lowered wages and dismissed their workers in large numbers. The unions, therefore, found it exceedingly difficult to retain their organizations in the face of such conditions. Thanks, however, to the efforts of John Doherty, an Irishman, there was founded, in 1830, a National Association for the Protection of Labor, with a membership of about a hundred thousand. For a while, Doherty's efforts attracted considerable attention; but in 1832, because of labor's apathy, the National Association disappeared.

The Roman Catholic Question

During the course of these disputes parliament and the nation had their attention directed toward the Roman Catholic question. It will be recalled that the Toleration Act of 1689 had granted no concession to Romanists. Catholics, moreover, were subjected to additional penalties over and beyond the Elizabethan Penal Laws and the Test Acts of Charles II. They might not inherit or purchase property nor could they send their children abroad for education. Beginning with

George II's reign, however, a more liberal policy was inaugurated by the government. Greater relaxation followed during the reign of his son. Catholics were allowed some freedom of worship and education; offices in the army and navy were thrown open to them. Existing prohibitions as to purchasing property were also removed. Similar concessions were accorded the Romanists of Ireland and Scotland. Civil disabilities, however, remained. A Catholic was not allowed to vote, hold a seat in parliament, or be a judge of a high court. Greater freedom might have been granted but for the Gordon Riots of 1780. These disturbances had been fomented by Anglican and Protestant opposition to a Catholic relief act then before parliament. More significant than vested interests or bigotry in checking Catholic emancipation was the fact that most of the Catholics in the United Kingdom were Irish. Every time, therefore, that the Roman question was raised, it became involved in Irish affairs which no ministry seemed anxious to settle. There was considerable truth in the charge made by the Irish leader, Daniel O'Connell, that "the English do not dislike us as Catholics; they simply hate us as Irish."

O'Connell's efforts to bring an economic, political, and religious peace to Ireland met decided opposition at first. Several bills introduced in parliament by his friends were either thrown out or defeated by large majorities. Wellington, moreover, who became prime minister in 1828, announced that Catholic relief was not a cabinet issue. The next year, however, two events occurred which forced Wellington to change his position. First, Lord John Russell, a Whig, championed the cause of the Protestants by advocating the repeal of the Test and Corporation Acts. Russell was able to carry this measure through parliament, and Protestants were given full and complete civil freedom. No concession, however, was afforded the Catholics. The example set of relieving the Protestants argued strongly for Catholic emancipation. The drift in this direction was furthered by the election of O'Connell to parliament in 1828. By existing law, O'Connell, a Catholic, was debarred from the Commons. His sweeping victory, however, convinced Wellington that England had to choose between emancipation and an Irish uprising. Wellington wished to avoid the latter, but George III strenuously objected to Catholic relief and Wellington resigned. George was unable to form a new ministry and was forced to take Wellington back on his own terms. A Catholic relief act speedily passed parliament. Full political and civil rights were given the Catholics with but few exceptions. Before holding any office of state, however, a Catholic was required to take an oath renouncing the temporal power of the Pope in England and swearing allegiance to the English king. Roman priests were forbidden seats in the House of Commons, and no Catholic was to become king of England, hold the office of Lord Chancellor of either England or Ireland, or be Lord Lieutenant of Ireland. Roman Catholic marriages, moreover, were not yet considered legal.

The Conservative Defense of Vested Interests

In reviewing the progress of events which led to the passage of the Catholic Emancipation Act and the various other reforms noted in labor and trade, one is forced to conclude that further changes in England's organic laws were bound to occur. The English governing classes of 1830, however, were convinced that additional reforms were neither expedient nor necessary. On the other hand, liberal and radical opinion, while anxious to promote change, was not oversanguine as it viewed the entrenched power of the conservative group. Many of the Whigs, moreover, refused to believe that human welfare or government could be enhanced by tampering with the English constitution. The Anglican Church was of the same opinion. Sincere as these groups were, their attitudes and ideals were predicated upon the retention of vested interests and privileges. An aristocracy of wealth and power was in control of government.

Most of the governing classes were the proud possessors of large estates which yielded handsome revenues to their owners. Many lived like princes. Their palatial homes, equipped with the best of furnishings and the latest comforts, were surrounded by ornate gardens and walks, which led to closed hunting preserves. Extravagant parties and balls were routine affairs, while the hospitality afforded the numerous guests was astonishing. Forty people, so Mr. Christie reports in his *The Transition from Aristocracy,* "sat down to dinner every day," at the Duke of Devonshire's home, "and about one hundred and fifty servants in the steward's room and servants' hall." In 1834, Lord Egremont feasted six hundred persons on one occasion, his home becoming a hotel for the time being. "Everybody came when they thought fit and departed without notice or leave-taking." Another writer reports that the hunt at Woburn was a brilliant success. "In five days we killed 835 pheasants, 645 hares, 59 rabbits, 10 partridges and 5 woodcocks." Virtue and morality often were lacking at these social gatherings. Men and women drank and gambled quite shamefully. Profanity and the telling of obscene stories were common. "God d—n it!" cried William IV, when the Belgian King asked for a glass of water at a state dinner, "Why don't you drink wine?"

The immense wealth of these people enabled them to direct the conduct of government. They dictated elections, bribed and intimidated the electorate and placed pliable servants in local and national offices. They saw nothing wrong in this procedure. For centuries their families had enjoyed these rights. Property and birth, so their political creed ran, endowed them with monopolistic powers of government. Those who were of humble birth or trafficked in business were debarred from participation in government.

The Attitude of the Manufacturers and Laborers Towards Reform

The class without property, however, flatly rejected this assumption and was determined to bring about a change, cost what it might, to the established order. The backbone of this opposition was English labor, though its ideology was furnished by men like Francis Place, Charles Hall, William Cobbett, Francis Burdett, Thomas Spence, and Earl Grey. Many who aimed at fundamental reorganization of society were not unfriendly to the cause of parliamentary reform. In all probability the rank and file of the opposition were better acquainted with Cobbett's *Register,* Carlile's *Republican,* Wades' *Gorgon,* and other radical weeklies than they were with the more refined publications of Bentham and the Clapham Sect. Others, moreover, had been members of those interesting labor associations disguised under the name of the Hampden Clubs, whose mother society was organized at London in 1811 and included among its members men of intellect and property. It was distinctly an aristocratic affair, no one being eligible for membership unless he had an annual income of £300 from land. In spite of this restriction, the London society and its many branches agitated for parliamentary reform in an effective manner. Petitions to parliament, signed by thousands throughout the realm, requested the adoption of measures which would provide for freer elections and the extension of the franchise to all direct taxpayers. Although the Hampden Clubs disappeared by 1817, their influence in stimulating parliamentary reform was extensive. One should not forget, either, the activities of the manufacturers in respect to a broader franchise.

Many of these manufacturers, though possessed of wealth, were not qualified voters. It will be remembered that elections to the House of Commons were based upon county and parliamentary borough constituencies. In the former, suffrage was restricted to those who qualified under the forty-shilling freehold clause of 1430. Freehold tenures, while relatively common in the fifteenth century, had become less numerous by 1830, and in many cases were completely under the domination of a local noble or politician. Thousands of individuals held property, the income from which was far greater than forty shillings; but because they did not have freeholds, they were not entitled to vote. Similar conditions prevailed among the limited number of parliamentary boroughs whose suffrage requirements depended upon the terms of a royal charter. As indicated in a previous chapter, the elections in both constituencies were held in the open and were attended by considerable corruption, intimidation and fraud. A voter, moreover, had to register his choice of candidates verbally. This exposed him to bodily injury or loss of employment. The House of Commons, elected upon this narrow and corrupt system, was subject to the same evil forces. Privilege and wealth dominated at Westminster and refused to listen to those who advocated greater social, political, and economic equality for the mass of the people.

England Faces Revolution

Labor, however, was bent upon a redress of grievances, and seemed prepared to gain its ends by force. Mob violence broke forth in various parts of England. At Bristol many homes, public buildings, and the bishop's palace were stormed and burned. At Reepham the crowd set fire to buildings and pelted the magistrates who tried to restore order. Abuse, ridicule, and foul language greeted the privileged classes wherever they appeared. In some instances the gentry armed themselves and their retainers and dispersed the rioters, while in other cases special commissions indicted hundreds of men and sentenced them to fine or imprisonment. It is likely that further disturbances would have followed had there been anything like a revolutionary organization. Wellington and the Tory ministers, however, believed that Jacobin societies were in existence, and predicted an armed uprising. The dread fear of a violent revolution spread among the governing classes. Greville, a prominent member of parliament, records in his Journal that many believed a "revolution in this country inevitable." It was for this reason that the privileged classes finally, but reluctantly, consented to alter the organic law and "not because they think concession will avert [revolution] but will let it come more gradually and with less violence."

The determination to yield was hastened by a Whig victory in the election of 1830. The success of this party was due in no small measure to internal dissensions among the Tories. The revolutionary upheaval of that year in France added zest to the reformers in England. More significant, however, was the skill exercised by the Whig campaign managers. Many a borough was bought from its owner and then resold to a candidate pledged to reform. Others were made secure by exacting from the candidates a promise to support reform. Edward Porritt, who examined the sources dealing with this election, concludes that, "Had it not been for this borough mongering . . . and for the pledges which Whig borough owners . . . exacted from their nominees . . . the Reform Act could not have been carried." The greater share of the Whig members of parliament, however, were as aristocratic as their Tory opponents. They glorified themselves as the defenders of liberty but actually preferred the company of the Tories to their popular ally, labor. They were not ready, therefore, to scrap the constitution and allow the masses a voice in government. On the other hand, they realized the necessity of reform and were prepared to introduce a moderate measure. Whig political traditions and history argued strongly for reform. Their birthright rested upon the achievements of the Glorious Revolution, and their orators and publicists continually recalled England's debt to the Whigs.

The Reform Act of 1832

Under the leadership of Earl Grey, whose devotion to parliamentary reform antedated the French Revolution, a measure was introduced in the Commons providing for a redistribution of seats and an extension of the franchise. Conservative opinion considered this proposal too extreme and was able to defeat it in April, 1831. Grey immediately appealed to the nation in a general election, his slogan being, "The Bill, the whole Bill and nothing but the Bill." Using the same campaign tactics of the year before, the Whigs won and introduced a new measure which passed the lower house by a large majority. The Lords, however, rejected the bill. Thoroughly convinced that the country supported him, Grey proposed another measure which, after passing the Commons, was defeated by the Lords. An unrepresentative upper house largely composed of aristocratic Tories once again had defeated the will of the nation. Grey appealed to William IV to create new peerages sufficient to secure the passage of a new bill. William refused and the Whig ministry resigned. Wellington then undertook to form a Tory government but found this impossible in the face of the Whig majority in the Commons. With great reluctance, William invited Grey to return and assured the latter that if necessary, new peers would be created. Although conservative opinion agreed with Lord Eldon that if "the bill passes, the Monarchy and the Peers of the realm will not as such survive," the Lords yielded to the persuasions of the King and Wellington and absented themselves in large numbers when a new bill appeared in the House of Lords. With the opposition thus weakened, the Reform Act passed and became law, July 7, 1832.

The enactment of this measure illustrated the effectiveness of the cabinet system of government. With the Whigs solidly entrenched in the lower house, and having the backing of the electorate in two recent elections, it was impossible for the

Tories to form a ministry which could have insured a continuation of orderly government. Although a group of "bitter enders," especially the spiritual lords, refused to approve of the measure, good judgment convinced Wellington and a hundred peers that they must accept the verdict of the nation and the operation of the cabinet system.

According to the terms of the Reform Act of 1832, the suffrage requirements were altered so as to give the vote to the middle class. The forty shilling freehold clause was retained in the counties, though copyholders and leasers were enfranchised provided their income equaled ten pounds a year. In the boroughs, most of the obsolete requirements were abolished and the vote given to all who paid an annual rental of ten pounds. The act, moreover, destroyed the franchise rights of a number of boroughs and reduced the representation of others. Altogether one hundred and forty-three seats were vacated in this manner and allotted to towns heretofore unrepresented. Special measures provided for a redistribution of seats and an extended franchise in Ireland and Scotland.

The changes effected by the Reform Acts were not so extensive as their strongest promoters desired. Corruption and bribery had been reduced but not abolished; and while the shopkeepers and industrialists were given the vote, the rank and file of English labor, whose agitations and threats of revolution had forced the passage of these measures, were left unenfranchised. The House of Lords had been chastened but not subjected to the will of the nation. On the other hand the cabinet system was more securely entrenched than before and the power of the landed aristocracy transferred to the manufacturing and trading classes. In spite of the moderation of the acts, the conservative groups predicted the speedy abolition of the monarchy and the founding of a republic. Their fears were strengthened by the decisive defeat sustained by the Tories in the election of 1832. An analysis of the returns, however, showed that the great majority of the victorious

Whigs were men of education and judgment. They were not fierce, wild-eyed Jacobins bent upon a Reign of Terror and the confiscation of private property. It is true that many were unfamiliar with parliamentary procedure and etiquette. Others lacked modesty and Eton breeding. Despite some lack of social grace and refinement, however, they exhibited an intense desire to further legislative reforms.

Whig Government, 1832–1837

One of the first measures introduced by the new Whig government, headed by Earl Grey, concerned Ireland. Irish voters had aided the Whigs in passing the reform acts and now expected compensation for their services. Their demands centered about the Established Church of Ireland. Three fourths of the Irish were Roman Catholics, while of the remainder only a little more than one half were Episcopalians. In other words, nearly seven million people were taxed to support a church which had less than a million communicants. Had the average Irishman not been burdened by an oppressive economic order which kept him close to perpetual starvation, the tithes which he gave for the Established Church would have been of little importance. As it was, he challenged the existing order, and having received no redress, resorted to violence in 1831. The action of the Whig ministry, in 1832, was a bitter disappointment to the Irish. Instead of abolishing or reducing the tithes, the government used force to collect arrears. Coercion, however, failed; and the ministry was compelled to meet the expenses of the Irish Church from other funds. In part, this explains why the size of the Irish episcopate was reduced in 1833, though not until 1837 did parliament authorize a land tax as a substitute for the tithe.

In the same year that witnessed the reduction of the Irish episcopate, parliament passed a measure abolishing slavery throughout the colonies and established a new factory act.

According to the latter, the employment of children under nine years of age was forbidden, while the total working hours per week for older children was restricted. Attendance at school for two hours a day was provided for all children under thirteen, and government inspectors were created to enforce the measure. No night work was to be engaged in by those under eighteen years of age. Unfortunately the act was limited to the textile industries and largely ignored the lot of adult laborers. The reports of the inspectors, moreover, revealed that no suitable method existed for determining the exact age of the children employed, and that the local officers were not inclined to punish violators; as long as the government had no adequate educational system, the schooling of children was out of the question. The schools maintained by the manufacturers were of little value, some of the teachers being unable to read or write.

In 1834 parliament enacted a new Poor Law. Heretofore the relief of poverty rested largely upon the Elizabethan measure, which was inadequate and obsolete for an industrial England. In an attempt to correct conditions, parliament in 1795 and 1796 had provided money allowances for those who were not inmates of the almshouses. Actually these provisions made matters worse, for they tended to make paupers out of some and allowed employers to keep wages close to the relief rate. The expense of maintaining this system, moreover, fell upon the local property holders, who in many cases could ill afford to pay these charges. The taxpayer could find no justice in a system which increased the allotment for mothers of illegitimate children. The act of 1834 attempted to remedy the situation. Illegitimate children were to be supported by their mothers, money allowances except for medical aid were abolished, poorer parishes were grouped with wealthier ones so as to spread more equitably the cost of relief, and a commission was appointed to supervise the enforcement of the act.

In the meantime the Whigs had suffered from repeated attacks of vested interests and had been torn by internal dissensions. In 1834 Grey resigned and was succeeded first by Lord Melbourne, who failed to command the confidence of the Commons, and then by Robert Peel, whose endeavors to promote a settlement of the Irish problem led to his downfall. Melbourne returned to office in 1835 and was sponsor for the passage of the Municipal Reform Act. The acts of 1832 had not touched the local governments, which generally were affected with corruption and inefficiency. According to the act of 1835 all boroughs and cities, with the exception of London and some very small units, were to be governed by a mayor, a board of aldermen, and a council. The councilors were to be chosen by the qualified voters of each borough. They, in turn, were to elect the mayor and board of aldermen.

The Municipal Reform Act of 1835 was the last important reform passed during the reign of William IV (1830–1837). A number of less significant changes were made, such as the conversion of English tithes for the support of the Established Church in England from payments in kind to an annual land tax. An attempt was also made to lower the qualifications for membership in the House of Commons and to extend the franchise. These matters, however, together with the perennial Irish problem, were left unsolved when William IV died in 1837. His reign had been short, but within that period the English constitution had been profoundly altered. Important concessions had been made to the industrialists, and labor organizations had been declared legal. Numerous changes in the conduct of trade and industry had taken place. The old aristocratic order, which had governed England for centuries, gave way to middle class domination.

SELECTED BIBLIOGRAPHY

Many of the references for the preceding and succeeding chapter may be consulted with profit. In addition the following are of value for political and constitutional affairs: Edward and Annie G. Porritt's *Unreformed House of Commons* (Cambridge, 1909); C. Seymour's *Electoral Reform in England and Wales* (New Haven, 1915); W. Bagehot's *English Constitution* (London, 1915); J. R. M. Butler's *Passing of the Great Reform Bill* (London, 1914); O. F. Christie's *The Transition from Aristocracy, 1832–1867* (New York, 1928), and J. A. Roebuck's *History of the Whig Ministry of 1830* (London, 1852). G. M. Trevelyan's *Lord Grey of the Reform Bill* (London, 1920), G. Wallas' *Life of Francis Place* (London, 1918), and A. Aspinall's *Lord Brougham and the Whig Party* (Manchester, 1927) are standard biographies. Religious matters are covered by R. Dunlop's *Daniel O'Connell* (New York, 1900) and B. N. Ward's *Eve of Catholic Emancipation* (London, 1911–1912). See also S. Maccoby's *English Radicalism 1832–1852* (London, 1935).

E. Halévy's *A History of the English People, 1815–1830* (New York, 1924) and S. Walpole's *History of England from the Conclusion of the Great War in 1815* (London, 1910–1913) are standard general histories for this period. Economic and social affairs are stressed in P. Blanshard's *Outline of the British Labor Movement* (London, 1923); G. D. H. Cole's *Short History of the British Working Class Movement* (London, 1927); Max Beer's *History of British Socialism* (London, 1919–1920); S. and B. Webb's *History of Trade Unionism* (London, 1920); W. Page's *Commerce and Industry* (London, 1919); B. L. Hutchins and A. Harrison's *A History of Factory Legislation* (Westminster, 1903), and W. Smart's *Economic Annals of the Nineteenth Century* (London, 1917). The works by Prothero, Barnes, and Slater are of value for agriculture and the corn laws.

CHAPTER XXX

Labor Agitations and Reform, 1837-1867

WILLIAM IV died childless and was succeeded by Victoria, daughter of Edward, Duke of Kent, the youngest son of George III. She began her reign amid conditions which many critics believed would lead to the abolition of monarchy. At her death in 1901, however, monarchy was more deeply entrenched than before, and a nation and empire mourned her loss with the sincerest of feelings and regard. Englishmen everywhere had come to love this simple woman who was not five feet in height or overattractive in looks. Her lack of ostentation, her intense domesticity and the personal interest which she showed in the fortunes of her subjects, endeared her to the nation and empire. Those who served the Queen as ministers realized how seriously she took her royal duties. Between the two, a relationship was established which often aroused the admiration and love of the latter. Lords Melbourne and Disraeli became personally attached to the Queen and won her confidence and friendship. On the other hand she disliked Lord Palmerston and William E. Gladstone, and frequently made their conduct of government embarrassing. Upon the former's death in 1865, she declared that "he was very vindictive, and personal feelings influenced his political acts very much." As for Gladstone, she believed that "he will ruin the country if he can." At times, her influence exceeded her constitutional powers. She never fully understood or accepted the basic essentials of responsible government. She refused to believe that the sovereign should give complete effect to the mandate of the electorate by installing Gladstone as Prime Minister after the election of 1892. At first she tried to prevent his accession to power and when she found herself thwarted, she endeavored to dictate as to his selection of ministers.

In spite of her reluctance to coöperate with some of her ministers, she never sought to override the organic law of the nation. The enhanced position of monarchy, therefore, was due, in no small measure, to the personality and character of Victoria. More significant was the fact that she offered no serious opposition to the political and economic reforms which were enacted during her long reign of sixty-four years. At times, she advised against certain measures, but she never refused to approve what her ministers and parliaments wanted. Many of these reforms profoundly altered the structure and purpose of the English constitution. A republic, in all but name, was consummated; however, monarchy continued and became the sign and symbol of English democracy. Patriotism and loyalty to Victoria were the bond which linked a far-flung empire into a political unit of great solidarity.

During the earlier half of her reign, the Whig and Tory Parties fought for control of government. Most of the time, the Whigs were in power under the leadership of ministers like Melbourne and John Russell. A liberal attitude was shown by these ministers as well as by Robert Peel, the great Tory leader. Fundamentally, however, both parties were essentially aristocratic and opposed to many of the reforms advocated by labor. A more conciliatory policy would have lessened labor's demands for political reform, since labor primarily wished improved economic and social conditions. Not able to convince the government of the justice of its demands, labor agitated for enfranchisement and representation in parliament. Give us the vote and seats in the House of Commons, so the argument ran, and we will abolish starvation wages, the employment of women and children, and all the abuses which undermine life and destroy happiness.

The Chartists

Labor, however, lacked definite organization and was hopelessly split upon a number of vital questions. Although parliamentary reform appealed to the working classes, many viewed it as an abstraction and argued for economic emancipation. Labor's strength, therefore, was dissipated, and the cause of parliamentary reform was represented singly by the group known as the Chartists. They secured their name from the "Charter" which, in imitation of Magna Carta, set forth their rights and objectives. An examination of this document reveals that its friends desired (1) universal manhood suffrage, (2) the secret ballot, (3) the abolition of property qualifications for membership in the House of Commons, (4) the payment of a salary to members of the lower house, (5) equal electoral districts, and (6) annual parliamentary elections. None of these seem radical or extreme from a modern point of view, but to the governing classes of the 1830's and 1840's they bordered upon revolution and treason.

Chartism had its inception in a Working Men's Association founded at London in 1836 by William Lovett, a Cornishman. Labor, in many parts of the realm, was attracted by the aims of this society and formed similar associations to further the campaign for parliamentary reform. Manufacturers and industrialists became interested in the movement, not because the latter were concerned with labor's political objectives, but because they hoped to use the Chartists' organization as a device to secure certain reforms in currency. The activities of the Birmingham Political Union may be cited as an example of this support given Chartism. The working classes in the Birmingham area, however, soon dominated the Political Union and immediately dropped the currency question. This led to the withdrawal of middle-class support. Lovett gained further assistance from northern labor leaders like J. R. Stephens and Fergus O'Connor. The Chartists held several conventions, at which considerable diversity of opinion developed as to how the organization might gain its ends. O'Connor wished to use force, while Lovett advocated peaceful coercion through petitions to parliament. While Lovett was busily engaged in obtaining signatures to a petition, O'Connor sought to agitate labor to riot. During the summer of 1839, Lovett's petition, bearing over a million signatures, was presented to parliament. Conservative opinion, alarmed over the violent agitations fostered by O'Connor, rejected the petition, whereupon the radical Chartists resorted to a general strike. Lacking adequate organization and facing public condemnation for their violence, the Chartists were no match for the superior strength of the government. A great number of the Chartist leaders were arrested, tried, and sentenced either to prison or to transportation.

The Chartist movement collapsed in 1839 but was revived the next year. For a time Lovett and his friends dominated, but by 1842 O'Connor had assumed leadership. O'Connor's victory resulted in the immediate withdrawal of liberals like Richard Cobden and Joseph Sturge, who had joined hands with Lovett in a united front to gain an extension of the suffrage and the repeal of the corn laws. O'Connor inflamed the masses and fomented street riots at London, Canterbury, and elsewhere. In the meantime (1848), a mammoth petition signed by three million people was presented to parliament. Investigation showed that many of these names were fictitious, and the foes of Chartism now accused O'Connor of both fraud and violence. Parliament rejected the petition while hundreds of special police patrolled the streets in the interest of law and order. Among the many constables was the future Napoleon III of France, then a political refugee living in King Street, London.

Trade Unionism and Robert Owen

Chartism never recovered from the unfortunate tactics followed by O'Connor. Radical leadership ruined the entire affair and postponed the political emancipation of the masses for several decades. Had labor been united, parliamentary reform would have been achieved much earlier. As it was, thousands of workers preferred to support other movements. Large numbers, for example, endorsed trade-unionism, the origins of which were mentioned in the previous chapter. Although Doherty's National Association had disappeared in 1832, local and national trade unions multiplied. Thousands in the textile, mining, building, and pottery trades organized and agitated for reform. The most important of these societies was the Builders' Union, which won a number of victories over the masters and contractors in 1832 and 1833. Although many of the leading newspapers condemned the union and bitterly complained about the tyranny of labor, the Builders' Union increased in size and influence. In November, 1833, it assembled in convention at Manchester. At this gathering Robert Owen, a prominent manufacturer and pronounced liberal, appeared and argued for a new social and moral order founded upon the socialistic concept of coöperation. Owen had two definite plans in mind: first, that the Builders' Union should accept his idea of coöperative stores, where labor might buy and sell at an advantage to itself; and second, that the Union seize control of the nation's entire building activity. Owen's suggestions were not new to the Builders' Union, as many of its members had been partners in the coöperative exchanges which Owen had founded as early as 1824. Accordingly, the convention accepted Owen's leadership and forgot its former program of improving conditions of employment.

The Builders' Union immediately enlisted the support of other societies and bound all together in the Grand National

Consolidated Trades Union. For a time it looked as though English labor had forgotten its differences and had united under one standard. Private interests, however, blasted the Consolidated. The master contractors struck a telling blow at the Builders' Union when they announced that no union man would be employed in their works. Moreover, unless labor already in their employ agreed to withdraw from the Builders' Union it could seek employment elsewhere. This device, known then as the "Document," was similar to the modern "Yellow-dog ticket." For a time the Builders' Union urged its members to stand firm, but in the face of continued unemployment and the lack of funds in the Union, desertions took place by the hundreds. Certain crafts, like the masons, withdrew from the Union. By the winter of 1834 the Builders' Union was a thing of the past.

Several months before, the Grand National Consolidated Trades Union had fallen to pieces. The Union, under Owen's leadership, had adopted the coöperative idea of exchanges and had sought to stimulate labor's control over all industry. Owen's plan called for the abolition of private capitalism and for the regulation of industry by the coöperative system of trade unions. Parliament, so he reasoned, would disappear; and in its place there would arise a national assembly of laborers. To meet this attack, industrialists adopted the "Document," as used by the building contractors, and forced thousands to desert the Consolidated. The government, moreover, lent a willing hand by striking fiercely under Melbourne's leadership at the Friendly Society of Agricultural Laborers in Dorset. This organization, like many others, had sought to keep its membership pure and intact by exacting from all candidates a strict oath of allegiance. To make the oath more impressive, an elaborate and secret ritual was devised. Webb, in his history of trade-unionism, describes the scene as follows: "Besides the opening prayer and religious hymns . . . these initiation pacts consisted of questions and responses . . . in quaint doggerel and were brought to a close by the new members' taking a solemn oath of loyalty and secrecy. Officers clothed in surplices, inner chambers to which the candidates were admitted blindfolded, a skeleton, drawn sword, battle axes, and other mystic properties enhanced the sensational solemnity of this fantastic performance."

The surprising thing is not that labor resorted to practices which remind one of the modern college fraternity but that the government viewed them as evidence of a plot to overthrow the constitution and establish a republic of workers. Conservative opinion became panicky and looked upon these mysteries as indicating the presence of communism. Availing himself of a law that had been passed in 1797 to forbid the taking of secret oaths, Melbourne instituted legal proceedings against the Dorset society. Six men were arrested, tried and transported for seven years. The Grand Consolidated struck back by petitions to parliament, parades, strikes, and the elimination of the offensive oaths. Individual members, moreover, resorted to violence. The government met these attacks with force and soon broke all forms of resistance. Without funds, the Grand Consolidated could not meet the joint attack of the government and the industrialists. By the fall of 1834, it had collapsed.

The failure of the Grand Consolidated did not mean the breakup of trade-unionism. Local societies, decreased in size and importance, continued to function, and frequently resorted to strikes to gain their ends. By 1841 there were distinct signs of a revival of the national union idea, and under the leadership of Martin Jude there was formed the Miners' Association of Great Britain. Other national unions developed; but until the establishment of the Amalgamated Society of Engineers in 1851, little real enthusiasm was shown. The Society of Engineers, like the many other unions modeled after it, did not seek to gain its ends by political methods. Rather, it sought so improve working conditions and to provide services and assistance to its members during strikes and periods of unemployment. In contrast to the amalgamated unions were those like the Spinners' Association, which, while providing services, agitated for legislative regulation of industry. Finally, one should notice the Miners' Associations, which generally followed the policies of the textile unions.

Trade-unionism, while not unfriendly to the ideals of Robert Owen, was unwilling to endorse his entire program. Owen was born in 1771, the son of a poor Welsh ironmonger. He received but little schooling, and at an early age became an apprentice in a Stamford drapery shop. Frugality and perseverance carried him through these critical years and placed him, while still a young man, as the manager of one of Manchester's largest manufacturing plants. Later he became the owner and partner of a large Scottish concern. Owen was a self-made man. He had encountered many a thorny problem and had stood plenty of hard knocks. He had seen his fellow workers exploited and had witnessed their fruitless attempts to battle private capitalism. His heart opened to labor's sufferings and complaints, and though wealth came his way, he never lost his compassion for the working classes. His unbounded enthusiasm often led him astray, and his philosophy was marred by an expanding imagination. Moreover, he was essentially a credulous individual and frequently accepted fiction as truth. These faults, however, were of little importance when contrasted with his many virtues.

In his own factory at New Lanark, he assumed that the well-being of his workers was as vital to him as to them. He lowered hours of work, increased wages, afforded educational opportunities to the children, and provided better homes for his help. All of this meant smaller profits and there was always the risk that free competition might force him to the wall. Astute management, however, prevented failure; and in spite of the costs of his social program, he amassed a respectable fortune. He accepted Bentham's utilitarianism and viewed labor as a productive factor in industry. He was a socialist; and from his writings and activities, British labor received its first instruction in Utopian socialism. Militant methods he deplored, and he saw little value in strikes or sabotage. Labor, he declared, could save itself from degradation only through coöperative methods. Educate against ignorance, he said, and economic emancipation would follow.

The Rise of Coöperative Societies

In 1824 Owen went to America and founded a coöperative society at New Harmony, Indiana. The experiment failed, and Owen returned home having lost heavily in the undertaking. His enthusiasm, however, overcame this disappointment, and by 1833, he had interested the trade unions in his ideas. Much of the strength shown by trade-unionism at this time was due to Owen. Organized labor, however, was not fundamentally interested in his socialism and parted company with him in the winter of 1834. Owen continued his work and was able to establish several coöperative societies which aimed at the foundation of a socialistic state. His idea of coöperative stores and exchanges spread. Foremost among the groups which endorsed this concept were the Rochdale Pioneers, founded in 1844. This society sought to establish retail stores for groceries, clothes, and other necessities, and to build homes and recreation centers. Previous organizations of this type had failed because the proprietors had operated on a cost basis. The Rochdale Pioneers sold at the market price and returned earnings to the members in proportion to their purchases. They controlled their own supplies and eliminated the middleman's profit. Moreover, there was no speculative buying, no accumulation of surplus stock, and very little advertising. Most of the management of these stores was furnished by volunteers.

Similar organizations were established elsewhere. As the

movement extended, the demand arose among the members for legal protection against the loss of funds and for the right of incorporation. In 1846 these groups were allowed to register as Friendly Societies, and in 1852, they were given limited rights of incorporation. Ten years later greater concessions were granted. This led to the establishment of national coöperative organizations. Shortly thereafter, further consolidation took place in the founding of the Coöperative Wholesale Society, which unified local efforts and brought the movement under one general management. Stock in this society was held by the local units and not by individuals, while profits were distributed by the local branches to their respective members. The movement spread rapidly, and by 1873 the society was manufacturing goods for its members. Plants and factories were established throughout the realm, the empire, and in foreign countries. Later, the society enlarged its services by acting as a banking and insurance company.

Conservative opinion viewed with concern the extension of these coöperative societies, trade-unionism, and socialism. Its philosophy, already well established by the *laissez-faire* teachings of Adam Smith and the population theory of Malthus, had been stimulated somewhat by the findings of Ricardo. Ricardo's law of wages, it will be recalled, was based in part upon Malthus' ideas, and afforded a justification for the low returns paid labor. Ricardo, however, believed in free trade, and through his law of profits pointed out that increased wealth and prosperity would accrue to the landlords at the expense of labor and the industrialists.

The Repeal of the Corn Laws

Although Ricardo had no intention of stimulating an attack upon the landed classes, his philosophy encouraged labor to challenge the former's control over rents and food prices. Labor wanted cheaper bread and believed that the corn laws, except in times of great scarcity, prevented the free importation of foreign wheat. In the contest to secure the repeal of these laws, labor secured the support of the industrialists, who saw that cheaper bread would enable them to lower wages at the cost of the favored landed classes and with no advantage to labor. At the same time those who argued for free trade joined in condemnation of the corn laws. Continued agitation by labor, the industrialists, and the free traders, particularly in the Manchester area, led, in 1838, to the formation of the Anti-Corn Law League under Richard Cobden and Robert Bright. Thousands of dollars were raised to promote the league's work, which was furthered by a number of tracts and pamphlets and by able speakers in every district of England.

The movement spread rapidly, and in spite of the determined resistance of the landed classes, it secured certain modifications in the corn laws. In 1841, for example, parliament had enacted a sliding scale of duties which permitted greater foreign importations as the domestic price of corn increased. Whig and Tory alike had united in support of this measure, but neither party, in spite of a decided free trade minority, was willing to abandon the idea of protection. During the next three years, however, the anti-corn law agitation received greater support. Motions for repeal in 1842 commanded ninety votes; in 1843, one hundred and twenty-five, and in 1844, one hundred and twenty-four. In 1845 a more determined attack was made against the landed classes, the occasion being a potato famine in Ireland and England. A shortage in potatoes was a serious affair to the average laborer, who had come to depend upon this vegetable for most of his daily food. The government recognized the seriousness of the situation and rushed through parliament measures of relief. In so doing, however, they raised the general question of the corn laws.

The Anti-Corn Law League welcomed the opportunity presented by the potato famine and stormed the country in favor of immediate repeal. Popular meetings were held throughout the realm. At these the landed classes were condemned and the merits of free trade extolled. Doggerel verses, of which the following is a striking example, appeared.

> Bread-tax eating absentee,
> What hath bread-tax done for thee?
> Crammed thee from our children's plates,
> Made thee all that nature hates,
> Filled thy skin with untaxed wine,
> Filled thy purse with cash of mine,
> Filled thy breast with hellish schemes,
> Filled thy head with fatal dreams,
> Of potatoes basely sold
> At the price of wheat in gold
> And of Britain's styed to eat,
> Wheat-priced roots instead of wheat.

Peel, who was Prime Minister at the time, utilized these demonstrations to further the introduction of a repeal measure in the Commons in January, 1846. The bill called for drastic reductions of the rates for the next three years, so that by February, 1849, only a nominal revenue tax would remain. The landed classes, supported by many prominent Tories and Whigs, rushed to meet the attack. The debates in parliament continued for twelve days and attracted considerable attention throughout the country. Peel argued effectively that past reductions had brought no great loss to the agriculturists, that the nation had prospered, and that the general well-being of the laboring classes was necessary for continued national development. Others attacked the landed classes, calling them "Drones in the hive." "Drones in the hive, INDEED!" came a spirited reply. "From the moment the great captain of the age, the illustrious Wellington, landed in the Peninsula, who were the most eager to rush to the battlefield? . . . Who composed the elite of that great commander's personal staff?"

From the voice of a free trader came the answer, "The landed aristocracy. Yes, the last to bid the cry of warfare cease, the first to make a monopoly of peace. For what were all these country patriots born (but) to hunt and vote and raise the price of bread?" Disraeli and Lord George Bentinck waved these jibes aside, and while admitting the necessity of extending relief to Ireland saw no reason for abandoning the principle of protection. Moreover, they declared, Peel had not investigated the extent of the potato famine or the alleged shortage of wheat. The cabinet was "an alarmist cabinet . . . fright was stamped upon their every forehead." Peel's mouldy potatoes, Disraeli said, were a myth; and no justification existed for the repeal of the time-honored corn laws. In spite of Disraeli's brilliant oratory, Peel's cold logic carried the measure through the Commons.

Peel and his followers expected the Lords to offer a determined resistance. Vested landed interests were securely lodged in the upper house and seemed bent upon thwarting the will of the nation. Fortunately for all, the measure was supported by Wellington. The Duke detested Peel for his advocacy of free trade and declared that the latter had been stampeded by "rotten potatoes." On the other hand, Wellington recognized that the nation wanted repeal and that no ministry could function on any other basis. He realized the imperative need of orderly government; he sensed the value of the cabinet system and saw the futility of resisting the inevitable. Accordingly, as one writer put it, "he sat in the House of Lords as a Free Trade Minister, 'with his hat down over his face.'" Wellington's support was decisive and the measure passed the Lords and shortly thereafter became law.

Free Trade and Financial Reform

Peel's advocacy of repeal rested fundamentally upon the theory of free trade. Here he followed in the footsteps of

Huskisson, who had done much toward breaking the monopolistic tendencies of English trade and commerce. Time after time during the early 1840's Peel lent his support to measures calling for reduction in the protective tariff. On one occasion in the Commons, he declared that England had taken as her motto, "Advance or Recede." Other countries were watching her example, and the presence of liberal groups in these states was sufficient proof that England need not expect free trade to be met by hostile tariffs. "What was it England had to dread? . . . Iron and coal, the sinews of manufacture, give us advantages over every rival. . . . Our capital exceeds that which they can command. In ingenuity, in skill and energy we are inferior to none. . . . And is this the country to shrink from competition? Is this the country which can flourish only in this sickly, artificial atmosphere of protection?" Others were of the same opinion, and in spite of Disraeli's oratory a measure was passed in 1845 bringing about a consolidation of the navigation acts and the entire abolition of export duties. Later, in 1849, parliament declared England's foreign trade open to all nations, and in 1853 allowed foreigners to engage in the coastwise trade.

Peel's ministry (1841–1846) is important also for certain reforms that were made in the nation's banking and financial structure. Labor disputes, business depressions, harvest failures, and foreign affairs had played havoc with the country's credit and gold supplies. Large supplies of gold had been shipped to Europe to purchase foodstuffs and to maintain the value of the pound. Additional export had taken place when the Bank of Belgium closed its doors and threatened a financial crisis in France. Clearances had been made to America also. The accumulative effect of these withdrawals from the Bank of England had weakened the gold reserves of the nation and had created a panic. Although French bankers prevented a collapse of England's economic structure by exporting large amounts of gold, almost a hundred provincial banks were forced to suspend payment. To prevent a repetition, Peel persuaded parliament to enact the Bank Charter Act of 1844. According to this measure, the further issue of bank notes was denied to all except the Bank of England, which has ever since enjoyed a monopoly in the issuing of notes. These notes were to be secured by bullion reserves and securities valued at £14,000,000. Finally, the banking functions, as opposed to the issuing of notes, were made a separate and distinct department of the bank.

Three years later another panic was caused by heavy gold exports abroad and overspeculation in railroad development. People believed that the Bank of England, restricted as it was in the issuing of notes, would be unable to meet its obligations, and they proceeded to hoard their currency. The government met the situation by suspending the Act of 1844 and promising to allow the Bank of England to increase the volume of its notes. The crisis was abridged in this manner, but another panic was caused in 1857 by the discovery of gold in America and the resultant rise in prices and overspeculation in American securities. Once again the Act of 1844 was suspended, and over two million pounds of notes were issued. Later, because of questionable banking practices between banking houses and building contractors, another crisis took place. Many mercantile firms and banks closed their doors, the firm of Overend, Gurney and Company failing, in 1866, with liabilities that exceeded £18,000,000. The Bank of England advanced large loans to various houses and promised to issue additional notes. These activities quieted the public and no new notes were issued. The panic, however, had cost the nation more than £50,000,000, and had revealed the extent of the country's dependency upon the Bank of England. In view of the monopoly possessed by this bank in respect to the issuing of notes, local banks increased their business by stimulating checking accounts and the use of bills of exchange. By 1864 the greater share of all mercantile transactions were conducted by these devices. These local banks expanded rapidly and established branches in most of the important cities.

Factory and Mining Acts

Meanwhile the government interested itself in labor conditions in the mines and factories. The Factory Act of 1833, it will be recalled, had left many abuses untouched. This was due in part to a faulty understanding of the situation and to advocates of *laissez faire,* who strongly resented governmental interference. It was argued, moreover, that continued regulation would increase operating costs and force capital out of the country. English reformers declined to accept these assumptions, and through Lord Ashley, the father of the Act of 1833, kept agitating for improved labor conditions. Thanks to his efforts, parliament, in 1842, undertook a thorough investigation of the mines and factories. The findings of this committee shocked the sensibilities of the nation. It was discovered that there were some children only four years old, who were employed in the mines in minor capacities. Others, slightly older and of both sexes, crawled on their hands and knees drawing trucks of ore. Most of these, stripped to the waist and wearing but a simple loin cloth or burlap skirt, pulled the carts through passageways which were but two feet in height. Often these passages contained more than a foot of standing water. Curses and a knotted whip hurried these unfortunates through a working day which extended from four in the morning to five in the evening. Moral conditions were appalling. "No brothel can beat it," declared a member of parliament. Sickness, accident, and death were common among both children and adults. When informed of an accidental death, the average operator thought, "Oh, it is only a collier."

Conservative opinion declared that abuses of this type were not common and, when the Mine and Collieries Bill was introduced, used all its influence to defeat the measure. The Earl of Radnor was opposed to the act because it interfered with the market of labor and because it attempted to "enforce morality by an act of parliament." The Duke of Hamilton declared that the measure "touched on that right which every man and woman ought to enjoy of disposing of their labor in what way they thought proper. . . . The poor females so employed did not deserve to be relieved from it. It was sweet to them, because by it they were enabled to maintain themselves or perhaps a parent or a child." In spite of this protest, the Mine and Collieries Act, which prohibited the employment of women and children in the mines, was passed in 1842.

The parliamentary committee of 1842 also revealed terrible conditions in the factories. Peel was determined to enact corrective legislation but encountered such bitter protest from the manufacturers and vested interests that he threatened to resign. Fearing that a new ministry might advocate greater regulation, conservative opinion yielded and allowed the passage of the Factory Act of 1844. In the future no woman was to work more than twelve hours a day, while children under thirteen were to be employed for but six and a half hours. Safety appliances were to be installed on dangerous machinery. Later, in 1847, women and children over thirteen years of age were not to be employed for more than ten hours. During the next two decades parliament passed a number of laws which affected those industries not covered by the former measures, as well as manufacturing in private homes and small workshops employing at least fifty hands. Later, in 1867, the Workshops Regulation Act extended these provisions to shops employing less than fifty. The enforcement of these acts was not so vigorous as it could have been. On the other hand, considerable progress had been made toward improving working conditions since the passage of the Reform Act of 1832.

The Reform Act of 1867

Under the provisions of this celebrated act a total of 217,386 voters had been added to the electorate. Altogether, about 900,000 men out of a total male population of 5,000,000 enjoyed the right to vote. Expressed differently, but one man out of six was enfranchised. Labor, in short, whose strength had forced the passage of the Act of 1832, was not given the vote. At the same time there were many growing towns still unrepresented in parliament, while county representation had not kept pace with the nation's growth. Cornwall, for example, with only a fraction of the population of Middlesex, had a larger representation. In spite of these apparent defects, neither Whig nor Tory seemed inclined to consider further reform. Labor, however, continued its agitation. The collapse of the Chartist movement caused many workers, particularly in the textile industries and mines, to give their support to trade-unionism and coöperative enterprises. Labor never lost sight of the need for parliamentary reform, but was generally not interested in any proposal which fell short of complete manhood suffrage. This, neither Tory nor Whig was ready to grant. During the two decades that followed the breakup of Chartism, trade-unionism sought to gain its ends by organizations and strikes. Distinct progress was made, but by the middle of the 1850's the unions came to realize that further gains could be made only through parliamentary reform.

Numerous petitions and measures advocating an extension of the franchise appeared in parliament. Few of these bills satisfied labor, although at times it expressed a willingness to follow the suggestion of its chief advocate in parliament, John Bright, and accept what was offered. Conservative strength, however, defeated Hume's moderate measure of 1848, Russell's bills of 1850 and 1852, Bright's proposals of 1859, and even Disraeli's bill of 1859. Parliament, however, did adopt one of the features of Bright's proposal, namely the abolition of the property qualifications for membership in the House of Commons.

Touched to the quick by the defeat of these moderate reform measures, labor embarked upon a campaign which was characterized by pressure, demonstrations, and publications. Trade unions, textile workers, and miners willingly gave their support to the movement. In 1862 certain prominent officials of the London Trades Council organized a "Junto," which succeeded in founding the Manhood Suffrage and Vote by Ballot Association. About the same time, the Manchester group of liberals and others headed by Bright and Cobden formed the Reform League, which in a short time became so powerful as to lead the Manhood Suffrage Association into its organization. Continued pressure of this type resulted in the introduction of further reform measures, notably one sponsored by Russell in 1866. Vested interests defeated Russell's bill and led to the downfall of the Whig Party in the same year.

Derby and Disraeli were then placed in control of the government, and sensing the inevitable, they proceeded to introduce a reform measure. In the meantime Bright, Gladstone (then entering upon a long political career), and others addressed the country in behalf of reform. Enthusiastic audiences greeted these speakers in all parts of the kingdom. Street demonstrations followed; and in July, 1866, an excited crowd tore down the closed gates of Hyde Park and, in defiance of governmental order, held a huge mass meeting. In the face of this agitation, the Tory government, convinced that if it did not yield the Whigs would return to power and pass a more radical measure, introduced a bill which after considerable debate passed parliament. According to the terms of the Reform Act of 1867, the suffrage was extended in both county and borough units to include a much larger proportion of the male population. The laboring classes in the towns generally

POLITICAL KIDNAPPING.

MRS. RUSSELL. "HI! HELP! P'LE—EEE—ECE! SHE'S A TAKIN' AWAY ME CHE-ILD!"

Reproduced by permission of the Proprietors of "Punch."

received the vote, though the greater share of the agricultural workers did not. The act also redistributed the seats in the House of Commons so as to reduce the number of representatives from boroughs of less than 10,000. Additional seats were granted to Scotland, while Birmingham, Leeds, Manchester, and Liverpool were given three seats each.

SELECTED BIBLIOGRAPHY

The volumes in the Hunt-Poole and Oman Series furnish general narrative accounts of value as do the following more specialized works: H. Paul's *History of Modern England* (New York, 1904–1906); J. McCarthy's *History of Our Own Times* (London, 1887), and S. Walpole's *History of England* (London, 1910–1913).

The period is rich in biographical works. S. Lee's *Queen Victoria* (London, 1902) and L. Strachey's *Queen Victoria* (New York, 1921) are of interest. Vols. I and II of W. F. Monypenny and G. E. Buckle's *Life of Benjamin Disraeli* (New York, 1929); S. J. Reid's *Lord John Russell* (London, 1905); S. Walpole's *Life of Lord John Russell* (London, 1891); C. S. Parker's *Sir Robert Peel* (London, 1891–1899); W. M. Torrens' *Memoirs of the Right Honorable William, second Viscount Melbourne* (London, 1878); G. M. Trevelyan's *Life of John Bright* (London, 1925); J. Morley's *Richard Cobden* (London, 1881), and G. D. H. Cole's *Robert Owen* (London, 1925) are standard works of merit.

Chartism has appealed to many writers of whom the following may be consulted with profit: B. F. Rosenblatt's *Social and Economic Aspects of the Chartist Movement* (New York, 1916); M. Hovell's *The Chartist Movement* (Manchester, 1918); P. W. Slosson's *Decline of the Chartist Movement* (New York, 1916), and R. S. Gammage's *History of the Chartist Movement* (London, 1894). Each of these studies also gives some attention to trade-unionism, socialism, and the repeal of the corn laws. Specialized treatment of these subjects may be found in the works by P. Blanshard, G. D. H. Cole, and Max Beer. J. F. Wilkinson's *Friendly Society Movement* (London, 1886); G. J. Holyoake's *History of Coöperation in England* (London, 1906); S. and B. Webb's *History of Trade Unionism* (London, 1920); J. L. and B. Hammond's *The Age of the Chartists* (London, 1930), and F. E. Gillespie's *Labor and Politics in England, 1850–1867* (Durham, 1927) are noteworthy studies. G. J. Holyoake's *History of the Rochdale Pioneers* (London, 1893) and A. Andreades' *History of the Bank of England* (London, 1909) are of help.

Parliamentary reform is admirably handled by C. Seymour's studies; E. Allyn's *Lords versus Commons* (New York, 1931), and J. H. Park's *The English Reform Bill of 1867* (New York, 1920). W. H. Hunt's "Factory System of the Nineteenth Century," in *Economica*, No. 16, is of value.

CHAPTER XXXI

Labor and Reform, 1867-1914

THE extension of the franchise, in 1867, to the laboring classes in the towns was the logical result of social and economic forces which had been operating since the close of the Napoleonic wars. Conservative opinion had been compelled to alter the organic law in the interest of the English people. The Act of 1867, however, should be viewed in the light of the future as well as the past. It marked the culmination of one order and became the source from which new reforms sprang. It also brought about a new alignment in parties. The respective retirements of Russell and Derby from politics in 1867 and 1868 allowed Bright and Gladstone to assume leadership among the Whigs or Liberals and Disraeli to direct the fortunes of the Tories or Conservatives. Increasingly, the latter party became the political refuge for those of aristocratic or conservative opinion. Many an individual who before 1867 had marched under the Whig banner of Russell forsook his former allegiance and became a Tory.

On the other hand the Whig or Liberal Party embraced not only the more radical followers of Russell but also the rank and file of labor, which had benefited by the Act of 1867. Labor willingly entered this alliance, knowing only too well that it lacked any political solidarity of its own and was totally deficient in experience. For several decades this arrangement continued. Ultimately, labor grew in stature, wisdom, and experience, and gradually drifted away from Liberal ranks and formed a party of its own. The schooling which it received during the life of this alliance was of lasting value. Labor, however, had not been a docile pupil, nor had it always followed the suggestions of its teacher. Much of the social legislation which the Liberal Party enacted during the next two decades after 1867 came as the result of labor influence and votes. In the meantime the Tory Party was altered definitely by the pressure exerted by labor. Labor votes were worth capturing; and the Conservatives, especially during the 1870's became sponsors of many a measure for political and party reasons. The Conservative Party became more moderate in nature and philosophy. It encouraged slow, orderly growth and paved the way for the Tory democracy of the late nineteenth and twentieth centuries. Labor's rôle in politics is illustrated by an examination of the several political and economic reforms which were enacted between 1867 and the death of Victoria in 1901.

Agricultural Advances

Historians often have called the period from 1853 to 1870 the "Golden Age" of English farming. Several factors combined to produce this prosperity. First in importance were the improvements that had been made in agricultural economy. Extensive drainage operations, begun as early as 1823, cleared many a swamp or fen and increased both the size and value of arable land. Mechanical devices such as haymakers, horse-rakes, and steam-driven machines for threshing, pumping, and grinding were introduced. Chemical research provided nitrate, potash, and mineral phosphates as fertilizer. The foundation of the Royal Agricultural Society in 1838 did much to inform the English farmer of these discoveries and improvements. The rapid extension of railroads and steamship service afforded better transportation facilities. The discovery of gold in California raised farm prices, while the Crimean War, in 1854, closed a Russian grain trade and gave advantages to the English producer. The trade expansion, which followed the repeal of the Navigation Acts, and the rapid increase in the country's birth rate stimulated domestic consumption of English wheat. Finally, nature was exceedingly kind and provided a series of good seasons.

Except in the dairying industry, where the foot and mouth disease and cattle plague caused much damage, agricultural prices remained high and brought splendid profits to the landed class in rents and sales. On the other hand the agricultural laborer did not share in this prosperity. Wages rose slightly but were too low to maintain a respectable standard of living. Higher wages might have been paid had labor limited its operations and reduced its birth rate. Workers were to be had in great abundance and seemed willing to accept starvation wages. In order to provide the farmers with cheap labor, there developed what was known as the Gang System. Contractors or middlemen managed this system and furnished the landed class with gangs of workers, chiefly women and children, at low prices. The effects of the Gang System were numerous. Throngs of laborers were moved about the country by the contractors. The home life of the worker was disrupted, and immoral conditions developed. Little by little the abuses inherent in the Gang System became public, and in 1868 parliament removed many of the most patent evils. Children under eight years of age, however, might still be employed. The passage of the Education Act of 1876 remedied this somewhat by forbidding the employment of children under ten years. Since the landed class was restricted by these acts to the labor of older children and adults, higher wages were paid, though at no time was the amount received sufficient to maintain a decent standard of living.

Throughout the period from 1815 to 1870, agricultural wages remained low. The repeal of the Corn Laws actually caused wages to decline; and when food prices rose after 1850, wage increases were kept low by higher rents, by the employment of women and children, and by the use of labor-saving machines. The lot of the agricultural laborer during the "Golden Age" was not one of milk and honey. Poorly educated and intent on keeping body and soul together, the farm workers gave much less attention to political matters than they should have. Intensely individualistic, they were slow to see the advantages of organization; and while they had agitated for the reforms of 1832 and 1867, they made little impression upon the conservative classes. It took an agricultural depression in 1870 to awaken the farm workers to the need of further political action.

Hoping to better their conditions, the rural workers organized themselves into the National Agricultural Laborers under the leadership of Joseph Arch. The union demanded higher wages and shorter hours. The landed class, taken by surprise, had to yield ground. Later, however, it attacked the union, broke up its meetings, intimidated individuals, and secured severe court sentences. Non-union labor poured into the affected areas. The local clergy often supported the landlords and condemned Arch for having destroyed the friendly relations which had existed between labor and capital. The Bishop of Bristol went so far as to suggest that the labor leaders be thrown into the millpond. Against these attacks the union distributed over £30,000 in strike pay, but was unable to continue the unequal fight as it dragged into 1874. Had the union been able to keep a united front and had the farmers not substituted machines for human labor, it is possible that the agricultural union might have survived for a longer time. As it was, the movement collapsed without having gained its ends. Only in Norfolk did the union continue to show any signs of life. In 1885 it was strong enough to send Joseph Arch to the House of Commons. Arch associated himself with the reforming element in the Commons and kept agitating the cause of the agricultural laborers.

British Labor Demands Political and Economic Reform

In the meantime the industrial workers in the towns were agitating for further political and economic reforms. For a brief period, 1860 to 1867, British labor flirted with the communist ideas of Karl Marx, a political exile from Germany, who had made London his home. Here he studied working conditions, and here he propounded his revolutionary concept of a proletarian uprising. The abolition of private capitalism and the establishment of labor governments were his immediate goals. Later, in 1867, he published his monumental volume, *Das Kapital,* which ever since has been the bible and text book of communists the world over. British labor listened with definite interest to Marx's appeal and coöperated in founding the First International Working Men's Association at London in 1864. In all probability, English labor did not grasp the full significance of Marx's philosophy. His statements were interpreted as expressions of internationalism, and English workers endorsed his efforts in much the same manner as they had greeted the political exiles from Italy and Poland. As the revolutionary nature of Marx's ideas became more apparent, British labor withdrew from the First International. Although Marx complained bitterly about the apathy of English workers, he was unable to convert the latter to communism.

Having rid itself of the International, British labor agitated for a modification of the laws affecting the legal status of workers. Its first attack was against the Master and Servant Act of 1824, which subjected labor to punishment for violation of contract or for quitting a job unfinished. An employer, under this act, might present evidence incriminating a laborer, though the latter was not permitted to furnish evidence against the former. A single justice, often an employer himself, might hear a case and impose punishment. The entire procedure was unfair to labor, and trade unions throughout

Britain joined in a spirited attack upon this law. In 1867 their efforts were rewarded by a new act, which largely removed these unfair practices.

The passage of this act came in the same year as the Reform Act of 1867. The following year there was a general election, and for the first time in English history a large number of manual workers were allowed to vote. Liberal and Conservative alike sought to capture this vote by promising to remedy labor conditions. Most of these promises were forgotten, but continued pressure on the part of labor forced the government to take some action. In 1869 the practice of employers' tapping union funds for alleged damages sustained through strikes was stopped, while in 1871 complete legal status was given to all trade unions. This latter privilege was extended, a few years later, to the Friendly and Coöperative Societies. The right of peaceful picketing was granted in 1875, while no act of organized labor was punishable unless it could be established as criminal when done by an individual member. During the same decade a number of other measures were passed to regulate the condition of workers in the mines, factories, and shipyards. Increased educational facilities were promoted, housing conditions were somewhat improved, and local governments were empowered to raise the general health standards of their communities. The Supreme Judicature Act of 1873, by reorganizing and consolidating the courts of the realm, afforded better justice to English labor. Never since the days of the Reform Act of 1832 had there been such a wave of social legislation, most of which was supported by a Conservative Government. Conservatives had supported these measures because they realized the need of reform, and at the same time, by passing such legislation, the Conservative Party hoped to win the votes of a grateful electorate.

The combined effect of these reforms in industry, education, health, and agriculture prepared the way for a further extension of the franchise. The agricultural laborer had not received the vote in 1867, and it was in his behalf that measures were ·introduced in 1872, 1875, and 1877. The landed classes, fearing that an extension of the suffrage to this group of workers might lead to a Liberal victory, defeated each of these bills. The reforming group, however, was not discouraged and went to the polls in 1880 intent on replacing Disraeli with Gladstone. The Liberals won the election and were reminded immediately that they owed their success to the reformers. Gladstone, because of other considerations, was unable to introduce a franchise measure until 1884. After considerable debate the bill passed parliament. By this measure the vote was given to the agricultural laborers and to certain urban groups which had not been covered by the Act of 1867. Universal manhood suffrage, except for those having no established residence and bachelors living with their parents, was secured by the Act of 1884.

The following year a redistribution bill passed parliament. This provided for single-member constituencies except for London and those boroughs whose population ranged between 15,000 and 165,000, which were given two representatives. The measure also increased the size of the House of Commons from 658 members to 670. In passing this act the Liberal Party actually carried out two of the six planks of the Chartist group, namely, universal manhood suffrage and equal electoral districts. The Chartist demand for the removal of property qualifications for membership in the House of Commons had been granted in 1858, while in 1872 the Australian secret ballot was made legal. In the meantime, obsolete restrictions on Roman Catholics, in respect to religious liberty and education, were removed; and in 1833 Quakers, Moravians, and Separatists were allowed representation in the lower house. Three years later, civil registration of births, deaths, and marriages was established; and in 1858 Hebrews were admitted to parliament.

British Labor Enters Politics

The passage of these numerous social, political, and economic reforms was made possible by labor activities within and without parliament. As early as 1830, labor captured its first parliamentary seat by Henry Preston's election from Preston. Oldham returned William Cobbett in 1832, and between 1847 and 1857 several Chartists won seats. In 1852 the first trade-unionist, William Newton, entered the House of Commons. With the death of Chartism, labor's interest in representation waned. In 1867, however, the London Working Men's Association undertook to revive the idea of working-class representation. In spite of internal disagreements among the various trade unions, the movement spread, and in 1869, the Labor Representation League was formed. It was not until 1874, however, that anything definite was accomplished. In that year fifteen labor candidates ran for office, two of whom, Thomas Burt for Morpeth and Alexander Macdonald for Stafford, were elected. Although these men may be called Labor members, they were counted and voted as Liberals in the House of Commons. In 1880 Henry Broadhurst, secretary of the Labor League, was returned; but he also was considered a Liberal in parliament. Shortly thereafter the League fell to pieces. At no time had this organization sought the formation of a separate workers' party, and it was not until 1893 that such a group was founded.

The genesis of an independent labor party is traceable to the socialistic teachings of Robert Owen and Karl Marx, who thought in terms of a labor parliament and government. Greater stimulus was afforded by the establishment, in the 1870's, of working men's clubs. The personnel of these groups was recruited from those laborers who suffered as a result of a business depression which swept England at that time, and who realized that the Liberal-Labor alliance in parliament was not accomplishing all it could for the manual worker. One of the leaders of this movement was Henry M. Hyndman, a writer of some reputation and a friend of Karl Marx. Hyndman united the working men's clubs by founding the Democratic Federation in 1881. At first, the Federation avoided socialism and sought, through independent party action, to achieve manhood suffrage, payment of members in the House of Commons, the abolition of the House of Lords, and other objectives which were distinctly Chartist in nature. The Federation, however, was unable to hold the radical working clubs together, especially as trade-unionism refused to join in the movement. Hyndman was forced to change his tactics and in 1883 molded the Federation into a militant socialist group. The Federation declared for nationalization of land, railroads, and banking, for reduced taxation, for state aid in housing and education and for the establishment of workshops to care for the unemployed. It published the *Justice,* the first modern socialist paper in Britain, and renamed itself the Social Democratic Federation.

The Federation attracted orthodox socialists, radical trade-unionists, anarchists, communists, and idealists like William Morris, a wealthy poet and craftsman. All these groups agreed in attacking the trade unions for their refusal to join in the movement, but quarreled among themselves over leadership and the question of forming a political party. As a result of these differences, Morris withdrew and founded the Socialist League, which sought to educate the masses to socialism before undertaking independent party action. It included within its limited ranks most of the anarchists who, by 1889, ousted Morris from the editorship of the *Commonweal,* the official organ of the League. Shortly thereafter, Morris retired, and the Socialist League disappeared.

Hyndman's society, however, continued to function, and laid stress on the necessity of political action. Three of its members ran for office in the election of 1885, but the total votes received by all amounted to but 667. The business depression from 1884 to 1886 increased the strength of the organization, and by the close of that decade, it was reaching the ears of the average laborer through a number of tracts, pamphlets, and newspapers. In addition to the *Justice* and *Commonweal,* there appeared *The Miner,* edited by Keir Hardie, *The Labour Elector,* founded by H. H. Champion, and the *Link,* by Annie Besant. Not all these papers were organs of the Social Democratic Federation though they gave attention to it in their columns. The Federation, however, under Hyndman's domineering leadership alienated many of the socialistic tendencies because of its strong Marxian tone. In brief, the Federation became increasingly doctrinal in its policies and teachings and failed to satisfy men like Tom Mann, who advocated a conversion of trade-unionism rather than constant attacks upon it. By 1890 the Social Democratic Federation had waned in influence and had given ground to a new movement headed by Keir Hardie.

Hardie ran for office in 1888, and though defeated, was instrumental in founding, in 1889, the Scottish Labor Party. Two years later the London Trades Council established the London Labor Representative Committee, which succeeded in forming throughout England branches pledged to the idea of an independent labor party. In the meantime a number of papers like Robert Blatchford's *Clarion* appeared, all decidedly socialistic. Equally significant were the numerous tracts published by the Fabian Society. The latter organization was founded in 1883 and included among its followers intellectuals and liberals like George Bernard Shaw and Mr. and Mrs. Sidney Webb. The *Fabian Essays* were written for upper and middle class readers and converted many to socialism. The net result of this propaganda was shown in the election of 1892, when Hardie, John Burns, and Havelock Wilson were elected to parliament. Twelve others, including Joseph Ash, were returned as Liberal-Laborites.

These victories encouraged the socialists and led to the

formation of the Independent Labor Party in 1893. The avowed objectives of this party included the passage of new labor laws, such as an eight-hour working day, and the collective ownership of the means of production, distribution, and exchange. The Fabians endorsed these ends but preferred to gain them by exerting pressure upon the Liberal and Conservative Parties. On the other hand the Social Democratic Federation, with its emphasis upon Marxism and revolution, viewed the Independent Labor Party as too moderate in its program. The trade unions, however, thought the new organization too socialistic. Hardie and his associates deplored this dissension among the workers, as they realized only too well that a socialist party could win only by trade union coöperation. In spite of these difficulties, the Independent Labor Party grew in strength and succeeded in gaining the support of the younger and more active trade union leaders. In the general election of 1895, however, not a single Independent Labor candidate was returned. This setback was due to conservative leadership among the trade unions, which in their convention of 1899 intimated that they were not interested in the Independent Labor Party or any working man's party.

The trade union convention of 1899, however, did authorize the formation of a committee to devise means for increasing the number of labor members in parliament. This committee met in February, 1900, and included representatives of the Independent Labor Party, the Social Democratic Federation, the Trade Union Congress and the Fabian Society. Bernard Shaw, Ramsay MacDonald and Keir Hardie were among its more prominent members; and because of their leadership, the committee secured an alliance between trade-unionism and socialism. In the future, the Labor Representation Committee, as the new organization was named, was to support any party which promoted labor legislation. In this fashion, trade-unionism might elect a candidate of the Independent Labor Party without necessarily indicating its belief in the socialism of that party. MacDonald was chosen secretary of the new organization, and it was largely owing to his efforts that the Labor Representation Committee remained intact during the first few years of the new century. Ultimately, in 1906, the Committee changed its name to the Labor Party and in the election of that year won twenty-nine seats in the House of Commons. In the same election, the Independent Labor Party returned seven members, making a grand total of thirty-six labor votes in the Commons. In 1910 there were forty labor votes, while by 1914 there were almost fifty.

In spite of these pronounced gains, labor was in no position to force its ideas upon parliament. It was only a weak minority. Parliament and the country, moreover, were too concerned with Irish, colonial, and foreign affairs to devote much attention to labor. Moreover, the miners' strike of 1912 and that of the London dockers and transport workers in the same year alienated public opinion and led temporarily to a labor setback. On the other hand labor, by strengthening the hand of the Liberal Party, gained through the passage of several important measures. In 1906, for example, parliament passed a Trades Dispute Act which protected the funds of trade unions. The cause for this act was the decision handed down by the House of Lords in the Taff Vale Case, which involved the liability of a trade union for acts of damage committed by its members. The Lords decided that the members of the union were liable "singly and collectively for acts committed under the auspices of the Union." The Trades Dispute Act of 1906 set aside this decision and freed the unions from liability for any action taken by them during a strike. Three years later the Lords, in the Osborne Case, ruled that it was illegal to use funds raised by compulsory contributions for the payment of a salary to a member of the Commons. Labor resented this, as few of its representatives were financially able to serve in parliament without this pay. Accordingly, when the opportunity presented itself in 1911, labor influenced the

Liberal Party to pass a measure providing for the payment of £400 a year to all members of the Commons.

Liberal Reforms Under Asquith and Lloyd George

Thanks to labor support, the Liberal Party was able to pass other acts of social and constitutional importance. The election of 1906 had been a landslide for the Liberal Party. Under the leadership of Campbell-Bannerman, Asquith, and Lloyd George, the Liberal Party proposed a number of measures which the House of Lords considered too radical and extreme. Considerable ill-feeling developed between the two houses. Matters reached a crisis in 1909 when Lloyd George, Chancellor of the Exchequer, proposed the passage of a budget entailing the expenditure of £162,000,000. This sum of money was necessary, so he declared, if the country was to maintain the usual military and civil costs of government, adequate naval defense in the face of Germany's bid for sea power, and if the cost of the Workingmen's Compensation Act of 1906 were to be met. According to this act employers were liable for all accidents (except those willfully caused) to all laborers, including domestic servants earning less than £250 a year. In 1908, moreover, there had been passed an Old Age Pension Law, which provided for the payment of one to five shillings a week to every person over seventy years of age, provided he had been a subject for twenty years, a resident for twelve years, and was not a criminal. To meet these extraordinary expenditures, the Liberal Party advocated a tax program which fell heavily upon the wealthy classes. This program included a higher tax on unearned incomes, an increase in the license fees required of hotels, a graduated assessment on motor vehicles, a gasoline tax, and a levy on what was termed the "unearned increment." The latter assessment was based upon the theory that land values had risen in the past few years, and that in general this increase had come about by improved standards of living and not by any additional investment on the part of the owners of property. As a result of these increased values landowners were acquiring profit, chiefly in the form of higher rents and sales, that represented a gain which the owner had not caused and therefore was not entitled to. Society, so it was argued, should receive a share of this additional profit or "unearned increment." Accordingly, when the budget reached the Lords, bitter opposition was aroused. Many of the Lords declared that the measure was more than a budget; it was "a revolution." The taxes seemed altogether too high and in some cases called for the adoption of measures which the Lords had refused to pass. The nation, so it was declared, did not approve of these expenditures and the Liberal Party had no right to force them through parliament. The budget, therefore, was defeated by a decided majority.

In rejecting this bill the Lords raised the constitutional question of their rights over a money bill. Since 1678 the upper house had not amended money bills. On the other hand the right of the peers to veto a finance measure was an established power though it had long since fallen into disuse. The House of Commons, however, lost no time in passing, by a vote of 349 to 134, the following resolution: "That the action of the House of Lords . . . is a breach of the Constitution and a usurpation of the rights of the Commons." Edward VII, who had become king on the death of Victoria in 1901, expressed a similar sentiment when, in a private conversation with the chief clerk of the Privy Council, he remarked that "[he] thought the Lords mad." A day later, December 3, 1909, Edward dissolved parliament, and in the course of his speech complimented the Commons on its financial arrangements and regretted that the provisions had not passed.

The general election which followed was characterized by considerable bitterness. The Liberals won 275 seats to the Tories' 273 and had to depend upon the seventy-one Irish

votes and forty Labor members to retain control of government. The election, which had been fought in part on the
issue of curbing the powers of the peers, was not so reassuring as
the Liberals had desired. Actually, they had lost a hundred
seats. Asquith indicated that he intended to introduce measures which would reform the upper house but proceeded so
cautiously and slowly that he aroused bitter feelings on the
part of the Irish and Labor members as well as among many
of his own party. The death of Edward on May 6, moreover,
tended to delay matters. On the 10th of the same month,
however, the Liberal Party introduced the following resolutions: (1) all money bills (and the determination of what constituted a money bill was left to the Speaker of the Commons)
were to be presented to the king for his signature within one
month after they had passed the Commons, regardless of the
action of the Lords; (2) all other measures were to be referred
to the king, irrespective of the wishes of the Lords, provided
they had passed the Commons in three consecutive sessions
and provided they had been presented to the Lords one month
prior to the close of a session and that two years had intervened since the measure was first introduced; (3) the life of
parliament should be five instead of seven years as established
by the Septennial Act of 1716. These resolutions passed the
Commons by a vote of 362 to 241.

In the meantime, the Lords introduced resolutions of its
own. Most of the peers recognized the seriousness of the
situation and listened with considerable interest to the plea of
Lord Lansdowne, a prominent Conservative, for a reorganization of the upper house. Lansdowne proposed that the house
be reduced to approximately 350 members, one hundred of
whom were to be chosen by the peers, while another hundred
were to be appointed by the Crown from the membership of
the Commons or from the outside. One hundred and twenty
others were to be chosen by a system of electoral colleges made
up of Commoners. All three groups were to serve for twelve

years, one fourth retiring every three years. Provision was also made for the election of seven bishops, including the primates of York and Canterbury, by the episcopacy, while those peers not elected or chosen were to be eligible for membership in the Commons. The great majority of the Lords found one fault or another with these proposals, and though they passed the second reading, they were not brought up for final action.

By this time the Commons bill was before the Lords and had become the object of bitter attack. It became evident that the Lords would not approve the measure. Asquith asked the Crown to dissolve parliament. The election which followed resulted in no material change in the structure of the Commons; and in February, 1911, a new bill was introduced. Commons passed it without much difficulty and forwarded it to the Lords, where it underwent radical amendment. Asquith refused to accept these changes and informed the Lords that the Crown was ready to create enough new peerages to secure passage of the bill. Lansdowne and some 300 peers abstained from voting, and the measure passed the Lords, 131 to 114.

The result of the Parliament Act of 1911 was to deprive the Lords of all legislative power in respect to finance. In view of the fact that the Lords since the late seventeenth century had approved without material change all money bills, the new measure was not so radical as it seemed. It is evident, however, that in respect to other measures the Lords lost its power of absolute veto, though it still retained a suspensive veto. On the other hand, since the last decade of the nineteenth century the House of Lords had pulled a weak oar in legislation; and the restriction imposed in 1911 amounted to but little more than a recognition of existing procedure. Nevertheless the act has and does prevent the Lords, an unrepresentative body, from checking the will of the English people. It stands as the culmination of democratic forces which materially trans-

THE INTERIOR OF THE HOUSE OF LORDS. In the background is the King's Throne; in the foreground is the Woolsack, the official seat of the Lord Chancellor.

formed the monarchy from an aristocratic institution to a political democracy.

It is of interest to note that in the passage of the Act of 1911, thirteen bishops, including the primates of York and Canterbury, supported the Liberal government. Had these ecclesiastics voted against the bill, as many expected, the measure would have been defeated. The attitude of the bishops toward reform had changed considerably since the opening of the nineteenth century. Before this date the Anglican Church was the established religion of Ireland, Wales, and England, while in Scotland, Presbyterianism was the established faith as provided for in the Act of Union of 1707. Outside Scotland, however, the Anglican Church maintained an official position which afforded it considerable power and influence. In Ireland this was particularly true, though the great majority of the people were Romanists. Ultimately, in justice to the Irish, the Church in Ireland was disestablished in 1869. Wales, however, though predominately nonconformist, remained a stronghold of Anglican power until 1914, when the Welsh Church was disestablished. Because of the outbreak of the World War, the act disestablishing the Welsh Church was suspended, and did not become operative until 1920.

The social and political reforms of the nineteenth and early twentieth centuries profoundly affected the structure and operation of the British constitution. The extension of the franchise and the redistribution of parliamentary constituencies destroyed an old order in which vested interests and property rights predominated. Official recognition of trade-unionism, the establishment of coöperatives, and the steady growth of socialism had placed British labor in a most advantageous position. Through its influence and its representatives in parliament, labor was able to secure the passage of measures which improved the social and economic lot of most Englishmen. The day was not far distant when labor was to be entrusted with the management of His Majesty's Government. The steady decrease of royal power and the waning influence of the House of Lords placed the conduct of government in the House of Commons. To all intents and purposes, political sovereignty had passed from the Crown to the Commons. Although all laws continued to be made in the name of the king, the legislative, as well as the executive and judicial, powers of the Crown were subject to the authority of the House of Commons. Ministerial responsibility to the Commons had become an integral part of the organic law. The cabinet system of government, conceived in the eighteenth century, was rounded and fashioned in the interests of the British people. The institution of monarchy was not destroyed. As a symbol of local and imperial authority, monarchy was stronger than in the days of George III. At the same time a political transformation had taken place. In lieu of royal authority and government by a privileged few, there had emerged the constitutional monarchy of 1914. England was a democracy in all but name.

SELECTED BIBLIOGRAPHY

A large number of the works cited for the previous chapter contain material pertinent to the period from 1867 to 1914. In the field of biography the following volumes may be read with profit: G. Cecil's *Life of Robert, Marquis of Salisbury* (London, 1921); A. G. Gardiner's *Life of Sir William Harcourt* (London, 1923); E. T. Raymond's *Life of Arthur James Balfour* (Boston, 1920); H. Spender's *The Prime Minister* (New York, 1920); E. T. Raymond's *Mr. Lloyd George* (New York, 1922); Earl of Oxford and Asquith's *Fifty Years of British Parliament* (Boston, 1926); Grey of Falloden's *Twenty-five Years* (New York, 1925); S. Lee's *King Edward VII* (New York, 1927); J. Arch's *The Story of His Life* (London, 1898); J. Morley's *Recollections* (New York, 1917); J. W. Mackail's *Life of William Morris* (London, 1922), and J. L. Garvin's *The Life of Joseph Chamberlain* (London, 1932–1934).

R. H. Gretton's *A Modern History of the English People, 1880–1910* (Boston, 1913) is a useful narrative account. A. L. Lowell's *Government of England* (New York, 1910); T. E. May's *Constitutional History of England* (London, 1873), and W. S. McKechnie's *The Reform of the House of Lords* (Glasgow, 1909) furnish good accounts of the political reforms of the nineteenth and twentieth centuries. The *Contemporary Review,* the *English Historical Review,* the *American Historical Review,* the *Fortnightly Review,* and the *Nineteenth Century* have many articles dealing with the status of parliament.

Social, economic, and labor problems are treated in C. Hayes' *British Social Politics* (New York, 1913); H. B. Gibbins' *English Social Reformers* (London, 1902); E. R. Pease's *The History of the Fabian Society* (New York, 1926); J. R. MacDonald's *The Socialist Movement* (New York, 1911), and R. E. Prothero's *English Farming, Past and Present* (London, 1912).

CHAPTER XXXII

The British Empire

ENGLAND'S interest in colonial and imperial expansion was at a low ebb following the American Revolution. Considerable time and effort had been spent in founding and rearing the Thirteen Colonies only to have them break away from the Mother Country. The theories of mercantilism and the Old Colonial System, upon which the eighteenth-century policy had been built, were discredited by the revolt of the American possessions. A keener perception and a more enlightened colonial policy was to follow, but at that time public opinion registered disdain and apathy. Some, like the Dean of Gloucester, agitated for the relinquishment of all colonies on the ground that imperialism led to costly wars, entailed expensive administration and returned little if any profit to the nation. Develop the domestic market, so the argument ran, and increase the sale abroad of the superior and low-priced commodities produced by efficient English workmen and manufacturers. Others, like Adam Smith, endorsed the Dean's views, except for giving up the colonies. Smith advocated an extension of trade and political privileges which would create an empire of self-governing colonies. The emergence of this new colonial philosophy coincided with the eighteenth-century industrialization of England. Unfortunately little was accomplished toward creating a new order because of the advent of the French Revolution and the Napoleonic Wars. Britain's back was to the wall and there was neither time nor thought to be wasted upon untried theories and assumptions.

Further delay followed the return of peace in 1815. Foreign complications plus industrial and social difficulties at home demanded immediate attention, while the agitation for parliamentary reform captured the zeal of liberal opinion which otherwise might have been directed to colonial matters. Imperialists, moreover, received but little encouragement from the government's financial statements, which revealed the great expense of colonial administration and a steady decline in the national income from these possessions. Why bother about colonial expansion in view of the mounting costs and risks of war? Again, the economic losses, which critics had prophesied would follow American independence, had not taken place. Statistics proved that the United States bought British goods more freely than before and provided England with greater quantities of raw materials. Imperialists also had to admit that as long as England's colonies continued to be stocked by alien peoples and British convicts, Englishmen of the better type could not be persuaded to undertake colonization. Without an exodus of free British labor, little improvement could take place in the colonial world. The contemporary literature of the early decades of the nineteenth century abounds with expressions of this nature. Economists, political scientists, journalists, and statesmen showed but little interest in colonial and imperial expansion.

By 1830, however, a new attitude showed itself. The rapid increase in England's population, the growth of cities, the constant warfare between labor and capital, and the social abnormalities of the industrial revolution revived an interest in colonies. The migration of a surplus population to the plantations, so it was argued, would relieve the situation at home and develop markets of great value. Foremost among those who advocated an imperial program was Edward G. Wakefield, whose writings and speeches attracted the attention of men like Charles Buller, member of parliament, John Stuart Mill, one of England's greatest minds, George Grote, an eminent historian, and Jeremy Bentham, the utilitarian. The philosophy of these imperialists envisioned the migration of thousands of Englishmen to the plantations, the adoption of *laissez faire* in colonial trade and commerce, and the extension of political and social rights to the colonists. In the future, colonies were to be given local self-government and a respectable place in a greater British Empire. The experience in the Thirteen Colonies was at last bearing fruit.

At the close of the American Revolution the British Empire included British North America, certain sections of India, a few scattered trading posts in Africa, several small holdings in Central America, a number of islands in the West Indies and Atlantic Ocean, and Australia and New Zealand, which Captain James Cook had discovered in 1769 and 1770. Economic forces plus the conquests made by Britain during the French Revolution and the Napoleonic Wars increased the size of the empire. Approximately one fourth of India, as well as Ceylon and a number of islands in the Indian Ocean, was in British hands. In the Mediterranean, the important naval base of Malta had been acquired, while in Africa, Cape Colony had been won from the Dutch and a sphere of influence established in Egypt. Several new islands had been added in the Atlantic and Pacific Oceans, while British Guiana had been gained in South America. During the remainder of the nineteenth century and the first two decades of the twentieth century, additional territory was acquired in Africa, Asia, and in the Pacific and Atlantic areas. This imperial growth was caused in part by wars fought with native princes and rulers as well as by treaties with foreign states. The development of British authority in India illustrates the importance of these forces.

British Expansion in Asia and Africa

At the opening of the nineteenth century, English interests in India were handled chiefly by the East India Company. The parliamentary acts of 1813 and 1833, however, had transferred most of the governing powers enjoyed by the company to the British government. Later, in 1858, the Indian Act was passed, whereby all the remaining rights of the East India Company were forfeited to the Crown. In the meantime British authority was extended over large sections of the peninsula. Further gains were made during the years that followed, with the result that by 1914 more than one half of India was directly under English rule. Native princes control the remainder, which includes, however, but one fifth of the total population of the peninsula. The superior military and naval strength of England, plus the rapid penetration of British capital, largely explains English domination in India today.

England's active annexationist policy in the Near East and in India brought her into conflict with Russia. In 1854 England became involved in the Crimean War which was caused in part by Russian activity in Turkey and the Suez Canal area. Russia's defeat removed any immediate danger to the British trade routes through these areas but did not lessen the pressure upon India itself. By 1880 Russian imperialism had penetrated Persia and Afghanistan and was threatening British power in India. Although several irritating encounters occurred between the two in Afghanistan, into which British troops had advanced, war was avoided. Had Russia kept aloof from European politics, she might have offered stronger resistance. Her fear of a German war, however, moderated her Eastern policy and led to the Anglo-Russian agreement of 1907. Russia recognized British influence in Afghanistan on the understanding that England would not annex this native state and would allow Russian traders full rights in this area. By the same treaty, the two countries ironed out their differ-

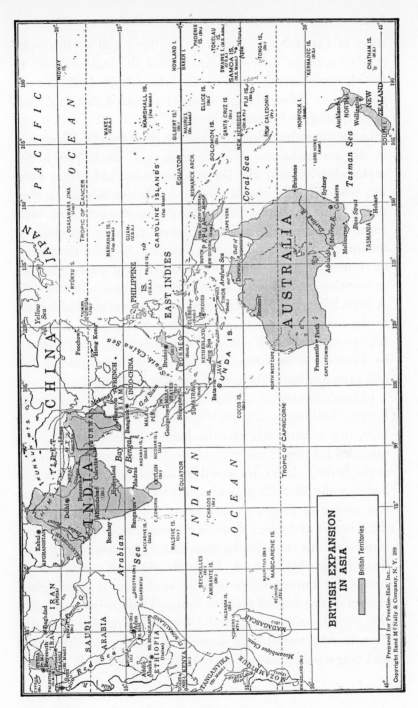

BRITISH EXPANSION
IN ASIA

British Territories

Prepared for Prentice-Hall, Inc.
Copyright Rand McNally & Company, N. Y. 289

ences in Persia by allocating the northern half of this independent state to Russian influence and the southern part to British exploitation. Both nations also admitted China's authority over Tibet, though Russia recognized Britain's paramount influence in that territory.

In the meantime Britain's holdings in Africa had increased in size and influence. This increase was due in part to the explorations of men like David Livingstone and Henry Stanley, who disclosed the heretofore hidden wealth of Darkest Africa and stimulated Englishmen to gain control of these resources. England's activities, however, were matched by the imperialist states of Western Europe. Between the powers there arose bitter disputes as to boundaries and prior rights and in one case nearly caused a war between France and England. A French expedition seized Fashoda, an important trading post in the Sudan, but a few weeks before the English arrived to take possession of the same. Fortunately, war was prevented by France's relinquishment of her claims in return for Britain's recognition of the former's power in Tunis.

Britain's interest in the Sudan arose out of her position in Egypt. Following Bonaparte's withdrawal from Egypt in 1799, that country fell into the hands of Mehemet Ali, who extended his power into the valley of the Upper Nile, known as the Sudan. Later, his grandson Ismail aided the French in building the Suez Canal, and secured from Turkey, the nominal owner of Egypt, recognition of his hereditary rights as the Khedive of Egypt. Ismail's extravagance and debts forced him to sell his stock in the Suez Canal Company to Disraeli, then Prime Minister of England. Disraeli's act was of paramount importance to Britain, as it secured for England control of the shortest route to India. Had Disraeli not taken this step, Ismail's shares would have been purchased by the French, who would have acquired a monopoly of the canal and thus would have endangered Britain's position in the Near and Far East. British public opinion applauded Disraeli and hailed him as a wise and far-sighted statesman.

Shortly thereafter Ismail created an Egyptian crisis by repudiating his debts. France, which claimed an interest in Egypt, immediately joined with Britain in seeking to protect Ismail's European creditors, and when this failed, induced the Sultan to depose Ismail in favor of his son, Tewfik. The latter's willingness to coöperate with France and England gave these powers an opportunity of establishing a dual control in 1880. Egyptian nationalism resented this alien domination and attempted to set up an Egyptian government of its own. At this juncture, France, because of political disturbances at home, dissolved its partnership with England, and the latter was left to deal with Egypt as it wished. By 1882 the Egyptian nationalists were defeated, Tewfik was restored to his throne, and England's control was made more secure. England announced that it had no intention of permanently occupying Egypt but for the time being would manage affairs so as to protect her investments and the Suez Canal. Lord Cromer was appointed British agent in Egypt and from 1884 to 1907 did much to advance England's influence. Numerous social and political reforms were undertaken, and in 1903 the Assouan Dam was completed. The Assouan Dam, located close to the Sudan, provided Egypt with a water supply which made possible the cultivation of thousands of acres of land.

British imperialism not only clashed with the interests of European governments but involved England in many a conflict with native populations. These disputes arose out of the natural desire of the natives to resist alien exploitation and domination. More significant, however, was England's interference with their social, political, and economic institutions. The stubborn resistance of the Sudanese, the Kafirs, and the Dutch settlers in South Africa illustrates the importance of these factors. In the case of the Sudanese, the situation was complicated by the expansionist policy of Egypt under Ismail. Thanks to the military skill of the English adventurer, Charles Gordon, Egyptian authority was maintained in the Sudan. When Ismail was deposed in 1879, however, the Sudanese rose in revolt, defeated an Egyptian army, and exterminated Gordon and his garrison at Khartoum. Following these disasters the Egyptian government, acting under British advice, retired from the Sudan. Later, this policy was reversed, and in 1896 the Khedive dispatched a large force under the future Lord Kitchener to conquer the Sudan, the control of which was necessary if Egypt was to have an adequate water supply. Kitchener did his job well. He defeated the Sudanese, notably at Omdurman in 1898, and restored the authority of the Khedive. The Sudan was placed under the joint control of Egypt and Great Britain, where it has remained ever since.

South African Problems

Britain's interest in Egypt was based fundamentally upon her control over the Suez Canal, which afforded an easy approach to India. At the opening of the nineteenth century, prior to the building of this canal, English traders to India had to sail around Africa, the southernmost part of which was a Dutch colony. Napoleon's annexation of the Netherlands in 1806 transformed the Dutch colony into a French possession. England's road to India, therefore, was endangered. In order to prevent the French from occupying this important possession, a British force was dispatched to South Africa. The conquest was an easy affair, and in 1814 the Congress of Vienna formally recognized England's authority in South Africa.

During the course of the next decade the British found colonization and expansion a difficult affair. In 1815 the population of Cape Colony was less than a hundred thousand, of which the greater share were Dutch, the remainder consisting of slaves, Negroes, and a few thousand Englishmen. The presence of a colored and enslaved group as well as the expense entailed in developing agriculture checked British migration, though by 1822, five thousand emigrants had settled at Port Elizabeth and Grahamstown. At the same time the British did little to understand the attitudes and aspirations of the Dutch, known as Boers, who resented English domination and the inroads of British colonists. To these troubles was added the problem of the Kafirs, a native tribe to the east of Grahamstown. Boundary disputes and border clashes led to a series of wars which taxed the resources of the local British population and caused the home authorities much trouble. By 1835 the English colonists had defeated the Kafirs and established a new boundary further to the east. The British government, however, refused to honor this arrangement and restored the conquered land to the Kafirs.

The Cape Colony authorities were amazed at this action, while the Boers interpreted it as a sign of weakness and sentimentality toward the blacks. Further irritation arose when London granted to the Hottentots, the Negroes within the colony, what amounted to legal equality with the whites. The British colonists approved of this humanitarian step; but the Boers, who looked upon the black man as the American had upon the Indian, were disgusted. In 1833, slavery was abolished over the protests of the Boers, who received but small compensation for their losses. As a result, the Boers migrated across the Orange River and by 1840 had wrested from the natives an area later known as the Orange Free State. Hardly had they settled in their new home when trouble developed between them and Cape Colony. The latter accused the Boers of harboring runaway criminals and of provoking the natives to the northwest. The Cape Colony authorities solved the problem by seizing the Boer territory. Immediately, many of the Boers crossed the Vaal River and formed a new state known as Transvaal. The English, however, soon discovered the difficulty of preserving order in the Orange River area, and, in 1852 and 1854, by two conventions with the Boers, accorded independence to the latter in the Orange Free State and Transvaal.

In the meantime Cape Colony had increased in size by the annexation of the Kafir territory, Basutoland and Griqualand. A British colony, moreover, was established in Natal. The discovery of diamonds in Griqualand in 1871 led to an influx of miners and investors, many of whom penetrated the adjoining Orange Free State. The Boers resented this infiltration and joined with the Transvaal authorities in defeating the troops which Cape Colony had dispatched to protect the English within their territory. Peace was restored by the Pretoria Convention of 1881, which practically admitted the independence of the Orange Free State. Further concessions were granted in 1884, at which time the British recognized the South African Republic, the new name for Transvaal. The success of the Boers stimulated their fellow countrymen throughout South Africa to agitate for federation. An organization, the Afrikander Bond, ultranationalistic in nature, was formed to achieve this end and to restrict British influence in the future.

While this movement was getting under way, gold was discovered in Transvaal. Immediately there was a "rush" to these gold fields, which converted a pastoral community into a rich and prosperous mining area. The Boers were delighted but resented the rapid influx of emigrants from Cape Colony and Natal. The ancient grudge between the Boer and Englishman flared up on many occasions. Had the latter been less aggressive and domineering, and had the Boer been more generous in his treatment of English settlers, a compromise might have been effected. As it was, the Boers insulted the English by calling them Uitlanders and by adopting measures which restricted the political and economic rights of the latter. Failing to secure any concessions from the Boers, the British settlers

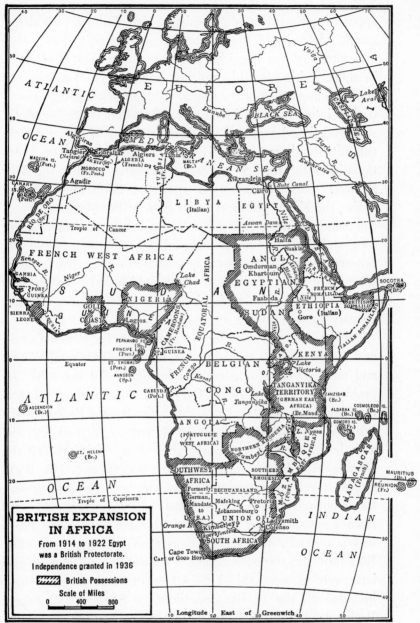

**BRITISH EXPANSION
IN AFRICA**

From 1914 to 1922 Egypt
was a British Protectorate.
Independence granted in 1936

///// British Possessions

Scale of Miles

0   400   800

Prepared for Prentice-Hall, Inc.

Copyright Rand McNally & Company, N. Y. 289

629

appealed to Cecil Rhodes, premier of Cape Colony. Rhodes, a staunch defender of British nationalism, agreed to lend assistance provided the English in Transvaal precipitated a revolt. Without waiting for this uprising, however, Dr. Jameson, the commanding officer of the military intended for the expedition, dashed into Transvaal in January, 1895. The Boers promptly surrounded and captured Jameson's entire force. The net result of this ill-conceived affair was an inflation of Dutch nationalism and further repressive measures against the Uitlanders. Germany showered upon the Boers approval and praise, the Kaiser going so far as to wire President Kruger of the South African Republic, "I express to you my sincere congratulations that without appealing to the help of friendly powers you and your people have succeeded in repelling with your own forces the armed bands which have broken into your country and in maintaining the independence of your country against foreign aggression."

Britain promptly disavowed responsibility for Jameson's raid and forced Rhodes to resign his office at Capetown. These and other gestures of good will eased but did not solve the problem in South Africa. The Boers continued to mistreat the Uitlanders, and the latter kept agitating for English intervention. By the summer of 1899, matters reached a crisis; and the South African Republic, which by then included the Orange Free State, precipitated the Boer War. The Boers gained several important initial victories over the Cape Colony forces but ultimately were defeated upon the arrival of troops from England under Lords Roberts and Kitchener. Peace was restored by the Treaty of Pretoria in May, 1902. The Boer provinces were placed under control of Cape Colony and later were incorporated in the Union of South Africa, which included all the British possessions in South Africa except Bechuanaland and Swaziland. Since 1902 the Dutch population has adjusted and integrated itself satisfactorily. Many prominent Boers have been active in the government.

Difficulties in India and Australia

British inability to appreciate or understand the attitudes and *mores* of native populations also caused considerable trouble in India. Moreover, the rapid extension of British power and the subsequent changes which took place in India's political, economic, and social structure fostered native dissension and revolt. England's interference with the religious practices of the Indians, such as the custom of burning the widow at the funeral of a husband, aroused considerable trouble. Finally, in 1857 the pent-up opposition burst forth in what is known as the Sepoy Mutiny. Cartridges greased with the fat of cows and pigs touched the religious sensibilities of the Hindu and Mohammedan soldiers employed by the British in India. The former considered the cow as a sacred animal while the latter viewed the pig as unclean. As a result, a number of these soldiers, known as Sepoys, mutinied in May, 1857. All India was inflamed and rose against British authority. By the middle of the next year the rebellion was put down, though the native opposition to English practices continued throughout the remainder of the century.

Britain also experienced some trouble with the native tribes in Australia, where British control and settlement advanced rapidly. Before the end of the eighteenth century, a colony had been planted on the site of the modern city of Sydney, and the area known as New South Wales had been explored. Coal was discovered here about the same time, while by 1825 large herds of sheep imported from Spain grazed upon the fertile lands of the interior. The island of Tasmania, to the south of New South Wales, was settled in 1804. Abundant pasture land led to sheep raising, there being nearly two hundred thousand sheep as early as 1821. Queensland was occupied in 1826, as was Victoria in 1830, while Western and South Australia were opened about the same time. The subsequent discovery of gold and copper in these areas did much to promote the early development of these colonies. Later, thanks to the efforts of Wakefield, six separate colonies were planted in New Zealand.

Except in New Zealand, the bulk of the colonists were British convicts. Between the prisoners and the free settlers considerable trouble arose, while the presence of convicts did much to discourage English migration. The British authorities in these colonies recognized this difficulty and endorsed the petition of the free inhabitants for the abolition of convict settlers. With the elimination of this practice in 1868 and the gradual emancipation of those convicts already there (each convict usually became free after seven years), Australia rapidly increased in value.

Canadian Problems

In the meantime Britain experienced some difficulty in administering Canada. It will be recalled that in 1791 parliament divided Canada into the provinces of Upper and Lower Canada, each having a Council and an Assembly. The Council was an unrepresentative body appointed by and responsible to the king, while the Assembly, which possessed but limited powers, was elected by property owners. Finally, there was a governor from England. In both provinces, trouble arose between the Council and Assembly. Religious differences caused additional annoyance, as did the war with the United States in 1812. More significant, however, was the dispute in Lower Canada between the French and English colonists over the disposition of public funds and the rights of the French population. By 1834 the French, under the leadership of Papineau, refused to vote supplies until the Assembly was given complete control over finances, and the Council was made an elective body. In Upper Canada, William Mackenzie of Toronto championed similar demands and agitated in behalf of the Protestant groups whose rights had been subordinated to the Roman and Anglican communions by the Act of 1791. Neither Mackenzie nor Papineau was able to move the Councils or influence the Mother Country in their cause, and as a result they resorted to force. Papineau failed to enlist the support of the French settlers, who were restrained by their local priests, while Mackenzie was forced to flee to the United States.

By this time the British government had become aware of the seriousness of the situation, and after suspending the constitution of Lower Canada in 1838, it sent Lord Durham to investigate conditions in both provinces. Durham was a Whig of liberal tendencies and had accepted the colonial views advocated by Wakefield, Buller, and Mill. As a result of his background and his examination of Canadian conditions, Durham recommended a union of the two provinces and the establishment of responsible government. In 1840, parliament united Upper and Lower Canada under a new constitution. The assembly, whose membership was divided evenly between the two former provinces, was to be elected; the governor and council were to be appointed by the Crown.

Responsible government was not given to Canada by this act, but the wise administration of Lord Elgin finally established the principle that ministers should be chosen by the majority party. Racial and religious differences were smoothed over, while economic conditions were improved by the repeal of the Navigation Acts and a commercial treaty with the United States. Conditions in the Maritime Provinces (Prince Edward Island, Nova Scotia, and New Brunswick), which were not subject to the Act of 1840, also showed decided improvement. By 1860 a group of leaders throughout Canada and the Maritime Provinces favored a revision of the Act of 1840. They placed their ideas, which called for confederation and the establishment of responsible government, before Lord Monck, who recognized the merits of the proposals and summoned a conference to meet at Quebec in October, 1864. Representatives from Canada and the Maritime Provinces drafted resolutions which were to become the basis of a new constitution. Shortly thereafter, a committee visited London and secured the passage of the British North America Act of 1867. According to this measure the present provinces of Quebec, Ontario, Nova Scotia, and New Brunswick were formed into the Dominion of Canada. Provision was made for the admission of Prince Edward Island, Newfoundland, and the territories to the west and northwest of Ontario. By 1905 all of Canada proper, except the Yukon, the Northwest Territories, and Newfoundland, were included as provinces within the Dominion of Canada. The Yukon and Northwest Territories were subject to the authority of the Dominion, but Newfoundland remains apart to this day. In 1885 Newfoundland was given a dominion status of its own.

The government of the Dominion of Canada, as set forth in the Act of 1867, provided for a Governor-General appointed by the king and possessed of a theoretical veto power over the acts of the legislature, which included a Senate and a House of Commons. The Senate, endowed with limited powers, was composed of members appointed by the government of the Dominion. The House of Commons was an elected body, with seats allocated to the provinces in respect to population, and was given the same general powers as enjoyed by the Commons in England. The ministry was made responsible to the House of Commons, whose majority leader was to be known as the Prime Minister. Each province was to have a Lieutenant-Governor appointed by the Governor-General, in fact by the Dominion Government, and a ministry responsible to a popularly elected assembly. All the provinces adopted unicameral legislatures except Nova Scotia and Quebec, which retained the traditional upper and lower house. The Act of 1867 also defined the distribution of powers between the Provincial and Dominion Governments.

The passage of the Act of 1867, which reflected the English

parliamentary and cabinet system, was a significant event in the annals of British history, although it attracted little attention in England at the time. It marked the complete abandonment of the Old Colonial System of government and afforded Canada local self-government and a respectable place in a greater British Empire. The lesson of the American Revolution had not been forgotten; and the imperial program, as advocated by Wakefield, Grote, Mill, Durham, and others, formed the basis upon which a New Colonial System was built. Not only did the Act of 1867 stimulate the political and economic development of Canada, but it served also as an incentive for the passage of similar measures for Australia, New Zealand, and South Africa.

Political Reform in Australia and New Zealand

During the first half of the nineteenth century, the various Australian colonies were governed by a British military governor, who, in New South Wales, was assisted by a local council chosen in part by the colonists. The rapid economic development of these colonies and the separation of Victoria from New South Wales in 1850 argued for more local self-government, and in 1850 the British parliament passed the Australian Colonies Act. Victoria, New South Wales, South Australia, and Tasmania were given local assemblies with power to determine the franchise, revenue, and customs. Provision was made also for the adoption of local constitutions, which by 1855 were in force in all the colonies. Later, in 1859, Queensland, which heretofore had been governed by New South Wales, was given a constitution of its own. In 1890 a similar concession was granted to Western Australia.

The Act of 1850, moreover, provided for the future federation of the colonies. Not until 1880, however, was there any sentiment favorable to federation. By this time each of the colonies had come to see the advantages of unification. The existence of a number of problems common to each, as well as the presence of a potential enemy in the German settlement in New Guinea, stimulated an active interest in federation. As a result, representatives of the colonies gathered in 1880 and 1883 and endorsed the federal idea. Overtures were made to England, which wisely permitted the establishment of a Federal Council. The Council, however, lacked power and never had the unanimous support of the colonies, though it continued to meet every two years. General dissatisfaction with this arrangement led to further discussion and conferences. Finally, in 1899 a federal constitution was submitted to each of the colonies for adoption. With the exception of Western Australia every colony voted for the new arrangement, which was approved by Britain in 1900, and on January 1, 1901, the Commonwealth of Australia came into being. The government of this dominion consisted of a Senate and a House of Representatives, both chosen in much the same manner as in the United States. Unlike America, however, Australia does not have a president. The executive power is lodged in a cabinet chosen by the majority party in the House of Representatives. The Senate, moreover, may not thwart the will of the Representatives. Any measure which has been vetoed by the upper house three times may become law if it gains a majority vote of the two houses meeting jointly. All questions of constitutionality are settled by a supreme court.

The new government worked reasonably well and was soon joined by Western Australia. Northern Australia was governed by the Commonwealth until 1911, when it was given territorial status and some degree of local self-government. Like Canada, the Commonwealth of Australia has a Governor-General, appointed by the king, and local administrative and legislative bodies for each of the states of the Dominion. New Zealand is not a member of this federation, though its political growth paralleled that of Australia. Representative government was accorded the colonies in New Zealand in 1852, and in 1907 parliament created the Dominion of New Zealand. Both countries have been extremely liberal in government. In 1879, for example, New Zealand approved of universal manhood suffrage, and in 1893 gave the vote to women. Labor governments have predominated in both states, but at no time have they or their people lost the feeling of attachment to England. During the World War and after, Australians and New Zealanders have coöperated in promoting the union of the British Empire.

Political Growth in South Africa and in the Crown Colonies

Dominion status was also given to South Africa. By 1853 the colony at Capetown had been given representative government. In the same year Natal received the same privilege, and in 1872 Cape Colony was accorded responsible government. Following the Boer War and the annexation of the South African Republic, which secured legislative independence by 1906, local opinion throughout South Africa agitated for dominion status. England granted this request in the fall of 1909 and established the Union of South Africa. British interests were to be protected by a Governor-General, while a local legislature was placed in charge of South African affairs. An executive cabinet was made responsible to this legislature, which consisted of a Senate, appointed jointly by the Governor-General and the provincial assemblies, and a House of Representatives elected by popular vote. The wisdom of granting responsible government was shown by the loyal support which South Africa gave Britain during the World War.

In addition to the Dominions, the British Empire overseas included by 1914, India, the Crown colonies, and the protectorates. The Crown colonies, consisting of such possessions as Malta, Gibraltar, Ceylon, the British West Indies, and St. Helena, varied as to the nature of their governments but were alike in that they did not have responsible government. They may be defined as holdings of the Crown, and are subject to the authority of parliament, a Secretary of State for the Colonies, and a local Crown appointee. Assisting the latter is a council which, though appointed by the Crown, usually consists of residents of the colony. In a few cases, such as the Barbados, there is also a bicameral legislature, the lower house being elected by the qualified voters of the colony. In the case of Jamaica and a few others, the lower house is partially appointed and partially elected. In Gibraltar, military reasons explain why the British governor assumes entire control.

Many differences in government also exist among the protectorates, which are subject to the Crown, parliament, and a governor. All acts of parliament relative to colonial affairs are applicable to the Crown colonies but not to the protectorates, for which special legislation is necessary. As the name implies, a protectorate represents a loose form of connection between a conquered area and England. Native rulers were more willing to accept British protection and government by an agreement which classified their states as protectorates, than by an act of parliament which annexed territory out and out. England, moreover, preferred this arrangement, as it allowed her to abandon such an area when pressed by the claims of foreign states. Annexed territory on the other hand, perhaps could not be surrendered without an act of parliament. The local administration of a protectorate is lodged in a governor who may be assisted, as in Uganda, by a council and an assembly. In the case of the Federated Malay States, authority is placed in the hands of a High Commission; while in certain other protectorates the resident British official merely advises the native rulers.

British naval and military resources as well as skill in commercial, industrial, and financial activities were important factors in the development and unification of the Empire. More significant was the extension of political rights to the dependencies, colonies, and dominions. Since the American Revolution, England has lost no possession of any size or value in spite of native uprisings and foreign wars. Before that event and prior to 1830, Britain viewed its colonies from a narrow and selfish point of view. Colonies enhanced the national ego and were exploited in the interest of land speculators, capitalists, traders, and imperialists. Humanitarian forces, though present, played but a small rôle in a colonial policy which rested upon the theory that colonies existed for the profit of the Mother Country. Although England granted greater political freedom to her eighteenth-century empire than other states, these concessions did not run counter to the accepted principles of mercantilism. The American Revolution, however, taught British statesmen a lesson which gradually became the cardinal factor in the New Colonial System of the nineteenth and twentieth centuries. In the future, colonies were to be viewed as an integral part of a British world and were to be endowed with the rights and privileges of English law. The colonies, therefore, became active partners in a common cause. England, indeed, became the Mother of a parliamentary and representative system which was carried to all parts of the world. Democracy, Britain's greatest contribution to government, transformed a disjointed and loosely knit colonial world into the proud and powerful British Empire of 1937.

In 1811, a writer in the *Quarterly Review* stated that the "sun in its daily course never sets upon Englishmen." British imperialism of the nineteenth and twentieth centuries demonstrated the truth of this proud boast. Thousands upon thousands of square miles, brilliantly colored red in the modern atlas, were acquired by discovery, exploration, and conquest. Alien peoples, ranging from civilized Europeans to the wild tribes of Borneo and New Zealand, came under the domination of England. Valuable trade routes and naval stations were established, and investments of millions were made by British traders and capitalists. Imperialism, however, brought trials and tribulations. Numerous contests, such as the Kafir and Indian Wars, were fought to protect these investments and maintain British power and influence. More significant were the conflicts with Russia in the Crimea and with Germany in 1914. English life and treasure have been spent in generous quantities to retain this empire. The total income derived by the British government from the empire is considerably below the cost involved. On the other hand, British culture and democracy have been carried to all parts of the world. Possibly these social and spiritual values, enjoyed by millions of people, will prove to be greater assets than trade and commerce. The union of English-speaking peoples represents a remarkable achievement in democracy and in preserving the peace of the world.

SELECTED BIBLIOGRAPHY

Howard Robinson's *The Development of the British Empire* (New York, 1936) is by far the best single study of English expansion overseas. H. E. Egerton's *Short History of British Colonial Policy* (London, 1913); C. H. Currey's *British Colonial Policy, 1783–1915* (Oxford, 1916); A. J. Herbertson's *The Oxford Survey of the British Empire* (Oxford, 1914); E. Jenk's *The Government of the British Empire* (Boston, 1918); A. B. Keith's *Responsible Government in the Dominions* (Oxford, 1912), and R. Jebb's *Studies in Colonial Nationalism* (London, 1905) are standard works.

For India, the following provide detailed information: P. E. Robinson's *History of India under the Government of the Crown* (Oxford, 1920); J. Chailley's *Administrative Problems of British India* (London, 1910); V. Chirol's *India* (New York, 1926); Lord Curzon's *British Government in India* (London, 1925), and W. W. Hunter's *Marquess of Dalhousie* (Oxford, 1895). Canadian affairs are handled by C. Wittke's *History of Canada* (New York, 1933); H. E. Egerton's *Canada under British Rule* (Oxford, 1917); J. L. Morrison's *British Supremacy and Canadian Self-Government* (Glasgow, 1919); G. Smith's *Canada and the Canadian Question* (New York, 1918); E. Porritt's *Evolution of the Dominion of Canada* (New York, 1918), and D. W. Prowse's *History of Newfoundland* (London, 1896).

South Africa, Egypt, Sudan, and Africa in general are treated in C. Hallberg's *Suez Canal* (New York, 1931), Lord Milner's *England in Egypt* (London, 1892), Lord Cromer's *Modern Egypt* (New York,

1916), E. Sanderson's *Great Britain in Modern Africa* (London, 1907), H. H. Johnstone's *History of the Colonization of Africa* (Cambridge, 1913), J. S. Keltie's *Partition of Africa* (London, 1895), H. C. Thomson's *Rhodesia* (London, 1898), C. Eliot's *The East African Protectorate* (London, 1895), W. J. Leyd's *The Transvaal Surrounded* (London, 1919), W. S. Blunt's *Secret History of the English Occupation of Egypt* (London, 1907), and P. F. Martin's *Sudan in Evolution* (London, 1921).

For the Crown Colonies and protectorates see W. J. Gardener's *History of Jamaica* (New York, 1909); A. W. Tilby's *Britain in the Tropics* (London, 1912); H. Johnston's *Uganda Protectorate* (New York, 1902); E. D. Morel's *Nigeria* (London, 1911); V. F. Boyson's *Falkland Islands* (Oxford, 1924); S. Baring-Gould's *History of Sarawak* (London, 1909), and G. H. Scholefield's *The Pacific, Its Past and Future* (London, 1919).

CHAPTER XXXIII

Foreign Affairs, 1815-1901

THE French Revolution and Napoleonic Wars had drenched Europe with blood and had burdened governments and peoples with exorbitant taxes and debts. On the other hand, the spirit and ideals of the Revolution—liberty, equality, and fraternity—had been carried far and wide. France indoctrinated European peoples with these ideas. She exalted, as no country had before, the concepts of nationalism and self-determination. Fearful as European monarchs were of the imperial armies of France, they trembled as these ideas silently invaded their domains. They felt reasonably certain that the military strength of a combined Europe might defeat Bonaparte in time, but would these alien philosophies, so dangerous to divine right monarchies, be stamped out once Europe was rid of Napoleon? The first and more immediate problem had been to defeat the Emperor. By 1815 Napoleon was on the rock-bound island of St. Helena and the victors gathered at Vienna to divide the spoils.

Reaction and Repression

At this notable gathering every important and unimportant Continental king and prince was present. England was represented by Lord Castlereagh. Even defeated France had its agent in Talleyrand, Bonaparte's onetime minister of foreign affairs. On the other hand the laboring classes of Europe, whose lives and fortunes had made Waterloo possible, were not represented, and not a single voice was raised in their behalf. Thinking only of themselves, the members of the Congress endorsed the general principle of legitimacy, whereby most of the French conquests were returned to their former rulers. The map of Europe was remade, with the lion's share going to Austria, Prussia, and Russia. European peoples were traded by these self-interested rulers, regardless of national feelings and desires.

More significant than these territorial changes, which the Prussian Blücher described as a cattle fair, was the defiance of the principle of nationality and the establishment of a policy of reaction and repression. The Congress did not outline any general formula but expressed itself through the individual actions of its members on their return home. Europe was to be a safe place for kings and emperors; there was to be no more preaching and talking about the rights of man. Representative government, in so far as Europe was concerned, was abolished; and those who advocated forbidden and heretical reforms were silenced by imprisonment or death. The arch protagonist of the new order was Metternich, the Austrian minister, who hated revolutionary equalitarianism and viewed it as "gangrene which must be burned out by the hot iron." He pledged his country to the idea of political immobility and conservatism, unmindful that the common folk could not forget the concepts of liberty which the French armies had spread throughout Austria. Russia and Prussia endorsed Metternich's ideas of reaction and repression, as did many of the smaller states. England accepted them in principle but never sought to force them upon her nationals as did European monarchs. England was not a party to the Holy Alliance, that piece of "sublime mysticism and nonsense," advanced by Alexander of Russia shortly after the Congress of Vienna. Practically every other European state joined this "brotherhood" of nations and pledged itself to work for universal peace.

Metternich called the Alliance a "sonorous nothing" and accepted it only because he thought it wise to humor Alexander. The Holy Alliance accomplished nothing and was a dead issue before the year 1815 was over. The Quadruple Alliance signed in November, 1815, by Russia, Prussia, Austria, and Britain had entirely different results. According to this agreement the contracting parties agreed to intervene in the event of another revolution which might upset the peace of Europe. Frequent meetings of the Alliance were to be held, and at these gatherings plans were to be discussed for meeting any European uprising. The Quadruple Alliance, therefore, and not the Holy Alliance, became the armed machine through which reaction, repression, and immobility were to be preserved in Europe. England interpreted her obligations somewhat differently from her allies. Existing sovereign and territorial rights, as defined by the Treaties of Vienna, were to be maintained. Wars of aggression between European states were to be prevented, but at no time would England interfere in the domestic and internal affairs of another country. Castlereagh made known England's position at the Congress of Aix-la-Chapelle in 1818, much to the disappointment of Austria and Prussia, who wanted joint action against liberal and revolutionary societies in central Europe.

In 1820 Europe experienced a series of popular revolts in Spain, Naples, and the Piedmont area of Italy. Continued oppression on the part of the rulers had led to criticism, dissension, and ultimately to revolution. Metternich immediately summoned the members of the Quadruple Alliance to meet him first at Troppau and again at Laibach and Verona. Metternich so completely dominated these gatherings that he gained from Russia and Prussia their consent to armed intervention. Armed forces sent into these troubled areas destroyed the revolution and restored absolutism. England's rôle at these conferences was not so clear or decisive as domestic opinion desired. In order to quiet hostile criticism at home, the British agents talked loudly against intervention. Privately, however, Metternich was given to understand that England would not stand in his way.

Having placed the Spanish Bourbons back in power, the Alliance was asked to assist Spain in a war to recover her lost colonies in the New World. A series of revolutions had taken place in these possessions as early as 1810, when Spanish authorities had been driven out and independent states established. Immediately, English and American traders made capital out of the situation and established valuable trade connections. Political considerations also explain why these two countries recognized the independence of the South American republics. Neither England nor America desired an extension of Spanish power in the New World. Spain's demand, therefore, that her colonies be restored was a challenge to the existing political and economic order which had developed since 1810. Canning, the British foreign minister, invited the United States to join in resisting European aggression, but President Monroe wisely declined the offer. Acting upon the advice of John Q. Adams, the President firmly informed Europe, in the famous Monroe Doctrine, that the United States would consider any step to change the *status quo* in the New World as an unfriendly act. Britain, in the meantime, had told the Alliance that the English fleet would be used against any aggressor. As a result, Spain had to abandon its plans of conquest and the Quadruple Alliance was forced to beat a hasty retreat.

Europe, moreover, had troubles of its own. In 1821 the Greeks, who had been subject to Turkish domination for a long time, rose in revolt. British sympathy was entirely with the Greeks, though Austria saw no reason for intervention. Russia, on the other hand, was anxious to aid the revolutionists, unmindful of the rôle she had played in suppressing liberal movements elsewhere in Europe. Russia wanted to drive Turkey out of Europe, dominate the Black Sea, control Constantinople, and play a major rôle in Mediterranean affairs. England, however, had no desire to allow a Russian fleet to patrol Near Eastern waters or to endanger British trade routes to India. Accordingly, after recognizing the Greeks as belligerents in 1823, England tried to induce Turkey to grant concessions to the revolutionists. The Sultan spurned these suggestions and induced the Pasha of Egypt to send an army under his son Ibrahim to stamp out the Greek rebellion.

Ibrahim performed his task in true military style and by 1826 had scattered the revolutionists. In the meantime horrible tales of brutality and persecution reached Europe, and hundreds of individuals volunteered for service in the Near East. Others formed themselves into Hellenic societies and raised huge sums to aid the Greeks. Ibrahim's continued success brought England to the point of armed intervention. France was moved to lend her support, and in 1827 a conference between representatives of Russia, France and England demanded that Turkey should concede local self-government to the Greeks. The Sultan refused, and war followed. Within two years the Turks were defeated; and in September, 1829, Greece was accorded complete independence by the Treaty of Adrianople.

Metternich had taken little interest in the affair but became considerably alarmed over the spread of liberalism in France, Belgium, Germany, Poland, and Italy. During the early summer of 1830, a middle class uprising swept Charles X out of France and placed upon the throne Louis Philippe of the Orleanist house. England recognized the new government at once, believing that Louis would be more friendly to Britain than the exiled king. Metternich, checked by England's action, was forced to recognize Louis Philippe. The success of the French revolutionists was felt immediately in Belgium, which since 1815 had been an integral part of the Kingdom of the Netherlands. Street riots in August were followed by armed rebellion against the Dutch authorities. When Wellington heard of the withdrawal of Dutch troops from Brussels he remarked, "it is a devilish bad business, the most serious affair for Europe that could have arisen." A successful revolution was bound to bring Belgium close to France and might lead the latter to annex Belgium, which was largely Catholic and pro-French. With France dominating the Lowlands and in control of the navigation of the Scheldt, England's position was endangered as it had been in 1792. Anxious to prevent a general European war, England summoned a congress of the leading powers and secured their consent to the establishment of an independent Belgium kingdom. Leopold of Saxe-Coburg was offered the throne, and in 1832 the present Belgium monarchy was formally installed.

Chinese, Crimean, and Italian Problems

During the following fourteen years, Britain had little to worry over in so far as Europe was concerned, nor was she greatly concerned over a war with Afghanistan concerning Indian affairs. Trouble, however, did arise in China. The British trade to China prior to 1833 was in the hands of the East India Company, which transacted its business through a gild of Chinese merchants of Canton. The Peking government put no restriction upon the East India merchants except a prohibition on opium imports. A licensed trade, however, was permitted through Canton. In 1833 parliament abolished the East India's trading monopoly and opened the Chinese trade to all English merchants. China refused to deal with the latter, insisting that all commerce should be conducted through the Canton merchants as before. Britain tried to negotiate directly with Peking, hoping to establish ordinary diplomatic relations and thus to abolish the older method of dealing through the East India Company and the Canton gild. China rebuffed several British agents and used military force to stop the illegal importation of opium. England's pride was touched to the quick, and a British fleet opened hostilities in 1840. China was no match for England, and by the Treaty of Nankin, August, 1842, permitted British traders free access to Canton, Shanghai, and three other ports. Hong-Kong was ceded to England, and an indemnity was given to those British traders whose opium had been destroyed by the Chinese. In the light of available evidence, it would seem that England's motives for the Chinese War were based upon the opium trade.

During 1842 England ironed out a prolonged dispute with the United States over the Northeastern Boundary. The Ashburton Treaty settled this matter, which for a time had prompted the inhabitants of Maine to use force to defend their rights in the Aroostook area. Fortunately, Webster and Ashburton, the British minister to the United States, made mutual concessions. Ashburton was also called upon to handle the more difficult problem of the Oregon boundary. Both England and America claimed this area on the basis of discovery, settlement, trading posts and treaty rights. In 1818 the two countries had agreed to a joint occupation of the Oregon area and to an extension of the 49° parallel as the boundary line between United States and Canada, from the Lake of the Woods to the Rocky Mountains. The arrangement in so far as Oregon was concerned proved unsatisfactory and led to increased friction between England and America. By 1845 it looked as though the jingoists might force a war. Peace societies in both countries conducted an active campaign against a war, while Ashburton patiently sought a diplomatic settlement. Finally, in 1846, it was agreed to extend the boundary of 49° to Vancouver Sound and from there along the middle of the channel to the ocean. The navigation of the Columbia River was opened to both nations.

In view of the alarming situation which had developed in the Near East, England was pleased to have the Oregon question settled. The trouble started over the religious question as to whether the Greek or Roman Catholic Churches should have control over the Holy Places in Palestine. France, under Louis Napoleon, nephew of the former emperor, supported the Roman cause on the basis of an agreement with Turkey in 1740. By this treaty France had been given the custody of the Holy Places but since the French Revolution had exercised no control at all. Russia then stepped in and advanced the influence of the Greek Church. No one questioned Russia's action until the middle of the nineteenth century, when a religious revival in Western Europe induced France to assume its rightful power under the treaty of 1740. Anxious to consolidate his position at home, Louis Napoleon championed the Roman cause, while Nicholas of Russia defended the Greek position. The Sultan, not wishing to offend either party, proposed a compromise, but neither France nor Russia accepted it.

By this time, Nicholas was determined to settle the Near Eastern problem once and for all. Nothing would have pleased the Czar more than to extend his empire over the entire Turkish domain, which seemed on the point of breaking. England, of course, would resist; but possibly Britain, so Nicholas argued, might be willing to share in the spoils. Overtures of this nature were made in 1844 and 1853, but the British foreign office offered no encouragement. The storm center, however, suddenly shifted from London and St. Petersburg to Constantinople, where the respective agents of both nations had created a crisis. Lord Stratford emphatically refused to consider Menshikov's proposal that Russia be given a guardianship over Greek Christians in Turkey. Stratford knew that such a concession was equal to recognizing Russian domination over Turkey. Menshikov, however, would not take no for an answer, and he embodied this demand in the form of an ultimatum to Turkey. The Sultan, accepting Stratford's advice, rejected Russia's proposal, and late in October, 1853, Russia and Turkey were at war. England might have remained neutral but for the fact that a Russian victory would endanger her position in the Near East and India. Accordingly, England made a pact with France and Piedmont, and on March 28, 1854, the three states declared war on Russia. England entered the war to prevent Russia from gaining control of Constantinople and to protect the trade routes of her merchants. France hoped to unite her people under Louis Napoleon, who in 1852 had become Emperor. Piedmont hoped to use the war as a means of attracting Europe's attention to Austrian policy in Italy.

The Crimean War, as this contest was called, lasted until March, 1856, and was characterized by several important military and naval encounters and by costly blunders on the part of both commands. England equipped its infantry with muskets made in the Napoleonic period, forgot to supply others with knapsacks, clothing, and medical supplies, was tardy in providing decent shelter or hospital facilities, and allowed its transport department to fall almost to pieces. Considerable waste in life and treasure followed, the greater share of which might have been saved had there been intelligent leadership and management. The only bright light in the dreadful carnage which took place was the humane activity of Florence Nightingale and an understaffed group of nurses and doctors. By March, 1856 both sides were ready to talk peace. Prussia and Austria were invited to join the belligerents at Paris. The Conference finally agreed to the following, known as the Peace of Paris: mutual restoration of conquered territory, recognition and European guarantee of Turkey's independence, closure of the Black Sea and the Dardanelles to warships, and adequate protection for Christians in the Sultan's domains. The Conference also adopted the Declaration of Paris, which provided that blockades to be effective must be binding, that the neutral flag protected enemy's goods except for contraband, that neutral goods, except contraband, were not subject to capture under either neutral or enemy flag, and that privateering was to be abolished.

What had England gained from the war? In the first place, Russian designs upon Turkey and the Near East were frustrated, and an opportunity was afforded for England to bolster its influence in Greece and the Mediterranean. At the outset of the war, the British national debt amounted to roughly $3,375,000,000, which was larger than the combined debts of all Europe, while at the close it had risen approximately another billion. Future generations had to meet this charge, which would have been much more burdensome but for the government's determination to make that age pay for most of the war. No reliable estimate exists for the loss of life, though modern research has placed deaths from all causes at the huge figure of 600,000, of which about 25,000 were English. For every Englishman who died from wounds, four died from sickness. England quickly forgot these losses in the tremendous increase which followed in trade and industry. This prosperity was unchecked by continued disturbances in Afghanistan, another Chinese war in 1857, and a serious uprising in India.

In 1859 England's attention was turned toward Italy, where a war had broken out between the Austrian government and the Kingdom of Sardinia. Sardinia, or Piedmont as it was also called, had been allowed to raise the Italian question at the Conference at Paris in 1856. At this gathering, Cavour, the Sardinian representative, briefly but cautiously charged Austria, the "arch-enemy of Italian independence," with responsibility for the turmoil in Italy. Cavour returned home without having secured more than a hearing before the great powers, but his indictment of Austria attracted the attention of all Europe. The British foreign office recognized the seriousness of the situation, particularly as Louis Napoleon appeared inclined to offer military assistance to Sardinia. A Franco-Sardinian alliance threatened both the peace of Italy and Europe, and the Treaties of 1815. A scrapping of these treaties would enhance Napoleon's prestige in France, which

smarted under the sting and disgrace of 1815, and might lead
to another Napoleonic Empire in Europe. At the same time
the British government realized that the Austrian policy of
reaction and repression had produced maladministration in
Italy from the Alps to the Mediterranean. Good government
existed only in Sardinia, from which a steady stream of liberal
thought and propaganda flowed through the peninsula. England, therefore, hoped to avert war by influencing a liberal
program in Italy and by insisting upon the maintenance of
the Treaties of 1815.

In the meantime Cavour continued to court Louis Napoleon.
In July, 1858, these two met at Plombières, a spa in the Vosges
mountains, and agreed upon joint military action in case
Austria were to attack Sardinia. In return for this aid, France
was to receive Savoy and possibly Nice. By January of the
new year both France and Sardinia had intimated that they
intended to provoke a war, while Austria seemed not unwilling
to accept the challenge. England tried to mediate by proposing that France and Austria jointly undertake reform measures
in Italy. As neither seemed inclined to accept the suggestion,
England tried to weaken Austrian military preparations by
announcing a policy of neutrality in the event of war. Austria
refused to be quieted and in the spring of 1859 declared war
upon Sardinia. By May of the same year, Louis Napoleon led
his armies into Italy and in coöperation with the Sardinian
troops drove the Austrians out of Lombardy. Then, without
consulting his ally, the Emperor made peace with Austria at
Villafranca, July 11, 1859. These preliminaries received a definite treaty form at Zurich, November 10, 1859. Lombardy was
given to Sardinia, while an Italian Confederation was to be
created under the presidency of the Pope. Realizing that he
had actually deserted his ally, Napoleon never raised the question of Savoy or Nice and exerted his entire influence to prevent a political unification of the Italian states under Sardinia.
Napoleon failed; and by 1861 a Kingdom of Italy under Vic-

tor Emmanuel embraced every state except Venetia and Rome, which were added in 1866 and 1870 respectively.

The American Civil War

At the outbreak of the Franco-Austrian War, Palmerston and the Liberal Party had come into power. Palmerston found himself not only burdened with maintaining a policy of neutrality in this war but was faced with a serious North American problem. The outbreak of the Civil War in the United States touched England to the quick. Although a few voices were raised in defense of the institution of slavery, the great majority of the English nation was opposed. But had the North a right to force the Southern States to remain in the Union? Many of the merchant, trading, and laboring classes said yes; the upper social classes, including the chief leaders of both Liberal and Conservative Parties, supported the Southern States, whose culture and traditions were more like those of England than the North. Privately and in an unofficial manner, Palmerston and his finance minister, Gladstone, spoke in behalf of the South, encouraging the latter, thereby, to believe that England would recognize the independence of the Confederacy. England's public position, however, was announced in May, 1861, when a policy of strict neutrality was established. Although the South gained recognition as a belligerent, much to the disappointment of the British laboring classes and the Federal Government of the North, she did not secure the status of an independent state.

Late in the same year England almost declared war upon the United States as a result of the Trent Affair. Among the passengers on board the British mail ship *Trent* were two Confederate agents, Mason and Slidell, en route from Havana to Europe to gain British and French assistance for the South. While on her way, she was stopped and boarded by Captain Wilkes of the American vessel *San Jacinto,* who seized the

Confederate commissioners as prisoners of war. The news of the seizure reached England on November 29th and was followed by further dispatches which told of the praise and honor which American papers were showering upon Wilkes. English opinion was outraged and interpreted the affair as an insult. Palmerston, who but a few days before had assured the American minister, Charles F. Adams, that in the event of such an occurrence England would raise no question as to the legality of the seizure, now threw himself into an ultra-patriotic pose. It is reported that as he entered the Cabinet meeting on hearing of the affair, he exclaimed, "I don't know whether you will stand it, but I'll be damned if I do." The ministers felt as he did, and proceeded to draft a strong note to Washington and secret instructions to Lord Lyons, the British minister to the United States. Palmerston showed both communications to Victoria and her husband, the Prince Consort. As a result of their intervention, the notes were softened so as to afford President Lincoln an opportunity of finding a way out of the crisis and at the same time to inform him of the feelings of the British government. Shortly thereafter, troops were sent to reinforce the garrisons in Canada.

By the time Lord Lyons received these dispatches, American opinion had cooled. Lyons appreciated the situation and believed that Lincoln was anxious to get out of the difficulty without violating American honor. Lyons, therefore, merely informed Lincoln of Britain's injured feelings, saying that England could not believe that America intended to insult Great Britain and that an expression of regret would be appreciated. The kind and gracious gesture was met by the prompt disavowal of Wilkes' act and the release of the prisoners. America claimed that the capture was legal in itself as the agents were contraband of war, but that Wilkes had erred in not bringing the *Trent* into port for a judicial review. England accepted the American position and considered the episode closed.

Liberal opinion in England applauded the action of both countries. In the meantime, however, the American blockade of Southern ports had reduced materially the cotton exports to Britain and had closed many of the English textile mills. Unemployment mounted and the government was forced to devise temporary poor relief. Conservative opinion questioned the wisdom of these actions and pressed for a recognition of the South so as to break the blockade by armed force. The British government showed clearly that it favored the Confederacy; but in the face of stern protests on the part of British labor, which supported the North even though the cotton shortage had thrown it out of work, England decided to remain neutral. The government, however, did little to prevent speculators from running the blockade and allowed domestic ship builders to construct privateers for the Confederacy. The American Minister repeatedly pointed out that these cruisers were not intended for neutral service, but he was unable to secure British coöperation. Particularly significant was the case of the *Alabama,* but no steps were taken to detain her until it was too late. The *Alabama* continued to prey upon American commerce, and not until 1864, on June 19, was she destroyed by the American navy. By this time the cotton shortage had been relieved by importations from India and Egypt. Lincoln's Emancipation Proclamation, moreover, showed England that the United States was waging a war to destroy slavery, and in the face of this pronouncement British opinion would not support plans to preserve an institution which was profoundly hated. Three days, therefore, before England received news of Lee's defeat at Gettysburg, the British government decided to drop all consideration of Southern independence. At a later date the ministry showed a distinct willingness to pay an indemnity for the ravages committed by the *Alabama*. America, irritated by Britain's past actions, insisted upon reparations to the amount of $2,000,000,000. England refused to accept these figures and after considerable discussion agreed to submit the case to arbitration. An international tribunal, selected by both nations and three neutral states, met at Geneva in 1872 and awarded damages to the United States amounting to about $15,500,000.

During the course of the Civil War, the British received overtures from France proposing European mediation by France, England, and Russia. England rejected the suggestion because it recognized that Napoleon III intended to use mediation as a means of extending French influence. England, however, did coöperate with France and Spain in sending a fleet to Mexico, which was in a state of revolution, to protect Europeans and to secure payment of loans made to Mexico. Once these objectives were gained, Britain withdrew, flatly refusing to join Bonaparte in a conquest of Mexico. Napoleon undertook the adventure alone, but by the spring of 1867 withdrew his armies before the victorious troops of the Mexican Republic and the pressure of the United States.

Diplomatic Encounters with Prussia

England's interest in Bonaparte's Mexican schemes was slight in contrast with her concern over a situation which had arisen in the Danish Peninsula. Since the fifteenth century, the two southernmost provinces of the peninsula, Schleswig and Holstein, had been governed by the Duke of Schleswig-Holstein. The relationship between this dukedom and Denmark was personal and not political, the Danish king being but the duke of the provinces. Schleswig, the northern province, was predominantly Danish, while Holstein was largely German. The Danish population desired political unification with Denmark, while the Germans wished that

Schleswig, like Holstein, might become a member of the Germanic Confederation which had been founded in 1815. Continued agitation led to the London Protocol of 1852, agreed to by Prussia and Austria, whereby the personal relationship between the provinces and Denmark was retained on the express understanding that the two never should be united politically. Eleven years later, however, the Danish Parliament, acting under the advice of its king, Frederick VII, annexed Schleswig and gave local autonomy to Holstein. Prussia declared this act illegal and proceeded to take action.

Prussia's interest in the question was based upon her desire to unite the various German states into a single nation, free of foreign domination. Bismarck, the Prussian Chancellor, realized that this might lead to a war with Austria, who since 1815 had dominated the Germanic Confederation and thwarted the national aims of the German people. The Schleswig-Holstein question, as raised by the annexation of Schleswig, afforded Bismarck the opportunity of abrogating the London Protocol and of forcing Austria into a situation which might cause her withdrawal from central Germany. His first move, however, was to induce Austria to join in an ultimatum to Denmark demanding that Schleswig be restored to its former status within forty-eight hours. Bismarck knew that the Danish parliament was not in session, that it could not be assembled within the stated time, and that the Danish king had no constitutional authority to accede to the ultimatum. Accordingly, Austrian and Prussian troops attacked the Danes at the end of forty-eight hours.

England realized that Denmark was no match for Prussia and Austria, and that these powers would dictate a peace dangerous to the European balance of power. Moreover, Britain was interested on dynastic grounds, the Prince of Wales having just married the daughter of the Danish king. On the other hand, Victoria's eldest daughter was the wife of the Prussian heir apparent. Victoria's sympathies were with her daughter. Moreover, she believed that England was obligated to support the London Protocol. The British foreign office, however, and the majority of the nation were for Denmark, and wished to intervene in favor of the latter. Victoria was able to prevent this, and Austria and Prussia won the war. A European conference followed at London. Palmerston wanted to support the Danes but was balked by Victoria's determination to remain neutral, and by French apathy. As a result the conference accomplished nothing, and Denmark's fate was settled at Vienna in October, 1864. Denmark ceded the provinces to the victors and agreed to abide by whatever disposition Austria and Prussia should make concerning Schleswig-Holstein.

Having accomplished his first objective, Bismarck rapidly sought to bring about an Austrian war. He refused to accept the latter's proposal that Schleswig-Holstein should become an independent state, but did agree to an arrangement by which Austria was to administer the affairs of Holstein, and Prussia the affairs of Schleswig. His next move was to secure a promise of neutrality from Napoleon III in the event of a Prussian-Austrian war, and an alliance with Italy, to whom was promised Venetia in case a war took place. Austria, moreover, was irritated purposely by Bismarck's open criticism of the former's administration of Holstein, and was provoked to bring the Schleswig-Holstein question before the Germanic Confederation in June, 1866. Prussia declared this a violation of her understanding with Austria, and when the latter induced the Confederation to vote war against Prussia, withdrew from the Confederation and opened hostilities. During the course of these events, England had sought to prevent war by offering mediation; but Bismarck, bent on achieving German unification, refused the opportunity. England could find no friends in Europe to help her and was forced to stay out of the conflict. Prussia won the war; Venetia was ceded to Italy, and the German states, including the provinces of

Schleswig and Holstein, were organized into a North German Confederation under Prussian leadership. Austria, moreover, was not given membership in the Confederation and had to retire from the dominant position she had held in central Europe since 1815. England accepted the situation, and for many years to come remained aloof from European problems. At the outbreak of the Franco-Prussian War of 1870, Britain, having had her offer of mediation repulsed, remained neutral. Moreover, owing to Bismarck's diplomacy with Russia, England was compelled to accept the latter's abrogation of the clause in the Treaty of Paris (1856), which excluded Russian men-of-war from the Black Sea.

During the remainder of Victoria's reign (1837–1901), England remained neutral whenever European difficulties arose and concentrated her energies on domestic and imperial problems. In 1875, under a spirited imperial policy fostered by Disraeli, England acquired control of a large block of shares of the Suez Canal Company, checkmating France's endeavors to dominate the Canal and to extend her influence in Egypt and the Near East. In the future Egypt was to be subject to English power, and the valuable trade routes to India by way of the Suez were secured for Britain. Indicative of British imperialism was Disraeli's next move of having parliament proclaim Victoria Empress of India.

Near Eastern Problems

About the same time, the Near Eastern or Turkish problem was reopened as a result of a series of uprisings on the part of the peasantry in Herzegovina, a Turkish province west of Serbia. Similar revolts arose in Bulgaria. Murad V, the Sultan, suppressed the Bulgarian insurrections with such brutality that European sensibilities were shocked to the utmost. Gladstone declared that the situation demanded joint European action. The "unspeakable Turk," he insisted,

should be expelled from Europe "bag and baggage." Disraeli, however, who was in charge of the government at the
time, recognized that any movement against Turkey would
raise the greater question of Russian expansion. Had the Turk
not massacred so freely, Disraeli might have offered the Sultan
English support; but in the face of public opinion, which had
been aroused by the Turkish atrocities, he could do nothing.
In July, 1876, the situation was made more acute by a declaration of war against Turkey by Serbia and Montenegro and by
continued insurrections in Bulgaria. In April of the next
year, Russia entered the contest against Turkey. Peace was
declared March 3, 1878, by the Treaty of San Stefano. Serbian, Montenegrin, and Rumanian independence was recognized by Turkey, while Bulgaria, much enlarged, was given
local self-government under Turkish direction.

None of these arrangements pleased the various Balkan
states; nor did they satisfy the powers of western Europe,
who believed their consent necessary to any map making in
Europe. England in particular resented the growth of Russian influence in the Near East, while Austria was desirous of
gaining Turkish territory for herself. Under Disraeli's leadership a strong protest was raised against the Treaty of San
Stefano. Russia was in no position to resist and agreed to a
general European conference, which met at Berlin in the
summer of 1878. The result of this gathering was the famous
Treaty of Berlin, by which the national aspirations of Greece
and the Balkan states were given greater security. Bulgaria
was divided into three parts, Macedonia to remain Turkish,
Eastern Rumelia to become an autonomous state under
Turkish authority, while Bulgaria proper was accorded practical independence of Turkey, the latter retaining but nominal
control. Russia secured Bessarabia from Rumania, thereby
gaining the ill will of that state, while Austria was allowed
to occupy and govern the Turkish provinces of Bosnia and
Herzegovina. Much of the success of this conference was due

to the brilliant diplomacy and leadership of Disraeli, who, by a separate agreement with Turkey, gained the island of Cyprus. In return, England promised to protect the Asiatic provinces of Turkey from Russian attack.

The Venezuelan Boundary Dispute

During the remainder of the nineteenth century, while Bismarck was fashioning the Triple Alliance (1879–1882) between the German Empire (which had been founded at the close of the Franco-Prussian War), Austria and Italy, and while Russia and France had come to a mutual understanding, England continued her imperial growth and development. Only in the closing years of the century did any serious problem arise in the field of foreign affairs. England became involved with Venezuela in a boundary dispute. Realizing the futility of a war, Venezuela appealed to the United States. The American government through its Secretary of State, Richard Olney, informed Britain that the Monroe Doctrine limited English action but that the boundary dispute itself could and should be settled by arbitration. Britain opposed America's interpretation of the Monroe Doctrine and at first refused to submit her case to arbitration. Whereupon, President Cleveland secured authority from Congress to appoint a committee to investigate the rival claims of Venezuela and Britain, the findings of which were to be considered final. The war spirit ran high in America, but neither the United States nor Great Britain was anxious to start a conflict. Ultimately, the British government agreed to arbitration. In October, 1899, the tribunal, composed of two Englishmen, two Americans, and one Russian, unanimously agreed to accept most of the British claims. By agreeing to arbitration, England practically recognized America's prior rights in the New World, though she did not acknowledge, in so many words, the implications of the Monroe Doctrine. From this time on, both countries seem to have become aware of the growing solidarity of their relations. A policy of good will and peace was developing between the two great English-speaking nations. A demonstration of this feeling was given by Britain in the spring of 1898 when she checked a general European alliance against the United States in the course of the Spanish-American War.

SELECTED BIBLIOGRAPHY

The general histories referred to in the past five chapters furnish brief accounts of British foreign affairs during the nineteenth century. The biographies of Disraeli, Gladstone, Salisbury, and the other English leaders have pertinent material of value. The *English Historical Review*, the *American Historical Review*, and the *Journal of Modern History* have a number of specialized articles of distinct merit. R. B. Mowat's *History of European Diplomacy, 1815–1914* (New York, 1922) and R. J. Sontag's *European Diplomatic History, 1871–1932* (New York, 1933) are general works, as is G. P. Gooch's *History of Modern Europe, 1878–1919* (New York, 1923).

C. K. Webster's *Foreign Policy of Castlereagh* (London, 1925); W. A. Phillip's *Confederation of Europe* (New York, 1914); H. Temperley's *Foreign Policy of Canning, 1822–1827* (London, 1925); W. P. Cresson's *The Holy Alliance,* and D. Perkins' *The Monroe Doctrine* (Cambridge, Mass., 1927) are standard works for the period immediately following Waterloo. J. Hall's *England and the Orleans Monarchy* (New York, 1912); J. A. R. Marriott's *Eastern Question* (Oxford, 1918); A. W. Kinglake's *Invasion of Crimea* (New York, 1868–1899); F. A. Simpson's *Louis Napoleon and the Recovery of France* (New York, 1923), and B. K. Martin's *Triumph of Lord Palmerston* (New York, 1924) are of value for the Crimean War. England's diplomacy in the Italian, Danish, Austrian-Prussian, and Franco-Prussian Wars may be found in W. R. Thayer's *The Life and Times of Cavour* (New York, 1914); C. G. Robertson's *Bismarck* (New York, 1919); L. D. Steefel's *The Schleswig-Holstein Question* (Cambridge, Mass., 1932); H. Oncken's *Napoleon III and the Rhine* (New York, 1928); R. H. Lord's *Origins of the War of 1870* (Cambridge, Mass., 1924); D. N. Raymond's *British Policy and Opinion during the Franco-Prussian War* (New York, 1921); K. R. Greenfield's *Economics and Liberalism in the Risorgimento* (Baltimore, 1934), and E. M. Carroll's "French Public Opinion on War with Prussia in 1870" in *American Historical Review,* Vol. XXXI.

The Bulgarian Question and the Treaty of Berlin are treated by G. Hanotaux's *Contemporary France* (New York, 1903–1909); N. Forbes' *The Balkans* (Oxford, 1915); R. W. Seton-Watson's *Rise of*

Nationality in the Balkans (London, 1917); T. W. Riker's *Making of Roumania* (Oxford, 1931); F. H. Skrine's *Expansion of Russia* (New York, 1915), and Lord Eversley's *Turkish Empire, Its Growth and Decay* (New York, 1917).

Foreign relations with the United States are handled by W. A. Dunning in his *British Empire and the United States* (New York, 1919); E. D. Adams in his *Great Britain and the American Civil War* (New York, 1925), and T. L. Harris in his *The Trent Affair* (Indianapolis, 1896).

CHAPTER XXXIV

The World War

EDWARD VII ascended the English throne in January, 1901. Contemporary sources describe him as having a genial disposition and a distinct flair for dress and court ceremony. During childhood and early manhood he had been tied to his mother's apron strings and subjected to many restrictions. He disliked this rigid discipline and evidenced a decided inclination against serious reading and education. His mother, moreover, was not disposed to allow him a rôle in government, and it was not until the last decade of her life that he became informed of the domestic and foreign affairs of the empire he was to govern. By this time, however, he had shaken off the guiding hand of Victoria and had become a man. His cheerful nature asserted itself, and he devoted much time to play, recreation, and travel. The theater and race track fascinated him, while a summer's cruise or a visit to gay Paris brought to light characteristics which pleased and confounded his friends and future subjects. Gossip questioned his actions and magnified many an innocent diversion. Surely, the heir apparent ought to be more circumspect about his company and should not be seen in certain places. He cared little about these comments, traveled freely throughout the Empire and Europe, learned much about diplomacy, and made warm friends with sovereigns, princes, and government officials. Actually, he knew little and cared less about state secrets and duties, which seemed boresome and intricate to one who wished a free and unhampered life.

He inherited from Victoria many thorny domestic problems which he willingly entrusted to his ministers. In foreign affairs, however, he showed greater interest and encouraged the ending of the Boer War in 1902. It is probably true that foreign affairs intrigued him because of the social contacts and opportunities for travel rather than any love for diplomacy itself. His visit to France in 1903, however, was crowded with meaning for the future. The imperial and colonial aspirations of both governments had clashed at Fashoda, and war seemed imminent. Edward's genial disposition and his ease at making friends soothed the irritated feelings of the French nationalists. Edward, moreover, induced the French President to come to England in July of the same year. This move did much to create a better understanding between the two countries. Lansdowne, Britain's foreign minister, utilized these visits and friendships to forestall a war. Delcassé, the French minister of foreign affairs, realized the need of retaining England's good will, in the face of Germany's military strength, and coöperated with Lansdowne in concluding the *Entente Cordiale* of April, 1904. Britain's paramount position in Egypt and the Sudan was recognized, as was France's influence in Morocco. As a result of these activities the imperial interests of both were satisfied, and war was prevented. More significant was the fact that the two nations were brought closer together in all future European controversies.

Lansdowne's European Policy

Four years prior to the *Entente Cordiale*, Lansdowne had strengthened the historic ties with Portugal and had won Italian good will in spite of the Triple Alliance of Italy, Germany, and Austria. Moreover, in 1902, a defensive alliance had been concluded with Japan. Lansdowne's foreign policy marked a distinct change in England's attitude toward European affairs. Generally speaking, British statesmen of the nineteenth century had adopted a hands-off policy in respect to Europe. This does not imply that England had no interest in Continental affairs as the Crimean War illustrates Britain's participation in European politics. At no time, however, did her ministers bind England to any defensive or offensive alliance. Rather did they seek to meet each problem as it arose and intervened only when British interests were at stake. Lansdowne reversed this policy. He believed that England should play a more active rôle in the face of European imperial activities. He realized that Britain's far-flung empire would be drawn into every major European problem and, as any one of these might lead to war, it was England's duty to forestall the same. To this end, Lansdowne entered into a series of agreements with France and Italy and tried to effect an understanding with Germany. In pursuing a policy of friendship toward Germany, Lansdowne was following a program initiated by Victoria in the 1860's and 1870's and which Salisbury had continued during his ministry. The German foreign office, startled by the growing Anglo-French accord, thoroughly misunderstood Lansdowne's overtures. The *Entente Cordiale* was interpreted as having closed the door against German expansion in Morocco. Lansdowne tried to correct this interpretation by indicating that the agreement of 1904 merely concerned Britain's relations with France in North Africa. Germany refused to accept this point of view and continued to look upon England as a doubtful friend.

The German Empire, at this time, was in the hands of Kaiser William II who had ascended the throne in 1888. The Kaiser gloried in his country's accomplishments and was eager to make it the arbiter of European and world affairs. He identified himself with the ultra-nationalist group, believing, as some of them did, in the divine mission of the German people, the superiority of German art and science, and the need of a large army and navy. In 1890, he parted company with the aged Bismarck. He failed to retain Russia's friendship, which

Bismarck had cultivated, and preferred to hold fast to the Triple Alliance as the best protection for peace in Europe. William, moreover, supported the German financial and trading interests which were seeking investments in Turkey and the Near East. In 1889, the Emperor visited Constantinople and allowed German officers to train and modernize the Turkish army. German business houses were accorded special considerations, and Turkey bought large quantities of German manufactures. Later, in the same century, the Kaiser visited the Sultan again and alarmed Europe by a bombastic speech in which he told the Turkish people to trust in his friendship and protection against any enemy. This was followed by a series of negotiations which resulted, in 1903, in the formation of the Bagdad Railroad Company. For a long time German traders had been casting wishful eyes upon a railroad from Berlin to the Indian Ocean. Because of Germany's alliance with Austria, whose interest in such a highway was manifest, no difficulty was encountered in that country, and Turkey was more than willing to please its benefactor and friend. England realized the danger, as did France and Russia, of an Austro-German corridor from Berlin to Bagdad and sought to restrict construction of the road until the question of terminals and European rights were settled. Seemingly, Britain did not wish to irritate Germany by blocking the project. Numerous conversations slowly removed existing difficulties and permitted, in the spring of 1914, the acceptance of a treaty which provided for the completion of the road.

During the course of Germany's penetration into the Near East, Russia became involved in a war with Japan (1904–1906), which ended in a victory for the latter. Russian morale and influence were so shattered by this defeat and subsequent internal dissensions that she lost caste and standing in European politics. Taking advantage of Russia's weakened condition, Germany registered a strong protest against French policy in Morocco. Berlin claimed that Morocco was becoming a

French protectorate and that German interests in North Africa were being ignored. Hoping to check further French expansion, the Kaiser visited Tangier in the spring of 1905. Posing as a defender and benefactor of Morocco, William II announced that, in his determination to maintain Moroccan independence, he would tolerate no interference by any power. France was startled by this threat of war and sought to discover Britain's attitude. England refused to take sides but did inform Germany that British opinion would be incensed by any act of aggression in Morocco. Accordingly, William agreed to settle the dispute by conference. A meeting was held at Algeciras in January, 1906. Here Germany admitted the right of France and Spain, the latter also having interests in Morocco, to handle the police and fiscal policies of that state. Morocco, however, was to be considered an independent state. The net result of the episode was a recognition of paramount French influence in Morocco and a tightening of the *Entente Cordiale*. At the same time Germany's prestige was enhanced. Germany, in brief, had forced France and England to admit her right to be consulted in all future colonial developments. Britain sensed this fact and realized that Germany intended to play a more dominant rôle in European politics. Accordingly, England ironed out its difficulties with Russia in India, Persia, and Afghanistan. By 1907 the *Entente Cordiale* had become the *Triple Entente* of France, Russia, and Britain. German policy had forced England to join hands with Russia.

When the *Entente Cordiale* was announced in 1904, many people interpreted it as an arrangement for bringing to an end England's quarrels with France. This is most certainly accomplished. Lansdowne, however, viewed it as something more than a device to establish friendly relations. He considered it a political weapon whereby Britain might affect the balance of power in Europe. England, in brief, was drawn into the European system and had taken sides against Germany. During the Morocco crisis of 1905, there were military and naval conferences between the French and the English. These consultations gave a peculiar significance to the diplomatic coöperation. The *Entente Cordiale* became an alliance.

Imperial Germany Demands a Place in the Sun

Germany was conscious of the steel bands which surrounded her, of the Anglo-Japanese alliance of 1902 and 1905, and of the friendly relations which existed between England and the United States. She was confident, however, that she could snap these bands asunder whenever she wished. Ever since her smashing victory over France in 1870, German pride in the Fatherland had grown to great heights. School teachers, philosophers, and historians deluged the country with ultra-nationalist ideas and literature. "Our age is an iron age," wrote the historian Treitschke, and "if the strong conquer the weak, it is the law of life." "Wars are terrible," Kuno Fischer maintained, "but necessary, for they save the State from social putrefaction and stagnation." Simple farmers, shopkeepers, traders, and factory hands were reared in this "iron age" and viewed their Emperor as one upon whom the "spirit of God has descended." William II was as ardent a protagonist of German Kultur as ever lived. Backed by a regimented people, a loyal army and a haughty landed class, he proceeded to strike out for new markets for the capitalists, and colonies for the imperialists. A Pan-German League, organized in 1886, advocated the union of all German-speaking peoples in Holland, Austria, Belgium, Russia, and Scandinavia into one superstate.

Germany was not alone in her enslavement to nationalism and imperialism. Cecil Rhodes, in his last will, declared, "The British race is the finest which history has yet produced." His contemporary, Chamberlain, held, "The Anglo-Saxon race is infallibly destined to be the predominant force in the history and civilization of the world." "France," Victor Hugo exclaimed, "the world depends upon your existence." France, England, Russia, the Netherlands, and practically every world state believed in the righteousness of its aspirations and policies. Each in turn insisted that it could do no wrong and that it was justified in defending national honor against the attacks of others. Nationalism and patriotism exalted the state above the individual citizens, who could do nothing better than die in battle so that the nation might live. Those who advanced these views controlled government and influenced the press, church and schools. Conditioned by such an environment, the manhood of Europe goose-stepped to the front, in 1914, believing the Fatherland in danger. Later in 1917, Americans, similarly trained, entered the trenches to make the world "safe for democracy."

Not every German or Englishman believed in these concepts and ideals. There were thousands who questioned the existence of national honor. Only a biological entity, so they declared, could experience the emotional reaction known as honor; and a nation was not a human organism, but a descriptive title for a group of kindred people, possessing a common historical heritage, and living within certain political and geographic boundaries. Wars were fought to protect individual interests and honors. One could not die so that the nation might live when such a thing as a living nation did not exist. Others declared that wars were fought by those who did not cause them, while those who caused war remained at home, made profits, and died in bed. War, moreover, was a denial of Christ, and no Christian might, by God's command, "resist evil by force." Views of this kind were scattered by peace societies, by non-resistant organizations, and by certain religious groups, notably the Friends. Their voices, however, were drowned by the tramping feet of the military and by Christians singing "The Son of God goes forth to War."

The Kaiser's prestige and that of the ultra-German nationalists had been inflated by the Morocco episode of 1905. Three years later William donned his shining armor and rattled the sword in defense of Austria, who since her ejection from central Europe in 1866 and 1870 had sought imperial power in the Balkans. The Berlin Conference of 1878 had given to Austria the administration of the Turkish provinces of Bosnia and Herzegovina, which in 1908 were threatened by the national aspirations of the Young Turks. Convinced that Turkey needed governmental reform and a reunion of her former European provinces, the Young Turks precipitated a movement which endangered imperial Austria. Accordingly, Vienna announced in October, 1908, the annexation of the two provinces, while the autonomous ruler of Bulgaria proclaimed the independence of that state, including Eastern Rumelia. Russia, whose interest in the Balkans was as great as Austria's, viewed the Slavic populations in that area as her wards. She protested against Austria's act and might have gone to war had Britain been willing to come to her aid. England, however, did not care to enhance Russia's influence in the Near East. The net result was that the Sultan had to yield to the military strength of Austria and Germany, relinquish authority over Bosnia, Herzegovina, and Bulgaria, while Germany gained new laurels. Turkey's feelings toward Germany were at first alienated by the Kaiser's actions; but in a short time he was able to convince the new Ottoman government, dominated by the Young Turks, that he was their best friend in Europe.

Flushed by these successes, William II in 1911 called France to account for having used military force in the suppression of a rebellion in Morocco. The Kaiser claimed that France had violated the spirit of the Algeciras Conference and was injuring German rights in Morocco. In July of that year he dispatched a gun boat to Agadir to protect German rights. War seemed imminent and hurried military preparations were made in Germany and France. Realizing that Russia had not

recovered from her defeat in the Far East and could not carry
out her treaty with France, France turned to Britain for help.
England quickly informed Germany that she would not remain neutral if her interests and treaties with France were
violated. In the face of this pronouncement, William II recognized French political domination in Morocco. In return,
he secured territorial concessions in the Congo region and free
economic opportunities in Morocco for the German imperialists.

The Dismemberment of Turkey

About the same time, the Italian government, reflecting the
national aspirations of her capitalists and imperialists, launched
a war against Turkey for the sole purpose of gaining the Sultan's provinces of Tripoli and Cyrenaica. The Ottoman government dispatched a number of troops, recently drilled by
German officers, to defend these African possessions. During
the course of this war, the nationalists of Greece, Bulgaria,
Serbia, and Montenegro seized the opportunity of attacking
Turkey. Their objective was to drive the Turk out of Europe
and divide the spoils among themselves. Russia had encouraged them to undertake this war, which, if successful, would
lessen German influence in the Near East, advance Russian
power, and possibly result in her gaining Constantinople. The
Turkish defense, weakened by the Italian war, crumbled before the swift offensive of the Balkan states. So rapid had
been the course of events that the governments of Western
Europe had no chance of preventing the conflict. All that
could be done was to rearrange the map of the Near East so
as to satisfy the victors and prevent a situation which might
endanger the peace of Europe. The interested parties met at
London and after much discussion accepted the Treaty of London (1913), which failed, however, to satisfy the imperialists
of Serbia and Bulgaria.

Serbia's demand that she be given the territory known as Albania had been denied. An enlarged and pro-Russian Serbia was not to the liking of Austria, which was already disturbed over Serbian propaganda among the Slavs of Bosnia and Herzegovina. Italy, which opposed Serbia's demand for territory on the Adriatic, and Germany supported Austria at London, while France and Russia backed Serbia. A world war seemed imminent and was prevented only by the establishment of the independent state of Albania. The settlement of this problem, however, raised another issue which immediately aroused Bulgarian resentment. Serbia, it seems, had been promised a portion of Albania by Bulgaria. Not having gained this at London, Serbia demanded as compensation that section of Macedonia which had been given to Bulgaria by the Treaty of London. Bulgaria, supported by Austria, refused to yield, and in June, 1913, was attacked by Serbia and her allies, Greece and Rumania. Turkey also entered the war, hoping to regain some of the territory which had been taken away by the Treaty of London. The conflict, known as the Second Balkan War, was over within a month; Bulgaria was decisively defeated. The Treaty of Bucharest, August, 1913, reduced Bulgaria's size and influence and enlarged the territories of Greece, Serbia, Rumania, and Turkey. In the meantime the Italian-Turkish war had come to an end, Italy securing the Sultan's provinces of Tripoli and Cyrenaica.

The gravity of the European situation was appreciated by all the great powers. The dismemberment of Turkey had resulted in a league of Balkan States, Bulgaria not included, which stood as a barrier to German-Austrian advance in the Near East. Italy had become a Mediterranean power and was anxious to gain control of Albania and certain portions of the Austrian Alps. Austria resented Italy's activities and turned to Germany for aid. The latter knew that Italy had never forgiven her for German support of Turkey in the recent Italian-Turkish war. Any definite endorsement of Austrian policy, therefore, would disrupt the Triple Alliance and force Italy to join the *Triple Entente*. Delay and compromise were all that Berlin could offer for the time being. On the other hand, William II supported Austria wholeheartedly in the latter's determination to check Russia's advance in the Balkans. Russia, it was believed, was behind every overt act of Serbia, which for several years had been flooding Bosnia and Herzegovina with Pan-Slavic literature and propaganda. The future integrity of the Austrian state demanded the immediate suppression of Serbian activities and the destruction of Russian power in the Balkans. Russia realized that her endorsement of Serbia might lead to a general European war, but she did little to prevent such a disaster. A strong front was maintained in the Balkans while military preparations were hastened at home.

And what of England? In general her policy was to keep the balance of power intact. On the other hand her statesmen were alarmed over the Kaiser's conduct in Morocco and Turkey and viewed with concern the growing naval strength of Germany. In an effort to retain Germany's good will and prevent a world war, Lord Haldane was sent to Berlin in 1912. Haldane assured the Kaiser that the English government had no thought of being a party to an unprovoked attack upon Germany and proposed a naval holiday. William II, however, questioned the sincerity of this statement and in return for Germany's friendship demanded Britain's promise to remain neutral in the event of a Franco-German war. England was not ready to surrender the benefits of the *Entente* and answered the Kaiser's bid for naval supremacy by continuing to build two ships for every one constructed by Germany.

The Outbreak of War in 1914

By the early summer of 1914, Europe had become a turbulent sea heavily mined with dangerous explosives. Low speed and skillful piloting were needed if war was to be prevented. Unfortunately, opposite tactics were employed; and on June 28, Francis Ferdinand, heir to the Austrian throne, and his wife were assassinated at Serajevo by a Serbian subject of Austria. Every European capital felt the impact of this blow and expressed its deepest sympathy to the aged emperor, Francis Joseph. At Vienna, however, a spirit of revenge manifested itself from the first. Berchtold, the foreign minister, immediately determined to use the incident as a means of punishing and humiliating Serbia. His secret service informed him that Serbia in no way was responsible for the crime, though as a matter of fact Serbia's prime minister had prior knowledge of the plot but had not seen fit to warn Francis Ferdinand. Berchtold did not know of this and, disappointed over the reports of his police, deliberately lied when he informed the Emperor and the Kaiser that he had definite proof of Serbian guilt. Later, during the course of further discussions with Berlin, Berchtold asked for and received William II's promise to aid Austria even if a war with Russia resulted. Having given his word, the Kaiser departed on his annual summer cruise not realizing that he had taken a step which would lead to a world war. As an indication of what might happen, Russia, on July 18, informed Austria that she "could not permit Austria to use menacing language or military measures against Serbia."

In making this statement, St. Petersburg did not know what had taken place between Vienna and Berlin. Paris and London also were uninformed. Had France known, it seems quite unlikely that President Poincaré and Foreign Minister Viviani would have risked a sea voyage to St. Petersburg, where they were the guests of the Czar, July 20 to July 23. Berchtold deliberately concealed his actions and intentionally withheld issuing an ultimatum to Serbia until Poincaré and Viviani had started for home. According to this ultimatum Serbia was given forty-eight hours to promise (1) a suppres-

sion of anti-Austrian texts in Serbia's schools, (2) a censorship
of all anti-Austrian societies and publications, (3) the removal
of certain officials, to be named by Austria, and (4) to allow
Austrians to coöperate with Serbian officials in stamping out
anti-Austrian activities. European opinion was shocked by
the severity of the Austrian demands. The Berlin *Vorwaerts*
stated in its columns that they could "only be intended deliberately to provoke war." On July 25, while every diplomat
in Europe was on tiptoe with excitement, Serbia answered by
accepting most of Austria's demands and agreeing to abide by
the decision of the Hague Tribunal as to the rest. The Austrian minister at Belgrade understood that Berchtold would
reply by a declaration of war, and within less than a half hour
after receiving Serbia's answer he was speeding by train to
Vienna.

Between July 25 and July 28, Sir Edward Grey, Britain's foreign minister, made every effort to prevent a war between
Serbia and Austria, and proposed that Italy, France, Germany,
and England confer so as to check further complications.
Italy and France accepted the invitation, but Germany refused
on the ground that Austrian honor demanded war and that
England should join with Germany in seeking to "localize"
the dispute. Berlin, in brief, wished to prevent a general
European war but would do nothing to restrain her ally from
attacking Serbia. The Austro-Serbian war began on July 28
and was followed by feverish military activity in Russia. The
Kaiser became alarmed and warned Berchtold against the
danger of a Russian war. William, moreover, informed the
latter that Germany would not be drawn into a conflict caused
by Austria's refusal to accept German advice. Berchtold ignored the Kaiser's warnings, knowing that if Russia did attack
Austria, Germany would have to fulfill its obligations under
the Dual Alliance. Accordingly, after Russia had mobilized
on July 30, Germany declared war against the former and demanded that France observe neutrality or face German attack.

BRAVO, BELGIUM!

Reproduced by permission of the Proprietors of "Punch."

France replied by mobilization, and on August 3 a state of war existed between these two nations. Italy found a technical reason for not joining her allies and announced neutrality, as did Rumania.

In the meantime Sir Edward Grey had tried to check an

impending world conflagration. On the other hand he prepared the mind of England for the worst. The frequent
visits of French military officers confirmed the rumor that Britain's resources might be utilized in defense of France. The
concentration of the Grand Fleet in the North Sea had by
chance occurred before Austria's ultimatum to Serbia. Continued concentration revealed a determination on the part of
the government to protect English interests. Grey, however,
hoped to avoid war, and inquired on July 29 as to Germany's
intentions in the event of a Franco-German conflict. Berlin's
reply was to the effect that she had no designs on French territory in Europe but refused to bind herself as to the French
colonies. Grey informed the Kaiser that England would not
remain neutral on such terms. On July 31, however, he asked
both France and Germany whether, in the event of war, they
would respect Belgian neutrality, which Europe in general
had promised years before. France said yes, but Germany
would promise nothing. Two days later, Germany demanded
that Belgium choose between allowing the passage of German
troops or war. Belgium immediately appealed to England,
which on August 4 asked Germany to respect Belgian neutrality
or face the consequences. By midnight of the same day, London heard that Germany would make no promises. The British government immediately proclaimed a state of war with
Germany and hastened to fulfill her obligations to France and
Belgium.

Sir Edward Grey has been criticized by some writers who
believe that the World War would have been prevented had
he told Germany by July 28 that Britain would support Russia
and France in case the Serbian issue provoked Germany to action. It is true that Grey's actions were not as decisive as
they might have been; but it is difficult to see how, under the
British parliamentary system of government, he could have
issued such a statement to Germany. On the other hand
Grey's inquiry of July 29 and his ultimatum of August 4 in-

dicated what England might do. The financial, commercial, and industrial classes of Germany realized the possibilities of an English war and questioned how long Germany would survive before the superior naval and economic resources of Britain. These groups, however, were unable to shake the Kaiser's confidence in his armies, whose generals assured him that France could be defeated within six to eight weeks. Years before, the German general staff had studied the question of a French war and had come to the conclusion that England could not possibly prevent a speedy and smashing victory over France. With France out of the way, Russia could be dispatched in short order, which, in turn, would render England helpless before the united front of the Dual Alliance. The German military, in brief, did not think it decisive whether or not England came into the contest, and the charge that Grey might have prevented war loses its effectiveness.

Militarism, Nationalism, and Imperialism

German militarism is much more responsible for the war than Grey's diplomacy. During the last ten days preceding the outbreak of hostilities, the German military lords completely eclipsed the civilian authorities in the conduct of government. Similar situations arose in Austria and Russia, and to an extent in France. Professionally trained in the arts of war, these men dominated the councils of Europe and seemed more than anxious to precipitate a crisis which would afford them an opportunity of displaying their skill and advancing their power. Preparedness for war, they had argued for decades as had their prototypes since the dawn of history, was the best security for peace. "How many people in the British Isles," wrote Maude in his *War and the World's Life,* "realize that Germany and France owe their security from invasion to the latent threat of their enormous armies?" Most of the military honestly believed in this theory, though few, if any, sought to test it in the light of history. Mutual fear and distrust was engendered by the presence of huge armies and navies, while the diplomat often became but the pawn for the military class. In Russia, the war lords proclaimed that their country's honor had been insulted by Austria's attack upon Serbia and forced the Czar to declare war upon Austria and Germany. German militarists took the same ground as did those in France. Closely allied to the militarists in purpose were the munition makers, whose proud statements about national patriotism and sacrifice were more than balanced by the profits they made from war. English soldiers, for example, were shot down in the World War by cannons made in England and sold to Germany. Militarism stands indicted as a powerful factor in bringing on the carnage of 1914.

Nationalism also shares great responsibility. The exaltation of the state as a superentity, which must defend itself against aggression, found expression by writers and speakers of all countries. "Anybody who is threatened," spoke the German Chancellor on August 4, "as we are threatened, and is fighting for his highest possessions, can have only one thought—how he is to hack his way through." This was the language of a nationalist and patriot and evoked prolonged cheers from the German people who believed as he did. Similar speeches were made in London, Vienna, Paris, Belgrade, and St. Petersburg to a populace who demonstrated their support by singing national hymns and parading through the streets. Each belligerent maintained that his national honor had been insulted, and that he was engaged in a life and death struggle. Realistically speaking, the "honor" and "highest possessions" continually referred to were but the "honor" and "highest possessions" of individual diplomats, generals, imperialists, and economic interests. One may well question whether the honor or property of the Czar-ridden peasant or factory hand of Birmingham was affected. Had the peasant or factory hand any grievance against the workers of Austria and Germany? He had been made to think so, and following the command of the powers that be, went forth to war while those who urged him on remained safe at home. The existence of the phenomenon of nationalism looms large as one of the antecedents of the World War.

Nationalism, so its defenders never tired of saying, demanded the territory and markets of others for full and complete national satisfaction. "Let us cease our wretched efforts to apologize for Germany," wrote Maximilian Harden. "Germany is carrying on this war because she wants more room and larger markets for the products of her activity." "Colonization is for France a question of life and death. Either France will become a great African state or she will in a century or two be a second-rate power," was the prediction of Leroy-Beaulieu. At times this frank note was disguised, as in the following extract from an American publication: "The imperialism of the American is a duty and credit to humanity. He makes beautiful the land he touches, beautiful with moral and physical cleanliness. . . . Such expansion . . . is an inalienable right and in the case of the United States it is a particular duty, because we are idealists and are thereby bound by establishing protectorates over the weak to protect them from unmoral Kultur." In England a great poet expressed the same idea in a poem entitled "The White Man's Burden." Each of these quotations illustrates the generally accepted theory that imperialism was vital, moral, and necessary for nations. History, however, shows that while individual capitalists and traders have reaped profit, their governments have actually lost, while the citizenry at large have been taxed to maintain the economic investments of a privileged few.

The World War and Its Consequences

The World War lasted from the summer of 1914 to the late fall of 1918. During the course of these years a large number of European, Asiatic, and American countries entered the conflict on the side of England and her allies. Germany, on the other hand, secured assistance from Bulgaria and Turkey. Treaty arrangements as well as political and economic ties explain the actions of most of these nations. Italy, for example, deserted her allies, Germany and Austria, in July, 1915 and joined hands with England and France because the latter promised more Austrian territory than Austria could be expected to surrender. In the case of the United States, which entered the war in the spring of 1917, the situation was quite different. At the outbreak of the conflict in 1914, the American Republic pledged itself to a policy of neutrality, and immediately found itself enmeshed in a tangle similar to that which preceded the War of 1812. England's rigid blockade of North German ports, her constantly enlarging list of contraband, and her interpretation of the doctrine of continuous voyage strained Anglo-American relations almost to the breaking point. Britain's blockade, moreover, cut so seriously into Germany's food supply and undermined her morale so effectively as to cause the latter to embark upon an extensive submarine attack upon her enemies and their overseas supplies. Germany realized that American life and property would be endangered by submarine warfare but hoped the United States would suffer these losses with patience. The war lords, moreover, were confident that no military aid of any importance would come to England in the event of America's entrance into the war and encouraged the German government to wage a relentless submarine campaign against British shipping.

In May, 1915, the British merchant ship *Lusitania* was sunk off the Irish coast with the loss of life of a hundred and fourteen American citizens. American opinion, which had become increasingly anti-German because of the latter's brutal treatment of non-combatants and neutrals, protested in most emphatic terms against this sinking. Although Germany promised the United States in May, 1916, that she would not sink merchant ships without warning, for the time being, relations between the two states remained unsettled. Late in January, 1917, however, believing that she could starve Britain within six months, Germany informed America that she would sink at sight all ships bound to and from the ports of her enemies. America broke diplomatic relations at once and, on April 7, 1917, declared war on Germany.

In spite of America's action, Germany destroyed about four million tons of Allied shipping during the first half of 1917. Improved naval operations on the part of Britain, however, diminished these losses to less than two million tons during the first half of 1918. Newly launched ships, moreover, increased so rapidly by 1918 as to balance the tonnage destroyed by submarines. Germany had staked all upon the success of her submarine campaign and had failed. In the meantime, her armies had overrun much of Western France, occupied most of Belgium, forced Russia and Rumania to surrender in March, 1918, and all but defeated Italy. The failure of her submarine campaign, the increased rigors of the blockade, the stubborn resistance of the English and French troops on the Western Front, and the arrival of fresh armies from the United States was too much for Germany. Finally, on November 11, 1918, after witnessing the collapse of Bulgaria, Turkey, and Austria, and her own armies' retreat toward the Rhine, Germany agreed to an armistice, which was followed in January, 1919, by the Treaty of Versailles. The World War was over.

England retired from the conflict breathless and badly wounded, and in her wake staggered the dominions and colonies beyond the seas. Various estimates have been made as to loss of life sustained by the British Empire. The following is probably the most accurate: total mobilized forces, 8,904,467; killed and died, 908,371; wounded casualties, 2,090,212; prisoners and missing, 191,652; and total casualties of all types, 3,190,325. Approximately thirty-six per cent of the enlisted strength of the Empire died in the course of the war, only a million and three hundred thousand less than the total suffered by all countries in the European wars of the nineteenth and twentieth centuries. Were one to add the loss sustained through the decrease in birth and the civilian deaths caused by sickness, lack of food, and malnutrition, the figure would be much higher. One authority estimated that if the British dead in the war were to parade, twenty abreast, down Fifth Avenue in New York City, it would take ten days, from sunrise to sunset, for the procession to pass the Public Library. Many more days would pass before the halt and the blind, the widows and orphans, the unemployed and paupers, the war babies and the criminals would pass in review, and in their wake would limp disorganized institutions of learning and social service. Increased vice and immorality would then follow, and the parade would close with countless thousands singing "Hymns of Hate."

Governmental authorities would see to it that little publicity would be given in this death march to the money expenditures and property losses caused by the war. English wars from 1688 to 1763 cost the paltry sum of $1,070,000,000, less than half of which was met by taxation, the balance being raised by loans for future generations to pay. Britain's national debt in 1763 amounted to $622,500,000, which the American Revolution and Napoleonic Wars raised to $4,300,000,000. Economic growth decreased this amount as the century progressed, but the Crimean, Colonial, and Boer Wars counterbalanced these gains to a marked degree. On March 31, 1914 the gross national debt stood at $3,538,270,000. By March 31, 1919, the British people (not including those in the dominions and colonies) had paid taxes to the amount of $48,025,000,000, while the government had raised, by loans at home and abroad, $33,925,895,000, which was added to the national debt. The gross national debt amounted to $37,464,165,000. Although the years noted exceed the duration of the war and include charges not related to this conflict, the fact remains that the World War accounts for most of the taxes paid and debts contracted. Only astronomers, who talk in terms of millions of light years, can appreciate the figure of 350 billions spent by all countries in the conflict, to which must be added billions more in interest charges, pensions, bonuses, hospital care, and rehabilitation work.

Compensating benefits offset to a degree this terrible toll in life and treasure. Petty factional disputes disappeared for the time being and the English people gained valuable experience in unity of action and national control of industry. Labor knew, as never before, its immense economic and political strength, while the British Empire was welded into a more compact political organism. Chemistry and medicine expanded their fields of knowledge, and man's conquest of the air was hastened. Finally, the British government could claim *victory* as another asset. As one analyzes the terms of victory as they appear in the Treaty of Versailles, one questions the value of this asset. The German military and naval machines had been destroyed, and the German bid for empire was blasted by the division of German colonies among the Allies. The acquisition of these possessions added increased governmental expenses and responsibilities for the benefit of English imperialists and capitalists, who gloried in the elimination of German trade and manufactures *Made in Germany* from the markets of the world. The new map of Europe, moreover, by dismembering Austria and reducing and dividing German territory in Europe raised many thorny problems which the victors claimed would be settled either by the League of Nations, President Wilson's contribution to European politics, or the strong arm of France, Italy, and Britain. In addition, provision was made to have the defeated nations pay the entire costs of the war, though little thought was given as to how reparations might be gained from the conquered, already saddled with war debts of their own and denied, by the victors, an opportunity to sell their products and services. Finally, victory was predicated upon the assertion that Germany had caused the World War, a conclusion which appears in the Treaty of Versailles but which impartial history cannot accept.

SELECTED BIBLIOGRAPHY

The literature dealing with the antecedents, characteristics and results of the World War is legion and perplexing in its conclusions. Of general interest are the chapters in the *Cambridge History of British Foreign Policy* (New York, 1923); G. P. Gooch's *History of Modern Europe, 1878–1919* (New York, 1926); H. E. Barnes' *Genesis of the World War* (New York, 1926); M. Montgelas' *The Case for the Central Powers* (New York, 1925), and F. L. Schuman's *International Politics* (New York, 1933).

European expansion is treated by J. A. Hobson in his *Imperialism* (New York, 1905). H. E. Barnes' *World Politics in Modern Civilization* (New York, 1930); I. Bowman's *The New World, Problems of Political Geography* (New York, 1928); C. Hodges' *The Background of International Relations* (New York, 1931); P. T. Moon's *Syllabus of International Relations* (New York, 1925); L. Woolf's *Economic Imperialism* (New York, 1921) and *Imperialism and Civilization* (New York, 1928); W. C. Abbott's *The Expansion of Europe* (New York, 1928); N. D. Harris' *Europe and Africa* (New York, 1927); R. L. Buell's *A History of Ten Years* (New York, 1928) and *International Relations* (New York, 1929); A. Woolf's *Empire and Commerce in Africa* (New York, 1920), and H. Feis' *Europe, the World's Banker* (Oxford, 1930) are standard works on this subject.

Nationalism, War, and Society (New York, 1916) by E. B. Krehbiel is a convenient guide for a study of nationalism. C. J. H. Hayes provides a careful analysis in his *Historical Evolution of Modern Nationalism* (New York, 1931). P. T. Moon's *Imperialism and World Politics* (New York, 1926); R. Muir's *Nationalism and Internationalism* (Boston, 1917); J. F. Scott's *Patriots in the Making* (New York, 1916); M. S. Wertheimer's *The Pan German League* (New York, 1924); H. S. Chamberlain's *The Foundations of the Nineteenth Century* (New York, 1910); A. J. Toynbee's *Nationality and the War* (New York, 1915); K. Francke's *The German Spirit* (New York, 1916), and J. L. Stocks' *Patriotism and the World State* (New York, 1920) are also of value.

W. L. Langer's *European Alliances and Alignments, 1871–1890* (New York, 1931) and *Diplomacy of Imperialism* (New York, 1935) are good for the diplomatic background of the World War. G. L. Dickinson's *International Anarchy, 1904–1914* (New York, 1926), E. Brandenburg's *From Bismarck to the World War* (Oxford, 1933); S. B. Fay's *Origins of the World War* (New York, 1928); E. M. Earle's *Turkey, the Great Powers and the Bagdad Railway* (New York, 1924); A. F. Pribram's *Secret Treaties of Austria-Hungary, 1879–1914* (Cambridge, 1920–1921); R. Hoffman's *Great Britain and the German Trade Rivalry* (Philadelphia, 1934); J. V. Fuller's *Bismarck's Diplomacy at its Zenith* (Cambridge, 1922), and B. E. Schmitt's *Coming of the War* (New York, 1930) and *Triple Alliance and Triple Entente* (New York, 1934) are also of value. Mention should also be made of F. R. Flournoy's *British Policy towards Morocco* (Baltimore, 1935); V. J. Puryear's *International Economics and Diplomacy in the Near East* (Stanford, 1935), and G. P. Gooch's *Before the War, Studies in Diplomacy* (New York, 1935).

The story of the World War is treated in the following: C. R. Cruttwell's *History of the Great War* (Oxford, 1934); J. Buchan's *History of the Great War* (New York, 1933); C. Lucas' *The Empire at War* (Oxford, 1921–1926); E. von Falkenhayn's *German General Staff and Its Decisions* (New York, 1926); W. Churchill's *World Crisis* (New York, 1923–1929); Viscount Jellicoe's *Grand Fleet, 1914–1916* (New York, 1919); C. J. H. Hayes' *Brief History of the Great War* (New York, 1920); C. Seymour's *American Diplomacy during the World War* (Baltimore, 1934), and T. G. Frothingham's *Guide to the Military History of the World War* (Boston, 1921). Germany, France, and Britain have published official histories of decided value.

Many of the above-mentioned works devote attention to the results of the war. In addition reference may be made to the numerous volumes published by the Carnegie Endowment Foundation under the general title *Economic and Social History of the World War*. The historical journals of all countries are rich in many articles dealing with more specialized topics. The bibliographies for Chapters XXXI, XXXII, and XXXV may be consulted.

CHAPTER XXXV

Ireland and the Empire After 1914

ENGLAND was enmeshed in a thorny Irish problem when the World War began in the summer of 1914. Although the Irish situation was novel in many respects, the fundamental difficulties between the two countries were much the same as in the seventeenth century. Irishmen resented English domination. Although politically joined to Great Britain by the Act of Union (1801), Irishmen chafed under an arrangement which afforded little chance for advancing their claims to local self-government. Had English statesmen given more thought to the economic life of Ireland, most of the nineteenth century difficulties might have been avoided. As it was, the greater share of the Irish were bound by a land tenure system which favored the proprietors, many of whom were absentee English landlords. Anxious to make profit, the landed class burdened their tenants with numerous taxes and high rents. Outside Ulster, where rents were based upon property values, landlords charged as much as the market would stand. Failure to meet these competitive rents frequently resulted in ejection, with the tenant receiving no compensation for improvements that he had made at his own cost. Fair rents and fixity of tenure would have reduced the economic distress of the Irish and made them more amenable to English control.

Inadequately informed and unwilling to believe the situation to be so bad as it was, the British government was startled from its complacency by the potato famine in Ireland during 1845 and 1846. Food depots were established, public works undertaken, and relaxations effected in the Corn Laws and Navigation Acts. In spite of these measures, conditions failed to improve; and in 1848 a rebellion broke out in the island. The uprising was speedily put down, but the factors which had caused it continued to plague both countries. Several years later, further revolt and dissension developed under the leadership of the Fenians (Champions of Ireland). The Fenian movement spread rapidly, but little was accomplished until the establishment of the Fenian Brotherhood in New York in 1858. The Fenian program offered nothing in the way of social, religious, or economic improvement but attracted thousands by its ideal of Irish independence. Hundreds of Irish-Americans subscribed liberally to the movement, and scores hurried to Ireland to join in armed rebellion. By 1868 the Fenian strength was spent, and British authority was supreme throughout the island. English statesmen, however, realized that further trouble would arise unless a more conciliatory policy was adopted by the government at Westminster.

Gladstone Tries to Solve the Irish Problem

William E. Gladstone was England's prime minister at this time. It was his belief that Ireland could be pacified if the British ministry would but solve the twin problems of land tenure and the Established Irish Church. Although the Irish had been relieved of tithes for the support of this church by the Temporalities Bill of 1835, the continued presence of the Anglican Communion with its elaborate organization and endowments was a source of annoyance to Irish nationalists and Catholics. Gladstone remedied this by securing the passage of a measure which disestablished the Irish Church. The Irish gained but little material advantage by this act, and the Anglican Church lost in money and jurisdiction. The measure, however, recognized that Ireland was a Catholic country. Equally significant was the fact that the Act of Union, which had saddled the Church on Ireland, had been altered. If it could be changed in this respect, it could be modified in other ways. Ireland welcomed this concession and did little to impede the work of the Anglican bishops and priests who remained on the island upon their own responsibility.

Having removed the Established Irish Church, Gladstone turned parliament's attention toward the land tenure system. The problem was difficult and required careful handling. For decades, Irish renters had protested against the unjust and high charges exacted by the landlords. Failure to meet these obligations had resulted frequently in arbitrary ejection with no compensation for improvements which the tenants had made. Any tinkering with this arrangement was bound to raise strong opposition from the landed class, yet this was what Gladstone intended doing. In spite of stubborn resistance, Gladstone gained the passage of the Irish Land Act of 1870, according to which no tenant could be ejected if he had paid his rents. When ejection for non-payment of rent did take place, the landlord was to make compensation for improvements. The owner, however, was not prevented from raising rents. Moreover, he could make compensation and then eject a tenant whom he thought undesirable. Gladstone's measure, therefore, failed to provide for fixity of tenure and fair rents.

Although the Fenian movement had fallen into disrepute, the bulk of the Irish believed in independence. On the other hand there were some, notably Isaac Butt and Charles Stewart Parnell, who argued for the establishment of a separate parliament for Ireland. Irish affairs were to be handled by this body and not by the parliament at Westminster. Ireland was to remain within the Empire and to have representatives in the House of Commons. Butt called this program *Home Rule for Ireland*. There were in Ireland, then, two different streams of thought—one insisting upon independence and the other standing for Home Rule. At first Butt's followers were outnumbered, but by 1874 they had won a majority of the Irish seats in the House of Commons. Realizing the hopelessness of their position in this body, which was predominantly anti-Irish, the Irish nationalists determined upon a filibustering program, with the hope of preventing parliament from doing anything until Irish requests were granted. English opinion was exasperated by these tactics, but Parnell and his followers were delighted.

In the meantime conditions in Ireland went from bad to worse, for little was being done by the Tory Party, which was in power, to improve matters. The general election of 1880, however, restored Gladstone to office. At first his attention was directed toward other problems, during the discussion of which he encountered Parnell's filibustering tactics. At the same time an organization of Irish cultivators known as the Irish Land League incited tenants to resist higher rents and to boycott those landlords who levied them. Although Gladstone frowned upon these practices and declared them illegal, he tried to correct the situation by carrying through parliament the Irish Land Act of 1881. This measure recognized that the occupier of land had rights which must be protected by law. A Land Court was established and empowered to fix rents which were to be binding for fifteen years. At the end of this period the tenure, subject to the approval of the Court, was to revert to the landlord. In the meantime the tenant might sell his rights either to his landlord or a prospective buyer. In case the occupier wished to purchase the holding, the British government would assist him by a long-term loan, amounting to three fourths of the sale price.

British and Irish opinion was hostile to this measure at first, but as time went on the public came to appreciate Gladstone's wisdom in trying to promote a large group of independent Irish farmers. In the meantime, the Irish clamored either for independence or Home Rule. Matters reached a crisis in May, 1882, when the British Secretary for Ireland was killed in Phoenix Park, Dublin. Gladstone retaliated by imposing more severe coercive measures than before, while Parnell disavowed all connections with the extreme Irish agitators. In return for his action, the Liberal Party in England intimated that they would support Home Rule. But shortly thereafter, Gladstone was succeeded by Lord Salisbury, who, during a brief period of Tory ascendancy, extended the loan system provided for in the Act of 1881. In February, 1886, Gladstone was back in office and revealed the policy of his party by introducing a modified Home Rule bill. The Tories, assisted by a number of Liberals, defeated this measure. Gladstone then resigned and the country was thrown into the throes of a general election over the question of Home Rule.

The electorate returned Salisbury and the Tories to power. Salisbury remained in office until 1892; and while he furthered loans to Irish tenants, he refused to believe that the latter were capable of governing themselves. The filibustering tactics of the Irish in parliament and the continued acts of violence in Ireland convinced him that he was right and that Home Rule was out of the question. Supporting evidence appeared in the April, 1888 issues of the London *Times*. Under the heading "Parnellism and Crime," Parnell was charged with being responsible for Irish unrest and with being implicated in the Phoenix Park Murder. A copy of a letter apparently written by Parnell seemed to establish his guilt. Parnell promptly denied these charges, while one of his friends, also indicted for the Phoenix Park Murder, sued the *Times* for libel. During the course of the investigation that followed, one Richard Pigott confessed that he had forged the letter in question. Immediately all charges were dropped, while the *Times* was required to pay heavy damages for the injury it had committed. Although Parnell was exonerated, the episode weakened his position and the cause which he advanced. Shortly thereafter, he was named as a corespondent in a divorce case which he did not contest. English opinion was outraged by his conduct and forced Gladstone, who at first declared himself no judge on such matters, to ask Parnell to retire from politics. Parnell refused; and the Irish nationalists, yielding to pressure, deserted in large numbers to a more respectable leader, Justin McCarthy. Parnell poured forth his wrath upon his former friends, but he was unable to regain control of the Irish nationalists. His death in 1891, however, was a serious loss to Ireland.

Home Rule for Ireland

Home Rule continued to attract Gladstone's attention even though public opinion had increased its hostility on account of Parnell's personal conduct. In spite of this opposition, Gladstone introduced a Home Rule bill in 1893. After a debate which lasted eighty-four days, the Commons approved of the measure by the bare majority of thirty-four votes. The Lords, however, turned down the bill. Gladstone was touched to the quick, and, although he continued to hold office for several months, it was this defeat which led to his retirement early in 1894. From then on to the close of the century, Home Rule for Ireland received little attention in England.

Gladstone's proposals for Home Rule materially weakened the historic Liberal Party and increased the strength of his Conservative opponents. In the division which attended the bill of 1886, ninety-three Liberals voted with the Conservatives. This desertion was enough to defeat the measure, though it did not deter Gladstone from trying again in 1893. Many of the Liberals, notably Joseph Chamberlain, questioned the wisdom of Gladstone's action and severed their connection with the party. For a time these dissenters pursued an independent course and were known in parliament as Liberal Unionists. Shortly after 1893 they joined the Conservative

Party which, in recognition, of their new allies and their determination to prevent Home Rule, assumed the name of Unionist. The Unionist Party also prevented Gladstone's attempt to check increased naval appropriations. The Liberal Party was shattered and the conduct of Irish affairs was placed in the hands of the Unionists who won the election of 1895 and continued in office, under Lord Salisbury and Balfour, until 1905.

In the meantime Ireland was distracted by the factional strife which developed between McCarthy's followers and those who accepted John Redmond, Parnell's successor. In dealing with this situation, the Tory or Unionist Government sought to "kill Home Rule by kindness." Additional loans were made to Irish cultivators, and in 1898 Ireland was given the same rights in local government enjoyed by England. Horace Plunkett's founding of the Irish Agricultural Society in 1897 also lulled Irish discontent. Through the establishment of coöperatives in farming, poultry raising, and dairying, the Agricultural Society increased the economic prosperity of the Irish. The advent of the Boer War, however, revived Irish interest in Home Rule and led to the union of the McCarthy and Redmond factions in 1899.

Six years earlier, Douglas Hyde, the son of an Irish country rector, founded the Gaelic League, which had as its objectives a revival of the Celtic language and the promotion of Gaelic culture. The movement spread rapidly and soon became the vehicle by means of which Irish agitators propagandized for independence. Ultimately many of the members of the League became ardent supporters of the Sinn Fein (we ourselves) movement, which advocated complete independence from England. Definite manifestations of Sinn Fein appeared in 1899 when Arthur Griffith began his agitations for the restoration of the Irish parliament which had existed in 1792. To gain his ends, Griffith advocated passive resistance to taxation and a boycott of English goods. He suggested also that Ireland should not elect representatives to the House of Commons. For a few years Griffith's group prospered, but by 1905 it was eclipsed by the radical Sinn Feiners. In the same year, the Unionists were swept out of office by the Liberals, who tried to pass a modified form of Home Rule. The Irish representatives refused to support this halfway measure and forced the Liberal ministry to drop the proposal.

The Liberal Party's reluctance to sponsor complete Home Rule was due to the hostile attitude of the Lords, who were ready to veto such a measure. As long as that body possessed the power of vetoing bills which passed the Commons, Home Rule for Ireland was out of the question. The ministry, moreover, was interested in furthering social and economic legislation and did not care to irritate the Lords by forcing Home Rule upon them. A crisis was reached in 1909 when the Lords rejected Lloyd George's budget. The general election of 1910 returned the Liberals but forced that party to depend upon Irish votes to enact their social program and the Parliament Act of 1911, which materially reduced the legislature power of the Lords. In return for Irish support and in keeping with a promise that had been made, the ministry introduced in January, 1912, a Home Rule bill which satisfied most of the Irish. Bitter opposition arose from the Tory members of parliament. Their position was strengthened by Ulster's attitude toward the bill. Under the leadership of Sir Edward Carson, the Protestant and Unionist population of Ulster declared their intention of resisting Home Rule by force. This declaration was followed by street demonstrations and gunrunning in Ulster. The Liberal Party, therefore, had to choose between modifying its bill to satisfy Ulster or facing a civil war in Northern Ireland. Although Redmond, speaking in behalf of the Irish nationalists, promised not to interfere with the religious and social life of Ulster in case the bill passed parliament, neither the Ulsterites nor the Unionists supported the original measure which passed parliament and was signed by the King in September, 1914.

Ireland During the World War

The advent of the World War altered the entire situation. Common sense dictated that England should not force Home Rule upon Ulster in the face of German attack. For this reason the measure was suspended. Redmond and the Irish nationalists realized England's difficulties and accepted the suspension in good grace, while the Ulsterites were appeased by the ministry's promise to amend the bill in their favor at a later date. The government, moreover, realizing the strong Sinn Fein sentiment which existed in Ireland, did not resort to conscription on the island. Voluntary enlistments were encouraged. Outside of Ulster there was little interest in the war except insofar as it gave Sinn Fein an opportunity to advance its plea for complete independence.

German diplomacy incited the separatists to action while Irish friends in the United States supplied Sinn Fein with funds. Among the leaders of the latter group none was more belligerent than Sir Roger Casement, who by the fall of 1914 had formed the Irish Volunteers. Working in close coöperation with Germany, the Irish Volunteers stormed and captured Dublin, April 22, 1916. Contrary to expectations, no aid was received from Berlin and within a week British authority was restored. Casement, Padraic Pearse, who had styled himself "President of the Provisional Irish Republic" and several others were charged with treason and executed. Irish opinion generally condemned these executions. This added only to the unrest existing on the island. Hoping to soothe injured feelings and to provide a basis for establishing Home Rule, Lloyd George summoned the leaders of Ireland to meet him at London. From July, 1917, to April, 1918, this gathering tried to find a formula which pleased all parties. The convention was doomed to failure when the Sinn Feiners withdrew and when England insisted that Ireland must accept conscription in return for Home Rule.

After the breakup of the convention, Ireland openly supported Sinn Fein and turned its back upon Redmond and the Home Rulers. In the general election of 1918, the latter won but seven seats, while the Unionists gained twenty-five and Sinn Fein seventy-three. The victors refused to attend the meeting of the British parliament, and in January, 1919, proclaimed the existence of the Irish Republic. At the time their leader, De Valera, was in prison; but in February of the same year he made his escape and appeared in Dublin, where he was hailed as President of the Irish Republic. British authority in Ireland was at a standstill, and rioting and conflict followed. Hoping to check Sinn Fein, the British dispatched an army to Ireland and passed a new Home Rule bill. According to this measure, separate Home Rule governments were created for Northern and Southern Ireland. Ulster accepted the offer, but Southern Ireland remained loyal to the Irish Republic. During the remainder of 1920 and the first half of 1921, English troops battled with the armed forces of Sinn Fein. Further bloodshed would have followed but for England's determination to settle the dispute by peaceful methods.

The Irish Free State

Late in June, 1921, Lloyd George met the leaders of Sinn Fein at London and after much discussion succeeded in bringing the war to an end. A treaty of peace was accepted, and Ireland was given dominion status within the British Empire. England, in short, was willing to tear up the Act of Union of 1801 and to accord Ireland independence subject to the following restrictions: (1) Ireland must assume its share of the

national debt; (2) judicial appeal to the English courts was to
be allowed; (3) an oath of loyalty to the British King was to
be required of all Irishmen; and (4) England was to retain,
in the interest of national defense, certain naval rights in Ireland. Ulster, moreover, might join the Irish dominion, which
was to be known as the Irish Free State, or remain a separate
entity as stipulated in the Home Rule Act of 1920. Ulster,
also known as Northern Ireland, decided to follow the latter
course, and today has its own parliament and responsible
ministry. Ulster, moreover, is represented in the British
parliament.

In the meantime, the treaty of 1921 had been submitted to
the British parliament and the Dail Eireann, the legislative body
of the Irish Republic. The former assembly accepted the
treaty without delay, but considerable opposition developed
in the Dail because of De Valera and his followers. De Valera
refused to vote for the treaty on the ground that it had not
recognized Irish independence. A majority of the members
of the Dail, however, differed with De Valera and the treaty
was ratified on January 7, 1922. De Valera immediately resigned his office of president and during the course of the year
attempted to incite rebellion against the Irish Free State.
Unable to gain his ends by force, he resorted to political
methods, and in the Irish elections of 1932 he gained a majority
of seats in the Irish parliament.

Immediately, an ultra-nationalist policy was fostered. For
the time being, De Valera was willing to consider the Free
State a member of the British Commonwealth of Nations.
He took steps, however, to secure the passage of measures
which forbade further payments on the British national debt,
abolished judicial appeal to English courts, and declared that
no Irishman should take the oath of loyalty to the British King.
Britain viewed these acts as violations of the treaty and sought
to punish the Free State by imposing tariffs against Irish
goods. The Free State retaliated with tariffs of its own.

While these anti-British tactics were approved by the bulk of the Irish electorate, there was considerable opposition to De Valera's economic program, which entailed an elaborate reorganization of Ireland's industrial and agricultural life. Heavy taxes and the increasing terrorism perpetrated by the Irish Republican army led finally to the organization of a semi-Fascist body of Blue Shirts under General O'Duffy. By the spring of 1934, O'Duffy had De Valera on the defensive, but because of internal dissensions among the Blue Shirts, De Valera regained control of the situation.

During 1935 De Valera continued his economic program in spite of strong opposition on the part of the landed and industrial classes of Ireland. Further unrest developed as the results of the tariff war between England and Ireland became apparent in a decline in Irish trade. Ireland's most profitable industry, the export of livestock, showed a decrease of over fifty million dollars. Early in 1936 the two governments agreed to a commercial pact which, it was hoped, would restore trade to a normal basis. Some improvement has taken place, but the results in general are far from satisfactory. In the meantime De Valera retained his narrow majority in the Dail and secured the enactment of measures calculated to hasten the day when the Irish Republic will be proclaimed. Children, for example, are to be taught to read, speak, and write Celtic, English having been abolished in the schools. Taking advantage of the constitutional crisis caused by Edward VIII's abdication in December, 1936, De Valera secured the Dail's consent to two bills which materially affected Anglo-Irish affairs. According to these measures, the internal affairs of Ireland became subject solely to the wishes of the Dail. On the other hand in the conduct of foreign affairs, the King was recognized as the head of the British Commonwealth of Nations. This concept was not expressed in explicit terms, but the evident meaning provided for Ireland's continued membership in the Empire. The King and Governor-General were removed from domestic affairs. In July, 1937, a majority of but 158,000 voters out of 1,212,000 accepted a new Irish constitution. At the same time, elections to the Dail reduced De Valera's control, and he may have trouble in securing the passage of acts necessary to initiate the new government. Although the constitution expounds Christian and social ideas, fairly echoes with expressions of Irish independence, and says nothing of the King, there is little that distinguishes it from previous arrangements. The new state is to be known as Eire and, if Northern Ireland consents, will include the entire island. It seems unlikely that Northern Ireland will accept the sovereignty of Eire, and it is certain that Britain will not tolerate any interference with the wishes of Northern Ireland. In world affairs, Eire will function as an independent state, though provision exists for coöperation with any group of nations. In this manner, Ireland's membership in the British Commonwealth of Nations will probably be maintained. Ireland, however, did not attend the Imperial Conference of 1937.

Imperial Conferences

Although Britain's relations with Ireland have been strained, happier contacts have existed with the other Dominions. The wisdom of granting local self-government to these possessions was shown on many occasions during the late nineteenth and early twentieth centuries. The presence of a common historical heritage, visits by members of the British royal family, the cruises of the British navy, and improved methods of transportation and communication represent ties which have bound the Dominions more closely to England than direct government from London. Conscious of the value of these connections, the Dominions have aided the Mother Country in time of war. Canada and Australia assisted Britain in the Sudan disturbances of 1885 and the Boer War, while all the Dominions furnished large supplies of life and treasure during the war with Germany. More significant were the coöperative efforts of the Dominions in promoting greater economic intercourse. Britain appreciated the value of trade connections as well as the problem of imperial defense, and she joined with the Dominions in building the British Commonwealth of English-speaking nations. The writings of James A. Froude, Sir Charles Dilke, and Sir John Seeley did much to stimulate imperial interest, as did the achievements of Cecil Rhodes and Sir George Grey. Liberal leaders like William E. Forster supported the movement which led in time to the foundation of the Royal Colonial Institute and the Imperial Federation League. It was the latter organization which suggested that a colonial conference should be held in conjunction with the Empire's celebration of Victoria's Jubilee of 1887.

During April and May of that year, representatives from Britain's colonies gathered at London and discussed matters of trade and defense. A decade later another meeting was held. Here the premiers of the Dominions vied with agents of the Crown colonies in advocating imperial unity. A third conference, held in 1902, agreed that further meetings should be held every four years. Because of political conditions in England, the next gathering took place in 1907. The delegates were so impressed by the importance of this meeting that they drafted a constitution for further Imperial Conferences. This document provided for the dissemination of news and the interchange of opinion between the sessions of the conferences. As a result, considerable preparation took place for the meeting of 1911. Several of the colonies proposed significant changes in imperial administration, that of an Imperial Council of State being the most important. The Dominions, however, jealous of their privileges within the Empire, were cold to this proposition. On the other hand their representatives anxiously discussed the foreign relations of Britain and sat on a special Committee of Imperial Defense, which had been established in 1907. The 1911 gathering was important also because of the request that the Dominions be supplied with confidential information on foreign affairs. It was suggested that the Dominions should follow Canada's policy, established in 1879, of maintaining agents at London so as to promote greater coöperation in world politics. Neither of these ideas had been accepted by the other Dominions when the World War broke forth in 1914.

The exigencies of the World War argued for greater coöperation. As a result, invitations were extended to the premiers of the Dominions to attend the regular sessions of the British War Cabinet which, in the interest of greater efficiency, had been established in place of the usual cabinet. India also was asked to attend this gathering, which convened for the first time as an Imperial War Cabinet, in the spring of 1917. Further conferences were held in 1918 and 1919, with the war as the most important problem under discussion. The meeting of 1919 was significant in that the Dominions, for the first time in history, had a voice in shaping the peace terms of that year. From a constitutional angle, the resolutions adopted in 1918 were more important. At this gathering it was agreed that the governments of the Dominions might communicate directly with the British prime minister on all matters of cabinet importance. During the interval between the meetings of the Imperial Conferences, each Dominion was to be represented at London either by its own premier or by a Dominion minister. According to the Treaty of Versailles the Dominions were recognized as nations and granted separate representation in the assembly of the League of Nations. Later, in 1921, Canada, Australia, and New Zealand attended the Washington Arms Conference as members of the Empire delegation. The Canadian Government, moreover, now maintains a resident minister in Washington, Paris, and Tokyo.

The experiences of the Imperial Conferences held before and after the World War argued for a new constitutional arrangement between the Dominions and the Mother Country.

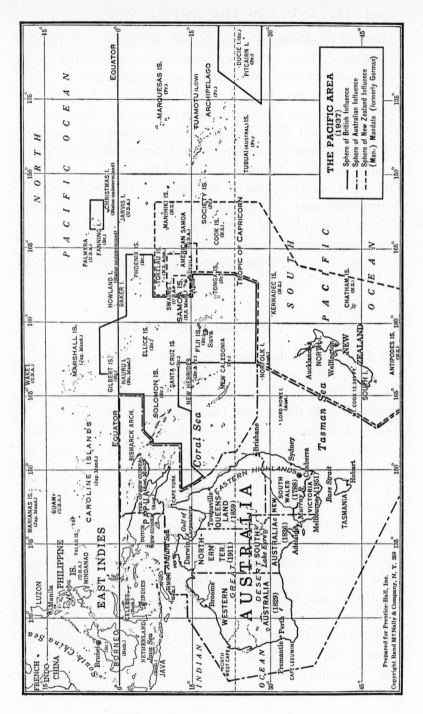

THE PACIFIC AREA
(1937)

——— Sphere of British Influence
—·—·— Sphere of Australian Influence
— — — Sphere of New Zealand Influence
(Man.) Mandate (formerly German)

Prepared for Prentice-Hall, Inc.
Copyright Rand McNally & Company, N. Y. 289 135

Each of the Dominions had become conscious of its national existence. Their sacrifices during the war constituted actions of which they were proud. Their agents had signed the Treaty of Versailles, were in the League of Nations, and spoke freely as equals at war cabinet meetings at London. South Africa, Australia, and New Zealand, moreover, acquired mandates from the League for certain former German colonies in Africa and the Pacific. Britain recognized the national aspirations of the Dominions, and at the Imperial Conference of 1926 generously met the demand of these self-governing states. Formal recognition of Dominion nationalism was granted and each state was accorded equality of status in domestic and foreign affairs. Further discussion of dominion status took place at the Imperial Conference of 1930.

The Statute of Westminster

As a result of these meetings the British parliament, in December, 1931, passed the Statute of Westminster which gave formal effect to the resolutions of the past two conferences. According to this act the Dominions were recognized as independent states within a British Commonwealth of Nations. Each was to direct its own foreign affairs and thus could not be embroiled in conflicts without its own consent. The British parliament was to have no authority over the Dominions nor could it disallow any act of a Dominion parliament. The authority of the Canadian parliament, however, was not to encroach upon the powers of the Canadian provincial assemblies. It was the provinces themselves which insisted upon the retention of the British North American Acts. Should a dispute arise between the provinces and the Dominion Government as to the constitutionality of a Dominion act, the matter is referred to the King's Privy Council for final settlement. Early in 1937 the Privy Council declared several acts of the Dominion unconstitutional. Although the authority for this decision, as well as for the Statute of Westminster, rests upon an enactment of the British parliament, it is inconceivable that any Dominion "would be refused any alteration in her fundamental law which her government and people really desired." Moreover, since an appeal to the Privy Council rests "not upon the British North America Acts, but upon other Imperial Statutes, it can be abolished . . . by the Dominion Parliament." Each Dominion recognized the existence of the British King as sovereign, an agent of whom was to preside in the Dominion but to possess only nominal power. The British parliament, moreover, was not to alter the line of succession or royal titles without the consent of the Dominions. Finally, it should be noted that Australia and New Zealand have not accepted as yet the Statute of Westminster.

The Statute of Westminster, in brief, transformed a large part of the empire into a British Commonwealth of Nations. Economic forces, cemented by sentimental ties and a common historical heritage, laid the basis for the Imperial Conferences and the Statute of Westminster. The latter merely gave authoritative status to an established fact. It can not be interpreted, as a few critics have asserted, as foreshadowing a dismemberment of the Empire and the collapse of British imperial solidarity. Loyalty to the Mother Country was patent before the passage of the Statute of Westminster and, since 1931, has grown in quality and significance. The Honorable B. S. B. Stevens, Prime Minister of New Zealand, recently remarked, "The problem of the Dominions, in so far as foreign policy is concerned, is not such a difficult one; and in practice there have been no great divergences of opinion that might conceivably have split the Empire. I am convinced that, even if we thought that Great Britain had made a mistake, the citizens of the overseas Empire would never consent to wash their hands of the consequences. The tie of sentiment has a very real value under these conditions." The Prime Minister also stated that "it is an Empire of the spirit, its bonds are above self-interest or legal exactitudes, its ties defy rational or juridical explanations, it is a unity accepted without question, in a fashion so inevitable as to be almost mystical."

Although no political connection of any value exists between Britain and the Dominions or among the Dominions themselves, the solidarity of the Commonwealth is beyond all question. The recent death of George V in January, 1936, was felt as keenly in Melbourne as in London, while Edward VIII was deluged with congratulatory messages from the Dominions. Edward VIII's abdication produced some discussion concerning the Dominions' rôle in the Empire. Each of these states, however, coöperated with the Baldwin ministry in the solution of the problem which resulted in George VI's accession to the throne. Similar sentiments were expressed in Newfoundland, which had been given self-government in 1855. Owing to financial difficulties caused in part by the World War and the depression, Newfoundland, at its own request, was reduced in 1933 from an autonomous government to a Crown colony. Although there were demonstrations in St. Johns during the fall of 1935 in favor of restoring self-government, conditions at present do not appear favorable to such a step. A happier story may be told of Southern Rhodesia, which in 1923 was granted local self-government.

An Enlightened Indian Policy

In the meantime India's position in the empire was altered. Between 1861 and 1909 India was governed by a British Viceroy, an executive council, a legislative assembly, and a series of provincial councils. The legislative assembly included the Viceroy, the executive council, and a group nominated by the native and European elements. The provincial councils had very restricted powers, as did the legislative assembly, while the franchise was limited to about thirty thousand people. With the opening of the twentieth century, a demand for greater rights arose among the native population. Most of this centered in the All Moslem League, founded in 1906, which voiced the national aspirations of over sixty million Mohammedans. A separatist group developed in 1907. This group sought to advance Indian independency by acts of violence. Others tried to injure Britain by boycotting English goods. The British government met these attacks by coercive legislation. Kindness, however, softened the enforcement of these measures; and in 1909 parliament passed an act by which the native population was given greater control in local matters and increased membership in the executive council. No further change was made until 1919.

During this interval, Indian nationalism demanded greater rights. Anxious to retain the friendship of the Indians who had helped Britain in the World War, the English government undertook an exhaustive study of the Indian problem. The results of this investigation formed the basis for the Government of India Act of 1919, whereby the powers of the provincial assemblies were enlarged and the total electorate increased to over five million. Britain was proud of this act and hailed it as a step toward Indian self-government. The Indian nationalists, however, registered their disappointment by renewed agitation for Home Rule.

The strength of the nationalists was shown at the 1920 sessions of the All-India Congress, founded in 1885, by those who advocated self-government. At the 1920 meeting the extremists gained control and elected to the presidency Lajpat Rai, a prominent lawyer and follower of Mohandas Gandhi. Gandhi was born in 1869 of Hindu parents who were pro-British in politics. He was educated in England and practiced law in India and South Africa. His professional duties brought him into contact with the British authorities and the lower classes of Indian society. English indifference to the sad lot of the "untouchables," the lowest caste in the social and religious system of the Hindus, and to the Indians, in general, convinced him that the hope of his country was in India and not in Britain. Accordingly, he preached and taught resistance to British authority. Gandhi realized the futility of armed resistance and urged his followers, who joined him by the thousands, to ignore and disobey the English government. Non-resistance and civil disobedience became the methods whereby he hoped to emancipate his country from British rule. In 1920 he staged a nation-wide demonstration. Loyal followers withdrew their children from the schools, boycotted English goods, and refused to recognize the judicial and executive actions of the British Indian government. So successful was the attack that Indian nationalists hailed Gandhi as Mahatma, or the Great Soul of India.

The All-India Congress of 1921 voted to support Gandhi in promoting civil disobedience. The religious differences, however, between the Hindus and Moslems plus Gandhi's attack upon the caste system retarded progress. At the same time some of Gandhi's disciples committed acts of violence which gave the British an opportunity of striking at the nationalist movement. In 1922 Gandhi himself was arrested and thrown into jail on the charge of inciting sedition among the Indians. True to his convictions, Gandhi refused to recognize the legality of the sentence and sought to resist it by going on a hunger-strike. By this time the nationalist cause had been seriously weakened by the withdrawal of most of the Moslems. These desertions, rather than the hunger-strike, probably explain why the British released Gandhi in 1924. Gandhi's influence had been lessened, and the British felt they could afford to adopt a tolerant attitude.

During the course of the next four years the nationalists, under Gandhi, continued to agitate for Home Rule, though the economic and social reforms introduced by the British convinced many Indians that English control was preferable to local self-government. In 1928 Sir John Simon visited India to undertake a survey of the political situation, with a view of altering the Act of 1919. The nationalists informed him that nothing short of Dominion status would satisfy them. On the other hand, wealthy Indians, native princes, Moslem leaders, and self-interested English capitalists, deluged Simon with reasons why Britain should reject the nationalists' demands. Simon returned to England and submitted certain recommendations to the British ministry. These led in turn to a conference on India in 1930. To this meeting came representatives of all the Indian factions except the nationalists. Nothing positive was accomplished by this gathering or those held in 1932 and 1933. Indian nationalism and British imperialism could not be reconciled, nor could any middle course be found which pleased both Moslem and Hindu. Indian princes, moreover, were opposed to any further extension of self-government which might interfere with their own absolute powers.

In spite of these conflicts the British ministry was determined to alter the Act of 1919 in the interest of India. Immediately, the ministry was bombarded by opposition both in India and at home. The government remained firm, and in 1935 succeeded in passing a new constitution for India. According to this measure, all of British India, except Burma, was to be divided into eleven states. These, together with the native states, were to form a federated government for India. Each of the various constituent units were to have a local assembly, while a federal parliament was to exist for all India. The Viceroy's council was to be transformed into a ministry responsible to the national parliament, which was to be elected on a broad and liberal franchise. In lieu of a Viceroy, India was to have a British Governor-General, responsible to the British Cabinet. Through this officer, Britain was to have all control over military and foreign affairs and on occasion might settle religious, judicial, financial, and minority problems. Beyond these restrictions, India was to have local self-government.

A detailed examination of this act would reveal that the

British government by concessions here and there had endeavored to find a formula which would satisfy most of the Indian factions and parties. The Moslems and the native princes, for example, were won over to the measure by the granting of greater rights and representation than their numbers justified. The All-India Congress Party, however, was not satisfied. Its leader, Mr. Nehru, called the Act of 1935 a "charter of slavery," and urged India to agitate for independence. Gandhi was less violent but stated that Britain should have granted Dominion status. The Governor-General, Lord Linlithgow, therefore, met stiff opposition in establishing the new government. In February, 1937, the elections to the assemblies in a majority of the provinces were won by the Congress Party. At first, this party refused to form ministries but, in July, following Gandhi's advice, assumed office. Later Gandhi and Lord Linlithgow conversed informally about India, and the way was cleared for the meeting of the Federated Parliament in August. At this gathering the Congress Party showed a willingness to coöperate. Careful leadership by Linlithgow, plus Gandhi's influence, appears to have ushered in a new day for India. Ultimately, Britain must grant Dominion status, which is what Gandhi has worked for, and which most Indians, except for certain radicals, desire.

Egyptian and Near Eastern Problems

The rising tide of nationalism, fostered by the World War, caused trouble for Britain in Egypt. When Turkey entered the war in December, 1914, as an ally of Germany, England proclaimed the separation of Egypt from Turkey and established a protectorate over the former. Egyptian nationalists disliked the arrangement and broke forth in a rebellion which England finally smashed by 1919. Four years later, Britain promulgated a constitution which provided for the establishment of an Egyptian kingdom under King Fuad. The nationalists interpreted this act as a recognition of Egyptian independence, but Britain viewed Egypt as a dependency. During the decade that followed, King Fuad tried to promote the welfare of his kingdom without offending Britain or his nationalistic subjects. He succeeded in so far as England was concerned, but the violence of the nationalists toward his government was shown on many an occasion. In 1930 Fuad sought to silence the opposition by issuing a new constitution which practically destroyed the legislative powers of the Egyptian parliament. The nationalists, however, continued their agitation and forced Fuad to abolish the organic law of 1934 and restore that of 1923. The internal situation was complicated still further by Italy's attack upon Ethiopia in 1935. Britain, moreover, aggravated conditions by sending troops into Egypt to protect her interests there and in the Sudan against Italy. Egyptian nationalists claimed that England had violated the constitution of 1923 and resorted to riots and demonstrations. As the situation became more critical, Britain suspended the law of 1923 and assumed full control of Egypt. Conditions failed to improve. Fearing an Egyptian uprising in the face of a possible Italian war, England reversed its policy and in December, 1935, restored the constitution of 1923. England's position in the Sudan and the Mediterranean demanded that she continue her hold over Egypt. The presence of British authority was objectionable to Egyptian nationalists, yet without English support, Egypt realized she might find herself embroiled in a conflict with imperialist Italy. To satisfy Egyptian nationalism and to safeguard British interests was a problem that seemed insoluble. The strength of the nationalists was shown by the rioting which took place following Fuad's death and burial in April, 1936, and by their gaining control of the Egyptian parliament in the elections of May, 1936.

In the meantime the British ministry undertook a series of negotiations with the Egyptian government which finally resulted in the Anglo-Egyptian Treaty of December, 1936. Egypt was recognized as an independent state. England agreed to withdraw her garrisons from Cairo and Alexandria within eight years but retained the right to police the Canal Zone. The military clauses relative to the Canal Zone may be revised within twenty years, or earlier if both parties agree. In the Sudan, an Egyptian force reorganized under English officers, will coöperate with the British in mutually protecting the interests of both states. The Egyptian Treaty has extricated Britain from a maze of uncertainties and absurdities which charac-terized that country's status in Egypt for the past fourteen years. An alliance between independent states has placed Anglo-Egyptian relations on a firm and friendly basis.

Nationalism caused Britain trouble in those areas over which she had acquired mandates as a result of the World War. According to the Treaties of Versailles and Sèvres, the victorious powers received territory formerly owned by Germany and Turkey. Generally, these possessions were held by the powers as mandates of the League of Nations, to which they were to give an account of their stewardship. German East Africa was divided between Belgium and England, the latter receiving the larger share. Togoland and the Cameroons were divided between France and Britain, while Mesopotamia, Palestine, Trans-Jordania, and Naura Island were awarded to England. South Africa received German Southwest Africa as a mandate; Australia, German New Guinea; and New Zealand, Western Samoa. The Ottoman Empire viewed with much concern the dismemberment of her Near Eastern territory but was helpless before the superior strength of the victors. The Turks, however, under their nationalist leader, Mustafa Kemal, showed their resentment by attacking and deposing Sultan Mohammed VI in 1922. Immediately, Mustafa Kemal tore up the Treaty of Sèvres and forced the powers concerned to agree to a new peace settlement known as the Treaty of Lausanne (1923). According to this arrangement Turkey received territory which Sèvres had allotted to Greece, Italy, and France, but recognized the British mandates of Palestine, Trans-Jordania, and Mesopotamia, the independent Arabian kingdom of Hejaz, and the French mandate of Syria. She also agreed to demilitarize the Straits and open them to the commerce of all nations.

Hardly had the Treaty of Lausanne been signed than nationalist feeling against Britain appeared in Mesopotamia and Palestine. Most of this centered in Hejaz, whose King, Hussein, aided the Arabian nationalists in the British mandated territory. Although England had allowed Feisal, one of Hussein's sons, to become King of Mesopotamia (Iraq), and another, Abdullah, to become the head of Trans-Jordania, Britain continued to view these as her mandates and sought to thwart any attempt on the part of the Arabians to knit these areas into a unified Arabian state. Rioting and street conflicts characterized the relations between the Arabian nationalists and England until 1930, when Britain, by the Treaty of Bagdad, recognized the independence of Mesopotamia. Two years later Mesopotamia was admitted to the League of Nations, and in 1935 the British troops were withdrawn from this area. In the meantime Abdullah had been trying to gain independence for his state of Trans-Jordania. In 1928, Britain agreed to the creation of a council and an elective assembly under Emir Abdullah but retained general control over that area.

In the territory west of the Jordan, known as Palestine proper, the Arabians sought to advance their nationalistic program but came into conflict with Britain and the Jewish population, which wanted the establishment of an independent Hebrew state. The Jews believed that England was friendly toward this objective, particularly after Lord Balfour had publicly announced England's willingness to aid in the founding of a Jewish state in Palestine. Jews from various parts of the world migrated to Palestine, while Sir Herbert Samuel, a Jew, undertook to govern this area as a British mandate. The Arabians, who outnumbered the Hebrews in Palestine, resented these actions and refused to coöperate either with the British or the Jews. England tried to bring the Jews and Arabians together but was unable to satisfy the national aspirations of either group. Frequent clashes took place, chiefly in Jerusalem, between the Jews and Arabians. It was only the superior military strength of the British that prevented war. At present, England retains her mandate at the point of the sword, much to the disgust of the Jews, who feel that Britain has violated Balfour's promises. Arabian nationalism, moreover, views the existing arrangement as impossible, and impatiently waits for the establishment of another independent Arabian state. Early in 1937, a British Commission visited and studied the situation in Palestine. In July, this body rendered a report which offered the following proposed solution: Trans-Jordania is added to Palestine and the enlarged area is divided into (1) a Jewish state which includes most of the coastal plain, the Valley of Galilee, and the upper waters of the Jordan; (2) a smaller British mandate around Jerusalem, with a corridor to the sea; (3) an Arabian kingdom which includes the highlands of Palestine, the desert of Gaza, and the area east of the Jordan. Parliament accepted the report and submitted it to the League of Nations. The League, after some study, appointed a neutral committee to coöperate with England in arranging for a partition. Certain Arabians have criticized the proposal, but the chief opposition arises from the Jews, who feel that they have been sacrificed so as to appease Arabian nationalism.

In her other mandates Britain has experienced far less trouble. New Zealand, Australia, and the Union of South Africa also have had good results in their mandates. The chief difficulty which has arisen in these areas has centered about the imperialistic program of Japan in the Pacific and the desire of Germany to regain her former colonies. The aggressions of Italy in the Mediterranean and North Africa have caused some trouble in Malta, while racial and religious disputes between India and the British Protectorate of Kenya have been productive of some unrest. A militant Japan, the penetration of communism into China, and the breakup of the Chinese Empire into several warring factions has caused England some concern in Hong Kong and Singapore. Elsewhere, British authority in the Empire remains undisputed. Most of the crown colonies, protectorates and dependencies are governed in a manner which satisfies the English, European, and native populations. Britain, moreover, has in some cases advanced the degree of self-government enjoyed by these peoples, and stands ready, at present, to aid in further political growth.

SELECTED BIBLIOGRAPHY

The general histories referred to in Chapters XXXI–XXXIV have pertinent material relative to Ireland and the Empire. H. Robinson's *Development of the British Empire* is invaluable. For Ireland, the following are recommended: S. L. Gwynn's *The History of Ireland* (New York, 1923); J. O. Connor's *History of Ireland, 1798–1924* (London, 1931); J. E. Pomfret's *The Struggle of Land in Ireland, 1800–1923* (Princeton, 1931), and D. R. Gwynn's *The Irish Free State, 1922–1927* (London, 1928).

C. H. Van Tyne's *India in Ferment* (New York, 1923) is favorable to England, while Lajpat Rai's *Young India* (New York, 1916) and *Political Future in India* (New York, 1919) are partisan in their treatment. Social affairs are treated in K. Mayo's *Mother India* (New York, 1927). M. K. Gandhi's *Young India, 1919–1922* (New York, 1923) represents the Indian nationalists. V. A. Smith's *The Oxford History of India* (Oxford, 1923) and E. A. Horne's *Political System of India* (Oxford, 1922) are of value. W. S. Blunt's *Secret History of the English Occupation of Egypt* (New York, 1922) and V. Chirol's *Egyptian Problem* (London, 1920) are of value for Egypt.

W. P. Hall's *Empire to Commonwealth* (New York, 1928); A. Zimmern's *Third British Empire* (London, 1926), and H. D. Hall's *The British Commonwealth of Nations* (London, 1920) are standard histories. Detailed studies may be found in A. B. Keith's *Responsible Government in the Dominions* (Oxford, 1928) and *The King and the Imperial Crown* (London, 1936). A. J. Toynbee's *Conduct of British Empire Foreign Relations since the Peace Settlement* (Oxford, 1928) and K. C. Wheare's *Statute of Westminster* (Oxford, 1933) are of value. The *Imperial Gazetteer* of India, the *Round Table*, and the *Times, Weekly Edition,* are current publications of value.

CHAPTER XXXVI

Domestic Affairs, 1914-1937

DURING the course of the World War, the English government conducted internal affairs so as to secure a victory over Germany. Factional strife was largely forgotten, the Home Rule Act of 1914 was suspended, and the cabinet was reorganized in the interests of national unity. The appointment of Lord Kitchener as Secretary for War added to the ministry a non-party man and led to a truce between the Liberals and their opponents, the Unionists and the Laborites. The arrangement worked rather well for several months but by 1915 signs of unrest had appeared. Conservatives and Laborites, alike, argued that their support warranted positions in the cabinet, especially as those in control seemed to lack an aggressive war policy. Matters reached a crisis by the spring of 1915, when the opposition demanded an explanation for military defeat abroad and the appalling lack of munitions. The Liberals, under Asquith, met the attack by admitting eight Conservatives and one Laborite to the cabinet but within a short time found themselves no better off. The addition of new members had increased the size but not the efficiency of the cabinet. Asquith, moreover, was unable to coördinate the activities of the cabinet members. The allocation of important duties to an inner group helped somewhat, but failed to produce the unity needed to conduct the war successfully.

Administrative Problems During the World War

The coalition cabinet, however, carried on, in spite of internal weakness and hostile criticism, until the close of 1916. By this time Lloyd George had shown his abilities as Minister of Munitions in so able a manner as to convince many that he should become the Prime Minister. Charles P. Scott, editor of the influential *Manchester Guardian,* expressed this thought in a letter to his friend L. T. Hobhouse. "I have a growing conviction," he wrote, "that with the present men we shall *not* win the war, and that the utmost we can hope for is a draw on bad terms. Hindenburg has changed the whole aspect of affairs for the Germans. George *might* do something of the same sort for us. . . . Of course, he has from our point of view great defects . . . but it is a question of alternatives and of the immediate use of his practical and efficient qualities for a definite purpose."

Lloyd George believed that no prime minister could act as the nation's executive, party leader, and chief cabinet officer at one and the same time. Accordingly, he tried to reorganize the ministry so as to relieve Asquith of the burden of directing the war, a duty which Lloyd George was willing to assume. The latter was convinced that Germany could not be defeated by continued pressure on the western front, and argued for increased activity in the Balkan area. Asquith, supported by the chief of the general staff, was opposed to this idea. Many of the Conservatives agreed with Asquith and questioned the wisdom of allowing a politican to supersede the views of the general staff. Fortunately for Lloyd George, aid came from an unexpected quarter in the person of Bonar Law who was anxious to keep the Conservative Party intact. This alliance paved the way for an arrangement which would have created a war committee, of which the Prime Minister would not have been a member. Asquith, however, was to remain as Prime Minister. In the meantime, Asquith had tried to settle his differences with Lloyd George. These conversations having failed, Asquith received the King's commission to form a new ministry. Bonar Law refused to serve if the "War Committee (without Asquith) was not set up." Asquith would not consent to this. Whereupon Lloyd George resigned. Realizing that he could not conduct affairs without Lloyd George, Asquith also resigned. Bonar Law was asked to form a ministry but was unable to gain the required support. The net result of these factional disputes was to elevate Lloyd George to the post of Prime Minister in December, 1916. George V's conduct in this ministerial crisis was beyond reproach. He quite willingly accepted the duty imposed upon him and installed Lloyd George without question. The King realized the need of keeping political unity at home as a means of defeating Germany. Moreover, he understood, as Victoria had not, the essential principles of ministerial responsibility. Neither George V nor his father, Edward VII, ever acted as Victoria had toward the ministers.

George V also consented to a complete alteration of the cabinet. Instead of an unwieldly body of twenty-two, a War Cabinet of five was established, most of whom were to devote their entire time to the problems incident to the war. Later, one or two others were added to this inner group in whose hands the remaining phases of the war rested. Assisting the War Cabinet were a large number of ministers who were in charge of specialized activities such as food control, shipping, and labor. By the close of the war the ministry consisted of the War Cabinet and some eighty-eight different bureaus or departments. In addition there were over four hundred committees and commissions handling matters of minor importance.

Although the traditional cabinet system had undergone modification, the idea of ministerial responsibility remained intact. The experiences of the World War, moreover, tended to increase the power and efficiency of that body. Heretofore, no precise or full statement of cabinet discussions and decisions was made. In seeking to discover how cabinet meetings were conducted, the historian had to depend upon such scraps of information as might appear in a biography of some minister, the official letters of the prime minister, and the brittle minutes of the Privy Council Register. Although the latter contains valuable data, such as decisions as to points of law and orders in council, there is no statement as to how these were arrived at or what arguments were advanced by the ministers. The prime minister's letters, moreover, were seldom shown to his colleagues. Nor were the activities of the various departments articulated in a manner conducive to proper coöperation and mutual understanding. During the early months of the war these shortcomings caused considerable trouble and impeded orderly progress of the government. Under the War Cabinet the chief clerk of the Council was instructed to include within the minutes a full summary of every discussion. This practice was discontinued after the close of the war. Since then the clerk has presented a digest of the documents on which the ministers were asked to make a decision. The minutes also contain any statement of fact made by a member and a complete record of all decisions. The cabinet members, therefore, have at their disposal an adequate record of their activities to which they may turn for guidance and precedent without having to rely upon memory. The old, informal system has given way to a businesslike organization. The decisions and orders appear as principles of action which have the complete support of the cabinet. The advice offered by the cabinet to the sovereign has become a definitive act of government in a manner that was not so apparent twenty years ago.

During the course of the war, the cabinet was frequently criticized for its conduct of that conflict, but at no time did the opposition try to unseat the ministry; nor was there any serious protest to the suspension of the Quinquennial Act of 1911. According to this measure, the parliament elected in December, 1910, should have been dissolved in 1916. The prospect of a general election in the midst of war did not appeal to many, and the parliament elected in 1910 voted to continue its sessions until the close of the war. Shortly after the Armistice of 1918, parliament was dissolved and writs were issued for a new election. The retiring parliament left an enviable record. Among its many achievements was the Franchise Act of 1918, which extended the vote to women.

Women Demand the Vote

Advocates of woman suffrage appeared as early as the eighteenth century. One of the first to favor this reform was Thomas Spence, who, in a tract published in 1798, argued for giving women the vote. William Thompson, a labor leader, did the same in 1825, while the London Working Men's Association considered placing it in their platform. During the passage of the Reform Act of 1832 there was some agitation in favor of extending the franchise to women, and in August of that year a petition to that effect was presented in parliament. Later, in 1867, John Stuart Mill spoke in support of woman suffrage in the House of Commons. In the meantime local societies became the basis for the National Union of Women's Suffrage Societies. During the remainder of the nineteenth century, a number of suffragette petitions appeared in parliament, and at least seven bills were introduced. In 1888, for example, a measure granting the vote to single women, who qualified as householders, was defeated in the Commons by but fifteen votes.

Outside of parliament, the suffragette movement grew in size and strength. Tracts and pamphlets were distributed, and the press gave increasing attention to the problem. By the opening of the twentieth century the question had become one of major importance, especially after Mrs. Pankhurst injected a militant note into the movement. At the same time the

Women's Social and Political Union was formed. In contrast to the older societies, which had appealed chiefly to the intellectual classes, the new organization enlisted the support of the women workers and the wives of laborers. The success of these tactics was shown during the 1906 session of parliament, when street parades and demonstrations took place in London. From the Ladies' Gallery in the Commons a heckling program was begun, while noisy bands of women besieged the homes and offices of the ministers. During the early winter, several of the women were arrested for rioting and, when they refused to pay their fines, were sent to jail.

Although the general public took more interest in the skating matches held indoors on artificial ice in midsummer, the government realized that the jailing of a few suffragettes had not broken the strength of the movement. Continued demonstrations and arrests took place until the fall of 1914. Acting under their energetic leader, Mrs. Pankhurst, the advocates of woman suffrage resorted to violence, rioting, and destruction of property. Since the government would not listen to reason and grant the vote to women, the suffragettes believed that a policy of frightfulness would force an extension of the franchise. Accordingly, windows were smashed, suburban railroad stations fired, golf greens ruined, telephone communications destroyed, and public buildings bombed. Birmingham Cathedral was whitewashed, and the church at Walgrave was burned to the ground. Parliamentary procedure and decorum was interrupted; and during the church litany service, suffragettes injected prayers for votes. On one occasion, a lady being presented to George V greeted him with the cry, "Your Majesty, won't you stop torturing women?"

What might have happened had the World War not intervened no one knows. At the outbreak of that conflict the suffragettes dropped their agitations and worked to win the war. Thousands of them became nurses, hotel clerks, porters, and workers in the munition plants. The net result of their valuable service, which released men for duty abroad, was the Franchise Act of 1918. All women over thirty years of age who were entitled to vote in local elections (this privilege had been granted in 1907) or whose husbands were qualified voters were given the vote. The act also removed the restrictions which the Reform Act of 1884 had not repealed, and gave the franchise to all men over twenty-one who had a fixed residence or place of business. The measure also abolished plural voting, which had been possible under the former law. In a few cases, graduates of Oxford and Cambridge, for example, were allowed to vote for their university, which enjoyed representation in parliament, as well as for their place of residence or business. Finally, the act redistributed the seats in the House of Commons and increased the number from 670 to 707. The establishment of the Irish Free State in 1922 reduced the size of the Commons to 615. In 1928 another act placed women on an equal status with men in respect to voting and established single unit constituencies, with some few exceptions, for every seventy thousand inhabitants. The size of the House of Commons was kept at 615. Women, moreover, by a measure passed in 1918, were allowed seats in the Commons, the first woman member being elected in 1919. Although the Lords have recognized women as peeresses in their own rights, they have not been granted membership in that body.

Labor Problems Since 1914

During the course of the war the British government had several sharp clashes with organized labor. Although the latter generally supported the conduct of the war, they frequently differed with the ministry on matters concerning labor conditions. Moreover, while they applauded the government's policy of controlling the railroads and mines and eagerly accepted trade agreements, they kept asking for further concessions and increased regulation of industry. Many were thoroughgoing socialists and desired a reorganization of society and government, which would eliminate private capitalism in favor of proletariat control. Higher wages, shorter hours, improved housing conditions, compensation for accidents, and national ownership or control of industry were demanded. Others, influenced by the Soviet Revolution of 1917, advocated a system of national gilds. According to this program, local and national labor committees were to manage each particular trade, and the industrial life of the nation was to be regulated by representatives of labor. Attempts were made by some of the munition workers to install this system; but the owners, supported by the government, were able to check these efforts.

In the meantime the British Labor Party had appointed a committee to investigate existing conditions and draft recommendations for a reconstruction of England's economic and political order. The committee reported in favor of placing the control of government in the hands of the workers, regardless of sex, whether the labor was performed by hand or brain. Private capitalism was to be supplanted by state capitalism. Realizing that such an arrangement could not be secured at once, the report advocated continued governmental control over the mines and railroads. In addition, steps should be taken to reduce unemployment, provide compensation for accident and sickness, establish a minimum wage, increase the taxes on profits and luxuries, further educational and cultural activities, and give labor a greater voice in industrial management. The report also emphasized the need of conducting foreign affairs more openly. Some of these suggestions had appeared already in the so-called Whitley report, submitted under the authority of the Ministry of Reconstruction created in the summer of 1917. The Whitley report was significant in that it advocated joint industrial councils, representing both employer and laborer, for the management of all trade and industry.

The agitations of the national gild advocates, the findings of the Whitley committee, and the recommendations of the British Labor Party were reflected in the election of 1918. Shortly after the Armistice, Lloyd George brought about a dissolution of parliament and appealed to the country to return the Coalition Government. He had selected a time when the country "was, as it were, disarmed and all political parties but its own at a disadvantage and in disarray, in order to seize power." The Labor Party, however, saw no valid reason why the Coalition should be continued now that the war was over. Moreover, it doubted that such an arrangement would be favorably disposed toward the demands of labor. The liberal and conservative supporters of Lloyd George tried to convince labor that suitable provision would be made for the working classes. Housing and labor conditions, so it was said, would be improved, a minimum wage established, the land system reformed, and employment secured by legislation protecting British industries and markets from foreign competition. Labor was also told that the expense of the war would be borne by the German people, who were responsible for the war, and that the Kaiser would be punished. Organized labor rejected these overtures and tried to influence the electorate by showing how "reckless and vulgar" were the "paltry" issues advanced by the government. The Coalition, however, had things much their own way. The election which followed was known as the "khaki" election because those in service were allowed the vote. The result was a disappointment to Labor for it captured but fifty-nine seats to the four hundred and eighty-three won by the Coalition.

No one had expected such a smashing victory for the Coalition, and while Labor had increased both its popular vote and seats in the Commons, it was far from being a formidable rival. Labor's outstanding leaders, Ramsay MacDonald, Philip Snowden, and Arthur Henderson, moreover, had been defeated in their constituencies. The nation had given its support to the Coalition and had rejected the socialism and pacifism of the Labor Party. England had gone Unionist, as most of the Coalition's strength came from that party, and the Liberal domination was broken. Finally, it should be noted that the Sinn Feiners, who had won seventy-three seats, absented themselves from parliament. As a result, the Coalition had a clear majority in the Commons. Labor, however, had the distinction of becoming His Majesty's Opposition.

The Unionist-Liberal Coalition continued to dominate until the fall of 1922. During this interval the prewar cabinet system was restored. Headed by Lloyd George, this body handled many delicate problems. In addition to Irish and foreign affairs, which are discussed elsewhere, considerable thought was given to trade and industry. Preferential arrangements facilitated trade within the Empire, while a moderate tariff shut off foreign competition in certain basic industries. British manufacturers profited from this policy as well as from an increased export trade. Wages, particularly in the coal trade, rose beyond what they had been in 1914. Experts realized, however, that this boom would stop as soon as Europe had replenished its exhausted supplies, and that prices and wages would have to decline. Trade-unionists appreciated this fact but were determined to prevent wage reductions. After considerable negotiation with the owners and the government, the railroad workers secured an agreement which protected them against a return to the 1914 level. Greater difficulty was encountered by the miners. At the outbreak of the war the government had taken over the mines as a war measure and had instituted a survey of mining conditions. The findings of the Royal Coal Commission had resulted in a recommendation, made in 1919, that the government should nationalize the mines. The Coalition Government refused to take this step and later announced that wartime control would cease in March, 1921. Shortly thereafter, the mine owners declared that economic conditions warranted a wage reduction. Labor protested, and having failed to secure any consideration, went on strike. Peace was restored in July. Labor received its former wages through governmental subsidies, but lost its demand for the creation of national boards to regulate wages.

Mine owners generally questioned the expediency of this arrangement. Europe, so they said, was in no position to continue its heavy purchases of British coal, while increased tariffs in the United States prevented the sale of British goods to that country. English manufacturers were of the same opinion and argued for a return to the price and wage level of 1914 as the only sensible road to recovery. In many industries, wages fell sharply after the boom years of 1919 and 1920; and although prices declined, they lagged behind wages. The purchasing power of the shilling, moreover, was less than it had been during the war. The miners' strike of 1921 had lessened their ability to buy needed supplies. Unemployment increased as did the dole, a system of money payments by the government to those out of work.

Tories and Laborites alike criticized Lloyd George for his handling of these problems. Many of the former believed that higher tariff protection should be given to British trade and industry. The Labor Party complained about the tardy and inadequate housing program, demanded government ownership (nationalization) of industry, and increased taxes upon profits and capital. Individuals, moreover, disliked Lloyd George's domination and manipulation of patronage, while others found fault with the dole. The conduct of foreign affairs also was criticized. Some disliked the settlement of the Irish question, the reparation question, and the Washington Arms Conference of 1921. More significant was the government's failure in the Near East. After encouraging the Greeks to attack the Turks in Asia Minor, Lloyd George had left them helpless before the victorious troops of Mustafa Kemal. Finally, in January, 1922, the Unionists announced that while they would support a coalition ministry, they intended to contest seats as an independent party at the next election. As the Irish problem had been settled, the Unionist Party assumed its former name, Conservative. Lloyd George tried to conciliate this group, but admitted failure when he resigned in the fall of 1922. Bonar Law immediately formed a wholly conservative government. Late in October of the same year, parliament was dissolved.

Labor rushed into the campaign with a splendid organization and, although it did not expect to win, believed it might double its strength in the Commons. Because of the establishment of the Irish Free State, the number of seats to be contested numbered but 615. Labor placed candidates in 412 constituencies. The Conservatives contested every Labor candidate on the ground that the latter advocated a socialist government comparable to Soviet Russia. The Liberals weakened themselves by splitting into two groups: the National Liberals, who supported Lloyd George; and the Independent Liberals under Asquith. In addition to these four major parties there were five relatively unimportant groups. The election was won by the Conservatives under Bonar Law. This party gained 344 seats to the 142 won by Labor and the 114 gained by the Liberals, of which 61 went to the National Liberals. The popular vote, however, gave the combined opposition, including the minority parties, a majority of over three million votes. Actually, the Conservatives polled less than forty per cent of the popular vote. Labor almost doubled its vote of 1918 and increased its strength in the Commons by eighty-three seats. Neither wing of the Liberal Party fared well in respect to the Commons. On the other hand there was a wide disproportion between the seats won and their popular vote. The combined vote of the National and Independent Liberal Parties amounted to over four million votes, but this gained only 114 seats in the Commons. The Conservatives, however, polled five and a half million votes which gave them 344 seats, of which 42 had been uncontested.

The Conservatives, however, claimed control of government. No one contested this claim, and the new ministry assumed office under Bonar Law. Failing health forced Bonar Law to resign in favor of Stanley Baldwin, who served as Prime Minister from May, 1923 to January, 1924.

During the period from October, 1922, to January, 1924, the Conservatives remained entrenched in office. Late in October, 1923, Baldwin created a crisis within his party by advocating increased tariffs as a means of decreasing unemployment and restoring prosperity at home. Many of his followers refused to follow him in this retreat from free trade, while the Liberals and Laborites grasped at the opportunity of forcing an election. Baldwin accepted the challenge, and in December, the electorate was asked to decide upon the issue of free trade versus protection. During the course of the campaign, the two factions in the Liberal Party merged and supported Asquith as their leader. Fierce tirades were delivered against the Conservative scheme of protection, and Labor was denounced for its proposed levy on capital, whereby capital reserves would be transferred by taxation from private individuals to the state. Baldwin realized that he faced a hard battle but did not expect defeat. The results of the election showed that the Conservatives gained five and one-half million votes and 258 seats. The opposition, however, polled more than nine million votes, with the Liberals in control of 159 seats to Labor's 191. The Conservatives, therefore, could not argue that they were entitled to form a ministry as in 1922. Baldwin appreciated the situation and quite properly waited defeat at the hands of parliament when it assembled in January of the new year. This procedure was in keeping with the cabinet system of government, which recognized ministerial responsibility to the Commons and not to the electorate. George V had to choose between Lloyd George and Ramsay MacDonald. MacDonald had a better claim for selection than Lloyd George. He was the recognized leader of the Labor Party whereas

Lloyd George somewhat divided that honor with Asquith. Lloyd George recognized MacDonald's claim and refused to press his own rights. Moreover, he believed that if Labor were given office and failed that the Crown might ask him to form a ministry. It was relatively simple, therefore, for George V to commission MacDonald to form a ministry.

Britain Under a Labor Government

For the first time in British history, England was under a Labor Government. Realizing that he did not have a Labor majority in the Commons, MacDonald did not try to advance any of the extreme proposals of his party. A generous policy toward organized labor was maintained, and an extensive program of housing reform was proposed. In the main, MacDonald believed that prosperity could not be returned to England until the European situation was quieted. Negotiations with France led to a "treaty of mutual understanding," and in February, 1924, Soviet Russia was recognized. Public opinion questioned the expediency of the arrangement with France and generally condemned recognition of Russia. There was also criticism of MacDonald's handling of domestic issues. Dissatisfaction finally centered on the government's attitude toward the editor of the *Worker's Weekly*. Radical editorials in praise of Soviet Russia had led the Labor Government to bring suit against the owner of the *Worker's Weekly*. Later these charges were dropped under pressure, so it was said, of Labor members in parliament. Liberals and Conservatives united in condemning MacDonald for this action, and voted for a parliamentary inquiry. MacDonald interpreted the latter as a vote of no confidence and immediately resigned. The real reason for the dissolution of parliament was the growing conflict between a socialist government and a non-socialist majority in the Commons. Labor, moreover, wanted to carry certain bills, such as nationalization of the mines and railroads, but this could not be done until it had a complete majority in the Commons.

The Conservative Party Encounters the General Strike

The Conservatives swept the country in the election of October, 1924, gaining nearly eight million popular votes and capturing 412 seats. Labor won but 151 seats and the Liberals 40. The combined popular vote of the opposition, however, numbered more than eight million, of which the Communist Party polled over 100,000. Both of the major opposition parties failed to hold the positions they had enjoyed in the previous parliament. An analysis of the returns showed a more pronounced disproportion of votes than in the 1923 election. Each opposition seat, including sixteen uncontested constituencies, averaged more than forty-two thousand votes. On the other hand, each Conservative seat, including sixteen uncontested districts, averaged less than twenty thousand votes. Critics pointed to this defect in the electoral system, and voices were raised in favor of electoral reform and proportional representation. Nothing, however, was done to correct the situation and the Conservatives, under Stanley Baldwin, remained in office until May, 1929.

During these years the British government tried in vain to settle the question of reparations, interallied debts, and the restoration of peace to distracted Europe. Considerable fault was found with Baldwin's handling of these complicated problems, as well as with his domestice program of increased tariffs. Profound differences of opinion also existed as to the dole and the condition of the mining industry. In spite of these disturbing factors the general economic condition of England was better than it had been when the Tories took office. Unemployment, while still serious, had decreased; the export trade had grown; and the purchasing power of the English people had improved. These gains, however, were wiped out when the mine owners announced that beginning August 1, 1925, wages would be reduced and hours of work increased. Labor immediately threatened a strike; and the government, wishing to avoid industrial warfare, subsidized the mine operators in order to continue existing wages for nine months. During this period a Royal Coal Commission studied

Courtesy Assoc. British and Irish Railways, Inc.

BUCKINGHAM PALACE, LONDON. Erected by John Sheffield, Duke of Buckingham-shire; purchased by George III in 1761. The London residence of the Sovereign since 1837.

the mining situation and reported in favor of government ownership of the mines. Realizing that nationalization could not take place at once, the Commission suggested that for the time being wages should be lowered somewhat, but that no change be made in the hours of work. The owners were willing to operate on this basis, but the miners refused to accept reduced pay. The owners proceeded to make necessary reductions, and, when labor refused to work on this basis, declared a lockout. On the same day, May 1, 1926, the miners went out on strike. At the same time the miners established contact with the transport, railroad, engineering, and ship-building unions and gained from them a promise to strike on May 3. Last minute attempts to prevent a general strike failed; and at midnight, May 3, the country was in the throes of a strike which promised to paralyze the life of the nation.

Public opinion condemned the strike as an attack upon society and government, while thousands of volunteers kept the railroads, trams, and other utilities in operation. In the meantime the conservative labor leaders, who opposed militant action, were seeking to mollify the left wing element which had caused the strike. Their efforts were successful; and on May 12, all the strikers except the miners returned to work. During the months that immediately followed, the Miner's Union witnessed a depletion of their strike funds and the return of individual miners to their former jobs. Reduced pay was better than starvation. Finally, in November of the same year, the Miner's Union rescinded the order to strike and tried to negotiate with the mine owners. Labor was defeated and suffered from reduced wages. More significant were the disastrous consequences of the strike upon industry and trade in general. Purchasing power was decreased, and the closing of unproductive mines sent some 200,000 miners into the army of the unemployed. Hoping to prevent a repetition of the general strike, parliament passed the Trades Dispute and Trade Union Act of April, 1927, which declared general strikes illegal.

Although the left wing of labor resented the passage of this measure and criticized Baldwin for severing diplomatic relations with Russia in May, 1927, the British Labor Party and the General Trade-Union Councils sought to improve relations between capital and labor. These organizations publicly repudiated communism and continued to coöperate with the industrial conferences which the ministry had established to deal with all labor disputes. During the course of 1928, the Baldwin ministry attempted to balance the budget and to improve the lot of labor. Boards were created to handle more carefully the question of relief and to reduce unemployment. More significant was the passage of a social security act which provided pensions for the aged, widows and orphans, the enactment of the Franchise Bill of 1928, and the construction of new houses to relieve the shortage which had existed since the war.

MacDonald Becomes Prime Minister

Toward the close of 1928 the various parties were preparing for the general election which, according to the Quinquennial Act, would take place before the fall of 1929. Labor realized that the effects of the general strike, the reduced numbers in the trade unions, and the split which existed between the right and left wing members had lessened their chances of winning the election. MacDonald believed that the Labor Party had a fighting chance, provided no extreme utterances were made during the campaign. Accordingly, the party platform repudiated communism and declared in favor of "ordered progress and democratic methods." Instead of advocating nationalization of industry, it argued for national control and promised to amend but not to repeal the Trades Dispute Act. Nothing was said about a capital levy, though a pledge was given to promote industrial development by a works program and the establishment of a National Economic Committee of workers and owners. In the meantime the Liberals under Lloyd George tried to capture the voter by promising peace at home and abroad, a reduction of unemployment, and jobs for all without increasing the cost of government a single penny. "Safety First" became the slogan of the Tories, who repeatedly stressed the wisdom of their acts. More effective was their argument that a Tory defeat would bring to England either socialism or political stagnation, owing to Labor's inability to control a majority in the Commons as in 1924.

The result of the election, which was held May 30, 1929, was a surprise to both Conservatives and Liberals. Although the latter polled over five million votes, they captured but fifty-nine seats instead of the one hundred they had expected. The Conservatives gained 8,656,473 votes but won only 260 seats. Labor, however, elected 288 members and had 8,389,512 popular votes. Although the electorate, in general, rejected socialism, the majority showed its dislike for Conservative administration. Aside from the closeness of the Conservative and Labor vote the most striking fact in the election was the drift back to a two-party system of government. The Liberals had increased their popular vote by over two million and had gained a few additional seats in the Commons but failed to make any dent upon their opponents, who also increased their hold on the electorate. Although Labor did not have a majority in the Commons, Baldwin admitted that a Labor Government would have to be formed, and he resigned on June 4. The following day, MacDonald became Prime Minister.

Labor remained in office for two years. MacDonald's foreign policy, which is discussed elsewhere, was generally successful, though his opponents found fault with it in many respects. In domestic affairs, he tried to bring about an improvement by continuing public works, the dole, and a reorganization of the coal industry. In spite of these, the economic condition of the country went from bad to worse. Unemployment and the dole increased. Left wing Laborites clamored for drastic social and economic legislation, but MacDonald checked their efforts, though in doing so he earned the ill will of that section of the Labor Party. Bad as the situation was, it might have improved had foreign states been able to purchase English goods. Every country, because of the world-wide depression, was limiting its purchases abroad, restricting imports, and concentrating upon production for domestic markets. English statesmen pursued the same general tactics. Various suggestions were made as to how English trade and industry might be revived. One group argued for general retrenchment by reducing the costs of relief and education and by funding the national debt. Others suggested that the interallied debts and reparations be canceled and that drastic reductions be made in military and naval expenditures. Tories, in large numbers, called for higher tariffs, while those in financial circles insisted upon lowering the value of the pound sterling. To gain the latter, Britain would have to abandon the gold standard; but the result, so it was said, would enable foreigners to buy English goods because of the increased purchasing power their money would have in a country whose currency had been reduced in value. A devaluated pound, moreover, would lower production costs and permit British merchants to sell abroad.

MacDonald Forms the National Party

The MacDonald ministry considered these suggestions but was unwilling to support any one in particular. Economic conditions, moreover, failed to improve throughout the world. Suddenly, in the spring of 1931, the Bank of Austria failed, and a world-wide financial panic was under way. English, French and American bankers threw large credits here and there in the hope of keeping Europe solvent. Gold withdrawals from England added only to MacDonald's difficulties. Gradually, MacDonald came to realize that his political views did not coincide with those of his party. He believed that the Labor Party must alter its socialist aims and adopt a policy more moderate in scope and action. By the summer of 1931 it became evident that his middle-class liberalism had rent the party asunder. His refusal to follow his party's program and his insistence upon governmental economy created a cleavage within the cabinet. Various conferences followed between MacDonald and the King, as well as between the Prime Minister and the opposition leaders. Late in August the Cabinet was informed that its resignation had been accepted and that George V had commissioned MacDonald to form a

National Government. The greater share of the Labor members immediately deserted MacDonald and accepted Arthur Henderson as the leader of the British Labor Party. The National Government, which consisted of two Liberals, four Conservatives, and four Laborites, carried on under Prime Minister MacDonald.

Parliament assembled in September of the same year and supported the National Government in reducing social services, education, and unemployment benefits. In the meantime the effect of the withdrawal of gold to meet obligations abroad and to bolster financial conditions in Europe reached a point where it was necessary for parliament to authorize the abandonment of the gold standard. MacDonald was unwilling to take any additional steps without a mandate from the people. Accordingly, parliament was dissolved and the Nationalists appealed to the electorate to return them on the understanding that the government could take any steps it wished for recovery.

With the exception of the Conservative Party, which formed the backbone of the National Party, all of the major parties underwent disintegration in the election. Most conspicuous was the secession of the Independent Labor group from the Labor Party. The election was also of interest for the appearance of a Fascist organization, under Sir Oswald Mosley, known as the New Party. The Conservative forces were led by Baldwin, the National Liberal by Sir John Simon, National Labor by MacDonald, the Liberal by Sir Herbert Samuel, Labor by George Lansbury, the Independent Liberal by Lloyd George, and the Independent Labor Party by James Maxton. The election of 1931 was a decided victory for the coalition, which captured all but sixty-one seats in the Commons. The Liberal Party was reduced to Lloyd George and three others, while Labor considered itself fortunate in view of MacDonald's retirement from that party, to win fifty-two seats. Five seats were gained by independents. MacDonald's position, however, was somewhat anomalous, as he still viewed himself as a Laborite but was at the head of a ministry predominantly Conservative.

The remainder of 1931 showed an improvement in the economic situation. Further gains were registered during the next four years. By September, 1934, the gold reserves of the Bank of England had reached the highest peak in its history, while commodity prices were higher than they had been since the election. Industry, particularly in the southern part of the island, earned increased profits; shippers carried a larger share of the world trade; and agriculture, thanks to government aid and new methods of organization, prospered. The textile and coal industries were still below the level of 1919 and 1920. Unemployment had decreased, though it still remained a serious matter for thousands of families. The National Government claimed, with some justification, that its policies were responsible for this improvement. The enactment of higher tariffs, a moderate revival of the old corn laws, the stimulus afforded to trade within the Empire, a continuation of the housing program, and the Unemployment Bill of 1934 were achievements of the National ministry. The Unemployment Bill amended and coördinated the unemployment insurance acts of 1920 and 1933 and recognized national responsibility for all uninsured and insured workers.

In spite of these gains, the political situation reflected an anti-government trend. Several vacancies in parliament were filled by Labor members; and in the municipal elections of 1933, the Labor Party won over half of the contests. The decline in the government's prestige was attributed to the lack of aggressive leadership on the part of the ministers in foreign and domestic matters, and to the belief, on the part of others, that the tariff and imperial preferences had not been successful. The Labor Party, however, showed the effects of MacDonald's desertion to the Nationalists and was bothered by the drastic proposals of its left wing members. On the other hand the

Liberals were split into two groups: one found a place in the National Government; the other, headed by Sir Herbert Samuel and Lloyd George, sought to keep intact the traditions and policies of Liberalism. Considerable unrest also existed among the Conservatives, a large group demanding the dissolution of parliament so as to permit the severance of the National Coalition. MacDonald's influence in the cabinet, though it had become but nominal, was a source of annoyance to orthodox Conservatives. Although a group of Laborites supported the National ministry, the bulk of that party remained faithful to labor principles. At its annual party meeting in 1933, labor passed resolutions pledging the next Labor Government to assume control of the banks and chief industries with compensation for individual owners.

During 1935 the political situation drifted toward a dissolution of parliament. In June, MacDonald retired from the post of Prime Minister and was succeeded by Baldwin, who announced that there would be a general election in the autumn. The rank and file of the Conservatives approved of this change and prepared for the coming campaign. Labor also was satisfied and undertook to wage a determined contest in the election which was to be held in November. Although the Baldwin Coalition forces were returned, their majority in the Commons was cut to 251, Labor increasing its position from 52 seats to 154. The Liberal Party showed signs of renewed vitality by winning twenty seats, while the Communist Party captured one seat. Since the 1935 election, British politics have centered about the conduct of foreign affairs. Public opinion has criticized the Conservative policy toward Germany and France, and has found much fault with the handling of the Ethiopian question and Britain's relation to the League of Nations. More recently there has been active debate over the Spanish problem. In spite of this opposition the Conservative Party was able to strengthen its position in government. In part this was due to Labor's inability to iron out its own internal dissensions or to formulate any clear-cut program in respect to foreign affairs. Labor's sympathies in the Spanish revolution, for example, were with the Spanish loyalists. On the other hand Labor realized the danger which might arise out of any overt act in favor of the Madrid Government. For this reason they supported the non-intervention policy of the Baldwin ministry and have mildly encouraged increased armaments to meet any threat of war from either Germany or Italy.

To meet the expenses incident to military preparedness, the Conservative Party raised the income taxes, increased the import duties, notably on tea, and have taken steps to float an enormous loan. Some opposition to this program arose within the Conservative Party, and voices were heard against Baldwin's continuance in office. It was believed by some that a younger and more aggressive Conservative should be placed in power. Baldwin's ill health also argued against him. During the early fall of 1936, Baldwin, upon the advice of his doctors, took an extended holiday. It was during this vacation that a constitutional issue was precipitated over Edward VIII's love for Mrs. Simpson. No one questioned the King's right to marry. On the contrary there seems to have been a nation-wide sentiment in favor of his marriage. The fact that Mrs. Simpson was an American may have prejudiced some, but to the great majority of Englishmen that did not appear to be a matter of great importance. The public, however, did disapprove of Mrs. Simpson because of a prior divorce gained in an American court and because she had but recently obtained another divorce in an English court from her present husband.

Edward VIII's Abdication

Realizing the gravity of the situation, Baldwin called on Edward to discuss the problem in an informal manner. Later, Edward sought the advice of his ministers and asked them to sponsor a bill permitting a morganatic marriage. Edward was aware that the Conservative Government, the Anglican Church, and the great majority of his subjects would not approve of a marriage which would make Mrs. Simpson queen. Had Edward forced the issue in this manner, he might have been deposed. Hoping to retain the throne, Edward suggested a marriage which would have recognized Mrs. Simpson as his wife, but would not make her queen. Any issue of this marriage, moreover, would have been denied succession to the throne. The Baldwin Government declined to sponsor such a measure and a statement to this effect was made in parliament. While Edward was debating as to his next move, Baldwin informed the Dominion Governments of what had transpired. According to the Statute of Westminster of 1931, the Dominions' consent was necessary for any change in the line of succession, and both Edward's proposal and Baldwin's refusal to support a morganatic marriage implied a change in succession. Shortly thereafter Edward notified the cabinet of his intention to abdicate so that he might marry the woman he loved. Edward's act of abdication was presented to parliament and on December 12, 1936, a bill was passed which sanctioned his abdication and provided that Edward's heirs should have no right to the throne.

The Abdication Act recited that Australia, New Zealand, South Africa, and Canada assented thereto. The Irish Free State is not mentioned; nor did it act until December 13. On that day, the Dail deleted the King's name from the Irish constitution. During this interval, therefore, Edward was King of Ireland, though he had ceased to be the ruler of Great Britain, the other Dominions, and the Empire. In addition to the issue raised by the action of the Irish Free State, another constitutional problem arose. George VI's children, Elizabeth and Margaret Rose, are girls. According to English law, but not Scottish, when the issue is limited to females, the estate is divided equally. But the British throne is not divisible, and it has been suggested that both girls would ascend the throne upon the death of George VI. The present government, however, upon advice of its lawyers, holds that the throne is not the King's property, and that Elizabeth is the sole present heir. Parliament, however, in the spring of 1937 enacted a Regency Bill which provided: (1) that if the sovereign is under eighteen years of age, the royal functions shall be performed in his name by a regent, who must be of legal age and a resident of Great Britain (a regency is ended when the sovereign attains eighteen years); (2) that in the event of the illness or absence from Britain of either the sovereign or the regent, a Council of State, composed of five adult members of the royal family, shall administer certain royal duties. The act in no way concerns the succession or title to the throne; hence no action by the Dominions is needed.

The solidarity of the British Empire was shaken by Edward's abdication. Had he pursued a different course, a definite cleavage might have resulted. Had he married Mrs. Simpson, the Baldwin ministry probably would have resigned. In such an event, the British Labor Party could not have commanded a majority in the Commons, and Edward would have had to call a general election. Edward could not have campaigned in this election, and there would have been few who would have risked their political careers in his cause. Constitutional and moral issues, moreover, would have been aired with frankness, and the Baldwin ministry would, in all probability, have been returned. Edward would then have had to yield, and, had he refused, he might have been deposed. Edward knew this and wisely selected a course that endangered the Empire as little as possible. Although the entire affair is to be regretted, it is evident that the Empire has weathered the crisis and that orderly government has been restored in Britain and the Dominions.

On the basis of the election of 1935, it would appear that England has returned to the two-party system, and that future contests will be fought between the Conservative and Labor Parties. The former is well entrenched in the rural areas and in most of the towns and cities outside of London and the mining districts. Property and vested interests have confidence in the National Government. One may expect the latter to safeguard the former. The Conservative Party, however, is not unwilling to advocate social reform provided no fundamental change is made in the economic and political structure of England. One may reasonably expect this party to endorse government ownership in those fields where private individualism no longer seems able to function. A step in this direction was taken late in April, 1937, when the Conservative Government announced that it would introduce measures designed to establish government ownership of the mines. It will also promote greater economic security for the masses by continuing old age insurance and unemployment benefits. To meet the expenses incident to these undertakings as well as for increased military preparation, the Government's budget calls for additional taxes, the burden of which will fall heavily upon the property and wealthy classes. Such a program invites the support of the middle class. Moreover, it steals some of the thunder of the Labor Party and lessens the prospect of another Labor Government. Baldwin's resignation in May, 1937, on account of advancing age, and the elevation of Neville Chamberlain to the post of Prime Minister, has not materially altered the policy of the National Government.

The Present Status of the Labor Party

The Labor Party faces a difficult and uncertain future. It increased its popular poll over that of 1931 by over a million and a half votes, and almost equaled its poll of 1929. It also gained greater representation in the Commons. Leaders in this party have pointed out the fact that the combined opposition vote was within four and one-half per cent of that cast for the Government, and yet the latter won two and one-third times as many seats. A system of proportional representation would give Labor greater representation in the Commons. Labor does not suggest any change in the electoral law but points to the disproportion between the total poll and the seats won. If Labor wishes to remain as His Majesty's opposition and if it hopes to gain control of government in the near future, it probably must revamp its organization and clarify its program. In respect to the first it must convince the electorate that its leaders possess the skill and ability to govern. Its present chairman, Mr. Clement R. Attlee, is not a national figure and does not command the respect of the country as did Mr. Lansbury and Sir Strafford Cripps, who dominated Labor a short time ago. Labor must also encourage its younger members to enter public life by allowing them to stand for election to the Commons in those constituencies which normally return a Labor candidate. At present they are forced to compete in hotly contested areas. As a result most of Labor's representation is limited to older heads and little opportunity is afforded the younger members to acquire skill in debate in the Commons. Finally the Labor Party must decide whether it is to be a socialist group or a party concerned chiefly with social reform. If it follows the latter course it must pursue a program that will not frighten the middle class, and, at the same time, must be aggressive enough to win support from the laboring classes. Such a policy implies a frank disavowal of Marxian ideas, and there must be no talk of a United Front with extreme socialism or communism. Adherence to social reform may transform the Labor Party into something like the Liberal Party of Gladstone's age. And should it gain sufficient popular support, it may acquire control of the government. "When that day comes it can begin, in the piecemeal fashion characteristic of the British love of compromise, the task of constructing the socialist state."

Some of the younger Labor leaders have adopted a policy of advocating social reform. They condemn private capitalism but limit their condemnations to academic and theoretical discussions. No frontal attack is contemplated. Others, like G. D. H. Cole, stress the dangers of fascism and boldly claim that the aim of the National Party is to build a fascist state. To prevent the latter, Cole and his group are willing to cease advocating socialism. Only through a union of radical and liberal opinion, so it is claimed, can Britain be saved from fascism, but this does not imply acceptance of a United Front composed of Communists, Liberals, and the Socialist League. The latter group was formed to replace the Independent Labor Party as a propagandist organization within the Labor Party. Its success was shown in January, 1937, in the establishment of a United Front, whose strength is limited to six Commoners and a handful of the electorate. Labor officially repudiated the United Front, disaffiliated the Socialist League, and threatened its members with expulsion from the Labor Party. The League met this attack by dissolution only to reappear as a Labor Unity Committee within the Labor Party. Tactics will be altered, but objectives will be unchanged. The Labor Party dreads fascism more than the United Front and looks with concern upon Mosley's New Party, a fascist group, which appears to be less active now than it was in the spring of 1937. British Labor refuses to believe that either the New Party or the United Front can solve national problems. Educate the electorate to the meaning and purpose of socialism, so many argue, and Labor will win. A frontal attack upon private capitalism may, therefore, be Labor's best chance of controlling government. Will it follow this course or will it pursue a policy of social reform? No one knows. In the opinion of some critics, Labor must choose one of these two roads. If it follows the latter, it must do more than make a case against the government. It must clarify its foreign and domestic policies so that the electorate

THE CHOIR IN WESTMINSTER ABBEY. The fine woodwork of the choir was executed in 1848.

will know what to expect from a Labor Government. In the last election it failed to do so, and the country rejected Labor's bid for power. Moreover, it has not shown any surprising strength in recent bye-elections, though in London it increased its majority in the March, 1937, elections to the London County Council.

Labor's attitude toward the monarchy is friendly. Although some of its more radical members have talked about abolishing this institution, there seems to be little support for so drastic a step within the Party itself. The Party willingly co-

THE HOUSES OF HANOVER AND WINDSOR

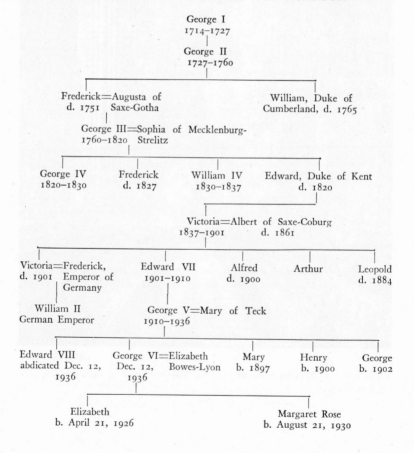

operated with the Government at the time of Edward VIII's abdication and participated in the coronation of George VI on May 12, 1937. In respect to the recently formed Chamberlain ministry, Labor has been less troublesome than was expected. It dreads the prospect of a world war and favors collective security. At the same time it has supported the defense program of Chamberlain. It realizes the need of rearmament, closer contacts with the Dominions and America, and, as a result of the rearmament program, that unemployment has decreased and that many of its members enjoyed a summer holiday in 1937 for the first time in many years. Mr. Attlee and others question the wisdom of coöperating with the National Party, believing that anything which implies approval of the latter will weaken Labor. He and his followers, however, were overruled at a July meeting of Labor's Executive Committee and at the October conference of the Party at Bournemouth.

SELECTED BIBLIOGRAPHY

H. L. Gray's *War Time Control of Industry; the Experience of England* (New York, 1918); W. P. Maddox's *Foreign Relations in British Labor Politics* (Cambridge, 1934); Sir Edward Grey's *Twenty-Five Years, 1892–1916* (New York, 1925); David Lloyd George's *War Memoirs* (Boston, 1933–1936); R. H. Gretton's *Modern History of the English People* (New York, 1930), and J. A. R. Marriott's *Modern England, 1885–1932* (London, 1932) are standard works. The current files of the *Fortnightly* and *Contemporary Review* reflect the ideas of the governing classes. Reference might also be made to the weekly editions of the *Times* and *Manchester Guardian* as well as to *Current History, English Historical Review, American Historical Review, Canadian Historical Review, Economic History,* and *Economica.* A. L. Bowley's *Prices and Wages in the United Kingdom, 1914–1920* (Oxford, 1921); W. A. Orton's *Labour in Transition* (London, 1921), and Gilbert Stone's *The English Coal Industry* (London, 1919) are specialized studies. The *Annual Register* and *The Statesmen's Year Book* are of value. See also J. L. Hammond's *C. P. Scott* (New York, 1934).

CHAPTER XXXVII

Foreign Affairs, 1919-1937

THE Armistice of November, 1918, marked the end of the greatest armed conflict the world had ever seen. The imperial wars of the Greeks and Romans, the religious and dynastic contests of the sixteenth and seventeenth centuries, and the economic and nationalist conflicts of more recent date were minor affairs in contrast with the magnitude of the World War. "The war to end war" was over, and mankind turned its attention toward reconstruction and the fashioning of a new world order. The actual determination of the terms of peace and the building of security for the future rested with the diplomats who gathered at Paris early in 1919. What these gentlemen would decide no one knew, though it was rather clear that some had well-defined ideas about reparations and distribution of conquered territory. Had a worldwide poll been taken, an overwhelming majority would have said, "This must not happen again." Expert opinion in the fields of history, economics, and political science showed the utter futility of the past war, indicated how close civilization had approached to destruction, and pleaded for a peace which would reflect the rights of the vanquished as well as the victors.

The Treaty of Versailles

On the other hand the allied nations in general accepted the idea that Germany had caused the war and must be made to pay the costs of that conflict. The British election of 1919 had, in one sense, been contested on that issue; and the return of the Coalition Ministry under Lloyd George reflected the wishes of the electorate. Peace was to be made and future international conflicts were to be prevented, but Germany must pay for having disturbed the peace of the world. Lloyd George accepted the mandate of the English people. Germany, he insisted, had caused the war and must be treated as a criminal. A confession of guilt must be signed, territory must be ceded, the Allies' war costs must be met, and Germany must accept whatever terms the Allies might impose. Moreover, one has only to read the Treaty of Versailles to appreciate that similar motives actuated the diplomats of the allied nations.

Britain's wartime friendship with France was as evident as her resentment towards Germany. The latter was forced to restore Alsace and Lorraine to France, reduce her army and navy to a police basis, admit sole responsibility for the war, permit for a limited time a military occupation of the Rhineland, restrict her commercial and industrial activities in a manner which benefited British and French capitalists, pay the victors an impossible indemnity, and allow the Saar Basin to be held in custody by the League of Nations. Since Germany had unwarrantedly devastated the French coal fields, those of the German Saar were to be placed at the disposal of France, under the League's supervision, for a number of years. At the same time Britain restrained France from imposing further burdens upon Germany. However, when France demanded, by way of compensation, a treaty between France and England, and another between France and the United States to defend her frontiers against any future German attack, England used her good offices to secure such agreements. Although parliament ratified the treaty between England and France, the King never signed it because of the failure of the American Senate to take any action on the Franco-American treaty. America's rejection of this understanding, as well as of the Treaty of Versailles, left the French frontier unprotected and weakened the future effectiveness of the League of Nations.

President Wilson shares, with other contemporary liberals, the honor of establishing the League of Nations. More than any other, however, he deserves the credit for placing the Covenant of the League in the Treaty of Versailles. According to this Covenant there was to be an Assembly, composed of representatives of all signatory powers, and a Council in which the five great victorious powers were given permanent seats while the lesser states were to have rotating membership. Definite duties were assigned to both bodies in a manner which distinctly favored the Council. Provision was also made for a World Court. In spite of many searching criticisms of the League, its sponsors hoped that it might prevent future wars. The effectiveness of the League was weakened at the outset by the refusal of the United States to accept the Covenant unless it were amended to suit America. At a later date the League discussed the amendments proposed by America and submitted to that country an arrangement whereby it might join. These overtures, although endorsed by several presidents, have been repeatedly rejected by the Senate. The United States has coöperated with the League, however, on several occasions. Moreover, it has sent observers to its sessions, has contributed to its cost, and has exercised considerable influence upon the activities of the League. With America out of the League, the success of that body was restricted from its inception. Germany, of course, was not admitted to membership in 1919, nor was Soviet Russia, which was viewed as an outlaw nation. What the League could accomplish without the coöperation of these three great powers was a question which no one seemed able to answer at that time.

Reparations and Debts

In one sense the success of the League depended upon the solution of the twin problems—reparations and interallied debts. Huge sums were owed England by her Continental allies, while Britain as well as these states were heavily obligated to the United States for wartime loans. It was hoped that German reparations would permit a prompt settlement of these debts as well as the expenses of the war. The German government and the German people, however, were not disposed to meet these reparations, which in 1921 had been fixed at thirty-two billion dollars and apportioned among her many creditors. Germany argued that she had not caused the war and that her promise to pay had been forced upon her and therefore was not binding. On the other hand she was in no position to resist, so she adopted the policy of delay. Moreover, in making payments in coal, machinery, and other commodities, as ordered by the allied nations, considerable difficulty arose. The allied producers of these goods protested against these payments on the ground that their activities were being hampered by the import of German commodities. As a result, further payment in kind was stopped and Germany was asked to remit in cash. How could Germany do this in the face of tariff restrictions which prevented the sale of her goods abroad? Unless Germany could obtain an income from the sale of her products, there was little chance of her meeting reparations. Moreover, the loss of her colonies and the failure of Russia to purchase German goods, owing to the economic collapse of Russia, excluded Germany from markets that had been valuable in the past. Hoping to ward off impending disaster, the German government resorted to inflation; but by 1922 this expedient had failed. Accordingly, Germany informed the Allies that she could not meet her obligations and asked for a two-year moratorium.

British opinion was inclined to grant this request, but France took the position that Germany could pay, and that force should be used to compel her to meet her obligations. In spite of British opposition and advice, France marched an army into the Ruhr, the industrial heart of Germany, and announced she would occupy the area and collect the revenue arising from industry and business until Germany fulfilled her promises. The German manufacturers and workers in the Ruhr, supported by their government, resorted to a general strike which paralyzed business, while throughout Germany sharp protests were raised against France. By the fall of 1923, France was convinced that Germany could not meet her debts and that she was on the verge of economic dissolution. Out of necessity, therefore, France had to consider a reversal of policy and a return to the conciliatory methods proposed by England a year before. At this juncture it was proposed that an international committee of experts examine the German situation and make recommendations for the future. France and the Allies accepted the idea, and in 1924 a commission headed by the American, Charles Dawes, visited Germany. The Dawes report did not reduce the amount of the reparations but arranged for smaller payments over a longer period of time. The Allies and Germany accepted this arrangement and France withdrew her troops from the Ruhr.

German unwillingness and inability to pay reparations prevented the Allies from meeting their own obligations. The question of interallied debts, therefore, was bound up with that of reparations; and since Germany had defaulted, the Allies did likewise. The British proposal that the interallied debts be canceled was rejected by America. English opinion had hoped that the United States would view these debts as expenses incurred by all in the common cause of war. America thought otherwise and insisted that these debts had been entered into on a business basis and must be met as a business proposition. Britain then suggested that the United States scale down the amounts owed her, but this was also rejected for the same reason. England then proposed that she be given a longer time to meet her obligations. America accepted this proposition and immediately made similar arrangements with her other debtors. For a time the plan worked; but as German reparations dwindled, the dual question of interallied debts and reparations was revived. Germany contended that her obligations must be reduced, and England was willing to do so, but France and her Continental allies would not give their consent until the United States pared her demands. America refused; and in 1929 another committee of experts, headed by Owen Young of the United States, investigated Germany and recommended that the reparations be reduced from thirty-two billion to eight billion dollars and that the Allied troops be withdrawn from the Rhineland. Accordingly, these suggestions were accepted by the Allies at The Hague in 1930.

By this time a world-wide depression was in progress. Germany was forced to stop payments, as were those states which owed the United States. Finland alone managed to meet her small debt to America. At Lausanne, in 1932, the Allies finally agreed to reduce reparations to seven hundred million dollars. The fulfillment of this treaty between the Allies and Germany rested to a great extent upon the United States. The signatory nations knew that no definite settlement could be reached unless the United States would coöperate by lowering her demands. Accordingly, at Lausanne, the allied nations entered into a gentlemen's agreement whereby their ultimate ratification of the treaty would depend upon America's attitude. The United States refused to reconsider its position. Since that date neither Germany nor the allied states, with the exception of Finland, have made any payments. To all intents and purposes reparations and interallied debts have been wiped off the international slate, though America continues to remind her debtors of their obligations.

Rampant Nationalism Creates New Problems

Had America and the European states been more reasonable in their treatment of Germany at Versailles, had they not
erected impossible tariff walls against German goods, Germany might have met a larger part of the reparations. It
should be noted, however, that Britain's attitude was much
more conciliatory than that of France. England realized that
her own economic recovery depended to a large degree upon
reëstablishing her former trade connections with Germany.
Not wishing to jeopardize her friendship with France, Britain
tried to steer a middle course. This failed to satisfy either
France or Germany and did little to improve economic conditions at home. In the face of cleavage between Britain and
France and in spite of the efforts of the League, considerable
friction developed in Europe. Internal difficulties plus insecurity in national and international finance raised obstacles
to peace and economic stability. Although the victors had
forced Germany to disarm, they did not reduce their own
military and naval establishments. Nationalism was more
aggressive than in 1914, and there was no feeling of security
except as it rested upon force. Russia with its communistic
government was feared, and those states which bordered upon
her frontiers raised huge armies to resist a possible Russian
attack. Germany resented the presence of Allied troops on
the Rhine, proclaimed her innocence of the war, suspended
reparations, and frowned upon the Polish Corridor, which
separated East Prussia from the rest of the Fatherland. She
also claimed that the Allies had promised to reduce armaments
after the war, and that since this promise had been broken she
should be allowed to arm, particularly because of Soviet
Russia.

France, however, in view of German actions since 1919 and
America's refusal to guarantee her frontier against a German
attack, increased her military establishment, built elaborate

fortifications, and entered into defensive alliances with Belgium and the new states of Jugoslavia, Poland, and Czechoslovakia, created by the Treaty of Versailles. She refused, moreover, to allow Austria, which was predominantly German as to language, race, and traditions, to enter into a customs union (known as the Anschluss) with Germany. A union of this type would have facilitated the economic recovery of central Europe and might have led to a more peaceful settlement. France feared Germany as it was, and did not care to face what might have become a greater Germany. In the final analysis France would agree to nothing which would not accord her a favored position in respect to Germany. Her policy weakened the League and tended toward a rift in Anglo-French relations. At the same time Japan embarked upon an imperialist program in the Far East, augmented her army and navy, and seemed bent upon disturbing the peace of the world. Imperialist Italy aggravated the situation, as did America with her tariffs, increased navy and unrelenting attitude toward her European debtors.

The Washington Arms Conference and the Geneva Protocol

Expensive armaments, colossal debts, rampant nationalism, a dissatisfied citizenry were problems which seemed to point to another war. Britain, although anxious to maintain her position, was eager to reduce the factors leading toward war. Not only did she support the League of Nations, but she played an important rôle at the Washington Arms Conference of 1921. At this gathering, which was called by the United States, representatives from Japan, France, Italy, China, and the Netherlands joined with those from America, Britain, and the British Dominions in discussing naval affairs and the question of the Pacific. As finally agreed upon, Britain and the United States were to have equality in capital ships. A ratio was established between these nations and the other powers on the basis of 5–5 for England and America, 3 for Japan and 1.75 for France and Italy. France, England, Japan, and the United States also promised to construct no new fortifications or naval bases in the Pacific; and all accepted the "open door" policy in China, whereby equality of trade and business was to exist for all. Every nation concerned was able, in view of this understanding, to reduce materially the staggering burden of naval costs. England, moreover, relinquished her time-honored supremacy of the sea when she admitted parity with America, while the latter denied herself a supremacy which her resources would have given her in the event of a naval race between the two powers.

Having arrived at an understanding relative to naval affairs, the English government under Lloyd George sought to solve the problem of security for France. Early in 1922 the British offered a limited guarantee in lieu of the ill-fated agreements between France and England, and France and the United States. France appreciated the offer but declined it because it did not give her the security she believed herself entitled to. Shortly thereafter, Germany defaulted in reparation payments, and in spite of British opposition the French marched troops into the Ruhr. When military demonstrations failed, France altered her policy. She accepted the Dawes report and entered into lengthy discussion with England relative to implementing the Covenant of the League of Nations. This document did not define what constituted an act of aggression nor did it specify precisely what sanctions might be imposed against an aggressor. Ramsay MacDonald, who had become Prime Minister in January, 1924, admitted the justice of the French position and agreed to a "treaty of mutual guarantee." Later this treaty was revised and submitted to the members of the League as the "Geneva Protocol." The "Protocol" stipulated that all international disputes should be settled either by conciliation or arbitration, and that the state which refused to abide by the award was to be defined as the aggressor. Joint economic or military action, under League supervision, might then take place against the offending nation.

Many students of international relations have viewed the "Geneva Protocol" as the most practical expedient against war which has been conceived since the establishment of the League. They applaud the diplomacy of MacDonald and the willingness of France to change its policy toward Germany. Their hopes were stimulated when the Assembly of the League adopted the "Protocol" and submitted it in turn to the governments of the member nations for ratification. Shortly thereafter, MacDonald was forced out of office; and the new ministry under Baldwin refused to approve of the "Protocol." Had the Labor ministry under MacDonald remained in power, it is possible that England would have ratified the "Protocol" and would have used her influence to secure adoption by the other powers. Tory opinion, strongly supported by sentiment in the Dominions, opposed an agreement which called for military and naval action on Britain's part whenever and wherever the peace of the world was disturbed. The League of Nations, so Foreign Minister Austin Chamberlain declared, would be converted by the "Protocol" into a "Super-State with police powers over the Nations of the World." As Britain's interests were world-wide, she refused to assume the duty of policing the world.

The Locarno Pact

Having erased the work accomplished by MacDonald, the Tory ministry was obliged to foster proposals of its own. Fortune favored the new government. Early in 1925, when the Dawes plan was operating smoothly, the governments of Berlin and Paris showed a willingness to discuss their differences. Britain immediately encouraged this trend and gained Italy's consent to join in a general conference which resulted in the Locarno Pact of October, 1925. According to this agreement Germany recognized the existing boundaries of Western Europe and promised to arbitrate any dispute that might arise between her and France, Belgium, Poland, or Czechoslovakia. She reserved the right, however, to settle peacefully the question of her eastern frontier. In return for these concessions, Germany was given a permanent seat in the Council of the League. At the same time England and Italy promised to give armed assistance to either France, Belgium, or Germany in case one of them violated the pact. The Locarno Pact did much to stabilize Western Europe, and for a few years France believed herself secure from German attack. In 1928 further security was gained by the Kellogg-Briand Pact, which outlawed war. Every nation of the world, with but few exceptions, ratified this Pact. Pacifists hailed it as the final renunciation of force. Pessimists, on the other hand, greeted it with ridicule and derision. Public opinion, in general, viewed it as a pious gesture and pointed to the increased naval appropriations in America, the country that had sponsored the treaty.

Naval and Financial Problems

In the meantime the Tory ministry had been agitating for a limitation of land armaments. Other nations were interested, and in 1925 the League appointed a commission to study the problem. When a report, in the form of a Draft Treaty, was submitted in 1931, it was evident to all that no general understanding could be reached as long as rampant nationalism held sway in Europe. How to satisfy the demands of those states which wanted to preserve the status quo, and how, at the same time, to meet the requirements of others who were opposed to existing arrangements was but one of the many problems the commission did not solve. A similar failure followed a meeting of Britain, Japan, and the United States at Geneva, in 1927, for a discussion relative to cruisers and light craft not covered by the Washington Arms Conference. The next year Britain made a separate agreement with France, whereby the latter was accorded an unlimited submarine program in return for which England was given an advantage in light cruisers.

In June, 1929, the British electorate returned the Labor Party to office. In foreign affairs, the Prime Minister, Ramsay MacDonald, favored a revision of the Dawes plan and supported the adoption of the Young plan, which provided for a marked reduction in the amount of German reparations and for a withdrawal of the Allied troops from the Rhine. MacDonald also negotiated with America concerning naval affairs and conversed with President Hoover at Washington. These conversations resulted in the calling of the London Conference of 1930, which was attended by all the principal naval powers. Britain, Japan, and the United States discussed cruisers and settled differences which had not been covered by the Washington Arms Conference. France and Italy, however, rejected the cruiser ratios offered them at this gathering. This was due in part to England's determination to maintain her superiority in the Mediterranean, which might have been endangered by an increase in the cruiser strength of either France or Italy. Moreover, if the cruiser strength of these powers were increased, Britain would have to increase hers; and this would have upset the arrangements made with Japan and America. More important, however, was France's refusal to admit parity with Italy. As a result neither power would accept the London Agreement, which extended the life of the Washington Arms Conference treaty to 1937 and established a ratio as to cruisers and auxiliary ships. MacDonald's interest in promoting a peaceful solution of international problems was also shown in his dealings with Russia. MacDonald maintained that the Russian people, regardless of their communistic views, had established a government and were entitled to a place in world affairs. He refused to accept the theory that Russia should be outlawed because of its governmental forms and philosophy. Moreover, he recognized the immense value which would follow from trade relations. Accordingly, Britain recognized the Soviet Government. In return, Leningrad agreed to cease communistic propaganda in the British Empire and to discuss the question of Russian debts to Englishmen.

MacDonald's interest in foreign affairs was predicated upon the assumption that economic recovery and prosperity were impossible as long as Europe seemed bent upon appealing to the sword. The reduction of military and naval armaments, the establishment of good will, the strengthening of the League of Nations, faithful adherence to treaties and pacts signed since the World War, and friendly commercial relations were the chief planks in his platform. Gain these ends, he declared, and England's economic recovery as well as that of other nations would be secured. The resignation of the Labor ministry in August, 1931, the formation of the National Government, and the general election of the same year caused no great change in Britain's foreign policy, for MacDonald retained the post of Prime Minister.

German Politics 1919–1933

Many Europeans, however, viewed MacDonald's internationalism as more evident in speech than in action. England, so it was said, had yielded little in accepting naval parity with America. Capital ships and cruisers had been limited; but Britain's naval supremacy over every other power was not a source of comfort to Japan, Italy, or France. Amply protected against hostile attack, MacDonald's pleas for military reduction seemed out of place to those European states who wanted as much security on land as England had on sea. They were willing, however, to discuss the question of military reduction, even though the League's Commission of 1925 had revealed how impossible it was to satisfy the demands of the various

powers. Since that date the situation had become more complicated by reason of the National Socialists' victories in Germany under Adolf Hitler. Hitler, like thousands of other Germans, resented the humiliations imposed upon the Fatherland
by the Allies after 1918. Germany, he insisted, had as much
right to exist as any power; and the shackles which had been
imposed by the Treaty of Versailles must be removed. Although Hitler was but expressing the hopes and ideas of most
of his countrymen, it was not until 1920 that he secured any
large following. In that year he founded the National Socialist Party, which advocated repudiating the Treaty of Versailles, regaining Germany's lost colonies, rearming and uniting all Germans, particularly those in Poland, Austria, and
Czechoslovakia, into a greater Fatherland. The National
Socialists, commonly known as Nazis, also wished to purge
Germany of Communists and Jews.

At that time Germany was a republic under the presidency
of the former Field-Marshal, Paul von Hindenburg. Although
his sympathies were with the former Kaiser, his sense of duty
was so strong that he did nothing toward restoring the Hohen-
zollerns. Moreover, he supported his ministers in trying to
abide by the Treaty of Versailles. The success of this program
was shown by a gradual business recovery. More significant
were the victories gained in foreign affairs, under the guiding
hand of Gustav Stresemann. Stresemann convinced the
French foreign minister, Aristide Briand, that Germany might
be trusted. As a result the French troops were withdrawn
from the Ruhr and steps were taken for the evacuation of the
Rhineland. Stresemann's diplomacy assisted in the signing
of the Locarno Pact and gave the Fatherland a place in the
Council of the League. The constant attack of the Nazis
under Hitler, and the Communists under Ernst Thälmann,
endangered further development. Both of these parties were
bitterly opposed to Stresemann's policies, and both gained
strength in the elections of 1924 and 1928. Unless Hindenburg

and Stresemann could check and overcome this opposition, further continuation of their policies was out of the question. Stresemann's death in 1929 made Hindenburg's task more difficult and disclosed the inherent weaknesses of the German Republic. In a desperate attempt to bolster the declining fortunes of the Republic, Hindenburg entrusted affairs to Heinrich Brüning, one of the ablest men in Germany. Brüning continued Stresemann's policies but was not able to retard the growth of the Nazis and Communists. In the election of 1930, the latter gained over a million votes and the Nazis almost six million. Further gains were made two years later. At this juncture Hindenburg made the mistake of dismissing Brüning and appointing Franz von Papen as Chancellor. From that moment things went from bad to worse. Von Papen's reactionary program actually strengthened the Nazis and Communists. Hoping to stave off the collapse of the Republic, Hindenburg replaced von Papen by an ultraconservative, General Kurt von Schleicher. The general was able to do little, and in January, 1933, Hitler succeeded him to the chancellorship. The elections which followed gave Hitler the whip hand. Accordingly on April 1, the Reichstag, at the request of Hindenburg, voted overwhelmingly to delegate its powers for four years to Hitler. To all intents and purposes the Republic had been abolished; and a Nazi dictatorship was enthroned in Germany.

In the meantime the Allies had been watching Hitler's rise with much concern. They realized that a Nazi dictatorship might endanger the peace of Europe. Hoping to stave off this disaster, the League of Nations had gathered at Geneva a world conference on reduction of armaments. All the powers, including Russia and the United States, were in attendance. At the outset France refused to reduce its forces to the level which Germany demanded, while the latter stubbornly insisted upon parity with France. British diplomacy did its best to find a formula which might be acceptable to both parties. The efforts, however, were in vain, particularly after Hitler had become dictator in April, 1933. Finally, in October of that year Germany withdrew from the conference and announced that it might resign its membership from the League and proceed to arm. "If the world decides," Hitler stated, "that all weapons are to be abolished, down to the last machine gun, we are ready to join in such a convention. If the world grants to each nation certain weapons, we are not prepared to let ourselves be excluded from this concession as a nation with inferior rights." At the same time he blamed France for Germany's actions. Between the two powers, Hitler said, there could exist no cause for war. This was an implied recognition of the Locarno Pact; and since Germany would abide by this agreement, what possible danger could France expect from a German army which was no larger than that of France?

Imperial Japan Threatens War

The British government tried valiantly to bring France and Germany together. Among other things it proposed a limitation of the forces of all the great powers to 200,000 men, and "a progressive approach" to this level by Germany. Hitler scorned this suggestion and viewed it as a denial of the Fatherland's sovereign right to arm as she wished. The World Disarmament Conference had failed. Although it continued to meet for several months, it accomplished nothing. Britain recognized the existence of this impasse, and in the summer of 1934 announced her intention of augmenting her air and military forces. At the same time Japan informed England and America that she would not consent to a renewal of the Washington Arms agreement, which was to expire in January, 1937, unless she were given parity with these powers. In the face of this pronouncement, the naval conversations of these three states at London, early in 1936, amounted to nothing. Britain was willing to make some concessions, but America refused to grant parity to Japan. Ultimately England sided with the United States, and Japan withdrew from the conference. In the meantime France and Italy, who had not signed the London Agreement of 1930, had increased their naval establishments, while Germany and Russia showed signs of doing the same.

The demands of the various powers for military and naval security rested, to a great extent, upon economic conditions. Considerable disparity existed among the nations of the world. Some controlled enormous supplies and resources while others were lacking in basic goods and commodities. The monetary and credit policies of the various countries, their tariffs, debts, and management of production and distribution were so conflicting as to lead to world disorder. Conditions had been bad enough before the World War, and the depression which followed created a crisis more formidable than that of armies and navies. The Lausanne Conference of 1932 recognized the need for economic recovery and recommended that the League of Nations convoke a World Economic and Financial Conference. The Council of the League endorsed this proposal; and in June, 1933, the world powers gathered at London to consider "restoring currencies to a healthy basis . . . and of facilitating the revival of international trade." A number of proposals were introduced and discussed, but at no time were the delegates prepared to "embark on any ambitious project in international planning." They were unwilling, too, to apply deflationary policies in respect to currency either at home or abroad. As a result the London Conference adjourned in July without accomplishing what its advocates had expected. The collapse of the Economic Conference and the World Disarmament Conference at Geneva was followed by the failure of the naval discussions of 1936. The world was plunged into uncertainty and international chaos.

Had Japan not asked for naval parity it is altogether likely that the Washington Arms Agreement might have been extended for a number of years. Japan's imperial program in the Far East, however, necessitated a different course. The World War had given Japan an unusual opportunity to extend her influence and power. The rapid disintegration of China which followed this conflict raised problems which Japan could not ignore. In the first place, her capitalists wished to acquire greater financial and economic control in China, and her imperialists had visions of territorial gains. In the second place, Japan feared Russia, which, taking advantage of China's weakness, had acquired a sphere of influence in Outer Mongolia and had spread communistic doctrine throughout the Far East. As a result, Japan brought about a quarrel with China and proceeded to conquer Manchuria and establish, in 1933, the puppet state of Manchukuo. China protested against this action and appealed to the League for help. A committee which investigated the situation reported that Japan had broken the Covenant of the League and was an aggressor nation. None of the European powers, however, was willing to impose sanctions, though the United States, which claimed Japan had violated the Nine Power Pact of 1921, signified her desire to take action. Britain did not feel that her interests in the Far East were sufficiently disturbed to warrant her joining America in resisting Japanese aggression. Moreover, the European situation was so troublesome as to make England pause before the dangers in the Orient. At the same time she refused to recognize Manchukuo and, early in 1936, strengthened her naval base at Singapore.

Fascist Germany and Italy Flout the League

In the meantime Japan renewed her activity in North China. She withdrew from the League and informed England and America that she would not renew the naval agreements of 1921 and 1930. If Japan could flout the League, others might do the same; and in March, 1935, Hitler renounced the military provisions of the Versailles Treaty. Since the Allies had broken this agreement by not reducing their armies, Hitler claimed Germany might rearm. Surrounded by the superior forces of France and her allies and by Soviet Russia, Germany felt that her security demanded a large and effective army and navy. France viewed the future with alarm and called upon allied powers to use force against Germany. Japan showed no interest. On the other hand Britain sought a middle course. Her economic recovery argued for increased trade with Germany. At the same time she supported the League's condemnation of Germany but would not approve of military sanctions. A balance of power between Germany and France was far better than disturbing the peace of Europe. Left alone, France had to content herself with coöperation between the powers. French diplomacy, however, scored two notable victories over Germany. First, France gained a five-year pact of mutual assistance with Russia; and second, she bound Italy to join her against German annexation of Austria and any further revisions of existing treaties. On the other hand she witnessed a widening of the breach between herself and Britain when the latter agreed to allow Germany to have a navy about one third the size of England's.

The Franco-Italian Entente of 1935 disturbed England's position in the Mediterranean. Anxious to preserve Italian friendship in Europe, France had given Italy certain rights in Tunis and some forty-four thousand square miles of territory which bordered upon Libya and British Sudan. Italy also gained territory in French Somaliland and a share in the railroad from Addis Ababa, the capital of Ethiopia, to the Gulf of Aden. More significant was France's promise not to interfere with Italian activities in Ethiopia.

Italian interest in North Africa dates back almost to the unification of Italy in 1871. During the eighties the coastal areas of Eritrea and Italian Somaliland were acquired, though an attempt to conquer Ethiopia was checked by the Abyssinian victory at Adowa in 1896. As a result of the Turco-Italian war of 1911–1912, Italy gained Libya. Further expansion was delayed by the World War and the deplorable economic conditions that followed. The inability of the Italian monarchy to restore order and the rapid growth of communism paved the way for the establishment of a Fascist dictatorship under Benito Mussolini. Skillful administration, combined with force, quieted domestic discord and permitted a stronger foreign and imperial program. Italy, according to Mussolini, possessed too much vitality to warrant being tied to the cart wheel of European diplomacy. Italy needed markets for an expanding industry and territory for an excess population. The Mediterranean must be dominated by Italy. French opposition was reduced by the Entente of 1935 while British attention was focused upon Germany, Japan, the Near East, and Egypt. The time to strike was at hand, and Ethiopia was chosen as the victim to satisfy Fascist imperialism. Mussolini found a cause for war, and late in 1935 Fascist troops marched into Ethiopia.

Immediately Ethiopia appealed to the League, which proceeded to investigate the situation. In spite of Mussolini's blustering protests and threats, the League found Italy guilty of having caused the war and of endangering the peace of the world. Britain's rôle in this unhappy episode was fraught with difficulty. The smaller nations looked to her to preserve the dignity and very existence of the League. England answered this call by attempting to persuade Italy to withdraw its troops. Mussolini curtly refused and threatened England by increasing his forces in Libya. England became alarmed, as an Italian victory over Ethiopia might undermine Britain's prestige in Egypt, the Sudan, and the Near East, and endanger her position in the Mediterranean. British diplomacy, therefore, had to protect the interests of her imperialists and capitalists as well as the millions of Englishmen, who supported the action taken by the League. Keeping a watchful eye on Germany, the British ministry allowed its representative at Geneva to endorse the imposition of economic sanctions upon Italy. On October 19, 1935, the League referred the following proposals to the members for adoption: (1) the prohibition of the export of arms and munitions; (2) the prohibition of loans and credits to the Italian government or its citizens; (3) the prohibition of the importation of Italian goods; and (4) an embargo upon certain exports to Italy. By December 11 the more important nations had accepted these proposals, the absentees being chiefly among the Latin-American states.

In the meantime, totally unknown to the other members of the League, Sir Samuel Hoare, the British Foreign Minister, had been negotiating with M. Laval, Premier of France. On December 8 the two ministers signed an agreement whereby peace was to be restored by a partition of Ethiopia. Europe was dumfounded by the news, and the British press condemned Hoare's action. Britain, it was said, had betrayed Ethiopia and the League, and had deserted the lesser states which, in September, had applauded England's determination to enforce the League's sanctions. Hoare realized the strength of public opinion, and not wishing to embarrass the Conservative Government under Stanley Baldwin, resigned his office. His place was filled by Anthony Eden, a staunch friend of the League and a determined advocate of economic sanctions. Hoare, in brief, had been forced out of office by the English people, who preferred an Italian war to the end of the League, which they believed would follow if the Hoare-Laval agreement were accepted.

This agreement reached Geneva at a time when a special committee was discussing the expediency of an embargo upon petroleum, coal, iron, and steel. There was no need for further debate if the Council of the League accepted the Hoare-Laval proposals. As a result the committee suspended its meetings until it heard of Hoare's resignation and the negative action of the Council. When the committee resumed its discussions, the situation had been eased somewhat by an understanding between France and England as to naval activities in the event of an Italian war. On the other hand nothing had been heard from America, where Congress was considering President Roosevelt's suggestion that oil exports to Italy be kept at their normal level, which represented less than eight per

cent of Italy's peacetime needs. Ultimately Congress rejected
Roosevelt's proposal but did place a ban upon the export of
arms and munitions. America's action made it practically impossible for the League to place an embargo upon petroleum,
for were this to be imposed, American exports would be increased. Moreover, any interference with American trade
might lead to difficulties with the United States, and the
League had no desire to increase its burdens. As a result both
France and England hesitated about enforcing additional sanctions, though the latter concentrated additional aircraft, battle-
ships, and troops at Malta, Gibraltar, and Egypt.

British imperialists approved of this change in Baldwin's
policy. They hoped this would bring to an end all talk of an
Italian attack upon Egypt. They did not know, however, that
when the British fleet anchored at Malta there existed no adequate defense against the superior Italian air force. On the
other hand the friends of the League were bitterly disappointed
over Baldwin's reluctance to impose further economic sanctions. The *Spectator,* a leading London paper, reflected the
attitude of this group when it wrote, "It is more and more
repugnant to the citizens of League States that Italy should be
continuing to carry on a lawless war on petrol supplied by the
favor of their governments. It is obvious, moreover, that the
Covenant plainly requires the stoppage of petrol supplies. In
all the circumstances the right course is to carry out the
Covenant. The League cannot lag behind America."

During the winter of 1935–1936, the Italian command in
Ethiopia encountered more serious opposition than it had expected. This, together with British naval activity in the Mediterranean and the talk of oil sanctions, aroused Mussolini to
greater efforts. Additional troops poured into Ethiopia and
every effort was made to finish the war before the rainy season,
which of necessity would retard operations. It is probable that
British diplomacy believed that Ethiopia would hold off the
invader and force a suspension of hostilities until the fall.
By that time the expense of the war plus the effects of the
sanctions already imposed might force Mussolini to listen to

reason rather than face an embargo on oil, coal, steel, and iron. Whether this assumption was valid or not, the fact remains that although the League continued to talk of sanctions, nothing was done during January and February, 1936. Ultimately no action was taken because of Hitler's interposition.

Taking advantage of the Ethiopian affair and sensing the lack of coöperation between England and France, Hitler suddenly, in early March, sent troops into the Rhineland in open violation of the Treaty of Versailles. If the League were now to place an oil embargo upon Italy and if Italy were to reply by war, as she said she would, the opportunity for Germany to attack France was greatly increased. France, therefore, forgot Ethiopia and directed its energies toward meeting the German challenge. England was forced to do likewise. Hitler's statement that the recent Franco-Russian alliance had invalidated the Locarno Pact spread consternation throughout Europe. Hitler informed Europe, however, that Germany had no designs upon France and Belgium. To prove it he offered several different proposals, which if accepted would preserve peace. In the first place, he suggested the establishment of a demilitarized zone on both sides of the Franco-German and Belgo-German frontiers. A twenty-five year non-aggression pact, endorsed by Britain and Italy, would then be signed by France, Belgium, and Germany. Non-aggression pacts would also be offered to those states bordering on Germany's eastern frontier, and an air pact would be arranged for the western frontier. Accept these proposals, Hitler said, and Germany would return to the League. But how could any nation have faith in a man whose hands had torn up the Versailles and Locarno Pacts? If Hitler could find an excuse for occupying the Rhineland, he could also invent a reason for violating a non-aggression pact. How could France agree to demilitarize her western front, which she had fortified at an enormous cost and which offered her reasonable security against German attack? Furthermore, France could not sign a non-aggression pact without deserting Russia, with whom Hitler would make no treaty and for whom he had nothing but provocative words.

Britain was agitated by Hitler's action but proceeded to re-build the shattered fabric of European security. She softened France's belligerent attitude and tried to modify Germany's position by suggesting a general discussion of the points raised by Hitler. It was evident that England did not want to scrap the Locarno Pact and the Covenant, yet she could not deny that Germany had a case as well as France. Some new for-mula, satisfactory to both parties and favorable to England, would have to be found. Veiled suggestions were made about a Russian-German non-aggression pact and a general confer-ence to consider a revision of both the Locarno and Versailles agreements.

Late in July, 1936, England, France, and Belgium jointly invited Italy and Germany to attend such a conference. The invitation was accepted, but because of the Spanish Civil War, no further step was taken until late September, when the Brit-ish suggested a meeting at London in October. France and Belgium endorsed the proposal. Italy accepted in principle, but suggested that a diplomatic exchange of views should pre-cede the fixing of the date. Germany replied that unless the discussions were limited to Western Europe, she would be reluctant to agree as to a date. Germany, in brief, did not want the Russian problem dragged into the conference; and yet it is difficult to see how, in view of the Franco-Russian Treaty, any agreement could be reached which did not affect Russia. England was disappointed but continued to work in the interest of a settlement. In the meantime, she redoubled her military, naval, and air activities, increased the tax burdens of her people, and maintained friendly relations with the United States.

Hitler's bold thrust in March, 1936, greatly strengthened Mussolini's hand in Ethiopia. The Italian command pushed its operations so speedily that by May 5 it had entered Addis Ababa. Italy had won the war and actually occupied more Ethiopian territory than the Hoare-Laval proposals had offered her in January. Not waiting to see what Europe might say or do, Mussolini proclaimed the annexation of Ethiopia and announced that what Italy had conquered she would defend to the last man. At the same time he assured England that Italy had no designs on the Sudan or any British territory in Africa. Although Britain did not recognize the Italian conquest of Ethiopia and continued to talk about sanctions, she proceeded to make the most of a bad situation. English diplomacy had suffered a defeat, and her prestige in Africa and the Near East had suffered. In Palestine the Arab situation continued with loss of life and property, and England partly blamed Italian propaganda for these uprisings. Nevertheless the British ministry showed a willingness to treat with Italy.

Rumor had it that the sanctions would be dropped. The return of Hoare to the ministry, as First Lord of the Admiralty, lent support to this rumor. Ultimately the League members revoked their economic sanctions but refused to unseat the Ethiopian representatives. Officially the League considered Ethiopia a sovereign and independent state. Germany, however, in October, 1936, recognized the Italian Empire in Ethiopia and thus complicated the situation still further. Since then Britain has taken no steps towards recognition of Italy's African empire. On the other hand the tangled state of diplomacy in Spain, China, and Germany argues for a change in Britain's position. In the opinion of some, Britain will recognize Italian power in Ethiopia so as to forestall any dispute which might involve her Mediterranean interests.

The Spanish Civil War

Germany's action may be explained in part by the similarity in government which exists in Fascist Italy and Nazi Germany. Both states, moreover, have a profound hate for Soviet Russia, the ally of France. More significant than either of these two factors in bringing about an Italian-German understanding was the unhappy situation which developed in Spain during the summer of 1936. In April, 1931, the Spanish monarchy under Alphonso XIII had been overthrown and a republic established in its place. The new government adopted an anti-clerical policy and passed a number of measures that were decidedly socialistic in nature. Communism, moreover, gained many followers. As a result, the monarchists, Catholics, and property classes joined together, and in the summer of 1936 resorted to armed force. A civil war followed. Considerable sympathy for the rebels appeared in Germany and Italy, whose dictators viewed the Spanish contest as a war against communism. At the same time Russia and France expressed interest in the cause of Republican Spain. British labor, moreover, went on record as favoring the existing government. With Europe taking sides, it was not long before charges were made that military assistance was being given both warring factions by their European friends. Hoping to silence these rumors, Britain supported France in proposing a non-intervention agreement.

At this juncture Hitler informed his millions of supporters that Soviet Russia was Public Enemy Number One. Germany's economic and political future depended upon the annihilation of communism, and Hitler suggested that Germany needed the industrial and agricultural sections of Soviet Russia. The world was stunned by this announcement. Russia replied by increased military activity and by accusing Germany and Italy of having aided the Spanish rebels. She informed Europe, moreover, that she might have to take sides in the Spanish war. Immediately France and England joined hands in trying to prevent an overt act that might lead to a world war. The non-intervention committee, which was meeting at London, redoubled its efforts. Immediate success was checked by German and Italian recognition of the Insurgent forces and by well-established evidence of German and Italian "volunteers" in Spain. Many of these troops had seen service at home and were well equipped with military supplies and arms. In spite of these difficulties a non-intervention agreement was reached but in the face of gunrunning and the presence of foreign troops this understanding became an international joke. Non-intervention became a game of international hide-and-seek. Germany took advantage of the situation by announcing an anti-communist pact with Japan. About the same time

Britain and Italy came to an understanding concerning their difficulties in the Mediterranean. France, moreover, announced that it would resist an unprovoked attack upon Britain, while England informed Europe that she would do likewise in respect to France.

The diplomatic weather then turned from storming to fair. Italy and Germany expressed a willingness to adhere to a policy of strict non-intervention, provided the other powers would do the same. Britain's reply came in the form of an order which warned its citizens that enlistment in either Spanish armies was a criminal action. France followed by an act which forbade further volunteering. This measure was to become effective when the other powers agreed to stop enlistments for Spain. None of the other states, however, had taken action by the middle of January, 1937. Italy and Germany had little confidence in either France or Russia and seemed unwilling to take the first move. Both Italy and Germany had pledged their prestige to assure an Insurgent victory and believed that their armed forces in Spain would bring this result, provided French and Russian aid was stopped. In brief, they required positive evidence that these two governments had abandoned Madrid before they would adhere to a non-intervention agreement. Late in February, 1937, the European states finally agreed upon joint action. Troops were to be stationed along the frontiers of Spain, and Spanish waters were to be patrolled so as to prevent military supplies and men from reaching either the Loyalists or Insurgents. Several incidents, however, such as an alleged Loyalist attack upon a German warship, led Italy and Germany to withdraw their patrols, thus largely negativing the aims of the non-intervention committee.

Further trouble arose in the summer of 1937, as the result of submarine activity in the Mediterranean. Several British and Russian ships carrying supplies to the Spanish Loyalists were attacked and sunk. Britain at once increased her naval units in this area and instructed their officers to fire upon any attacking submarine. Hoping, however, to preserve peace, Britain joined with France in summoning a conference of certain European powers to meet at Nyon, Switzerland. Italy and Germany expressed interest but refused to attend when Russia boldly charged Italy with being responsible for the submarine attacks. At the Nyon Conference, held in September, it was agreed: (1) that Britain and France would patrol the main Mediterranean trade routes; (2) that the smaller powers would guard their own waters; (3) that Russia and

Ewing Galloway.

PARLIAMENT BUILDING AND WESTMINSTER BRIDGE, WITH BIG BEN AT RIGHT.

the Black Sea nations would protect their interests in their area; and (4) that Italy would be invited to help France and Britain. Italy accepted and, together with these powers, is patrolling the Mediterranean. More recently, Britain and France asked Italy to confer with them regarding the withdrawal of Italian soldiers serving in Spain against the Loyalists. Although France intimated that she might open her southern frontier to volunteers who wish to aid the Loyalists, if this offer was not accepted, Italy refused.

In the meantime, Japan found an excuse for sending a punitive expedition against China, whose governing officials Japan charged with being pro-Russian. Peiping was captured in

August, as well as some northern territory; but at Shanghai, Chinese resistance has checked several determined attacks. British and neutral property have been endangered and destroyed by artillery and aircraft fire, and sharp protests were presented to Japan and China, between whom no declaration of war has been announced. In the course of these encounters, the British Ambassador to China was seriously wounded by what appears to have been an unwarranted attack by Japanese aviators. A sharp note to Japan brought no apology until September, while no satisfactory statement has been received relative to Britain's protest against Japanese bombing of defenseless areas. Throughout the affair, Britain has tried to prevent the war from spreading and joined with America in asking both countries to seek a peaceful solution for their differences. China was willing, but Japan curtly refused. In September, the League of Nations reviewed the situation and invited America to join in a conference on the Far East. The United States accepted. Shortly thereafter, President Roosevelt challenged Japan's actions and intimated that sanctions might have to be imposed. Within two days, both the League and the United States declared Japan to have been the aggressor and a violator of the Nine-Power Pacific Pact and the Briand-Kellogg Pact. Whether Britain, in view of the Spanish trouble, will advocate economic sanctions in the Far East, remains to be seen.

The effect of these events did little to ease a troubled situation. Britain still talks about a revised Locarno Pact, but until the Spanish and Chinese problems are settled, there seems to be little hope for promoting collective security. Britain is hopeful but is not blind to the realities. She is concerned over the accord which exists among Germany, Italy, and Japan; the agreement recently announced between Russia and China; and is decidedly interested in Germany's attitude toward Czechoslovakia. Should Germany attack the latter, it is possible that Russia would consider it an act of war. In such an event, France might be drawn into the conflict, and England would have to side with France. Should Russia aid China,

Japan might attack the former, and this might lead Germany into the war. Anticipating the worst, Britain has increased her military and naval preparations. The European situation and its relation to the Empire was a major topic of discussion at the Imperial Conference of May, 1937. Were England to accept Italy's invitation to join the anti-communist pact, it is likely that more friendly relations might be established in Europe. But England refuses such an alliance. She places her trust in democratic government, and will enter into no agreement which might endanger her priceless heritage. Moreover, she believes that the Dominions will support her and hopes that the United States will use its force to preserve democratic government. What the future has in store no one knows.

SELECTED BIBLIOGRAPHY

Many of the references for the preceding two chapters may be used with profit for this chapter. In addition the following are of value: C. K. Webster's *League of Nations in Theory and Practice* (New York, 1933); M. O. Hudson's *The World Court* (Boston, 1934); R. L. Buell's *Europe, a History of Ten Years* (New York, 1928); F. H. Simond's *Great Powers in World Politics* (New York, 1935); R. L. Buell's *Washington Conference* (New York, 1922); J. W. Wheeler-Bennett's *Disarmament and Security since Locarno* (New York, 1932); G. H. Blakeslee's *The Pacific Area* (Boston, 1929); C. H. Peake's *Nationalism and Education in Modern China* (New York, 1932); K. S. Latourette's *Development of China* (New York, 1929); A. Hitler's *My Battle* (New York, 1933); W. H. Dawson's *Germany under the Peace Treaty* (New York, 1933); H. G. Daniel's *Rise of the German Republic* (New York, 1928); K. Heiden's *History of National Socialism* (New York, 1934); S. de Madariaga's *Spain* (New York, 1930); P. Vaucher's *Post-War France* (London, 1934); H. E. Goad's *Making of the Corporate State* (London, 1932); M. I. Currey's *Italian Foreign Policy, 1918–1932* (London, 1932); W. R. Batsell's *Soviet Rule in Russia* (New York, 1929); L. Trotsky's *History of the Russian Revolution* (New York, 1932); H. Finer's *Mussolini's Italy* (New York, 1935); J. S. Barnes' *The Universal Aspects of Fascism* (London, 1929), and A. Werth's *France in Ferment* (New York, 1935).

CHAPTER XXXVIII

Religion, Education, and Science

SINCE the World War, British foreign policy has been complicated by domestic issues and party politics. Had the MacDonald ministry of 1924 remained in office, it is likely that the *Geneva Protocol* would have been adopted and an earlier understanding reached with Russia. The Ethiopian question, moreover, might have been solved more advantageously for England had Sir Samuel Hoare remained in the cabinet. Hoare's retirement was caused in part by public condemnation of his retreat from the pacific principles of the League of Nations. England had become peace-minded and was unwilling to return to the older ways of settling international disputes even though adherence to the League might cause an Italian war. In that case it would have been a war waged by the League. International rivalries, so many insisted, should be solved by international coöperation and not by the Hoare-Laval method. Similar sentiments greeted Anthony Eden in June, 1936, when he proposed to the Commons that the sanctions against Italy be lifted. Friends of the League interpreted this suggestion as a retreat from Geneva, and condemned Eden and the Tory Party in no uncertain terms. Although the Baldwin Government easily carried a motion endorsing Eden's proposal, hostile criticism continued. When on July 15th the British sanctions were dropped, considerable opposition was shown.

Pioneering for Peace

British loyalty to the League rests fundamentally upon the conviction that international disputes have not and cannot be settled by the sword. The genesis of this concept antedates the Ethiopian question by several centuries. Although the Roman Church did little during the medieval period to combat war, the pacific teachings of Christ have influenced thought and action. As early as the fourteenth century, Wycliffe uncompromisingly opposed war. Wycliffe's views were endorsed by More in his celebrated *Utopia* and by Erasmus in his *Praise of Folly* and *Complaint of Peace*. Later the Brownists, a separatist sect, followed these anti-war traditions and influenced the thinking of George Fox and Robert Barclay, founders of the Society of Friends. Quaker condemnation of war was also shown by Penn's *Plan for the Permanent Peace of Europe,* in which an international tribunal was suggested. Penn's ideas reappeared many times during the eighteenth century. On the other hand the Continental wars of this century and of the early nineteenth checked the peace crusade.

In one sense these conflicts actually strengthened the peace movement. The enormous loss of life and the rapidly mounting costs of war convinced many of the evils of war and the merits of peace. In 1811, for example, an unknown writer in the *Monthly Magazine* condemned the existing war and advocated the establishment of a National Court of Arbitration. Later, on June 14, 1816, a prominent Friend named William Allen founded the British Peace Society. Additional stimulus came from America, where similar peace activities had been undertaken by David Low Dodge and Noah Worcester. Most of the early English peace leaders were Friends. In 1819 they sought to advance their cause by founding the *Herald of Peace,* which is still in existence. Of the auxiliary societies formed in various parts of the kingdom, that at Birmingham, founded by the Quaker Joseph Sturge, was the most influential. Prom-

inent manufacturers like Edward Baines and humanitarians
like Joseph Hume became members of the peace society and
supported the movement within parliament. Baines' work
was significant, as he was the owner of the *Leeds Mercury* and
Staffordshire Mercury. In the issues of these papers and several others appeared editorials and news in favor of peace.

By the late 1830's the British society was championing the
idea of arbitration and a congress of nations. Moreover, it
supported the American proposal for a Universal Peace Convention, which met at London in June, 1843. In the decade
that followed, other meetings were held at Brussels, Paris,
Frankfort, and London. The growing strength of the peace
movement, which gained recruits from Free Traders like
Richard Cobden and Non-Conformists like Henry Richard,
was shown by the numerous peace meetings held throughout
the kingdom and by the many anti-war petitions to parliament.
Convinced peace men believed the time ripe for action; and on
June 12, 1849, Cobden moved on the floor of the Commons
that the Government should coöperate with other nations in
establishing a world system of arbitration. Roebuck, Hume,
Ewart, and Gibson, prominent liberals and reformers, supported Cobden. On the other hand Palmerston and Russell
opposed the motion on the ground that existing conditions did
not warrant such a step, however sound it might be in theory.
Cobden's motion was defeated by 176 votes to 79.

During the course of the next two decades the peace movement was torn by internal dissensions and by the wars in India
and with Russia. Thanks to the untiring efforts of Henry
Richard, W. E. Darby, W. R. Cremer, Joshua Rownstree, and
W. T. Stead, the agitation against war survived these conflicts.
Added stimulus came from foreign peace societies. More
significant was the action of the Czar in August, 1898, in inviting the governments of the world to participate in a general
peace conference. The British Peace Society seized this opportunity, and W. T. Stead toured Europe in behalf of the

Czar's suggestion. Ultimately a conference was held at the Hague from May 18 to July 29, 1899. No understanding was reached as to armament limitation. The use of expanding bullets, gas, and projectiles from balloons was forbidden; and steps were taken to codify international law and establish a world court of arbitration.

Within a few months of the Hague Conference, England became involved in the Boer War. British feeling ran high and scoffed at Stead and other pacifists. Public opinion failed to answer the criticism of foreigners who wanted the South African dispute referred to the Hague Court. Joseph Chamberlain, England's outstanding imperialist, captured the public by his war speeches and was "feted even by the Wesleyan pacifists." The British Peace Society, moreover, became nationalistic in its attitude and refused to support Stead's movement to "Stop the War." In spite of this dissension the crusade against war gained strength after the Treaty of Pretoria. It supported the Anglo-American Arbitration Treaty of 1903 and argued for a peaceful settlement of all international disputes. Valuable recruits were gained from organized labor, notably Ramsay MacDonald; and in 1912 the Labor Party discussed the possibility of a general strike in case of war. British opinion in general was suspicious of the peace movement, and at the outbreak of war, in 1914, rallied to the colors. Defection and desertion within the peace groups followed to such an extent that the movement lost caste and influence. Those who remained loyal to their anti-war ideals did little to check the course of the conflict.

Following the World War the British peace movement regained most of the ground it had lost during that contest. The establishment of the League of Nations was chiefly responsible for this renewed interest, which showed itself in the formation of several new anti-war societies. An alert branch of the War Resisters' International and the Council of Christ and Peace Campaign joined with the older organizations in stimulating a peace movement. The Baptist, Congregational, Presbyterian, and Methodist Churches, as well as the Society of Friends, endorsed the platform of the Council of Christ, which declared that its members "would not countenance any war nor encourage their countrymen to serve in any war with regard to which the Government of their country had refused to offer to submit the dispute to pacific methods of settlement." The British League of Nations Union and the Royal Institute of International Affairs encouraged these pacific attitudes; and the Labor party, the Trades Union Congress, and the Coöperative Congress pledged themselves to war resistance. Finally, in 1935, a house-to-house campaign conducted by the British League of Nations Union secured the signatures of several million Englishmen against war.

The accumulative effect of these forces upon Britain's foreign policy was shown when Sir Samuel Hoare retired from the cabinet in 1936. Undoubtedly further gains will be made, though the peace movement, if it would gain its ends, must do more than support the League of Nations. It must make Englishmen conscious of the basic antecedents of war and must educate for peace. It must enlist the support of the Established Church. Although the Council of Christ and Peace Campaign was founded by the Bishop of Chichester and has secured the endorsement of many prominent clergy and thousands of laymen, no official action has been taken by the Church of England.

Recent Trends in Religious Life

At the opening of the nineteenth century the Established Church was experiencing a religious revival known as the Wesleyan movement. Those in control of the Church refused to sanction this evangelical renaissance, and as a result drove thousands into the Methodist communion. Conservative principles and leaders maintained the historical catholicity of the

Established Church. The higher clergy, recruited from the noble and wealthy classes, continued to deliver pompous and scholarly sermons which, in all probability, some of the laity did not understand. Pastoral duties, except for formal visitations of their dioceses and the administering of confirmation, were usually neglected. On the other hand these prelates became skillful in business and reflected Tory attitudes in the House of Lords. Seldom was a clerical voice raised in defense of labor or in favor of parliamentary reform. The lesser clergy, though orthodox in theology, emulated their Protestant rivals in humanitarian and social reform. Though content with meager stipends, they questioned the large incomes enjoyed by the bishops and frowned upon the latter's neglect of duty. They did not approve of parishes being held by an underpaid cleric in behalf of some priest who absented himself for a political career. Objection to these practices was registered at the diocesan convocations, where earnest appeals were made in behalf of social reform. The greater clergy, however, were more than satisfied with existing conditions and turned a deaf ear to the pleas of the humble rectors.

In the meantime the Church was attacked by outside forces, and in 1828 and 1829 witnessed the repeal of the Test and Corporation Acts and the passage of the Roman Catholic Emancipation Act. The political and religious concessions granted by these measures weakened the power and influence of the Church of England. Romanists and Protestants, with but few exceptions, might hold any office; and as members of parliament, they might vote on all matters affecting the Established Church. The Reform Act of 1832 increased the number of non-Anglicans in parliament, and the Irish Temporalities Bill of 1833 decreased the Anglican episcopate in Ireland both as to size and power. Wellington viewed these measures as revolutionary and insisted that power had been transferred "from our class of society, the gentlemen of England, professing the faith of the Church of England, to another class of society, the shopkeepers, being dissenters from the Church." A nonconformist attitude, aided by an evangelical spirit on the part of the humble clerics of the church and by the return of Romanism to England, threatened the life of the Established Church.

Many of the lesser clergy and a few liberal bishops sought to save their beloved church by agitating for humanitarian and social reforms, and by developing a priesthood which carried the gospel of Christ into the heretofore neglected rural areas and factory towns. On the other hand, there was another group within the Church which believed that the historic English Church could be saved from disintegration by stressing the catholicity of its faith. Spiritual enthusiasm, so it was argued, would fire the mind and hearts of the laity. The crusade, which the latter group started, had its inception at Oxford and became known as the Oxford Movement. In its earlier stages it was distinctly a youth movement sponsored by a few earnest divinity students, but within a short time it had attracted several prominent professors and a large number of the English clergy. Those who joined in this religious renaissance firmly believed that the Anglican Church must justify its existence upon spiritual grounds and not upon the incident of the Reformation. The latter had given the Established Church shape and form, but its birthright rested upon religious forces apostolic in origin.

In order to advance their views, the leaders of the Oxford Movement published a number of pamphlets, notably a series known as the *Tracts for the Times*. As this series progressed, a decidedly Roman attitude appeared. Henry Newman, for example, rector of St. Mary's, Oxford, declared in Tract 90 that the Thirty-Nine Articles were doctrinally in tune with the Roman creed. Stout defenders of the Anglican Church condemned this thesis and forced Newman to resign his parish. Others encouraged Newman to continue his studies, with the result that in 1845 he and several other prominent men espoused the Roman faith. According to their point of view the English Church was a "schismatical offshoot of the true Catholic faith." Continued membership in the Established Church, therefore, was heretical. Newman's action disrupted the Oxford Movement. On the one hand there appeared within the English Church a High Church group, which stressed the apostolic and Catholic origins of the Anglican faith. More elaborate ritual and ceremony were introduced by this group into the services of the Established Church, and many a layman like Gladstone found peace and contentment within this medieval atmosphere. Others were stimulated by Newman's retreat to Rome to adopt a broader religious attitude. Loyalty to the Established Church was uppermost in their minds, though in doctrine and ritual they adopted a liberal position.

Since the Oxford Movement and Newman's conversion to Rome, the Anglican Church has become the honored faith of High, Low, and Broad Churchmen. In social, political, and economic affairs, the Established Church has followed a more liberal policy. Many prominent priests and laymen have labored in the slum areas and have brought improved living conditions to the poor and needy. The Church, however, is subject to the authority of the crown and parliament, which may alter its structure and creed regardless of ecclesiastical opinion or action. Protestants, Romanists, and skeptics within parliament exercise as much control over religious affairs as Anglicans. There are many within the Anglican Church who resent this civil domination, established by Henry VIII, from which the Anglican Church has not been able to free itself. Actually there have been but few occasions when the non-Anglican members of parliament have interfered with the faith or practices of the Established Church. Although this opposition rejects the doctrine of the Established Church, it honors and respects an institution which represents the best elements and traditions in English national life and history. The Anglican Church's utility to the state and nation is not questioned. Its revenue is large but is used chiefly for the benefit of the English people, and its parochial system places rectors of refinement and ability in the humblest parish. The laity, moreover, are not, as in most of the other denominations, taxed to support the clergy.

Among the Protestant faiths there has been continued growth and progress. Factional strife within each communion has given way to unity. The Congregational Union of England and Wales, the Presbyterian Church of England, the Methodist Church, and the Baptist Union of the British Isles represent, today, wholesome forces in the religious and social life of England. The Unitarians and Friends have made valuable contributions in social and intellectual activities; and the Salvation Army, founded by William Booth in 1865, has brought comfort and aid to thousands. More recently, the evangelical force known as the Oxford Movement has swept through the kingdom with astonishing success.

In the meantime the Roman Catholic Church renewed its activities in England. Following the repeal of the Test and Corporation Acts and the passage of the Roman Catholic Emancipation Act, Roman priests were allowed to officiate in Britain. Later, in 1832, Romanists were given the right to hold property, erect churches, and maintain parochial schools. As a result of these measures and the Oxford Movement, the influence and prestige of the Roman Church was increased. In 1850, the Pope established the Archbishopric of Westminster, thereby according official recognition of an English branch of the Roman faith. Since that date the Roman Church in England has grown in size and influence.

The presence of the Roman, Anglican, and Protestant Churches constitutes but one manifestation of the religious life of the English people. Other evidences may be found by surveying the moral tone and attitudes of the clergy and laity. Prior to 1870, Anglican and Protestant experienced the driving force of evangelicalism, which stressed the Bible as the living word of God and made the "English the 'people of a book.'" Man's life was viewed as a preparation for the Kingdom of Heaven or Hell. The former was pictured in exalted terms, while the latter was depicted as an eternal furnace of fire and brimstone. A sabbatical sanctity prevailed throughout England. Family prayers, weekday and Sunday services, and devotional readings were as characteristic of evangelicalism as were the gloomy and lengthy discourses of the clergy. Churchgoing was both a privilege and a duty. Attendance by every member of the family was strictly adhered to, and missionary offerings were made without stint. Relatively little emphasis was placed upon formal doctrine. The Lord's Supper, for example, was administered but twice a year. The infiltration of these ideas and practices within the Established Church led, as has been shown, to the Oxford Movement, which stressed the Catholic elements within that faith. On the other hand, many of the lesser clergy and most of the laity followed evangelicalism.

Nevertheless, evangelicalism had spent much of its strength by 1870. Not only did it yield ground to the Anglo-Catholic Movement within the Established Church, but it was forced to retreat before the attack of skeptics and freethinkers. Agnostics had existed before the nineteenth century, but their number and influence was greatly increased by the scientific discoveries of the Victorian age. Biblical miracles, like Jonah and the Whale and the Marriage Feast at Cana, were rejected. Although organized religion refused to depart from God's words in the Old and New Testament, many of the younger generation accepted these new views and withdrew from the churches. Science, moreover, through multiple devices, afforded new outlets for human emotions. Peaceful and sedate Sunday walks gave way to train excursions to some throbbing urban center or beach. Churchgoing decreased, and sermons and theological discourses, which had been the vogue when

Victoria ascended the throne, now slumbered in the libraries or gathered dust in the secondhand shops. Penny newspapers like the London *Daily Chronicle* and a countless assortment of cheap, popular fiction reflected a vital change in English literary tastes. Self-interest and self-indulgence manifested itself. Man thought less of eternity and gave more attention to earthly pursuits and pleasures. Sunday became a day of rest or merry-making. Evening parties, at which cards and wines were featured, decreased the attendance at evensong and Wednesday night prayer meetings. Football, cricket, croquet, tennis, golf, and cycling provided varied amusement and sport for both men and women. Athletic skill forced changes in costume. Loose short breeches, flannels, and shorts replaced the frock coats and full trousers of Wellington's day. Men no longer wore top hats when playing cricket. Although women shortened their skirts a trifle to engage in these games, they continued to wear bustles and corsets of steel or bone for many years.

Educational Problems

The waning influence of organized religion brought radical changes in education. Prior to 1870 the government paid little attention to education. The aristocratic and upper middle classes sent their sons to Eton, Oxford, and Cambridge; but the poorer people had to content themselves with the limited offerings of the Established Church and Non-Conformists. Organized religion considered education a vested interest and vigorously resisted outside interference. The conservative groups, moreover, feared an intelligent laboring class and defeated every attempt made in parliament to establish national elementary schools. The growing power of labor, and the increased interest in humanitarian activities, following the Reform Acts of 1832 and 1867, forced a change. In 1870, 1873, and 1876, parliament passed measures which provided elementary training for every child. By 1880 compulsory attendance was required of all between the ages of five and fourteen. Parents might send their children either to the church schools or to those maintained by the state. The latter were supported entirely by government grants and local fees, and were governed by popularly elected school boards. Church schools might receive similar assistance if they accepted state supervision. At first, instruction was limited to the "three R's," but by the close of the century more advanced subjects had been introduced. Kindergarten and technical training were also provided. The effect of these various measures was revealed by the school census of 1900, which showed nearly six million children in attendance in the church and state schools. In 1870 less than a million had received instruction.

In the meantime many of the school boards developed secondary schools. Although the Act of 1870 had not provided for higher grades, the government did not interfere. The type of instruction offered by the local boards "was wanting in breadth" and was below that which was given by the endowed grammar schools. Those who were interested in promoting education for children over fourteen years of age deplored the situation and pointed to the confusion which existed as to what constituted a liberal education. Various government commissions investigated conditions, but it was not until 1902 that any change took place. In that year parliament passed a measure which abolished the local school boards, except for London, and made the county councils the authorities for all elementary, secondary, and technical schools. Privately endowed grammar schools were not affected by the act. Although the Established Church retained the right of religious instruction, appointed its teachers, and furnished the necessary buildings, all expenses were to be met out of local taxes. Local taxes also provided the income for the support of the non-church or state schools. The Established Church welcomed this arrangement which shifted the cost of education to the local areas, but the Non-Conformist Churches protested on the ground that local taxes maintained Anglican schools and Anglican instruction. More significant was the criticism that in certain areas, chiefly in Wales, there was no school but an Anglican school. Non-Conformists wanted state schools to be established in these districts so their children would not have to attend those controlled by Anglicans. An attempt to amend the Act of 1902, in this respect, was defeated in the Commons, and the country was saved from the "folly of a patchwork covering the country with rival system."

Since 1902 there has been a steady and wholesome growth. Teacher training has been promoted and salaries have been raised. The curriculum and school equipment also has advanced. Many of the smaller grammar schools, moreover, have accepted government aid and supervision. In 1907 medical inspection was established; and in 1918, according to the Fisher Act, further financial aid was accorded the secondary schools. The Fisher Act also abolished the exemptions from school attendance for those under fourteen. No child under twelve years was to be excused from school so that he might work in the textile mills. Children between twelve and fourteen might be employed after school hours, but not after eight in the evening or before six in the morning. In addition, provision was made for nursery schools, physical training, playgrounds, better salaries, and special instruction for defectives. The expenses incident to this broad program were to be shared equally by the national and local governments.

Unfortunately, the expenses incident to the World War and the depression that followed were so excessive that the Fisher Act has not operated fully. In spite of this a decided improvement has taken place. Similar gains have been made by the institutions of higher learning. At the opening of the nineteenth century, collegiate training was limited to Oxford and Cambridge. Both of these universities were citadels of Anglicanism. At Oxford no one was admitted who would not declare his acceptance of the Thirty-Nine Articles. Cambridge allowed Protestants to matriculate, but subscription to these Articles was necessary for a degree. The establishment of London University in 1836, however, marked the beginning of a new order. Although this institution offered no instruction, it might, upon examination, confer degrees which were unen-

Courtesy Assoc. British and Irish Railways, Inc.

CHRIST CHURCH, COLLEGE CHAPEL, OXFORD.

cumbered by a religious test. In 1854 the Universities of Oxford and Cambridge were opened to Protestants, but the various colleges within these institutions continued to impose restrictions until 1871. Charles P. Scott, later influential editor of the *Manchester Guardian,* was denied admission by Queen's and Christ Church, Oxford, in 1864, because he could not furnish a certificate of baptism. Nearly all of the higher degrees, prizes, and college offices were opened in 1871. Since 1878, non-Anglicans have been admitted to all honors and degrees, except for the degrees and professorships of theology.

In the meantime other colleges and universities appeared at Durham, Manchester, Birmingham, Liverpool, and a score of other boroughs and cities. Equally important were the strides made in women's education. Queen's College, London, was founded in 1848; and the Cheltenham Ladies' College was opened in 1858. Later, Girton College was established at Cambridge, while Oxford added Lady Margaret Hall in 1878. At first none of the women attending these institutions were considered members of the university proper, though they were allowed to attend classes and receive degrees. These restrictions were removed in time, as were those which prevented the city and provincial colleges from giving formal instruction. In 1898, for example, parliament authorized the establishment of faculties and colleges at London University.

During most of the nineteenth century, classical and literary subjects comprised most of the curriculum at these institutions for men and women. Those who wished to study science either matriculated at a Scottish university or became members of the Royal Institution in London. Local "philosophical" and mechanical societies also gave instruction in the sciences. Few of the nationally known scientists studied at Oxford or Cambridge, while many like Sidney G. Thomas and Sir Joseph W. Swan, prominent inventors in the steel and electrical trades, were self-taught. Later in the century a number of technical colleges were founded. Since then considerable attention to science has been paid by all institutions of higher learning. The Imperial College of Science and Technology, the City and Guilds Engineering College, and the School of Mines, all parts of London University, illustrate the modern trend toward scientific training. Reference should also be made to the London School of Economics and Political Science, which was founded in 1895.

Earlier in the nineteenth century, Oxford and Cambridge undertook extension classes. Influenced by the American Chautauqua, these institutions also established summer schools.

In some cases these extension centers developed into city colleges which emphasized technical and vocational training. Other offshoots resulted in the formation of labor schools, of which the Worker's Educational Association, founded in 1904, was the most important. The Independent Labor Party, following the plan evolved by the Fabians before the World War, maintains summer schools. College students, as well as adults, attend these schools. Special week-end meetings for adults are also arranged. The Labor Party has no summer schools though its Research Department and Young People's Organization have sponsored educational activities. At first these labor schools gave instruction in economics and history, though, more recently, attention has been paid to general cultural and scientific subjects.

Scientific Development

The scientific development, which took place during the nineteenth century, was as remarkable as it was extensive. Great strides were made in the natural sciences, notably in biology. The concept of an evolutionary process in nature existed during the classical age, but those who believed in this theory were philosophers whose teachings in this respect dominated thought for nearly two thousand years. In the meantime, physiologists, naturalists, and chemists, particularly since the nineteenth century, had been collecting observational and experimental data which paved the way for discoveries made by men like Buffon and Lamarck. It seems quite unlikely that their conclusions were known to Thomas Malthus, author of *Essay on Population,* but it was Malthus who influenced Alfred R. Wallace and Charles R. Darwin to study evolution. Malthus' comments on the ratio which existed between population and food supply convinced these men that "under these circumstances favorable variations would tend to be preserved and unfavorable ones to be destroyed." This thesis was elaborated by Darwin in his *Origin of Species* and by Wallace in his *Natural Selection*. Although the latter contended that man was a "new and distinct order of being," both agreed that the different species which existed among plants and animals were the result of natural selection and continuous adaptation to environment. Students of science and learned doctors of divinity were confounded by this new theory of the origin and development of man. Ridicule and abusive language was hurled upon these scientists, who not only refused to retract a single word but were able to convince men like Thomas Huxley, Asa Gray, and W. B. Carpenter of the soundness of evolution. Ultimately the Darwinian theory became an accepted scientific fact, though later investigation has questioned the idea of inheritance of acquired characteristics.

The progress made in biology was matched by similar gains in physiology, bacteriology, anthropology, and organic chemistry. Development in one of these fields, moreover, proved increasingly useful to the others. The constant interchange of ideas stimulated new sciences, such as biochemistry and biophysics. Many astonishing discoveries resulted. Methodical microscopic investigation of animals and human bodies revealed structures and forms of inestimable value. Sir Frederick Hopkins, for example, a biochemist at Cambridge, announced that physical health depended upon a diet rich in certain properties later known as vitamins. The medical profession is heavily indebted to the scientists in these various fields.

During the nineteenth century important changes took place in medicine. The investigations of the Unitarian minister and physician, Thomas S. Smith, did much to remove the odium which former ages had attached to dissection. The passage of the Anatomy Act of 1832 followed, and students for the first time were allowed to dissect and explore the human organism. Smith's activities were equalled by Edwin Chadwick, who labored in the field of preventive medicine and hygiene.   Chadwick was instrumental in securing the passage of the Public Health and Nuisances Removal and Diseases Prevention Acts of 1848 and 1849.   Later, Sir John Simon, head of the General Board of Health, secured authority to abolish city cesspits, improve sewers and quarantine regulations, and to establish sanitation inspectors.   His work progressed so rapidly that the government in 1871 transferred the duties of the Board of Health to the Privy Council, and in 1917 created the Minister of Health.   Notable gains were also made in surgery, as a result of the discovery of anesthesia, antiseptic surgery, and the germ theory of disease.   The use of ether by William Morgan in the United States stimulated Sir James Simpson to employ chloroform.   Mention should also be made of John Tyndall, a prominent germ specialist, and Lord Joseph Lister, whose antiseptic dressings reduced deaths from operations.   J. J. Thompson, E. Rutherford, and F. Soddy, moreover, introduced England to the possibilities of radium.   Others experimented in the ductless glands and hormones and showed how the latter influenced mental processes and physical activity.   Typhoid, diphtheria, influenza, scarlet fever, and other similar diseases were checked by antitoxic serums.   In 1894, for example, diphtheria patients in the London hospitals had but four chances out of ten of surviving.   The following year antitoxin was administered, and the deaths dropped twenty per cent. By 1910 the mortality was reduced to about twelve per cent.

In the meantime the work of Florence Nightingale had revolutionized nursing and hospitalization.   Clinics were established and important medical data were collected which did much to improve the general health of the nation.   Much of this advance was owing to the important discoveries which the chemists and physicists had made.   Michael Faraday's electromagnetic experiments, based upon the findings of the Italian, Volta, led to the invention of the dynamo.   Clerk-Maxwell's investigations of electromagnetic waves, Sir Joseph Swan's invention of the incandescent electric light, and discoveries by William Thomson (later Lord Kelvin) in mathematics, electricity, and magnetism were scientific achievements of great importance.   J. J. Thompson and E. Rutherford advanced new concepts as to the structure of the atom, while others conducted extensive investigations as to the nature of the electron and the theory of relativity.

The general effect of these discoveries in science was to revolutionize man's knowledge of himself and the world. Physical and natural forces were harnessed and a new civilization appeared.   Oil, gas, and electricity generated motive power and energy to a point where time and space have been all but eliminated.   At the opening of the nineteenth century, a fast sailing vessel might cross from London to New York in six weeks.   Today, the *Queen Mary* lands its passengers in less than five days.   Air-conditioned cabins, refrigerated foods, and constant radio and wireless communication are standard features on first-class ships.   Comfortable trains, driven by oil or steam, make it possible for a resident of Bristol to attend a matinee in London and return home within the same day. The British ambassador at Washington may telephone London and inform the Prime Minister of events almost as soon as they are known in Chicago or Seattle.   Most of these advantages are at the disposal of the average Englishman.   His radio keeps him in touch with all parts of the globe.   Automobiles, electric refrigerators, tropical foods, and foreign newspapers are common in many homes.   Science, moreover, has made possible a much larger population, which is chiefly concentrated in cities like London, Liverpool, and Glasgow.   A complex and highly mechanized social order which requires much skill in management and control has developed.   Were the water, electrical, and transportation facilities of London to be cut off for a single day, the consequences would be appalling.   Finally, it may be noted that science with its emphasis upon a material universe has challenged some of man's earlier concepts as to the "soul" and the life hereafter and, for many people, has forced a reorientation in religion.

SELECTED BIBLIOGRAPHY

Britain's rôle in science is treated in A. Schuster and A. E. Shipley's *Britain's Heritage of Science* (London, 1917); G. J. Romanes' *Darwin and After Darwin* (London, 1892–1897); F. Darwin, ed., *Life and Letters of Charles Darwin* (New York, 1891); A. N. Whitehead's *Science and the Modern World* (New York, 1925); A. S. Eddington's *Nature of the Physical World* (New York, 1928), and J. Jeans' *This Mysterious Universe* (New York, 1931).

For religious development see Dean R. Davidson's *Life of Archbishop Tait* (London, 1892); A. C. Benson's *Life of Edward White Benson, Archbishop Benson* (London, 1899); H. C. G. Moule's *The Evangelical School in the Church of England* (London, 1901); E. S. Purcell's *Life of Cardinal Manning* (London, 1896); S. Paget's *Henry Scott Holland* (London, 1921); A. W. Harrison's *The Methodist Church* (London, 1932); R. Jones' *Later Periods of Quakerism* (London, 1921); A. Peel's *Three Hundred Years: A Centenary History of the Congregational Union of England and Wales* (London, 1931), and R. W. Church's *The Oxford Movement* (London, 1891).

Education is handled in Sir G. Balfour's *The Educational Systems of Great Britain and Ireland* (Oxford, 1903); J. W. Adamson's *English Education, 1789–1902* (New York, 1930); F. Smith's *A History of English Elementary Education, 1760–1902* (London, 1931), and Sir G. W. Kekewich's *The Education Department and After* (London, 1920).

CHAPTER XXXIX

Modern Art and Literature

THE romantic movement in English literature had all but disappeared when Victoria ascended the throne in 1837. In its place there arose a group of writers who selected their themes from the democratic, scientific, and social activities of that age. Poets, dramatists, and novelists utilized their skill to depict life as they found it. Many frankly admitted an ulterior purpose for writing and flooded the market with works that were distinctly propagandist in nature. At the same time impassioned free traders, socialists, pacifists, and imperialists appealed for reform in government or society. Romanists, Protestants, and Anglicans vehemently defended vested interests and evidenced a blind partisanship toward social and political questions. A proposed change in the country's educational system immediately aroused the divines and unleashed a bitter attack against those who assailed their sacred portals. Darwin's theory of evolution also aroused considerable feeling. Prejudices were appealed to, and man was urged to denounce this or that evil in society and to protect his rights against the insidious tongue of the proletariat. Although literature for literature's sake continued to attract the skill of many writers, a large share of the books published showed a bias and prejudice which reflected a machine age.

Scientific, Political, and Philosophical Writings

At the opening of the Victorian era, most of the titles listed in the trade journals of the publishers were religious in nature.

Today fiction predominates.   Scientific and political treatises, histories, biographies, and hundreds of works on art, economics, dress, business, and sport also attest the change in literary tastes since 1837.   In the field of science one notices a brilliant array, from W. R. Grove's *The Correlation of Physical Forces* and T. H. Huxley's *Man's Place in Nature* to Sir J. H. Jeans' *Eos, or the Wider Aspects of Cosmogony.*   Bertrand Russell, R. G. Collingwood, A. N. Whitehead, and Sir Ernest Rutherford are others who have written scientific works of distinction. David Ricardo's *Principles of Political Economy,* S. Dowell's *History of Taxation and Taxes in England,* Sir Robert Giffen's *Case Against Bimetallism,* and E. T. Powell's *Evolution of the Money Market* illustrate the writing in economics.   G. D. H. Cole, Sidney and Beatrice Webb, Sir W. H. Beveridge, Ramsay MacDonald, Mrs. Bernard Bosanquet, and many others have contributed impressive volumes on poverty, labor, housing, and social security.   Talbot Baines' *The Industrial North,* J. H. Clapham's *Economic History,* R. E. Prothero's *English Farming, Past and Present,* and many other works by Gilbert Slater, William Page, and E. Lipson illustrate the interest that has been given to commerce, agriculture, and industry.   Albert Peel, John H. Newman, Bishop Bell, Archbishop Davidson, and Dean Inge have produced religious treatises that stress historical growth and applied Christianity rather than formal theology.   Scores of others, like Sir W. R. Anson, A. V. Dicey, Walter Bagehot, F. W. Maitland, Sir H. S. Maine, and W. S. Holdsworth, have written in the field of government and politics.   Attention has also been paid to internationalism, arbitration, war and peace, and the League of Nations.

Many of these writers were historians, and the interest they showed in economic and social development was in marked contrast to the political histories of the eighteenth century. Monographs and specialized studies dealing with the genesis and growth of institutions appeared in large numbers.   Historians no longer patterned their narratives after a Hume or

Gibbon. Time and energy did not exist for an elaborate study like the *Decline and Fall of the Roman Empire*. Accuracy in research forced the historian of the nineteenth century to focus his attention upon a narrower phase of human development. At the same time the scope of history was widened to include every phase of man's activity. Histories of the frozen meat trade, nursing, feudal incidents, the Black Death, town life, medieval gilds, and diplomacy appeared. On the basis of these studies, many of which were microscopic in nature, broader works like G. M. Trevelyan's *England in the Age of Wycliffe* and the *Cambridge Modern History* were written. George Grote, Bishop Stubbs, S. R. Gardiner, J. A. Froude, and W. E. Lecky were prominent nineteenth-century historians. Modern writers include such well-known names as G. P. Gooch, R. W. Seton-Watson, and R. B. Mowat.

Few historians, however, have equalled the literary skill of Thomas B. Macaulay, J. A. Froude, and Thomas Carlyle. Macaulay's writings, notably his articles in the *Edinburgh Review,* glorified the wisdom and statesmanship of the Whig Party, of which he was a member, in promoting parliamentary reform. Carlyle, though as partisan as Macaulay, took keen delight in throwing thunderbolts at preconceived notions. He rescued Cromwell from the calumny which eighteenth-century writers had fastened upon this Puritan, and struck telling blows at those who belittled spiritual values in favor of a mechanized society. His style was vivid; and his brilliant delineation of dramatic events, as depicted in his *French Revolution,* marked him as a master in narration. Froude's unfolding of the march of Elizabethan England reads almost like a novel. At times both Carlyle and Froude allowed literary excellency to overshadow historical accuracy. Carlyle, moreover, often introduced passages which were highly philosophical in nature.

In the field of philosophy, England produced several outstanding writers, notably John Stuart Mill, Herbert Spencer, and Sir William Hamilton. Mill accepted the utilitarian concepts of Jeremy Bentham, whose watchword, "the greatest happiness of the greatest number," profoundly influenced nineteenth-century thought. Bentham's interest in philosophy was purely practical; he preached as a means to social and political reform. Mill, on the other hand, stressed the theoretical aspects of Utilitarianism, though he was by no means blind to the need of social reform. To what extent, Mill asked, may government interfere with the liberty of the sovereign individual? His answer was, "The only purpose for which power can be rightfully exercised over any member of a civilized community, against his will, is to prevent harm to others." Every additional function of government strengthens bureaucracy and "bureaucracy is the grave of individuality." Mill, however, did not believe that the state could not interfere with the economic freedom of the individual, provided it were for the common good of all. Individual liberty, he stated, was not involved in the question of free trade; and government might regulate commerce in exactly the same way as it might insist upon sanitary precautions. Spencer was also a disciple of Bentham, but, like Mill, was interested in the theory of Utilitarianism. Spencer devoted his skill to the task of trying to fathom the principle of evolution. In doing this he believed that he had discovered the existence of a single identical phenomenon in all fields of human knowledge, and this phenomenon was that of evolution. In respect to government and its penetration of individual rights, he was even more emphatic than Mill. The state, he believed, was necessary during "man's apprenticeship" in society, and its chief duty was to protect the individual and his rights. To do more constituted a violation of nature. Accordingly, he did not hesitate to condemn the social legislation of his age. He believed that evolution was leading man from a condition where the state was everything and the individual nothing, to an order where the individual would be all and the state nothing.

The Victorian Stage

In the meantime there appeared a number of learned treatises on various aspects of English literature. General histories of literature, specialized studies, and philological works were produced by Edmund Gosse, W. P. Ker, Walter Raleigh, G. Saintsbury, and W. J. Courthope. Others, like F. A. Swinnerton, H. G. Wells, Bernard Shaw, and Henry James, contributed drama, verse, and essays in which philosophical concepts often appeared. During the Victorian era little progress was made in the English theater. Most playwrights were under the iron domination of managers who presented either their personal revisions of the Shakespearean plays or cheap melodramas, often borrowed from the French stage. The theatergoing public seemed to enjoy these presentations, and the manager's interest in profits checked the individual art of playwrights. By 1880 a change had taken place. Henry A. Jones and A. W. Pinero, for example, won considerable commendation for having had the courage to write plays which the managers had to produce in spite of their attitude toward anything new or modern. It was not until the present century, however, that the stage was emancipated from the domination of the managers and producers. Brilliant plays were written by Barrie, Shaw, Galsworthy, and many others. The high standards established by these writers was shown by the applause they received at home and abroad. Broadway not only opened its theaters to these plays but publicly recognized the leadership of the British dramatists. Although the audiences appreciated the literary excellency of these productions, what actually pleased them most was the simple fact that the play itself was a discussion of some social problem and not a recitation by the actors. Tradition and taboos were discarded; and themes depicting divorce, war, socialism, property rights, and laboring conditions were staged with great success. Not all the plays were necessarily serious in nature. Comedy and humor softened many a drama which was designed primarily for a serious purpose. Musical comedies and farces were also presented in large numbers. At the same time England did not ignore its greatest playwright, Shakespeare, whose tragedies and historical plays were produced with a fidelity unknown in the nineteenth century.

Into the very heart of this theatrical renaissance came a serious rival in the form of the motion picture. At first the films depicted English themes by English actors. The public hailed this new form of entertainment and packed the cheap show houses, which adapted themselves to the situation as well as might be expected. Later, specially constructed cinema halls were opened, and the British motion-picture industry was on the road to success. The outbreak of the World War checked this growth, and many of the studios were forced to suspend operations. American producers seized this opportunity of presenting stars like Mary Pickford, Charles Chaplin, and Douglas Fairbanks. During the last decade, however, British producers and actors have gained in popularity. Vaudeville, which often borders upon burlesque, also has its followers.

Prose and Poetry

In the field of poetry, Alfred Tennyson, Robert Browning, and Algernon Swinburne were the great Victorian writers. Tennyson sought for and gained perfection of form. In well-ordered verse he glorified the conventional standards of his age, as may be seen in either his *Idylls of the King* or *Maud*. Most critics praise him for his excellency of form and meter but become somewhat bored by his repeated and fanciful effusions. The latter characteristics were lacking in the verses of Robert Browning and his wife, Elizabeth Barrett. Browning delighted his readers by an unrivaled skill in depicting human motives and dramatic events. He was also able to translate into words the spirit and soul of music and the fine arts. Possibly his *Pippa Passes* and *The Ring and the Book* are his best-known works. Later in the nineteenth century, a group of new writers like Rudyard Kipling, Thomas Hardy, and W. B. Yeats rose to fame. Kipling's earlier work gained little recognition, because of his refusal to follow approved form. Critics spoke harshly of the man who had "no poetic diction." He did appeal, however, to the imperialist, colonist and humanitarian. The former liked Kipling, as did the latter, for his concept of England's duty to carry Britain's standards and British culture to "heathen lands." The colonist moreover, applauded Kipling for his immortal *Recessional,* which ranks today next to *God Save the King* and *Britannia Rules the Waves* as a national anthem. Hardy's poems, on the other hand, never received the recognition they were entitled to, and would have been tossed aside were it not for his reputation as a novelist. Yeats fared better, in spite of his devotion to Irish scenes and characters, because of the lyrical nature of his verses.

Generally speaking, none of the late nineteenth-century poets earned any reputation in their own age. The public cared little for innovation and gave homage to those who adhered to conventional forms and rules. No recognition was given to Oscar Wilde, for the simple reason that his private life was weighed down by irregularities which outraged the good and pure. When the floodgates of human emotion were opened by Edward VII, a decided change took place and the rejected poets received prolonged applause. A group of younger poets, moreover, who threw aside the traditional themes and forms, appeared at this time. Robert Bridges, D. H. Lawrence, and Walter de la Mare were the leaders in this movement which sought to forget iambic pentameters and the like. Lyrical and free verse predominated, and a definite attempt was made to establish an understanding and communion of sound and rhythm.

Many of the British poets of the nineteenth and twentieth

centuries were novelists of note. Most of the earlier writers
employed realism in their works, though a few followed the
romantic trend of the Georgian era. Political, social, and
economic themes predominated. Disraeli, for example, used
his skill to depict the aims and hopes of the Tory Party and
the Established Church. To him, the novel was but a means
of presenting political views. *Conningsby* is a splendid
delineation of Tory attitude toward the Reform Act of 1832,
and *Sybil* describes middle-class views according to the results
of the Industrial Revolution. Charlotte Brontë's *Shirley* centers
about the Luddite Riots of 1812, George Eliot's *Adam Bede*
shows what happens to man when he disregards morality, and
Charles Dickens' *Bleak House* illustrates the complexity and
red tape of the Court of Chancery. Dickens was a keen
observer of life, and filled his numerous novels with detailed
descriptions of sordid housing conditions, human frailties, and
eccentricities. Although his popularity has declined, today's
screen versions of his novels have created a new interest in
this great Victorian author.

Less popular than Dickens was William M. Thackeray,
whose *Vanity Fair* depicted the frivolity and shallowness of
the immortal Becky Sharpe. While men were dying for
God and King at Waterloo, Becky Sharpe was dying for her
breakfast. Thackeray was a master in ferreting out the in-
nermost thoughts of man and in analyzing character. His
greatest historical novel was *Henry Esmond*. Thackeray appealed to the intellectual classes more than did Dickens, though
neither captured the popular mind as did Charles Kingsley,
Captain Marryat, and Charles Lever. History and adventure
abound in the writings of these authors. Charles Reade's
Cloister and the Hearth also illustrates the trend toward historical fiction. Other writers, like Wilkie Collins, wrote mystery stories; and Mrs. Gaskell delineated the misfortunes of
the poor.

Later in the nineteenth century, George Meredith, Robert

Louis Stevenson, and Thomas Hardy enjoyed considerable popularity. Meredith drew his stories from the life of the upper classes. Hardy and Stevenson, however, were more concerned about the conditions of the ordinary person. Hardy has been criticized for drawing depressing and horrible pictures. Even as late as 1910, many American libraries refused to purchase some of his novels. *Jude the Obscure,* for example, was condemned on the ground that it was immoral and morbid. In striking contrast were the boisterous and adventurous scenes in Stevenson's *Kidnapped* and *Treasure Island.* The literary excellency of these writers did not appeal to the masses, who took keen delight in reading the soul-gripping novels of Mrs. Henry Wood, whose *East Lynne* was one of the best sellers. Rider Haggard's *King Solomon's Mines* and *She* were equally popular. Later, the average reader found interesting content in the stories by Hall Caine and Marie Corelli.

Most of these authors wrote primarily for men, but with the extension of education to women a decided change took place. Women, moreover, had more leisure than men; and as the writers were interested in the sale of their novels, they naturally cultivated this new audience. Arnold Bennett, John Galsworthy, H. G. Wells, and George Moore wrote of women for women. Love and adventure replaced masculine greatness, and sex problems were discussed with a frankness which displeased many of the critics. The prim Victorian days, however, were gone; and the Edwardian age enjoyed the new fiction. Other writers like John Buchan, at present Governor-General of Canada, delineated English life during and after the World War. D. H. Lawrence viewed sex as the most important problem in the modern age. *Aaron's Rod* and *Lady Chatterly's Lover* are perhaps his best known novels. James Joyce's *Ulysses* has also been roughly handled by the censors, but in the opinion of many critics has profoundly influenced recent literature. Joyce's realism was matched by the dramatic sea stories of Joseph Conrad.

Newspapers, Magazines, and Tabloids

Most of the Victorian novelists wrote for the middle and upper classes. There were writers, however, who catered to the shopgirl and factory hand. Love, travel, mystery, and adventure appealed to these readers, who also took great delight in the cheap story magazines and newspapers. At the opening of the nineteenth century the British press was restricted by a stamp, advertisement, and paper tax, and by a law of libel which prevented hostile criticism of the government. With the passage of the Reform Act of 1832 a change took place. Political repression was discarded, and by 1861 parliament had removed the various taxes. Since then there has been complete freedom of expression save as to obscenity and defamation of character. By 1870 every important borough and city had a newspaper which sold for as low as two cents a copy. These papers gave considerable attention to government affairs, though space was devoted to religion, sensational law cases, sports, and business. Little attempt was made to doctor the news, and headlines were few in number. Most of the owners of these papers prided themselves on the high quality of editorials and news items. These intellectual standards, however, did not appeal to the masses whose reading knowledge was limited to short sentences and simple words. George Newnes sensed the situation and proceeded to make capital out of it by founding, in 1880, a weekly paper known as *Tit-Bits*. In order to increase his circulation, Newnes resorted to prize competitions, and was the first "to give his readers a free insurance, though it was only a modest policy against railway accidents."

Newnes' success prompted Alfred and Harold Harmsworth,

later Lords Northcliffe and Rothermere respectively, to found *Answers to Correspondents* and *Comic Cuts*. Later, the Harmsworth brothers purchased the *Evening News* and the *Daily Mail*. Both of these London papers, under their new owners, catered to the lower classes and were sold for but one cent a copy. Within a year the circulation of the *Daily Mail* was twice as large as that of any other London paper. Early in the present century Alfred Harmsworth started the *Daily Mirror*, designed primarily for women; and when that failed, he organized it into a cheap tabloid. In 1908 he purchased the London *Times*. He increased its circulation by lowering its sale price from six to two cents and by introducing into its columns a more popular note. The *Times*, however, retained its former intellectual standards, and together with the *Manchester Guardian* and *Liverpool Daily* represents the British press of today at its best.

In addition to these papers which provided general news, there appeared a number of others devoted to some special group or interest. Many of these were the organs of the trade unions, workers, and Labor Party. The *Poor Man's Guardian*, the *Voice of the People*, the *Crisis*, and the *Pioneer and Official Gazette* were popular in the nineteenth century. The *Daily Herald* and *Daily Citizen* illustrate the so-called radical press of today. Finally, there is the London *Gazette*, founded in the seventeenth century, which serves as the official newspaper for the British government.

The influence of the press upon public opinion has been enormous. Particularly is this true in respect to political questions. The conduct of a British election is different from American practices. Here, presidential elections occur every four years. During most of the intervening period no extensive campaign is undertaken. It is only after the party conventions have been held that any serious attempt is made to educate the electorate. In England, however, elections may take place at any time and frequently are held within a month after parliament's dissolution. British parties, therefore, must be ready to wage a campaign at almost a minute's notice. For this reason they rely upon their own periodicals and newspapers to keep the voter informed of political activities. The *Conservative Home and Empire,* which has over two hundred and fifty thousand subscribers, is the organ of the Conservative Party. The Liberal Party sponsors the *Liberal Magazine,* and Labor publishes the *Labour Magazine.* Tracts and pamphlets are distributed in great abundance. In the brief campaign of 1931, the Labor Party issued over five million copies of its Election Manifesto, twenty-one million leaflets and over a hundred thousand digests for speakers. Each party also publishes several books setting forth its aims and ideals.

Weekly, monthly, and quarterly papers and magazines also appeared in large numbers. At the opening of the last century the *Edinburgh Review, Quarterly Review,* and the *Gentleman's Magazine* were the leading periodicals which every politician and gentleman read and to which the best literary writers contributed. Those interested in literature alone, also read the *European Magazine* or the *Repository of Arts,* which tried to increase their sales by the use of prints and colored illustrations. The *Agricultural Magazine* and *Farmer's Magazine* illustrated the interest in husbandry. Later there appeared the *Fortnightly Review,* ably edited by John Morley, the *Spectator,* and *Saturday Review.* Many of the daily papers, like the *Times* and *Manchester Guardian,* have, during the last two decades, published illustrated weeklies. Special publications exist for those interested in sport, design, religion, industry, and trade. Most of the learned societies, moreover, publish monthly or quarterly magazines. In the field of history, for example, there are several scholarly publications, notably the *English Historical Review, History,* and the *Cambridge Historical Quarterly.* Political science and economics are well represented by *Economica,* the *Political Quarterly,* and the *Economic Journal.*

The Fine Arts

All these publications reflected the great interest shown by the public in politics, industry, and science. This interest, however, did not extend to the fine arts, which were actually retarded by the results of the Industrial Revolution. The idealistic creations of Joseph Turner or the landscapes of John Constable were characteristic of early nineteenth-century painting. Constable's scenes were but careful reproductions of natural objects. Portrait painters also copied the exact likeness of their models. Skillful as these artists were in the use of color and perspective, there was little in the way of emotional expression. The artist did not seek to express his own feelings, nor did he aim at stimulating an emotional response on the part of those who praised his skill. Complete objectivity and realism dominated the efforts of men like Watts, Rossetti, and Burne-Jones. The invention of the camera, however, created a rival in reproduction which the greatest masters could not equal. Although the French painters met the challenge by resorting to imagery and interpretation, the English artists refused to alter their methods. They ridiculed those who utilized color and line to convey perception and emotion. Ruskin, one of England's greatest art critics, characterized the new art as a "pot of paint," and applauded those who continued to reproduce what they saw in nature. British painting, however, was influenced by the French school, particularly after Whistler, an American who had studied in Paris, made his home in England. English impressionistic painters became more numerous, and by 1890 were exhibiting their sketches in the great art galleries of the kingdom. During the twentieth century, cubists and symbolists have appeared. Generally speaking, British painting of today still adheres to older styles.

Conventional methods were also employed by the sculptors. Precise representation of dress, stature, and face was the sole object of the artist. Alfred Stevens and Thomas Woolner, however, were the last great sculptors to follow these methods. Influenced by the French, Hamo Thornycroft resorted to interpretation without offending the aesthetic tastes of his patrons. Later, J. M. Swan and others emphasized the decorative side of sculpturing, while F. W. Pomeroy excelled in statuettes. During the present age, Sir George Frampton has shown a conversion to Greek archaism and Jacob Epstein has illustrated the possibilities in impressionistic work. Frampton's *Edith Cavel* and Epstein's *Christ,* though examples of the modern trend in sculpturing, have not altogether pleased the British public.

Early Victorian architecture, furniture, and costume were tawdry and ugly. Prior to the nineteenth century, British builders, cabinetmakers, and designers produced graceful homes, public buildings, household equipment, and dress. A native art which was in keeping with English traditions existed. The eighteenth-century home, moreover, harmonized with the landscape about it. The industrial Revolution did not destroy this artistic sense but emphasized cheapness rather than quality. Mass production and improved methods of transportation profoundly influenced these arts. Cheap brick and iron supplanted stone, slate, and timber. Row upon row of ugly homes, cheaply built and quickly put together, rose in every city and village. Pretentious public buildings and mansions clashed with Wren's churches and the picturesque Elizabethan manor house. Instead of trying to make the mass of the building light and pleasant, with low, hidden roofs, and windows that were large simple openings trimmed with graceful sashes and slender bars, the architect of the machine age reared shops, stores, and homes that reflected wealth and poor taste. The curved bay windows and embowed fronts were discarded in favor of a design which demanded utility rather than art.

Within these houses and shops, stiffly and uncomfortably

dressed people applauded the machine age which had given them silk and plush upholstery. The latter was far more comfortable than the Georgian furniture, but it was totally lacking in beauty. The public did not seem to find fault with the squeaky springs—one of the many conveniences which resulted from the Industrial Revolution. By 1870, however, a definite revolt manifested itself against these tendencies in household equipment and architecture. T. G. Jackson was one of the first architects who dared to reject the English Gothic in favor of the more pleasing Renaissance style. Unfortunately many of the new public buildings reflected classical or medieval influences which were out of tune with the demands of modern life. For example, the new home constructed in 1889 for Scotland Yard looked "like a French early-Renaissance chateau (with some touches of a German castle) transported from the Loire to the Thames." Better designs characterized the homes of the well-to-do, though the dwellings of the middle and lower classes continued to be but ugly boxes of bricks. Since the close of the World War, many of the squalid tenement areas have been destroyed or abandoned. Simple homes reflecting the strong individualistic nature of the English have been constructed in the suburban areas. Much remains to be done, as there is a distinct housing shortage. The British government has given much thought to this problem, and it is likely that utility and beauty will characterize the homes of the next few decades.

In spite of the tremendous improvement which had taken place in science and mass production, the average home of the nineteenth century was lacking in modern conveniences. If cleanliness is next to godliness, Victorian England was a heathen country. Bathtubs, sanitary toilets, adequate illumination, and respectable kitchen equipment were to be found only in the homes of the wealthy. Any American, who visited England after the World War, wondered how these things could be tolerated. Some of the better hotels provided their guests with running water or private baths, but the great majority lacked these facilities. The average restaurant offered little in the way of fresh fruits, vegetables, or desserts. Although the food served was wholesome, it was not always well-prepared, and the costuming of the waitresses was sloppy and dirty. The use of refrigeration was not common, and the open milk can invited the curiosity of the cat. Conditions have changed during the last decade. Many of the hotels now provide private baths. American methods and sanitation have penetrated the cafes, and a greater variety of well-cooked food is served by better-dressed waitresses.

Costuming Since 1837

British costuming of the early Victorian era followed past conventional standards. Women wore heavy silk, satin, or taffeta dresses which extended from neck to toe. Generous trains, sometimes more than a yard in length, dragged along the floor or were gingerly held up by hand. Bustles and hoops billowed the form into grotesque shapes, and steel or whalebone corsets narrowed the waist and extended the bust to alarming proportions. Seldom if ever did one see the heavy shoes or the formidable array of skirts and petticoats. Bodily movement was curtailed. Participation in outdoor games or play was out of the question except for croquet. In the eighties, a few had the courage to shorten their skirts so as to play lawn-tennis or ride bicycles. The corset and bustle continued to be worn until the present century. Mutton-leg sleeves became popular by 1890, as did separate skirts and blouses. About the same time, the knicker came in style as a substitute for the petticoat. These gains, however, were offset by various hats which were held on the head by inserting long and dangerous hatpins through knobs of hair massed on top of the head. During the last three decades these hats and pins have been abandoned. Lighter, cheaper, and less cumbersome clothes came into fashion. Skirts were shortened so as to expose both ankle and calf. Common-sense styles predominated and women were given an opportunity for engaging in a variety of outdoor sports.

At the opening of the Victorian age the well-dressed man was adorned with a dark frock coat, wide trousers, and an imposing top hat. The influence of sports altered this style and introduced short trousers and jackets. White flannels were worn for tennis. In general, men's clothes were much simpler and more hygienic by 1880. Later, ready-made clothes brought further changes. Top hats disappeared, except for formal wear. The imposing beards and moustaches were shaved off, and man looked more like a human being than a wild animal. Among the working classes there was a gradual abandonment of garbs which reflected occupation. The farmer gave up his smock, and the artisan discarded corduroy. The ready-made clothes were too attractive for these classes to ignore, especially as they provided greater body freedom and permitted their wearers to dress like the middle and upper classes.

British Music

Dressed in this fashion they did not appear out of place when they attended the cinema, theatre, opera, or music hall. British music was at a low ebb when Victoria ascended the throne. Most Englishmen enjoyed the revival songs of the Methodist Church and the instrumental music commonly used by the Established Church. Select audiences, moreover, continued to listen to Handel's *Messiah* and the many national operas which had been so popular in the eighteenth century. The growing dominance of spoken dialogue in opera lessened the influence of the latter. Generally speaking, the English cared little for music and were far behind the standards maintained in Europe. Scant recognition was given to domestic composers, and men like Sterndale Bennett were known only to a small number of music lovers. Bennett's work was not forgotten. His pupils, notably Parry and Sullivan, continued to stress good music in the Royal Academy of Music. Later in 1880, courses in music were offered by the Royal College of Music. About the same time a group of German artists toured England and did much to stimulate a revival in music. Light opera advanced rapidly, owing to the brilliant compositions by Gilbert and Sullivan. During the nineties, a number of new composers like Edward Elgar rose to prominence. Queen's Hall was opened and became the center of orchestral music. Grand opera, sung entirely by foreigners, was presented at Covent Garden. Further gains have been made during the present century. Opera, under the skillful direction of Thomas Beecham, has become more popular; and many English singers of note have been attracted to this field of music. Probably the greatest single advance came in folk songs, though the symphonies by Elgar, Williams, and Broughton were notable achievements. The invention of the gramophone displaced the old music box and brought popular and classical compositions to the masses. Later came the "talkies," which permitted all classes to see and hear musical plays, light opera, and opera.

SELECTED BIBLIOGRAPHY

The *Cambridge History of English Literature* and R. Garnett and E. Gosse's *English Literature, an Illustrated Record* (London, 1903–1904) furnish general information as to the chief writers of the nineteenth and twentieth centuries. F. A. Swinnerton's *The Georgian Literary Scene* (New York, 1935); F. M. Ford's *Joseph Conrad* (New York, 1924); H. G. Well's *Experiment in Autobiography* (London, 1934); E. C. Stedman's *Victorian Poets* (Boston, 1903); W. L. Cross' *The Development of the English Novel* (New York, 1933); G. P. Gooch's *History and Historians in the Nineteenth Century* (New York, 1913); E. Barker's *Political Thought from Herbert Spencer to the Present Day* (New York, 1915); J. Seth's *English Philosophers and Schools of Philosophy* (London, 1912), and J. W. Cuncliffe's *English Literature*

During the Last Half Century (New York, 1919) are convenient guides. R. A. Scott-James' *The Influence of the Press* (London, 1913) and G. B. Dibblee's *The Newspaper* (London, 1913), *A Newspaper History, 1785–1935* (London, 1935), and *The Times* (London, 1935) furnish information about the press. The legal aspects of printing and publishing are referred to in any standard constitutional history.

The Oxford History of Music and Sir G. Grove's *Dictionary of Music and Musicians* (New York, 1927–1928) are standard works. C. Nicholson and C. Spooner's *Recent English Ecclesiastical Architecture* (London, 1911); Sir W. Bayliss' *Five Great Painters of the Victorian Era* (London, 1902); J. W. Mackail's *Life of William Morris* (London, 1899); J. and E. R. Pennell's *The Life of James McNeill Whistler* (London, 1908), and Joseph Holbrooke's *Contemporary British Composers* (London, 1925) are of value. The works on dress and costuming cited elsewhere may be used with profit.

APPENDIX I

List of Prime Ministers

Date of Installation	Party	Duration Years	Duration Days	Prime Minister
Mar. 20, 1721	Whig	20	326	Sir Robert Walpole
Feb. 11, 1742	Whig	1	9	Lord Wilmington
July 26, 1743	Whig	2	226	Henry Pelham
Feb. 10, 1746	——	—	2	Earl of Bath
Feb. 12, 1746	Whig	8	22	Henry Pelham
April 21, 1754	Whig	2	205	Duke of Newcastle
Nov. 16, 1756	Whig	—	142	Duke of Devonshire; Wm. Pitt, actual head.
June, 1757	Whig	4	335	Duke of Newcastle; Pitt in control until Oct. 1761,
May, 1762	Tory	—	319	Earl of Bute
April, 1763	Largely Whig	2	85	George Grenville
July 12, 1765	Whig	1	20	Lord Rockingham
Aug. 2, 1766	Coalition	3	176	Duke of Grafton; Pitt, actual head.
Jan. 28, 1770	Tory	12	48	Lord North
Mar. 20, 1782	Whig	—	104	Lord Rockingham
July 3, 1782	Whig	—	273	Earl of Shelburne
April 2, 1783	Coalition	—	259	Duke of Portland
Dec. 23, 1783	Largely Tory	17	79	William Pitt, the Younger
Mar. 17, 1801	Largely Tory	3	55	Viscount Sidmouth
May 15, 1804	Largely Tory	1	253	William Pitt, the Younger
Feb. 11, 1806	Whig	1	43	Lord Grenville
Mar. 31, 1807	Tory	2	243	Duke of Portland
Dec. 2, 1809	Tory	2	161	Spencer Perceval
June 9, 1812	Tory	14	39	Earl of Liverpool
April 12, 1827	Tory	—	106	George Canning
Sept. 5, 1827	Tory	—	125	Lord Goderich
Jan. 25, 1828	Tory	2	295	Duke of Wellington
Nov. 22, 1830	Whig	3	236	Earl Grey
July 18, 1834	Whig	—	128	Lord Melbourne
Dec. 26, 1834	Tory	—	108	Sir Robert Peel
April 18, 1835	Whig	6	144	Lord· Melbourne
Sept. 6, 1841	Tory	4	296	Sir Robert Peel
July 6, 1846	Whig	5	230	Lord John Russell

Feb. 27, 1852................Tory	—	293	Lord Derby
Dec. 28, 1852................Whig	2	33	Lord Aberdeen
Feb. 10, 1855................Whig	3	10	Lord Palmerston
Feb. 25, 1858................Tory	1	106	Lord Derby
June 18, 1859..............Whig	6	122	Lord Palmerston
Nov. 6, 1865................Whig	—	232	Lord John Russell
July 6, 1866.................Tory	1	234	Lord Derby
Feb. 27, 1868................Tory	—	279	Benjamin Disraeli
Dec. 9, 1868................Liberal	5	70	W. E. Gladstone
Feb. 21, 1874...............Tory	6	59	Benjamin Disraeli
April 28, 1880.............Liberal	5	56	W. E. Gladstone
June 24, 1885.............Conservative	—	221	Marquess of Salisbury
Feb. 1, 1886................Liberal	—	175	W. E. Gladstone
July 26, 1886.............Conservative	6	23	Marquess of Salisbury
Aug. 18, 1892.............Liberal	1	196	W. E. Gladstone
Mar. 3, 1894................Liberal	1	118	Lord Rosebery
June 29, 1895.............Unionist	7	12	Marquess of Salisbury
July 12, 1902..............Unionist	3	146	Arthur Balfour
Dec. 5, 1905...............Liberal	2	125	H. Campbell-Bannerman
April 8, 1908...............Liberal; Coalition from May, 1915	8	243	Henry Asquith
Dec. 7, 1916...............Coalition	5	320	David Lloyd George
Oct. 23, 1922...............Conservative	—	212	A. Bonar Law
May 22, 1923.............Conservative	—	244	Stanley Baldwin
Jan. 22, 1924..............Labor	—	287	Ramsay MacDonald
Nov. 4, 1924...............Conservative	4	213	Stanley Baldwin
June 5, 1929...............Labor	2	80	Ramsay MacDonald
Aug. 24, 1931.............Nationalist	3	287	Ramsay MacDonald
June 7, 1935...............Nationalist			Stanley Baldwin

APPENDIX II

List of Parliaments of the United Kingdom

Date of Meeting	Date of Dissolution	Duration Years	Days
Jan. 22, 1801	June 29, 1802	1	158
Nov. 16, 1802	Oct. 24, 1806	3	342
Dec. 15, 1806	April 29, 1807	—	135
June 22, 1807	Sept. 29, 1812	4	99
Nov. 24, 1812	June 10, 1818	5	198
Jan. 14, 1819	Feb. 29, 1820	1	46
April 21, 1820	June 2, 1826	6	42
Nov. 14, 1826	July 24, 1830	3	252
Oct. 26, 1830	April 23, 1831	—	179
June 14, 1831	Dec. 3, 1832	1	172
Jan. 29, 1833	Dec. 29, 1834	1	334
Feb. 19, 1835	July 17, 1837	2	148
Nov. 15, 1837	June 23, 1841	3	189
Aug. 19, 1841	July 23, 1847	5	337
Nov. 18, 1847	July 1, 1852	4	226
Nov. 4, 1852	Mar. 21, 1857	4	137
April 1, 1857	April 23, 1859	2	22
May 31, 1859	July 6, 1865	6	36
Feb. 1, 1866	Nov. 11, 1868	2	284
Dec. 10, 1868	Jan. 26, 1874	5	47
Mar. 5, 1874	Mar. 24, 1880	6	19
April 29, 1880	Nov. 18, 1885	5	202
Jan. 12, 1886	June 26, 1886	—	164
Aug. 5, 1886	June 28, 1892	5	328
Aug. 4, 1892	July 8, 1895	2	337
Aug. 12, 1895	Sept. 25, 1900	5	44
Dec. 3, 1900	Jan. 8, 1906	5	36
Feb. 13, 1906	Jan. 10, 1910	3	332
Feb. 21, 1910	Nov. 28, 1910	—	281
Jan. 31, 1911	Nov. 25, 1918	7	299
Feb. 4, 1919	Oct. 26, 1922	3	265
Nov. 20, 1922	Nov. 16, 1923	—	361
Jan. 8, 1924	Oct. 9, 1924	—	266
Dec. 2, 1924	May 10, 1929	4	159
June 25, 1929	Oct. 7, 1931	2	105
Nov. 3, 1931	Oct. 25, 1935	3	356
Nov. 26, 1935			

Index